Memory
in animals and humans

The Comparative Psychology of Animals and Humans

Series Editor: Professor W. Sluckin, University of Leicester

The comparative perspective — viewing animals and human beings side by side — is best suited to a range of topics within psychology. The nature/nurture issue has traditionally been considered in this way, and more narrowly circumscribed areas of study, such as conditioning, have for a long time been investigated in animals as well as in humans. In more recent times, developments in the related fields of ethology and sociobiology have focused attention on the comparative approach to selected psychological topics.

The aim of this series is to produce books dealing in a comparative manner with a variety of topics. The multiple authorship of each book ensures a thorough and in-depth coverage of the topic, while at the same time great care is taken that the chapters cohere according to an overall structure provided by the book's editor. Each volume is under the separate editorship of a specialist in the given field. All the books review and evaluate research in the respective fields, and give an up-to-date summary of the present state of knowledge.

Memory
in animals and humans

Some comparisons and their theoretical implications

Edited by

Andrew Mayes

Department of Psychology
Manchester University

 Van Nostrand Reinhold (UK) Co. Ltd.

Published by Van Nostrand Reinhold (UK) Co. Ltd.
Molly Millars Lane, Wokingham, Berkshire, England

Library of Congress Cataloging in Publication Data
Main entry under title:

Memory in animals and humans.

    (The Comparative psychology of animals and
    humans)
    Includes bibliographies and index.
    1. Memory — Physiological aspects. 2. Memory,
Disorders of. 3. Physiology, Comparative. I. Mayes,
Andrew Richard. II. Series. [DNLM: 1. Memory.
2. Psychology, Comparative. BF 371 M533]
QP406.M45   1983   156'.312   82-8617
ISBN 0-442-30524-9   AACR2

Typeset by Colset Pte Ltd, Singapore.

Printed in Great Britain at the University Press, Cambridge

Preface

In recent years, many books have been published which attempt to review the current state of our knowledge of human memory. This volume is not intended as an addition to such a list. Although it contains some chapters which concentrate on memory processes which may be special to human beings, there has been particular emphasis on the investigation of memory activities which animals and humans may share. Appropriate animal models of human memory systems offer powerful means for elucidating the physiological mechanisms underlying memory. Consideration of what these mechanisms are constitutes a second major theme of the book. The stress on animal comparisons and physiological mechanisms illustrates what may be regarded as the volume's leitmotif. This is the view that any basic advances in our theories of memory will depend on the adoption of a 'convergent operations' approach. Such an approach represents not merely a reaction to the excessive and isolated exploitation of highly specific paradigms. It is concerned not only to use and relate findings, derived from several experimental paradigms, selected because they are believed to depend on common memory processes, but, more widely, it aims to identify the underlying mechanisms of such processes by developing animal models of human memory. More precise psychological and physiological knowledge can then provide effective constraints for the construction of information processing models, which can be tested by computer simulation.

Surprising though it may be, it is unusual to see considered, in one context, research drawn from work on intact humans, intact animals and organisms which have undergone some physiological or biochemical manipulation. In this volume the three areas are juxtaposed and some of the implications of this juxtapositioning are assessed. In the opening chapter, Andrew Mayes introduces the idea of the 'convergent operations' approach to memory research and illustrates it with examples drawn from human neuropsychology and work on intact animals and humans. David Oakley then views memory in an evolutionary framework, and proposes a tentative, comprehensive scheme for classifying the varieties of human and animal memory. In the third chapter, Peter Meudell reviews research on the ontogeny of memory, focusing on those periods of poor memory, or even amnesia, associated with the early and late stages of the life cycle. The discussion involves comparisons of the phenomena in animals and humans. Andrew Mayes then tries to interpret the evidence about the nature of the consolidation of memory. Inevitably, his review concentrates on the animal literature, but studies on humans are included in relation to views about how memory changes over long periods of time, and also in relation to recently expressed ideas that, even in animals, the traditional consolidation period of a few seconds or minutes may involve psychological activities, such as rehearsal. In the fifth chapter, Graham Hitch first describes the current state of knowledge and thinking about human short-term memory processes, and then contrasts and compares this with the more inchoate state of research on animal short-term memory. There then follows a chapter by Andrew Mayes and Peter Meudell, which critically reviews current theories of human amnesia and assesses the extent to which light is thrown on these by comparisons with apparently similar amnesias in animals. The last two substantive chapters concentrate on human memory. In the first, Michael Gruneberg reviews recent research on rehearsal, 'feelings of knowing' and the use of mnemonics. The emphasis here is on processes which are likely to be unique to humans — the processes involved being dependent on some degree of self-knowledge. Michael Eysenck then critically reviews work which relates human memory to personality dimensions, like anxiety and introversion, and cognitive factors, such as verbal and spatial ability.

Although the individual difference approach can be fruitfully applied to animal research, there has unfortunately been little use made of it, as Andrew Mayes points out in the final chapter. In this overview chapter, he selects a number of themes and discusses them in terms of the 'convergent operations' approach, paying special attention to the interpretive difficulties that arise.

A number of topics occur incidentally or centrally in several chapters. These include ideas about familiarity, short-term memory, arousal and abstract or semantic memory. Lack of complete agreement among the contributors may act as a salutary warning about the present immature state of memory theory. The book is intended for advanced undergraduates, postgraduates and research workers in the field of memory. Nevertheless, the writing should be readily intelligible to the non-specialist who is seeking an integrated compendium of memory research and theory.

Andrew Mayes

Contents

CHAPTER 1

Human and Animal Memory: Some Basic Questions

Andrew Mayes

1.1 Memory and Other Psychological Processes

Memory stands at the centre of the web of psychological processes. For this reason, as the functions underlying memory phenomena are so intimately inter-dependent, their elucidation has created intractable difficulties. The ancient division of memory processes into registration, storage and retrieval implicitly demonstrates the salience of perception, attention and thinking to remember-ing. How information is registered depends on how it is perceived, attended to and related by thinking to what is already known. Success in retrieval depends on reconstructing the ambience of initial registration through the activities of thinking and perception. In turn, the richness of registration depends on the ability to interpret new information by retrieving other information already in storage.

Explanations of memory phenomena are hard to achieve therefore, because the effects of registration, storage and retrieval are not mutually independent. Nevertheless, such explanations are the goals of memory research. A given kind of memory is characterized by the way in which the relevant information is registered, stored and later retrieved. The characterization comprises several detailed points. First, what kinds of process underlie registration, and what kinds of information are eventually stored? Second, what are the processes initiated by registration, which consolidate memory storage? How can these processes be modified and what is their time course? Third, where in the brain is the information stored and what inter-neuronal organizational processes are involved in its storage? Fourth, and related to the two previous points, what neuronal and sub-neuronal processes mediate storage? Fifth, what are the processes which enable the information to be retrieved after a delay?

In typologies of memory, each kind of memory is, in principle, identifiable in terms of these five points. A typologist proposes a kind of memory on the basis of the sort of information he thinks is being stored, and attempts to corroborate his suggestion by showing that the remembering of this information is uniquely characterized by the five points. For example, it can be argued that verbal and visuospatial memories are distinct because they show differences in the mode of registration, in what is registered, in where storage occurs and the organization this requires, and possibly in the mechanisms of retrieval. Even so, the two kinds of memory will share many processes. This suggests that memory may be as fruitfully classified into distinct registration, storage and retrieval functions, as it is, at present, into types based on the kind of information being stored. This former course is still probably impracticable, however, because we know too little about these basic memory functions.

1.2   A Convergent Operations Approach to Memory

It has proved particularly hard in memory research to develop concepts and explanations which advance significantly beyond what has been available to common knowledge for millenia. Research has tended to be paradigm-bound, with the result that a number of phenomena have been minutely explored, and theories developed which do not readily generalize across situations. There is remarkably little 'cross-talk' among memory researchers, simply because their methods usually do not try to achieve general explanations.

In response to this predicament, Hitch (1979) proposed a 'convergent operations' approach to the models developed by cognitive psychologists. This approach involves the examination of putative memory processes from a wide range of perspectives to see whether these yield implications which are mutually consistent, or reveal hitherto unseen confusions and complexities. It is argued here that Hitch's proposal should be extended beyond the confines of research into the memories of intact humans to include brain damaged people and the related memory systems of animals. Putative memory processes can be better characterized by tests using many paradigms, and animal models can then be used to identify more precisely the physiological activities involved. These sources of knowledge can then provide the constraints on further theorizing. Such theorizing about the processing and storage of information falls within the domain of artificial intelligence (AI) research and generates theories whose complexities can only be tested by computer simulation modelling.

This three-stage activity therefore requires that memory abilities are properly characterized by testing over many paradigms, that their underlying physiology is illuminated where possible by animal models, and that the information so gained provides constraints in the development of computer simulated AI models. In more detail, the first stage involves the examination of a range of memory tasks, which putatively depend on the operation of given memory processes. These tasks may be used to test both human and animal memory. A fuller description of the processes may then be found by looking at the effects of ageing, brain damage and individual differences on performance of the various tasks. These factors, like the variables which influence task performance in intact humans, should affect the hypothetical processes in unique ways. A major problem in defining the features of putative memory processes is the fact that different kinds of people and other animals may perform what is nominally the same task in radically differing ways. Special attention to uniquely human memory activities, such as those associated with self-awareness and awareness of memory itself, should help to reduce this kind of problem.

Researchers, therefore, need not only to explore parametrically particular tasks in humans, but also to find other tasks which bear conceptual similarities to the former, and to see whether these are similarly affected by comparable task variables, and by the effects of age, brain damage and individual differences. Attempts to identify similar memory abilities in other species will then be more securely based. In this book, Chapter 5 illustrates this approach and its problems as it applies to short-term memory abilities. Chapters 3 on ageing, 6 on brain damage, and 8 on individual differences indicate the extent to which these factors differentially affect putatively different kinds of memory. Chapter 7 reviews the phenomena which may be unique to human memory, and which make cross-situational and cross-species comparisons trickier.

Clearer determination of the kinds of memory and their underlying physiology requires research into both the neuropsychology of human memory and animal memory. In general, neuropsychologists have analysed the effects of different brain lesions to corroborate the picture of memory abilities and processes derived from studying intact humans. Some lesion effects on memory do not seem to fit into this framework, however. For example, the retrograde amnesia for pretraumatic memories, in which older memories seem to be relatively spared, has no adequate explanation in terms of current theories. Such phenomena should stimulate the emergence of novel theories. In humans, the predominant approach of using lesions to fractionate memory processes in accordance with the notions of cognitive psychology is understandable, as it is very hard to gain precise knowledge of the underlying physiology. This problem does not apply, however, to animal neuropsychology, and even human neuropsychology can now draw on techniques which measure electrophysiological, blood flow and metabolic changes associated with learning and remembering.

These physiological techniques are complemented by rapidly increasing knowledge of the brain's micro- and macro-anatomy. It therefore becomes possible to plot the flow of information through the brain as various memory processes operate on it. If sufficient details are discovered, the development of computer-simulated AI models of memory abilities becomes a reasonable objective. Unfortunately, most extant AI theories have been based on an inadequate number of psychological, physiological and anatomical constraints.

The next two sections briefly examine the impact of animal and human neuropsychology on attempts to classify the different kinds of memory. Chapter 2 reviews a provisional classificatory scheme for memory within an evolutionary framework and based largely on animal research, whereas Chapter 6 mainly considers the role of limbic system structures in complex human memory.

1.3 Varieties of Memory in Humans and Animals

Views about the relationship between animal and human memory have swung between extremes. On the one hand, theorists like Watson and Skinner have maintained an atomistic position, which sees no essential difference between simple and complex learning processes. In the long run, according to this position, it will be shown how complex behaviours like speech are compounded of conditioned sequences of simpler behaviour. This kind of view has caused a reaction so that some workers act, in practice, as if there is little or no relationship between the simpler processes of animal memory and the complex ones of human memory. The truth surely lies between these extremes. Many human memory processes have their animal counterparts, although identification may prove difficult as these common processes are often overlaid, in humans, with functions unique to our species.

In the past, the predominant influence of the atomistic position led to the importation into human memory research of notions drawn from animal research. An example is the significance which has been attached to reinforcement in human learning. More recently, however, the direction of flow of ideas has reversed. This is illustrated by the use of the ideas of rehearsal and short-term memory, originally derived from research on human verbal memory, and now used to explain phenomena in animal conditioning and habituation (for example, see Wagner *et al.*, 1973). Such approaches assume that animal and human memory share organizational characteristics in registration, storage and perhaps retrieval, even though the animal memory is much simpler. When such organizational commonalities are lacking, it remains possible that the microscopic changes within neurons, mediating storage of simple memory in animals, are very similar to the changes underlying the storage of complex human memory. Animals can, therefore, be used to model human memory at the organizational (macroscopic) and the neuronal (microscopic) levels.

Successful adoption of animal models of organizational processes in human memory depends on a taxonomy of memory, like that offered by David Oakley in this book. In general, an animal model should be of the same kind of memory as the human memory which the researcher wishes to illuminate. Exceptions to this rule may, however, be made when organizational processes are believed to mediate several kinds of memory, as has been argued for rehearsal (see Wagner *et al.*, 1973).

Oakley postulates four levels of information gain and storage, the last three of which constitute what is conventionally regarded as memory. Within the third level, four major kinds of memory are distinguished: event, associative, representational and abstract memory. Second-level memories, such as those for imprinting, are distinguished because they can only be acquired during critical stages of development and only permit experience to modify the behaviours involved in a limited number of ways. The fourth level of information gain is only distinguished by the fact that the source of the gain is from culturally acquired experience. Such culturally acquired memories will be stored within third-level systems.

Most, if not all, neural tissue has the capacity to show plastic change in response to environmental contingencies, and learning abilities probably emerged very early in the course of evolution. David Oakley argues that new learning capacities depend on the emergence of new modular brain systems. These systems perform the operations which make the new kinds of learning possible. He contrasts this view with the now largely discredited notion of encephalization, according to which functions are transferred from phylogenetically older structures, like the tectum, to more recently evolved ones, like the neocortex. If functions are properly characterized, the excephalization view can be seen to be false. For example, in mammals the neocortex plays a central role in vision, whereas in amphibia and reptiles this role is taken by the tectum. In all three groups, however, the tectum performs basically similar functions — perhaps involving simple visual analysis, visual attention and control of orientation toward stimuli — which in mammals are integrated with sophisticated, new functions of the neocortex.

Oakley's conception is therefore one in which distinct neural modules mediate the kinds of memory constituting the 'cells' of his taxonomy. He attempts to define distinct kinds of information processing and then show that memory for each kind depends on the activity of separate neural modules. As the modules are concerned with registration, storage and retrieval, this approach suggests that these processes may be basically different for the various kinds of memory. It does not, however, prove it. For example, it has long been disputed whether classical and instrumental conditioning are fundamentally different kinds of associative memory. Do they involve basically distinct kinds of registration, storage and retrieval processes? Their operational definitions are distinct. In classical conditioning, reinforcement with the unconditional stimulus is not contingent on performance of the conditioned response, whereas this is the case with instrumental conditioning. The presence or absence of contingency is often hard to determine, as conditional responses may affect the perceived quality of the unconditioned stimulus in a task, which is supposedly one of classical conditioning. Conversely, with autoshaping, behaviours which appear to be under the control of instrumental contingencies may, in reality, be not contingent on reinforcement (see Mackintosh, 1978).

Assuming that classical and instrumental tasks have been correctly identified, there is considerable evidence that learning and memory of the former is less dependent on neocortical mechanisms (Oakley, 1981). The reasons for these possible neurological differences still need to be unveiled and may not reflect the operation of different memory processes. They are, anyway, not clearcut, as Oakley argues that instrumental tasks may be performed not only in the absence of neocortex, but also even in spinal preparations and simple invertebrates. This observation itself raises another interpretive difficulty. What has provisionally been defined as one kind of memory may, on analysis, subdivide into several kinds. Although several subvarieties may coexist in complex species like mammals, cross-species comparisons will be hard as more primitive species (like mammalian spinal preparations) may only show simpler varieties of the relevant kind of memory. The same point applies to comparisons of human and animal memory.

Provisional evidence that two kinds of memory are really distinct is available when brain lesions disturb them in a way that doubly dissociates, i.e. lesion A disturbs memory 1 but not memory 2, and lesion B disturbs memory 2 but not memory 1. A single dissociation is inadequate, as one kind of memory may be harder and use more of a general resource, like attention, which the lesion disturbs. If the kind of memory is believed to be common to several species, then comparisons need to ensure that tests tap apparently similar abilities and that lesions are of homologous brain regions. This analysis would be greatly helped by knowledge of the relevant neuroanatomy to determine the sequence of information processing and storage. Such knowledge is critical in deciding whether spinal and neocortical conditioning are radically different.

What applies to instrumental conditioning also applies to Oakley's event memory and to habituation. Oakley introduces event memory because, he believes, an associate memory presupposes the existence of an ability to remember events. It seems likely, however, that this category is heterogeneous. Sensory event memory, manifested in abilities such as eidetic imagery, may be quite separate from the kind of event memory necessary for classical conditioning. Similarly, the habituation of the gill withdrawal reflex of the invertebrate Aplysia and of spinal responses in mammals may be distinct from habituation of the orienting reaction, which involves neocortical mechanisms. The latter kind of habituation involves the creation of a representation of past experience against which new experiences can be matched. Evidence suggests that when matches occur the orienting reaction is inhibited by limbic system mechanisms. Lesions to these structures impair habituation without affecting the orienting reaction itself (see Williams *et al.*, 1974). All such neurological differences must, however, ultimately be analysed in information processing terms.

As the structure of a memory taxonomy depends on similarities in registration, storage and retrieval, it must remain an open question whether possible subvarieties of conditioning, event memory and habituation have less in common with each other than they do with apparently more distant forms of memory on Oakley's scheme. Cross-species comparisons and the scheme's neatness are also threatened by the occurrence of convergent evolution, in which two species display a similar memory ability, which has evolved independently and involves separate mechanisms in the two cases. The scheme will be made more complex by the occurrence during evolution of many remarkable learning adaptations. An example of such an adaption is bait shyness, a form of classical conditioning which may occur in one trial even when several hours separate conditioned and unconditioned stimuli. These and other features of bait shyness have led some researchers to argue for species-specific laws of conditioning and learning (see Seligman & Hager, 1972). It seems more likely that bait shyness depends on mechanisms additional to those found in the forms of conditioning, which require multiple trials and close spatiotemporal proximity of the stimuli to be associated. In this kind of case, evolutionary divergence may have led from a single, inchoate adaptation in an ancestral form to many specific adaptations, each with unique organizational features.

The preceding paragraphs pinpoint some of the pitfalls which memory taxonomists must face. If successful, a taxonomist will show how closely two operationally defined kinds of memory are, initially in terms of mediating brain structures, but ultimately in terms of the mechanisms of registration, storage and retrieval. Even when two kinds of memory differ with respect to such organizational processes, their storage may depend on similar microscopic changes within neurons. Such changes index storage and will be critical in deciding to what extent phenomena, like learning and forgetting, implicate registration, storage or retrieval mechanisms. At present, because storage strength cannot be indexed directly by physiological measures, it is exceedingly hard to decide, for example, whether forgetting is caused by changes in storage, retrieval, or both.

Knowledge of the microscopic changes mediating storage is important in constructing a memory taxonomy. Thus, David Oakley distinguishes between long-term and short-term reference memory in his scheme. The distinction is supported by many others, who believe it reflects different long- and short-term storage mechanisms. Many theorists believe that the microscopic changes initiated by learning, which underlie long-term memory storage, take time to complete, and that during this consolidation period memory is held by one or more short-term storage mechanisms. It is unclear, however, whether these consolidation short-term stores correspond to Oakley's. Oakley's postulation of short-term representational stores depends on evidence that forgetting for some kinds of information is very rapid under some conditions and that this forgetting may be differentially affected by factors like brain lesions. Such short-term abilities may well reflect rapidly changing retrieval conditions rather than unique storage mechanisms. In turn, the retrieval changes may depend on the adequacy of initial registration. If they exist, consolidation short-term stores occur with many kinds of memory and across many animal groups. For example, retrograde amnesia caused by a physiological disruption, which is taken as evidence for slow long-term memory consolidation and the need for short-term storage, is found not only in mammals but also in invertebrates like honey bees (Erber, 1976). It remains to be proved, therefore, that short-term representational memory reflects specialized storage adaptations, rather than inadequate registration with an associated rapid deterioration of retrieval conditions. The structure of Oakley's scheme will depend of the resolution on this issue.

1.4   The Neuropsychology of Human Memory

Some of the problems inherent in cross-species comparisons can be avoided in studies of the neuropsychology of human memory. The effects of brain lesions on human memory do suggest a crude classificatory scheme for memory processes. Memory breakdown or its absence may be divided into four categories: simple learning skills, exemplified by Oakley's associative memory, which are largely unaffected; disturbances of specific kinds of complex memory; disturbances of those kinds of memory dependent on sophisticated voluntary strategies of registration and retrieval; disturbances of all kinds of complex memory (global amnesia).

Limbic system lesions, which cause global amnesia for complex memory, have often been reported to leave motor learning, perceptual learning, classical and instrumental conditioning unimpaired (see Chapter 6). Similarly, anencephalic children, with little functional neocortex or limbic system, can show normal classical conditioning (see Chapter 2). These kinds of learning are largely independent of forebrain mechanisms. Little is known, however, about the brain stem and cerebellar lesions which may selectively impair these kinds of memory. These must be explored if the organizational processes underlying simple memory are to be understood. Some mechanisms will, no doubt, be shared with complex memory. For example, the role of the reticular formation in generating arousal may have similar effects with most kinds of memory.

Specific disorders of complex memory are consequences of lesions to particular neocorical regions. The kinds of complex memory affected comprise Oakley's representational and abstract memory, but probably also kinds of sensory event memory. In his sense, representational memory involves multi-event representations of the environment, in which spatiotemporal relations are specified. Abstract memory, on the other hand, stores the accumulated pool of general knowledge, which is abstracted when events in representational memory recur. Oakley likens this distinction to Tulving's (1972) episodic/semantic dichotomy, in which episodic memories are specified by their spatiotemporal contexts, whereas semantic memories provide a mental dictionary and encyclopedia, independent of such contexts.

De Renzi (1982) has recently described specific memory failures for colours, faces and geographical locations. The patients seemed to have normal intelligence and memory except for these specific kinds of information. New learning and memory for the relevant material was very poor although old (as opposed to more recent) pretraumatic memories were preserved. For example, patients with topographical amnesia could not learn new routes although they might remember ones learnt long ago. De Renzi argued that these patients had effectively normal cognition and registration abilities. For example, his patients who could not remember faces were able to decide whether frontal and side views were of the same person.

Other specific amnesias have been reported by Ross (1982), who described a patient with damage to the neocortical regions concerned with vision. This patient's vision was good, apart from some blind fields, but he had a selective loss of memory for all recent visual events. He was unable to draw a plan of the apartment to which he had recently moved although his drawing of the room plan of his parents' house, where he had lived before his stroke, was very accurate. Examination of the lesion suggested that the stroke may have disconnected the visual neocortex from important memory-mediating structures lying in the limbic system deep beneath the temporal lobe.

Both De Renzi and Ross therefore suggest that specific amnesias (in which poor new learning and memory is associated with good remembering of old pre-traumatic memories) are caused when select neocortical regions are disconnected from limbic system memory mechanisms. Each neocortical region processes particular kinds of information whereas the limbic structures some-how boost the storage of the relevant material. It has, however, been difficult to prove that patients with specific amnesias do not have subtle perceptual-cognitive problems, which could lead to deficient registration and hence poor memory. Nevertheless the proposal implies a scheme in which the neocortical mosaic is divided into many specific information processing systems, each connected with the limbic storage boosting mechanisms. Another plausible assumption implicit in the scheme is that if a neocortical region processes a given kind of information it will also store it.

Provisional support for this assumption is given by the effects of other neo-cortical lesions. Thus, Warrington (1975) described several patients with cortical atrophy, who displayed object agnosia. These patients seemed to have lost much knowledge about the significance of objects and words. Their ability to learn most things was severely impaired. Warrington argued, however, that when learning placed minimum demands on semantic interpretation (as in memory for abstract pictures) their performance reached normal levels. The lesions may have degraded the storage of long-established semantic information. More recently, Warrington (1982) has reported patients with other neocortical lesions, whose syndromes suggest that storage of semantic information may be highly differentiated. One patient had a selective problem in solving simple arithmetical tasks. Althouh he understood concepts like quantity, and operations like multiplication, he solved problems slowly, inconsistently and inaccurately. He seemed to have lost his knowledge of over-learned, arithmetical facts like '2 × 3 = 6', without which even simple problems become tricky. Warrington (1981) has described other patients whose syndromes suggest that abstract and concrete words may also be stored separately in the neocortex.

The final category of memory disorder caused by neocortical lesions comprises the short-term memory failures. Of these, the best known is the sub-variety of conduction aphasia in which there is a selective loss of auditory, phonemic short-term memory (see Shallice & Warrington, 1970). This disorder doubly dissociates from the severe long-term memory failure caused by limbic system lesions. It is also associated with good visual short-term memory, which immediately suggests that there may be other short-term memory systems. Although incompletely characterized, Warrington and Rabin (1971) reported a syndrome in which patients with posterior neocortical lesions showed impaired visual 'spans of apprehension' for both verbal and non-verbal material. The patients had normal digit spans to auditory presentation. Similar modality-specific short-term memory impairments have been described by Butters *et al.* (1970) and Samuels *et al.* (1972). They found that right parietal cortex lesions impaired memory for visually presented material in the Peterson task. Recall of verbal and non-verbal material was equally affected but remained intact for auditorily presented material. In contrast, left parietal lesions caused selective short-term memory impairments for both visual and auditory modalities of presentation.

The short-term memory failures are usually interpreted as disturbances of specific short-term stores because comprehension is generally relatively intact. This interpretation is a speculation with the less documented syndromes, and another view of the auditory, phonemic short-term memory syndrome is possible. It may arise from subtle processing deficits for phonemic information under conditions of rapid presentation. Although processing and storage deficit interpretations are hard to separate, the former should predict problems in phoneme discrimination when memory requirements are minimized, and also long-term memory impairments for meaningless phonemic sequences. Partial phonemic analysis is sufficient to extract meaning, which explains why semantic information is well retained in multitrial learning.

The third variety of memory disorder is caused by lesions of the frontal neocortex and involves frank disturbances of registration and retrieval. Basic cognitive and memory functions are well preserved in patients with these lesions, but they cannot spontaneously initiate and execute detailed plans for registering and retrieving information. They may, however, be able to execute such plans when carefully guided. For example, Signoret and Lhermitte (1976) reported how the deficit in learning paired-associate words, shown by some frontal patients, can be alleviated if the patients are told how to form mediating images. Frontal patients also have difficulty in retrieving episodes which may have been experienced decades before their traumas. For example, Albert *et al.* (1980) found that patients with Huntington's chorea, who have atrophy in the frontal neocortex as well as the neostriatum, have retrograde amnesia for public events and faces stretching back for decades. This contrasted with the memories of patients with limbic system lesions, which were better for very old memories.

If information can be registered and retrieved automatically with little attentional involvement, memory for it is less affected by frontal lesions. A possible exception to this generalization arises from the observation that frontal patients have particular problems making judgements about the relative recency of events (Milner, 1971). Such judgements are thought to depend on automatic registration and retrieval processes (see Chapter 6). Even so, the frontal neocortex is best conceived of as a system which integrates and elaborates the information initially processed by the specific neocortical association areas. This elaboration requires planning and considerable attentional resources.

The fourth variety of memory disorder constitutes the limbic system amnesias discussed in Chapter 6. Patients with this disorder may show poor learning and memory for most, if not all, kinds of complex information (anterograde amnesia), some abnormal forgetting of pretraumatic information (retrograde amnesia), together with good intelligence and normal short-term memory. This syndrome may not be a unitary disorder. It may be subdivided in two ways. First, unilateral limbic system lesions seem to cause memory deficits, which are not global but specific to classes of information, not unlike the neocortical amnesias. Thus, Milner (1971) associates lesions of the left side of the hippocampus and limbic system with amnesia for verbal material, whereas right-sided lesions impair memory for visuospatial and other non-verbal materials. Patten (1972) claimed that dominant hemisphere lesions may cause gustatory amnesia whereas minor hemisphere lesions may cause an olfactory memory deficit.

Second, there is also preliminary evidence that differently placed bilateral lesions of the limbic system cause different kinds of amnesia. Thus, some evidence suggests that lesions of the medial temporal lobes cause both slow learning and more rapid forgetting even when learning is increased to match that of controls. In contrast, amnesics with diencephalic lesions learn slowly but forget at a normal rate (see Huppert & Piercy, 1979 and Chapter 6 for a discussion). There is also some evidence that retrograde and anterograde amnesia are dissociable. Goldberg *et al.* (1981) have described an individual with a selective retrograde amnesia. Although his anterograde amnesia resolved over two years so that his learning and memory fell within normal limits, he continued to show a profound retrograde amnesia. This extended back over two decades and affected school learning, so that he could not recall that Paris was France's capital or that Shakespeare wrote Hamlet. CT studies showed that damage was concentrated in the midbrain with hypodense regions, including locus coeruleus projections into the medial forebrain bundle and the ventral tegmental pathway, which forms part of an ascending cholinergic reticular pathway projecting to the limbic system. Although other cases of selective retrograde amnesia have been reported, clear cases of anterograde without any retrograde amnesia remain to be established (but see the reference to Winocur *et al.* in the last chapter).

Mishkin (1982) has argued that normal storage and retrieval requires that neocortically processed information pass through two or more parallel cortico-limbo-thalamo-cortical circuits. One circuit involves the amygdala and dorso-medial thalamic nucleus and the other involves the hippocampus and anterior thalamic nuclei. Mishkin has reported that there needs to be damage to both circuits if monkeys are to show severe amnesias as evinced by their performance in delayed non-matching to sample tasks. Although it is polemical to what extent lesions of the amygdala circuit add to the effects on memory of lesions of the hippocampal circuit (see Squire & Zola-Morgan, in press), Mishkin's view is compatible with the limbic system performing several memory-related functions. Cohen and Squire (1980a) have suggested that the limbic system is an extrinsic memory modulatory system. Such a system influences the storage and retrieval of memories, but does not store them or affect what is registered. These latter functions are performed by an intrinsic system, which in this case corresponds to the neocortex.

Possible functions of the limbic memory structures are discussed in Chapter 6, but it remains unclear whether these functions are correctly construed as extrinsic. It has been suggested that limbic memory functions include the elaborate registration of information (Butters & Cermak, 1975) or, contrastingly, the registration of more automatically encoded information (Hirst, 1982). Indeed, a dominant view of limbic system amnesia is that it is caused by the inability to use spatiotemporal and other kinds of contextual information.

10

There is also a possibility that parts of the limbic system may act as temporary memory stores. The phenomenon of long-term potentiation in the hippocampus shows that plastic changes, lasting for days, may be related to the temporary storage of information (see Tsukahara, 1981).

It has also been argued that limbic structures affect storage of episodic but not of semantic memory. Comparison of the two is confounded, however, by the fact that semantic memories are usually grossly overlearnt relative to episodic ones. Overlearnt memories may indeed be less vulnerable to limbic lesions, but overlearning is an incidental feature of semantic memories. Even so, although semantic memory seems to be little affected in retrograde amnesia, learning and retention of new semantic material is drastically impaired by limbic lesions. On the other hand, Cohen and Squire (1980b) found that amnesics learned and retained normally the skill of reading mirror-reversed words although they could not remember the words used in acquiring the skill. They proposed a distinction between declarative and procedural memory. Declarative memories comprise both semantic and episodic memory (and, presumably, Oakley's abstract and representational memory) and concern memories which, in principle, the rememberer could describe in verbal terms. In contrast, procedural memories, which are cognitive, perceptual and motor skills, can only be displayed in action. Cognitive procedural memory (as for reading mirror-reversed words) should not be confused with semantic memory, and like other kinds of 'simple' memory, seems to be independent of the limbic system.

Despite many unresolved issues, a picture does emerge from this section. There is a variety of kinds of simple memory which do not involve the neocortex and limbic system. These are registered, stored and retrieved by older brain regions. There are other more complex forms of procedural memory which are processed and perhaps stored by the neocortex, but do not require limbic system activity. Other complex information, for both episodic and semantic material, is processed in a highly articulated fashion by the neocortex. Information processed in a given neocortical region is probably also stored there, although frontal cortex function is important in integrating information processed by separate regions. All neocortical processing regions send information through parallel limbic system loops, which appear to boost neocortical storage and retrieval in several poorly understood ways.

1.5 Individual Differences in Memory

If the above picture is correct, one would expect individuals to differ not only in some overall memory ability, but in a number of specific memory abilities corresponding to the efficiency of various neocortical regions. Evidence for such specific abilities is derived from questionnaire studies and direct memory tests. Herrmann and Neisser (1978) gave a battery of questions to 205 students, asking how good they thought their memories were in various areas. The results were factor analysed and eight specific abilities were identified in addition to a general factor. These included rote memory, memory for names, memory for people and their faces, memory for conversations, memory for lists, like errands, and memory for places. The students' impressions of their memories seem to correspond reasonably closely to reality. For example, Woodhead and

Baddeley (1981) have shown that people with exceptional memories for faces and pictures may only have average verbal memories.

More systematic testing of different kinds of memory has been largely confined within the framework of intelligence testing. These efforts have been described and interpreted by Guilford (1971, 1982). He indicates that even in the late 19th century Binet had cited evidence which differentiated visual memory for sentences, memory for musical tones, memory for colours, and memory for digits. Guilford's own work corroborates Binet's and identifies kinds of memory, like memory for colour and memory for shapes, which differ from each other in subtle ways. His model of intellect, which determines his classification of memory abilities, is unfortunately not easy to assess and has had little influence on memory research.

In his model Guilford (1971, 1982) distinguishes the mental operations of cognition, memory, divergent and convergent thinking. These operations can be reinterpreted as registration, storage, and divergent and convergent retrieval. His test batteries have led him not only to differentiate many memory abilities, corresponding to distinct mental contents and products, but also matching registration and retrieval abilities. He therefore argues that individual differences in memory for material, like sentences and pictures, depends on variations not only in the efficiency of registration, but also in the efficiency of storage and retrieval. According to this view, even retrieval comprises the separable abilities of searching memory in a focused manner for a uniquely specified target, and searching it repeatedly for loosely specified items.

Guilford's approach to memory is important although his conclusions are open to dispute as the close interdependence of registration, storage and retrieval make them hard to disentangle. For example, it is very likely that some processes are common to registration and retrieval, so it is no surprise that Hunt (1978) has found that people of high verbal ability not only learn verbal material (such as paired associates) more rapidly, but they also retrieve well established verbal memories more rapidly. Even so, the study of individual differences in memory gives preliminary support for the view that storage, registration and retrieval mechanisms are mediated by distinct brain mechanisms. Further investigation in this field could be advanced by examining individual differences in animal memory.

Studies of individual differences in animal memory offer the advantages of selective breeding and the greater ease of measuring biochemical and physiological variables. A recent computer search of *Psychological Abstracts*, performed for the author, revealed however that very few such studies have been carried out since 1967. There are some exceptions, which have attempted to correlate measures of limbic system function to memory performance. For example, Schwegler et al. (1981) have shown, with both unselected and selectively bred mice, that there is a negative correlation between two-way active avoidance performance and the number of mossy fibres synapsing on basal dendrites of hippocampal pyramidal neurons. Similarly, Berry and Thompson (1978) found that rabbits showing more hippocampal theta activity over the 2–8 Hz range, in the two minute period prior to learning, acquired a classically conditioned nictitating membrane response more rapidly when trained for several days.

One kind of hippocampal theta is sensitive to anticholinergic drugs and the structure is known to receive cholinergic innervation. It is therefore interesting that several studies suggest that there is a correlation between basal cholinergic metabolism and the acquisition and retention of conditioning tasks. (see Kammerer *et al.*, 1982). As these memory tasks are different from complex human memory, and as there is disagreement about the degree to which the limbic system mediates them, a study of Barnes (1979) is more relevant to the human situation. Barnes examined spatial memory in young and old rats. Spatial memory is a form of representational memory. He found that the poor memory of senile animals was associated with a less durable long-term potentiation of the hippocampus although development of potentiation was normal.

These studies, correlating constitutional measure of limbic activity with memory ability, leave open the question of how this activity relates to memory. Measured variations in limbic activity may, for example, be determining motivational and emotional differences, which in turn cause the memory differences. It is important to identify the presence of such indirect factors. The early work on the selective breeding of maze dull and maze bright strains of rat, for example, had to be reinterpreted when it was later found that there were emotional differences between the two strains (see Guilford, 1971). Future work not only needs to examine a range of memory and other tasks, but will benefit from a more detailed knowledge about information flow through the limbic system.

In Chapter 8, Michael Eysenck mainly focuses his attention on memory differences associated with variations in temperament and intellect. Studies in this area need to identify the mediating processes which influence memory. These processes include arousal, selective attention and poorly identified information analysing skills. Individual difference research is a means of determining the importance of such factors for different kinds of memory. Selective effects will reinforce the view that there are a number of basically distinct kinds of memory. Like the use of animal models, however, this kind of research will be advanced by a better knowledge of the physiology of the limbic system and other brain regions.

1.6 Information Flow, Processing and Storage in the Brain: A Prolegomenon

Knowledge of how the brain processes information depends on the use of animal models. These are critically dependent on accurate descriptions of the brain's anatomical connections, and examine not only lesion effects, but also the biochemical and electrophysiological correlates of memory. These techniques, still in their infancy, will be illustrated by considering work on the limbic system.

Cormier (1981) has recently suggested functions for the amygdala, hippocampus and septum largely on the basis of animal studies. As damage to these structures has been implicated in human organic amnesia, their functions in animals may be of critical significance. Cormier proposes that the amygdala somehow associates stimuli with reinforcers, whereas the hippocampus habituates stimuli which no longer are, or never were, associated with reinforcers. He emphasizes that these structures process different kinds of stimuli for different purposes. He also argues that the hippocampus not only processes stimuli so as to habituate them, but additionally it processes stimuli distantly

associated with reinforcers (secondary stimuli). These stimuli, which correspond to the contextual features studied in human memory, are not habituated
but acquire significance as discriminative cues. Cormier ascribes the supposedly greater sensitivity of human memory to hippocampal lesions to the far
higher proportion of secondary stimuli processed by humans.

Cormier's hypothesis is therefore a variant of the popular 'contextual processing deficit' view of human amnesia. It offers two advantages. First, it is
anatomically specific and detailed, as he postulates that the septum integrates
amygdala and hippocampal activity, with the medial septum feeding reinforcement information to the hippocampus and lateral septum receiving its output.
This precision is impossible to achieve in human amnesia research. Second, the
animal paradigms suggest ways of testing the capacity of human amnesics to
process secondary stimuli.

The hypothesis proposes a hippocampal role in processing contextual information, but as such information may also be processed elsewhere in the brain,
the precise hippocampal role in registering, storing or retrieving the information needs to be specified further. Cormier's general view of hippocampal
function is widely held. For example, Jeffrey Gray's (1982) theory of septo-
hippocampal function claims that the system compares perceived and predicted
events so as to modulate attention and action. His model involves a very
detailed description of how information flows through and is processed by the
microanatomy of the hippocampus, is modulated by the system's inputs, and
finally how it is transferred to other systems.

This kind of model can be critically assessed only through the use of physiological analysis of limbic system function. Such analyses are now burgeoning.
For example Deadwyler et al. (1981) recorded averaged sensory-evoked
responses from the outer molecular layer of dentate gyrus in rats, which were
being conditioned to respond to an auditory stimulus. They identified two
negative peaks, one of which was responsive to unexpectedness in stimuli and
the other of which was responsive to stimuli with acquired biological significance. They were able to show by the further use of selective lesions that
information about event unexpectedness was transmitted to the dentate from
the entorhinal cortex via the perforant path, whereas information about biologically significant events was transmitted to the dentate from the medial septum.
Buzsaki et al. (1981) have described how information about event unexpectedness may be modulated by hippocampal theta. They found that perforant
pathway stimulation evokes the greatest responses from the dentate during the
negative going phase of hippocampal theta. The medial septum is an important
generator of hippocampal theta so this finding supports the view that the dentate
gyrus integrates entorhinal and septal inputs. The dentate gyrus may assess
information along a dimension of significance and use this assessment to
determine the strength of memory storage.

Another impressive use of electrical recording techniques in elucidating the
nature of limbic-diencephalic memory mechanisms, discussed by Oakley, is the
work of Caan et al. (in preparation) and Perrett et al. (in preparation). This
Oxford group trained monkeys in a serial recognition task and found some
neural units which responded selectively to stimulus familiarity. The units
increased their firing rate within 200 ms of being re-exposed to objects shown
earlier in a session, whereas presentation of novel objects inhibited their firing.
The 'familiarity' response was acquired within a second or so of first exposure to

novel objects and the response declined after the last exposure in an exponential fashion. These properties of the effect suggest that behavioural and electrophysiological familiarity responses are closely matched. This impression is corroborated by the considerable degree of perceptual constancy shown by the familiarity units and by their failure to react differentially as a function of whether an object was associated with reward or punishment. In contrast, some neurons in the lateral hypothalamus and substantia innominata respond to a stimulus associated with food reward but not with saline. These units were insensitive to different degrees of stimulus familiarity. This electrophysiological double dissociation of familiarity and associative memory corresponds to Gaffan's (1972) claim that fornix lesions affect memory for familiarity, but not most forms of associative memory.

The Oxford group's research represents an attempt to chart how information is processed as it flows through the brain. They do this by identifying the characteristic eliciting stimuli for neurons at different stages in the neural pathway. The group needs to plot the characteristic eliciting patterns for neurons in other parts of the neocortical, striatal and limbic systems to discover how familiarity information is extracted. They have shown, for example, that there are a small number of familiarity units in the mammillary bodies. The majority have been found, however, in the medial region at the anterior border of the thalamus, but not in the anterior thalamic nuclear complex. This finding is not congruent with that of lesion studies, which have shown amnesia from lesions of the mammillary body, but not the anterior border of the thalamus. Further research may reveal that these latter neurons are not concerned with storing familiarity information, but with monitoring this information for unknown reasons. If so, then familiarity information must be stored and initially processed elsewhere in the brain.

Processed visual information is projected from the inferotemporal cortex to the hippocampus via the entorhinal cortex. It is interesting, therefore, that Fuster and Jervey (1981) have reported that neurons in monkey inferotemporal cortex discharge in a way consistent with their retaining visual information during a delayed response task. This suggested role in storing visual information is supported by the well known impairment of visual discrimination learning and memory caused by inferotemporal cortex lesions. Such lesions may, however, disturb registration rather than storage. Thus, Wilson and DeBauche (1980) found that anterior inferotemporal cortex lesions prevent monkeys from showing categorical perception of visual stimuli, which indicates that the memory problem is partially caused by an encoding problem.

Single and multiple unit recording studies allow researchers to plot information flow from neocortex through the limbo-thalamic circuits, so that the manner of its transformation can be plotted. Similar recording techniques can be used to plot how cortical, limbic and thalamic neurons change activity in the course of learning, storage and retrieval. In this way, the temporal organization of memory processes can be plotted as they stabilize during learning, and later during retrieval. Mayes (1981) discusses how Olds and his group used recording techniques to isolate where memory storage changes occur. The techniques have also been used by Gabriel et al. (1981) to study dynamic changes during learning. They used multiple unit recording to show that cingulate cortex neurons changed their activity during conditioning before anteroventral thalamic neurons. These latter neurons receive a cingulate input, and eventually showed changed activity which persisted even when the cingulate units no longer maintained their altered activity. This study used rabbits and a learning paradigm, which makes it hard to relate to limbic function in complex human memory, but it does indicate that some limbic circuits may act as temporary information buffers.

Physiological studies in humans have largely been confined to correlating EEG and evoked potentials with cognitive processes. Little is known about how such measures are related to neuronal activities in the neocortex and limbic system. Such knowledge depends on rarely used invasive techniques. Using such a technique, Halgren *et al.* (1980) reported that large field-potential and unit responses can be evoked from recording sites within the human hippocampus and amygdala, by infrequent, attended events. These evoked responses correlated with scalp recorded responses, such as N_2 and P_3, and these components have been associated with attention, so the argument linking the two limbic structures with attention, and indirectly memory, is also strengthened.

Despite the above example, elucidation of the physiology of human memory relies almost entirely on the selection of appropriate animal models, although this dependence may be reduced in the next decade as less invasive human techniques are refined which allow measurement of localized, neuronal metabolism. The examples given in this section show that precise tests of the physiological predictions of information processing theories, such as Gray's (1982) may be made, using animals. The behavioural implications can also be tested in animals. What these behavioural implications are in a model as complex as Gray's could fruitfully be determined by computer simulation. His model is powerfully constrained by current physiological and behavioural knowledge, but its postulated mechanisms' intricate interactions may best be revealed by the methods of AI.

The likelihood that animal models will accurately match human memory processes will be increased if those processes are examined in many situations. Separate memory abilities and processes can be identified in humans most convincingly by showing that the hypothetical abilities and processes vary characteristically in different paradigms, in response to selective kinds of brain damage, in different kinds of people, and as people mature and grow old. Such abilities and processes, specified across many paradigms, should be easier to match in animal models. In future, such models should provide more systematic physiological knowledge about memory processes to constrain the form taken by detailed information processing theories. The predictions of these theories will need to be determined by the computer simulation methods of AI. Current knowledge about memory abilities and their mechanisms is discussed in the other chapters of this book, across many paradigms, in various kinds of human being, and in many animal species. In the final chapter, a few illustrative problems are considered, which are associated with the degree to which tests of memory in different situations have convergent implications.

References

ALBERT, M.S., BUTTERS, N. and BRANDT, J. (1981) Patterns of remote memory in amnesic and demented patients. *Archives of Neurology*, **38**, 495–500.

BARNES, C.A. (1979) Memory deficits associated with senescence: a neurophysiological study in the rat. *Journal of Comparative and Physiological Psychology*, **90**, 74–104.

BERRY, S.D. and THOMPSON, R.F. (1978) Prediction of learning rate from the hippocampal EEG. *Science*, **200**, 1298–1300.

BUTTERS, N. and CERMAK, L. (1975) Some analyses of amnesia syndromes in brain-damaged patients. In: R. ISAACSON and K. PRIBRAM (Eds.) The Hippocampus. Volume 2, pp. 377–409. Plenum, New York.

BUTTERS, N., SAMUELS, I., GOODGLASS, H. and BRODY, B. (1970) Short-term visual and auditory memory disorders after parietal and frontal lobe damage. *Cortex*, **6**, 440–459.

BUZSAKI, G., GRASTYAN, E., GZOPF, J., KELLENYI, L. and PROHASKA, O. (1981) Changes in neuronal transmission in the rat hippocampus during behaviour. *Brain Research*, **225**, 235–247.

CAAN, W., PERRETT, D.I., ROLLS, E.T. and WILSON, F. (in preparation) Thalamic neuronal responses related to visual recognition. 1. Activity during performance of recognition and association tasks.

COHEN, N. and SQUIRE, S. (1980a) Learning of rules and procedures in amnesia. *International Neuropsychological Bulletin*, December 20.

COHEN, N. and SQUIRE, S. (1980b) Preserved learning and retention of a pattern analysing skill in amnesia: Dissociation of knowing how and knowing that. *Science*, **210**, 207–209.

CORMIER, S.M. (1981) A match-mismatch theory of limbic system function. *Physiological Psychology*, **9**, 3–36.

DEADWYLER, S.A., WEST, M.O. and ROBINSON, J.H. (1981) Entorhinal and septal inputs differentially control sensory-evoked responses in the rat dentate gyrus. *Science*, **211**, 1181–1183.

DE RENZI, E. (1982) Memory disorders following focal neocortical damage. *Philosophical Transactions of the Royal Society, London* B, **298**, 73–83.

ERBER, J. (1976) Retrograde amnesia in Honeybees (*Apis mellifera carnica*). *Journal of Comparative and Physiological Psychology*, **90**, 41–46.

FUSTER, J.M. and JERVEY, J.P. (1981) Inferotemporal neurons distinguish and retain behaviourally relevant features of visual stimuli. *Science*, **212**, 952–954.

GABRIEL, M., FOSTER, K. and ORONA, E. (1980) Interaction of laminae of the cingulate cortex with the anteroventral thalamus during behavioural learning. *Science*, **208**, 1050–1052.

GAFFAN, D. (1972) Loss of recognition in rats with lesions of the fornix. *Neuropsychologia*, **10**, 327–341.

GOLDBERG, E., ANTIN, S.P. BILDER, R.M. Jr., GERSTMAN, L.J., HUGHES, J.E.O. and MATTIS, S. (1981) Retrograde amnesia: Possible role of mesencephalic reticular activation in long-term memory. *Science* **213**, 1392–1394.

GRAY, J.A. (1982) *The Neuropsychology of Anxiety: An Enquiry into the Functions of the Septohippocampal System*. Oxford University Press, Oxford.

GUILFORD, J.P. (1971) *The Nature of Human Intelligence*. McGraw-Hill, London.

GUILFORD, J.P. (1982) Cognitive psychology's ambiguities: Some suggested remedies. *Psychological Review*, **89**, 48–59.

HALGREN, E., SQUIRES, N.K., WILSON, C.L., ROHRBAUGH, J.W., BABB, T.L. and CRANDALL, P.H. (1980) Endogenous potentials generated in the human hippocampal formation and amygdala by infrequent events. *Science*, **210**, 803–805.

HERRMANN, D.J. and NEISSER, U. (1978) An inventory of everyday memory experiences. In: M.M. GRUNEBERG, P.E. MORRIS and R.N. SYKES (Eds.) *Practical*

Aspects of Memory, pp. 35–51. Academic Press, London.

HIRST, W. (1982) The amnesic syndrome: Descriptions and explanations. *Psychological Bulletin*, **91**, 435–460.

HITCH, G.J. (1979) Developing the concept of working memory. In: G. CLAXTON (Ed.) *New Directions in Cognitive Psychology*. Routledge & Kegan Paul, London.

HUNT, E. (1978) Mechanics of verbal ability. *Psychological Review*, **85**, 109–130.

HUPPERT, F.A. and PIERCY, M. (1979) Normal and abnormal forgetting in amnesia: effect of locus of lesion. *Cortex*, **15**, 385–390.

KAMMERER, E., RAUCA, C. and MATTHIES, H. (1982) Cholinergic activity of the hippocampus and permanent memory storage. In: C. AJMONE MARSAN and H. MATTHIES (Eds.) *Neuronal Plasticity and Memory Formation*. pp. 387–395. Raven Press, New York.

MACKINTOSH, N.H. (1978) Conditioning. In: B.M. FOSS (Ed.) *Psychology Survey No. 1*, pp. 43–57. Allen & Unwin, London.

MAYES, A.R. (1981) The Physiology of memory. In: G. UNDERWOOD and R. STEVENS (Eds.) *Aspects of Consciousness. Volume 2. Structural Issues*, pp. 1–38. Academic Press, London.

MILNER, B. (1971) Interhemispere differences in the localization of psychological processes in man. *British Medical Bulletin*, **27**, 272–277.

MISHKIN, M. (1982) A memory system in the monkey. *Philosophical Transactions of the Royal Society* B, **298**, 85–95.

OAKLEY, D.A. (1981) Brain mechanisms of mammalian learning. *British Medical Bulletin*, **37**, 175–180.

PATTEN, B.M. (1972) Modality specific memory disorders in man. *Acta Neurologica Scandinavica*, **48**, 69–86.

PERRETT, D.I. CAAN, W., ROLLS, E.T. and WILSON, F. (In preparation) Thalamic neuronal responses related to visual recognition. II. Memory Characteristics.

ROSS, E.D. (1982) Disorders of recent memory in humans. *Trends in Neurosciences*, May, 170–173.

SAMUELS, I., BUTTERS, N. and FEDIO, P. (1972) Short-term memory disorders following temporal lobe removals in humans. *Cortex*, **8**, 283–298.

SCHWEGLER, H., LIPP, H.P., VAN DER LOOS, H. and BUSELMATER, W. (1981) Individual hippocampal mossy fibre distribution in mice correlates with two-way avoidance performance. *Science*, **214**, 817–819.

SELIGMAN, M.E.P. and HAGER, J.L. (1972) *Biological Boundaries of Learning*. Appleton-Century-Crofts, New York.

SIGNORET, T.L. and LHERMITTE, F. (1976) The amnesic syndromes and the encoding process. In: M.R. ROSENZWEIG and E.L. BENNETT (Eds.) *Neural Mechanisms of Learning and Memory*. MIT Press, Cambridge, Mass.

SQUIRE, L.R. and ZOLA-MORGAN, S. (in press) Neuropsychology of memory: Studies in man and sub-human primates. In: J.A. DEUTSCH (Ed.) *The Physiological Basis of Memory 2nd, edition*. Academic Press, New York.

TSUKAHARA, N. (1981) Synaptic plasticity in the mammalian central nervous system. *Annual Review of Neuroscience*, **4**, 351–379.

TULVING, E. (1972) Episodic and semantic memory. In: E. TULVING and W. DONALDSON (Eds.) *Organisation of Memory*. Academic Press, London.

WAGNER, A.R., RUDY, J.W. and WHITLOW, J.W. (1973) Rehearsal in animal conditioning. *Journal of Experimental Psychology Monograph*, **97**, 407–426.

WARRINGTON, E.K. (1975) The selective impairment of semantic memory. *Quarterly Journal of Experimental Psychology*, **27**, 635–657.

WARRINGTON, E.K. (1981) Concrete word dyslexia. *British Journal of Psychology*, **72**, 175–196.

WARRINGTON, E.K. (1982) The fractionation of arithmetical skills: a single case study. *Quarterly Journal of Experimental Psychology*, **34A**, 31–52.

WARRINGTON, E.K. and RABIN, P. (1971) Visual span of apprehension in patients with unilateral cerebral lesions. *Quarterly Journal of Experimental Psychology*, **23**, 423–431.

WILSON, M. and DE BAUCHE, B.A. (1980) Inferotemporal cortex and categorical perception of visual stimuli by monkeys. *Neuropsychologia*, **19**, 29–41.

WILLIAMS, J.M., HAMILTON, L.W. and CARLTON, P.L. (1974) Pharmacological and anatomical dissociation of two types of habituation. *Journal of Comparative and Physiological Psychology*, **87**, 724–732.

WOODHEAD, M.M. and BADDELEY, A.D. (1981) Individual differences and memory for faces, pictures and words. *Memory and Cognition*, **9**, 368–370.

CHAPTER 2

The Varieties of Memory: A Phylogenetic Approach

David A. Oakley

The process of biological evolution is one of the acquisition, storage and utilization of information and it is instructive to consider memory in that broader
perspective. The general outline for such a consideration has been presented
recently in two papers by Plotkin and Odling-Smee (Plotkin & Odling-Smee,
1979, 1981; see also Plotkin, 1981) and the first section of this chapter owes a
great deal to their account. Plotkin and Odling-Smee were primarily concerned
with the various processes of information gain and storage which could be
described in biological systems and laid particular stress on the evolution of
learning as an adaptive strategy. I take memory in its widest sense to mean no
more than the storage of information, and so memory, like learning, can be seen
as part of a more general evolutionary strategy.

2.1 Levels of Information Gain and Storage

In an unchanging and predictable world it is conceivable that the processes of
natural selection at the gene level, achieved by testing the fitness of a succession
of varying phenotypes, could equip a species with all the information it needed
for survival (Partridge, 1979; Waddington, 1969). Information gain in this case
would occur by the differential survival of the more reproductively successful
gene combinations in each generation until the optimal phenotype was
achieved. The resultant gene pool represented by the population as a whole is in
effect a storehouse of information reflecting all past adaptations and all past
environmental conditions. At conception each new member of that population
is 'simply a memory-store embedded in cytoplasm' (Plotkin, 1981, p. 381). A
phylogenetic information store, or memory, encoded at the gene level could
thus provide the basis for all the observed physical and behavioural adaptations
of a species. In behavioural terms the outcome would be a genetically coded
response repertoire which provides an appropriate reaction for every possible
situation.

The world, however, is not unchanging and this creates problems for the gene
pool when it comes to providing adaptations suitable for future environments.
There are several reasons for this. First, it is clear that the gene pool must
provide evolutionary fitness not only for the presently experienced environment
but also must provide potential fitness for the future (Thoday, 1953). Speaking
teleologically, the gene pool should ideally be able to predict the environmental
changes which are likely to take place. Some environmental changes *are*
predictable and can be built into gene-based phylogenetic memory — circadian
rhythms and the succession of seasons for example. Other changes, such as

those created by the continued evolution of other species or the precise location of food supplies on a short-term basis, may be less predictable from the perspective of a single evolving species. It is also the case that immediate fitness and potential fitness are best served by different, or even antagonistic, strategies. Immediate fitness is most clearly represented by a set of highly specialized adaptations. Potential fitness, on the other hand, requires a more general set of adaptations, suitable to a variety of possible environments. Where high degrees of environmental unpredictability exist the cost of providing sufficient specialist adaptations for every possible eventuality by direct genetic coding could be very high, perhaps prohibitively so. It nevertheless remains true that in any particular environment the product of the specialist strategy is likely to prove more efficient than its generalist counterpart, providing of course that the specializations are appropriate, which in turn means once again that the environment must be predicted. One way out of this dilemma is to abandon precise predictions and provide some potential for adaptation to future environments on a speculative basis. This type of strategy is embodied in the variation which occurs within each generation as a result of genetic recombination in the process of sexual reproduction as well as the possible contributions from mutations, inversions, deletions and translocations which can occur at the chromosomal level (Maynard-Smith, 1975). Apart from being wasteful in that many of these 'speculative variants' are not successful the method by which the variants are tested involves a delay, generational dead time, which limits its effectiveness as a strategy for coping with change. The gene combinations which are selected under one set of environmental conditions as being the most suitable for those conditions and are selectively passed on to the next generation may encounter a different set of environmental conditions, for which they are likely to be less suitable. The information in phylogenetic memories must inevitably lag behind environmental change by at least the time it takes to produce a new generation. Where rapid changes are combined with long periods of sexual immaturity during development the problem of generational dead time is a severely limiting one (Lorenz, 1969).

Given the limitations inherent in phylogenetic mechanisms when it comes to coping with change, species must either avoid or minimize changes originating in their environments or they must develop subsidiary mechanisms for dealing with them. It is difficult to see how environmental change could be avoided completely but several strategies exist for minimizing it. The most obvious one is for a species to occupy a geographical area which is buffered in some way from change — a deep ocean trench or a polar ice cap for example. There are in fact a number of classic 'living fossils' which have avoided the need to change. One of these is *Lingula*, a shellfish living buried in sand or mud, which has persisted unchanged for 600 million years since Cambrian times. Similarly *Limulus*, the horseshoe crab and the coelacanth, *Latimeria*, have not been significantly redesigned for some 400 million years. Avoiding change may involve a high degree of specialization. The nematode worm *Allantonema*, for example, spends its entire life as a parasite in the body and droppings of the bark beetle *Hylobius*, itself an occupier of a highly specific environment (Kerkut, 1961). It seems reasonable to suggest in fact that the majority of species adopt avoid-change strategies aimed at reducing environmental variation for at least parts of their lives. The selection of species-typical nesting sites and the construction of elaborate and stereotyped nests by some birds would be an example of a local avoid-change strategy. Similarly the critical stages in the early development of mammals are sheltered from change by the fact that offspring are nurtured within the homeostatically controlled environment of the mother's body. Despite its advantages, though, the avoidance of environmental change also imposes limitations, particularly on the exploitation of new or variably distributed resources. It prevents opportunism. It also makes the extinction of the species that much more likely if their environment, despite their precautions, does change.

If it is impossible, or strategically undesirable, to avoid environmental change the species must develop processes for coping with that change. As already noted, some changes, like the daily light–dark cycle, are sufficiently predictable for phylogenetic mechanisms to build into the species a schema or model to represent the change and so form the basis for adaptations which must be programmed in relation to it (Oatley, 1975, 1978). Where phylogenetic mechanisms cannot cope, however, subsidiary mechanisms must be evolved to provide the individual members of a species with a means of dealing with the particular environmental conditions which they encounter within their own lifetimes. One way of doing this is to provide the species with a variable, 'open' developmental programme, or set of programmes, so that the particular phenotype which emerges depends on the precise environmental conditions which the developing organism encounters. It must be stressed here that this is a very special provision which goes counter to the usual developmental strategy which depends on a 'closed' developmental programme which is buffered against environmental variation. This conservative rule of what Bateson (1982) calls 'developmental homoeostasis' is what normally ensures that the same developmental path is followed as far as possible in all members of the same species despite variations in, say, nutritional levels. See Plotkin (1981) for further discussion of open and closed programmes of development.

Variable development or, to use Plotkin and Odling-Smee's term, variable epigenesis constitutes a second level of information gain and storage. It is a capacity which is primed at the first, phylogenetic level. Variable epigenesis involves the specification by the gene pool not only of the likely range of environmental conditions but also the type of developmental trajectory which will cope most effectively with each of them. A much-quoted example of variable epigenesis is provided by the migratory locust, *Locusta migratoria* (Bateson, 1981; Dempster, 1963). Under conditions of low population density *Locusta migratoria* leads a relatively harmless existence as a solitary grasshopper. With increasing numbers, however, the offspring of these non-migratory individuals develop differently from their parents, becoming gregarious and migratory, often travelling long distances and causing incalculable harm if they invade cultivated areas. The behaviour, geographical distribution and physical appearance of the migratory and non-migratory forms of this insect are so dissimilar that they were at one time classified as different species. This is an example where the 'openness' of the developmental programme is limited to two distinct alternatives cued by a small range of environmental factors. A similar situation exists in the case of sexual differentiation in mammalian and avian central nervous systems though here the organizing factor is a hormonal influence during a critical period of development (Arai, 1981; Konishi & Gurney, 1982; Toran-Allerand, 1981). Variable epigenesis is also seen to occur with greater openness in the development of mammalian nervous systems and examples of the effects of environmental influences on the development of the visual system in particular are given below (also see Hickey, 1981). Behavioural development can also be shaped by environmental events in the process of imprinting. I shall return to a discussion of imprinting and related phenomena but for the moment it is sufficient to note that they are treated here, on account of their developmental status and relative irreversibility, as products of second level systems of information gain and storage. They represent stages in developmental programmes which are 'open' for a specified period in order to gain a particular class of information which is needed for their completion. I should also make it clear that on this point I am diverging from Plotkin and Odling-Smee's account as they consider imprinting as a product of third level systems.

Variable epigenesis frees the phylogenetic mechanism from the need to predict the specific environment that a given individual will encounter. It is limited, however, both by the need to predict and make provision for a range of environments and also by the fact that once a particular developmental pathway has been selected its trajectory is irreversible. Second level systems allow information gain during development in order to complete phylogenetically primed behavioural programmes which will subsequently be available to the animal as constant directives to action irrespective of subsequent experience. In this sense they are systems which are briefly open to information and then become closed systems. 'Development' for the present discussion can be seen as extending from conception to the time at which the individual becomes reproductively competent and so able to feed successful alleles back into the gene pool. The critical, or 'sensitive' period for second level information gain within a given behavioural programme may be very short and precisely timed or, in other instances, may represent a relatively large proportion of the total development period.

To be able to cope with environmental changes which are reversible, and possibly also short-lasting when compared to the lifetime of the individual species member, a third level of information gain and storage is needed. Examples of specialist subsystems at this level are those which subserve learning and memory. Another example is the immune system. Systems at this third level are developed to compensate for the shortcomings of mechanisms at the other two levels. Third level systems, like second level systems, operate within the lifetime of a given individual and their effects are limited to that lifetime in the sense that information gained and stored in them cannot be fed back into the phylogenetic information stores of the gene pool. That is to say, as far as we know at present, Lamarckian forms of inheritance do not exist (Partridge, 1979). Information held in the first level, phylogenetic memory stores, however, can be and, in the interests of efficiency, should be, fed forward and incorporated in third level systems. In practical terms this means that learning and memory systems, for example, will be designed with constraints as to what types of information can be acquired and stored, on the basis of their past utility to the species. The advantage of this is that they will be facilitated in collecting the full set of relevant information by the fact that they already possess phylogenetically stored information and are primed to attend to, encode and store the most salient stimuli, events and relationships in their environments. The price of this efficiency is paid for in that it is the genetic mechanisms which must once again determine what is relevant, salient, worth storing, etc., and this once more demands some prediction of the type of environment in which the species will find itself. An advance in third level systems which would free the species from this constraint would be the development of generalist, as opposed to specialist, information storage capacities. The enormous cost in terms of energy and space, not to say the futility, of providing a system which unselectively encoded and stored all possible information obtainable from its environment suggests that we should not expect to find an example of a truly generalist information collection and storage capacity in the animal kingdom. All third level systems are specialist and phylogenetically constrained, though some species may well have a greater array of specialist systems than others. They are all, however, seen as continually open systems in the sense that they retain throughout both development and post-developmental periods the facility for adding new information and for revising or updating already stored information in the light of later experience.

A major limitation of information gain and storage at the second and third levels is that the information so gained is restricted to a particular individual. It is true that the genetic instructions which gave rise to the systems involved will be selectively retained for future generations as a result of the increased fitness contributed by the information gained on an individual basis. The information itself will, nevertheless, be lost with the demise of the learner. In a sense this is how it should be, as individually gained information, however useful to that individual, if it were to be passed back into the gene pool would suffer the problems of generational dead time and failure to track change which beset first level systems. If, however, a mechanism were to exist for the direct transmission of individually acquired information throughout the members of a species then that information could be passed by extra-genetic means not only to the individual's peers but also to subsequent generations, provided of course that their life-spans overlapped sufficiently. In the case of humans, language has evolved to subserve information gain and storage at this fourth, cultural level and is deployed particularly effectively in the method of direct instruction. The ability of one individual to act as a source of information for other members of the species is not, however, limited to humans or by the presence of a natural language. The phenomena of social facilitation, observational learning and imitation all conform to this definition of cultural transmission of behaviour and are shown by a variety of species (see Davey, 1981, pp. 267–75; Galef, 1976; Manning, 1979, pp. 199–201). Perhaps the best known example of cultural transmission in non-humans is that of a group of Japanese monkeys who acquired the habit of washing sweet potatoes in the sea to rid them of sand. This behaviour was seen to originate with one female monkey and to then spread via her close relatives throughout the colony (Miyadi, 1964). Other examples include the stealing of milk from doorstep milk bottles, displayed by titmice in Southern England (Hinde & Fisher, 1952), local variations in the styles which oyster catchers adopt to open the shells of marine mussels (Norton-Griffiths, 1969) and the dialects found in the song of the American white-crowned sparrow (Marler & Tamura, 1964). It is worth noting here that though social facilitation, observational learning and imitation can be loosely classified together as types of cultural transmission, they may be mediated by very different processes and, furthermore, any one example of cultural transmission may be difficult to classify as depending exclusively on only one of them (See Davey, 1981, pp. 267–75 for a discussion). Social facilitation, as seen in instances where a whole flock of feeding birds will become airborn if one of its

24

members suddenly takes flight, is phylogenetically programmed and requires no individual learning on the part of the receivers of the transmitted information. The effects of each instance of social facilitation are thus transitory and there is no gain in information within the population. Social facilitation is most easily attributed to first level systems and is not considered in the present scheme as a true example of cultural transmission. Observational learning by contrast can lead to long-term changes in behaviour within a population. It is thus a fourth level process though it depends primarily on existing third level information-gaining systems. The ability to imitate the actions of others irrespective of context and to utilize the information gained as a basis for future action, as seen primarily in primates, has evolved specifically to serve fourth level, cultural, information-gaining and storing systems. It will be evident from later examples that cultural transmission also occurs in variable epigenesis during second level information gain as well as within the mammalian immune system in the case where, for example, individually acquired immunity is passed from parent to offspring in the maternal milk.

As with second and third level information storage, culturally acquired information cannot directly affect information stored at the first level in the gene pool. The capacity for transmitting and receiving cultural information, however, is specified genetically and is thereby constrained in terms of the types of cultural organization which can emerge to support it and in the nature and extent of information sharing. This also means that the biological mechanisms underlying the development of fourth level information-gaining systems are open to selection pressure. Equally, when a new habit is adopted on the basis of cultural transmission the fact that it can be possessed by the entire population and their offspring allows new selection pressures to operate at the gene level to produce anatomical as well as other behavioural adaptations which will increase the effectiveness of that cultural habit in future generations. So long as the acquisition and storage of information is limited to single individuals its presence in future generations is unpredictable. When the behaviour becomes reliably shared, however, it is sufficiently predictable for genetic mechanisms to operate on the basis of its presence. In this sense culturally stored behavioural adaptations may become as stable and predictable as phylogenetically stored relfexes or instincts.

2.2 Referents and Substrates

In order to clarify a number of points which may have already begun to concern the reader it is necessary to introduce, and to some extent adapt, Plotkin and Odling-Smee's notion of a 'referent' and to distinguish it from what I shall call a 'substrate'. For the purposes of this chapter a referent is an abstraction which identifies the global organizational unit which gains information. A substrate on the other hand is any entity, substance or structure which serves physically to store the information which has been gained and/or to express that information in anatomical, biochemical or behavioural form. Each level of information gain has its own referent, which is uniquely its own, but may operate via a variable number of substrates which can be shared across levels. The referent for the first level of information gain is the gene pool of a breeding population and is a product of phylogenesis. The information contained in the gene pool is expressed in physical terms first of all in the actual genetic endowment of the individual members of the population and, via epigenesis, in all the organ systems of those individuals. In the case of reflexes and innate or species-typical behaviours the final substrate involved is the central nervous system. The referent for the second level is embodied in the variable development of a phenotype from a genotype. The information gained and stored in variable epigenesis is represented in the final phenotypic form of the individual and may involve changes across a number of its organ systems, as in the case of the migratory locust, or may be more limited, as in the case of developmental plasticity in visual systems and in imprinting, where the substrate is the central nervous system. The third level referent is the autonomous capacity for information gain and storage possessed by an individual and which is available throughout its lifetime. Third level systems always occupy highly specific substrates. The immune system has its own unique mechanisms. Learning and memory are mediated by the central nervous system. (The interested reader will find that Plotkin and Odling-Smee, 1979, considered each of the specific third level systems as a referent in its own right, so that the central nervous system was a 'referent'. In my definition of a third level referent I have tried to maintain the distinction between referents and substrates.)

The referent for the fourth level is the accumulation of cultural information which occurs within a population. By analogy with the gene pool this fourth referent has been called the 'cultural pool' with its constituents (information, ideas, etc.) distributed throughout an interacting population. Like the gene pool its existence does not depend on individual members of the population, it is dynamic, constantly changing and to the same extent an abstraction. This similarity has also been noted by Dawkins (1976) in his suggestion that we consider ideas, fashions, tunes, etc., as units of cultural transmission or imitation. To heighten the analogy he calls his units memes, which are seen as interacting competitively in a meme pool. Fourth level systems depend on second and third level systems for their existence and share their substrates. The total immunity of a population for instance is stored in the immune systems of its members, though of course it transcends any individual. Individual nervous systems similarly form the major substrate for the pool of culturally transmitted learned information. Parts of the cultural pool, though, can exist independently of the nervous systems of the population which generated it in the form of information stored in libraries, computer memory banks, museums and so forth, as well as in the form of artefacts, machinery and tools with which the species surrounds itself. Substrates for the fourth level of information storage are thus unique in that they can be both biological and non-biological.

Before leaving the question of substrates I would like to comment on the question of distribution of function within the central nervous system, which has now been cited as a substrate for all four levels of information gain and storage. I believe that, where levels one, two and three are concerned, the phylogenetic approach adopted here would imply that functionally and anatomically distinct subsystems exist within the central nervous system to serve each level independently. Indeed, Plotkin (1981) has suggested that a difference in neurological substrate may be the only reliable means of distinguishing between the products of second and third levels of information gain. Such an arrangement would certainly be consistent with the principles of modularity in nervous system design which appear to operate within third level systems (see Section 2.5).

The major characteristics of the four levels of information gain and storage in living systems are summarized in Table 2.1.

2.3 Interactions Between Levels

It is assumed both here and by Plotkin and Odling-Smee that adaptations, and I am considering behavioural adaptations in particular, will be specified as fully as possible by first level systems and only when these prove inadequate will higher level systems develop. Second and third level systems can be seen as progressively finer tuning mechanisms which operate to refine the coarse-grained adaptations supplied genetically and, in particular, to compensate for the failure of first level systems to cope with unpredictability in future environments. The development of fourth level systems depends on the prior existence of second or third level systems and serves mainly as a means of amplifying the capacity of mechanisms operating at the lower levels by providing an alternative to the gene pool for trans-generational information gain and storage. In many ways the fourth level systems, as already noted, have similar properties to first level systems. It would follow from this account that, so far as the first three levels are concerned, information stored at any higher level can only be understood in terms of its relationship to the information available from lower systems.

2.3.1 Level One and Level Two

So far as the relationship between the first and second levels of information gain is concerned, one example has already been given of the emergence of a particular phenotype in the migratory locust as a result of variable epigenesis. This is an example of a rather crude switching between two developmental trajectories, both of which were fully specified at the first level. More subtle differences in the final form of structures within the mammalian nervous system could be given as examples of developmentally induced variations within a general range specified genetically. The neocortex, for example, develops a thicker structure with large neural cell bodies and more glial cells as well as having more densely branched dendrites with greater numbers of synaptic spines, when young animals encounter complex and stimulating environments (Greenough, 1978; Horn et al., 1973; Rosenzweig et al., 1972). Similarly, it has been shown that neurons in the visual cortex of cats may change their preferred orientation specificity from horizontal bar stimuli to vertical stimuli, or vice versa, depending on the predominant orientation of the stimuli which they encounter during critical periods of their development (Blakemore & Cooper, 1970; Hirsch & Jacobson, 1975). In both these examples it could be suggested that the general form of the particular nervous system structures was laid down on the basis of information stored genetically, but that the developmental programme was left sufficiently open for the final structure to be matched precisely to the environment which the developing individual actually encountered. Jacobson (1974) has suggested that the conflict between deterministic and probabilistic processes in central nervous system development

Table 2.1 The Characteristics of the Four Levels of Information Gain and Storage

Level	Referent (+ process) Supra-individual	Intra-individual	Substrates	Nature of stored[1] material	Reversibility[2]	Examples
4	*Cultural pool or Meme pool (Cultural transmission)*		CNS and Immune system. Non-biological information stores	Culturally acquired information	Yes if based on level 3 systems (open)	Imitation and observation learning. Potato washing in monkeys. Human education
					No once sensitive period is passed if based on level 2 systems (open then closed)	Dialects in white-crowned sparrow
3		*Autonomous capacity for learning and memory.* Mediated by specialist information gaining and storing subsystems (Learning and memory)	CNS and immune system	Individually acquired information	Yes (open)	Pavlovian and operant conditioning. Cognitive mapping. Learning set formation

2	*Variable epigenesis* (Variable development)	One or many organ systems including CNS	Developmentally acquired information Expressed as phenotype[3]	No once sensitive period is passed (open then closed)	Plasticity in developing visual system. Alternative phenotype in migratory locust. Sexual differentiation of CNS in mammals. Imprinting
1	*Gene pool* (Phylogenesis)	DNA and all organ systems including CNS	Genetically acquired information Genotype	No (closed)	Reflexes, 'innate' behaviours. Biological constraints on learning. Innate teaching mechanisms

[1] This refers to storage at an intra-individual level.
[2] Reversible (open) systems are those which allow change or updating in individual information stores.
[3] This includes the behavioural phenotype.
CNS = central nervous system.
DNA = Deoxyribonucleic acid, the genetic material.

which these examples imply, is resolved by the existence of two classes of neurons. One of which (Class I) develop first, under tight genetic control, while the others (Class II) show variable development in response to hormonal, sensory and other influences.

A similar solution to the deterministic/probabilistic problem is adopted in many instances where the development of behavioural adaptations is concerned. The gene pool can specify the general form of a behavioural pattern but frequently requires certain information, such as the precise colouration of the mother, for its complete specification, which is only available to the developing individual. In these cases first level systems specify a partially open developmental programme which can be closed by a particular type of experience during a critical period in development. The information stored in first level systems is thus completed by information gained and stored in second level systems. The supplementary information store is classed as second level as it forms the basis for an irreversible change in the developmental trajectory and results in a variety of (behavioural) phenotypes in the population as a result of environmental influences during development. It is an important aspect of this process that the gene pool specifies not only the timing of the second level information gain but also specifies within quite precise limits the nature of the information which should be encoded and stored.

Before giving examples of variations in behavioural phenotypes which emerge from interactions between first and second level information stores it is worth considering whether there are any examples of behaviours which are specified completely on the basis of genetically stored information. Basic bodily reactions such as tendon reflexes might be expected to be sufficiently predictable in terms of their utility and of the stimuli by which they should be elicited for first level systems to cope. This assumption may be premature, however, as other, apparently equally basic, responses do seem to require an additional experiential input during development to complete their programming. Reyniers (cited by Manning, 1967), for example, has provided evidence that neonatal rats require tactile stimulation of the genital region, normally provided by the mother post-partum, to initiate the reflex emptying of the bladder. If this environmental trigger is provided the bladder will subsequently empty reflexively when it is full, otherwise the reflex fails to develop. The environmental cue is presumably needed in this case because the developing rat's genetic programme is not in control of the time off its own birth and so needs to acquire that information via the mother rat's behaviour. As there are arguably two phenotypes involved, one with, and one (soon to die) without, a bladder reflex this seems to be an acceptable, if elementary, case of an interaction between the first two levels of information gain. It could be suggested by extension of this argument that all development involves just such an interaction. For any further analysis it may, as Gottlieb (1976) suggests, be essential to distinguish between experiential inputs during development which are inductive (channel development one way or another), and those which are facilitative (influence the timing or vigour of developmental processes) or serve a maintenance role (maintaining the integrity of what has already been achieved developmentally). The important point, however, is that in all three cases two distinct referents are involved in the process; the gene pool and the developing phenotype.

Perhaps the clearest examples of first and second level system interactions are those covered by the general label of 'imprinting' (Bateson, 1971; Davey, 1981, Ch. 8; Manning, 1979, Ch. 2). A number of species of birds and mammals can be shown to form a preference for the sight, sound or smell of objects encountered during a sensitive, or 'critical', period of their development (Bateson, 1981). The imprinted object is commonly the infant's own mother, though imprinting-like processes can also be detected in relation to food preferences and the home locality. In the case of the precocial young of ducks and geese, for example, the tendency to follow the imprinted object is strong ('filial' imprinting) and under unnatural conditions birds exposed to humans, cardboard boxes, balloons and the like during the sensitive period will show a positive preference for the imprinted object. Filial imprinting exhibits a degree of plasticity within the sensitive period and in the case of chicks imprinted on artificial stimuli it is possible to reverse the process if a second imprinting exposure occurs within 6 days of hatching (Salzen & Meyer, 1968). Later in life there is evidence that 'sexual' imprinting has also occurred, frequently to the same objects, and the artificially imprinted birds, particularly males, may show sexual advances to boxes, balloons or whatever. Under normal circumstances, then, the animal in this particular example is primed genetically to obtain and store information about the physical appearance of its mother and thereby of the female members of its species in order to complete behavioural programmes underlying following reactions or attachment in infancy and sexual behaviour as an adult. In other cases, such as that of the bullfinch, a more elaborate situation exists in which adolescent imprinting may override earlier experience in the determination of mate selection (Nicolai, 1956, cited by Hinde, 1970). The duration of the sensitive period for sexual imprinting clearly may vary widely among species but once it is passed the imprinting process appears to be irreversible (Immelman, 1972). There is evidence also that the choice of a mate by males is directed by first level systems to be slightly different (but not too different) from the mother and siblings who served as the imprinted objects in order to preserve a balance between inbreeding and outbreeding in the population (Bateson, 1982).

Where the need is for long-term, irreversible information stores and where these are to be formed during a delimited developmental period, the involvement of second level systems is clearly most appropriate. It would also follow that the substrates which serve these second level information-gaining processes should be highly specific and distinct from those subserving third level systems (see Plotkin, 1981). There is some preliminary evidence in fact to support the existence of such a dissociation. Imprinting in chicks, for example, is prevented by lesions of the intermediate part of the medial hyperstriatum ventrale (McCabe, et al., 1981) whereas the same lesion does not prevent chicks from learning a heat-reinforced visual discrimination (McCabe et al., 1982).

2.3.2   Level One and Level Three

Where the requirement is for information stores which are open on a longer-term basis so that new information can be added throughout the life of the individual, and in particular where the stored information itself must be modified or even reversed, interactions between first and third level systems will be involved. In fact in most instances interactions will be evident between first, second and third level systems, but for simplicity only the first and third level components will be considered. In the case of the immune system the ability to develop immunity is clearly genetically given and the range of antibodies which can be produced is limited, presumably by the range of important antigens which the species has encountered during phylogeny (Novikoff & Holtzman, 1976 pp. 244–7). Within these genetic constraints new immune responses can be acquired by the individual animal, usually with favourable results but sometimes with disastrous consequences for that individual in the case of degenerative diseases such a polymyositis and myasthenia gravis which may develop as the result of auto-immune reactions (Brain & Walton, 1969).

Where behavioural adaptations are concerned there is once more a compromise to be reached between the economy of supplying the majority of the information needed directly from phylogenetic stores and the flexibility which accrues from allowing the individual animal to acquire its own individually tailored information stores upon which to base its behaviour (Alcock, 1975, Ch. 9). Some behaviours have to be right the first time they are executed — the first flight of the young of a cliff-nesting gull for example. In other cases there is simply not time for the individual animal to gather the relevant information. The wasp *Philanthus triangulum*, for example, is a predator of honeybees and is better served in its short lifetime by an innate mechanism for identifying and attacking them than it would be by a capacity to select by trial and error from the hundreds of other available insect species the one which it was best suited to capturing (Alcock, 1975, p. 256). Even in cases of innate or instinctive behaviours, however, the possibility of subsequent improvement or modification by later experience and learning may not easily be excluded. The first flight is a notoriously clumsy affair in most birds compared to later performance. Whether first level systems leave only a little room for individual information gain and storage or a relatively large amount in any given instance, it is always the case that third level systems are constrained by first level information stores. The first level stores serve to guide information gain in third level systems and normally make them more efficient. They act as what Lorenz (1969, 1977) has aptly called 'innate teaching mechanisms', though, as we shall see later, under unnatural, experimental conditions the innate teaching mechanisms can be seen to lead the animals astray.

Some examples of improvement in 'innate' responses with repetition apparently involve no more than repeated exercise of the response itself and so are perhaps best regarded as examples in behavioural terms of the normal interactions which occur between the environment and the genotype to form a particular phenotype. One such is the development of feeding in the cuttlefish, where it is seen that the latency to initiate an attack on a shrimp decreases significantly over the first 10 such attempts by a newly hatched individual (Wells, 1958). This improvement occurs irrespective of whether the cuttlefish is rewarded with a shrimp, or punished for its attack with an electric shock and is still evident in older animals when first exposed to shrimps. In other instances a case can be made for the improvement of instinctive behaviours by third level systems of information gain and storage. The jackdaw, for instance, appears to have a genetic programme which leads it to bring a variety of materials to a prospective nest-site and to test the suitability of each item by bringing it into contact with the base and pushing it inwards with a vibratory motion (Lorenz, 1969, 1977). This 'tremble-shove' manoeuvre results in some materials becoming tightly wedged into the existing framework. The individual bird will thereafter select increasingly only those materials which produce the intrinsically reinforcing feedback of becoming firmly fixed. This system obviously allows for considerable opportunism in the selection of nesting material. The most bizarre objects recorded by Lorenz as being tried out by inexperienced nest-builders are pieces of glass, ice and the bases of old light bulbs. The failure of such objects to respond to tremble-shoving leads to their rejection and individual birds become specialists in selecting the most suitable material in their locality, taking only twigs from a particular type of tree for example. In industrial areas nests may be built in part of strips of metal waste or wire which though they produce excellent feedback from tremble-shoving, are unsuitable for the purpose to which they have been put by virtue of their properties as conductors of thermal energy. In this case the innate teaching mechanism has resulted in inappropriate behaviour because it has been unable to anticipate the occurrence of these particular human artefacts and serves as an example of the limitations of first level systems when faced with unpredicted environments.

Hailman (1969) has similarly claimed that food soliciting by infant gulls, that classic of 'innate' responses, is in fact a product of instinct–learning interactions. The accuracy with which the newly hatched laughing-gull pecks at the red beak of its parent to elicit regurgitated food improves rapidly over time, in part as a product of the maturation of sensory and motor systems. Some of the improvement, however, and the development of head rotation by the chick during beak pecking, Hailman suggests, is a product of individual learning. Similarly the preference which these chicks show for pecking at a red stimulus, particularly a vertically elongated one which moves horizontally, is generated by first level systems and serves to ensure that the majority of early pecks are directed at the parent's beak, but later changes in the beak pecking response seem to involve learning. Newly hatched laughing-gull chicks, for instance, do not differentiate between the beaks of their own parents and the rather differently marked ones of herring-gulls, nor for that matter do they seem to be affected by whether or not the beak has a head attached to it. By the time the chicks are a week old, however, they show what appear to be learned preferences for their own parents and are sensitive to detailed differences in the shape of head and beak. The selection of suitable food objects by the young herring-gull could also be a product of learning, in this case actively assisted by the behaviour of the parent bird. Initially the chick will peck the parent's beak even after food has been regurgitated on to the floor of the nest. Parent birds under these circumstances will eventually pick up the food, say a small fish, in their beaks and the chick, partly as a consequence of its early pecking inaccuracy, makes some pecks at the food itself. A related mechanism also exists in that newly hatched chicks will peck at the white tip of the bills of older chicks in the nest. If this occurs while the older chick is pecking regurgitated food some of the younger chick's pecks will also encounter the food. Under experimental conditions newly hatched herring-gull chicks were seen to find food sooner when tested with an experienced chick than if tested in isolation or with a companion who was equally naive about food. In this way perhaps, the herring-gull chick acquires and stores information concerning suitable food objects to guide not only its behaviour within the nest but also to direct its later behaviour as an adult. The reader will also have realized that this is an example of cultural transmission of information, based on third level systems and guided by information stored at the first level.

Instincts, in Hailman's terms, may be learned — or at least, partially so. The other side of this particular coin is represented by the recently recognized importance of considering the role of first level systems in experimental situations whose primary concern has been with third level learning and memory (Bolles, 1979, Ch. 9; Davey, 1981, Ch. 5; Garcia et al., 1972; Shettleworth, 1972, 1979; Seligman, 1970). In other words, to invert Hailman's phrase, all learning is instinctive — or at least, partially so. What is now a classic experiment in this field of so-called 'biological constraints' on learning was reported by Garcia and Koelling (1966). These authors found that if rats were made sick by X-irradiation or the injection of a toxin (e.g. lithium chloride) following the consumption of 'tasty' water (flavoured with salt or saccharin) they would reliably avoid that flavour in future. If, however, the water was made 'bright and noisy' by accompanying its consumption with a flashing light and a clicking relay, subsequent sickness did not make the rats avoid 'bright-noisy' water in future. Exactly the opposite outcome was seen when drinking either 'tasty' or 'bright-noisy' water was followed by foot shock — only the 'bright-noisy' water was avoided on subsequent trials. What is learned and remembered by the rat in this situation is evidently influenced by information stored at the first level. Under natural conditions it is more probable that a rat will be made sick by something it has eaten and the gene pool has reflected this likelihood by favouring a learning system which selectively registers tastes and subsequent physiological states as one of its specialist functions. Painful stimuli to the surface of the body, on the other hand, for the rat are rarely the result of ingesting substances with a particular taste though they may well be predicted by particular auditory and visual stimuli in its environment. Quite in line with this interpretation is the fact that quail, whose initial food selection is visuallly guided, will associate the colour of drinking water more readily than its taste with subsequent illness under conditions where rats make exactly the opposite associations (Wilcoxon et al., 1971). These experiments and related studies (see Davey, 1981; Shettleworth, 1972; Seligman, 1970, for reviews) are convincing evidence that the information which an animal gains and stores is determined by what its gene pool is able to predict will be useful. This once again hinges on the ability of phylogenetic mechanisms to predict the animal's future environment and the relationships which are likely to exist within it. The system of 'prepared' learning mechanisms (Seligman, 1970) by definition works well in predictable environments, but, as the above examples show, reliance on such mechanisms when the animal encounters a genetically unexpected environment may prevent it from learning what are in fact perfectly reliable and potentially useful bits of information.

In addition to tailoring learning systems to environmental needs, genetic mechanisms are admirably suited to providing economical solutions in situations where an appropriate response is required the first time an animal encounters an external aversive stimulus. Taking the rat as an example once more, Bolles (1970, 1979) has described two major species-specific defence reactions (SSDRs). One is quite simply the tendency to escape from, or subsequently to avoid, the aversive event by running away. If no escape route is evident, however, rats become immobile or 'freeze'. In an experimental situation where the rat is required to learn to produce a response which is consistent with its SSDRs it will do so with alacrity. Rats will learn to jump out of a box to avoid shock in a single trial or to run in a running wheel for shock avoidance in about 40 trials. Where the SSDRs are inconsistent with the appropriate response, however, such as when required to press a lever to avoid foot shock, most rats learn exceedingly slowly if at all, though they learn to produce the same response very rapidly to secure food. To make Bolles's list of SSDRs more complete it is worth noting that it has recently been shown that the rat will, if suitable material is available, return to the source of an aversive stimulus, such as a shock prod, and will bury it (Terlecki *et al.*, 1979; Wilkie *et al.*, 1979). This highly stereotyped response occurs reliably with a single exposure to the aversive stimulus and is another product of first level information storage which is incompatible with many of the responses which experimental psychologists have tried to teach rats as a basis for shock avoidance.

A tendency to approach and investigate stimuli which predict the occurrence of favourable events also appears to be genetically prescribed for many species. This type of behaviour has been demonstrated in the context of appetitive Pavlovian conditioning, where a distinctive stimulus (the conditional stimulus) reliably precedes the occurrence of a second stimulus (the unconditional stimulus) such as food. The phenomenon of conditional stimulus approach has been called autoshaping or sign-tracking (Hearst & Jenkins, 1974; Schwartz & Gamzu, 1977). Under normal circumstances this is presumably adaptive and the predictive stimulus bears not only a close temporal relationship to the unconditional stimulus but also a close spatial relationship. If the sign stimulus is separated from the food which it predicts by placing the conditional stimulus at one end of a long alleyway and the food hopper at the other end, however, pigeons will waste so much time tracking the conditional stimulus that they will miss the food reinforcement which it predicts and which is briefly available at the other end of the alley (Hearst & Jenkins, 1974). A similar, and equally maladaptive, persistence in sign-tracking can be seen, again particularly in pigeons, when any contact with the predictive stimulus is punished by the omission of the food reward on that trial (Williams & Williams, 1969). As in the case of some shock avoidance situations, then, the animals' preprogrammed reactions can be seen to take precedence over, and interfere with, adaptive performance in experimentally contrived appetitive situations. Similar types of 'misbehaviour' were described by Breland and Breland (1972) as products of 'instinctive drift' and appeared as genetically predisposed complications in attempts to train animals to perform in television commercials. In one such example pigs were trained to pick up large wooden coins and deposit them, for food rewards, into a large piggy-bank. Their subjects rapidly learned to perform this task and were happily depositing four or five coins for each reinforcement when the experimenters noted slow and incorrigible changes in the pigs' attitudes towards the coins. Instead of depositing their coins they began to drop them to the ground, root them along the ground, pick them up, drop them again, root and so on until eventually very few coins were reaching the piggy-bank and consequently very few rewards were being earned. Raccoons under similar circumstances 'drifted' into repeatedly 'dipping' their coins into the slot of the piggy-bank without letting go, and rubbing them together in a miserly fashion. With both the pigs and the raccoons it would appear that as the association between the coin and the food became stronger, genetically programmed food-gathering behaviours were ever more powerfully elicited by the coins and eventually disrupted the adaptive responses which had already been acquired on the basis of third level information gain and storage.

What I have hoped to show by this excursion into the biological constraints literature is, first, that what is learned and remembered by individual animals is a supplement to, and is guided by, information stored in first level systems. The second point is that, while this is normally a formula for rapid and appropriate learning, the interaction of information stores may be maladaptive in the short term if the learner encounters unusual environments, such as those presented experimentally. In this case first level systems may take precedence and either prevent the storage of relevant information by third level systems or may prevent its expression in behaviour even though the learner had clearly acquired and stored the information at an earlier stage of training.

2.3.3 Level Four

It has already been noted that cultural transmission of information at the fourth level of information gain and storage depends on the prior existence of second and third level systems and that both of these in turn are specified genetically and are consequently constrained by first level systems. The major attribute of fourth level systems is the massive increase in the amount of information which can be gained by an individual in its lifetime and the speed with which it can be gained, compared to intra-individual trial-and-error methods for instance. A further increase in both capacity and rate of acquisition is achieved, particularly in a species such as *Homo sapiens* by the development of a special language system and in the use of non-biological information stores. Fourth level systems vary also from the situation in which other animals act as passive 'teachers' — as, for example, in the case of food learning in herring-gulls, dialects in white-crowned sparrows (see below) or potato washing in Japanese monkeys — to the involvement of active teachers in the case of humans. In so far as fourth level information gain can be seen as a special case of second and third level mechanisms there is probably no need to posit special information stores — it is only the source of the information which is unique. There are, however, a number of special adaptations which are associated with the elaboration of fourth level systems. In the case of humans the development of language has meant that much, though by no means all, information gain and storage is mediated via that particular system. It is also worth mentioning that once it is developed, a language system is available for the representation of individually, not only culturally, derived information. In fact if this results in more flexible representations, then this could be a reason in itself for developing a language irrespective of the need to communicate to others. What is clear is that linguistic ability requires prodigious amounts of space in neural terms, not only for the reception and production of speech (Geschwind, 1979) but also for storing its generative rules and the elements (words, meanings, etc.) which compose it (Dimond, 1980, Ch. 12; Kolb & Whishaw, 1980, Ch. 16). The ability to copy the actions of conspecifics and the capacity to understand the significance of the actions being imitated would be expected to develop as specialized attributes to facilitate fourth level systems. This creates a category of active cultural learners as opposed to passive learners and would be most effective perhaps when associated with active cultural teachers, though by no means limited to the prior existence of such individuals. Again, specialized neural machinery would be expected to subserve such abilities and, by way of example, it may be noted that in humans one aspect of ideomotor apraxia resulting from lesions of the supramarginal gyrus in the dominant hemisphere is a specific inability to imitate the actions of others (Walsh, 1978). The transmission and perpetuation of cultural information would also be enhanced by the existence of stable and well organized social groups. Indeed it has been suggested that much of the pressure towards intellectual improvement in primates is a product of the need to maintain a social order which will provide a stable substrate for the perpetuation of subsistence technologies (Humphrey, 1976). One useful supplement to primate social interaction, particularly where reciprocal altruism is concerned (Trivers, 1971), is the ability to recognize individual faces. In man, specific damage to the underside of both occipital lobes extending forward to the inner surface of the temporal lobes can result in prosopagnosia, an inability to recognize faces (Geschwind, 1979). Similarly, specialized circuitry for face recognition has also been described recently in the monkey brain (Rolls, 1981). In the present context then, a number of highly specialized systems, particularly within primate brains, can be seen as dedicated to the improvement of fourth level information gaining and storage systems.

2.3.4   *Interactions at All Four Levels*

In the previous examples of interaction I have for the most part arbitrarily selected only two of the four levels of information gain for consideration. In this final subsection on the topic I would like to take the case of the development of birdsong to illustrate the way in which information gained at all four levels may have to be considered in any complete description of a particular type of behaviour. It should first of all be noted that the developmental profile for vocalization varies enormously in different species of birds (Marler, 1981). The account which follows is not, therefore, intended to be a general description but is based primarily on some very elegant work conducted on the development of dialects in the song of the white-crowned sparrow, with additional material from two closely related species (Konishi, 1965; Manning, 1979, pp. 54–60; Marler, 1981; Marler & Tamura, 1964). The white-crowned sparrow if reared in isolation can produce a recognizable, albeit generalized, 'white-crowned sparrow' song, but can only do so if it can hear its own vocal output. Deafened individuals produce only a series of disconnected notes as adults. It is as if the phylogenetic information store of the gene pool supplied a neural template of the song, which the bird, when adult, matches by comparing its own output with the model which it carries in its own nervous system. If, however, a young bird, up to 3 months of age, is exposed to a particular example of white-crowned sparrow song it will, when it begins to sing its own song several months later, produce a faithful copy of that version. Exposure to the sample song during the critical period can be seen as a form of auditory imprinting which modifies the stored template to match the sample. The modified template is stored as a long-term memory (up to 240 days in swamp sparrows) and, again provided the bird can hear its own output, serves as a model upon which the adult song is based. The process of template modification appears to be a permanent one — once the adult song matches the stored template the adult birds can go on singing it normally even if they are subsequently deafened. The tight control which first level systems exert over the information gain during development is exemplified by the fact that, in the case of the white-crowned sparrow at least, exposure to the song of other species during the critical period does not affect the stored template and the generalized song emerges just as in totally isolated birds. Perhaps even more impressive as an example of the selectivity built into such systems is the fact that in the period when templates are being modified the developing swamp sparrow will reject song sparrow chunks in a song-salad constructed experimentally from syllables taken from the songs of the two species.

The modification of song templates is clearly an example of second level information gain and forms the basis upon which local dialects in birdsong are built. In a wide-ranging species, such as the white-crowned sparrow, groups of individuals may occupy quite different ecological niches. The gene pool of each sub-population will vary in response to local selection pressures to suit individuals to that particular habitat. It may thus be an advantage to a male to remain in, or return to, the locality in which it was born to maximize its breeding success (Alcock, 1975). It could do this by seeking to occupy territory near to individuals singing the song which it heard as a fledgling. The transmission and preservation of dialects within populations are examples of a cultural tradition and as such represent a fourth level system. The fact that it is based on second level systems makes the culture more rigid than would be the case with cultures based on third level systems. The transmission of information is from adult to youngster during a critical period. The imprinted information is then passed on unchanged in turn to a subsequent generation, and so forth. Conservatism is exactly what is required in this case of course and is why a second level system is involved.

The 'white-crowned sparrow' picture is not yet complete, however, as elements of individual, autonomous learning emerge in adult song production, related perhaps to individual recognition. Marler (1981) in particular describes 'inventions' which are individually produced and retained within the songs of adult white-crowned sparrows. These examples of third level information gain are, however, partitioned off from the products of second level systems which constitute the invariables of the dialect. The fixed dialect components are contained within the 'trill' patterns of white-crowned sparrow song, which do not vary among the local population. The individually generated components appear in separate, whistled sections of the song. New dialects can thus only emerge via, presumably very rare, variations in trill components of adult song. The complex interplay between levels of information gain and storage which appears in birdsong has parallels in the development of human language and the potential fruitfulness of using the former as a model for the latter is increasingly stressed (e.g. Marler, 1981) especially as both show lateralized neural control (Nottebohm, 1981).

2.4 Varieties of Memory within Third Level Systems

Having, I hope, made a convincing case for seeing information storage as a widespread phenomenon in the evolutionary strategies of all animal species, occurring within up to four distinct levels, it is recognized that the other contributors to this volume are primarily interested in information storage capacities based on third level systems. It is also true, contributors to this volume excepted of course, that the majority of psychologists are even more selective and concern themselves exclusively with verbal memory in humans. While this is an understandable preoccupation it has led to a monolithic view of memory and has resulted in serious difficulties when data collected in animal studies are presented for comparison, particularly where human clinical data and animal lesion data are concerned (Oakley, 1981a). The earlier part of this chapter has argued that third level memory is a specialist information storage system which evolved to complement and interact with information stored at other levels. The emergence of third level systems presented the opportunity for differentiation into specialist subsystems to cope with particular environmental demands and for the development of increasingly sophisticated information-processing and storage capacities. There is, thus, every reason to expect at least as much diversity within third level memory systems as there is between levels. I would like, therefore, to consider now the range of information storage capacities which might be expected to have evolved to subserve third level systems and to present some comparative and neuroanatomical data as evidence of their existence.

I have chosen to limit my discussion to those third level capacities which have the central nervous systems as a substrate as this is assumed in the usual psychological definition of memory. The exclusion of the fourth level from consideration, especially in the context of human memory, requires a little more by way of explanation. The fourth level of information gain and storage has as its referent the shared knowledge, ideas, etc. (the cultural pool) of a population of individuals. The information gain and storage within an individual consequently cannot occur at a higher level than level three even though some of the information stored will originate in fourth level systems and will in turn represent part of the substrate for that level of information gain. (The gene pool is an abstraction in the same way as the cultural pool and so the same situation arises when considering the individual in relation to first level systems. Information gain can only occur within individuals at levels two and three.) The fourth level of information gain and storage is thus only relevant to individual learning and memory as a cultural reservoir from which information can descend to the third level systems of the individual learner to supplement his own direct experience of environmental events and relationships.

All information storage systems face two major design decisions, namely what to store and for how long it should be retained. To a certain extent the decision on duration of storage has already been made by the selection of level three systems. Essential information which must be acquired once and then retained unchanged for the entire lifetime of the individual is best served by level two systems. There is, nevertheless, still a wide range of storage durations open to third level systems and there is considerable evidence that both shorter- and longer-term storage capacities have evolved to expand the simplest memory capacity, which I will call *event memory*. In line with a terminology suggested by Olton (see for example Olton *et al.*, 1980) the specialized longer-term storage systems based on event memory will be referred to as *reference memory systems* and short, or limited, term memories which need only be retained until the completion of a current task are considered to be mediated by *working memory systems* (see Table 2.2). Concerning selectivity, it is first of all evident that much of the information potentially available to a given individual is not stored for the simple reason that it is never received. Phylogenesis has endowed particular species with a range of sensory capacities which is just adequate for their survival. Equally, as we have seen in the discussion on biological constraints,

Table 2.2   Varieties of Memory within Level Three Systems

1. *Event Memory*
The registration and storage of sensory and motor events.

2. *Reference memory systems*
Longer-term storage systems involving greater depth of processing than event memory. Subdivided into:

   (a) Association memory
   Detection and storage of likely causal relationships between sensory and motor events.
   Examples: Habituation, Pavlovian conditioning, instrumental learning and may include some aspects of skilled performance.
   (b) Representational memory
   Organization of sensory and motor events into spatial/temporal maps, environmental and social models, linguistic representations.
   Examples: Episodic or biographical memory, recognition memory, cognitive mapping (as in latent learning, 'reasoning' and detour problems), spatial reference memory (such as for the layout of a radial arm maze).
   (c) Abstract memory
   Extraction and storage of rules, meanings, etc., from the flow of sensory and motor events within representational systems and the establishment of a body of 'knowledge' without spatial or temporal context.
   Examples: Semantic memory, concept formation, learning sets, gnosis, extraction of performance rules including those underlying some aspects of skilled motor performance.

3. *Working memory systems*
Specialized short-term or limited-term information holding systems used to support a current task. Always work in conjunction with reference memory systems.
   Examples: Various control processes, human short-term memory, delayed response memory (as in delayed matching to sample), 'list' memory (such as for the arms already entered on a radial arm maze test).

only a proportion of the information which *is* received is actually stored. Again the selection is phylogenetically primed on the basis of limiting storage to that which has, on past evidence, a high probability of proving useful to the survival of the species. What we need to consider now is how to categorize the forms in which the information which passes both of these filters is stored. It is suggested that the categories which are identified may implicate quite separate storage systems within the third level (see Oakley, 1981a).

2.4.1   Event Memory

Events, both sensory and motor, are the basic units of all information storage in the central nervous system. In order to be processed further any given event must by definition be stored for at least as long as it takes for it to become engaged in the subsequent process. In Pavlovian conditioning, which depends primarily on association memory systems (see Section 2.4.2), the first stimulus event, for example, must be retained for at least 70–80 ms to be associated with the second stimulus event (the unconditional stimulus) where nictitating membrane conditioning is concerned, and the optimal inter-stimulus (or inter-event) interval is 250 ms. In the case of heart-rate conditioning the optimal inter-stimulus interval is longer, in the region of 6–7 s, and for learned taste aversions the interval between the initial sensory event and subsequent sickness may be from 30 min to several hours in the case of taste stimuli (see Bolles, 1976; Mackintosh, 1974, pp. 66–70). Event memory could be seen as no more than a restatement of Hull's (1943) notion of a 'stimulus trace', though it must now be added that these 'traces' can be remarkably persistent if we are to encompass taste aversion conditioning in the same framework as other forms of Pavlovian conditioning (Dickinson, 1980, Mackintosh, 1974). In human memory research event memory is represented in the visual domain in the first instance as iconic memory with a duration under normal circumstances of 500 ms or less. With the entry of these basic visual sensory data into a short-term visual memory based on pattern recognition the effective store is extended up to 25–30 s (Baddeley, 1976). Long-term retention of what appear to be purely visual images is sometimes reported in humans, particularly in children, as eidetic imagery, in which the original scene can be re-visualized outside the subject's head and scanned for information (Haber, 1969). Eidetic imagery of sufficient intensity and accuracy to form one-half of a quasi-random dot stereogram giving the illusion of a raised square has been demonstrated over a 24 h period in one, perhaps exceptional, subject (Stromeyer & Psotka, 1970). There seems in fact some justification for claiming that the normal Western education process, stressing linguistic skills and representations, results in the suppression or abandonment of eidetic imagery skills. Eidetic imagery is more prevalent in school children than in adults and is seen more often in retarded and autistic children than in their normal siblings (P. Eames, 1981 personal communication; Siipola & Hayden, 1965). Similarly, the remarkable powers of memory displayed by Luria's subject 'S' (Luria, 1968), which appear to have depended on a form of eidetic imagery, seem to have been a mixed blessing. S reported frustration at not being able to erase images which were no longer useful and found that they interfered with the process of abstract reasoning and with his comprehension of written material. For humans, then, eidetic imagery may represent a primitive form of long-term visual event memory to be supplanted as soon as possible by more efficient storage techniques based on language. In other animals, however, no equivalent option may be open and eidetic imagery or its equivalent may be of far greater significance. Rather similar statements to those offered above for vision can be made for auditory and tactile memory in humans, though considerably less interest has been shown in them than in vision (Baddeley, 1976). Even more neglected in the human literature is olfactory memory. This is no doubt justified in terms of the relatively poor olfactory capacities of our own species but should not blind us to the fact that the olfactory worlds of other species may be as rich as our own pre-eminently visual one. Even so, olfactory memory is known to be remarkably persistent in humans. Literature and personal experience attest that for many people childhood memories, often with a strong emotional tone, are associated with odours rather than with auditory or visual images. The experimental evidence, too, in humans is that though initial recognition of odours may be poorer than for visual and auditory stimuli they are retained in memory without decrement for up to 3 months (Engen & Ross, 1973). At this point it is perhaps worth reiterating that smells and tastes, particularly in combination, may also be uniquely persistent as images in other animals, as the taste aversion literature indicates for rodents (Palmerino *et al.*, 1980).

So much for sensory events, but what is the evidence for memory for motor events? It is first of all important to distinguish what I am calling motor memory here from the acquisition and retention of motor skills, which will be considered later. One contender as an animal paradigm for studying motor memory is the delayed alternation procedure in which the animal, typically in a T-maze, is rewarded only if it turns in the opposite direction at the choice point on successive trials. On any given trial the animal has only the memory of the response it made on the previous trial to guide its behaviour and the procedure has consequently been used recently as a model for short-term memory in the rat (e.g. Grant, 1981). It is clear, however, that the animal need not rely on motor memory and could solve the problem on the basis of sensory or 'place' information. The fact that damage to septo-hippocampal complex, which has been implicated in polysensory spatial cognitive mapping (O'Keefe & Nadel, 1978), impairs delayed alternation behaviour is consistent with the latter interpretation (Thomas & Brito, 1980). The experimental literature, however, has provided a less ambiguous paradigm than delayed alternation for demonstrating that animals are not only aware of the nature of the last response they made but are able to utilize the memory of that response to form the basis for a future action. Rats, for instance, can be taught to use their own behaviour, typically washing, rearing or scratching, as a cue to which lever in a multi-lever Skinner box will deliver a food pellet when pressed (Beninger *et al.*, 1974; Morgan & Nicholas, 1979). Equally, the fact that response learning occurs in situations where a passive movement, such as forced wheel running, or a discrete spontaneous act, such as body scratching or grooming, is followed by a reinforcer, implies the persistence of memory for that motor event at least until the occurrence of a reinforcing event (Annable & Wearden, 1979; Mackintosh & Dickinson, 1979; Morgan & Nicholas, 1979; Pearce *et al.*, 1978). Humans also can retain information about recently completed movements, such as running a finger a set distance along a surface with their eyes closed, sufficiently well to repeat the movement accurately, though accuracy drops to an asymptotic low level within 60–80 s of completing the act (Adams & Dijkstra, 1966).

I hope that it has become clear from the above that I am treating an event as deriving from a relatively low level of sensory or motor processing — the onset of a light in a conditioning experiment, the production of a particular motor response or the visual characteristics of a room at a given moment in time. I do not mean to include here memories for more structured 'events' such as eating breakfast this morning or 'The Royal Wedding of 1981'. These are mediated by another memory, representational memory in fact, which is discussed later.

2.4.2 Reference Memory Systems

(a) Association memory. An animal which can monitor and store information about events originating in its own body and in the environment will be assisted

in its commerce with that environment if it can detect causal relationships between such events. To be successful the animal needs to assess the causal texture of its world. The simplest formal example of such a process lies in the formation of event–event associations and has been extensively studied as Pavlovian conditioning and instrumental learning (see Dickinson, 1980, 1981, for excellent summaries of recent thinking in this area). To adopt Dickinson's (1980) notation, associations can be written as $E1 \rightarrow E2$, where the events (Es) can be either sensory or motor. In the case of stimulus events the limiting condition where an event E1 has no consistent predictive relationship with any other event results in the animal ceasing to respond to it. This is the process of habituation, and E1 will subsequently be less available for incorporation into other $E1 \rightarrow E2$ associations. The process underlying the latter effect has been termed latent inhibition, though 'learned irrelevance' would probably be a better term. Where a reliable relationship does exist between two stimulus events, and the second is an important biological stimulus (e.g. food or shock) the procedure is that of Pavlovian conditioning. The development and storage of an $E1 \rightarrow E2$ association in this case can be demonstrated by the emergence of a conditional response to E1 which is similar to the unconditional response normally elicited by E2 and which can be elicited by the presentation of E1 alone at a later time. For response events, in a situation in which a particular motor act (E1), or set of actions, has no effect on the occurrence of other important events (typically aversive events such as foot shock) the animal learns the irrelevance of its actions and will subsequently show this in the form of 'learned helplessness'. That is the animal.will fail to use motor acts in other situations where they would in fact affect the occurrence of E2. The more usual experimental situation involving motor events as E1 is that of instrumental learning, or operant conditioning, in which the animal's actions *do* reliably predict the occurrence of an important stimulus event (again food or shock would be suitable examples). The persistence of an $E1 \rightarrow E2$ association in this case is revealed by a subsequent change in the probability of the motor act E1 in conditions where its predictive relationship to E2 has been established.

Experimental work in the area of Pavlovian conditioning and instrumental learning has been prodigious in humans and other animals but has generally been framed in terms of the acquisition of associations rather than their storage (see Bolles, 1976, pp. 21–48; Davey, 1981, Ch. 10, pp. 276–99). At a practical level though, experimental psychologists know that animals will produce the appropriate Pavlovian conditional response or instrumental act days, months or even years after it was originally acquired, though the retention is seldom perfect and, when the retention interval is long, may occasionally be quite poor (Gleitman, 1971; Mackintosh, 1974, pp. 472–6). Nevertheless, and despite the reluctance of learning theorists to study retention, it seems to be established that event–event associations once formed are entered into long-term storage. Association memory, then, consists of the storage of information about event–event relationships, though as noted above this storage is only likely to the extent that the relationships are causal ones. In part some decisions as to the likely causality between events are made phylogenetically in the form of biological constraints on learning. Equally, however, the degree of correlation between events and, therefore, the likely causality of their relationship, can be determined from the animal's own experience. An $E1 \rightarrow E2$ association would be expected to form only when E2 occurs more reliably after E1 than it does at other times for example (Dickinson, 1980, 1981; Rescorla, 1968).

I have argued elsewhere that the ability to form $E1 \rightarrow E2$ associations emerged at a very early phylogenetic stage and can be mediated very adequately by older subcortical mechanisms in vertebrate brains (Oakley, 1979a, 1979b). Many of the data relevant to this conclusion have been collected from mammals with neocortex surgically removed (neodecorticated) and in addition to acquisition neodecorticates show apparently normal retention of the underlying associations. Pavlovian nictitating membrane conditioning has been shown to be retained over a period of 7–8 weeks in neodecorticated rabbits for instance (Oakley & Russell, 1977) and instrumental bar pressing over 18–26 days in neodecorticated rats (unpublished observations). The suggestion that association memory represents not only an early evolutionary development but is anatomically as well as functionally distinct from other types of memory derives from clear dissociations of lesion effects on the various types of memory (Oakley, 1981a). Examples of lesions which affect some memory systems but leave association memory intact in humans and other animals are given later when other memory types are discussed.

Before moving to other types of memory, however, I would like to consider the possibility that certain aspects of motor skills involve association memory processes. The acquisition as well as the execution of motor skills is embedded within longer-term aspirations and goals and the original learning of a particular motor skill may be guided by conscious cognitive processes. Human skills, in particular, seem to be assembled in the first place by a laborious process of consciously stringing together the required motor movements, often with linguistic mediation, though simply copying the actions of another may in many cases be the more efficient strategy (see Harvey & Greer, 1980; Reason, 1977). The sequences of movements on repeated juxtaposition become fused into longer and more economic motor acts. The process may perhaps be envisaged as one in which the animal's cognitive/representational systems (see below) present a series of events for the association system to form into longer sequences for eventual automatic execution. Given the modular organization of the central nervous system it is not, I hope, unreasonable to imagine that the cognitive/representational systems are capable of programming another system to carry out routine functions. Once acquired then, the controlling mechanisms of a skill may be reducible in part to a series of event–event associations. In particular if an animal can represent its own actions to itself, and if the $E1 \rightarrow E2$ formulation has complete generality, two motor events could be engaged sequentially via the associative mechanism. A more traditional view would be in terms of sensory and motor event (i.e. stimulus–response or S–R) associations and it is true that skills are executed in relation to external stimulus events otherwise their adaptiveness under changing conditions would be limited. It is also true that all motor acts have their sensory consequences and these could be seen as serving to elicit the next response in the skilled act. Either or both types of association may be involved, though, to repeat the point, it is clear that an analysis of skills solely in these terms can only be part of the story.

In terms of their storage characteristics some skills are noted for their apparent insensitivity to the passage of time while others are less resistant to the effects of disuse. It appears to be the case that 'continuous' skills, such as those involved in swimming or cycling, are stored without decrement on a very long-term basis. On the other hand, 'discrete' skills, such as typing, where separate responses must be made to a series of more or less unitary stimuli, are much more prone to impairment if they are not practised (See Baddeley, 1976, pp. 255–62). This observation alone indicates that different types of skill may be mediated by different mechanisms and that 'skills' is not a unitary category. It is similarly possible that skills should not be classified under association memory and are perhaps sufficiently unique to require a separate heading. What is clear, however, is that, particularly in humans, the acquisition and storage of motor skills is an important part of the animal's information gaining and storing strategy. It is also the case that brain damage which affects other sorts of memory leaves motor skills intact. This has been particularly noted in cases of so-called 'global' amnesia in humans, where everyday experiences in particular are rapidly forgotten but skills such as those involved in mirror drawing, jigsaw puzzles and rotary pursuit can still be acquired and retained on a long-term basis (Meudell & Mayes, 1982; Newcombe, 1980; O'Keefe & Nadel, 1978). Association memory in the form of Pavlovian eyeblink conditioning (Weiskrantz & Warrington, 1979) and instrumental visual discrimination (Gaffan, 1972) is also intact on human amnesics. In this respect association memory and motor skill memory are similar and I shall use this similarity to justify having treated both of them together here.

(b)   Representational memory.   The ability to store information concerning the likely causal relationships between events in the form of $E1 \rightarrow E2$ associations represents an important step forward in providing a basis for individual animals to cope with their environments. A more significant advance in central processing would be to organize sensory and motor events into more complex, multi-event representations of the environment (Jerison, 1973, 1976, 1982; Oatley, 1978). The events held in such a system would be entered into a matrix which represented the perceived relationships between each of them. The first and most fundamental relationships to be represented in this way would perhaps be spatial and temporal ones (Downs & Stea, 1977; O'Keefe & Nadel, 1978). The process then, is one of environmental mapping or modelling and the underlying storage system I have called representational memory (Oakley, 1981a). For maximum efficiency accurate environmental models should be formed in anticipation of the need to use them and it is assumed that animals which are capable of forming representational memory stores have an innate predisposition to collect the relevant information irrespective of their current needs. That is, the animals in question will show curiosity and will explore their environments even when they have no evident homoeostatic needs and will later use the information they have gained in the satisfaction of those needs when they arise. Changes in the environment are particularly important and animals with representational memory systems can be expected to react to novelty with exploration, changing their internal environmental representations accordingly. They will also be expected to show routine exploration of familiar environments in order to detect change and update their representations.

Before expanding on, and hopefully clarifying, what is meant by representational memory systems two points should be made. First, what is being said here has its antecedents in Tolman's (1932) view of learning with its emphasis on 'cognitive maps', 'latent learning', 'expectancies' and so forth (see Bolles, 1979, Ch. 5 or Bower & Hilgard, 1981, Ch. 11). Second, it is worth noting that some authors (for example Davey, 1981; Dickinson, 1980) talk of central representations of stimulus and motor events and consider the association $E1 \rightarrow E2$ itself as a representation of the correlation between these two events. I prefer, however, to ascribe the storage of the latter to association memory and to reserve the term representational memory for the storage of multi-event maps and models in the brain. As a further point it must be stressed that where important $E1 \rightarrow E2$ relationships exist they will be stored not only in association memory but will be re-represented as points within a larger representational memory system if one is available.

Perhaps the simplest way to portray some of the more fundamental attributes of representational memory and its advantages is to adopt an example given by O'Keefe and Nadel (1978) with respect to spatial mapping. If we wished to direct a friend to point X in the countryside we could present him with a route to follow — down Station Road, turn left just before Sainsbury's, along Galley Lane until the stile, etc. That is to present him with a series of directives based on prominent stimuli and the appropriate responses to them. Provided our route was accurate this may be a very efficient procedure. Alternatively we might give him a map of the entire area including his destination. This might take up more space and would require the understanding of a few simple rules and conventions, but would have several distinct advantages. The spatial information in a map is non-egocentric and so our map user could find his destination from any point of entry within the mapped area and from any given point could use a variety of alternative paths to his goal. The route-user is, literally, lost if he deviates from his instructions and will have difficulty in locating his goal if the route is blocked, or if the information is ambiguous at any point. He also cannot take short-cuts or a detour which will take in a local beauty spot. There is a long history of debate in the field of animal learning as to whether animals use routes, based on stimulus–response associations, or cognitive maps when they are, for example, traversing a maze (See Bolles, 1979, Ch. 5 or Bower & Hilgard 1981, Ch. 11). The rat in fact seems to use whichever of the two is best suited to the particular situation and may change strategy as its experience with the maze increases. Along with O'Keefe and Nadel (1978) I am assuming that routes are mediated by association memory systems or, as they prefer to call them, taxon systems.

In addition to representing environmental space the existence of central modelling processes underlies our perception of objects in the world (Oatley, 1978). One dramatic demonstration of our own ability to construct and manipulate a perceptual representation was provided by Shepard and Metzler (1971). These authors presented human subjects with line drawings of complex, three-dimensional objects and asked them to match them with other drawings of the same objects rotated in depth. Correct solution required the subjects to rotate mentally the object represented by the original figure and this they were apparently able to do. A similar process underlies our ability to recognize a table, for example, as the same object irrespective of the angle at which we view it. Once representational systems have developed there is a further possible advance in that it is possible to manipulate or interact with the representation itself. To some extent this was evident in our hypothetical map-user. If central representations include all known relationships between objects and events they are available for creating hypotheses, for reasoning about one's environment and for carrying out safe internal experiments and observing the likely outcomes. Shepard and Metzler's subjects were in effect experimenting with what each object would look like from below or from the other side. They could have gone further and mentally taken some part away, added something new or imagined the consequences of dropping it from a high building.

So far representations have concerned inanimate objects, but other members of the animal's own species are also suitable objects for cognitive modelling in order to frame hypotheses about their behaviour, to anticipate their likely reactions to the animal's own behaviour and so forth (Humphrey, 1976, 1980). Representations of the self, which underlie self-recognition in chimps and man (Gallup, 1977) and self-image in man (Crook, 1980; Slobodkin, 1978) are also powerful determinants of action. The importance for human behaviour of observing and modelling the behaviour of the self and others and of forming working hypotheses to give a consistent account for the causes of such behaviour has long been recognized in psychology. The view of Man as a Scientist continually using his experience of the world to form, and revise, hypotheses in order to make predictions about future events is fundamental to Kelly's influential Personal Construct Theory (Kelly, 1955 — see Fransella, 1981). Implicit personality theories are involved in the formation of stereotypes and powerfully affect first impressions of others (e.g. Kelley, 1950). Attribution theory (see Buck, 1976, Ch. 9; Weiner, 1972, Ch. 5 and 6) has charted the bases upon which humans decide the likely causes of the behaviour of others (e.g. Kelley, 1967) and by a process of self-observation, or self-perception, form hypotheses about their own behaviour and attitudes (Bem, 1972). In interpersonal perception there is a clear bias towards dispositional attributions, that is for the observer to attribute a particular behaviour to the attitudes or personality of the actor, rather than making a situational attribution even when the situational pressures on the actor are quite evident (e.g. Jones & Harris, 1967). In the case of intrapersonal perception the observer is more prone to attribute his own behaviour to situational factors (Jones & Nisbett, 1972). Changes in behaviour without adequate situational pressure, however, can result in a dispositional attribution and if necessary a consequent adjustment in beliefs or attitudes, as shown in many experiments generated by cognitive dissonance theory (e.g. Festinger & Carlsmith, 1959). Individual differences in the tendency to form predominantly situational or predominantly dispositional attributions about the causes of one's own behaviour have also been noted and have been related to measures of differences in perceived locus of control (Rotter, 1966).

A further refinement of representational systems involves the possibility of coding experience into another, more economical, form and then using these re-representations of reality as the basis for interactive modelling, reasoning, etc. Human language is such a higher order representational system. The view that understanding passages of written prose, for instance, involves the creation, modification and evaluation of a mental representation of what the passage is about is currently a focus of attention (see for example Green *et al.*, 1981). Clearly, to be useful, linguistic representations in common with others must not only be created but must be stored and so contribute importantly to the total memory store in humans. Finally, in so far as temporal information is encoded into representational memories they will act as an autobiographical store, a life history, in which items can be ordered in terms of recency. Adequate temporal coding should protect the stored items to some extent from interference by events of a similar sort which occurred either before or after the event in question. It is this ability to recall events as having happened to the individual at a particular time in the past, to have 'personal' memories, which is one of the subjectively most compelling aspects of normal human memory. Tulving identified this type of memory, particularly in relation to linguistically mediated information stores, as 'episodic' memory (Tulving, 1972).

I believe that the development of neocortex and the development of flexible representational systems are closely related in mammals (Oakley, 1979a, 1981a) and there is considerable evidence that older cortical structures, represented by the hippocampus, are particularly involved in spatial mapping (O'Keefe & Nadel, 1978). This does not deny, of course, the possibility that similar abilities may be mediated by the development of other structures in non-mammalian species. In birds and reptiles, for example, there is a clear phylogenetic expansion of the neostriatal/hyperstriatal complex and of the dorsal ventricular ridge respectively, which are homologues of mammalian neocortex (Northcutt, 1978). Moreover, there is good reason to believe that the ability to form and store environmental maps is not restricted to vertebrates. A somewhat time-worn example of cognitive mapping, or latent learning, in invertebrates concerns the digger wasp (see Alcock, 1975). Having constructed a burrow the female digger wasp performs a brief orientation flight before departing in search of prey. When she returns she is able to locate the burrow rapidly on the basis of environmental landmarks. If the landmarks have been changed experimentally in the meantime she goes to the wrong place, but to a place which could be predicted on the basis of the new positions of the landmarks. Similarly, rapid mapping also appears to occur in the establishment of temporary territories in various species of butterfly (Baker, 1972). Even more impressive, however, is the fact that one species of wasp, *Ammophila pubescens*, can maintain up to 15 nests simultaneously and provision them differently depending on the state of maturation of their larvae as a result of a single visit to each nest site at the beginning of each day's foraging. It is clear that phylogenesis has invested heavily, of necessity, in this particular ability for this type of wasp. The maps formed are also curiously rigid, in so far as once the daily inspection visit is complete the wasp provisions the nest for that day on later visits irrespective of changes in the contents of the nest, such as substitution of an older larva or the removal of existing provisions.

Rats not only learn spatial locations readily even in the absence of local cues (Morris, 1981) but are apparently able to use their cognitive maps more flexibly than the wasp. For example, once rats have learned the layout of an apparatus consisting of three distinct tables joined by runways into a Y-shape they can run directly to a table on which they have just been fed, when placed on either of the other two tables. This is despite the fact that the tables themselves are screened from view from the runways and that whenever the test is repeated the baited table and the start table are chosen at random so that the rat cannot learn any particular route to food (Ellen, 1980; Maier, 1932; Stahl & Ellen, 1974). This was originally seen as a test of 'reasoning' (Maier 1932; Stahl & Ellen, 1974) as the animal cannot solve the problem without integrating the knowledge which it has previously gained about the layout of the apparatus with the independent information which it has just received concerning which table is baited. More recently the original experience of exploring the three tables and their interconnecting alleys has been described as essential to the formation of a cognitive map upon which later solution of a series of different baited-table problems can be based (Ellen, 1980). In a similar vein, chimpanzees in the so-called 'travelling salesman problem' display an impressive ability to devise a new, economical route to collect up to 18 items of food which they have seen hidden by an experimenter who had deliberately used a circuitous and inefficient path (Menzel, 1978). This again has been seen as an example of the formation of a cognitive map by the animal, which it then uses to plan its route.

If items in representational memory are entered in terms of their temporal as well as spatial and other relationships, a basis is provided for recognizing recently entered items and distinguishing them clearly from similar, or the same, items encountered on previous occasions. The fact that we consciously recognize an event as having been experienced by us at some definite time in the past is an important aspect of our biographical or episodic memory systems. The case for the existence of recognition memory, and its distinction from habituation or associative mechanisms, has been plausibly argued by Gaffan (1976, 1980) in both rats and monkeys. The monkeys were required on a retention test to select 'junk' objects which they had previously seen in association with a food reward. Under 'recognition' conditions the items were presented alongside novel items so that familiarity as well as association with food reward were relevant cues. In the 'association' condition the previously rewarded objects were presented alongside equally familiar objects which had not been associated with food. This second condition was, therefore, a test of association memory. Gaffan found that his animals performed much better under the 'recognition' condition than the 'association' condition. This he took as evidence for a powerful recognition memory system which was separate from association memory. This belief was strengthened by the fact that lesioning the fornix in these animals impaired performance in the recognition tests but not on those tests involving association memory alone. Rolls (1981) has reported microelectrode recording studies in monkeys which further substantiate the distinction between recognition and association memory. In these studies monkeys were presented with a series of objects or coloured slides and received fruit juice if they responded only to stimuli which they had seen before on that experimental session. Each stimulus occurred only twice each day and up to 16 other stimuli (taking approximately 15 min to present) could intervene between the first and second presentation of a particular stimulus. Neurons in the anterior thalamus, close to the fornix, were found to fire only to stimuli which were familiar to the animal. The increase in firing anticipated the animal's response and could even be seen on trials where a familiar stimulus was presented but the animal failed to respond. Conversely, increased firing in the 'recognition' neurons was not seen on trials where the animal incorrectly responded to a novel stimulus object. In a separate discrimination test the same neuronal firing was seen to all familiar stimuli irrespective of whether or not they had been associated previously with food reward. Again the implication is that recognition memory is distinct from association memory. Its relationship with other types of memory has yet to be established experimentally. Much of the interest in these studies stems from the fact that damage to systems closely associated with the fornix and anterior thalamus in man results in an amnesic syndrome in which recognition memory is particularly impaired (Gaffan, 1976, 1980; Warrington, 1976). The particular interest for this chapter is that recognition memory is seen as a product of representational systems and is anatomically distinct from other memory systems. In addition to providing a basis for normal feelings of familiarity the specialized recognition system, if it is activated at an inappropriate time, may account for the false attachment of familiarity to current experience in the form of the déja vu phenomenon, which may occur spontaneously as well as during electrical stimulation of the brain and in association with temporal lobe epilepsy (Kalat, 1981; Walsh, 1978).

The notion that one function of representational memory systems, especially perhaps in man, is to provide a biographical record of life experiences raises one final question — that of the capacity of such a system. At the extreme it might be supposed that all events, experiences and their accompanying effects are permanently stored in all their detail. This, however, would not fit the general principle that animals should be highly selective not only in the events they monitor but also in what they retain in storage. The more practical approach would be to retain only the most significant events in store and perhaps to wipe out even those after a predetermined period of potential utility. The human brain, while it may not adopt the former extreme approach to storage, is apparently less practical than the latter would suggest. There is certainly a considerable amount of evidence to suggest that far more episodic material is stored than is normally available to, or needed by, the individual. The apocryphal return of early memories in old age, for example, or the ability of subjects to re-experience vividly earlier experiences containing apparently long-forgotten material under hypnotic age regression (e.g. Hilgard, 1977) suggest that material once entered into long-term episodic storage may remain there for a lifetime. In a similar manner the classic observations of flashback experiences described by Penfield (1969) during electrical stimulation of the temporal lobe in conscious human patients could be taken to suggest a permanent experiential record. As the electrode was placed Penfield's patient became suddenly 'aware of all that was in his mind during and earlier strip of time' as though 'the stream of former consciousness [was] flowing again' (Penfield, 1969, p. 152). For the most part the experience reported was neither significant nor important to the subject. The possibility that the permanent experiential record may extend to almost incidentally acquired information is further raised by the numerous reports, albeit many of them in popular form, of hypnotic regression to former lives (Iverson, 1976; Moss & Keeton, 1979). If paranormal explanations are to be excluded for the accurate knowledge which some hypnotized subjects display of obscure and often mundane historical details when asked to go back to a time long before their birth, it must be assumed that the relevant information was gained during the subject's own lifetime and was being used to create a fictitious, though subjectively very vivid, previous incarnation. As the majority of subjects have no special historical knowledge or training and are not able to account themselves for the material they produce when regressed the explanation must lie in long-forgotten historical novels, school lessons, documentary programmes and the like. The immense potential capacity of the human brain for retaining information is also attested by the feats of the various mnemonists who have undergone scientific evaluation (e.g. Hunt & Love, 1972; Hunter, 1962; Luria, 1968) and in view of their achievements the idea of a complete life-record seems less implausible. It is generally suggested, however, that, apart from a certain notoriety, the mnemonists themselves found their memories of little practical use (e.g. Baddeley, 1976, Ch. 14). Most of us it seems are protected from our memories not by limited storage capacity but by a limited capacity (or willingness) to retrieve what is there. Methods for improving our memories have accordingly centred on techniques for improving retrieval, such as the method of loci and first letter mnemonics, rather than on any intention to increase storage capacity (Gruneberg, 1978). From a biological point of view the notion of a virtually unlimited storage capacity coupled with a highly inefficient (or selective) retrieval mechanism appears to be very wasteful of neural space. The fact that material cannot be brought to conscious recall does not, however, necessarily mean that it cannot be used to control and inform behaviour outside consciousness (Dixon & Henley, 1980).

(c) Abstract memory.   The recurrence of similar series of events in representational memory allows the possibility that common factors may be abstracted from them and stored as part of an accumulating pool of general information or 'knowledge'. The abstraction process can be envisaged as generating two broad types of stored information (Premack, 1978). On the one hand repeated sensory events which have common features — all dogs, all vegetables, all sneezes, etc. — can be stored in abstract memory as sensory prototypes which retain the central features of, and so represent, that class of objects or events (Rosch, 1975). In human verbal memory a similar process occurs in the formation of what Bartlett (1932) called 'schemata'; organized masses of information representing themes, attitudes and ideas, which serve to represent and organize the common elements of past experience (see Oatley, 1978, Ch. 6). The core themes and cultural norms embodied in folk literature, for example, are represented in abstract memory systems and are used by human subjects to fill out the gaps left by failures of representational memory to create an acceptable narrative when they are asked to recall a particular story such as the now classic *War of the Ghosts* (Bartlett, 1932). Abstraction on the other hand can result in the identification or generation of rules which define relationships, provide strategies for the solution of a class of environmental problems and, in humans, underly the production and understanding of speech.

It is recognized of course that repetition of events in representational memory is not the only way in which animals, humans in particular, may gain the sort of information which, it is suggested, fills abstract memory. Cultural transmission, for example, can allow the individual to gain facts and rules based on the repeated experiences of others and non-biological stores of such items in libraries, computer data banks and so forth provide a powerful short cut to gaining abstracted information. Equally, a single experience may be the basis for generating a rule, or at least an hypothesis, for storage in abstract memory, though repetition of the experience is needed if it is to be tested. In cases where information enters abstract memory via a single experience there is more likelihood that the corresponding episodic memory can be retrieved. We may remember the book in which we read a particular novel piece of information for example, or the occasion on which we first heard a new word. With further exposure to, or possibly rehearsal of, the same fact or word the biographical details which accompany it are lost to recall and it enters a pool of general information. For the purposes of this chapter, however, the basic mechanism by which information enters abstract memory will be assumed to involve repeated experience of events in representational systems.

An issue which a consideration of the animal literature will raise is that of the relationship of association memory to abstract memory. I have already suggested above that the situation which forms the basis of E1→E2 associations is also entered as biographical data into representational systems where these are present. In cases where some higher order information or rule is abstracted from a situation in which associative learning is taking place it seems likely that abstraction is occurring via the representational system and not directly via association memory. Similarly, some aspects of skilled performance where rules are involved may be represented in abstract memory via representational systems and not simply on the basis of E1→E2 associations.

A final point before considering examples of abstract memory concerns the need to develop a system of this sort in the first place. This is a particularly important question in view of the suggestion above that episodic memory has, if not unlimited, vast and underexploited storage capacity. The major disadvantage of relying on representational storage would be in speed of access to information. It would be necessary to extract a relevant fact or rule from a mass of irrelevant biographical detail on each occasion that it was required. A considerable advantage can thus be imagined for a system which stored the abstracted information separately for future use. It is likely that species will vary in the types of information which will form the basis of abstractions but in view of the potential utility of such a process it is suggested that a wide variety of species will 'connect *relatable* experiences and construct abstractions for the resulting set' (Premack, 1978, p. 426). To take Premack's own example of a simple abstraction, consider the case of an animal which preys on another species which habitually occupies the darkest available areas of the objects upon which it lives. The predator will experience successful prey capture on the darker side of these objects, though the absolute values of darkness may vary over a wide range. Indeed, the darker side in some situations may be lighter than the lighter side in other places. On a return visit our predator could find its prey by memorizing the specific locations or the specific brightness values associated with prey capture in the past. Either strategy would be limiting and could lead to incorrect choices if ambient light levels changed over time. If, however, the animal were to abstract the concept 'darker than' it could not only allow for local fluctuations in light levels and angles of incidence, but could identify an unlimited number of other potential prey sites outside those already sampled. In this example it is assumed of course that the predator in question is not a member of a species which has always found its prey on the darker side of objects. If that were the case phylogenesis would have provided, via first and second level systems, the appropriate behavioural hypothesis in the form of an innate predisposition or at least would have primed the animal to form the 'darker than' hypothesis very quickly on the basis of very few exemplars, possibly via a developmental critical period. There is thus a case to be made for the usefulness of a separate system for extracting items of general information from the stream of experience. A major support for such a distinction between abstract and representational systems derives from the fact that various lesions appear to damage them separately (see below and Oakley, 1981a).

The most discussed example of an abstract memory system is that of semantic memory (Tulving, 1972), which is concerned with the knowledge necessary for the use of language and in particular, as its name implies, with the storage of, and access to, the meaning of words. The interrelatedness of representational (particularly episodic) and semantic memory systems is evident here in the sense that speech which forms a large part of our daily experience is dependent for its production on the contents of semantic memory. Conversely, episodic memory is involved not only in the formation but also in the revision of the information we have about the meaning of words. See Morris (1978, Ch. 5) for a review of interrelations in semantic and episodic memory and of the major theories of human long-term memory which take them into account. The importance of neocortex in humans in the mediation of both receptive and expressive aspects of language is widely documented (e.g. Geschwind, 1979) though the role of subcortical sites, particularly the thalamus, in linguistic functions is increasingly stressed (Dimond, 1980, Ch. 12). More significantly for the present discussion, there is also evidence from clinical studies of humans with cortical injuries that semantic storage systems can be selectively damaged and are consequently to be seen as anatomically as well as functionally distinct from representational systems, particularly those mediating episodic memory (Warrington, 1975, 1979).

The nearest approach to a study of semantic memory in animals is that embodied in several recent attempts to teach language to chimpanzees and gorillas. So far it is clear that these animals show a remarkable ability to use plastic symbols (Premack, 1971), American Sign Language (Gardner & Gardner, 1969) and a computer keyboard (Rumbaugh & Gill, 1976) to represent objects, logical relationships, concepts and actions. They have also been attributed with some ability to combine symbols in a meaningful way and to respond appropriately to changes in word order (See Davey, 1981 for a brief review). At the moment it seems reasonable to conclude that, under these rather artificial conditions at least, some non-human primates are capable of acquiring a large repertoire of 'words' and learning their meanings. Claims that their language also embodies rules similar to those forming the basis of grammatical structure in human language, however, have been criticized on the grounds that a careful analysis of multi-sign utterances in one signing chimp reveals no good evidence that 'word order' is governed by the semantic role of the signs used. Much of the semantic look in sign combinations in fact seems to be contributed by the chimp's tendency to imitate its human teacher's immediately preceding utterance (Terrace et al., 1979). There are as yet no data on the anatomical substrates of acquired linguistic abilities as displayed by these sub-human primates but recent studies have led to the claim that certain pre-linguistic abilities, as embodied in an auditory delayed symbolic matching to sample task and in the perception of conspecific sounds, are mediated by areas of neocortex in the left hemisphere in monkeys (Dewson, 1977; Nottebohm, 1979; Weiskrantz, 1977).

The term semantic memory is restricted for the purposes of this chapter to abstract memory systems underlying language functions and word meanings and is a special case of the more general role of abstract memory systems in supplying meaning to environmental events. The failure to attach meaning to stimuli, where this failure cannot be accounted for in terms of sensory impairment, defective perceptual analysis, general intellectual deterioration or language deficit, constitutes the long-recognized clinical condition of agnosia. Perhaps the most striking feature of agnosia is the specificity of the symptoms which may be shown in any one case (see, for example, Ratcliff & Ross, 1981; Shallice, 1981; Walsh, 1978; Warrington, 1975, 1979). Visual, tactile and auditory agnosias, for example, have all been described as isolated entities and argue for the existence of modality-specific abstract systems. Supporting such an interpretation Shallice (1981) notes that in some cases tactile recognition of objects is almost perfect where the patient need not verbalize but naming objects from touch results in large numbers of errors. Visually guided naming on the other hand is almost perfect in these patients, indicating that the deficit is not one of general naming, leading Shallice to the conclusion that the symptoms are a product of differential disruption within, or between, specific tactile and verbal abstract memory subsystems. In addition to modality specificity, agnosias may involve limited categories of stimuli. Agnosias for letters and words have been described relatively frequently, less common are agnosias for colours and faces and cases of agnosia for objects are rare, but important in that they occur at all. Even more circumscribed agnosias, such as the inability to produce or understand the names for parts of the body are also occasionally described (e.g. Dennis, 1976, cited by Dimond, 1980, q.v.).

Warrington (1975) has reported observations of three patients with agnosias for both objects and words and it is instructive to consider her analysis of their condition in a little detail to give some idea of the profundity and specificity of the cognitive deficits involved and of the organization of abstract memory systems which they reveal. All three patients were in their late 50s or early 60s and were diagnosed as suffering from general cerebral atrophy. They nevertheless scored at average or above average levels on IQ (WAIS) tests and tests of reasoning (Progressive Matrices), were able to converse fluently, albeit with a reduced vocabulary, and could comprehend syntactically complex messages based on a high frequency vocabulary (Token Test). Reading was 'remarkably well preserved' in these patients and even words which were meaningless to them could be correctly read and written. On sensory and perceptual tests all three patients were shown to have normal vision and hearing, they performed well on shape discriminations and object matching tasks. For the latter test objects were photographed from a conventional and an unconventional viewpoint and the subject was asked to say whether two different photographs presented to him were different views of the same object or represented two different objects. These patients could perform successfully on this task even when the objects were ones for which they were agnosic. One patient for instance, on being shown a table-tennis bat viewed from a normal angle, previously having been shown an unconventional view of it, was able to tell the experimenter that he had already been shown a photograph of the same thing from a different angle and had already said that he had no idea what it was. It would appear that the patients could form accurate representations of the objects in question, transform those representations between orthodox and unorthodox views and classify them as the same or different objects quite independently of their ability to provide a verbal semantic classification for the object. It is worth noting here that Ratcliff and Ross (1981) report one patient shown to have visual object agnosia who, when tested with pictures, did not perform adequately on the object matching test though he could copy drawings very accurately indeed. Ratcliff and Ross concluded that this patient's agnosia could be explained in terms of an inability to create a 3-D model from a 2-D visual representation and a consequent failure to access the appropriate semantic memory system. The conclusion to be drawn from this is either that this particular patient, with what appears to be primarily a representational system deficit, should not be considered an agnosic as there is no need to assume a deficit in semantic memory systems or conversely, if the label is to be retained, that not all cases of 'agnosia' necessarily involve abstract memory systems directly.

Agnosia for objects, in Warrington's (1975) patients, was evident in tests where familiar objects (scales and sledge were two of the least familiar ones used) were presented as line drawings for naming and identification. In an alternative version of the test the name of the same object was spoken for the subject to provide a description or definition. One interesting outcome of these tests, which we will return to in a moment, was that the extent of the agnosia which they revealed varied on a modality-specific basis between subjects. Two of the patients were worse on the visual version than on the auditory version, while the reverse was true in the third patient. On items for which they failed to provide a definition the subjects claimed that the object was 'familiar' but that they had forgotten what it was — possibly indicating an intact recognition memory for these semantically 'forgotten' items. Similarly, in later tests of short-term memory it was evident that 'unknown' common three-letter words were being processed differently than matched nonsense syllables even though the subjects regarded the words as meaningless and later could not distinguish the real words from the nonsense syllables on a forced choice test. The latter is perhaps surprising given that real words should engender the cue of 'familiarity' but the indication again is that the deficit under investigation is located within a specialized subsystem and is not a product of a general deficit which prevents all mnemonic processing for the 'unknown' objects or their verbal representations. In contrast to their clear object agnosia all three patients could identify letters, colours and numbers without difficulty.

More specific testing of the agnosia for words, which all three showed to some extent, revealed a further specificity, where lower frequency words were concerned, along an abstract–concrete dimension. In one patient fewer, or less accurate, definitions were given for concrete than for abstract words, the reverse was the case in the second patient and the third patient was equally impaired in both categories. The patient AB, for example, was able to give acceptable definitions for 'arbiter', 'vocation' and 'pact' but responded to the concrete words 'poster', 'needle' and 'acorn' with 'No idea!', 'Forgotten!' and 'Don't know!' respectively. One plausible explanation for this outcome is that separate semantic stores exist for abstract and concrete words or concepts. All three patients were at a loss when asked to explain common proverbs, though evidently for different reasons. AB's difficulty, as might be anticipated, lay in his inability to understand some of the concrete words and in response to 'Too many cooks spoil the broth' he claimed that he expected that he would be able to explain it if only he knew what 'broth' meant.

Tests of other varieties of memory in the same patients revealed no deficit in short-term working memory (see below) when they were asked to repeat strings of five, three-letter words which they had just heard spoken, irrespective of whether the words were 'known' or 'unknown' — the latter indicating the independence of working memory systems mediating word-span from semantic systems. All three were impaired, however, on tests of delayed recall of short stories and of word lists and when asked to produce visual designs from immediate memory, but unlike amnesics their biographical episodic memory was normal. They were in touch with ongoing events, were well oriented in time and space, their conversations were not repetitive and they could refer forwards and backwards to detailed events of importance in their life. Amnesics for their part do not show agnosias for words or objects.

The observation that these patients had unequal difficulty where visual and verbal representations of objects were concerned could be accounted for in terms of a disconnection syndrome by suggesting that access to semantic memory stores was differentially affected in the two modalities involved (visual and auditory) and Geschwind (1965) has suggested that object agnosia should be seen as part of a disconnection syndrome. Warrington, however, believes that her data are more consistent with the view that, in these three cases at least, the agnosia is caused by damage directly within the semantic systems themselves and not within access routes. There are two major reasons for this. First, it was seen that the semantic deficit in these three patients was not total and frequently the words which were not adequately defined could be correctly allocated to superordinate semantic categories, though not to subordinate categories. When, for example, the word 'canary' was spoken the patient might correctly categorize it as 'living', 'animal' and 'bird' but could not identify it as 'yellow', 'small' and 'pet'. Apart from indicating the hierarchical organization of semantic memory systems this suggests that the correct information was reaching the semantic systems but was being treated in a deficient manner once there. Second, the repertoire of known and unknown words was importantly determined by semantic rather than physical or physiological variables. The dissociation between concrete and abstract words being an obvious example of a semantic determinant. If this analysis in terms of a semantic memory deficit, rather than a selective dissociation syndrome, is correct it would seem to imply that visual and verbal semantic memory systems are separate in functional and anatomical terms. Warrington concludes that a particular concept may thus be represented in two abstract memory hierarchies, one primarily visual, the other primarily verbal. Later studies have indicated that damage to the left temporo-occipital region of the cerebral cortex is critical in producing the agnosic syndrome displayed by these patients (Warrington, 1979).

Compared to the enormous human clinical literature on the subject, agnosia has received little attention in animal research. This is partly due of course to the fact that agnosia is by definition a cognitive deficit and it is far easier to ask a human what he sees, knows and understands than it is to devise a test which will provide the same information for an animal (see Benton, 1978). In its turn the 'commentary' approach to clinical investigation is not without its pitfalls as Weiskrantz (1977) has noted, and may conceal data which are directly available in animal studies. Despite its potential for clarifying issues in human agnosia research, animal agnosia has not emerged as a coherent area in modern experimental psychology and for direct statements on the matter it is necessary to look back as far as the writings of Munk in the late nineteenth century (see Benton, 1978). Munk described a dog after removal of areas of occipital cortex outside the primary visual area as behaving in a manner which suggested 'mindblindness', a term which was later dropped in favour of 'visual agnosia'. The dog, Munk said, could evidently still see and could use his visual ability to move around his environment without bumping into obstacles, but the animal no longer knew or recognized what he saw. In Munk's opinion the dog had lost the 'visual ideas' or 'memory images' which he formerly possessed and so saw but did not understand. The mindblindness was in fact transitory and in a few weeks was no longer evident, but during its presence the dog failed to respond to the sight of human companions whom he had previously greeted joyfully, he paid no special attention to the sight of his food bowl even when he was hungry and food itself elicited no response unless he could smell it. Equally, the dog no longer performed the trick of presenting a paw in response to a hand waved before his eyes, though he would respond immediately and appropriately on hearing the word 'paw'. Munk's dog appears to have been suffering from visual object agnosia and it is significant that this and a number of other visual agnosias are also associated with occipital lesions in man (Walsh, 1978).

In order to consider a number of other studies in connection with agnosia it is necessary to offer the speculation that the primary visual cortex (striate cortex or area V1) is important in preparing visual inputs for processing by representational and abstract systems. There is now ample evidence that areas outside primary visual cortex are capable of mediating visual sensory processing of a high order in terms of acuity and stimulus detection (Humphrey, 1974; Weiskrantz, 1977, 1980). In humans with striate cortex lesions this residual visual ability includes the capacity for discriminating a cross from a circle and between horizontal, vertical and diagonal line gratings on a forced choice test. The visual inputs do not, however, reach consciousness and the fact that the subject continues to deny his visual capacity while performing well on visual discrimination tasks has led to the label 'blindsight' for this peculiar condition (Weiskrantz, 1977, 1980). Accepting that vision is to some extent spared in these cases it is predictable on the basis of the above speculation that without primary visual cortex the subject will be agnosic with respect to his visual capacity. The absence of conscious awareness of the visual experience in humans makes an interpretation on this issue difficult but in the case of monkeys the prediction appears to be supported. Weiskrantz (1980), for instance, refers to what he identifies as agnosia in a monkey with unilateral removal of primary visual cortex which was tested by Cowey and himself (Cowey & Weiskrantz, 1963). This animal showed good sensitivity to brief and to small stimuli within its 'blind' visual field but ignored the appearance of a strange doll until it was moved into the region of normal vision, at which the animal cried out in surprise and refused to be tested further. More extensive observations (Humphrey, 1974) are also available for a monkey with bilateral removal of primary visual cortex which showed a number of symptoms which Ratcliff and Ross (1981) conclude are 'similar to visual agnosia in man'. This particular monkey, Helen, after a long period of recovery and experience of both laboratory and rural life in Cambridgeshire was able to perform visual tasks with remarkable accuracy. She was able, as was Munk's dog, to avoid obstacles when moving rapidly and seemed on the basis of a variety of control tests to be using vision for this purpose. Helen was able to catch live, and lively, cockroaches, which she ate, as well as to pick up currants from the floor. On the latter her prowess was considerable; 25 currants randomly scattered over an area of 5 m^2 were retrieved in around 55 s. Acuity was so good in this animal in fact that she would detect small specks of dirt on the floor and would pick them up and try to eat them. In fact she appeared, despite her fine acuity, to be unable to distinguish food objects from non-food and treated any small object as a potential titbit. Humphrey suggested that this and related evidence pointed to a failure of 'object recognition'. Helen's visual agnosia, if it is accepted as such, would of course be expected on the initial speculation to be accompanied by other deficits, notably those based on impaired visual representational memory. In this respect it is worth noting that Helen was indeed deficient in spatial mapping where vision was concerned. She would for instance return repeatedly to try and pick up a piece of black tape stuck to the floor without learning to ignore it on the basis of its relationship with other objects surrounding it. Each time she moved away and then caught sight of it again she would return to the tape and investigate it.

Helen's condition is similar in many ways to a deficit seen in other monkeys after massive damage to the temporal lobe, including damage to hippocampus and the amygdalar nuclei (Klüver & Bucy, 1939). One of the major symptoms in these animals was 'psychic blindness' or visual agnosia. Like Helen, Klüver and Bucy's monkeys seemed, in their words, 'unable to detect the meaning of objects on the basis of visual criteria alone', and would pick up edible and inedible objects alike to examine them orally before rejecting the non-edible items. They would also examine the same inedible object repeatedly within the same session or on repeated sessions as if encountering it for the first time. Objects which in normal monkeys caused fear or excitement appeared to have lost their emotional significance for these animals, who would approach and examine a hissing snake or the mouth of a cat just as readily as they would a piece of food. Equally, objects such as a human or another monkey, which formerly elicited aggressive reactions no longer did so even under provocation. The monkeys also showed elevated and indiscriminate sexual behaviour much as though they no longer recognized the biologically appropriate releasing stimuli for such activity. The monkeys had no evident visual sensory deficits, could perform visual discriminations and generalize across dimensions of size, brightness, colour and shape. Their inability to recognize the significance of visual stimuli is thus not easily attributable to sensory loss. Though visual agnosia was their main concern, Klüver and Bucy in fact noted from incidental observations that their animals seemed to be agnosic for auditory and tactile stimuli as well and, again, there was no apparent impairment in sensitivity in either of these channels. If this is true and the only channels left with access to abstract systems in the monkeys were those of olfaction and taste it is not surprising that they explored the meaning of their world by mouth and nose. The Klüver–Bucy syndrome is not species specific as similar cases have been described in humans, albeit rarely. Perhaps the most complete example was that reported by Marlowe et al. (1975) of a 20-year-old man who had suffered gross bilateral damage to his temporal lobes as a result of a viral infection. In addition to showing hypersexuality he tended to examine food and non-food objects orally and repetitively, apparently unable to gain information by tactile or visual means alone. He was unable to recognize a wide variety of common objects and when handed his razor, for example, would stare at it in a bewildered fashion. He was able, however, to copy the actions of another patient using a razor and succeeded by this means in shaving himself. His ability to distinguish food from non-food items visually was limited and he is reported as having ingested among other strange dietary elements, dog food, ink, cleaning paste and plastic bread wrappers, showing a preference for liquids or soft solids.

The lesions responsible for the Klüver–Bucy syndrome and its attendant agnosias involve a variety of structures and a number of later studies have shown that certain symptoms result from more restricted lesions. The indiscriminate hypersexuality and loss of aggression to normally adequate stimuli have been seen after lesions of the amygdalar nuclei in cats (Schreiner & Kling, 1953) and in monkeys, with appropriate changes in dominance hierarchies (Pribram, 1962; Rosvold *et al.*, 1954). The importance of temporal cortex itself, however, has also been underlined by Meyer (1958) in monkeys with temporal lobe lesions in which every effort was made to restrict the lesion to the surface of the hemisphere. With bilateral lesions Meyer's animals showed an inability to differentiate visually between food and such inedible items as nuts and bolts. Rubber snakes, which frightened the normal animals, had no great significance for the lesioned monkeys and one of them succeeded in taking the model from Meyer's hand and biting off its head. What Meyer calls 'the laboratory triumvirate of negative objects' — net, water hose and broom, had similarly lost their meaning for animals with temporal lobe lesions.

If, as I have suggested, abstract memory in mammals is closely associated with neocortex and if agnosia is a product of damage within, or in access to abstract memory systems then total removal of neocortex should produce among other symptoms a 'global' agnosia. The only sensory system which might be exempted is olfaction and it is possible that olfactory abstract memory systems may be extraneocortical. Neodecorticated mammals, as noted earlier, do not appear to be impaired in their ability to use association memory systems and consequently perform well in situations which emphasize associative learning. Pavlovian conditioning (Oakley & Russell, 1977), autoshaping (Oakley *et al.*, 1981) and alleyway running (Oakley, 1979c) are all tackled as well, or even more efficiently, in neodecorticate as in normal rats and rabbits. There are as yet no direct assessments of sensory capacity in totally neodecorticated animals but both their sensory and motor abilites are adequate to mediate Pavlovian light-tone discriminations (Oakley & Russell, 1976), to detect and respond to both moving and to illuminated levers in an autoshaping situation (Oakley *et al.*, 1981) and preliminary work indicates that they are capable of performing well in a horizontal/vertical stripe discrimination (Oakley, 1981b). They are certainly capable of running around detours in a chicane alleyway and of finding and responding to a variety of manipulanda in Skinner boxes. Despite their apparent sensory and motor competence in these types of situation, however, neodecorticates are impaired in a variety of ways compared to normal animals in operant bar pressing. The most likely reason for this is that, though it could solve the problem using association memory alone, the normal animal makes use of both representational and abstract memory systems whenever possible. What the neodecorticate lacks is 'cognitive overlay' and it is obvious to an observer, as I have noted before (Oakley, 1979a), that the neodecorticate performs the objectively appropriate response without giving the impression of insight or that it really knows what it is doing. Lest this subjectivity seems overly self-indulgent I would like to add to my own comments some of Lashley's observations drawn from his studies of neocortically lesioned rats in latch boxes (Lashley, 1935). Lashley noted, for instance, that though there were no differences in terms of trials taken to solve the problem using two-latch boxes, the neocortically lesioned animals had 'less insight', showed 'less initiative' and were generally more 'stereotyped' in their behaviour. One possible way in which abstract memory systems might prove an advantage in a Skinner box is if the animal came to the situation with a concept along the lines of 'objects to be manipulated for reward' or at least developed the equivalent of such a concept in relation to the particular manipulandum. In fact this is precisely what

59

Lashley suggested. Talking again of the latch-box problems, he noted that the normal rat, unlike the neodecorticate, appeared to dissociate the latch from the other parts of the problem and later to react to it 'as an object to be manipulated in a certain way'. I have used a simple test of manipulandum identification in neodecorticate rabbits which involved moving the treadle to a different part of the Skinner box once the animal had learned to press it for food (Oakley, 1978). The neodecorticates, in fact, found the manipulandum in its new position and it exerted some stimulus control over their actions inasmuch as they produced the treadle-press response towards it. Unlike the normals, however, they did not go on to use the treadle in its new position in the way they had previously to obtain reinforcement, instead they treated the situation as though it represented a totally new problem and devised a new solution to it. There are of course a number of other possible reasons for the neodecorticate's failure to transfer its response to a new manipulandum position and it would be overstepping the data to claim to have identified 'manipulandagnosia' in these animals. Such a label, however, would sum up exactly my feeling about the neodecorticate rabbit's behaviour as I watched during the transfer tests. I offer these observations as an indication that a condition akin to agnosia is detectable in rats and rabbits as well as in primates, cats and dogs, after neocortical damage. There is clearly a need, however, to clarify the criteria to be used for identifying agnosia in subprimates and in designing appropriate tests to assess the underlying abstract memory deficit.

Abstract memory systems have been more extensively studied in animals in situations where a performance rule must be abstracted from a series of test trials which embody that rule. (For general reviews see Davey, 1981, Ch. 11; Riopelle & Hill, 1974; Warren, 1974.) A few studies of this sort have assessed the ability of animals to abstract common elements from environmental stimulus displays and to develop appropriate concepts of, for example, shape or form. One notable example is that of Fields (1932) who, after many training exposures to a variety of triangles, was able to get rats to display at least a limited concept of 'triangularity' and to respond appropriately to triangular shapes irrespective of their size or orientation and whether they were solid, outline drawings or composed of dots. More recently pigeons have been shown to learn the concept of an 'A' and to apply it appropriately to different typefaces and handwritten letters (Morgan et al., 1976). Similarly, in delayed matching to sample problems, the animal must not only use its working memory to remember which item it has just seen but must also know the rule by which to form its choice, i.e. it must choose the stimulus which is the same as the sample. That this embodies a rule and is not a self-evident product of the situation is indicated by the fact, as Owen and Butler (1981) point out, that monkeys typically find it easier to learn the non-matching version of the problem, where they have to choose from the two-object stimulus set the object which was not presented as the sample. The abstracted rule can in fact be quite complex. In an 'oddity' discrimination the animal typically must select from a three stimulus array the stimulus which is 'odd' in the sense that it differs in some definite way from the other two stimuli, which in turn are similar to each other. Correct performance on oddity problems has been shown in chimpanzees (Nissen & McCulloch, 1937), rats (Wodinsky et al., 1953), pigeons (Urcuioli & Nevin, 1975; Zentall & Hogan, 1974) and canaries (Pastore, 1954). In conditional oddity problems, which rhesus monkeys can solve, the appropriate solution is indicated by some second cue such as the colour of the tray on which the three objects are presented. When the stimulus tray is white, for example, the odd coloured object should be selected but if the tray is dark the odd shaped object is correct (Harlow, 1943 cited by Davey, 1981).

Further evidence for the extraction of performance rules is that as problems of the same sort are repeated the animal may develop what Harlow (1949) called a learning set, enabling it to apply the rule more rapidly to each new problem in the series (see also Oakley, 1979a). A well documented example is that of reversal learning set formation. Oakley (1979d), for example, trained rabbits to press one of two treadles in a Skinner box for food reward. Once the animals were pressing reliably only the reinforced treadle, the reinforcement conditions were reversed and food was given only for pressing the previously non-reinforced treadle. It took the animals longer in fact to reverse their treadle press performance than it had taken them to learn to press only one treadle in the first place. Once they had learned to press the new treadle exclusively, the reinforcement conditions were reversed once more, and so on until 15 response reversals had been completed. By the final reversals the rabbits were switching very rapidly to pressing the other treadle as soon as the experimenter changed the reinforcement conditions, often taking only one or two presses to decide which was the reinforced treadle for that session. Learning sets of this sort culminating in very rapid solutions to new examples of a familiar problem have been shown in a variety of other two-choice situations, such as object quality discriminations in a range of primates as well as cats, mink, ferrets, skunks and chickens (see Warren, 1974, for a review). With two-object discriminations the animal can only be correct on the first trial of a new problem on a 50 : 50 basis but can be 100% correct on the second trial by adopting a win–stay : lose–shift strategy. Riopelle and Chinn (1961) reported an interesting variation on this theme by always placing the correct object in the same position, say always on the left, on the first trial of each new problem. The monkeys in this study could thus use trial one to identify the correct object for the new problem on a positional basis but had to choose thereafter on the basis of the object itself irrespective of its position. They were eventually able to perform at around 80% correct on trial one of each new problem and over 90% correct on the second trial. The combination of rules underlying this strategy could clearly only be abstracted over a series of such problems.

The ability to form learning sets, reversal learning sets in particular, was proposed by Bitterman (1965a, 1965b) as an index of phylogenetic advance-ment. This conclusion was based on his earlier observation that fish (goldfish and African mouthbreeders) did not form reversal learning sets with either visual or spatial problems, whereas birds (pigeons) and mammals (rats) did so on both types of problem. Reptiles (turtles), on the other hand, were appro-priately intermediate in their performance and formed reversal learning sets on spatial problems but not on visual problems. The reality of this phylogenetic hierarchy has since been questioned by studies such as that of Squier (1969) using two fish of the species *Astronotus ocellatus* (Oscars) which were able to form good learning sets in between 9 and 12 reversals of a visual discrimination (see Warren, 1974, for further discussion). Even more difficult to accommodate into Bitterman's hierarchical scheme is the fact that Morrow and Smithson (1969) have shown the development of a spatial learning set over nine reversals in a T-maze by the invertebrate *Porcellio scaber* (an isopod, closely related to the woodlouse) and another invertebrate, the octopus, forms visual reversal learning sets (Mackintosh, 1965). While the formation of learning sets is clearly an ability which is more widely distributed in the animal kingdom than Bitterman supposed, there is still a case to be made for the wider occurrence and greater efficiency of learning set performance in mammals, and in primates and cetaceans (dolphins, porpoises, etc.) in particular (Mackintosh, 1974, pp. 610–19; Jerison, 1982; Passingham, 1981). There is the further possibility that improvements over a series of reversals in non-primates depend on factors other than the development of generally applicable strategies, which seems to be the case in rhesus monkeys and chimps (see Sutherland & Mackintosh, 1971, especially pp. 318–36 and Ch. 12). Bitterman (1965a) also suggested as part of his rationale for the hierarchical view that mammalian learning set performance was mediated by neocortex. There is in fact evidence for a strong relationship between neocortex and efficiency of learning set formation in mammals. The ability to form visual reversal learning sets appears to be abolished by temporal neocortical lesions in the tree shrew (Diamond & Hall, 1969) and by the removal of around 70% of neocortex in the rat (Gonzalez et al., 1964). Decortication also severely impairs, but does not completely prevent, spatial reversal learning set formation in the rat (Gonzalez et al., 1964; Kolb & Whishaw, 1981) and the rabbit (Oakley, 1979d). The greater sensitivity of visual reversal learning set performance to neocortical damage implied by these data is also consistent with Bitterman's suggestion based on the phylogenetic series that in vertebrates the ability to form spatial reversal learning sets is phylogenetically older than visual learning set ability and is less dependent upon neocortex or its homologues. This in turn suggests that separate functional and anatomical systems may be involved in learning set formation when spatial or visual stimuli are involved and is similar to the possibility of modality-specific abstract memory systems which emerged from the earlier discussion of agnosias. Evidence from Warren (1966, cited by Sutherland & Mackintosh, 1971) further indicates that in primates at least an additional, non-modality-specific process is involved as rhesus monkeys show positive transfer of reversal learning set ability from spatial to visual problems. Cats in the same study showed no such transfer. This outcome suggests either that cats, unlike monkeys, do not extract a rule such as win–stay : lose–shift or that, if they do, it shows far more situational specificity.

Evidence from transfer studies has also been used by Premack (1978) to suggest that pigeons, which show good evidence of learning the correct response in matching and non-matching to sample problems, do not generate a relational rule of sufficient strength to transfer to new examples of the same problem. The pigeon's performance on transfer tests appears to be more directly influenced by the absolute values of the original stimulus set than by a truly abstract relational concept of 'same' or 'different' (see Wright & Sands, 1981, for a model of pigeon matching to sample performance which is consistent with this view). Premack (1978) suggests a possible basis for a new phylogenetic hierarchy of behavioural competence in terms of the weightings which each species places on absolute versus relational factors in processing environmental information. Dolphins and primates again rise to the top with high weightings on the relational factor; a position, incidentally, which would be expected on the basis of their comparable, high evolutionary grade as determined on the basis of encephalization quotients (a measure of relative brain size — see Jerison, 1973,

1976, 1982; Russell, 1979). Chimpanzees in fact seem to categorize environmental objects and events quite spontaneously on the basis of very few experiences of them. To take one of Premack's own examples; the chimp Sarah on being introduced to a visitor wearing a soft wool skirt, touched the skirt and then ran to touch her crib blanket, which was of a similar texture. A more formal example of spontaneous conceptual clustering was seen when one of the chimps was handed a sample of nine items for later matching. The sample was a mixture of three items of dolls clothing, three food items and three toys which were sorted by the chimp and handed back to the experimenter clustered into these conceptual groups. Despite the low weighting assigned to absolute factors in chimps, however, they may occasionally override relational factors on transfer tests. Four young chimps trained to match to sample using toys failed to transfer on to a set of mixed toys and natural objects (sticks, plants and flowers). They based their decisions on absolute factors from original training and chose a toy on all trials irrespective of the sample being a toy or a natural object. When all toys were removed, however, and only natural items were used, the original match to sample rule was once more correctly applied and continued to control performance even when toys were reintroduced on later tests.

Where more natural concepts are concerned the pigeon fares rather better in assessments of its conceptual abilities (see Davey, 1981; Premack, 1978 for brief reviews). Herrnstein *et al.* (1976) for instance have shown pigeons slides of a variety of objects and scenes and have found that they can reliably learn to peck a response key whenever an exemplar of a tree or part of a tree appears or, in other subjects, when water is shown in any of its natural forms (streams, lakes, seashores, puddles, etc.). It has so far proved impossible to determine which features or combination of features define the concept of 'tree' or 'water' for the pigeon and simple associative processes based on individual attributes or on generalization appear to be ruled out. Premack (1978) concludes that, as pigeons do not seem to recognize water soon after hatching, they are programmed genetically to form a general concept of water on the basis of a very few examples from the vast potential array. Clearly, in evolutionary terms this is a very attractive notion and fits well with the discussion of levels of information processing in the earlier part of this chapter, especially where such obviously pigeon-relevant features as water and trees are concerned. It is less easy, though not impossible, to imagine the origin of a biological disposition which underlies the ability to recognize a particular young human female from all other people, which pigeons are also capable of acquiring. At the moment then the possibility of truly abstract concepts must be acknowledged for the pigeon. They would, however, seem to be limited, and perhaps innately so, in their range compared to the more open ability to create conceptual classes which is seen in cetaceans, in higher primates in general and in humans in particular. It is tempting to equate this expanded capacity for deriving and storing abstracted information with the obvious expansion of neocortex which has occurred in the latter groups.

2.4.3 Working Memory Systems

Reference memory systems have been defined above as being concerned with the storage of information which retains its relevance to the animal over relatively long time intervals. Some aspects of the total information pool available to any one individual are, however, relevant only on a shorter-term basis. In particular some types of information need only be stored for as long as it takes to complete a specific task and it would clearly be wasteful to store on a long-term basis information which is only useful in the short term. Indeed, there may be positive advantages to removing that information from the system once it has served its purpose. It would be equally wasteful, on the other hand, to abandon the contents of reference memory too readily. Shorter-term and longer-term memories would thus seem to demand separate handling and storage facilities. The specifically task-oriented nature of the shorter-term stores is emphasized by grouping them together under the general label of 'working memory' and it will, I hope, be evident from what follows that working memory systems do indeed have a degree of both functional and anatomical independence from longer-term memory stores. It will equally be evident that efficient performance depends on integrating information from both types of store.

Both the need for working and reference memory systems and the relationship between them can be illustrated in relation to naturally occurring food-searching behaviours. When discussing representational memory it was noted that cognitive mapping of the environment may assist animals in returning to a nest site or known food source by a variety of routes and in devising the most economical route to visit a series of food sites. There is a further consideration, however, in relation to foraging behaviours which makes slightly different demands on the memory systems. The source of food for some species occurs locally in large quantities which can be repeatedly exploited. This situation is seen in fruit bats, who will return to exploit the food supply on a particular tree over several days (Morrison, 1978) and has an experimental analogue in the traditional laboratory maze with food always supplied in the same goal box. A long-term cognitive map of the maze would be sufficient for the animal to find food reliably not only from the start-box, as is usual, but from any other point in the maze (e.g. Olton, 1979). For other species, or in other situations, however, food may occur in small amounts distributed widely throughout the home range and it may be advantageous for the animal not to visit any one location too often. This is particularly the case if the source requires time to be replenished. Optimal foraging for species with this type of food supply should involve win–shift strategies, where food rewards are concerned, coupled with a good working memory for recently visited food sites. Foraging performance which corresponds to this pattern has been identified experimentally in ring doves (Wilkie et al., 1981) and in rats (e.g. Olton, 1978) and has been seen in natural or semi-natural conditions in a nectar-feeding bird, Loxops virens, (Kamil, 1978), in bumblebees (Pyke, 1979) and in the rat (Olton et al., 1977b). An appropriate apparatus for studying this type of foraging is a maze consisting of a number of symmetrically placed arms radiating from a central point like the spokes in a wheel. A single item of food is placed out of sight at the end of each arm and to be efficient an animal must visit each arm only once. Using radial arm mazes of this sort rats have been shown to have a working, or 'list', memory for up to 17 items (Olton et al., 1977a) and ring doves up to 14 items (Wilkie et al., 1981). Work with a hierarchical version of the maze indicates that the rat's capacity for storing spatial information in working memory may be as high as 32 units (Roberts, 1979). In contrast to these impressive figures preliminary work on the ferret, a mustelid carnivore, suggests that it performs rather poorly on the radial arm maze, which is consistent with the view that it is a win–stay forager (D. Einon, 1981, personal communication).

Performance in the radial arm maze by rats seems not to depend on cues within the maze or on response patterns or strategies but on extra-maze cues. This suggests that the rat's solution of the problem may be based on a cognitive map of the entire apparatus in relation to its environmental context, which serves on a long-term basis for subsequent tests, plus a shorter-term working memory of alleys entered which can be used in conjunction with the map to ensure that re-entries are avoided within a test session. It would seem to be important for the win–shift forager that working memory be limited in some way as there is an increasing probability as time passes that any given location may have been replenished. The duration and capacity of working memory will thus be expected to vary widely across species depending on the distribution and rate of replenishment of food sources. The specification of durational and capacity aspects of working memory will also be expected to vary within species, and within individual members of that species, in relation to different resources. Food and water sources for instance are likely to have different distribution and replenishment characteristics and so require either different strategies (win–shift or win–stay) or working memory systems with different duration and capacity characteristics to ensure their efficient exploitation. It is worth noting also that rats escaping from water adopt win–stay strategies from the outset of testing, in contrast to the marked win–shift tendency they show in food searching behaviour (Morris, 1982). In the radial maze Olton (1978) suggests that efficient performance is maintained by resetting working memory and clearing it of its contents at the end of each experimental session, though this does not explain how the timing of resetting is determined under more natural conditions.

In addition to assessing the capacity of working memory in animals, a number of studies have been concerned with the duration of storage of single items within it. One of the most common procedures involves delayed matching to sample (D'Amato & Cox, 1976; Honig, 1978; Roberts & Grant, 1976: Ruggiero & Flagg, 1976). In a typical delayed matching to sample procedure a sample stimulus or display is presented to the animal and then, after a delay with no stimuli, two stimuli are presented, one of which is the sample already seen. The animal's task is to select the sample stimulus, usually for a food reward, with only the memory of the original stimulus as a guide. Pigeons can produce respectable performances with delays between sample and test stimuli of up to 60 s and a well-trained monkey up to 9 min (Honig, 1978). Solution of this type of matching to sample requires the combination of a working memory for the particular sample shown on a given trial with a simple performance rule held in reference memory (i.e. something like 'choose sample'). Working memory is allied to more complex performance rules in conditional delayed matching to sample problems. D'Amato and Worsham (1974) for example, devised a delayed conditional matching task in which the sample (a red disc or a vertical line) was followed by a two-stimulus display (a triangle and a circle). If the red disc had been the sample the correct choice was the triangle and when the sample had been the line, the circle was correct. The monkeys in this study handled the problem as easily as the conventional delayed match to sample procedure.

If working memory is used by an animal in conjunction with reference memory to guide its behaviour it is possible that the nature of the reference memory system itself has some influence on the characteristics of working memory. There is some evidence in fact that this is the case and, to anticipate the following discussion, it would appear that far more efficient and more durable working memories may be available for use in conjunction with representational memory than with association memory. With this in mind one particular study by O'Keefe and Conway (1980) is worth considering in a little detail. These researchers tested rats in an elevated + -shaped maze set in a curtained enclosure, on the walls of which were placed six distinctive cues bearing a constant relationship with the goal arm containing food. A number of earlier studies had indicated that rats can use these extra-maze cues to run directly to the goal arm irrespective of the arm in which they are placed at the start of any given trial. Furthermore, it appears that the animals do not base their solution on turn strategies or on simply approaching any particular cue. The latter would be an example of what O'Keefe and Nadel (1978) have called a 'guidance hypothesis' based on association systems. The rat in fact appears to use representational systems to form a cognitive map of the maze in relation to all six extra-maze cues. The condition where the cues are all present as the animal makes its choice of goal arm is referred to as the 'perceptual' version of the task. The same experimental situation can serve as a basis for a working memory test by simply removing all six extra-maze cues after the animal has been placed in the start-arm and allowed time to register their location. The animal is then allowed to exit from the start-arm after a variable delay period in the absence of the extra-maze cues and so must choose the goal-arm on the basis of its memory of the cue locations on that trial. This working memory plus representational memory version O'Keefe and Conway term a 'despatch' task as a mnemonic for *delayed spatial choice*. They found with this procedure that rats could still choose the goal-arm with delays of up to 30 min even if they were forced to make a detour en route. In fact there was no evidence of any fall in performance as the delay was increased to this value, which was the longest they tested. This contrasts with the very much shorter values obtained for working memory in the delayed matching to sample studies mentioned above but is consistent with other studies which have tested the rat's working memory for spatial locations where accurate retention over delays of 50 min (Olton, 1972) and even 135 min (Sinnamon *et al.*, 1978) has been seen.

In a second study reported in the same paper by O'Keefe and Conway (1980) one group of animals was encouraged to use association memory as the reference memory in its solution of the spatial choice problem by having all the extra-maze cues clustered at the end of the goal arm. All that was required for correct performance thus was to approach any one, or any combination of cues. The first surprise was that these rats took significantly longer to solve this apparently simple problem compared to the rats which were trained with distributed cues. Rats, it would seem, are more prepared to learn about spatial locations on the basis of widely dispersed cues, that is to use a cognitive mapping strategy, than to use the intuitively simpler method of approaching a set of cues associated with food. What was even more interesting was that none of the animals which learned the perceptual task under the clustered cues (association memory) condition were able to perform the working memory version of the same task. They did not seem to be able to recall where the cues had been once they had been removed from view. Successful solution under conditions of response delay after associative learning depends on working memory bridging the gap between cue registration and the opportunity to perform the response. The working memory capacity available to the animals under these conditions was apparently unable to mediate even the shortest of delays. Long-term memory for the association between food and the cues, on the other hand, was clearly present in view of the fact that these animals could learn the perceptual version of the clustered cue task, in which the cues remained in sight while they were making their response.

As a final demonstration of the importance of cognitive mapping O'Keefe and Conway (1980) sectioned the fornices in several of the animals which had already learned the distributed cue version of the task. This lesion, which disrupts communication within the septo-hippocampal system, they believed would impair or prevent cognitive mapping (see O'Keefe & Nadel, 1978). This appears to be exactly what happened as the animals not only forgot the solution to the distributed cue problem but took very many more trials to re-solve it than they had originally. Moreover, they were no longer able to perform the working memory version of the distributed cue problem. These final observations can be used to suggest that the fornix-damaged animals solved the distributed cue problem post-operatively by using an associative memory strategy (approaching one of the cues for example.) On this latter point it can be noted that an occasional normal animal also appears to use association memory to solve the distributed cue problem, taking very many more trials than usual, and is then unable to perform in the working memory version. Furthermore, fornix lesions do not affect performance of the perceptual version of the distributed cue task in these aberrant animals, which is consistent with the view that this type of lesion does not affect association memory (Oakley, 1981a). Overall it would appear not only that the rat learns more rapidly in this type of maze using cognitive mapping strategies than it does using associative mechanisms but also that information is better retained in working memory within the context of representational memory systems than it is in conjunction with association memory. As to the role of the hippocampal–septal complex it should be noted that though I have followed O'Keefe and Conway's view that fornix lesions impair cognitive mapping directly there is evidence from other test situations to suggest that the major effect is on working memory systems themselves (Olton et al., 1980). For further discussion and an experimental analysis of working-memory and spatial-mapping views of hippocampal function see Morris (1982).

The figures which have been quoted above for the capacity of working memory and durability of items within it in animals contrasts rather sharply with the brief retention periods (of the order of a few seconds) and the limit of six to seven items claimed for working (or short-term) memory capacity in the modal (e.g. Atkinson & Shiffrin, 1971) model of human memory (see Baddeley, 1976). More recent theoretical developments in human memory, however, have moved towards the opinion that a unitary view of short-term memory systems is inappropriate. Increasingly a variety of short-term memory systems are described in relation to speech perception, speech production, reading, arithmetical calculations, problem solving, etc., which are seen as part of a more extensive working memory system (e.g. Hitch, 1980, and this volume). In view of the animal literature it may perhaps be anticipated, especially if human working memory systems outside the traditional verbal area are included, that different subsystems may have different capacities and durations depending on the tasks for which they are serving as control processes.

Whatever the final decision concerning the range of processes to be included as part of human short-term memory systems there is already a well-established clinical literature which attests to the appropriateness of drawing a general distinction between short- and long-term memory processes on both anatomical and functional grounds. Detailed testing of human amnesics in particular has shown that the operation of long-term storage systems can be impaired while short-term memory mechanisms remain largely unaffected (e.g. Baddeley, 1976; Kolb & Whishaw, 1980, Ch. 15; Mayes & Meudell, this volume; Milner, 1970; Warrington, 1979). Damage to the hippocampus and related structures has traditionally been implicated as a critical factor in producing this effect though there is currently renewed debate on this issue (Mayes & Meudell, this volume; Squire, 1980) as well as on the precise nature of the long-term memory deficit itself (Meudell & Mayes, 1982). The converse syndrome of impaired short-term memory with sparing of longer-term storage systems has also been described following, in this case, left parieto-occipital lesions in man (Warrington & Shallice, 1969, 1972; Warrington, 1979). As a parallel to this literature, Owen and Butler (1981) have recently described an analogue of the human amnesic syndrome in which long-term memory is selectively impaired in monkeys with fornix lesions. The basic procedure they used was that of delayed non-matching to sample, which is similar to the delayed matching to sample procedures described above except that the subject must choose from the two-object stimulus set that object which was *not* previously presented as the sample stimulus. Monkeys find the non-matching version the easier of the two. Owen and Butler also included a test of the effects of visual distraction by maintaining the animals in either a brightly lit cage or in darkness during the delay period. When the stimuli used in this type of problem are drawn from a very large set so that the individual stimuli are seen infrequently (less than once per week in this study) monkeys show good long-term retention (over 24 h) with very little sensitivity to interference by irrelevant stimuli. When the stimulus set is small (only two stimuli in Owen and Butler's study), however, a normal animal's memory for which stimulus was the sample on a given trial declines rapidly over time and performance is highly susceptible to interference effects. Delayed non-matching to sample with a restricted stimulus set has thus been claimed as analogous to tests of human short-term memory. The fornix-lesioned animals were severely impaired in the large stimulus set version of the task in the Owen and Butler study if the delay was in excess of 70 s, but performed like normal animals at all delay intervals (10, 70, 130 s) when a restricted sample set was used. In the latter case both groups showed a rapid decline in performance as the delay interval increased. The authors concluded from this that the fornix lesions had introduced a selective impairment in long-term memory mechanisms.

The importance of Owen and Butler's result is clear from the point of view of differentiating long-term and short-term memory capacities but it is less easy to interpret in detail. One likely candidate for the mechanism mediating long-term performance in the large sample tests is recognition memory which, as noted above, has been shown by Gaffan (1976, 1980) to be impaired by fornix lesions. The residual, but still high, levels of performance by the fornix lesion group on the large sample tests could be mediated by association memory as the stimulus sample was reinforced at the time of its presentation, though of course the animal must select the non-sample item for its subsequent choice to be correct. Visual short-term memory is contraindicated by the fact that performance of neither group of animals was affected by visual distraction on these tests. Performance in the restricted sample version, however, is less suitable for mediation by recognition memory as both of the stimuli forming the set are seen frequently with very little difference in their recency. This appears to predispose both normal and lesioned animals to use an alternative, shorter-term and less efficient strategy. This interpretation is of course strengthened by the fact that fornix lesions do not affect performance on the restricted sample test. Association memory is also inappropriate as both stimuli had been equally and recently associated with reward. Owen and Butler concluded that delayed non-matching to sample with restricted stimulus sets is based on neither recognition nor association memory but 'is mediated by a third, that is to say, short-term mechanism' (Owen & Butler, 1981, p. 122). In view of the task demands of this test, the relatively short durations of delay which could be bridged and the deleterious effects of visual distraction on performance, it seems possible that the short-term process involved with small stimulus sets could be event memory. Whatever the finally preferred interpretation of the Owen and Butler study it supports the distinction between short-term and longer-term processes in memory and stands as a further evidence of the need not only to consider memory as composed of a number of distinct purpose-built subsystems but also supports the belief that they will prove to be anatomically distinct entities.

Working memory then, is a generic term for a variety of shorter-term control processes. In terms of the classification of varieties of memory in this chapter, working memory subsystems may vary according to the demands of the task itself and in relation to the particular reference memory system which is employed concurrently. It also seems likely, as suggested in relation to the Owen and Butler (1981) study, that event memory could serve as a simple working memory system in some instances. It is perhaps also worth noting here that eidetic imagery which, as discussed earlier, can be seen as a very long-term event memory is of limited value as a form of working memory, especially where familiar material is concerned, unless the image can be located accurately within a temporal framework. The mnemonist described by Luria (1968) for instance, could retain and read off information from what were apparently eidetic images, but in order to do so he had to bring back to mind the entire occasion on which he saw the original items. The process took some time and, in the context of what has been said above, would seem to imply that the eidetic image was being used as an unusual form of working memory in conjunction with episodic memories encoded via representational systems.

2.5 Modularity in Memory Systems

A strong case has been made for the advantages of modular designs in information processing systems whether these are artificial systems designed by humans or biological systems emerging by the process of evolution (Marr, 1976; Shallice, 1981). A similar case has been made on anatomical and physiological evidence that the brain, or more specifically neocortex, is organized in a modular fashion as a series of columns or barrels, each of some 2500 neurons and organized as an independent processing unit (Eccles, 1980; Mountcastle, 1978). A modular system is one in which as many as possible of the processes or sub-processes are carried out as independently as possible, preferably by physically separate mechanisms. A major advantage with this type of design is that new or extended facilities for information processing and/or storage could be added, or an existing one modified, without redesigning the whole system. This type of argument has a certain intuitive appeal, particularly when applied in the context of the evolution of vertebrate central nervous systems. One distinct advantage is that this line of reasoning provides an alternative to the early, but persistent view of nervous system evolution embodied in the principle of encephalization or corticalization of function. The latter held that as more rostral structures developed, the functions of phylogenetically older parts of the central nervous system were transferred, presumably in improved form, to more recently developed areas. This type of thinking has received increasing criticism of late on both theoretical and empirical grounds and is being discarded in favour of the view that once structures develop in a particular functional context they retain that ability (see for example Oakley, 1979a; Russell, 1980; Warren & Kolb, 1978; Weiskrantz, 1977). Newer structures, or elaborations of existing structures, in this view reflect the development of additional abilities rather than the transfer of existing functions to new substrates. The more recent view is of course easily accommodated by the principle of modularity.

An even more powerful reason for accepting the notion of modularity, however, is that it is consistent with, not to say demanded by, a vast amount of empirical evidence, particularly that from human neuropsychology (e.g. Geschwind, 1979; Luria, 1973). The modular view of brain organization predicts that damage may impair functional subsystems selectively, frequently not preventing the operation of the system as a whole but affecting its mode of operation in a systematic way and rendering it less efficient. A modular organization also means that damage to one subsystem will leave other subsystems within the same functional domain unaffected. An obvious example of a functional system displaying these characteristics is that of language, composed as it is of groups of dedicated neurons forming subsystems at separate anatomical loci (e.g. Geschwind, 1979). An elegant argument for the modularity principle has also been offered recently in the demonstration of separate functional subsystems within the, already specialized, domain of reading (Shallice, 1981).

The account of memory put forward in this chapter also embodies the modularity principle. In very gross terms the information gain occurring in levels one to four is mediated by functionally and physically separate systems or subsystems. Clearly the information gained by the gene pool is not stored in the same form or at the same anatomical location as that derived via variable epigenesis or learning. The systems are interactive of course and hierarchically arranged. There can be no level four cultural information gain without the participation of second or third level systems for instance. What is claimed, though, is that as each level of information gain and storage emerged during the evolutionary process it was mediated so far as possible by new systems or subsystems which were functionally and anatomically distinct from each other and from those already in existence. The advantage of the new systems being of course that they increased the information gaining and storage power of the organism as a whole and thereby increased its evolutionary fitness.

Modularity is more conventionally evident within a given level. In terms of

70

level three systems I have suggested at least five types of memory, all of which I have claimed are functionally and anatomically separable, though once again the memory systems are interactive and hierarchical. Abstract memory systems for instance were said to be impossible without the mediation of the dynamic aspects of representational systems, though interestingly, the storage of abstract memory and representational memory of the episodic sort is clearly independent. I have tried to give examples not only of the different types of memory in animals and man but also of instances in which lesions can be shown to affect one type of memory without affecting others (see Warrington, 1979 for more examples of dissociations between memory systems). Neodecortication, for example, was considered to abolish abstract memory, to impair representational memory to an extent which has not yet been determined, but to leave association and event memory completely intact (see also Oakley, 1981a). Similarly abstract memory can be impaired in agnosics without the losses in representational memory which result in the amnesic syndrome. One study which exemplifies the discrete damage which can occur within level three memory systems is a particular favourite of mine as it contains evidence relating to function in all five varieties of memory within level three systems. Weiskrantz and Warrington (1979) trained two human amnesics in a very impressive-looking Pavlovian conditioning apparatus which delivered a compound light and tone conditional stimulus followed by an air puff directly into the subject's eye as the unconditional stimulus. Despite their inability to retain information for everyday events for more than a few minutes, both subjects acquired a clear eyeblink to the conditional stimulus and were able to retain this conditional response over 10 min and 24 h breaks in testing. This clearly suggests intact event and association memory systems, though as no normal control subjects were run it does not exclude the possibility that eyeblink conditioning was not as rapid as normal in the two amnesics. In striking contrast to the retention of the conditional responses, neither subject when questioned in full view of the apparatus could remember even within 10 min of the end of a long conditioning session what the equipment had been used for or what they had been doing in it. Representational memory systems were thus severely impaired in so far as retrieval of episodic or biographical information was concerned. Abstract memory though would seem to have been intact both from before the onset of the patients' amnesic symptoms, as revealed by their IQ scores (WAIS, full scale scores of 116 and 123 respectively) and during the conditioning tests. The latter is indicated in an incidental comment made by one of the patients. This patient was talking casually about himself after one of the conditioning sessions and among other things mentioned that he had a weak right eye 'because someone had once blown air into it'. I take the latter to be an instance in which information entered an abstract memory store as a 'fact' devoid of the spatial/temporal context which would be expected of representational memory, especially as the subject never mentioned an air puff in connection with the apparatus or his experience with it. Short-term memory is also intact in this type of amnesic patient.

Finally, there is modularity within the five memory types. In the case of event memory I would anticipate modality-specific subsystems and for association memory both modality-specific and paradigm-specific systems. Different substrates may be expected to underly habituation (E1 → no E2 associations), Pavlovian conditioning (E1 → E2 associations where both events are sensory), instrumental learning (traditionally E1→E2 associations where either E1 or E2 is a motor event and the other event is sensory) and motor chaining (E1→E2 associations where both events are motor). My category of representational memory covers a variety of possibly distinct subsystems covering recognition memory, spatial mapping and episodic or biographical memory, and within each of these subsystems there is the possibility of modality, or some other, specificity. Equally, within abstract memory systems, those dealing with abstracted rules and those storing word meanings or concepts need not be the same. Indeed, if the modularity which exists even within semantic memory at both sensory and category levels is considered it would be surprising if modularity were not the rule generally in abstract memory systems. Working memory has equally been portrayed as a system of specialized control mechanisms which vary in their duration and capacity specification according to the type of task and reference memory system which they support.

The truth is that once a modularity principle is adopted, as seems to be the case for biological information gaining and storage systems, there is no limit to its potential expression. Each functionally and anatomically distinct subsystem becomes a candidate for further development in a modular fashion into sub-subsystems and so forth. Warrington's (1975) distinction between agnosia for concrete words and agnosia for abstract words is thus not an oddity of the peculiar arrangement of semantic memory but embodies a design principle which governs the entirety of information-gaining and storage systems. Cognitive psychologists should not, therefore, be shy about proliferating small boxes in their models of memory functions, as this would seem to be the way that evolution has improved its own product. They should, however, look to phylogenetic or neuropsychological evidence for the existence of any new box which they wish to introduce.

Acknowledgements

I am grateful to Lesley Eames, Laura Goldstein, Henry Plotkin, Andrew Mayes and R.E. Rawles for their comments on earlier versions of this chapter.

References

ADAMS, J.A. and DIJKSTRA, S. (1966) Short-term memory for motor responses. *Journal of Experimental Psychology* **71**, 314–318.

ALCOCK, J. (1975) *Animal Behavior: An Evolutionary Approach.* Sinauer Associates, Sunderland, Massachusetts.

ANNABLE, A. and WEARDEN, J.H. (1979) Grooming movements as operants in the rat. *Journal of the Experimental Analysis of Behavior,* **32**, 297–304.

ARAI, Y. (1981) Synaptic correlates of sexual differentiation. *Trends in Neurosciences,* **4**, 291–293.

ATKINSON, R.C. and SHIFFRIN, R.M. (1971) The control of short-term memory. *Scientific American,* **225**, 82–90.

BADDELEY, A.D. (1976) *The Psychology of Memory.* Harper & Row, London.

BAKER, R.R.B. (1972) Butterfly territories. *Journal of Animal Ecology,* **41**, 453–469.

BARTLETT, F.C. (1932) *Remembering.* Cambridge University Press, Cambridge.

BATESON, P.P.G. (1971) Imprinting. In: H. MOLTZ (Ed.) *Ontogeny of Vertebrate*

Behavior, pp. 369–378. Academic Press, New York.

BATESON, P.P.G. (1981) Ontogeny of behaviour. *British Medical Bulletin*, **37**, 159–164.

BATESON, P.P.G. (1982) Behavioural development and evolutionary processes. In: King's College Sociobiology Group (Eds.) *Current Problems in Sociobiology*. Cambridge University Press, Cambridge.

BEM, J. (1972) Self-perception theory. *Advances in Experimental Social Psychology*, **6**, 1–62.

BENINGER, R.J., KENDALL, S.B. and VANDERWOLF, C.H. (1974) The ability of rats to discriminate their own behaviors. *Canadian Journal of Psychology*, **28**, 79–91.

BENTON, A. (1978) The interplay of experimental and clinical approaches in brain lesion research. In: S. FINGER (Ed.) *Recovery from Brain Damage: Research and Theory*. Plenum Press, New York, pp. 49–68.

BITTERMAN, M.E. (1965a) Phyletic differences in learning. *American Psychologist*, **20**, 396–410.

BITTERMAN, M.E. (1965b) The evolution of intelligence. *Scientific American*, **212**, 92–100.

BLAKEMORE, C. and COOPER, G.F. (1970) Development of the brain depends on the visual environment. *Nature*, **228**, 477–478.

BOLLES, R.C. (1970) Species-specific defense reactions and avoidance learning. *Psychological Review*, **79**, 394–409.

BOLLES, R.C. (1976) Some relationships between learning and memory. In: D.L. MEDIN, W.A. ROBERTS and R.T. DAVIS (Eds.) *Processes of Animal Memory*, pp. 21–48. Lawrence Erlbaum Associates, Hillsdale, NJ.

BOLLES, R.C. (1979) *Learning Theory: Second Edition*. Holt, Rinehart and Winston, New York.

BOWER, G.H. and HILGARD, E.R. (1981) *Theories of Learning: Fifth Edition*. Prentice-Hall, Englewood Cliffs, NJ.

BRAIN, W.R. and WALTON, J.N. (1969) *Brain's Diseases of the Nervous System: Seventh Edition*. Oxford University Press London.

BRELAND, K. and BRELAND. M. (1972) The misbehavior of organisms. In: M.E.P. SELIGMAN and J.L. HAGER (Eds.) *Biological Boundaries of Learning*, pp. 181–186. Appleton-Century-Crofts, New York. (Reprinted from *American Psychologist*, 1961, **61**, 681–684)

BUCK, R. (1976) *Human Motivation and Emotion*. Wiley, New York.

COWEY, A. and WEISKRANTZ, L. (1963) A perimetric study of visual field defects in monkeys. *Quarterly Journal of Experimental Psychology*, **15**, 91–115.

CROOK, J.H. (1980) *The Evolution of Human Consciousness*. Clarendon Press, Oxford.

D'AMATO, M.R. and COX, J.K. (1976) Delay of consequences and short-term memory in monkeys. In: D.L. MEDIN, W.A. ROBERTS and R.T. DAVIS (Eds.) *Processes of Animal Memory*, pp. 49–78. Lawrence Erlbaum Associates, Hillsdale, NJ.

D'AMATO, M.R. and WORSHAM, R.W. (1974) Retrieval cues and short-term memory in capuchin monkeys. *Journal of Comparative and Physiological Psychology*, **86**, 274–282.

DAVEY, G.C.L. (1981) *Animal Learning and Conditioning*. Macmillan, London.

DAWKINS, R. (1976) *The Selfish Gene*. Oxford University Press, Oxford.

DEMPSTER, J.P. (1963) The population dynamics of grasshoppers and locusts. *Biological Reviews*, **38**, 490–529.

DENNIS, M. (1976) Dissociated naming and locating of body parts after left anterior temporal lobe resection. An experimental case study. *Brain and Language*, **3**, 147–163.

DEWSON, J.H. (1977) Preliminary evidence of hemispheric asymmetry of auditory function in monkeys. In: S. HARNAD, R.W. DOTY, L. GOLDSTEIN, J. JAYNES and G. KRAUTHAMER (Eds.) *Lateralization in the Nervous System*, pp. 63–71. Academic Press, New York.

DIAMOND, I.T. and HALL, W.C. (1969) Evolution of neocortex. *Science*, **164**, 251–262.

DICKINSON, A. (1980) *Contemporary Animal Learning Theory*. Cambridge University Press, Cambridge.

DICKINSON, A. (1981) Conditioning and associative learning. *British Medical Bulletin*, **37**, 165–168.

DIMOND, S.J. (1980) *Neuropsychology: A Textbook of Systems and Psychological Functions of the Human Brain*. Butterworths, London.

DIXON, N.F. and HENLEY, S.H.A. (1980) Without awareness. In: M. JEEVES (Ed.) *Psychology Survey No. 3*, pp. 31–50. George Allen and Unwin, London.

DOWNS, R.M. and STEA, D. (1977) *Maps in Minds: Reflections on Cognitive Mapping*. Harper & Row, London.

ECCLES, J.C. (1980) *The Human Psyche.* Springer, Berlin.

ELLEN, P. (1980) Cognitive maps and the hippocampus. *Physiological Psychology*, **8**, 168–174.

ENGEN, T. and ROSS, B.M. (1973) Long-term memory of odours with and without verbal descriptions. *Journal of Experimental Psychology*, **100**, 221–227.

FESTINGER, L. and CARLSMITH, J.M. (1959) Cognitive consequences of forced compliance. *Journal of Abnormal and Social Psychology*, **58**, 203–210.

FIELDS, P.E. (1932) Studies in concept formation: I. The development of the concept of triangularity by the white rat. *Comparative Psychology Monographs*, **9**, 1–70.

FRANSELLA, F. (1981) Personal construct psychology. In: F. FRANSELLA (Ed.) *Personality*, pp. 147–165. Methuen, London.

GAFFAN, D. (1972) Loss of recognition memory in rats with lesions of the fornix. *Neuropsychologia*, **10**, 327–341.

GAFFAN, D. (1976) Recognition memory in animals. In: J. BROWN (Ed.) *Recall and Recognition*, pp. 229–242. Wiley, London.

GAFFAN, D. (1980) Memory disorder. In: M. JEEVES (Ed.) *Psychology Survey No. 3*. pp. 51–61. George Allen and Unwin, London.

GALEF, B.G. (1976) Social transmission of acquired behavior: A discussion of tradition and social learning in vertebrates. *Advances in the Study of Behavior*, **6**, 77–100.

GALLUP, G.G. (1977) Self recognition in primates: A comparative approach to the bidirectional properties of consciousness. *American Psychologist*, **32**, 329–338.

GARCIA, J. and KOELLING, R.A. (1966) Relation of cue to consequence in avoidance learning. *Psychonomic Science*, **4**, 123–124.

GARCIA, J., McGOWAN, B.K. and GREEN, K.F. (1972) Biological constraints on conditioning. In: A.H. BLACK and W.F. PROKASY (Eds.) *Classical Conditioning II: Current Research and Theory*, pp. 3–27. Appleton-Century-Crofts, New York.

GARDNER, B.T. and GARDNER, R.A. (1969) Teaching sign language to a chimpanzee. *Science*, **165**, 664–672.

GESCHWIND, N. (1965) Disconnection syndromes in animals and man. Part II. *Brain*, **88**, 585–644.

GESCHWIND, N. (1979) Specializations of the human brain. In: *The Brain*, pp. 108–117. A Scientific American book. W.H. Freeman, San Francisco. (Reprinted from *Scientific American* 1979, **241**, No. 3, 158–168.)

GLEITMAN, H. (1971) Forgetting of long-term memories in animals. In: W.K. HONIG and P.H.R. JAMES (Eds.) *Animal Memory*, pp. 1–44. Academic Press, New York.

GONZALEZ, R.C., ROBERTS, W.A. and BITTERMAN, M.E. (1964) Learning in adult rats with extensive cortical lesions made in infancy. *American Journal of Psychology*, **77**, 547–562.

GOTTLIEB, G. (1976) Conceptions of prenatal development: Behavioral embryology. *Psychological Review*, **83**, 215–234.

GRANT, D.S. (1981) Intertrial interference in rat short-term memory. *Journal of Experimental Psychology: Animal Behavior Processes*, **7**, 217–227.

GREEN, D.W., MITCHELL, D.C. and HAMMOND, E.J. (1981) The scheduling of text integration processes in reading. *Quarterly Journal of Experimental Psychology*, **33A**, 455–464.

GREENOUGH, W.T. (1978) Development and memory: The synaptic connection. In: T. TEYLER (Ed.) *Brain and Learning*, pp. 127–145. D. Reidel Publishing Co., Dordrecht, Holland.

GRUNEBERG, M.M. (1978) The feeling of knowing, memory blocks and memory aids. In: M.M. GRUNEBERG and P. MORRIS (Eds.) *Aspects of Memory*, pp.186–209. Methuen, London.

HABER R.N. (1969) Eidetic images. *Scientific American*, **220**, 36–44.

HAILMAN, J.P. (1969) How an instinct is learned. *Scientific American*, **221**, 98–106.

HARLOW, H.F. (1943) Solution by rhesus monkeys of a problem involving the Weigh Principle using the matching-form-sample method. *Journal of Comparative Psychology*, **36**, 217–227.

HARLOW, H.F. (1949). The formation of learning sets. *Psychological Review*, **56**, 51–56.

HARVEY, N. and GREER, K. (1980) Action: The mechanisms of motor control. In: G. CAXTON (Ed.) *Cognitive Psychology: New Directions*, pp. 65–111. Routledge & Kegan Paul, London.

HEARST, E. and JENKINS, H.M. (1974) *Sign-tracking: The Stimulus-reinforcer Relation and Directed Action*. The Psychonomic Society, Austin, Texas.

HERRNSTEIN, R.J., LOVELAND, D.H. and CABLE, C. (1976) Natural concepts in pigeons. *Journal of Experimental Psychology: Animal Behavior Processes*, **2**, 285–302.

HICKEY, T.L. (1981) The developing nervous system. *Trends in NeuroSciences*, **4**, 41–44.

HILGARD, E.R. (1977) *Divided Consciousness: Multiple Controls in Human Thought and Action*. Wiley, New York.

HINDE, R.A. (1970) *Animal Behaviour: A Synthesis of Ethology and Comparative Psychology. Second Edition*. McGraw-Hill, New York.

HINDE, R.A. and FISHER, J. (1952) Further observations on the opening of milk bottles by birds. *British Birds*, **44**, 393–396.

HIRSCH, H.V.B. and JACOBSON, M. (1975) The perfectible brain: Principles of neuronal development. In: M.S. GAZZANIGA and C. BLAKEMORE (Eds.) *Handbook of Psychobiology*, pp. 107–137. Academic Press, New York.

HITCH, G.J. (1980) Developing the concept of working memory. In: G. CAXTON (Ed.) *Cognitive Psychology: New Directions*, pp. 154–196. Routledge & Kegan Paul, London.

HONIG, W.K. (1978) Studies of working memory in the pigeon. In: S.H. HULSE, H. FOWLER and W.K. HONIG (Eds.) *Cognitive Processes in Animal Behavior*, pp. 211–248. Lawrence Erlbaum Associates, Hillsdale, New Jersey.

HORN, G., ROSE, S.P.R. and BATESON, P.P.G. (1973) Experience and plasticity in the central nervous system. *Science*, **181**, 506–514.

HULL, C.L. (1943) *Principles of Behavior*. Appleton-Century-Crofts, New York.

HUMPHREY, N.K. (1974) Vision in a monkey without striate cortex: A case study. *Perception*, **3**, 241–255.

HUMPHREY, N.K. (1976) The social function of intellect. In: P.P.G. BATESON and R.A. HINDE (Eds.) *Growing Points in Ethology*, pp. 303–317. Cambridge University Press, Cambridge.

HUMPHREY, N.K. (1980) Nature's psychologists. In: B.D. JOSEPHSON and V.S. RAMACHANDRAN (Eds.) *Consciousness and the Physical World*, pp. 57–75. Pergamon Press, Oxford.

HUNT, E. and LOVE, T. (1972) How good can memory be? In: A.W. MELTON and E. MARTIN (Eds.) *Coding Processes in Human Memory*, pp. 237–260. Winston/Wiley, Washington, DC.

HUNTER, I.M.L. (1962) An exceptional talent for calculative thinking. *British Journal of Psychology*, **53**, 243–258.

IMMELMAN, K. (1972) Sexual and other long-term aspects of imprinting in birds and other species. *Advances in the Study of Behavior*, **4**, 147–174.

IVERSON, J. (1976) *More Lives Than One?* Souvenir Press, London.

JACOBSON, M. (1974) A plenitude of neurons. In: G. GOTTLIEB (Ed.) *Studies on the Development of Behavior and the Nervous System, Vol. 2*, pp. 151–166. Academic Press, New York.

JERISON, H.J. (1973) *Evolution of the Brain and Intelligence*. Academic Press, New York.

JERISON, H.J. (1976) Palaeoneurology and the evolution of mind. *Scientific American*, **234**, 90–101.

JERISON, H.J. (1982) The evolution of biological intelligence. In: R.J. STERNBERG (Ed.) *Handbook of Human Intelligence*. Cambridge University Press, Cambridge.

JONES, E.E. and HARRIS, V.A. (1967) The attribution of attitudes. *Journal of Experimental Social Psychology*, **3**, 1–24.

JONES, E.E. and NISBETT, R.E. (1972) The actor and the observer: Divergent perceptions of the causes of behavior. In: E.E. JONES, D.E. KANOUSE, H.H. KELLEY, R.E. NISBETT, S. VALINS and B. WEINER (Eds.) *Attribution: Perceiving the Causes of Behavior*. General Learning Press, Morristown, New Jersey.

KALAT, J.W. (1981) *Biological Psychology*. Wadsworth Publishing Co., Belmont, California.

KAMIL, A.C. (1978) Systematic foraging by a nectar-feeding bird, the Amakihi (*Loxops virens*). *Journal of Comparative and Physiological Psychology*, **92**, 388–386.

KELLEY, H.H. (1950) The warm-cold variable in first impressions of persons. *Journal of Personality*, **18**, 431–439.

KELLEY, H.H. (1967) Attribution theory in social psychology. In: D. LEVINE (Ed.) *Nebraska Symposium on Motivation, Vol 15*, pp. 192–237. University of Nebraska Press, Lincoln, Nebraska.

KELLY, G.A. (1955) *The Psychology of Personal Constructs*. Norton, New York.

KERKUT, G.A. (1961) *Borradaile, Eastham, Potts and Saunders' The Invertebrata, Fourth Edition*. Cambridge University Press, Cambridge.

KLÜVER, H. and BUCY, P.C. (1939) Preliminary analysis of functions of the temporal lobes in monkeys. *Archives of Neurology and Psychiatry*, **42**, 979–1000.

KOLB, B. and WHISHAW, I.Q. (1980) *Fundamentals of Human Neuropsychology*. W.H. Freeman, San Francisco.

KOLB, B. and WHISHAW, I.Q. (1981) Decortication of rats in infancy or adulthood produced comparable functional losses on learned and species-typical behaviors. *Journal of Comparative and Physiological Psychology*, **95**, 468–483.

KONISHI, M. (1965) The role of auditory feedback in the control of vocalization in the white-crowned sparrow. *Zeitschrift für* Tierpsychologie, **22**, 770–783.

KONISHI, M. and GURNEY, M.E. (1982) Sexual differentiation of the brain and behaviour, *Trends in Neurosciences*, **5**, 20–23.

LASHLEY, K. (1935) Studies of cerebral function in learning. XI. The behavior of the rat in latch-box situations. *Comparative Psychology Monographs*, **11**, 5–40.

LORENZ, K. (1969) Innate bases of learning. In: K.H. PRIBRAM (Ed.) *On the Biology of Learning*. pp. 13–93, Harcourt, Brace and World, New York.

LORENZ, K. (1977) *Behind the Mirror*, Methuen, London.

LURIA, A.R. (1968) *The Mind of a Mnemonist*. Basic Books, New York.

LURIA, A.R. (1973) *The Working Brain*. Penguin, Harmondsworth, Middlesex.

MCCABE, B.J., CIPOLLA-NETO, J., HORN, G. and BATESON, P.P.G. (1982) Bilateral lesions in hyperstriatum ventrale after imprinting in the chick. *Brain Research*. In Press.

MCCABE, B.J., HORN, G. and BATESON, P.P.G. (1981) Effects of restricted lesions of the chick forebrain on the acquisition of filial preferences during imprinting. *Brain Research*, **205**, 29–37.

MACKINTOSH, N.J. (1965) Discrimination learning in the octopus. *Animal Behaviour. Supplement 1*. 129–134.

MACKINTOSH, N.J. (1974) *The Psychology of Animal Learning*. Academic Press, London.

MACKINTOSH, N.J. and DICKINSON, A. (1979) Instrumental (Type II) conditioning. In: A. DICKINSON and R.A. BOAKES (Eds.) *Mechanisms of Learning and Motivation*, pp. 143–169. Lawrence Erlbaum Associates, Hillsdale, New Jersey.

MAIER, N.R.F. (1932) Cortical destruction of the posterior part of the brain and its effect on reasoning in rats. *Journal of Comparative Neurology*, **56**, 179–214.

MANNING, A. (1967) *An Introduction to Animal Behavior*. Edward Arnold, London.

MANNING, A. (1979) *An Introduction to Animal Behaviour*. *Third Edition*. EDWARD Arnold, London.

MARLER, P. (1981) Birdsong: The acquisition of a learned motor skill. *Trends in Neuro Sciences*, **4**, 88–94.

MARLER, P. and TAMURA, M. (1964) Culturally transmitted patterns of vocal behavior in sparrows. *Science*, **146**, 1483–1486.

MARLOWE, W.B., MANCALL, E.L. and THOMAS, J.J. (1975) Complete Klüver-Bucy syndrome in man. *Cortex*, **11**, 53–59.

MARR, D. (1976) Early processing of visual information. *Philosophical Transactions of the Royal Society of London. Series B.*, **275**, 483–519.

MAYNARD-SMITH, J. (1975) *The Theory of Evolution*. *Third Edition*. Penguin, Harmondsworth, Middlesex.

MENZEL, E.W. (1978) Cognitive mapping in chimpanzees. In: S.H. HULSE, H. FOWLER and W.K. HONIG (Eds.) *Cognitive Processes in Animal Behavior*, pp. 375–422. Lawrence Erlbaum Associates, Hillsdale, New Jersey.

MEUDELL, P. and MAYES, A. (1982) Normal and abnormal forgetting: Some comments on the human amnesic syndrome. In: A. ELLIS (Ed.) *Normality and Pathology in Cognitive Function*. Academic Press, London. In Press.

MEYER, D.R. (1958) Some psychological determinants of sparing and loss following damage to the brain. In: H.F. HARLOW and C.N. WOOLSEY (Eds.) *Biological and Biochemical Bases of Behavior*, pp. 173–192. University of Wisconsin Press, Madison, Wisconsin.

MILNER, B. (1970) Memory and the medial temporal regions of the brain. In. K.H. PRIBRAM and D.E. BROADBENT (Eds.) *Biology of Memory*, pp. 29–50. Academic Press, New York.

MIYADI, D. (1964) Social life of Japanese monkeys. *Science*, **143**, 783–786.

MORGAN, M.J., FITCH, M.D., HOLMAN, J.G. and LEA, S.E.G. (1976) Pigeons learn the concept of an 'A'. *Perception*, **5**, 57–66.

MORGAN, M.J. and NICHOLAS, D.J. (1979) Discrimination between reinforced action patterns in the rat. *Learning and Motivation*, **10**, 1–22.

MORRIS, P. (1978) Models of long-term memory. In: M.M. GRUNEBERG and P. MORRIS (Eds.) *Aspects of Memory*, pp. 84–103. Methuen, London.

MORRIS, R.G.M. (1981) Spatial localization does not require the presence of local cues. *Learning and Motivation*, **12**, 239–260.

MORRIS, R.G.M. (1982) An attempt to dissociate 'spatial-mapping' and 'working-memory' theories of hippocampal function. In: W. SIEFERT (Ed.) *Molecular, Cellular and Behavioural Neurobiology of the Hippocampus*. Academic Press, New York. In press.

MORRISON, D.W. (1978) On the optimal searching strategy for refuging predators. *American Naturalist*, **112**, 925–934.

MORROW, J.E. and SMITHSON, B.L. (1969) Learning sets in an invertebrate. *Science*, **164**, 850–851.

MOSS, P. and KEETON, J. (1979) *Encounters with the Past*. Penguin, Harmondsworth, Middlesex.

MOUNTCASTLE, V.B. (1978) An organizing principle for cerebral function: The unit module and the distributed system. In: G.M. EDELMAN and V.B. MOUNTCASTLE (Eds.) *The Mindful Brain*, pp. 7–50. Mit Press, Cambridge, Massachusetts.

NEWCOMBE, F. (1980) Memory: A neuropsychological approach. *Trends in Neuro sciences*, **3**, 179–182.

NICOLAI, J. (1956) Zur biologie und ethologie des gimpels (*Pyrrhula pyrrhula* L.). *Zeitschrift für Tierpsychologie*, **13**, 93–132.

NISSEN, W.H. and MCULLOCH, T.L. (1937) Equated and non-equated situations in discrimination learning by chimpanzees. I. Comparison with unlimited response.

Journal of Comparative Psychology, **23**, 165–189.

NORTHCUTT, R.G. (1978) Forebrain and midbrain organization in lizards and its phylogenetic significance. In: N. GREENBERG and P.D. MACLEAN (Eds.) *Behavior and Neurology of Lizards*, pp. 11–64. National Institutes of Mental Health (DHEW Publication No. (ADM) 77–491). Washington, D.C.

NORTON-GRIFFITHS, M. (1969) The organization, control and development of parental feeding in the oystercatcher (*Haematopus ostralegus*). *Behaviour*, **34** 55–114.

NOTTEBOHM, F. (1979) Origins and mechanisms in the establishment of cerebral dominance. In: M.S. GAZZANIGA (Ed.) *Handbook of Behavioural Neurobiology. Volume 2.* Plenum, New York.

NOTTEBOHM, F. (1981) Laterality, seasons and space govern the learning of a motor skill. *Trends in NeuroSciences*, **4**, 104–106.

NOVIKOFF, A.B. and HOLTZMAN, E. (1976) *Cells and Organelles. Second Edition.* Holt, Rinehart and Winston, New York.

OAKLEY, D.A. (1978) Manipulandum identification in operant behaviour in neodecorticate rabbits. *Physiology and Behaviour*, **21**, 943–950.

OAKLEY, D.A. (1979a) Cerebral cortex and adaptive behaviour. In: D.A. OAKLEY and H.C. PLOTKIN (Eds.) *Brain, Behaviour and Evolution*, pp. 154–188. Methuen, London.

OAKLEY, D.A. (1979b) Neocortex and learning. *Trends in NeuroSciences*, **2**, 149–152.

OAKLEY, D.A. (1979c) Learning with food reward and shock avoidance in neodecorticate rats. *Experimental Neurology*, **63**, 627–642.

OAKLEY, D.A. (1979d) Instrumental reversal learning and subsequent fixed ratio performance on simple and go/no-go schedules in neodecorticate rabbits. *Physiological Psychology*, **7**, 29–42.

OAKLEY, D.A. (1981a) Brain mechanisms of mammalian memory. *British Medical Bulletin*, **37**, 175–180.

OAKLEY, D.A. (1981b) Performance of decorticated rats in a two-choice visual discrimination apparatus. *Behavioural Brain Research*, **3**, 55–69.

OAKLEY, D.A., EAMES, L.C., JACOBS, J.L. DAVEY, G.C.L. and CLELAND, G.C. (1981) Signal-centered action patterns in rats without neocortex in a Pavlovian conditioning situation. *Physiological Psychology*, **9**, 135–144.

OAKLEY, D.A. and RUSSELL, I.S. (1976) Subcortical nature of Pavlovian differentiation in the rabbit. *Physiology and Behaviour*, **17**, 947–954.

OAKLEY, D.A. and RUSSELL, I.S. (1977) Subcortical storage of Pavlovian conditioning in the rabbit. *Physiology and Behaviour*, **18**, 931–937.

OATLEY, K. (1975) Clock mechanisms of sleep. *New Scientist*, **66**, 371–374.

OATLEY, K. (1978) *Perceptions and Representations.* Methuen London.

O'KEEFE, J. and CONWAY, D.H. (1980) On the trail of the hippocampal engram. *Physiological Psychology*, **8**, 229–238.

O'KEEFE, J. and NADEL, L. (1978) *The Hippocampus as a Cognitive Map.* Clarendon Press, Oxford.

OLTON, D.S. (1972) Discrimination reversal performance after hippocampal lesions: An enduring failure of reinforcement and non-reinforcement to direct behavior. *Physiology and Behavior*, **9**, 353–356.

OLTON, D.S. (1978) Characteristics of spatial memory. In: S.H. HULSE, H. FOWLER and W.K. HONIG (Eds.) *Cognitive Processes in Animal Behaviour*, pp. 341–373. Lawrence Erlbaum Associates, Hillsdale, New Jersey.

OLTON, D.S. (1979) Mazes, maps and memory. *American Psychologist*, **34**, 588–596.

OLTON, D.S., BECKER, J.T. and HANDELMANN, G.E. (1980) Hippocampal function: Working memory or cognitive mapping? *Physiological Psychology*, **8**, 239–246.

OLTON, D.S., COLLISON, C. and WERZ, M. (1977a) Spatial memory and radial arm maze performance of rats. *Learning and Motivation*, **8**, 289–314.

OLTON, D.S., WALKER, J.A., GAGE, F.H. and JOHNSON, C.T. (1977b) Choice behavior of rats searching for food. *Learning and Motivation*, **8**, 315–331.

OWEN, M.J. and BUTLER, S.R. (1981) Amnesia after transection of the fornix in monkeys: Long-term memory impaired, short-term memory intact. *Behavioural Brain Research*, **3**, 115–123.

PALMERINO, C.C., RUSINIAK, K.W. and GARCIA, J. (1980) Flavor-illness aversions: The peculiar roles of odor and taste in memory for poison. *Science*, **208**, 753–755.

PARTRIDGE, L. (1979) The evolution and genetics of behaviour. In: D.A. OAKLEY and H.C. PLOTKIN (Eds.) *Brain, Behaviour and Evolution*, pp. 1–27. Methuen, London.

PASSINGHAM, R.E. (1981) Primate specialization in brain and intelligence. *Symposia of the Zoological Society of London*, **46**, 361–388.

PASTORE, N. (1954) Discrimination learning in the canary. *Journal of Comparative and Physiological Psychology*, **47**, 389–390.

PEARCE, J.M., COLWILL, R.M. and HALL, G. (1978) Instrumental conditioning of scratching in the laboratory rat. *Learning and Motivation*, **9**, 255–271.

PENFIELD, W. (1969) Consciousness, memory and man's conditioned reflexes. In: K. PRIBRAM (Ed.) *On the Biology of Learning*, pp. 129–168. Harcourt, Brace and World, New York.

PLOTKIN, H.C. (1981) The evolution of closed and open programmes of development. In: D.R. GARROD and J.D. FELDMAN (Eds.) *Development in the Nervous System: British Society for. Developmental Biology. Symposium 5*, pp. 379–389. Cambridge University Press, Cambridge.

PLOTKIN, H.C. and ODLING-SMEE, F.J. (1979) Learning, change and evolution: An enquiry into the teleonomy of learning. *Advances in the Study of Behavior*, **10**, 1–41.

PLOTKIN, H.C. and ODLING-SMEE, F.J. (1981) A multiple-level model of evolution and its implications for sociobiology. *The Behavioral and Brain Sciences*, **4**, 225–268.

PREMACK, D. (1971) Language in chimpanzees? *Science*, **172**, 808–822.

PREMACK, D. (1978) On the abstractness of human concepts: Why it would be difficult to talk to a pigeon. In: S.H. HULSE, H. FOWLER and W.K. HONIG (Eds.) *Cognitive Processes in Animal Behavior*, pp. 423–451. Lawrence Erlbaum Associates, New Jersey.

PRIBRAM, K.H. (1962) Interrelations of psychology and the neurological disciplines. In: S. KOCH (Ed.) *Psychology: A Study of a Science: 4*, pp. 119–157. Mcgraw-Hill, New York.

PYKE, G.H. (1979) Optimal foraging in bumblebees: Rule of movement between flowers within inflorescences. *Animal Behaviour*, **27**, 1167–1181.

RATCLIFF, G. and ROSS, J.E. (1981) Visual perception and perceptual disorder. *British Medical Bulletin*, **37**, 181–186.

REASON, J.T. (1977) Skill and error in everyday life. In: M.J.A. HOWE (Ed.) *Adult Learning: Psychological Research and Applications*. Wiley, London.

RESCORLA, R.A. (1968) Probability of shock in the presence and absence of CS in fear conditioning. *Journal of Comparative and Physiological Psychology*, **66**, 1–5.

REYNIERS, J.A. (1953) Germ-free life. Lancet, **9**, 33–34.

RIOPELLE, A.J. and CHINN, R.McC. (1961) Position habits and discrimination learning by monkeys. *Journal of Comparative and Physiological Psychology*, **54**, 178–180.

RIOPELLE, A.J. and HILL, C.W. (1974) Complex processes. In: D.A. DEWSBURY and D.A. RETHLINGSHAFER (Eds.) *Comparative Psychology*, pp. 510–546. Mcgraw-Hill Kogakusha, Tokyo.

ROBERTS, W.A. (1979) Spatial memory in the rat on a hierarchical maze. *Learning and Motivation*, **10**, 117–140.

ROBERTS, W.A. and GRANT, D.S. (1976) Studies of short-term memory in the pigeon using the delayed matching to sample procedure. In: D.L. MEDIN, W.A. ROBERTS and R.T. DAVIS (Eds.) *Processes of Animal Memory*, pp. 79–112. Lawrence Erlbaum Associates, Hillsdale, New Jersey.

ROLLS, E.T. (1981) Processing beyond the inferior temporal visual cortex related to feeding, memory and striatal function. In: Y. KATSUKI, M. SATO and R. NORGREN (Eds.) *Brain Mechanisms of Sensation*. Academic Press, New York. In Press.

ROSCH, E. (1975) Cognitive representations of semantic categories. *Journal of Experimental Psychology: General*, **104**, 192-233.

ROSENZWEIG, M.R., BENNETT, E.L. and DIAMOND, M.C. (1972) Brain changes in response to experience. *Scientific American*, **226**, 22-29.

ROSVOLD, H.E., MIRSKY, A.F. and PRIBRAM, K.H. (1954) influence of amygdalectomy on social behavior in monkeys. *Journal of Comparative and Physiological Psychology*, **47**, 173-178.

ROTTER, J.B. (1966) Generalized expectancies for internal versus external control of reinforcement. *Psychological Monographs*, **80**, 1-28.

RUGGIERO, F.T. and FLAGG, S.F. (1976) Do animals have memory? In: D.L. MEDIN, W.A. ROBERTS and R.T. DAVIS (Eds.) *Processes of Animal Memory*, pp. 1-19. Lawrence Erlbaum Associates, Hillsdale, New Jersey.

RUMBAUGH, D.M. and GILL, T.V. (1976) Language and acquisition of language-type skills by a chimpanzee (*Pan*). *Annals of the New York Academy of Sciences*, **270**, 90-123.

RUSSELL, I.S. (1979) Brain size and intelligence: A comparative perspective. In: D.A. OAKLEY and H.C. PLOTKIN (Eds.) *Brain, Behaviour and Evolution*, pp. 126-153. Methuen, London.

RUSSELL, I.S. (1980) Encephalization and neural mechanisms of learning. In: M.A. JEEVES (Ed.) *Psychology Survey No. 3*, pp. 92-114. George Allen and Uwin, London.

SALZEN, E.A. and MEYER, C.C. (1968) Reversibility of imprinting. *Journal of Comparative and Physiological Psychology*, **66**, 269-275.

SCHREINER, L. and KLING, A. (1953) Behavioural changes following rhinencephalic injury in the cat. *Journal of Neurophysiology*, **16**, 643-659.

SCHWARTZ, B. and GAMZU, E. (1977) Pavlovian control of operant behavior: An analysis of autoshaping and its implications for operant conditioning. In: W.K. HONIG and J.E.R. STADDON (Eds.) *Handbook of Operant Behavior*, pp.53-97. Prentice-Hall, Englewood Cliffs, New Jersey.

SELIGMAN, M.E.P. (1970) On the generality of the laws of learning. *Psychological Review*, **77**, 406-418.

SHALLICE, T. (1981) Neurological impairment of cognitive processes. *British Medical Bulletin*, **37**, 187-192.

SHEPARD, R.N. and METZLER, J. (1971) Mental rotation of three dimensional objects. *Science*, **171**, 701-703.

SHETTLEWORTH, S.J. (1972) Constraints on learning. *Advances in the Study of Behavior*, **4**, 1-68.

SHETTLEWORTH, S.J. (1979) Constraints on conditioning in the writings of Konorski. In: A. DICKINSON and R.A. BOAKES (Eds.) *Mechanisms of Learning and Motivation*. pp. 339-416. Lawrence Erlbaum Associates, Hillsdale, New Jersey.

SIIPOLA, E.M. and HAYDEN, S.D. (1965) Exploring eidetic imagery among the retarded. *Perceptual and Motor Skills*, **21**, 275-286.

SINNAMON, H.M., FRENIERE, S. and KOOTZ, J. (1978) Rat hippocampus and memory for places of changing significance. *Journal of Comparative and Physiological Psychology*, **92**, 142-155.

SLOBODKIN, L.B. (1978) Is history a consequence of evolution? In: P.P.G. BATESON and P.H. KLOPFER (Eds.) *Perspectives in Ethology. Volume 3*, pp. 233-255. Plenum, New York.

SQUIER, L.H. (1969) Reversal learning improvement in the fish *Astronotus ocellatus* (Oscar). *Psychonomic Science*, **14**, 143-144.

SQUIRE, L.R. (1980) The anatomy of amnesia. *Trends in NeuroSciences*, **3** 52-54.

STAHL, J. and ELLEN, P. (1974) Factors in the reasoning performance of the rat. *Journal of Comparative and Physiological Psychology*, **87**, 598-604.

STROMEYER, C.F. and PSOTKA, J. (1970) The detailed texture of eidetic images. *Nature*, **225**, 346-349.

SUTHERLAND, N.S. and MACKINTOSH, N.J. (1971) *Mechanisms of Animal Discrimination Learning*. Academic Press, London.

TERLECKI, L.J., PINEL, J.P.J. and TREIT, D. (1979) Conditioned and unconditioned defensive burying in the rat. *Learning and Motivation*, **10**, 337–350.

TERRACE, H.S., PETITTO, L.A., SANDERS, R.J. and BEVER, T.G. (1979) Can an ape create a sentence? *Science*, **206**, 891–902.

THODAY, J.M. (1953) Components of fitness. *Symposia of the Society for Experimental Biology*, **7**, 96–113.

THOMAS, G.J. and BRITO, G.N.O. (1980) Recovery of delayed alternation in rats after lesions in medial frontal cortex and septum. *Journal of Comparative and Physiological Psychology*, **94**, 808–818.

TOLMAN, E.C. (1932) *Purposive Behavior in Animals and Men*. Appleton-Century-Crofts, New York.

TORAN-ALLERAND, C.D. (1981) Gonadal steroids and brain development, *in vitro veritas? Trends in NeuroSciences*, **4**, 118–121.

TRIVERS, R.L. (1971) The evolution of reciprocal altruism. *Quarterly Review of Biology*, **46**, 35–57.

TULVING, E. (1972) Episodic and semantic memory. In: E. Tulving and W. Donaldson (Eds.) *Organization of Memory*, pp. 381–403. Academic Press, New York.

URCUIOLI P.J. and NEVIN, J.A. (1975) Transfer of hue matching in pigeons. *Journal of the Experimental Analysis of Behavior*, **24**, 149–155.

WADDINGTON, C.H. (1969) Paradigm for an evolutionary process. In: C.H. WADDINGTON (Ed.) *Towards a Theoretical Biology 2: Sketches*, pp. 106–128. Edinburgh University Press, Edinburgh.

WALSH, K.W. (1978) *Neuropsychology: A Clinical Approach*. Churchill Livingstone, Edinburgh.

WARREN, J.M. (1966) Reversal learning and the formation of learning sets by cats and rhesus monkeys. *Journal of Comparative and Physiological Psychology*, **61**, 421–428.

WARREN, J.M. (1974) Learning in vertebrates. In: D.A. DEWSBURY and D.A. RETHLINGSHAFER (Eds.) *Comparative Psychology: A Modern Survey*, pp. 471–509. McGraw-Hill Kogakusha, Tokyo.

WARREN, J.M. and KOLB, B. (1978) Generalizations in neuropsychology. In: S. FINGER (Ed.) *Recovery from Brain Damage: Research and Theory*, pp. 35–48. Plenum Press, New York.

WARRINGTON, E.K. (1975) The selective impairment of semantic memory. *Quarterly Journal of Experimental Psychology*, **27**, 635–657.

WARRINGTON, E.K. (1976) Recognition and recall in amnesia. In: J. BROWN (Ed.) *Recall and Recognition*, pp. 217–228. Wiley, London.

WARRINGTON, E.K. (1979) Neuropsychological evidence for multiple memory systems. In: *Brain and Mind (Ciba Foundation Symposium n.s. No. 69.)*, pp. 153–166. Elsevier, Amsterdam.

WARRINGTON, E.K. and SHALLICE, T. (1969) The selective impairment of auditory verbal short-term memory. *Brain*, **92**, 885–896.

WARRINGTON, E.K. and SHALLICE, T. (1972) Neuropsychological evidence of visual storage in short-term memory tasks. *Quarterly Journal of Experimental Psychology*, **24**, 30–40.

WEINER, B. (1972) *Theories of Motivation: From Mechanism to Cognition*. Rand McNally College Publishing Co., Chicago.

WEISKRANTZ, L. (1977) Trying to bridge some neuropsychological gaps between monkey and man. *British Journal of Psychology*, **68**, 431–445.

WEISKRANTZ, L. (1980) Varieties of residual experience. *Quarterly Journal of Experimental Psychology*, **32**, 365–386.

WEISKRANTZ, L. and WARRINGTON, E.K. (1979) Conditioning in amnesic patients. *Neuropsychologia*, **17**, 187–194.

WELLS, M.J. (1958) Factors affecting reactions to *Mysis* by newly hatched *Sepia*. *Behaviour*, **13**, 96–111.

WILCOXON, H.C., DRAGOIN, W.B. and KRAL, P.A. (1971) Illness-induced aversions in rat and quail: Relative salience of visual and gustatory cues. *Science*, **171**, 826–828.

WILKIE, D.M., MACLENNAN, A.J. and PINEL, J.P.J. (1979) Rat defensive behavior: Burying noxious food. *Journal of the Experimental Analysis of Behavior*, **31**, 299–306.

WILKIE, D.M., SPETCH, M.L. and CHEW, L. (1981) The ring dove's short-term memory capacity for spatial information. *Animal Behaviour*, **29**, 639–641.

WILLIAMS, D.R. and WILLIAMS, H. (1969) Automaintenance in the pigeon: Sustained pecking despite contingent non-reinforcement. *Journal of the Experimental Analysis of Behavior*, **12**, 511–520.

WODINSKY, J., VARLEY, M.A. and BITTERMAN, M.E. (1953) The solution of oddity problems by the rat. *American Journal of Psychology*, **66**, 137–140.

WRIGHT, A.A. and SANDS, S.F. (1981) A model of detection and decision processes during matching to sample by pigeons: Performance with 88 different wavelengths in delayed and simultaneous matching tasks. *Journal of Experimental Psychology: Animal Behavior Processes*, **7**, 191–216.

ZENTALL, T. and HOGAN, D. (1974) Abstract concept learning in the pigeon. *Journal of Experimental Psychology*, **102**, 393–398.

CHAPTER 3

The Development and Dissolution of Memory

Peter R. Meudell

3.1 General Introduction

The development of memory within an individual has, crudely, two stages, both of which are related in so far as they are both stages in an individual's memory where it may be poor relative to a mature 'high point' in development where memory works optimally. These two stages are, of course, early in life from birth to some point around adolescence and later in life from the years of middle age to senescence. This chapter will examine both these extremes of memory 'development' since they both represent relatively poor performance of mnemonic systems and since essentially similar psychological mechanisms have been proposed to underlie the improvement in memory in the early years of life and the dissolution of it in old age.

Since our immediate personal knowledge of poor childhood memory comes from the observation of the phenomenon of 'childhood amnesia' and since much recent work with animals concerned with the ontogeny of memory has concentrated upon this topic (Spear & Campbell, 1979), this represents a convenient point of departure.

3.2 Infantile Amnesia: The Development of Memory

3.2.1 Introduction

The first description of infantile amnesia is attributable to Freud as the phenomenon and its psychoanalytic explanation was an important part his theorizing about the influences of early experience upon subsequent adult behaviour. In 1905 he wrote:

> What I have in mind is the peculiar amnesia which, in the case of most people, though by no means all, hides the earliest beginnings of their childhood up to their sixth or eighth year. (Freud, 1905)

More recently Spear (1979) has illustrated the phenomenon as follows:

> . . . whereas a 20-year-old person would be quite unable to remember specific events accompanying her birth in hospital a 40-year-old can remember without difficulty a good deal about her stay in the hospital during an illness 20 years earlier; the greater forgetting for the infantile experience over the common 20-year duration defines 'infantile amnesia'. (Spear, 1979)

The inability to recall memories acquired in childhood has not only been 'documented' on the basis of personal intuition or casual observation, many questionnaires asking people to recall their first memories and their characteristics have also documented the dearth of memories before the ages of 5–6 years (e.g. Dudycha & Dudycha, 1941). Some of the characteristics of such memories that are reported are as follows. The first reported memory is typically when the child is about $3\frac{1}{2}$ years old with females reporting first memories a few months earlier than males. The memories reported are primarily 'visual' in form and appear to be affective in content rather than being of neutral events; they also cover the whole range of emotional experiences but with 'joy' being the most dominant followed by 'fear' (Waldfogel, 1948). There appears to be no relationship between the number of childhood memories recalled and adults' scores on intelligence tests, nor their scores on dimensions of personality tests, nor their scores on tests of current memory performance (Waldfogel, 1948).

Various hypotheses have been put forward to explain the phenomenon of childhood amnesia in humans. The most well known of these is Freud's suggestion that such memories are available to people but are made inaccessible to consciousness because some of them (and, by a process of 'guilt by association', most of the others also) would be too painful for us to cope with if we were to become aware of them. In other words the mechanisms of repression operate on early memories to produce a rather special kind of retrieval failure.

An alternative hypothesis originally put forward by Schactel (e.g. 1963) has recently been aired by Neisser (1967) and the particular hypothesis owes its flavour to the general idea that there are significant qualitative changes in cognition between infancy and adulthood — a view much favoured by developmental psychologists such as Bruner and Piaget. Although argued in somewhat different terms, the Schactel–Neisser hypothesis essentially states that infantile amnesia results from qualitative changes in encoding and subsequent retrieval strategies across the developing years. Since encoding and retrieval processes are different in the adult from what they were in the child (for example the characteristics of linguistic, temporal, relational, causative and spatial knowledge will change from birth to maturity) a mismatch will occur between the information encoded by the child and the retrieval plan devised by the adult to access that information: the result is a failure to retrieve adequately available information. Apparently implicit in both this view of infantile amnesia and of Freud's repression notion is the hypothesis that storage processes (for example the rate at which information might be lost from memory or how effectively memories are consolidated) do not differ in mature and immature organisms: development either leads to a change in the form of encoding and subsequent retrieval strategies on the one hand or to an active blocking of retrieval effectiveness on the other.

Whatever the merits of theories such as these for the understanding of the development of mnemonic processes (for they are very difficult to put to direct satisfactory experimental test), a major difficulty with research on childhood amnesia is the problem of the reliability of the data upon which the hypotheses are constructed. Since retrospective questionnaire studies necessarily have no control over what actually was experienced during infancy, people's recall, as adults, of these periods cannot be checked for omissions, distortions, substitutions, fabrications and reconstructions. Such data that are obtained from retrospective studies can, therefore, only give at best some suggestions that a phenomenon of interest may be occurring: prospective longitudinal studies are of course an alternative but it is unrealistic to assume that anyone would embark upon a 20-year research programme with no guarantee as to outcome. In view of these factors, other lines of approach to the study of infantile amnesia seem appropriate and two such lines can be seen as relevant. First, since developmental changes in storage or encoding processes would have clear implications for theories of childhood amnesia, comparisons can be made, cross-sectionally, between the actual memory performance of young children across the developing years and those of adults and, second, the phenomenon of childhood amnesia can be directly examined in non-human animals where the time period for longitudinal assessment is drastically shorter than that needed in man.

3.2.2   Memory in the Human Infant

(a)   Recognition memory in the first year of life.   It is obvious that separation anxiety, object permanence, attachment and related phenomena shown by the child of less than 1 year must depend to some extent upon the presence of reasonably effective mnemonic systems, but these are complex accomplishments in which memory may play a relatively trivial role in relation, for example, to the roles of the development of knowledge and understanding (but see Fox *et al.*, 1979). Accordingly more direct, rather than frankly inferential measures of memory are required. One productive indicant of memory in the pre-linguistic child has been the duration of eye fixations while the child examines novel stimuli or stimuli which have been exposed previously (and thus which might, or might not, have some representation in memory), the argument being that differences in fixation between new and familiar pictures at delayed test, relative to control conditions, indicates memory for the previously exposed stimulus. Two variations on this paradigm have been employed (Cohen & Gelber, 1975). First, in 'habituation' paradigms, fixation time is compared for a single stimulus on initial presentation (when the stimulus is novel) and a subsequent exposure when the infant may have some memory of it. Second, in 'paired comparison' paradigms, initial fixation duration of one of two simultaneously exposed novel pictures is compared with fixation time when that same member is later paired with another novel stimulus.

Using these techniques investigators were initially concerned with the demonstration of the *presence* of mnemonic abilities (as indicated by visual recognition indexed by changes in fixation durations) in pre-verbal children. With the habituation paradigm delayed recognition memory has been demonstrated in 6-week- and 8-week-old infants at retention intervals between 12 and 24 h (Weizman *et al.*, 1971) while Martin (1975) has shown similar results in 2-, $3\frac{1}{2}$ and 5-month-old babies. Martin's results are particularly interesting since while all three age groups showed habituation to stimuli shown initially 24 h earlier, there was a trend for it to be greater in the 5-month-old group than in either of the other two groups, both of which show approximately equal habituation. These results imply some improvement in memory between 3 and 5 months of age. Using the paired comparison paradigm Fagan (1970, 1973, 1978) has demonstrated delayed recognition memory in 6-month-old infants for retention intervals as long as 2 weeks after initial presentation.

There seems little doubt that babies of less than 1 year of age demonstrate considerable memory for visually presented information and, since changes in fixation between first and subsequent presentations of a stimulus might readily

8

be taken to indicate the *presence* of memory while the absence of a difference might not necessarily be taken as evidence of *absence* of memory, these durations of infant memory must be taken as minimum estimates.

Perhaps not surprisingly no studies using habituation or paired comparison designs have been reported with adults so direct comparisons between memory in infants and mature individuals, as indexed by looking behaviour, are not available. (Of course we know, however, that the *pattern* of looking at pictures is different in young and mature people (Mackworth & Bruner, 1970) but we do not know about their comparative rates of habituation and dishabituation.) Since adult performance in such paradigms may reflect factors other than memory (they may reflect aesthetic preference for example), comparisons between infants and adults may not, anyway, prove particularly meaningful. A paired comparison experiment has been reported, however, with older ($1\frac{1}{2}$–$3\frac{1}{2}$ years) children (Daehler & Bukatko, 1977) which showed clear development a trends in looking times at test, i.e. Daehler and Bukatko demonstrated that the older the child the less it looked at the previously exposed member of a pair of pictures, the one receiving the most attention being novel.

These results, combined with those of Martin (1975) strongly suggest that visual recognition memory continues to improve from 3 months to $3\frac{1}{2}$ years. Exactly what the differences in mnemonic ability are due to is, however, unclear, since we have no knowledge of how well the information was originally 'learned' by these infants of different ages — differences in retention (as indexed by differences in fixation durations) might therefore simply reflect differences in initial level of acquisition. Equating initial looking time is, of course, one solution to this problem but it is by no means clear that such looking time is systematically related to level of acquisition: we know from studies of adults, for example, that many orienting tasks take a long time to complete but yet lead to poor memory relative to other tasks which are quickly completed (e.g. Baddeley, 1979). In any event, for whatever reason, we do know that infants show progressively better visual recognition memory across the first months of life. Whether, if levels of acquisition were equated between babies and infants of different ages or even matched with adults, differences in retention would still be observed is an open question.

What is the infant remembering, or, put differently, what aspects of a stimulus do babies encode? McGurk (1970) has shown that, in 6- to 26-week-old babies, habituation to a stimulus in one orientation will 'recover' if the same stimulus is presented in a different orientation. In other words information about orientation must be available to the infant if a stimulus only differing from another in terms of orientation is treated by it as being novel. Similar effects occurred in paired comparison experiments. Under some conditions of paired comparison experiments 7-month-old infants show evidence of retaining the perceptual features defining the sex of a face (Fagan, 1976) and of the pose of a face (Fagan, 1976, 1978). Six-month-old babies also have been shown to remember the organization of elements in a pattern and the shape and colour of particular features in it (Miranda & Fantz, 1974). In an intriguing study Strauss and Cohen (1978) have shown that in 5-month-old children 'simple' aspects of stimuli such as orientation, colour and form are not only encoded by uch children, but, further, these features become unavailable at different rates. hey showed that while the orientation, colour and form of a stimulus parately showed habituation immediately after initial presentation (i.e. the infant looked at a novel stimulus, alike in two respects to the familiar stimulus, in preference to the latter), after a 24 h retention interval they showed habituation only to form (i.e. when the novel and familiar stimuli were alike in form and colour but not orientation, or form and orientation but not colour, then the infant looked at both patterns equally; if the two patterns differed in form, however, the infants predominantly fixated the novel pattern). As Kail (1979) has pointed out, however, studies with older children, not yet carried out, are important here especially since we know that, under ordinary learning conditions, different aspects of information about words which have been encoded in memory by adults are lost at the *same* rate (Bregman, 1968). Developmental changes in rates of loss of availability of features in memory are obviously of some importance but in view of the paucity of data, both from different age groups and from different types of material and features to be remembered, it must remain a tantalizing issue rather than an area where definitive statements can be made.

There are, of course, individual differences in infants' abilities to demonstrate visual recognition of stimuli. While sex is an important determiner of adults' face recognition performance — females being better than males (e.g. Ellis, 1975), it does not, however, appear to be a factor in face recognition (or indeed other types of visual recognition) in 4–7-month-olds (Fagan, 1979). On the other hand, general 'cognitive status' does appear to be a factor, even in 13-week-old babies, since Down's syndrome infants evidence less habituation to abstract shapes and faces than do normal babies (Miranda & Fantz, 1974): indeed this inferiority is 'maintained' at 10 to 12 years of age (Dirks & Neisser, 1977).

(b)   Recognition memory in pre-school and school children.   With the development of language, children's memory can be tested in ways practically identical to those used in the assessment of adults without the need for elaborate inferential methodology. Several early studies reported little difference in picture recognition memory between 4-year-old children and adults (e.g. Brown & Scott, 1971; Corsini *et al.*, 1969) and, in view of the claim that recognition memory was no worse in 60-year-olds than it was in 20-year-olds (Sconfield & Robertson, 1966) it might be assumed that recognition skills develop and mature rapidly from birth and, subsequently, are remarkably constant and resistant to dissolution. However, in both the developmental studies and in the ageing ones ceiling effects contaminated interpretation of the data and when these factors are removed recognition memory can be shown to continue to improve up to early adolescence (Dirks & Neisser, 1977) and to deteriorate with advancing age (Erber, 1974). There thus appears to be nothing special about recognition performance in the ontogeny of memory (see Section 3.4.3d for a further discussion of the relationships between recognition and other ways of assessing memory).

Are there qualitative as well as quantitative changes in the bases of recognition performance as children grow up? In a series of experiments (Mandler & Stein, 1974; Mandler & Robinson, 1978) Mandler and her associates have investigated development a changes in picture recognition in 7–11-year-olds by varying the kinds of 'foils' employed in recognition tests. Mandler and Robinson (1978) employed several different types of foil including ones which had elements which were deleted from, added to or moved in relation to a given target picture. Across a total of eight such types of foil, accuracy of performance was very similar across the age ranges tested: however, in comparison to adults, deletions of items from pictures proved very difficult for the children (i.e. in contrast to adults and relative to other types of foils, the children made many more false positive errors to foils which differed from targets in terms of the deletion of one element). A further qualitative difference between these age groups is in their ability to recognize organized scenes or unorganized collections of objects (Mandler & Robinson, 1978; Newcombe *et al.*, 1977). While adults were equally good at recognizing organized and unorganized scenes, 7–11-year-old children were all poorer at recognizing unorganized pictures (Mandler & Robinson, 1978): Newcombe *et al.* showed a similar pattern of results between 6-year-olds and 9-year-olds (i.e. the latter showed a trend to be differentially better with organized than unorganized scenes relative to the former).

In a related experiment, Carey and Diamond (1977) tested two alternative immediate face recognition memory when the 'new' face had irrelevent paraphernalia (such as glasses or a hat) which might be similar to the 'old' face. While 6-year-olds were fooled by irrelevant paraphernalia (i.e. they tended to select new faces which matched the old face in terms of paraphernalia), 10-year-olds were not so easily fooled. Carey and Diamond argue that while the younger child's memory depends upon a superficial analysis of faces the older child's depends upon a 'deeper' more configurational analysis of these stimuli. Accordingly the latter are not fooled by superficial irrelevant detail. This is the most frequently given interpretation of data such as these, i.e. it is argued that there are qualitative changes in encoding strategies, affecting both recognition and recall, as children develop. In more general terms Mandler has suggested that these developmental changes in memory are a consequence of the development of 'schemata'. Schemata refer to '. . . internal structures, built up through experience, that organize and give meaning to incoming information'. In other words, in comparison to adults, young children have poorer memory since they cannot employ, because they do not possess, those skills involved in the meaningful analyses of stimuli which, when employed by the normal adult, lead to good memory (see Cermak, 1978).

This view has been very influential not only as an explanation of the development of memory but also as a factor in the dissolution of memory with advancing years (see Section 3.4.3b) and in the pathology of memory occurring in alcholic Korsakoff's syndrome (see Mayes & Meudell, this volume). Much of the evidence used to buttress the hypothesis in the context of child development comes from the study of recall rather than recognition and it is, therefore, to a consideration of some of these studies that we now turn.

(c)   Recall in pre-school and school children.   Just like recognition memory, free recall performance improves as children grow up (e.g. Cole *et al.*, 1971) but, when initial level of performance is equated, 3-year-olds recall paired associates after 7 days as well as 9-year-olds (Hasher & Thomas, 1973). The most usual explanation for these age-related changes is that the development of more powerful cognitive skills leads to better memory: as Flavell (1971) has put it, anticipating the Craik and Lockhart (1972) depth of processing notion

Memory is in good part just applied cognition. That is, what we call 'memory

88

processes' seem largely to be just the same old, familiar, cognitive processes, but as they are applied to a particular class of problems.

While general intellectual change, leading to modifications in mnemonic strategies, is almost certainly related to memory performance, it is unlikely, however, that there is a direct equation between the two as both Craik and Lockhart and Flavell suggest since, for example, we know that Korsakoff patients, some of whose intellectual powers appear comparable to those of controls, nevertheless show profound disorders of memory (see Mayes & Meudell, this volume). Be that as it may, qualitative as well as quantitative changes have been reported in the acquisition processes of children of different ages and which, at least in part, might contribute to observed age-related improvements in free recall. These differences include reduced primacy effects in younger children in free recall tasks (Cole *et al.*, 1971), changes from 'passive' to 'active' role rehearsal strategies as children grow up (Ornstein *et al.*, 1977), an increase as youngsters develop in the use of organizational strategies, reflected in patterns of recall of categorized word lists (Hasher & Clifton, 1974) and a tendency for older children and adults to show greater release from proactive interference with changes in semantic category on 'shift' trials (Zinober *et al.*, 1975).

All these data have been interpreted as indicating that with increasing age there is an increase in the number and type of dimensions upon which stimuli can be analysed and thus encoded in memory. Since training in various forms of rehearsal improves an infant's memory (Turnure *et al.*, 1976) and, more significantly, elevates his performance differentially relative to older children (Moely *et al.*, 1969; Ferguson and Bray, 1976), at least at some ages the child's relatively poor free recall performance might reflect a spontaneous failure to employ appropriate acquisition strategies which are, in fact, available to him or, at least, usable by him. Not surprisingly these spontaneous encoding deficiencies are mirrored by related retrieval deficits at the times when memories are tested (Kobasigawa, 1974) and, of course, at very early ages the differences between the adult and the infant must be due to an *absolute* failure on the part of the very young child to encode and retrieve multiple and sophisticated aspects of stimuli: these skills being neither available nor usable by him.

(d) Implications for childhood amnesia. It is apparent that there are changes in acquisitional processes employed by children as they grow up and that those employed by the young child are qualitatively, not merely quantitatively, different from those employed by the adult. To the extent that the nature of retrieval plans also become modified in development (as a result of the same changes which induce modifications in encoding processes) and thus the form of the information encoded early in life will be different from that of the retrieval operations in later life which might be used to access it, childhood amnesia is a readily understood phenomenon. On the other hand the magnitude of effects of this type and the extent to which they are the sole cause of childhood amnesia are unknown. Since we have no knowledge of comparative rates of forgetting in, say, 2-year-olds and adults (although there is a trend for forgetting rates to decrease across the period of very early childhood) such encoding specificity deficits as there are may be merely superimposed upon a more basic (and possibly more substantial) difference in the strengths of memories or in rates of

loss of information from memory. Until such data are available (and in view of the technical difficulties involved in direct comparisons of this sort, it may never materialize) the Schactel–Neisser explanation of childhood amnesia in humans must be seen as simply explaining an unknown fraction of the difficulties adults have in recall of their infancy.

3.2.3   The Phenomenon in Animals

(a)   Methodological and related issues.   Comparisons of young and mature animals' memories probably has fewer methodological pitfalls than those associated with similar ones in humans. Nevertheless, even such animal comparisons are not free from factors which readily may complicate the interpretation of experiments on weanling versus mature members of non-human species. These problems include equating for initial level of learning before investigating forgetting rates — while at the same time avoiding floor effects in the infant and ceiling effects in older animals — and ensuring that the motivational states of young and mature animals are broadly comparable.

While some studies of comparative rates of forgetting in infant and adult rats have failed to ensure that the degree of initial learning was equated between the two groups (e.g. Campbell & Campbell, 1962; Coulter *et al.*, 1976), Feigley and Spear (1970) have been able to show that immature rats (21–25 days old) learned an active avoidance task to criterion at the *same* rate as mature (60–70 days old) animals but, when tested for relearning 28 days later, the young animals took more trials than the older ones to relearn the avoidance behaviour, i.e. the former rats showed greater forgetting than the latter ones. Although Potash and Ferguson (1977) have shown that with a more stringent learning criterion (i.e. more consecutive appropriate escape responses) young immature rats showed *less* rapid learning than mature ones, nevertheless the Feigley and Spear data appear to give clear support to the hypothesis that young animals do indeed forget at faster rates than mature ones given that the two groups of animals had similar initial standards of performance at levels unconfounded by the presence of floor or ceiling effects. Other experiments demonstrating the phenomenon of infantile amnesia in the frog, dog, mouse, chick and wolf as well as the rat, whether initial levels of learning have been equated or not, have been recently and fully reviewed by Spear (1978, 1979) and by Nagy (1979) and so will not be discussed further here.

Motivational factors are essentially imponderable but Campbell (1967) and Spear (1979) have argued that since, for example, forgetting is independent of shock intensity in an aversive conditioning task for both young and mature animals, at least under some circumstances it might be assumed that considerations of motivation should not play a large part in any explanations of differences between mnemonic performance in these two groups of animals. The major limitation of this research strategy is, however, that only those tasks in which shock intensity as the motivating factor is not a differential factor in infant and mature animals' performance can be used to assess retention in the two groups. These aversively conditioned escape and avoidance tasks may have special characteristics — such as the ability to attend to spatial cues — which might reflect a variety of factors none of which is directly related to memory and which may thus limit not only the generality of findings but also their specific interpretation (see Miller and Berk, 1979).

90

This latter problem raises a further general complicating factor in the study of infantile amnesia, namely that neurological changes in developing animals are not likely only to produce changes in mnemonic function: in other words while there may be neurological development of putatively critical mnemonic structures such as the hippocampus (e.g. Douglas, 1975) there may also be changes in other structures, not directly subserving memory functions but which, nevertheless, may influence aspects of performance in mnemonic tasks. Parts of the neocortex of handled rats, for example, show changes in cell pro-liferation for up to 41 days after birth (Altman *et al.*, 1968) and non-mnemonic factors related to cortical changes may cause interpretative problems, not only in the studies of the development of animals' memory (including human memory) but also in the study of pathological loss of memory in man in certain groups of patients (see Meudell & Mayes, 1982) and in the investigations of normal loss of memory in animals and men in old age (see Section 3.4.2).

In this connection it is worth while considering the so-called 'neurological change' theory of infantile amnesia (e.g. Campbell *et al.*, 1974; Spear, 1979) that suggests infantile amnesia reflects structural change with development in memory systems in terms of, for example, variations in neurotransmitter amounts or rates of turnover, mylenization and synaptogenesis (Campbell & Spear, 1972). This view is frequently contrasted with 'behavioural' theories of infantile amnesia — that it is due to differences in encoding, storage or retrieval processes between infant and mature animals. This seems a strange contrast since, presumably, differences in encoding, storage or retrieval processes (as evidenced by behavioural measures) are themselves reflections of neurological differences: the two views are not therefore in opposition to one another and what is needed is a relationship between particular neurological change on the one hand and the precise form of the behavioural change that is associated with it on the other. Given the assumptions that acquisition, motivation and effective task can be equated across species (Miller & Berk, 1979), the absence of infantile amnesia (i.e. the absence of any age-related differences in retention between youngsters and adults) in animals such as the guinea pig which are thought to be near full neurological maturity during the prenatal period (Altman & Das, 1967; Campbell *et al.*, 1974), obviously tends to implicate neurological development as a factor in the infantile amnesia of the rat and other animals showing age-related mnemonic improvement from birth to maturity.

A similar conclusion follows from related work by Douglas (1975). Douglas has shown that mnemonically related spontaneous alternation behaviour in the adult rat is abolished after hippocampal lesions and is also absent in immature animals in whom the dentate gyrus is subject to postnatal neurogenesis (Altman & Das, 1965). Further, Douglas noted that the precocial guinea pig — born with a relatively well developed dentate gryus (Altman & Das, 1967) — shows spon-taneous alternation behaviour at 10 days of age which is equivalent to that of adults. Douglas also reported that humans up to the age of 3 or 4 are impaired on an analogous spontaneous alternation task. This age may correspond to the period for maturation of the human hippocampus. Finally, there are well docu-mented developmental changes in the dendrites of cells in the hippocampus of the rat (the hippocampus conceivably being a structure involved in the media-tion of memory) which are generally only complete within 24–48 days after birth (Pokorny & Yamamoto, 1981), i.e. a continuation in neurogenesis up to and beyond he age at which rats are considered immature for experimental purposes (typically aboaut 24 days of age).

Neurological development seems almost certainly a factor in the infantile amnesia of altricial animals but whether these developments lead to changes in encoding, storage or retrieval processes is a separate question, and one to which we now turn.

(b) Encoding and storage deficits in immature animals. Much of the research on infantile amnesia in animals has been, until recently, largely concerned with establishing the existence of the phenomenon. Over the last few years, however, hypotheses have been put forward postulating differences between what is encoded by immature and adult animals as being casually related to the observed differences in retention. Gordon (1979) has argued, for example, that since there are changes in the sensory systems which guide rat pups' behaviour as they develop (from tactile and olfactory systems perinatally to the visual system in later development) this will in some way change what is encoded and what retrieval cues will be effective as the animal matures. In a similar vein Spear (1979) has suggested (as have others studying the relatively poor memory of the human infant and the human aged) that '. . . the immature animal's capacity for processing information is more limited than the adult . . . and . . . the number of events in an episode the immature animal attends to, perceives and hence learns will therefore be fewer than that of the adult within any single session of training' (Spear, 1979, pp. 93–4). We have already noted that this type of view is popular not only as an explanation of animal infantile amnesia but also of human infantile and aged memory impairment. However, the precise form of it that Spear describes appears to involve the notion that mature animals differ from immature ones only in terms of the *number* of attributes of an 'episode' that are encoded while the form espoused in the study of the memory of the human infant and the human aged more specifically suggests a qualitative change in the *kinds* of features encoded (i.e. in development from 'acoustic' to 'semantic' attributes and vice versa in the dissolution of memory with advancing years).

While the evidence for changes in encoding strategies as children develop seems well established (although the magnitude of their effects upon memory remains unclear) the evidence for quantitative let alone qualitative changes in encoding processes as animals develop is sparse and open to alternative inter-pretations. Thus the major piece of evidence cited by Spear (1979) as support-ing the encoding deficit notion is an experiment by Kessler and Spear (1979) demonstrating that infant rats' retention of a Pavlovian conditioned avoidance response after a 28 day interval was better after distributed training than after massed training but that this effect was smaller or absent for adult rats. This result has been interpreted as reflecting the fact that with distributed training a young animal may perceive (and thus learn) a different aspect of the situation than previously and so '. . . the immature animal given distributed training may represent, within its memory of an episode, more events of the episode than if an extended masses sessions were given'. There may be, however, several alternative explanations for such an effect. Thus the very similar 'spacing effect' in normal human memory, for example, has been attributed to context differences being highlighted with spaced as opposed to closely presented items within a list (e.g. Anderson, 1980) and failure of context encod-ing (Huppert & Piercy, 1978), of context retrieval (Winocur & Kinsbourne,

1978) and of susceptibility of degraded memories to contextual changes (Mayes *et al.*, 1981) have all been suggested as explanations for the greater forgetting of human amnesics. Given the greater forgetting of infant animals compared to adults the greater susceptibility to the effects of massed versus spaced practice in young animals seems unlikely to help in distinguishing its source. Further, since the beneficial effects of distributed training violates the total time law (see Baddeley, 1976), it is tempting to seek non-mnemonic explanations for its occurrence. Indeed Underwood (1970), describing the advantage of distributed practice in adult human verbal learning, specifically attributed it to an attentional deficit (i.e. not primarily, if at all, a mnemonic impairment) associated with massed repetition. Accordingly, differential benefit from distributed training in young rats relative to mature ones may conceivably reflect a non-mnemonic factor related to the development of the ability to sustain attention rather than to any ontogenetic changes in the effectiveness of mnemonic systems themselves. Of course it may be that such attentional deficits are themselves solely and uniquely responsible for infantile amnesia — as indeed has been suggested (Frieman *et al.*, 1969; Brennan & Barone, 1976). These workers argue that adult rats become relatively desensitized to stimuli that tend to distract young rats and thus the mature animals are better able to make appropriate responses to salient cues in learning situations. However, in man and in the rat, a variety of attentional deficits occur after frontal lesions which are not accompanied by severe memory deficits (see Kolb & Wishaw, 1980), so it may be that attentional deficiencies in the immature rat are not critically involved in its relatively poor memory and are merely a reflection of incomplete frontal development in addition to incomplete development of the structures specifically involved in the mediation of memory.

The basic observation that infant animals forget more rapidly than older maturer ones even when degree of initial learning has been equated is not incompatible with the hypothesis that there are differences in consolidation processes leading to variations in memory strength between immature and mature organisms, i.e. some form of storage difference (see Meudell & Mayes, 1982). Further, Sussman and Ferguson (1980) trained young and mature rats on active and passive avoidance learning and then tested their retention after 28 days: at this time the young rats took the same number of trials to relearn the task as did an untrained control group while the mature animals did show some memory — in terms of taking fewer trials to relearn the task than an appropriately old, but untrained, control group. However, even in the absence of memory for the escape response, the young rats obviously did retain elements of the learning situation since, compared to the same age untrained control group and relative to initial levels, the immature rats showed a reduction in activity when replaced in the testing apparatus 1 month after initial training. This suggests that some aspects of a memory trace (perhaps recognition of fearful experience) might be lost less rapidly than others (such as knowing exactly what to do about it). This phenomenon has been noted in human adult amnesics (the Claparède effect) and has recently been specifically attributed to differences between weak and strong memories in the availability of various features in memory at a given retention interval, (Meudell & Mayes, 1981).

The view that infantile amnesia might be a result of incomplete development of consolidation processes leading to weaker memory in immature compared to adult animals might gain less credibility, however, if it could be shown that retention failures could readily be alleviated by the presence of appropriate retrieval conditions.

(c)   Retrieval failure hypotheses of infantile amnesia.   One specific hypothesis that has been put forward to explain at least part of human childhood amnesia is that growth-induced size changes (along with concomitant changes in perception) from childhood to maturity cause difficulties at retrieval since what was originally encoded in infancy now no longer matches what is perceived at maturity (e.g. Hunter, 1957). There is no experimental evidence about this hypothesis in humans — one way or the other — but it has been investigated directly in rats by Feigley and Spear (1970). They showed that even when putative growth-induced perceptual changes were allowed for in young rats by testing their retention of a passive avoidance response in a larger apparatus than that used for initial training, retention loss after 28 days was still greater than that shown by mature animals. Further, there were no differences in retention between young rats trained and tested in apparatus designed to match approximately their growth and those trained and tested in the same apparatus. Perhaps the most critical evidence against the notion of 'growth-induced generalization decrements' (as the hypothesis has been termed), however, is that immature rats' retention is still poorer than that showed by mature animals when a conditioned suppression paradigm is employed in which the rats are required to stop responding whenever they hear a shock-associated signal (e.g. Miller & Berk, 1979). Since it is improbable that either the stimuli or the responses in such situations can be related to size changes, the demonstration of infantile amnesia in this paradigm makes the role of growth-induced physical changes in the poor retention of immature animals, at best, negligible.

In a series of experiments Spear and Parsons (1976), following Campbell and Jaynes (1966), investigated the hypothesis that 'reactivation treatments' (part of the original training procedure — such as the conditioned stimulus or the unconditioned stimulus alone — represented to the animal during a retention interval) would serve as reminders and thus, in some way, act as retrieval practice which might alleviate forgetting. If young animals are particularly prone to retrieval failure (for whatever reason) then such reinstatement procedures should differentially aid their retention relative to that of older mature ones. Spear and Parsons observed, however, that such procedures actually aided mature rats' memory *more* than the young ones, i.e. the converse of the result predicted on the hypothesis of a retrieval deficit in immature animals. This is a strange effect since the overall level of retention shown by the older rats was greater than that shown by the immature ones and, as Spear and Parsons themselves note, at least in human memory, the stronger the memory the less likely it is to be aided by retrieval hints (e.g. Mayes & Meudell, 1981a). On the other hand Spear and Parsons compared young and old animals trained and subsequently given reactivation treatment alone: perhaps a more appropriate comparison would be between animals given training and reactivation and animals given training but no reactivation treatment. However, when this has been done (Spear & Smith, 1978) similar results are obtained, namely, 7-day-old rats do not benefit at all from reinstatement procedures over a 24 h retention interval while 12-day-old rats gain significant benefit in terms of number of relearning trials to criterion. Unfortunately, no mature adult animals were included in this study so it still remains an open issue what the pattern of results

94

such mature animals would show relative to the 12-day-old rats. Further, floor effects contaminated the 7-day-old rats' data since, as Spear (1979) notes, these very young animals showed hardly any learning of the avoidance task employed. Although Bryan (reported in Spear, 1979) has shown that even these very young creatures show some benefit of reactivation treatments in a Pavlovian conditioning paradigm, no mature animals' data are reported, as they were not in Haroutunian and Riccio (1977), so it still remains unknown whether younger rats show greater or lesser effects of reactivation than do adult ones. To the extent that Solheim *et al.* (1980) have shown that young rats show greater retention loss relative to older ones if they are tested in a different situation to that in which they were trained (compared to retention losses obtained when testing and training took place in identical situations) and this 'context shift' phenomenon is known to be one which is characteristic of human memory made weak through the passage of time (Mayes *et al.*, 1981), it seems likely that considerations of memory strength may be as apposite a factor in considerations of animals' memory as it is of human memory.

A further way in which difficulty at retrieval might manifest itself is through the effects of interfering activity either before or after learning. In an early experiment Smith (1968) compared infant and mature rats' relearning performances on a four choice maze after intervening learning of competing responses (learning to go to different goal boxes within the same maze), i.e. a retroactive interference (RI) paradigm. While young rats showed a greater susceptibility to the interpolated learning than the mature ones (i.e. they took longer than adult animals to relearn the original task after the interpolated learning), there was no differential effect on the infant compared to adult rats of the similarity of the interpolated learning to the original learning (similarity was defined in terms of distance and orientation of the new and old goal boxes), nor was there any difference in the proportion of intrusion response errors made by the two groups. A similar result for active avoidance learning has been shown by Parsons and Spear (1972). Proactive interference ((PI) effects have also been investigated and similarly it has been argued that since infant rats showed an increase in the number of trials to learn an active avoidance response after previously having learned a passive avoidance task relative to older animals (Spear *et al.*, 1972), the young animals might be especially sensitive to the effects of proactive interference.

Once again, however, it is not clear whether such effects of PI and RI as there are, are the cause or the consequence of forgetting. If they are a result of the latter such that more forgetting is associated with greater susceptibility of memories to the effects of prior or subsequent experience, then differences between young and mature animals in terms of vulnerability to interference may be a reflection of differences between the two groups in terms of the states of their memories after a given retention interval (see Meudell & Mayes, 1982), rather than being attributable to a selective problem at retrieval in infant creatures.

3.2.4 Conclusions on the Development of Memory

The animal data, and to some extent the human data, tend to point to decreases in the rate of forgetting from early infancy to adulthood. The Schactel–Neisser view of infantile amnesia attributes the relative unavailability of early memories to gross changes in encoding and retrieval operations between birth and full maturity, but since rates of forgetting across the relatively brief retention intervals of days and months do tend to decrease within the period of infancy itself, proponents of this view would also have to argue that more subtle changes in encoding and retrieval, occurring across these much smaller time-spans, are responsible for the observed differences in rates of loss of availability of memories. Since the magnitude of such encoding specificity effects is largely unknown and since many of the data are currently interpretable in terms of a storage difference between young and mature animals, and men, possible changes in mnemonic efficiency due to alterations in encoding and subsequent retrieval strategies as animals grow up may be merely superimposed upon more significant differences in consolidation processes.

3.3 Changes in Memory from Infancy to Adolescence and Maturity

The years between infancy and adulthood are characterized by continued improvements in short-term memory as assessed by digit span and related techniques. Such changes, according to Chi (1976) are attributable not so much to alterations in the 'capacity' of a short-term memory structure, but simply represent continual improvement in grouping, recoding, elaborative and related strategies which are also responsible for the sustained improvement in long-term memory over the same period. These strategies seem not, however, to be responsible for variations in span *within* normal adults (Lyon, 1977). Interestingly, Belmont (1972) has observed that rates of forgetting in the Peterson and Peterson (1959) paradigm are not only unrelated to age in infants, adolescents and adults, once floor and ceiling effects are avoided, but also, at least across these developing years, rates of forgetting across short retention intervals are independent of gross intellectual function as assessed by IQ measures.

Two further factors may contribute to the continued improvements observed in memory through infancy and adolescence to adulthood.

One, related to the changes mentioned in encoding operations, is the development of knowledge. As Piaget and Inhelder (1973) note, how an event is interpreted depends on what an individual knows about the world and this will affect what is stored and what can later be reconstructed. That such differences in knowledge between people may well affect level of mnemonic function is clearly shown by a recent experiment by Chi (1978) who has shown that under some circumstances 10-year-olds can demonstrate better memory than adults. She showed that while memory for digits was superior in novice chess-playing adults to that observed in 10-year-old skilled chess players, the chess-playing children were superior to the tiro adults on a test requiring memory for the positions of chess positions taken from actual games. Changes in knowledge about all aspects of experience are therefore likely to affect the efficiency with which information is encoded and retrieved and such knowledge will almost certainly affect the level of an individual's mnemonic performance.

The other development which might affect memory through the period of schooling is the development of metamemory (see Gruneberg, this volume). Kail (1979) has recently reviewed some aspects of metamemory thought to be relevant to development. First, the child might need to become aware that memory tasks are a distinct class of processes associated with relevant cognitive activity and appropriate behaviour. Second, the awareness of the factors which might contribute to efficient memorizing needs to be developed and, relatedly, the infant may need to develop a consciousness of the status of information in his memory, i.e. he might well become able to monitor and predict performance in various mnemonic tasks. While even pre-school children are aware of the *need* to remember in certain situations, they have little consciousness of the factors which will affect their mnemonic performance; this latter information appears to be gained by about 8 or 9 years of age. Similarly, memory-monitoring abilities appear to improve systematically up to adolescence (see Kail, 1979). These metamnemonic factors were originally thought progressively to play a major role in organizing and directing mnemonic activities as children approached adolescence. Recent evidence, however, has shown that in children of less than 9 years there is very little relationship between mnemonic knowledge on the one hand and mnemonic performance on the other; above 9 years, however, it is claimed that metamnemonic wisdom increasingly becomes to be related to performance in actual tests of memory (see Flavell and Wellman, 1977). Whether, in the adolescent or the adult, both memory function and metamnemonic indicants are both simply related to the general efficiency of an individual's memory or whether, in some way, metamemory factors are necessary for, or even determine, memory performance, remains unclear.

3.4 Memory Changes in Senescence: The Dissolution of Mnemonic Processes

3.4.1 Human Ageing and Memory: Introduction

As mature people approach senescence some aspects of their memory appear to remain relatively unchanged. An individual's forwards digit span is barely different in his 60s from what it would have been in his 20s (Botwinnick & Storandt, 1974) and his ability to monitor aspects of his memory functions — so-called metamemory — is also claimed to be as effective as that of younger people (e.g. Lachman *et al.*, 1979). Reliably, however, older people show decrements on split span tasks (Inglis & Caird, 1963) and show more or less impairment on any *supra* span task (so long as ceiling effects are avoided), however this is assessed.

One might reasonably expect theoretical disagreement about the reasons for this *supra* span memory impairment and indeed this is the case but what one might not expect, *a priori*, is that many of the data on 'long-term memory' in older people are frankly contradictory and the theoretical battles appear to be fought on foundations of shifting empirical sand. Of course the minutiae of any experiments are sufficiently different so that with a little ingenuity some recon-ciliation between the occasional contradictory experiment in one particular area of research can easily be achieved. Unfortunately, in examining the literature of human ageing and memory, it appears that the experimental contradictions are neither infrequent nor limited to restricted areas of memory research.

The ubiquity of these experimental inconsistencies is such that their source might best be sought elsewhere than in microscopic analysis of experimental paradigms: in particular it seems most likely that individual differences within elderly populations are so large, relative to those within the young, that the assumption that quasi-random sampling of small numbers of people from an aged population who have 'no obvious physical or mental defect' will ensure comparability between different experiments is simply unrealistic. The variance in the elderly population is such that the constituents of one old group of people might well have quite different cognitive characteristics from those of another and experiments based upon the premise that all old people are more or less alike for experimental purposes may not be adequate, at least as they are currently reported, to make any useful statements about age and memory whatsoever.

Accordingly, the data upon which these comments are based will be presented in this section along with suggestions for future research along both 'standard' and somewhat different lines; because parallel experiments have frequently been carried out on amnesics these will also be commented upon where appropriate since similarities and differences between normal loss of memory through age and that through acute brain damage are clearly of some importance. Before turning to the main section, however, some methodological points, relevant to the study of the elderly memory system, will be presented.

3.4.2 Methodological Problems

(a) Sampling biases.   An obvious question which might be asked about human ageing and memory is 'does memory decline with age?' The answer to this deceptively simple question has been assumed to be positive both in folklore and in experimental psychology (e.g. Craik, 1977). In spite of a plethora of research on human learning and memory in old age, however, it is still not at all clear whether memory does become progressively impaired in senescence or, if it does, when the deterioration begins and what the magnitude of the decrement is.

The reason for these uncertainties lies in the almost exclusive use of cross-sectional designs in the reported research on human ageing and memory. It is known from the study of intellectual performance across different ages that cross-sectional studies of some aspects of intelligence tend to indicate a greater diminution of ability than do longitudinal studies of those same intellectual skills (e.g. Botwinnick, 1977). Further, recent investigations (Riegal & Riegal, 1972; Palmore & Cleveland, 1976) have shown that the smaller falls in intelligence noted in longitudinal research across the period from maturity to old age may all be attributed to cognitive changes occurring in people within 5 years of their death. That is, there may be *no* decline in some aspects of intellect beyond maturity except from a period shortly before death (the so-called 'terminal drop'). The apparent progressive decline in intelligence occurring across the later part of the life-span, observed even with longitudinal studies may, therefore, indicate simply that as a given cohort ages, progressively more people come within 5 or so years of their death and, accordingly, *group* intellectual performance apparently shows progressive decline from middle age onwards even though, in fact, the decrement occurs in individuals only during the very last few years of life.

Employing cross-sectional designs, research workers in human memory and ageing typically have selected two age groups, one young (usually 20 years to 30 years) and one old (usually 60 years to 80 years), and observed differences

98

between them. With some exceptions (to be discussed below) such studies almost invariably show poorer memory in the aged groups. However, if, as seems not unreasonable, the considerations of cross-sectional and longitudinal studies and of 'terminal drop' are as relevant for the study of memory as they are for the investigations of aspects of intelligence then, at least, the magnitude of mnemonic deficits occurring with age may be exaggerated by the routine employment of cross-sectional designs and, at best, may mean that memory deficits, like intellectual deficits, may only manifest themselves behaviourally shortly before death and may not occur *throughout* the period of life after maturity.

Since cross-sectional studies of rats (e.g. Barnes, 1979), of mice, (Kubanis *et al.*, 1981), and of monkeys (e.g. Bartus, 1979) have all shown mnemonic deficits in older animals it is clear, however, that cultural and related factors are unlikely to be, as some have argued (see Labouvie-Vief *et al.*, 1974), exclusively responsible for the age-related mnemonic deficits observed in cross-sectional studies of humans.

(b) Floor effects, ceiling effects and levels of performance. One problem with research on groups of people who have memory problems is that the use of short retention intervals which lift the impaired group's performance above floor levels tends to elevate the unimpaired group's performance to ceiling levels. Conversely, longer retention intervals, which tend to ensure that the unimpaired group shows performance which is below ceiling levels, tend also to depress an impaired group's performance to floor levels. It has been argued elsewhere (Meudell & Mayes, 1982) that one solution to this dilemma is differential testing of the impaired and unimpaired groups such that the impaired group is tested at shorter retention intervals than the unimpaired group.

An additional argument advanced by Meudell and Mayes (1982) was that differential testing of groups of people with impaired and unimpaired memory helps to overcome the problem that, even if floor and ceiling effects could be avoided, impaired and unimpaired groups frequently function at different levels of performance. Given different levels of performance it is not satisfactory to argue, as many researchers have, that unusual patterns of performance in impaired memory groups reflect a selective deficit in a particular stage of memory. This is unsatisfactory because Woods and Piercy (1974) among others (e.g. Squire *et al.*, 1978; Mayes & Meudell, 1981) have shown (by varying retention interval) that in normal young adults with unimpaired memory *pattern* of performance on some memory tasks is related to overall *level* of performance. Thus differences in the pattern of performance found in groups with impaired and unimpaired memory could result not because of qualitative differences (e.g. a selective impairment of a particular memory stage) but because of the quantitative differences in levels of performance. In other words the processes involved in forgetting may be identical in impaired and unimpaired groups but the impaired group rapidly achieves states of memory which are attained by unimpaired people after a longer interval of time. Equating the two groups' overall level of performance by differential testing, therefore, overcomes these problems.

These arguments were originally put forward by Meudell and Mayes (1982) in the context of research in human organic amnesia (e.g. Korsakoff's psychosis) and although the magnitude of the memory decrements observed in the normal elderly is likely to be less severe than those of organic amnesics, nevertheless the same considerations ought to apply to research on the nature of the memory deficit in the aged since such research involves comparisons of young people with good memory with old people with relatively poor memory. Indeed these types of problem crop up in many diverse areas of psychopathology (e.g. Chapman & Chapman, 1973).

(c) Neuropathological and neuropsychological changes in old age. Some amnesic patients can show grossly impaired memory in the face of apparently complete intactness of other cognitive functions. The minimal lesion responsible for this pure memory disorder is controversial (see Mayes & Meudell, this volume) but almost certainly involves single or combined lesions of the hippocampus, mamillary bodies, the fornix, the dorsomedial nucleus of the thalamus, the amygdala and possibly the temporal stem. A natural question to ask therefore is, 'do elderly individuals show deterioration in these structures?'

Unfortunately, for what are probably historical reasons, of the limbic and related structures only the hippocampus has been singled out for detailed investigation of age-related macroscopic and microscopic changes. In the normal elderly man the hippocampus shows many histopathological changes such as senile plaques and neurofibrillary tangles (Tomlinson *et al.*, 1968; Wisnieswki & Terry, 1976) and loss of dendrites and dendritic spines (Scheibel *et al.*, 1975). Similar changes in the hippocampus are also noted in the brains of Alzheimer's patients (i.e. those suffering from 'presenile' dementia). It might reasonably be assumed that changes such as these might lead to some manifestation in terms of impaired behaviour and indeed Blessed *et al.* (1968) have shown that a count of senile plaques (albeit sampled across much of the cortex of their elderly samples) was negatively correlated with scores on tests of intellectual function.

Although animals other than man appear not to show senile plaques or neurofibrillary tangles (Dayan, 1971), and reports of cell loss in the hippocampus are variable (see Kubanis & Zornetzer, 1981), the rat does show dendritic atrophy especially in the dentate gyrus (Geinisman & Bondareff, 1976) and, interestingly, this structure is the only one in the limbic system to show any change with age in cerebral glucose utilization (Smith, *et al.*, 1980). While electrophysiological recordings from hippocampal granule cells reveal only marginal changes in synaptic response rise times (Barnes & McNaughton, 1979) or in amplitude, latency, stimulation threshold or wave form (Landfield & Lynch, 1977) with low frequency stimulation, if aged and young hippocampal synapses are given high frequency repeated stimulation then aged animals, known to have memory problems, show deficiencies in high frequency potentiation (Landfield *et al.*, 1978; Barnes, 1979). While there is evidence that synaptic processes are related to performance on spatial memory tasks both between and within aged and younger samples (Barnes, 1979), it may be that potentiation is a property of other systems as well as the hippocampus and that aged animals show a general decline in this phenomenon. In view of the current uncertainty surrounding the site of the minimal lesion in amnesia — with the hippocampus as only one candidate — such recordings for other relevant areas are obviously necessary.

Biochemical research on neutrotransmitter systems in the young and elderly has recently focused upon cholinergic function. In general, as Kubanis and

Zornetzer (1981) point out in their review, the results of studies of the effects of ageing on the cholinergic synthetic enzyme, choline acetyltransferase (CAT) have been variable with differential declines in amount in the elderly being noted in the human hippocampus relative to the amounts obtained from the cortex, to no age-related changes being noted in the rat in either the hippocampus or the cortex. Variable results have also been obtained in the assessment of age-related amounts of acetylcholinesterase (AChE), the metabolic enzyme for acetylcholine, with decreases in levels of AChE being occasionally noted in the hippocampus as well as in the cortex of the mouse, rat and human. Interestingly, Kubanis and Zornetzer also point out that some recent human studies on the normal aged brain and on the brains of patients suffering from Alzheimer's disease during life, show that while decreased cholinergic receptor binding tends to be a characteristic of the normal elderly brain, it is sometimes claimed to be not characteristic of the presenile demented brain (see Perry, 1980; Davies & Verth, 1977). They further suggest that this might indicate differences in the type of memory losses which might be observed in the normal aged and in Alzheimers' patients. As yet, however, even if these recent reports of differences between the two groups are confirmed (for the reported changes are controversial — see Gibson et al., 1981), there is no clear behavioural evidence that mnemonic function is qualitatively different between the normal elderly and those with Alzheimer's disease.

Direct manipulation of cholinergic systems on memory in the human aged have been disappointing (Mohs et al., 1979), as have the effects of physostigmine in aged monkeys (Bartus, 1979), so while cholinergic systems may well play a role in age-related memory impairments, currently available agents cannot be reliably used for their alleviation.

In any event, there does seem to be a considerable body of evidence both from human and animal work to suggest that there is significant deterioration in the hippocampus with advancing age. However, changes in the brain with advancing years (unlike the acute lesions of some relatively young amnesics) are not confined to the limbic system let alone the hippocampus. Brody (e.g. 1976), for example, has reported that in addition to cerebellar degeneration, atrophy of the frontal, temporal and parietal lobes is readily noticeable in old age: similar atrophy has also been reported in animals (e.g. Ordy & Brizzee, 1975). As already noted, biochemical analyses of human and animal brains show decreased levels of cholinergic enzymes in the cortex of aged individuals as often as they show lowered amounts in the hippocampus. The effects of these widespread changes in senescent human brains is that not only is memory affected in old age but there are also changes in arousal level (Eisdorfer, 1968), in speed of response (Welford, 1977), in the ability to deal with irrelevant information (Rabbitt, 1965), in perceptual flexibility both in vision (Heath & Orbach, 1963) and in hearing (Obusek & Warren, 1973), in problem solving skills (Rabbitt, 1977) and in global intellectual changes as assessed by IQ measures (Botwinnick, 1977).

As a result of factors such as these the observed behaviour in senescent organisms (whether the expression of memory or otherwise) is necessarily a result of the complex interaction of areas or systems of the brain, each of which, to some unknown greater or lesser extent, is affected by ageing processes.

101

Unless normal ageing processes result in focal damage — which they patently do not — the search for the nature of isolated cognitive deficits in the old is almost certainly doomed to failure. The 'best' that could therefore be hoped for is that atrophy of critical mnemonic structures is relatively greater than that observed in other structures. The relationship between extent of atrophy and remaining function is unclear, however, and may not be consistent across all areas of the brain so it is not obvious that histopathological and related studies could, for example, answer the question of whether there is, in fact, relatively selective atrophy (and consequently relatively selective impairment of mnemonic function) in those regions of the brain involved directly in memory.

(d)   Matching and assessing young and old groups.   The widespread nature of the neurological and consequent cognitive changes that can be observed in the elderly means that disentangling behaviourally what are genuine age-related mnemonic deficits from what are memory problems occurring secondary to other cognitive changes (which happen to be age related) is not simple.

One research strategy which has been employed to disentangle these factors has involved matching young and old groups on the basis of *full* WAIS scores and then looking for differential memory impairment in the elderly group; the argument being that if the groups are matched on overall WAIS scores then any memory deficits cannot be attributable to intellectual impairment at least to the extent that the WAIS is a good guide to general intelligence. It has been argued elsewhere (Meudell & Mayes, 1982) that while this approach is sound for the study of *new* learning it may not be appropriate for the study of memory for older information acquired by an elderly group before senile decline began. The approach may be inappropriate since, if intelligence has declined in the later period of life, the elderly person would be required to access information acquired with one (relatively high) level of intelligence with currently a different (relatively low) level. The result of this 'encoding specificity' would be retrieval difficulties of a rather special kind. Matching an elderly group with a younger one in terms of current overall WAIS scores may, therefore, be appropriate for the study of new learning in the laboratory where information is acquired and retrieved with a constant level of intelligence (albeit, in the elderly one which may be below their more youthful optimum) but may be inappropriate for the assessment of memories stored before mental deterioration began.

While the observation of poor new learning in the elderly in the face of comparable full scale WAIS scores to a younger comparison group may be a satisfactory way of partialling out the contribution of gross changes in intellectual factors to their impaired memory, the widespread practice of equating groups on the basis only of the vocabulary scale of the WAIS may be quite inappropriate. The assumption lying behind the use of the vocabulary test appears to be that the vocabulary test is a good indicant of current general linguistic intelligence, i.e. it correlates highly with overall verbal IQ. Its use, therefore, appears to give a quick and efficient method of matching young and old groups in terms of verbal intelligence. Unfortunately, however, it is known that of the WAIS verbal subtests, vocabulary is remarkably stable over age (Yates, 1954) and, as such, is often used clinically as an indicant of premorbid function in some brain-damaged patients. Thus, while its use in young groups may well give a reasonable estimate of current linguistic intelligence, it might not do so for an elderly group where other aspects of verbal intellect (as assessed for example by the 'similarities' scale of the WAIS) may not have held up over time and, therefore, might be much poorer than the vocabulary scores would tend to suggest. Since it is known, for example, that similarities' scores within groups of younger people are related to memory scores (Stoff & Eagle, 1971), in those studies where elderly and younger groups have been matched solely on the basis of vocabulary scores, it is necessarily unclear whether any observed memory deficits are due to selective memory problems or whether they represent at least a partial consequence of some unknown amount of intellectual decline. Much variability in the results of similar experimental manipulations on memory in the elderly may well be attributed to unknown cognitive deficits, outside the direct realm of memory, but which nevertheless contribute to the overall level and pattern of memory performance.

The cognitive changes noted in older people may be due to small subclinical infarcts occurring randomly in an ageing population (Blessed *et al.*, 1968), in addition to differences in 'intrinsic' rates of ageing between individuals, and such factors may well account for the fact that not only do elderly groups of people show decrements in mean levels of performance relative to younger people they also show a massive increase in variance: in memory and reaction time studies, for example, mean scores change by about 20% across the mature life-span but the variability between subjects increases by about 160% across the same period (Rabbitt, 1980). The effect of this increased variance is that with suitable (or unsuitable) sampling procedures practically any type of experimental result is capable of being demonstrated in a small elderly group. Extensive general psychological assessment of older people is, therefore, indicated before the investigations of putatively specific functions, such as memory, can even be contemplated. Some suggestions as to minimum assessment requirements have recently been put forward by Albert and Kaplan (1980) and a knowledge of non-mnemonic capabilities of the individuals within a group of elderly people, in addition to their memory abilities, would enable us to see in what ways particular deficits (or absence of deficits) interact with memory to produce particular patterns of performance.

3.4.3 The Experimental Study of Mnemonic Deficits in the Human Elderly

(a) Introduction. In making comparisons between an elderly group and a younger one it is not sufficient merely to show that the older people are worse on some test of memory. Rather, if we are to make some sense of the *nature* of the mnemonic differences between old and young people, it must be shown first that, at least with some manipulations, the elderly are qualitatively as well as quantitatively different from a matched younger group and, second, as argued above, that a given qualitative difference does not merely arise through differences in overall level of performance between the two groups.

(b) The processing deficit hypothesis. A very influential way of conceiving of all the varied age-related changes in cognition is to assume that all the deterioration in high level processing is a manifestation of the same basic cause. Specifically the so-called 'processing deficit' hypothesis (Craik & Simon, 1980) suggests that all aspects of cognition which require effort are mediated by the same limited

103

capacity central system and that as people age the resources available to this system are diminished. Consequently, as we grow older, changes in effort-requiring tasks will progressively be observed. The widespread cognitive deterioration in old age, involving perception and thought as well as memory, is therefore not surprising since the same impaired system is involved in all our highest endeavours. Mnemonic impairment is thus a consequence of the fact that, according to the theory, good memory depends upon effortful analyses of stimuli — on this view there is nothing special about the memory deficit of the elderly since it is just one manifestation of the general processing deficit. The fact that memory impairments are the first failings that are noted in old age (as they are in presenile dementia) may not mean there is anything special about age and memory other than that mnemonic functions are more sensitive to slight changes in available resources than are other systems.

It is argued that the particular way in which memory is affected by the reduction in resources in old age is that the elderly economize on those semantic and related analyses of stimuli which are especially effort requiring. In other words older people have a semantic coding deficit and spontaneously tend to employ superficial or relatively effort-free analyses of information.

The evidence upon which semantic processing deficits have been attributed to the elderly will now be examined.

(i) Material type and recognition errors. One research strategy which has often been employed in attempts to demonstrate encoding deficits in the aged has been to vary the type of information that old and young groups are required to remember (e.g. Rowe & Schnore, 1971; Wittels, 1972; Witte & Freund, 1976; Wallach et al., 1980). It is not clear, however, what the logic is behind these studies. It is often claimed, for example, that if the elderly have a semantic coding deficit (i.e. they fail to engage in those meaningful analyses of stimuli which are necessary for good memory) then giving young and old subjects meaningless material should abolish any differences between the two groups which may be observed with meaningful information since in the former case both groups cannot impose effective semantic analyses on the stimuli. On the other hand, it is equally possible to argue that giving younger people meaningless material might force them to strive spontaneously to impose some sort of meaning upon what they are being required to remember: accordingly, if the elderly do not so strive, the difference between the groups may be exacerbated rather than reduced with meaningless material in comparison to stimuli which were rich in semantic content. How an individual responds to variations in stimuli which he is required to learn may be quite idiosyncratic (and not necessarily related to age) and thus it is not surprising that the results from experiments which have varied aspects of stimulus dimensions such as meaningfulness, concreteness, emotionality and list organization are frequently contradictory. Since both relative exacerbation and relative improvement in the elderlies' memories are predicted from encoding deficit theories in these experimental situations, they cannot anyway provide critical tests of where an age-related mnemonic deficit might lie.

Another approach to the study of encoding deficits in the elderly has been through investigations of the types of errors made in recognition memory experiments. Once again, however, the interpretation of the results from such experiments is problematical. If, for example, the elderly make more 'acoustic' than 'semantic' errors in recognition tests while a younger group make the opposite pattern of results, is this because the elderly initially encoded *less* semantic information than the young and are thus not prone to making semantic errors or is it because the aged individuals encoded *more* semantic information than the young controls and are thus less likely to make semantic errors since the richness of their encoded information ensures fine semantic discriminations? Empirically it appears that the pattern of semantic and acoustic recognition errors made by the elderly is similar to that made by young people (indicating no encoding deficit for these types of information) although, relative to neutral distractor items, the older age groups make more semantic and acoustic errors (Rankin & Kausler, 1979). However, since both the younger and older groups made less than 5% errors on the neutral distractor items, this latter result is most likely to be attributable to ceiling effects when the target and foil items were unrelated.

In the neuropsychological literature some alcoholic amnesics have been shown to be differentially impaired in their memory for particular classes of words (Cutting, 1978) and in their error patterns across various foils in recognition tests (Butters & Cermak, 1975). These interactions are in some respects similar to some of those reported between young and elderly normal subjects but their interpretations are, of course, just as problematical. Furthermore, with appropriate memory strength controls — not so far carried out with young/elderly comparisons — no difference between amnesics and controls in error patterns across recognition distractors has been found (Meudell & Mayes, 1980). Direct comparisons between pathological loss of memory in alcoholic amnesia and the normal memory loss occurring in old age on tests such as these are, therefore, currently not realistic; while such comparisons may well be of interest, in principal the interactions (or absence of interactions) under consideration cannot point to the source of the mnemonic deficit in either amnesic or elderly memory loss.

(ii) Variations in 'depth of processing'. In contrast to the above correlational studies, where processing strategies have been inferred from performance, experiments which directly manipulate encoding processes in groups of people would appear to provide a more critical test of processing deficits in the elderly. Specifically, if the old spontaneously fail to engage in extensive semantic analyses of stimuli under ordinary learning instructions, they should be differentially improved relative to a younger group (who might be expected to employ extensive elaborative analyses of items) when encouraged to analyse for meaning through the adoption of an appropriate orienting task (Prediction 1). Conversely, preventing the old from analysing the meaning of stimuli that they are required to remember should have relatively little effect upon their memory, relative to an ordinary learning condition, since they do not spontaneously encode for meaning when they are free to do so; the young, however, should be particularly disadvantaged when they are prevented from engaging in elaborative processing of stimuli (Prediction 2).

Some studies employing the depth of processing framework have failed to employ the critical control condition of ordinary learning instructions and thus, in the absence of this baseline, the results from such experiments are difficult to interpret. Some other studies have, however, manipulated encoding strategies through the use of appropriate orienting tasks and have also incorporated straightforward 'learn' condition. Unfortunately the patterns of results obtained from these experiments are far from consistent.

Table 3.1 summarizes the relevant data for each of four recently reported experiments using verbal material where it was possible to examine both predictions from the processing deficit hypothesis. It is clear that the results across experiments are highly variable. Eysenk's (1974) recall data and White's (1977) recognition data are consistent with both predictions from a processing deficit hypothesis — the old perform differentially better than the young when encouraged to analyse the meaning of words while the young do differentially worse that the old with tasks which make the extraction of meaning somewhat difficult. On the other hand Zelinski *et al.*, (1978) found no age by orienting task interaction at a retention interval similar to Eysenk's: at a longer (48 h) interval, however, such an interaction was observed but almost certainly this occurred as a trivial consequence of a floor effect for the older people at this long retention interval. White's data (cited by Craik (1977) and by Craik and Simon (1980) are frequently quoted as providing evidence for a processing deficit but full statistical analyses have not been formally reported and while there may be some suggestion that the younger group in her experiment were differentially impaired when semantic analyses were not encouraged, this might well be attributable to a floor effect for the aged group. A similar argument applies to Mason's (1979) data — a floor effect prevents the elderly group from showing as much drop in recall with the 'superficial' task as the young. Mason's results from orienting tasks where semantic analyses were encouraged showed that, if anything, the elderly improved *less* (in relation to ordinary learning instructions) than did the young control group: this might well be taken to mean that the old spontaneously engaged in relatively *more* semantic analyses than the young and consequently are not especially helped when ecouraged to do so, alternatively it might mean that the elderly sample had an *absolute* processing failure which was not remediable by forced semantic encoding. Another study, but using non-verbal material (Smith & Winograd, 1978), found the old were equally advantaged or equally disadvantaged as the young with orienting tasks which encouraged, respectively, deep analysis of faces or superficial analysis of them.

Two other studies employing variants of the depth of processing approach discussed above also deserve mention.

Following the observation made on younger people that the more decisions that are made about a word the better it is remembered (e.g. Ross, 1981), Barrett and Wright (1981) compared the young and the elderly (matched on the basis of number of years' schooling) on memory for words after one or after two semantic decisions about the words. They argued that if the elderly had an encoding deficit then the elderly should be differentially improved compared to the young when two decisions, rather than one, were overtly required. No such effect occurred, the old group improved by an identical extent to the young ones and thus their data are consistent with the notion of normal semantic processing in aged people.

Of course it is obvious that if the elderly do have a processing deficit then this will manifest itself at retrieval as well as at encoding. Accordingly Simon (1979) has argued that if the elderly spontaneously fail to analyse the semantic aspects of stimuli then giving them semantic hints at retrieval should not benefit their memory performance over free recall levels. Younger groups, however, who putatively do spontaneously encode for meaning, should benefit from semantic hints when memories are assessed. This is exactly the pattern of results found by

Table 3.1 Performance of Young (18–30 years) and Old (60–80 years) Subjects on Tasks that Prevent Efficient Extraction of Meaning ('Low') and Tasks that Encourage it ('High')

White's data are approximate proportions correct: the others are numbers of words correctly recalled. In White's experiment (a) refers to recall, (b) to recognition. Y indicates prediction was fulfilled, N that it was not. See text for predictions 1 and 2. 'Matching' refers to the reported non-mnemonic comparability of the groups.

Study		Orienting task (OR)			Type of OR		Matching	Predictions fulfilled	
		Low	Learn	High	Low	High		1	2
Eysenck (1974)	Y	6.5	19.3	17.6	Letter counting	Imagery	Vocabulary	Y	Y
	O	7.0	12.0	13.4					
Mason (1979)	Y	4.0	11.3	15.4	Case judgement	Category	Non	Y?[1]	Y[2]
	O	3.7	5.6	6.4					
Zelinski et al. (1978)	Y	4.5	9.5	8.5	Detect eg in words	Rate as pleasant/unpleasant	Verbal abilities/fluency	N	N
	O	2.5	5.5	5.5					
White (1977) (a)	Y	.11	.33	.30	Rhyme decision	Category	Non-reported	(a) N	?[3]
	O	.08	.17	.15					
(b)	Y	.35	.74	.57				(b) Y	Y
	O	.38	.33	.60					

[1] Greater improvement in young group.
[2] Floor effect?
[3] No ANOVAs reported.

Simon and is, or course, consistent with the notion of a general processing deficit in the elderly which manifests itself both at encoding and at retrieval. Simon's young and old groups were matched in terms of a vocabulary test but even if the effect were replicable on other groups of subjects, faith in this hypothesis might be enhanced if it could be shown that when the elderly are *forced* to analyse the meaning of words (which they were not in her study) and are then given semantic hints, they perform differentially *better* in relation to free recall than a younger group. According to the hypothesis this should occur since the younger controls should spontaneously employ encoding specific retrieval strategies while the elderly, in spite of adequate initial encoding, might not spontaneously employ relevant retrieval strategies and might thus benefit especially from semantic hints. A study which goes some way to meeting this specification (but only in part since although category cues subsequently given at retrieval were present during learning, the subjects were not forced to process the category–exemplar relationship) in fact *failed* to find that the old were differentially aided by semantic hints at retrieval in comparison to free recall (Smith, 1977).

Of course there may be many differences of detail between all these experiments which could conceivably be responsible for their different outcomes but a particularly relevant one may the differences in the kinds of orienting tasks employed. However, in so far as even when the orienting tasks are identical, as in the category judgement task of White (1977) and Mason (1979), the data are conflicting, the source of the discrepancies is most probably best sought elsewhere. Since the data on the characteristics of the samples involved in these studies are sketchy in the extreme the variability of the results appears to be readily attributed to: (a) differences in intellectual and related cognitive abilities between the young and old groups compared within a single experiment; and (b) differences between the elderly groups sampled and differences between the younger groups sampled between different experiments. Mild cognitive, affective or motivational disorders may well affect how effectively an orienting task is carried out and, since performance on orienting tasks has not been systematically reported in any of the cited studies, differences between various elderly groups in terms of their efficiency of execution of the orienting tasks may well be responsible for the conflicting patterns of data which have been obtained. That there are qualitative differences between elderly groups of the *same* age is shown (albeit in a rather obvious way) by the fact that the degree of release from PI with taxonomic shifts (often taken as an indication of the extent of encoding deficits) is greater in elderly groups in the community than similar aged people in the care of institutions (Puglisi, 1980). The latter group also have a poorer memory overall, than the old living at home (Klonoff & Kennedy, 1966).

Craik (1977) expressed the hope that depth of processing studies would prove useful in the evaluation of encoding processes in the elderly. There is still every reason to assume that such experiments will prove of value, but four factors need to be incorporated into any such investigation which varies type of processing through the introduction of various kinds of orienting tasks. These are:

1. an adequate description of the young and old samples;
2. measures of how well the two groups performed on the orienting tasks themselves;

3. at test the subjects should be reminded of the original learning conditions to avoid encoding specific retrieval difficulties;
4. the old should be equated with young in terms of level of performance under ordinary learning instructions: achieved by varying retention interval or by manipulating learning time.

Such factors as these are hardly likely to be important in depth of processing studies with subjects who are all young undergraduates, but when comparing groups who may differ in many respects other than chronological age they are mandatory. It is interesting to note that when all these controls are introduced in neuropsychological research on amnesia no interactions between alcoholic amnesics and age matched controls are observed (see Meudell & Mayes, 1982; Mayes & Meudell, this volume). It remains to be seen whether this is the case for comparisons of older and younger people's memories.

(iii) Preserved 'automatic' mnemonic abilities? A corollary of the processing deficit hypothesis is that tasks which do not require effort (and which thus are said to be automatically executed) should show no age-related decrement. The accuracy with which young normal people can make judgements from memory about the frequency of occurrence of items, for example, does not depend upon whether subjects know that such a judgement will ultimately be required and it is, therefore, argued that the information in memory upon which frequency estimates are made is acquired automatically without intention and without effort (Hasher & Zachs, 1979): accordingly elderly people should not show deficits on tasks such as these.

There are two sources of evidence which are relevant to this aspect of the processing deficit hypothesis. First, Hasher and Zachs (1979) have shown that elderly people's estimates from memory of the frequency with which items had been previously shown were very reliable although less accurate than those of a younger group. Second, and more importantly, in forced choice tasks where subjects are required to select which of two items had been shown more frequently, the elderly are not significantly impaired (Attig & Hasher, 1980) or are indistinguishable from younger groups (Kausler & Puckett, 1980). Since the latter recognition tests bypass criterion settings (which may be set more cautiously in the elderly) Attig and Hasher (1980) believe that they provide the critical evidence for normally efficient automatic encoding in the old.

These recognition data cannot be accepted uncritically, however. In Kausler and Puckett's experiment, although the old group performed identically to the younger controls on the frequency judgement task, the older group had significantly *higher* vocabulary scores than the younger one. Since there may be some relationship between vocabulary scores and judgements of word frequency (as indeed was reported for the younger although not for the older group) it might be speculated that had the two groups been equated in vocabulary the younger people might have outperformed the older ones. In the Attig and Hasher (1980) study, although the two groups were matched (at least in terms of years of education and place of residence), the elderly individuals showed a slight tendency ($p < .10$) to perform less well than the younger group on the frequency recognition task. If performance on so-called automatic tasks turns out to be not identical in young and old subjects but rather the elderly are merely less impaired on such tasks than they are in other putatively effortful tasks, then this may simply reflect the fact that it is easier (for unknown reasons) to make

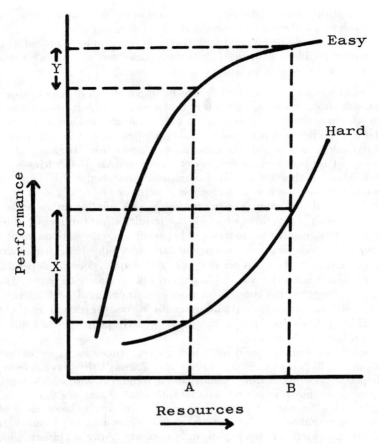

Fig. 3.1 Hypothetical performance–resources curves for two tasks, one easy (e.g. frequency recognition) and one difficult (e.g. item recall). If age results in a depletion of resources from **B** (young level) to **A** (old level), then even with a fixed fall in available resources, the easier task will be less affected (a drop of *Y* performance units) than the more difficult task (a drop of *X* performance units).

frequency and related judgements about an item than it is, for example, to recall the item itself. This would not necessarily imply that a processing deficit is an incorrect description of the elderly person's memory impairment since, on the contrary, if resources are depleted one might expect greater impairment in more difficult tasks relative to simpler ones depending upon the precise performance–resource functions for hard and easy tasks (Norman & Bobrow, 1975). It does mean, however, that a dichotomy between effortful and automatic processing may not be a valid one and that the elderly do not necessarily have a selective impairment of the former with preservation of the latter.

Even if we were to grant adequate methodological status to the Kausler and Puckett (1980) and Attig and Hasher (1980) studies and thus accept the data purporting to support the null hypothesis of no difference whatsoever between the young and the old in their ability to make frequency judgements, it is still not clear that a failure in effortful processing with intact automatic processing in the elderly would necessarily predict *no* difference in the accuracy of frequency recognition between the two groups. This is so since there is some evidence that, even if there is little difference between the accuracy of frequency judgements when people know or do not know that such information will ultimately be tested (Hasher & Zachs, 1979), subjects' memory for frequency information is improved by semantic orienting tasks during learning (Rowe, 1974) and that the processes mediating frequency judgements are sensitive to semantic variations within repeated words (Rowe, 1973). This suggests that frequency judgements may depend in part upon specific frequency information but also upon inferences from semantic relationships effortfully encoded during learning. Since the old are putatively deficient in the latter it might be expected that, even if specific frequency information were encoded automatically and as well as by younger people, their overall performance should be depressed relative to the young controls since they would lack the additional semantic information available to the young and which would provide further information upon which frequency decisions could be made.

At this stage, therefore, the logical status of the idea that the elderly have pre-served 'automatic' encoding abilities is very unclear. On the other hand, if it is assumed that there is not a dichotomy between effort-free and effortful processes but that all activities merely require more or less effort and have varying performance–resource functions like those illustrated in Fig. 3.1, then this causes no logical problems: however there is, as yet, no data which support or negate such a hypothesis. In addition to replications of the Kausler and Puckett and Attig and Hasher experiments with fully matched samples, varying depth of processing and ultimately testing frequency and other contextual information in elderly and young groups should prove especially informative.

In contrast to Hasher's hypothesis that the elderly have selective preservation of the abilities to encode frequency and related contextual information, Huppert and Piercy (1978) have argued that alcoholic amnesics have a selective *impairment* in encoding such information. The evidence for this view comes from experiments where amnesics, unlike age- and IQ-matched controls, are shown to confuse frequent items with recent items when asked to make recency judgements and, conversely, confuse recent items with frequent ones when required to make frequency judgements. Such patterns of performance are not shown by normal people even when their memory is made weak (Meudell & Mayes, in preparation) and thus may reflect a genuine amnesic deficit causally related to their memory impairment. On the other hand, frontal patients who are not densely amnesic have been reported to be impaired on recency discrimination (Milner, 1971) and since many alcoholic amnesics might be expected to have cortical as well as limbic damage, the amnesics' difficulties with recency and frequency discrimination may be unrelated to their memory problems. As well as a replication of the Huppert and Piercy (1978) study on patients with selective frontal lesions, a replication with matched young and old normal people would be of some importance partly since Hasher's hypothesis would predict no difference between the two groups and partly because reported elderly impairment on aspects of behavioural tests purporting to assess frontal function (Nelson, 1976; Albert & Kaplan, 1980) might lead to the contrary expectation that the old normal people may well perform differently from a younger control group.

(iv) Variations in processing time. A further research strategy which has been employed to investigate the locus of the memory impairment with advancing age has been through manipulation of the length of time that young and old groups have to learn or to retrieve information. The theoretical reason for varying encoding and/or retrieval times appears to be that if the elderly have an encoding deficit, or at least one which is speed related (Waugh & Barr, 1980), then *increasing* the time available for learning should disproportionately improve older people's memory relative to younger groups on the assumption that the benefit that younger people gain from longer exposure asymptotes relatively quickly. A similar argument would also apply to elderly speed-related deficits occurring at retrieval.

Several studies have systematically varied the time available for learning and the time available for retrieval and investigated their effects upon paired associate (PA) learning in young and old groups of individuals. While the total time hypothesis appears to hold for the elderly just as much as it does for the young, such that for a given period of learning it matters little how that time is made up (Kinsbourne & Berryhill, 1972), some studies have shown that increasing encoding time has differentially aided the older person's memory relative to young controls (Canestrari, 1968; Arenberg, 1965). Other studies have shown the opposite effect, namely, no disproportionate improvement in PA learning as the 'inspection' time increases but a relatively greater improvement in elderly performance compared to controls when the time available for making a response to the stimulus members of the PAs is increased (Monge & Hultsch, 1971; Treat & Reese, 1976), while another study failed to find any differential effect for the elderly at either encoding or retrieval (Hulika *et al.*, 1967). Even if some consistency of results could be achieved through adequate control of subject parameters (matching in these experiments was at best achieved through vocabulary measures, but even here the matching was sometimes unsuccessful), a somewhat more important demonstration would be, not to show that *level* of performance is raised in the elderly with increases in encoding and/or retrieval time, but to reveal that a *pattern* of performance shown by the young at a relatively brief learning or retrieval period is progressively shown by the elderly as either or both of these intervals is increased.

While such studies have yet to be carried out, a related experiment has recently been reported. Simon (1979) attempted to simulate an elderly pattern of performance by *restricting* the encoding time of young people, the argument being that such a restriction upon a healthy young person's learning period may render his encoded information in memory somewhat like that of an older person operating without time pressure. Simon's original observation was that with a relatively long exposure time for learning sentences, contextual and semantic cues given at retrieval were most effective for young controls while phonemic cues led to highest cued recall in her aged group. By reducing the encoding time of the young group she was then able to show that the normal young people behaved in a very similar way to the original group of older individuals. In spite of the fact that the young and old groups in the original experiment were only matched on vocabulary, the fact that the pattern of elderly performance could be simulated in younger people gives some support to its credibility and buttresses the hypothesis that certain semantic and related aspects of information are not encoded by the elderly under normal conditions nor by the young under duress.

Although restrictions on encoding time have not been systematically investigated in the amnesic literature, there is the occasional study, but since these are not comparable to those reported to the elderly and are discussed in Mayes and Meudell (this volume) they are not discussed here.

(v) Conclusions on the processing deficit hypothesis. The idea that the elderly suffer from a general reduction in resources which manifests itself across most cognitive activities is clearly an attractive one. The major problem with the hypothesis, however, is that, in view of the almost whimsical description of the old and young people involved in many studies, there is little evidence which unambiguously supports it.

Since complete tests such as the WAIS are rarely administered to young and old individuals in research on ageing memory there is always the possibility the elderly are operating at a lower intellectual level than their younger counterparts: differences between the two groups in mnemonic efficiency might then be attributable to age *per se* or to the effects of intellectual deterioration. Since we know that for a given age, level of mnemonic function and types of mnemonic strategies that are employed are related to IQ (e.g. Brown *et al.*, 1973), only when young and old groups are fully matched in terms of raw intelligence scores can it be discovered whether there are mnemonic impairments in the elderly which occur over and above any that are due to possible changes' acquisition and subsequent retrieval strategies consequent upon decreases in intellectual functioning.

There seem to be two obvious lines of future development given adequate descriptions of experimental groups. First, since the processing deficit hypothesis views aged mnemonic failure as a consequence of a more general cognitive failure occurring through reduced capacity, this should be investigated directly in the elderly through dual task paradigms where memory load is minimal but where the two tasks involved require substantial effort for their effective execution. Some such studies have already been carried out, especially with the dichotic listening paradigm (e.g. Clarke & Knowles, 1973), and they do show elderly impairment, but, since it is possible to argue (e.g. Shallice & Evans, 1978) that most aspects of cognition involve a general resource component (an executive planning and monitoring system) and a specific resource component (e.g. numerical or spatial ability), the dual tasks should be varied, in terms of their demands upon specific resources to assess the extent to which ageing reflects the loss of general resources, specific resources or a combination of both. Second, it can then be investigated whether, as a result of a reduction in capacity, the elderly fail to engage in those semantic analyses of stimuli which, in young people, are known to be effort requiring (Eysenk & Eysenk, 1979), especially through appropriate manipulation of encoding and retrieval strategies. In this connection it is pertinent to consider a recent report by Charness (1981). Charness has shown that when old and young chess players are matched in terms of their ELO score (a measure of a player's likely ability and, therefore, an indicant of the effectiveness of his chess-related encoding abilities), the young players remembered chess positions *better* than did the older ones. In other words, even when specific encoding skills are equivalent in the young and the elderly there still remains a memory deficit in the old people for information directly related to these encoding abilities: accordingly some factor in addition to, or instead of, encoding deficiencies may well be involved in elderly mnemonic impairment.

(c) *Storage failure hypothesis and rates of forgetting.* Do the old forget more rapidly than the young? At least over brief retention intervals the answer appears unequivocally to be negative. Over the 30 s or so of the Peterson and Peterson paradigm the old and the young forget at identical rates (Kriauciunas, 1968; Keevil-Rogers & Schnore, 1969). Moenster (1972) has shown that, after 10 min delay, retention of items from a story as indicated by recognition performance was similar in young and old groups and Wickelgren (1975) has demonstrated a similar effect over a 2 h period with memory for unrelated words. It is of interest that these experiments did not equate for degree of initial learning yet they still obtained parallel forgetting functions: when initial level of learning has been equated through training of paired associates to a specified criterion (Wimer & Wigdor, 1958), once again no age- related differences in rates of forgetting over a 15 min interval were observed.

Up to periods of minutes or hours after learning, therefore, the old appear to forget at much the same rate as the young and this parallel loss is apparently a robust phenomenon since it can be shown with several different measures of memory, with different types of material to be learned and whether initial degree of learning is similar or not. At longer retention intervals, however, a different and more uncertain picture emerges. Wimer (1960) showed elderly people demonstrated more forgetting of paired associates than young controls over a 24 h retention interval, similar results over a 48 h interval have been reported by Davis and Obrist (1966) and by Hulicka and Rust (1964) after both a 24 h and a 7 day interval. In contrast to these three studies, however, three other studies have failed to show faster rates of forgetting in the elderly when relatively long retention intervals have been employed. Hulicka and Weiss (1965) found retention of paired associates by young and old people to be identical 1 week after initial training to criterion, a similar result has also been reported by Desroches *et al*. (1966). Both of these studies employed rather older 'young' people, however (mean ages were 38 and 45 years respectively), and as Schonfield and Stones (1979) point out different results may well have been obtained with a somewhat younger control group. On the other hand, this argument does rely upon the notion that age-related deficits in memory may be well established by age 38 — an argument that many may not wish to accept uncritically. More importantly, Schneider *et al*. (1975) found identical rates of forgetting for 20- and 70-year-olds over a 7 day period for both story recall and for nonsense syllable recall even though initial level of performance was not equated.

While we can say with some confidence that retention over relatively brief retention intervals is very similar in young and old groups we cannot say with very much certainty what happens at longer intervals. It is not surprising, therefore, in view of the state of the data base, that while Craik (1977) cited studies which '. . . showed to age difference in retention . . .' Schonfield and Stones (1979) cited studies which led them to conclude '. . . the evidence strongly suggests that people of 70 show more forgetting within 24 hours than do young adults . . .'.

(d) *Retrieval deficit hypothesis.* (i) Cueing experiments. If the elderly have a

114

retrieval deficit then it has been suggested that providing appropriate hints at the time of memory testing should differentially improve their memory relative to young controls and in comparison to a largely 'hint free' condition such as free recall (e.g. Schonfield & Stones, 1979). Such an effect has been reported for one group of amnesics (e.g. Warrington & Weiskrantz, 1974), replicated on another (Mayes & Meudell, 1981b) and indeed has been demonstrated on a group of presenile dements with mild memory problems (Miller, 1975); the first two of these experiments used the initial three letters and the last the initial letter of previously presented words as prompts. Do the old differentially benefit from initial letter prompts at retrieval?

There are three studies in which cued recall performance with single letter prompts has been compared with free recall performance in young and old groups. Smith (1977) found that single letter prompts did not improve either his young or his old group's performance beyond free recall levels (a result also observed by Miller (1977) for his non-demented control group) and while Drachman and Leavitt (1972) did find both an elderly group and a younger one to improve marginally their performance with single letter prompts compared to free recall, the magnitude of the effect was identical for both sets of people. Since the two groups of individuals were matched on full WAIS scores by Drachman and Leavitt some faith must be expressed in their results. The study has been criticized, however, on the grounds that sharing 26 initial letter cues among the 35 words which were presented for learning hardly constitutes an effective retrieval cue for either group (Schonfield & Stones, 1979). On the other hand, contrary to the impression given by Schonfield and Stones, the advantage, albeit small, of such cueing was significant and, furthermore, Earhard (1977) has shown that there is no differential improvement in an older group, relative to a younger one, as the number of items that the cue delineates in the original list presented for learning is decreased. In terms of its relevance for theorizing about older people's memory the latter result must be treated with some caution, however, since Earhard's 'senior adults' had a mean age of 47.5 years and might be better termed middle aged rather than elderly. The effectiveness of initial letter prompts as aides to memory appears to be at best rather small and certainly is a rather labile phenomenon: what is clear, however, is that old people do not gain more advantage from such hints than do young individuals.

If we turn now to category cueing, which is known not to be obviously of disproportionate benefit to organic amnesic patients (Warrington & Weiskrantz, 1974), then two studies with normal elderly people show identical results to each other. Laurence (1967) and Hultsch (1975) have both shown that the elderly are differentially *aided* by the presence of category cues at recall compared to free recall conditions and in relation to younger people. As they stand such results clearly support the hypothesis that retrieval difficulties are a factor in elderly memory impairment and, since single letter hints are not especially helpful to old people, that this problem is one which is largely due to a failure to employ adequate semantic strategies at the time of test.

Taken together with the Simon (1979) data mentioned earlier, and with a study by Perlmutter (1979) which showed that th elderly were disproportionately aided by their own previously generated free association to a to-be-remembered word compared to an experimenter-determined normative associate when each was given as a retrieval cue, these experiments might be taken

115

to point to the idea that the old are deficient in employing appropriate semantic retrieval strategies which, in part, might reflect inadequate encoding strategies. However, even if this consistency of data is real, current evidence does not allow an unambiguous interpretation of the cueing experiments whether these have been carried out on elderly individuals, amnesics or dements. Elderly groups tend to perform less well overall than younger people at both category cueing and free recall. We need to know, therefore, what pattern of performance (specifically the relationship of cued to free recall) a younger control group would show when operating at the same level of performance as the older one. We know, for example, that three letter prompts are especially effective for normal young memories made weak through the passage of time (i.e when overall level of performance is low) compared to 'strong' memories where overall performance level is relatively high (Mayes & Meudell, 1981a). If such an effect holds for category cueing then cueing experiments cannot distinguish between the cause and the effect of memory deterioration in the elderly.

This argument is similar to one advanced earlier in the literature in the specific context of recall–recognition on comparisons in young and old subjects (McNulty & Caird, 1967). McNulty and Caird argued that the relative preservation of recognition performance in the face of rapidly deteriorating free recall performance as people age (e.g. Erber, 1974) does not necessarily provide evidence for a selective retrieval deficit as some had argued (e.g. Schonfield & Robertson, 1966) but might merely reflect the fact that decayed or impoverished memories may not be adequate to support recall but may be sufficient to support recognition. The current argument, therefore, simply extends the generality of the McNulty and Caird type of argument to any comparisons of retrieval methods be it recognition v. recall, recall v. cued recall or whatever.

(ii) Susceptibility to the effects of interference. While some workers in gerontology have considered any differential effects of interference on the memory of young and aged people to reflect storage differences in the two groups (e.g. Smith, 1979) it is perhaps more usual to consider that interference from memories acquired before or after a critical one are a reflection of the difficulties in discrimination of relevant from irrelevant information, i.e. at the time of retrieval. Of course this leaves open the question of whether this particular kind of retrieval difficulty is the root *cause* of an elderly person's problem or whether the interference occurs as a *consequence* of forgetting, such that the 'weaker' any memory becomes (the less information there is in a trace, for example) the greater is the disruptive effect of interference on the expression of such memories in performance.

Leaving these theoretical issues aside, what evidence is there to suggest the old are or are not especially susceptible to the effects of proactive and retroactive interference? Some experiments have shown that the elderly are differentially disadvantaged compared to controls when learning P-As of low associative strength compared to P-As of high associative strength (e.g. Gilbert, 1941; Zaretsky & Halberstam, 1968; Lair *et al.*, 1969; Winocur, 1981). Similar results have been obtained in amnesics (e.g. Winocur & Weiskrantz, 1976) and both sets of results have been interpreted as reflecting a greater susceptibility to interference in the two experimental groups. Equally, of course, such effect might reflect encoding differences, so that, while highly associated word pairs might easily 'prime' pre-existing relationships in memory, low associative pairs may require effortful analyses in order to link them together. Further, in the light of the fact that *young* people with memories made impoverished through the passage of time also find relatively lowly associated P-As differentially more difficult to recall than more highly associated ones compared to when their memories are new (Mayes, *et al.*, 1981), the original effects, both in the old and in amnesics, might simply be consequences of forgetting (i.e. some form of storage failure). Interesting as such interactions between the type of material to be learned and chronological age are, correlational studies of this sort cannot discriminate between various views about the locus of an elderly mnemonic deficit.

Apart from the interpretive difficulties that such experiments pose, methodologically some may be criticized for not equating degree of initial learning between young and old groups: even granting that the data might unequivocally be read as indicating heightened susceptibility to interference in the elderly (which they cannot), the effects may have arisen simply as a result of poor initial learning leading in the older groups to an apparently greater vulnerability to the effects of interference. An obvious experiment, therefore, suggests itself: equate for initial level of learning of young and old groups and then examine directly recall of this list of items after training to the same level of performance on an interfering set. Two such experiments using P-A learning that have been reported show a total absence of differential effects of retroactive interference in the elderly (Gladis & Braun, 1958; Hulicka, 1967). Unfortunately, there is another study (Traxler, 1973) which shows that although the old are not especially susceptible to the *type* of interfering P-A learning that is required after learning on original list to criterion (i.e. young and old people are affected in similar ways by interpolated A-C, C-B or C-D learning after acquisition of an A-B list), they nevertheless show greater susceptibility to interference overall than do a younger sample. Winocur (1981) has recently suggested two factors, both based upon the characteristics of the elderly samples involved, which might go some way to reconciling why some studies find especial sensitivity to interference in the elderly while others do not. First, pointing to the data of Gilbert (1941) Winocur has suggested that the more intellectually able are *less* likely to manifest excessive susceptibility to interference than the less bright and certainly one study which showed no differential effects of interference in old people employed subjects who were relatively clever (Canestrari, 1966). Second, Winocur points out that those studies which do not show differentially greater susceptibility to interference in elderly groups have tended to draw their old people from the community (i.e. those living at home). On the other hand those studies which do show the elderly to be particularly at risk from interference tended to select their subjects from the elderly living in institutions. Interestingly enough, Winocur actually reports exactly this pattern of results in a PI paired-associate learning paradigm. That is, he has showed that relative to a no prior learning condition, the institutional elderly are differentially more impaired at learning a second list after having previously learned an initial one, compared to both the old living at home and the young; the latter two groups being equally affected by the PI condition relative to the no PI condition.

This is a suggestive and important experiment and Winocur's approach in attempting to identify the subject characteristics which may be relevant for performance at various memory tasks is clearly one which is in sympathy with the present discussion. However, even if the complicating factor of an apparent ceiling effect for all three groups in the no PI condition in Winocur's experiment is ignored, it is not at all clear that IQ and institutionalization are critical factors in determining susceptibility to interference. In Traxler's (1972) study *greater* RI was observed in an elderly group not only in spite of the fact that the old sample were trained to the same initial level of performance as the young group, but also in the face of the facts that the old people were community based and were University Professors, 57% of whom had Ph.Ds! Although intelligence and the need for institutional care may well be relevant factors to be taken into account when evaluating elderly memory in general, it would appear that such factors may not be critical in determining the extent of retroactive interference in particular. Such attempts as Winocur's are, however, obviously along the right lines: mnemonic impairment cannot be studied independently of other cognitive and social factors in the old and individual differences in the elderly must be measured, presented and taken into account when assessing memory.

(e)   The fate of very old memories.   Any hypothesis, be it an acquisitional, storage or retrieval deficit one, which attempts to explain the old person's difficulty in learning new information should have implications for how well, relative to the young, the elderly should be able to remember events that happened in the past many years earlier. Simple mindedly, if the old have an acquisitional failure which is insidious in onset, then, relative to a younger group and within the limits of what the younger group might reasonably be expected to have experienced, the more distant a memory becomes in time the less impaired the elderly should become. A similar pattern of results should also occur if the old progressively manifest a storage disorder. If the aged person's difficulty in learning new information is a manifestation of retrieval disorders, however, then it might be expected that, relative to an appropriate younger control group, the elderly would not show selective preservation of older memories but that their memory performance should merely be depressed by a constant amount, proportional to the magnitude of the retrieval deficit, at all time periods tested be they recent or remote.

The assessment of memories acquired years or decades before entering the laboratory has invariably involved the use of various types of questionnaire techniques. Since it is not a straightforward matter to control for overlearning of older memories through repeated exposure, the composition of items in questionnaires is of critical importance. When 'item difficulty' has not obviously been taken into account across all the time periods tested (i.e. where the older memories tested may be easier to access since they might be rather better learned through overexposure), some studies tend to show that old people show better recall and recognition of remote memories relative to more recent ones in comparison to younger people (Poon *et al.*, 1979; Botwinnick & Storandt, 1980) while another has shown that they do not (Squire, 1974). When item difficulty is controlled (by a questionnaire assessing memory for TV programmes which were exposed for a fixed amount of time in any given recent or remote period) selective preservation of memory for remote programmes was again observed (Squire & Slater, 1975).

In view of the better controls involved in the last study the discrepancies between the other ones reported would seem most likely to be due to differences between the sensitivities of the tests to variations in item difficulty across the time periods assessed, and Squire and Slater's results are consistent with some form of progressive acquisitional or storage failure in the elderly but are not consistent with a retrieval failure. However, in direct contrast to Squire and Slater's (1975) results, Warrington and Sanders (1971) have shown that elderly people's recall and recognition of public events and photographs of famous people's faces was *not* differentially better than their memory for more recent ones relative to younger groups. A constant depression in performance across all time periods tested strongly suggests a retrieval deficit especially since Warrington and Sanders took pains to ensure that their items had roughly equal original exposure in each of the sampled time periods.

The type of questionnaire involved in a particular study is obviously critical for its outcome to the extent that, for example, Perlmutter (1978) has reported that on one questionnaire memory for 'facts' occurring between 1890 and 1969, the old were actually *better* than the young. Although a reconciliation of the Warrington and Squire studies in terms of questionnaire design is not easy, following recent work with amnesics, future questionnaires might fruitfully operationally equate for the difficulty of recent and remote memories in the manner of Albert *et al.* (1979). The conflict of data in the ageing literature is, in fact, mirrored by that in the amnesic literature but the balance of evidence in patients with profound memory deficits is that they do show selective preservation of older memories (see Meudell & Mayes, 1982). Whether Ribot's Law — that the older a memory becomes the more resistant it becomes to disruption — is an apposite description of the old person's memory performance, however, remains as much an unproved hypothesis today as it did when Ribot proposed it in 1882.

3.4.4 Conclusions on the Dissolution of Memory in Aged Humans

To point to individual differences between people as a source of differences in the way that they might perform on various tasks and which may thus reconcile conflicting experimental results in the literature is hardly revelatory. Nevertheless, it is not a trivial point since if we knew *what* extra-mnemonic cognitive factors were involved in particular memory tasks (and consequently if it could also be shown that their absence or malfunction in some individuals through the normal processes of ageing might qualitatively affect their memory in different ways compared to those people in whom they function effectively) we might not only reconcile the diverse findings of many experiments on ageing memory but also we might learn something of importance about how various cognitive factors interact with and determine levels and patterns of mnemonic performance.

The difficulty is, of course, that we do not yet know a great deal about exactly how extra-menmonic factors do influence memory and one cannot, therefore, specify completely in advance what parameters of elderly and young people should be measured in order to give satisfactory descriptions of the subjects concerned. In the absence of detailed information of this type, rather than merely attempting to compare young and old groups on tests of memory borrowed (sometimes uncritically) from cognitive psychology, another and different research strategy might be to investigate directly individual differences with groups of elderly people and to relate these differences to the quan- titative and qualitative variations, that they show in aspects of their memory performance. Some work along these lines has already been reported (Perlmutter, 1978) where performance on simple tests of memory was related to educational achievement, physical health, mental health and the acceptance or otherwise of stereotypical expectations about cognitive decline in old age. In view of the fact that we know memory to be related to neuroticism, anxiety, intelligence, personality and arousal even within homogeneous undergraduate samples (Eysenk, 1977, and this volume), detailed further studies of such relationships in the elderly with good memory and in the elderly with poor memory cannot help but be informative.

3.4.5 Memory in Aged Animals

Just as with comparisons of immature and mature animals' memory, comparisons of elderly and mature creatures is made difficult by the possible presence of motivational differences between the two groups. Unfortunately, unlike immature and mature rats, shock avoidance thresholds differ in young (mature) and aged rats (see Elias & Elias, 1977) and consequently, demonstrations of age-related mnemonic impairment by means of active and passive avoidance responses (e.g. Doty, 1966a; Thompson & Fitzsimons, 1976) may reflect the unequal effects of stressful experiences on the two groups rather than any differences in memory function. Differential dietary deprivation techniques have also been criticized as inadequate ways of controlling for motivational differences between young and elderly groups (e.g. Barnes, 1979). Nevertheless, as noted earlier, mnemonic deficits can be demonstrated in elderly animals where motivational factors are unlikely to play a large part. Thus, for example, Barnes (1979) 'took advantage of the tendency of rodents to avoid brightly lit, unenclosed surfaces and to seek darkened enclosed shelter [which] . . . does not require dietary alteration, electric footshock, stamina or speed' to assess the elderly rats memory. Using this tendency Barnes has been able to show an impairment in aged rats' memories for the location of such an enclosed shelter. Some memory impairments in elderly animals are, therefore, unlikely to be simply attributable to motivational factors.

The effects of massed versus distributed practice has been investigated in elderly rats just as it has been with immature infant animals, and, in contrast to the data on infant memory, one experiment has shown that elderly animals show no beneficial effects of distributed versus massed training on a 14 point maze learning task (Goodrick, 1973): if anything massed practice led to somewhat *better* performance in the aged rats, the converse being the case for the younger control animals. However, in view of the facts that the theoretical interpretation of the effects of massed versus distributed practice is unclear (see Section 3.2.3b) and, albeit in an avoidance learning paradigm, Doty (1966b) has demonstrated the opposite effect (namely that her elderly rats were particularly impaired when given massed as opposed to distributed training in comparison to yonger ones), it is not obvious what can be made of Goodrick's result.

Retention deficits in aged and young mature animals have recently been reviewed by Kubanis and Zornetzer (1980) and so will not be considered in detail here. Although Kubanis and Zornetzer cite many experiments showing age-related retention deficits most of them involve active or passive avoidance learning, which as has been noted, may well be contaminated by motivational factors. Nevertheless, as already mentioned retention deficits are observed in rodents' memory for the location of shelter — a task which might be little different in terms of motivational effects on young and old animals (Barnes, 1979; Barnes *et al.*, 1980).

Especial difficulties in reversal learning have recently been cited by some as evidence of some form of retrieval failure in humans with pathological loss of memory (Warrington & Weiskrantz, 1978). In rats no consistent deficits in aged subjects have been reported on the reversal trials for two choice water maze learning (Birren, 1962), for Y maze learning (Botwinick *et al.*, 1962), for circle/triangle discrimination learning (Kay & Sime, 1962) and for the learning of the position of an escape tunnel in a circular display (Barnes, 1979). In these studies initial learning on the pre-reversal trials was similar in young and old animals. On the other hand Bartus *et al.* (1979) have recently claimed that aged monkeys are especially impaired, relative to young controls, on the reversal trials of shape or colour discrimination problems. These data may point to proactive interference as a causal factor in the memory deficit in elderly monkeys. On the other hand, even though there was no significant difference between the five young and five elderly monkeys on initial learning trials, nevertheless there was a clear tendency for the older animals to be impaired overall in comparison to the young controls. Slight differences in level of initial learning, possibly leading to a greater susceptibility to PI effects might thus be responsible for the observed effects on reversal trials. In other words these effects in monkeys may reflect the consequences of poor memory in the aged animals and may provide no support for the hypothesis that in some way PI is causally involved in their deficits. Against this, however, must be set the fact that when young and elderly animals were matched on an individual basis in terms of their performance on the initial learning trials of the colour discrimination task, the aged animals showed a differentially large increase, relative to that shown by the young ones, in the number of trials to reach criterion on the reversal trials. Further, when level of performance in control conditions is made identical in young and old animals (by the method of testing younger animals at longer retention intervals than older ones), Bartus and Dean (1979) have shown that old monkeys were differentially impaired in their memory for the location of a visual stimulus if retention intervals were filled with interfering visual activity related to the event the animal was required to remember. It is conceivable, therefore, that the Bartus experiments do demonstrate a heightened susceptibility to the effects of PI and RI which are in some way causally involved in any mnemonic deficits in monkeys. As Bartus and his colleagues suggest, however, it may be that poor reversal learning accompanied as it is by response perseveration may have little directly to do with memory and may simply reflect, both in human amnesics and elderly monkeys, impairment of frontal lobe function since it is known that behavioural rigidity, inability to shift 'set' and perseveration are all characteristic of deficits in frontal performance in man (see Kolb & Wishaw, 1980) and in the monkey (e.g. Pribram, 1969).

Finally, it is worth while considering a currently fashionable view of elderly memory impairment, namely that the old are characterized by deterioration in hippocampal function (Barnes, 1979) that the hippocampus involves a spatial mapping of the environment (O'Keefe & Nadel, 1978) and that, therefore, the aged suffer particularly from impairments in spatial memory. This view of hippocampal function is, of course, theoretical and does not have universal support (see Olton *et al.*, 1979; Mayes & Meudell, this volume), but the empirical backing for the hypothesis of specific spatial memory deficits in the

121

elderly comes from a dissociation between tasks on which elderly animals are said to be unimpaired in learning and those upon which they show clear deficits. Specifically it is argued (Barnes *et al.*, 1980) that tasks which old animals perform poorly on have a strong spatial component (e.g. Barnes, 1979; Goodrick, 1968) while those they are said to perform as well as younger animals do not have such a factor (e.g. Stone, 1929; Kay & Sime, 1962). There is, of course, an alternative explanation, considered but rejected by Barnes *et al.* (1980), namely that those tasks upon which the old do quite well (and on which they thus show similar performance to young animals) are merely simpler than those tasks upon which a large difference between young and old memory can be demonstrated. In other words there is nothing special about the poor learning of spatial tasks by elderly animals other than such tasks might tend to be somewhat more difficult than, for example, learning to discriminate vertical from horizontal stripes — a task in which young and old animals perform similarly (Fields, 1953). Barnes *et al.* (1980) argue against this position on the grounds that a 'circular platform task (with only one "place" to remember) was equally effective in discriminating between age groups as [a] . . . radial 8-arm maze task (that had eight "places" to remember)', i.e. the former task is easier than the latter yet both cause similar decrements in aged performance. However, since no direct numerical comparison between the 'circular' and eight-arm maze is reported, while it certainly can be said that both caused an impairment in learning in the old compared to the young groups, it is difficult to see how it could be said that the two tasks were 'equally' effective in discriminating between them. All that can be said with confidence is that both tasks are ones in which old animals show impairment but the relative impairment caused by them is uncertain. Related comments apply to a recent experiment by Wallace *et al.* (1980). They showed that although there was no significant difference between young and old rats on a modified form of Kornorski's (1959) discriminated delayed response task (a situation not involving a spatial component), the old animals were impaired in an eight-arm maze task requiring spatial memory. The aged animals were, however, consistently even if insignificantly worse than their young counterparts in the Kornorski paradigm and once again, therefore, the observed 'dissociation' may simply reflect differences in difficulty between the non-spatial and spatial tasks.

The hypothesis of a differential spatial memory deficit in the aged animal is an interesting speculation but currently there is no compelling evidence to support it: in view of the difficulties noted above that old animals have on the reversal trials of shape and colour discrimination tasks (Bartus *et al.*, 1979), which have no obvious spatial component, there may well be clear evidence against it.

3.5 General Concluding Remarks

The similarities of methodological problems and of the difficulties in disentangling mnemonic from non-mnemonic function in the study of infant and senescent memory is striking. It is also apparent that the kinds of explanation advanced, both in the human and animal research, for the relatively poor memory of the young and the old are equally, very similar. In particular an especially influential view, running like a leitmotiv through this chapter, has been that in comparison to the memory of the normal adult in the prime of life, memory at the extremes of life is characterized by impoverished encoding techniques. Although the magnitude of the effects that these changes might have on the *level* of mnemonic function is unknown, there does seem to be little doubt that qualitative differences in encoding processes, relative to the mature individual, can be easily demonstrated in the human infant. While changes in encoding have been postulated in the study of animal infant memory, the evidence is ambiguous and although the idea that capacity limitations, leading to particular forms of encoding differences, is the most pervasive view of elderly memory impairment, the ubiquity of contradictory experimental findings (probably attributable to imprecise descriptions of the subjects employed in elderly samples) means that its status as an explanation of relatively poor aged memory function is unclear.

References

ALBERT M.S., BUTTERS N. and LEVIN J. (1979) Temporal gradients in the retrograde amnesia of patients with alcoholic Korsakoff's disease. *Archives of Neurology*, **36**, 211–216.

ALBERT M.S., and KAPLAN E. (1980) Organic implications of neuropsychological deficits in the elderly. In: L.W. POON, J.L. FOZARD, L.S. CERMAK, D. ARENBERG and L.W. THOMPSON (Eds.) *New Directions in Memory and Ageing.* LEA, Hillsdale, New Jersey.

ALTMAN J. and DAS G.D. (1965) Autoradiographic and histological evidence of post-natal neurogenesis in rats. *Journal of Comparative Neurology*, **124**, 319–336.

ALTMAN J. and DAS G.D. (1967) Postnatal neurogenesis in the guinea pig. *Nature*, **214**, 1098–1101.

ALTMAN J., DAS G.D. and ANDERSON W.J. (1968) Effects of infantile handling on morphological development of the rat brain: an exploratory study. *Developmental Psychobiology*, **1**, 10–20.

ANDERSON J.R. (1980) *Cognitive Psychology and its Implications*, pp. 212–217. Freeman, San Francisco.

ARENBERG D. (1965) Anticipation interval and age differences in verbal learning. *Journal of Abnormal and Social Psychology*, **70**, 419–425.

ATTIG M. and HASHER L. (1980) The processing of frequency of occurrence information by adults. *Journal of Gerontology*, **35**, 66–69.

BADDELEY A.D. (1976) *The Psychology of Memory*. Harper & Row, New York.

BADDELEY A.D. (1979) The trouble with levels: a re-examination of Craik and Lockhart's framework for memory research. *Psychological Review*, **85**, 139–152.

BARNES C.A. (1979) Memory deficits associated with senescence: a neurophysiological study in the rat. *Journal of Comparative and Physiological Psychology*, **90**, 74–104.

BARNES C.A. and McNAUGHTON B.L. (1979) Neurophysiological comparison of dendritic cable properties in adolescent middle aged and senescent rats. *Experimental Ageing Research*, **5**, 195–206.

BARNES C.A., NADEL L. and HONIG W.K. (1980) Spatial memory deficit in senescent rats. *Canadian Journal of Psychology*, **34**, 29–39.

BARRETT T.R. and WRIGHT M. (1981) Age related facilitation in recall following semantic processing. *Journal of Gerontology*, **36**, 194–199.

BARTUS R.T. (1979) Physostigmine and recent memory: effects in young and aged non-human primates. *Science*, **206**, 1087–1089.

BARTUS R.T. and DEAN R.L. (1979) Recent memory in aged non-human primates:

123

hypersensitivity to visual interference during retention. *Experimental Ageing Research*, **5**, 385–400.

BARTUS R.T., DEAN R.L. and FLEMING D.L. (1979) Ageing in the rhesus monkey: effects on visual discrimination learning and reversal learning. *Journal of Gerontology*, **34**, 209–219.

BELMONT J.M. (1972) Relation of age and intelligence to short-term color memory. *Child Development*, **43**, 19–29.

BIRREN J.E. (1962) Age differences in learning a two-choice water maze by rats. *Journal of Gerontology*, **17**, 207–213.

BLESSED G., TOMLINSON B.E. and ROTH M. (1968) The association between quantitative measures of dementia and of senile change in the cerebral grey matter of elderly subjects. *British Journal of Psychiatry*, **114**, 797–811.

BOTWINNICK J. (1977) Intellectual abilities. In: J.E. BIRREN and K.W. SCHAIE (Eds.) *Handbook of the Psychology of Ageing*. Van Nostrand, New York.

BOTWINNICK J., BRINLEY, J.F. and ROBBIN J.S. (1962) Learning a position discrimination and position reversals by Sprague–Dawley rats of different ages. *Journal of Gerontology* **17**, 315–319.

BOTWINNICK J. and STORANDT M. (1974) Memory, related functions and age. CHARLES C. THOMAS, Springfield, Ill.

BOTWINNICK J. and STORANDT M. (1980) Recall and recognition of old information in relation to age and sex. *Journal of Gerontology*, **35**, 70–76.

BREGMAN A.S. (1968) Forgetting curves with semantic, phonetic, graphic and contiguity cues. *Journal of Experimental Psychology*, **78**, 539–546.

BRENNAN J.F. and BARONE R.J. (1976) Effects of differential cue availability in an active avoidance CS for young and adult rats. *Developmental Psychobiology*, **9**, 237–244.

BRODY H. (1976) An examination of cerebral cortex and brain stem ageing. In: R.D. TERRY and S. GERSHON (Eds.) *Ageing: Neurobiology of Ageing*. Raven Press. New York.

BROWN A.L. and SCOTT M.S. (1971) Recognition memory for pictures in preschool children. *Journal of Experimental Child Psychology*, **11**, 401–412.

BROWN, A.L., CAMPIONE, J.C., BRAY, N.W. and WILCOX, B.L. (1973) Keeping track of changing variables: effects of rehearsal training and rehearsal prevention in normal and retarded adolescents. *Journal of Experimental Psychology*, **101**, 123–131.

BUTTERS N. and CERMAK L.S. (1975) Some analyses of amnesic syndromes in brain-damaged patients. In: R. ISAACSON and K. PRIBRAM (Eds.) *The Hippocampus Vol. 2*. Plenum, New York.

CAMPBELL B.A. (1967) Developmental studies of learning and motivation in infra-primate mammals. In: H.W. STEVENSON,, E.H. HESS and H.L. RHEINGOLD (Eds.) *Early Behaviour: Comparative and Developmental Approaches*. Wiley, New York.

CAMPBELL B.A. and CAMPBELL, E.H. (1962) Retention and extinction of learned fear in infant and adult rats. *Journal of Comparative and Physiological Psychology*, **55**, 1–8.

CAMPBELL B.A. and JAYNES J. (1966) Reinstatement. *Psychological Review*, **73**, 478–480.

CAMPBELL B.A. MISANIN J.R., WHITE B.C. and LYTLE L.D. (1974) Species differences in ontogeny of memory: indirect support for neural maturation as determinants of forgetting. *Journal of Comparative and Physiological, Psychology* **87**, 193–202.

CAMPBELL, B.A. and SPEAR, N.E. (1972) Ontogeny of memory. *Psychological Review*, **79**, 215–236.

CANESTRARI, R.E. (1966) The effects of commonality on paired-associate learning on two age groups. *Journal of Genetic Psychology*, **108**, 3–7.

CANESTRARI, R.E. (1968) Age changes in acquisition. In: G.A. TLLAND (Ed.) *Human ageing and Behavior*, Academic Press, New York.

CAREY S. and DIAMOND R. (1977) From piecemeal to configurational representation of faces. *Science*, **195**, 312–314.

CERMAK L.S. (1978) The development and demise of verbal memory. In: A. CARAMAZZA and E.B. ZURIF (Eds.) *Language Acquisition and Language Breakdown: Parallels and Divergencies*. John Hopkins, Baltimore.

CHAPMAN L.J. and CHAPMAN J.P. (1973) Problems in the measurement of cognitive deficit. *Psychological Bulletin*, **79**, 180–185.

CHARNESS, N. (1981). Visual short term memory and aging in chess players. *Journal of Gerontology*, **36**, 615–619.

CHI M.T.H. (1976) Short-term memory limitations in children: capacity or processing deficits? *Memory and Cognition*, **4**, 559–572.

CHI M.T.H. (1978) Knowledge structures and memory development. In: R. SIEGLER (Ed.) *Children's Thinking: What develops?* LEA, Hillsdale, New Jersey.

CLARK L.E. and KNOWLES J.B. (1973) Age differences in dichotic listening performance. *Journal of Gerontology*, **28**, 173–178.

COHEN L.B. and GELBER E.R. (1975) Infant visual memory. In: L.B. COHEN and P. SALPATEK (Eds.), *Infant Perception: From Sensation to Cognition. VI. Basic Visual Processes*. Academic Press, London.

COLE M., FRANKEL F. and SHARP D. (1971) Development of free recall learning in children. *Developmental Psychology*, **4**, 109–123.

CORSINI D.A., JACOBUS K.A. and LEONARD S.D. (1969) Recognition memory of preschool children for pictures and words. *Psychonomic Science*, **16**, 192–193.

COULTER X., COLLIER A.C. and CAMPBELL B.A. (1976). Long-term retention of early Parlorian fear conditioning in infant rats. *Journal of Experimental Psychology; Animal Behaviour Processes*, **2**, 48–56.

CRAIK F.I.M. (1977) Age differences in human memory. In: J.E. BIRREN and K.W. SCHAIE (Eds.), *Handbook of the Psychology of Aging*. Van Nostrand, New York.

CRAIK F.I.M. and LOCKHART R.S. (1972) Levels of processing: a framework for memory research. *Journal of Verbal Learning and Verbal Behaviour*, **11**, 671–684.

CRAIK F.I.M. and SIMON E. (1980) Age differences in memory: the roles of attention and depth of processing. In: L.W. POON, J.L. FOZARD, L.S. CERMAK, D. ARENBERG and L.W. THOMPSON (Eds.) *New Directions in Memory and Aging*. LEA, Hillsdale, New Jersey.

CUTTING J. (1978) A cognitive approach to Korsakoff's syndrome. *Cortex*, **14**, 485–495.

DAEHLER M.W. and BUKATKO D. (1977) Recognition memory for pictures in very young children: evidence from attentional preferences using a continuous presentation procedure. *Child Development* **48**, 694–696.

DAVIES P. and VERTH A.H. (1977) Regional distribution of muscarinic acetylcholine receptors in normal and Alzheiner's type dementia brains. *Brain Research*, **138**, 385–392.

DAVIS S.H. and OBRIST W.D. (1966) Age differences in learning and retention of verbal material. *Cornell Journal of Social Relations*, **1**, 95–103.

DAYAN A.D. (1971) Comparative neuropathology of ageing. *Brain*, **94**, 31–42.

DESROCHES, H.F., KAIMAN B.D and BALLARD H.T. (1966) Relationships between age and recall meaningful material. *Psychological Reports*, **18**, 920–922.

DIRKS J. and NEISSER U. (1977) Memory for objects in real scenes: the development of recognition and recall. *Journal of Experimental Child Psychology*, **23**, 315–328.

DOTY B.A. (1966b) Age and avoidance conditions in rats. *Journal of Gerontology*, **21**, 287–290.

DOTY B.A. (1966a) Age differences in avoidance conditioning as a function of distribution of trials and task difficulty. *Journal of Genetic Psychology*, **109**, 249–254.

DOUGLAS R.J. (1975) The development of hippocampal function: implications for theory and therapy. In: R. ISAACSON and K. PRIBRAM (Eds.) *The Hippocampus, Vol. 2*. Plenum, New York.

DRACHMAN D.A. and LEAVITT J. (1972) Memory impairment in the aged: storage versus retrieval deficit. *Journal of Experimental Psychology*, **93**, 302–308.

DUDYCHA G.J. and DUDYCHA M.M. (1941) Childhood memories: a review of the literature. *Psychological Bulletin*, **38**, 668–682.

EARHARD M. (1977) Retrieval failure in the presence of retrieval cues: a comparison of three age groups. *Canadian Journal of Psychology*, **31**, 139–150.

EISDORFER, C. (1968) Arousal and performance: experiments in verbal learning and tentative theory. In: G. TALLAND, (Ed.), *Human aging and Behaviour*. Academic Press, New York.

ELIAS M.F. and ELIAS, P.K. (1977) Motivation and activity. In: J.E. BIRREN and K.W. SCHAIE (Eds.), *Handbook of the Psychology of Aging*, Van Nostrand, New York.

ELLIS H.D. (1975) Recognising Faces. *British Journal of Psychology*, **66**, 409–426.

ERBER J.T. (1974) Age differences in recognition memory. *Journal of Gerontology*, **29**, 177–181.

EYSENCK M.W. (1974) Age differences in incidental learning. *Developmental Psychology*, **10**, 936–941.

EYSENCK, M.W. (1977) *Human Memory: Theory, Research and Individual Differences*. Pergamon, Oxford.

EYSENCK M.W. and EYSENCK, M.C. (1979) Processing depth, elaboration of encoding, memory stores and expended processing capacity. *Journal of Experimental Psychology, Human Learning and Memory*, **5**, 472–484.

FAGAN J.F. (1970) Memory in the infant. *Journal of Experimental Child Psychology*, **9**, 217–226.

FAGAN J.F. (1973) Infant's delayed recognition memory and forgetting. *Journal of Experimental Child Psychology*, **16**, 424–450.

FAGAN J.F. (1976) Infant's recognition of invariant features faces. *Child Development*, **47**, 627–638.

FAGAN J.F. (1978) Facilitation of infants' recognition memory. *Child Development*, **49**, 1066–1075.

FAGAN J.F. (1979) The origins of facial pattern recognition. In: M.H. BORNSTEIN and W. KESSEN (Eds.) *Psychological Development from Infancy: Image to Intention*. LEA, Hillsdale, New Jersey.

FEIGLEY D.A. and SPEAR N.E. (1970) Effect of age and punishment condition on long-term retention by the rat of active and passive avoidance learning. *Journal of Comparative and Physiological Psychology*, **73**, 515–526.

FERGUSON R.P. and BRAY N.W. (1976) Component processes of an overt rehearsal strategy in young children. *Journal of Experimental Child Psychology*, **21**, 490–506.

FIELDS P.E. (1953) The age factor in multiple-discrimination learning by white rats. *Journal of Comparative and Physiological Psychology*, **46**, 387–389.

FLAVELL J.H. (1971) First discussants' comments: what is memory development the development of? *Human Development*, **14**, 272–278.

FLAVELL J.H. and WELLMAN H.M. (1977) Metamemory, In: R.V. KAIL and J.W. HAGEN (Eds.) *Perspectives on the Development of Memory and Cognition*. LEA, Hillsdale, New Jersey.

FOX N., KAGAN J. and WEISKOPF, S. (1979) The growth of memory during infancy. *Genetic Psychology Monographs*, **99**, 91–130.

FREUD S. (1905) Three essays on the theory of sexuality. In: J. STRACHEY (Ed.) *The Standard Edition of the Complete Works of Freud. Vol 7*. Hogarth, London, 1963.

FRIEMAN J.P., ROHRBAUGH M. and RICCIO, D.C. (1969) Age differences in the control of acquired fear by tone. *Canadian Journal of Psychology*, **23**, 237–244.

GEINISMAN, Y. and BONDAREFF, W. (1976). Decrease in the number of synapses in the senescent brain: a quantitative electron microscopic analysis of the dentate gyrus molecular layer in the rat. *Mechanisms of Ageing and Development*, **5**, 11–23.

GIBSON G.E., PETERSON C. and JENDEN D.S. (1981) Brain acetylcholine synthesis declines with senescence. *Science*, **213**, 674–676.

GILBERT J.G. (1941) Memory loss in senescence. *Journal of Abnormal and Social Psychology*, **36**, 73–86.

GLADIS M. and BRAUN H.W. (1958) Age differences in transfer and retroaction, as a function of inter-task response similarity. *Journal of Experimental Psychology*, **55**, 25–30.

GOODRICK C.L. (1968) Learning, retention, and extinction of a complex maze habit for mature-young and senescent Wistar albino rats. *Journal of Gerontology*, **23**, 298–304.

GOODRICK C.L. (1973) Maze learning of mature-young and aged rats as a function of distribution of practice. *Journal of Experimental Psychology*, **98**, 344–349.

GORDON W.C. (1979) Age: is it a constraint on memory content? In: N.E. SPEAR and B.A. CAMPBELL (Eds.) *Ontogency of Learning and Memory*. LEA, Hillsdale, New Jersey.

HAROUTUNIAN V. and RICCIO D.C. (1977) Effect of arousal conditions during reinstatement treatment upon learned fear in young rats. *Developmental sychobiology*, **10**, 25–32.

HASHER L. and CLIFTON D. (1974) A developmental study of attribute encoding in free recall. *Journal of Experimental Child Psychology*, **17**, 332–346.

HASHER L. and THOMAS H. (1973) A developmental study of retention. *Development Psychology*, **9**, 281.

HASHER L. and ZACHS R.T. (1979) Automatic and effortful processes in memory. *Journal of Experimental Psychology, General*, **108**, 356–388.

HEATH H.A. and ORBACH S. (1963) Reversibility of the Necker-cube: IV. Responses of elderly people. *Perceptual and Motor Skills*, **17**, 625–626.

HULICKA I.M. (1967) Age differences in retention as a function of interference. *Journal of Gerontology*, **22**, 180–184.

HULICKA I.M. and RUST L.D., (1964) Age-related retention deficit as a function of learning. *Journal of the American Geriatric Society*, **12**, 1061–1065.

HULICKA I.M., STERNS H. and GROSSMAN J. (1967) Age group comparisons of paired-associate learning as a function of paced and self-paced association and response times. *Journal of Gerontology*, **22**, 274–280.

HULICKA I.M. and WEISS R.L. (1965) Age differences in retention as a function of learning. *Journal of Consulting and Clinical Psychology*, **29**, 125–129.

HULTSCH D.F. (1975) Adult age differences in retrieval: trace dependent and cue-dependent forgetting. *Developmental Psychology*, **11**, 197–201.

HUNTER I.M.L. (1957) *Memory*, pp. 269–280. Penguin, Harmondsworth.

HUPPERT F.A. and PIERCY M. (1978) The role of trace strength in recency and frequency judgements, by amnesic and control subjects. *Quarterly Journal of Experimental Psychology*, **30**, 346–354.

INGLIS J. and CAIRD W.K. (1963) Age differences in successive responses to simultaneous stimulation. *Canadian Journal of Psychology*, **17**, 98–105.

KAIL R. (1979) *The Development of Memory in Children*. Freeman, San Francisco.

KAUSLER D.H. and PUCKETT J.M. (1980) Frequency judgements and correlated cognitive abilities in young and elderly adults. *Journal of Gerontology*, **35**, 376–382.

KAY H. and SIME M.E. (1962) Discrimination learning with old and young rats. *Journal of Gerontology*, **17**, 75–80.

KEEVIL-ROGERS P. and SCHNORE M. (1969) Short-term memory as a function of age in persons of above average intelligence. *Journal of Gerontology*, **24**, 184–188.

KESSLER P.G. and SPEAR N.E. (1979) Distributional practice decreases infantile amnesia. Cited by Spear (1979).

KINSBOURNE M. and BERRYHILL J.L. (1972) The nature of the interaction between pacing and the age decrement in learning. *Journal of Gerontology*, **27**, 471–477.

KLONOFF H. and KENNEDY M. (1966) A comparative study of cognitive functioning in old age. *Journal of Gerontology*, **21**, 239–243.

KOBASIGAWA A. (1974) Utilization of retrieval cues by children in recall. *Child Development*, **45**, 127–134.

KOLB B. and WISHAW I.Q. (1980) *Fundamentals of Human Neuropsychology*, Freeman, San Francisco.

KORNORSKI J. (1959) A new method of physiological investigation of recent memory in animals. *Bulletin de l'Academie Polonaise des Sciences*, **7**, 115–117.

KRIAUCIUNAS R. (1968) The relationship of age and retention interval activity in short-term memory. *Journal of Gerontology*, **23**, 169–173.

KUBANIS P., GOBBEL G. and ZORNETZER S.F. (1981) Age related memory deficits in Swiss mice. *Behavioral and Neural Biology*, **32**, 241–247.

KUBANIS P. and ZORNETZER S.F. (1981) Age related behavioral and neurobiological changes: a review with an emphasis on memory. *Behavioral and Neural Biology*, **31**, 115–172.

LABOUVIE-VIEF G., HOYER W.J., BALTES M.M. and BALTES P.B. (1974) Operant analysis of intellectual behaviour in old age. *Human Development*, **17**, 259–272.

LAIR C.V., MOON W.H. and KAUSLER D.H. (1969) Associative interference in the paired-associate learning and middle-aged and old subjects. *Developmental Psychology*, **1**, 548–552.

LACHMAN J.L., LACHMAN R. and THRONESBERY C. (1979) Metamemory through the adult lifespan. *Developmental Psychology*, **15**, 543–551.

LANDFIELD P.W. and LYNCH G. (1977) Impaired monosynaptic potentiation in *in vitro* hippocampal slices from aged, memory-deficient rats. *Journal of Gerontology*, **32**, 523–533.

LANDFIELD P.W., McGAUGH J.L. and LYNCH G. (1978) Impaired synaptic potentiation processes in the hippocampus of aged, memory-deficient rats. *Brain Research*, **150**, 85–101.

LAURENCE M.W. (1967) Memory loss with age: a test of two strategies for its retardation. *Psychonomic Science*, **9**, 209–210.

LYON, D.R. (1977) Individual differences in immediate serial recall: a matter of mnemonics. *Cognitive Psychology*, **9**, 403–411.

McGURK H. (1970) The role of object orientation in infant perception. *Journal of Experimental Child Psychology*, **9**, 363–373.

MACKWORTH N.H. and BRUNER J.S. (1970) How adults and children search and recognise pictures. *Human Development*, **13**, 149–177.

McNULTY J.A. and CAIRD W.K. (1967) Memory loss with age: an unsolved problem. *Psychological Reports*, **120**, 283–288.

MANDLER J.M. and ROBINSON C.A. (1978) Developmental changes in picture recognition. *Journal of Experimental Child Psychology*, **26**, 122–136.

MANDLER J.M. and STEIN N.L. (1974) Recall and recognition of pictures by children as a function of organisation and distractor similarity. *Journal of Experimental Psychology*, **102**, 657–669.

MARTIN R.M. (1975) Effects of familiar and complex stimuli on infant attention. *Developmental Psychology*, **11**, 178–185.

MASON S.E. (1979) Effects of orienting tasks on the recall and recognition performance of subjects differing in age. *Developmental Psychology*, **15**, 467–469.

MAYES A. and MEUDELL P. (1981a) How similar is the effect of cueing in amnesic and normal subjects following forgetting? *Cortex*, **17**, 113–124.

MAYES A. and MEUDELL P. (1981b) How similar is immediate memory in amnesic patients to delayed memory in normal subjects? A replication, extension and reassessment of the amnesic cueing effect. *Neuropsychologia*, **19**, 647–654.

MAYES A., MEUDELL P. and SOM S. (1981) Further similarities between amnesia and normal attenuated memory: effects with paired associate learning and contextual shifts. *Neuropsychologia*, **19**, 655–664.

MEUDELL P. and MAYES A. (1980) Do alcoholic amnesics passively release verbal information? *Brain and Language*, **10**, 189–204.

MEUDELL P. and MAYES A. (1981) The Claparède phenomenon: a further example in amnesics, a demonstration of a similar effect in normal people with attenuated memory, and a reinterpretation. *Current Psychological Research*, **1**, 75–88.

MEUDELL P. and MAYES A. (1982) Normal and abnormal forgetting: Some comments on the human amnesic syndrome. In: A. ELLIS (Ed). *Normality and Pathology in Cognitive Function*. Academic Press, London.

MILLER E. (1975) Impaired recall and memory disturbances in presenile dementia. *British Journal of Social and Clinical Psychology*, **14**, 73–79.

MILLER E. (1977) *Abnormal Ageing: The Psychology of Senile and Presenile Dementia*. Wiley, London.

MILLER R.R. and BERK A.M. (1979) Sources of infantile amnesia. In: N.E. SPEAR and B.A. CAMPBELL (Eds.) *Ontogeny of Learning and Memory*. LEA, Hillsdale, New Jersey.

MILNER B. (1971) Interhemispheric differences in the localisation of psychological processes in man. *British Medical Bulletin*, **27**, 272–277.

MIRANDA S.B. and FRANTZ R.L. (1974) Recognition memory in Down's syndrome and normal infants. *Child Development*, **45**, 651–660.

MOELY B.E., OLSON F.A., HALWES T.G. and FLAVELL J.H.(1969) Production deficiency in young children's clustered recall. *Developmental Psychology*, **1**, 26–34.

MOENSTER P.A. (1972) Learning and memory in relation to age. *Journal of Gerontology*, **27**, 361–363.

MOHS R.C., DAVIS K.L., TINKLENBERG J.R., HOLLISTER L.E., YESAVAGE J.A. and KONNELL B.S. (1979) Choline chloride treatment of memory deficits in the elderly. *American Journal of Psychiatry*, **136**, 1275–1277.

MONGE R.H. and HULTSCH D.F. (1971) Paired associate learning as a function of adult age and the length of the anticipation and inspection intervals. *Journal of Gerontology*, **26**, 157–162.

NAGY Z.N. (1979) Development of learning and memory processes in infant mice. In: N.E. SPEAR and B.A. CAMPBELL (Eds.) *Ontogeny of Learning and Memory*, LEA, Hillsdale, New Jersey.

NEISSER U. (1967) *Cognitive Psychology*. Appleton-Century-Crofts, New York.

NELSON H.E. (1976) A modified sorting test sensitive to frontal lobe deficits, *Cortex*, **12**, 313–324.

NEWCOMBE N.E., ROGOFF B. and KAGAN J. (1977) Developmental changes in recognition memory for picture of objects and scenes. *Developmental Psychology*, **13**, 337–341.

NORMAN D.A. and BOBROW D.B. (1975) On data-limited and resource-limited processes. *Cognitive Psychology*, **7**, 44–64.

OBUSEK C.J. and WARREN R.M. (1973) Comparison of speech perception in senile and well preserved aged by means of the verbal transformation effect. *Journal of Gerontology*, **28**, 184–188.

O'KEEFE J. and NADEL L. (1978) *The Hippocampus as a Cognitive Map*. OUP, London.

OLTON D.S., BECKER J.T. and HANDLEMAN G.E. (1979) Hippocampus, space and memory. *Behavioral and Brain Sciences*, **2**, 313–365.

ORDY J.M. and BRIZZEE K.R. (Eds.) (1975) *Neurobiology of Ageing*. Plenum, New York.

ORNSTEIN P.A., NAUS N.J. and STONE B.P. (1977) Rehearsal training and developmental differences in memory. *Developmental Psychology*, **13**, 15–24.

PALMORE E. and CLEVELAND W. (1976) Aging, terminal decline and terminal drop. *Journal of Gerontology*, **31**, 76–81.

PARSONS P.J. and SPEAR N.E. (1972) Long-term retention of avoidance learning by immature and adult rats as a function of environmental enrichment. *Journal of Comparative and Physiological Psychology*, **80**, 297–303.

PERLMUTTER M. (1978) What is memory aging the aging of? *Developmental Psychology*, **14**, 330–345.

PERLMUTTER M. (1979) Age differences in adults' free recall, cued recall and recognition. *Journal of Gerontology*, **34**, 533–539.

PERRY E.K. (1980) The cholinergic system in old age and Alzheimer's disease. *Age and Ageing*, **9**, 1–8.

PETERSON L.R. and PETERSON J.J (1959) Short-term retention of individual verbal items. *Journal of Experimental Psychology*, **58**, 193–198.

PIAGET J. and INHELDER B. (1973) *Memory and Intelligence*. Basic Books, New York.

POKORNY J. and YAMAMOTO T. (1981) Postnatal ontogenesis of hippocampal CAi area in rats, I. Developemental of arborisation in pyramidal neurons. *Brain Research Bulletin*, **7**, 113–120.

POON L.W., FOZARD J.L., PAULSHOCK D.R. and THOMAS J.C. (1980) A questionnaire assessment of age differences in retention of recent and remote events. *Experimental Aging Research*, **5**, 401–411.

POTASH M. and FERGUSON H.B. (1977) The effect of criterion level on the acquisition and retention of a 1-way avoidance response in young and old rats. *Developmental Psychobiology*, **10**, 347–354.

PRIBRAM K.H. (1969) The primate frontal cortex. *Neuropsychologia*, **7**, 259–266.

PUGLISI J.T. (1980) Semantic encoding in older adults as evidenced, by release from proactive inhibition. *Journal of Gerontology*, **35**, 743–745.

RABBITT P.M.A. (1965) An age-decrement in the ability to ignore irrelevant information. *Journal of Gerontology*, **20**, 233–238.

RABBITT P. (1977) Changes in problem solving ability in old age. In: J.E. BIRREN and K.W. SCHAIE (Eds.) Handbook of the *Psychology of Aging*. Van Nostrand, New York.

RABBITT P. (1980) Cognitive psychology needs models for changes in performance with old age. In: A.D. BADDELEY and J. LONG (Eds). *Attention and Performance IX*, LEA, Hillsdale, New Jersey.

RANKIN J.L. and KAUSLER D.H. (1979) Adult age differences in false recognitions. *Journal of Gerontology*, **34**, 58–65.

RIEGAL K.F. and RIEGAL R.M. (1972) Development, drop and death. *Developmental Psychology*, **6**, 306–319.

ROSS B.H. (1981) The more, the better?: number of decisions as a determinant of memorability. *Memory and Cognition*, **9**, 23–33.

ROWE E.S. (1973) Frequency judgements and recognition of homonyms. *Journal of Verbal Learning and Verbal Behavior*, **12**, 440–447.

ROWE E.J. (1974) Depth of processing in a frequency judgement task. *Journal of Verbal Learning and Verbal Behavior*, **13**, 638–643.

ROWE E.J. and SCHNORE M.M. (1971) Item concreteness and reported strategies in paired associate learning as a function of age. *Journal of Gerontology*, **26**, 470–475.

SCHACTEL E. (1963) *Metamorphosis*. Routledge & Kegan Paul, London.

SCHEIBEL M.E., LINDSAY R.D., TOMIYASU U. and SCHEIBEL A.B. (1975) Progressive dendritic changes in ageing human cortex. *Experimental Neurology*, **47**, 392–403.

SCHNEIDER N.G., GRITZ E.R. and JARVIK M.E. (1975) Age differences in learning, immediate and one week delayed recall. *Gerontologia*, **21**, 10–20.

SCHONFIELD D. and ROBERTSON B. (1966) Memory storage and aging. *Caadian Journal of Psychology*, **20**, 228–236.

SCHONFIELD D. and STONES M.J. (1979) Remembering and aging. In: J.F. KIHLSTROM and F.J. EVANS (Eds.) *Functional Disorders of Memory*. LEA, Hillsdale, New Jersey.

SHALLICE T. and EVANS M.E. (1978) The involvement of the frontal lobes in cognitive estimation. *Cortex*, **14**, 294–303.

SIMON E. (1979) Depth and elaboration of processing in relation to age. *Journal of Experimental Psychology: Human Learning and Memory*, **5**, 115–124.

SMITH A.D. (1977) Adult age differences in cued recall. *Developmental Psychology*, **13**, 326–331.

SMITH A.D. (1979) Age differences in encoding, storage and retrieval. In: L.W. POON, J.L. FOZARD, L.S. CERMAK, D. ARENBERG and L.W. THOMPSON (Eds.) *New Directions in Memory and Ageing*. LEA, Hillsdale, New Jersey.

SMITH A.D. and WINOGRAD E. (1978) Adult age differences in remembering faces. *Developmental Psychology*, **14**, 443–444.

SMITH C.B., GOOCHEE C., RAPOPORT S.I. and SOKOLOFF L. (1980) Effects of ageing on local rates of cerebral glucose utilization in the rat. *Brain*, **103**, 351–365.

SMITH N. (1968) Effects of interpolated learning on the retention of an escape response in rats as a function of age. *Journal of Comparative and Physiological Psychology*, **65**, 422–426.

SOLHEIM G.S., HENSLER J.G. and SPEAR N.E. (1980) Age-dependent contextual effects on short-term active avoidance retention in rats. *Behavioral and Neural Biology*, **30**, 250–259.

SPEAR N.E. (1978) *The Processing of Memories: Forgetting and Retention*. (Especially Ch. 5). LEA, Hillsdale, New Jersey.

SPEAR N.E. (1979) Experimental analysis of infantile amnesia. In: J.F. KIHLSTROM and F.S. EVANS (Eds.) *Functional Disorders of Memory*, LEA, Hillsdale, New Jersey.

SPEAR N.E. and CAMPBELL B.A. (1979) *Ontogency of Learning and Memory.* LEA, Hillsdale, New Jersey.

SPEAR N.E., GORDON W.C. and CHISZAR D.A. (1972) Interaction between memories in the rat: the effect of degree of prior conflicting learning on forgetting after short intervals. *Journal of Comparative and Physiological Psychology*, **78**, 471–477.

SPEAR N.E. and PARSONS P. (1976) Alleviation of forgetting by reactivation treatment: a preliminary analysis of the ontogeny memory processing. In: D. MEDIN, W. ROBERTS, and R. DAVIS (Eds.) *Processes in Animal Memory.* LEA, Hillsdale, New Jersey.

SPEAR N.E. and SMITH G. (1978) Alleviation of forgetting in neonatal rats. Developmental Psychobiology, **11**, 513–529.

SQUIRE L.R. (1974) Remote memory as affected by ageing. *Neuropsychologia*, **12**, 429–435.

SQUIRE L.R. and SLATER P.C. (1975) Forgetting in very long-term memory as assessed by an improved questionnaire technique. *Journal of Experimental Psychology, Human Learning and Memory*, **104**, 50–54.

SQUIRE L.R., WETZEL C.D. and SLATER P.C. (1978) Anterograde amnesia following ECT: an analysis of the beneficial effects of partial information. *Neuropsychologia*, **16**, 339–348.

STOFF D.M. and EAGLE M.N. (1971) The relationship among reported strategies, presentation rate, and verbal ability and their effects on free recall learning. *Journal of Experimental Psychology*, **87**, 423–428.

STONE C.P. (1929) The age factor in animal learning. 1. Rats in the problem box and the maze. *Genetic Psychology, Monographs*, **5**, 1–130.

STRAUSS M.S. and COHEN L.B. (1978) Infant immediate and delayed memory for perceptual dimensions. Reported In: R. KAIL, *The Developmental of Memory in Children.* Freeman, San Francisco, 1979.

SUSSMAN P.S. and FERGUSON H.B. (1980) Retained elements of early avoidance training and relearning of forgotten operants. *Developmental Psychobiology*, **13**, 545–562.

THOMPSON C.I. and FITZSIMONS T.R. (1976) Age differences in aversively motivated visual discrimination learning and retention in male Sprague–Dawley rats. *Journal of Gerontology*, **31**, 47–52.

TOMLINSON B.E., BLESSED G. and ROTH M. (1968) Observations on the brains of non-demented old people. *Journal of the Neurological Sciences*, **7**, 331–356.

TRAXLER A.J. (1973) Retroactive and proactive inhibition in young and elderly adults using an unpaced modified free recall test. *Psychological Reports*, **32**, 215–222.

TREAT N.J. and REESE H.W. (1976) Age, pacing, and imagery in paired-associate learning, *Developmental Psychology*, **12**, 119–124.

TURNURE J., BUIUM N. and THURLOW M. (1976) The effectiveness of interrogatives for promoting verbal elaboration productivity in young children. *Child Development*, **47**, 851–855.

UNDERWOOD B.J. (1970) A breakdown of the total-time in free-recall learning. *Journal of Verbal Learning and Verbal Behaviour*, **9**, 573–580.

WALDFOGEL S. (1948) The frequency and affective character of childhood memories. Psychological Monographs, **62**, 1–39.

WALLACE J.E., KRAUTER E.E. and CAMPBELL B.A. (1980) Animal models of declining memory in the aged: short term and spatial memory in the aged rat. *Journal of Gerontology*, **35**, 355–363.

WALLACH H.F., RIEGE W.H. and COHEN M.J. (1980) Recognition memory for emotional words: a comparative study of young, middle aged and older persons. *Journal of Gerontology*, **35**, 371–375.

WARRINGTON E.K. and SANDERS, H.I. (1971) The fate of old memories. *Quarterly Journal of Experimental Psychology*, **23**, 432–442.

WARRINGTON E.K. and WEISKRANTZ L. (1974) The effect of prior learning on subsequent retention in amnesic patients. *Neuropsychologia*, **12**, 419–428.

WARRINGTON E.K. and WEISKRANTZ L. (1978) Further analysis of the prior learning effect in amnesic patients. *Neuropsychologia*, **16**, 169–177.

WAUGH N.C. and BARR R.A. (1980) Memory and mental tempo. In: L.W. POON, J.L. FOZARD, L.S. CERMAK, D. ARENBERG and L.W. THOMPSON (Eds.) *New Directions in Memory and Ageing.* LEA, Hillsdale, New Jersey.

WEIZMANN F., COHEN L.B. and PRATT J. (1971) Novelty, familiarity and the development of infant attention, *Developmental Psychology*, **4**, 149–154.

WELFORD A.T. (1977) Motor performance. In: J.E. BIRREN and K.W. SCHAIRE (Eds.) *Handbook of the Psychology of aging.* Van Nostrand, New York.

WHITE S. (1977) Cited by Craik (1977) and Craik and Simon (1980).

WICKELGREN W.A. (1975) Age and storage dynamics in continuous recognition memory. *Developmental Psychology*, **11**, 165–169.

WIMER R.E. (1960) A supplementary report on age differences in retention over a twenty-four hour period. *Journal of Gerontology*, **15**, 417–418.

WIMER R.E. and WIGDOR B.T. (1958) Age differences in retention of learning. *Journal of Gerontology*, **13**, 291–295.

WINOCUR G. (1981) Learning and memory deficits in institutionalised and non-institutionalised old people: an analysis of interference effects. In: F.I.M. CRAIK and S. TREHUB (Eds.) *Aging and Cognitive Processes.* In Press.

WINOCUR G. and KINSBOURNE M. (1978) Contextual cueing as an aid to Korsakoff amnesics. *Neuropsychologia*, **16**, 671–682.

WINOCUR G. and WEISKRANTZ L. (1976) An investigation of paired associate learning in amnesic patients. *Neuropsychologia*, **14**, 97–110.

WISNIESWKI H. and TERRY R.D. (1976) Neuropathology of the ageing brain. In. R.D. TERRY and S. GERSHON (Eds.) *Neurobiology of Aging (Vol. 3).* Raven, New York.

WITTEE K.L. and FREUND J.S. (1976) Paired associate learning in young and old adults as related to stimulus concreteness and presentation method. *Journal of Gerontology*, **31**, 186–192.

WITTELS I. (1972) Age and stimulus meaningfulness in paired-associate learning. *Journal of Gerontology*, **27**, 272–375.

WOODS R.T., and PIERCY M. (1974) A similarity between amnesic memory and normal forgetting. *Neuropsychologia*, **12**, 437–445.

YATES A.J. (1954) Validity of some psychological tests of brain damage. *Psychological Bulletin*, **51**, 359–379.

ZARETSKY H.H. and HALBERSTAM J.L. (1968) Age differences in paired associate learning, *Journal of Gerontology*, **23**, 165–168.

ZELINSKI E.M., WALSH D.A. and THOMPSON L.W. (1978) Orienting task effects on EDR and free recall in three age groups. *Journal of Gerontology*, **133**, 239–245.

ZINOBER J.W., CERMAK L.S., CERMAK S.A. and DICKERSON D.J.C. (1975) A developmental study of categorical organization in short-term memory. *Developmental Psychology*, **11**, 398–399.

CHAPTER 4

The Development and Course of Long-Term Memory

Andrew Mayes

4.1 Introduction

Seminal to the thinking of many psychologists is the notion that memory continues to change after initial learning. Much of this thinking is inchoate and loosely formulated, but includes ideas arising from the so-called consolidation hypothesis, Gestaltic and Bartlettian views about the qualitative evolution of complex memories and theorizing about the causes of forgetting. These groups of hypotheses may not be as unrelated as their traditionally separate treatment might suggest.

Consolidation is usually regarded as a sequence of physiological processes, triggered by learning and continuing for seconds, minutes or hours, which is necessary for the establishment of a stable, long-term memory. It is often presupposed that the long-term memory once formed is permanent and unchanged and forgetting is explained in terms of interference between the growing number of competing memories. The presupposition is unsupported, and although interference undoubtedly contributes to forgetting, it is probable that the physiological substrate of memory decays at a negatively accelerated rate over time, just as recall and recognition do. The way this deterioration affects recall of complex material, typified by stories or pictures or the occurrences of everyday life, is a matter of untrammelled guesswork. It is possible that different mnemonic features, such as semantic or visual aspects of stimuli, have their own characteristic rates of decay. Alternatively, decay rate for a given strength of input may be constant across features, varying only as a function of the deployment of attention at the time of acquisition. Either way, retrieval of the weakened memory may give the appearance of qualitative change from its original form. If the autonomous, physiological decay of memory is seen as a kind of extended consolidation process, which it has been by Wickelgren (1977), then consolidation, forgetting and the qualitative changes of memory over time, may be intimately associated.

Discussion of the variety of consolidation hypotheses forms the heart of this chapter. It is, therefore, only fair to point out that the fecundity of theorizing in this area is not matched by the ability to test the fruits critically. A tiro, reading the literature, is told by one authority that stable, long-term memories are formed in a fraction to a second, and by others that there is a precise series of changes, including protein synthesis, which take around an hour to complete. The nature of the evidence is such that both these positions are currently tenable although neither (unfortunately contrary to fact) should be confidently maintained. The nature of contemporary disputes can be clarified by outlining the main contending hypotheses.

Best known of the rival views is still the sequential, multi-store model, according to which learning activates a linked series of physiological, biochemical and structural changes which cumulate in the emergence of an enduring memory trace. As these changes continue well after active learning and as it is possible to remember during this interval, one or several short-term memory mechanisms have been postulated with different physiological bases and decay characteristics. These stores briefly coexist so retrieval may be from two or more of them, but essentially they are required for the continuity of memory. A famous example, is Hebb's (1949) suggestion that reverberatory neural activity is the basis of a short-term store and the initiator of a sequence of physiological processes which create a long-term memory. It is implicit to this kind of theory, and a *sine qua non* of its testability, that consolidation processes can be blocked by appropriate disruptive treatments with consequential amnesia. Demonstrations of experimental amnesia are not only vital for showing that the sequential theory is broadly correct, but their detailed form should provide insight into the particular consolidation processes and their time courses.

More recently, it has been suggested that learning simultaneously initiates both a short-term and a long-term memory trace. It is assumed that the short-term trace rapidly reaches full strength and quickly decays whereas the long-term trace requires much longer to develop. Although in the short-term retrieval must be possible from the transient trace, unlike with the sequential view, some information may also be retrieved from the gradually developing long-term trace. Clearly, however, the positions are similar and hard to disentangle experimentally.

Gold and McGaugh (1975) have advanced what they refer to as a single trace, dual process hypothesis. They argue that learning causes the rapid development of a memory trace, which will also rapidly decay, unless it is bolstered by a second set of relatively non-specific changes. These secondary processes, which continue after learning, are functions of the perceived significance of the events which gave rise to the memory. The hypothesis is, therefore, geared to explain why arousing, important events result in much more enduring memories. It also carries the interesting implication that no memory is intrinsically permanent, but has a durability related to its biological salience. Memories will be 'short-term' if the autonomous (and rapidly completed) consolidation processes are not boosted by non-specific arousal-related changes. The problem with the hypothesis is that disruptive treatments, applied after learning, may cause amnesia either because they disturb consolidation processes or because they disturb the non-specific activations. Although Gold and McGaugh have tried to specify these non-specific activations which include the release of hormones such as ACTH, vasopressin and adrenaline, many amnesic agents disrupt non-specific stress-related reactions, and also fundamental neural processes such as protein synthesis.

The single trace, dual process hypothesis is, therefore, difficult to distinguish from the sequential, multi-store view. Its suggestion that consolidation is very rapidly completed so that it is coterminous with learning, has been taken up by more severe critics of the traditional consolidation hypothesis, such as Miller (1978) and Lewis (1979). These theorists argue that the occurrence of amnesia following the administration of post-learning disruptive treatments, is compatible with a rapid consolidation process and a 'cognitive' organizing process which sets the basic memory in context and enables retrieval to operate efficiently. They claim that disruptive treatments do not usually affect consolidation of the basic memory but do prevent the performance of the subsequent 'cognitive' process, which they refer to misleadingly as retrieval.

This last hypothesis introduced a new dimension, not readily apparent in the three preceding hypotheses. All four views postulate physiological and biochemical consolidation processes, which occur automatically, even though they differ over the time-course of these processes. In addition, the last view postulates that relevant cognitive processes continue after the learning experience is finished. Such post-learning rehearsal and contextual appraisal is plausible in human memory, but Miller and Lewis make the interesting proposal that similar interpretive activities are also a feature of the simpler kinds of learning evinced by animals. Their suggestion emphasizes the point that active learning cannot clearly be said to end with the completion of the formally defined learning stage. Certainly, humans continue to rehearse and restructure their memories, not only for minutes after initial learning but for many years. This kind of mnemonic reorganization over an extended period is associated with the qualitative changes of memory, highlighted by Bartlett (1932).

As well as this active, cognitive reorganization of memory, Wickelgren (1979) has postulated that the negatively accelerated process of decay is the flipside of an extended consolidation activity, which continues for many years. Prolonged consolidation causes the decreasing fragility of the trace, as shown by reduced susceptibility to the action of disruptive physiological factors, such as concussion. This is important because Wickelgren relates consolidation not to increasing strength as measured by success in recall and recognition, but to decreasing fragility as assessed by vulnerability to physiological assault. Other theorists tend to relate short-term consolidation to memory strength, which may not correlate positively with decreasing fragility. Indeed, Wickelgren (1979) and Squire and Schlapfer (1981) argue that fragility only decreases as strength declines, and not just as a function of time.

Contemporary thinking, therefore, ranges from the view that consolidation is an almost immediate process, through the view that it may take up to an hour or so, to the view that some kind of autonomous change may extend for years. This gamut of positions is interlaced with speculations about short-term stores, the occurrence of post-learning cognitive activities in animals as well as humans, and the independent notions of memory strength and fragility. The contrast between autonomous consolidation and non-specific booster processes provides a further complication. Although most effort has been devoted to studying the nature and reality of these processes, they have also been used to explain other memory phenomena. For example, the facilitatory effect of high arousal, at the time of learning, and shortly after, on delayed recall, has been related to the kind of view advanced by Gold and McGaugh (1975), i.e. learning in these circumstances is well consolidated as a consequence of considerable non-specific boosting activity. Müller and Pilzecker (1900), often cited as the originators of modern consolidation theory, used the hypothesis to explain the disruptive effect of learning further verbal material on memory for what was acquired first. This idea that interference disturbs consolidation is currently unpopular, perhaps because interference works proactively as well as retroactively. If, however, the disruption is of post-learning cognitive activities rather than autonomous physiological activities, then this suggestion becomes more plausible. Posner and Konick's (1966) acid bath hypothesis is a recent example of this speculation.

The next sections consider experimental retrograde amnesia as a means of investigating the nature of consolidation. A subsequent section will review the complementary evidence provided by studies of the physiological and biochemical correlates of learning.

4.2 The Disruption of Memory in Animals

4.2.1 The Basic Phenomena of Experimental Retrograde Amnesia

Severe closed head trauma often causes permanent loss of memory in humans for events immediately preceding the accident. This effect gives plausibility to the view that there are physiological processes, which continue after the learning experience and which are required for the formation of stable memory. Since about 1949, the nature and time-course of these consolidation processes have been pursued by producing retrograde amnesia experimentally in animals through the application of various disruptive treatments in the period following learning. In its simplest form, the consolidation hypothesis predicts that effective treatments should produce permanent amnesia provided they are given so as to disrupt critical processes close enough to the time of learning. The amnesia may not develop immediately because memory may be retrieved from unaffected short-term stores, but it should appear after a fairly constant delay when such stores have faded. Researchers reasoned that the use of animal models would illuminate the time-course of the probably sequential changes, comprising consolidation. On the assumption that complex human and simpler animal memory were dependent on similar changes, at least at the cellular level, it was hoped that the conclusions could be extrapolated to humans.

If the simple interpretation is workable then similar disruptive treatments should give similar estimates of consolidation processes. Unfortunately this does not appear to be the case. Electroconvulsive shock (ECS), which produces amnesia in humans and animals, has been used as a disruptive agent in hundreds of animal studies. ECS usually causes amnesia for a one-trial passive avoidance task in rodents, only if applied within 10 s of training (see Chorover & Schiller 1965). Under apparently similar conditions, however, ECS may cause amnesia when given after delays of many hours. One factor which has been shown to extend the period of retrograde amnesia is ECS intensity (Gold *et al.*, 1973). This is difficult to reconcile with the view that ECS is disrupting a process which is completed within a short time after learning. At the opposite extreme, several researchers have claimed that pre-training familiarization with the learning environment can reduce the period of susceptibility to disruption by ECS to less than 0.5 s, although this claim is disputed (see Lewis, 1979, for a discussion). Similarly, amnesia caused by cycloheximide (CXM) a protein synthesis blocker, does not occur in chicks which are raised in isolation (De Vaus *et al.*, 1980). This isolation procedure is thought to be stressful and arousing to chicks. In contrast, group-reared chicks which are less stressed show maximum amnesia even when CXM is applied 10 min after learning. The great variability of retrograde amnesia gradients, even for a given disruptive agent, suggests that the time-course of consolidation processes cannot be gauged by the period of susceptibility to disruption, without making extra assumptions.

The onset of amnesia after disruptive treatments is not immediate. Although this kind of effect may be accommodated by the consolidation hypothesis by postulating unimpaired short-term stores, the detailed pattern of results makes this implausible. Geller and Jarvik (1968) found that ECS-induced amnesia for a passive avoidance task built up over a period of 3–6 h. Hughes *et al.* (1970) showed, however, that the build up could be over weeks rather than hours, and was a function of ECS intensity as well as the training–ECS interval. Agents which block protein synthesis, cause hyperpolarization or block sodium pump activity also cause amnesia with a delayed onset (Gibbs & Ng, 1977). The rate of forgetting produced by the last two kinds of agent is reduced in chicks, which have been stressed by rearing in isolation. Such variability of amnesia onset makes explanation in terms of accelerated loss of a single trace as plausible as the operation of one or more short-term stores.

Recovery from retrograde amnesia may sometimes be spontaneous (Mayes, 1973), but even when this is not so reminders or pharmacological treatments are often effective in restoring memory. Zinkin and Miller (1967) gave the first demonstration that ECS-induced amnesia for a one-trial passive avoidance task can be dissipated by placing the experimental animals back in the training apparatus. No shocks were given and control animals showed no pseudo-acquisition, but nevertheless experimental animals recovered their memories. Miller and his co-workers (see Miller, 1978) using a similar task, found that giving electric shocks in a completely different apparatus was also effective as a reminder, and that the delays between ECS and reminder, and between reminder and test were unimportant. These researchers also showed that allowing rats to drink saccharine-flavoured water in a different apparatus, acted as a reminder for an appetitively motivated one-trial task. In all cases ECS was applied within seconds of the training trial. Reminders are also effective with amnesia induced by protein synthesis blockers, such as CXM (Quartermain, 1976). There have, finally, been many demonstrations of recovery from experimental retrograde amnesia, following the administration of several pharmacological agents, including amphetamine, physostigmine, adrenaline, ACTH and vasopressin.

Although hard to reconcile with a simple interpretation of the consolidation hypothesis, all three of the phenomena described above are consistent with the existence of a labile period unique to the time following initial learning. This uniqueness has been challenged in the past decade (for examples, see Lewis, 1979; Miller, 1978). It has been claimed that amnesia for a task can be produced by a disruptive agent whenever memory for that task has just been activated. Whether the memory is a new one, activated for the first time, or an old one, which has previously been activated many times is unimportant, according to Lewis and Miller. An early demonstration of the cue-dependent amnesia was by Misanin *et al.* (1968). They trained rats to inhibit a response, signalled by a tone. Then a day later the animals were returned to the apparatus, and the presentation of the tone was immediately followed by ECS. A further day later these animals were amnesic for the task. Robbins and Meyer (1970) have provided a further dramatic example of cue-dependent amnesia. They trained rats on a series of three discrimination tasks, the first and third of which were motivated appetitively or aversively, and the second of which was motivated in a contrasting fashion. When acquisition of the last task was followed immediately by ECS, then the animals developed amnesia not only for it, but also for the first task, which was similarly motivated. There is some question about the generality of this amnesic effect as it has not always been found (Dawson & McGaugh, 1969).

4.2.2 Some Interpretations of the Basic Phenomena

The above data necessitate the deployment of more sophisticated arguments if they are to be construed as favouring prolonged consolidation activity. These arguments are plausible to mount on three main grounds. First, the retrograde amnesia gradient means that, in general, memory loss is greater the shorter the training–disruption interval. This suggests that disruptive treatments only partially block consolidation. If this is true then a weak long-term memory will emerge, which will dissipate more rapidly than normal memories. The time taken for it to become undetectable will depend on the degree of consolidation block, which is, in turn, a function of factors such as learning–treatment interval and treatment intensity. A memory, which is weakened but not destroyed, may also be strengthened by subsequent reminders or pharmacological treatments, which reactivate consolidation.

The great variability of retrograde amnesia gradients may be explained by two further arguments. The first is that different kinds of disruptive agent disturb different consolidation processes, which occur in sequence after learning. The second is that the rate of consolidation varies across different tasks and species, but more interestingly, as a function of level of motivation for the task and manipulations, which affect post-training arousal. These arguments are most fully developed in the work of Gibbs and Ng (1977). They propose that there are probably at least four sequentially linked consolidation processes, which are disturbed by separate groups of agents. ECS must be applied within seconds of learning to disturb reverberatory neural activity. The reverberation initiates a phase of hyperpolarization caused by potassium conductance, which is inhibited by monosodium glutamate or low concentrations of potassium chloride. These agents have to be applied within 5 min of learning to produce amnesia. Hyperpolarization may trigger prolonged sodium pump activity, which, in turn, is associated with the intake of amino acids essential for protein synthesis. Agents, which inhibit pump activity such as ouabain and ethacrynic acid, cause amnesia if applied within 15 or 20 min. Finally, neural protein synthesis gives rise to structural changes which underlie stable memory. When this activity is blocked by CXM or other antibiotics within about half an hour of learning, amnesia develops. De Vaus et al. (1980) have reported that the development of amnesia is delayed in chicks, reared in isolation, following the application of both potassium chloride and ouabain. They argued that noradrenaline release triggered by stress-inducing isolation extends those consolidation processes, disturbed by these agents. CXM may fail to cause amnesia in isolated chicks because the earlier stages are sufficiently extended for protein synthesis to occur when the drug has ceased to be effective.

The suggestion that amnesic agents partially disrupt one or more of a sequence of consolidation processes, whose rate of completion depends on factors such as arousal, only partly rehabilitates the simple version of the hypothesis. For example, great variations in the gradient of ECS-induced amnesia

138

have been described. Although this agent disrupts many physiological and bio-chemical processes in the brain, there is no direct evidence that gradient variations can be related to the blockade of different consolidation processes. Nevertheless it is possible that ECS does affect several memory processes in a differential fashion depending on its conditions of application. Radical critics of the notion of prolonged consolidation do not accept these *ad hoc* proposals, and argue that agents which cause amnesia do not act primarily by disrupting consolidation. Their position hinges on a different interpretation of the data about memory recovery following amnesia and the nature of cue-dependent amnesia.

Not only have Lewis *et al.* (1969) reported the absence of amnesia following ECS when animals have previously been familiarized with the training appa-ratus, but Azmitia *et al.* (1972) found none when animals recovered from ECS in the training apparatus. Lewis (1979) and Miller (1978) have interpreted these results as showing that consolidation of the core experience is almost instant, and is never disrupted by agents like ECS and antibiotics. In their view, ECS disrupts the cognitive elaboration of what is registered initially. Without the contextual retrieval cues provided by this elaboration the memory is rendered inaccessible. Reminders (which work both for ECS and antibiotic-induced amnesia) restore memory by enabling new retrieval cues to be linked to the core memories. They should be effective when amnesia has been complete and should not simply act as another learning trial. These claims are disputed by consolidation theorists who believe that ECS and other agents weaken con-solidation so that abnormally feeble memories develop. Thus, Gold and King (1974) reported that reminders do not work for animals with 'complete amnesia'. Lewis (1979), however, cites contradictory data and also claims that reminders have a greater effect than single learning trials. This latter point depends on comparisons between animals, weakly motivated at learning and others, strongly motivated, but which also receive ECS. For example, Wittman and De Vietti (1980) found that mesencephalic reticular formation stimulation followed by cue presentation, improved retention in ECS animals but actually impaired it in weakly trained animals. Improvement in the ECS animals was found only when they showed cardiac excitation when the cue was presented. More importantly, these workers argued that the reminder did not act as a learning trial because the weak memory group failed to display improvement. They suggest that ECS-treated animals do not, therefore, merely have weak memories, but qualitatively impoverished ones with normal core components.

Even if, as Lewis suggests, ECS prevents the encoding of experiences B,C and D, as well as core experience A, it may also disturb post-learning consolida-tion processes. Consolidation block may be rarely, if ever, complete. This possibility is supported by the observation (Mah *et al.*, 1972) that a second ECS, given 1 h after learning (which would normally have no effect) enhances the effect of a first ECS, given 5 min after passive avoidance training. This finding suggests that consolidation continues at a reduced rate following ECS. The resulting memory may also differ qualitatively from a poorly learned one because different kinds of memory consolidate at different rates or are differentially susceptible to ECS because they are stored in different parts of the brain. For example, Schneider (1975) has argued that ECS disrupts the classically conditioned, but not the instrumentally conditioned components of passive avoidance. He argued further that this selective disruption explains the reminder effect. One reason he gave was that classically conditioned rats, which were given ECS and later a reminder, subsequently showed avoidance despite not having learned this instrumental response previously. Whether or not Schneider is right in this specific case, it remains plausible that as memories are complex, different aspects of them may be differentially susceptible to consolidation disrupting agents. It should also be pointed out that ECS renders its subject unconscious and hence makes elaborative encoding impossible when given shortly after learning, whereas other agents do not appreciably impair consciousness (for example, learning itself can occur normally under the influence of protein synthesis blockers), so it is difficult to believe they impair encoding.

Lewis argues that amnesic agents do not disrupt a post-learning consolidation process and claims that it is recently activated memories which are particularly prone to disturbance, regardless of whether they are recently formed or old. To make this point convincingly it is important to show that ordinary (new learning) and cue-dependent amnesia are very similar, and second, to provide a plausible common mechanism for the loss of memory. There is little evidence relevant to the first point. Miller (1978) has reported that cue-dependent amnesia shows a temporal gradient of sensitivity, although Gordon (1977a) found this gradient to be steeper than that of new memories. Time-dependent memory facilitation induced by strychnine has also been found with reactivated memories just as has been shown previously with new memories (Gordon 1977b). Slight differences between gradients of amnesia for new and reactivated memories can always be explained in terms of hypothetical alterations of the latter which have occurred over time. If recently activated memories are susceptible to amnesic agents regardless of their age, then disruption of consolidation cannot be the mechanism of action.

Even the disturbance of elaborative encoding seems an implausible explanation of amnesia for established memories. Lewis (1979) seems to argue that the mechanism is similar to that which operates in associative interference. For example, he cites a study by Gordon and Spear (1973) in which cues for a well-learned task were presented while a competing memory was being simultaneously evoked. Animals showed considerable forgetting under these circumstances whereas they showed none when the established memory was not activated. Interference seems to operate between activated memories for active and passive avoidance tasks (Gordon & Feldman, 1978). Lewis proposes that active memories involve particular patterns of neural firing and that similar memories involve similar patterns. When similar patterns are activated at the same time, they interfere with each other, causing forgetting which arises not from destruction of the memory trace but from retrieval blocking. In his view agents like ECS also create a neural pattern of activity which interferes with the recently activated pattern of a memory.

This theory can only cope in an *ad hoc* fashion with why some agents facilitate and others disrupt reactivated memories, and with the effectiveness of different disruptive agents. More critically, Squire *et al* (1976a) found that, in humans ECT did not induce amnesia for recently retrieved, established memories whereas it did for newly acquired ones. Cue-dependent amnesia in animals may then not be an effect on memory but one on the motivation to perform certain tasks. This possibility needs careful investigation. Amnesia induced by ECS and other agents has been explained in terms of the disruption of physiological consolidation, the blocking of elaborative encoding, and the operation of interference. Even if, cue-dependent amnesia is a performance effect there is much evidence that hormonal and pharmacological factors can modulate amnesia, caused by ECS and protein synthesis blockers. Such evidence provides the basis of the view that there are non-specific processes which modulate memory in a time-dependent fashion.

4.3 Time-Dependent Modulation of Memory

4.3.1 The Basic Evidence for Time-Dependent Modulatory Processes

The grossness of ECS's effects stimulated attempts to develop more selective manipulations of memory. It was soon found that low-level electrical stimulation of many brain sites, including the midbrain reticular formation, substantia nigra, caudate nucleus, entorhinal cortex, hippocampus and amygdala, could either impair or enhance memory in a time-dependent fashion (see McGaugh et al., 1979). Similar effects were also reported with several drugs, which include picrotoxin, strychnine, metrazol and caffeine (McGaugh, 1966). When facilitatory these drugs could actually attenuate the amnesic effects if they were applied before learning (see McGaugh, 1966). The brain stimulation studies indicated that facilitatory or inhibitory effects on memory were functions of the degree of learning as well as stimulation parameters. The same type of stimulation improved memory subsequent to poor learning whereas it disrupted memory following good learning (McGaugh et al., 1979).

This kind of evidence led Gold and McGaugh (1975) to propose that learning is accompanied and followed by non-specific activational changes, which are consequences of the perceived significance of the learning and which modulate the consolidation of the learnt response. Their hypothesis states that there is an optimal level for such non-specific changes, above and below which retention is poorer. This claim is supported by Gold and Van Buskirk's (1976a, 1976b) data, which suggest that when non-specific hormonal stress reactions are considerable, increasing them with exogenous treatments causes a memory impairment. Gold and McGaugh do not specify what range of learning tasks are modulated by these non-specific activation reactions. Nevertheless, although the modulatory system may affect the consolidation of many kinds of learning, there will presumably be others which are much less influenced. Most effort has been devoted to determining what non-specific activations modulate memory, together with the mechanism of this modulation, in a rather narrow group of tasks.

Non-specific activation is associated with peripheral hormonal release, the increase in certain central hormonal or neurotransmitter agents and changes in electrophysiological activity. The last has not been pursued as much as the bio-chemical changes. Even so, Bloch (1970) has examined the effect of stimulating the midbrain reticular formation, the activity of which is central in non-specific arousal. He found that stimulating this structure shortly after learning can improve not only subsequent retention, but can compensate for amnesia induced by fluothane and anaesthesia (Bloch et al., 1970). Under different conditions, low-level reticular stimulation has been shown to cause at least a temporary disruption of memory (Kesner, 1977).

There is evidence for a relationship between reticular formation activity and a possible role of paradoxical sleep (PS) in modulating some kinds of memory. Amnesia for more complex, less 'prepared' kinds of learning has been reported when animals or humans are deprived of PS in the period following learning (see Fishbein, 1981, for reviews). Learning has also been reported to be followed by a selective increase of PS in animals and Bloch (1976) has claimed that the degree of learning is related to the size of this effect, which is greatest while learning is progressing. He has argued that PS causes an activated brain state necessary for the stabilization of memory. In support of this view he has found that reticular formation stimulation selectively abolishes the post-learning increase in PS and it also reverses the amnesic effect of post-learning PS deprivation. Similar effects with post-learning amygdala stimulation have been reported by Smith and Young (1980). The level of stimulation they used had no effect on the avoidance learning of rats which were not PS deprived.

Post-learning PS activity may only modulate memory for 'unprepared' kinds of learning and many theorists (see Kesner, 1977) believe the modulation is not of consolidation, but involves an elaborative stabilization of the memory. Whether this merely requires the elaborative encoding and 'cross-indexing' of the core memory or whether it primarily requires further physiological activity has not been clarified. Kesner has, in fact, speculated that post-learning PS activity is involved in a secondary modulation of memory which renders it independent of a hippocampal retrieval system (see Section 4.6.1 and Chapter 6). Whatever its precise role, PS modulatory function has been associated with both cholinergic and catecholaminergic activity. Skinner *et al*., (1976) found that amnesia for a passive avoidance task, caused by 3 days of PS deprivation prior to training, could be prevented by injecting a low dose of the anticholinesterase drug physostigmine 20 min following acquisition. The cholinergic system has been related to both sleep and memory (Jouvet, 1972; Deutsch, 1971). The link between the two may be the hippocampal theta rhythm, which is present in PS and has been associated with the consolidation period of memory. As the rhythm is, in part cholinergically mediated, it is notable that there are reports of hippocampal stimulation improving retention and of increases in hippocampal acetylcholine following learning (see Skinner *et al.*, 1976, for details).

Stern and Morgane (1974) have shown that the amnesic effects of PS deprivation can also be reversed by several treatments which raise brain catecholamine activity. This is particularly interesting as both central and peripheral catecholamine activation is found in non-specific arousal, and a great deal of other work has found that catecholamine and hormonal or neurotransmitter activities, associated with arousal, can affect memory in a time-dependent fashion. Many peptides have been shown to influence memory performance in this way. Evidence, to be discussed, suggests that some of the actions of these substances are mediated by one or more central catecholaminergic systems. Fragmented forms of many of these peptides exist, which only affect neural tissue and exert no peripheral hormonal effects. Both central and peripheral mnemonic effects of peptides (as well as of catecholamines, such as noradrenaline) have been described and it is likely that both peripheral and central peptide activation occurs in non-specific arousal. Furthermore, peripherally released hormones may have a mnemonic action directly on the brain. The modulatory system shows complexity and probably great redundancy as effects have been reported with ACTH, MSH, LPH, vasopressin, oxytocin, the endorphins and enkephalins, and substance P.

$ACTH_{4-10}$ and other fragments of $ACTH_{1-39}$, which only act centrally, were early shown to increase resistance to extinction for both aversively and appetitively motivated tasks when applied before testing (see De Wied & Bohus, 1979). They also reverse the active avoidance acquisition impairment caused by hypophysectomy without affecting such learning in control animals. More dramatically, $ACTH_{4-10}$ partially blocks the amnesia induced by CO_2 inhalation or ECS (Rigter & Van Riezen, 1975). As the restorative effects of ACTH fragments on hypophysectomized rats are only short-lived, Squire and Davis (1981) have suggested that the action, of the fragments at least, may be on performance rather than memory as such. In accord with Gold and McGaugh's (1975) hypothesis, however, it has been found that post-trial injections of the whole ACTH molecule impair or enhance retention of a passive avoidance, depending on the degree of initial learning (Gold & Van Buskirk, 1976b). Impairment is consequent on good initial learning and facilitation follows poor learning, and both effects are time dependent. It is uncertain whether centrally acting ACTH fragments have a similar effect. It seems likely, however, that even the effects of the whole ACTH molecule are on performance and not directly on memory. There are two reasons for arguing this. First, ACTH's antiamnesic action is unclear. Mactutus et al. (1980) found that injections of it only reversed hypothermia-induced amnesia when given 30 min before retention testing. Injections of the hormone had no effect when given 1 day before testing. Interpretation was made somewhat equivocal because combining ACTH injections with a task reminder (exposure to fear-related cues) restored memory recovery for a week. The combined treatments may have more fully reactivated the learning conditions and hence have acted as a better reminder cue for memory. The second reason for proposing that ACTH has an effect on performance and not on memory directly argues against this interpretation. Attempts to improve human memory by injecting this hormone have proved largely ineffective (see Squire & Davis, 1981), although increases in alertness as well as decreases have been reported. The matter is not resolved however.

Whether they modulate perceptuo-motor aspects of performance or some kinds of memory directly, ACTH and the antagonistically acting glucocorticosteroids achieve some of these modulations by a direct effect on the brain. Injections of corticosterone have been found to facilitate extinction (De Wied, 1967), and Van Wimersma Greidanus and De Wied (1969, 1971) found the same effect when the hormone was applied directly to the medial midline thalamus or the lateral ventricles. The retarding effects on extinction of $ACTH_{1-10}$ were most effectively achieved by direct applications to the rostral midbrain or caudal diencephalon. Micheau et al. (1981) found that immediate post-training injections of corticosterone into the cerebral ventricles improved retention of an appetitively reinforced discrimination task. Although interesting this finding could reflect a perceptual performance effect as the experimenters did not use the important control procedure of testing on the reversal of the discrimination. A mnemonic interpretation would predict better initial performance on this than a perceptual interpretation. The brain sites of action of these hormones include monoaminergic systems, so it is interesting that Telegdy and Kovacs (1979) have reported some effects of ACTH on limbic and striatal catecholaminergic as well as serotonergic activity.

The evidence relating vasopressin directly to memory modulation is more impressive and the hormone's effects are achieved by forms of the peptide, which have no classical endocrine action. Unlike ACTH, vasopressin has a long-lasting effect in increasing resistance to extinction and improving avoidance learning in hypophysectomized rats. In also protects against the amnesias caused by the protein synthesis blocker puromycin, CO_2 inhalation and ECS (see De Wied & Bohus, 1979). Discrimination learning, based on sexual reward, is also improved by vasopressin although learning mediated by food reward does not appear to be. Brattleboro strain rats, which lack the ability to synthesize vasopressin, show several impairments in learning and retaining avoidance tasks. For example, these animals retain a passive avoidance ability for 1 h but not for 24 h and their deficit is reversed by treatment with a form of vasopressin, which lacks antidiuretic action. A similar deficit is caused by giving intact rats post-training treatments with vasopressin antiserum, applied intraventricularly. Like ACTH, vasopressin injections given after training improve passive avoidance retention. The effect is dose dependent and decreases as the training–treatment delay increases beyond 3 h. Facilitation was also found if vasopressin was given within an hour of retention testing (see De Wied & Bohus, 1979, for a review). Rigter et al. (1974) reported a similar antiamnesic action, in which the hormone reversed CO_2-induced amnesia for passive avoidance when applied 1 h after learning or 1 h before testing. This suggests that the hormone may modulate retrieval as well as consolidation. Such mnemonic interpretations are supported by the finding of Weingartner et al. (1981), that nasal inhalation of vasopressin improves memory in healthy adult humans and in ECT patients. Squire and Davis (1981) discuss similar results with humans. As vasopressin improves performance on speed as well as memory tests, however, it remains uncertain whether its effects are mediated by improvements of attention and mood or by a more direct action on memory.

Vasopressin and oxytocin (which has on antagonistic mnemonic action), whether they are released by the posterior pituitary or in a 'fragmented' form by specialized brain regions, have their mnemonic effects mediated by direct actions on the brain. Thus, Van Wimersma Greidanus and De Wied (1976) found that intracerebroventricular injections of antivasopressin serum, given up to 2 h following learning, caused amnesia 1 day later for passive avoidance. Also, septal or hippocampal destruction has been reported to prevent the facilitatory action of vasopressin on memory, and microinjection of the hormones into the posterior thalamus modifies retention of an active avoidance task (see De Wied & Bohus, 1979). As with ACTH, these hormones affect the levels and turnover of monoamines in various brain regions in complex but mainly antagonistic ways corresponding to their mnemonic effects (Telegdy & Kovacs, 1979). Whereas oxytocin increases hypothalamic dopamine turnover and decreases dopamine and noradrenaline turnover in the striatum, vaso-pressin has an opposite effect.

If vasopressin's memory-modulating effects depend on its ability to increase septal and hippocampal noradrenergic activity, this may be mediated via the dorsal noradrenergic bundle, which projects to these and other limbic system structures. Rossor et al. (1981) have reported that vasopressin is present in the human locus coeruleus, which gives rise to the dorsal noradrenergic bundle. Consistent with this, Kovacs et al. (1979) have reported that the hormone's normal facilitation of passive avoidance retention is prevented by dorsal noradrenergic bundle lesions. It seems likely that the arousal caused by the perception of significant events triggers the release of vasopressin or related more fragmentary peptides from the posterior pituitary and also from local brain regions, and this influences activity in the locus coeruleus, which affects the memory-modulating structures in the limbic system. How directly this final modulation acts on memory remains uncertain.

The opioid peptides have also been implicated in memory modulation. It has been reported that post-training injections, given subcutaneously or intracerebrally, of heroin, morphine, the enkephalins and the endorphins impair retention of aversively motivated tasks, whereas the opioid-blocker naloxone facilitates retention (see Kapp & Gallagher, 1979; Squire & Davis, 1981, for discussions). Opposite effects on aversive tasks have been found but are hard to assess because the drugs were active at the time of testing and involved high dose levels (see Squire & Davis, 1981). Met-enkephalin has been found to improve retention for maze learning in rats and discrimination reversal learning in monkeys (see Squire & Davis, 1981). Kapp and Gallagher (1979) found that disruption of retention for avoidance was only found with microinjections into the amygdala and not other opioid-rich structures. These workers have suggested that opioid peptides may reduce noradrenergic activity in the amygdala by presynaptic action. They have found a time-dependent improvement in passive avoidance retention following post-training application of an alpha adrenergic antagonist to the amygdala (Gallagher & Kapp, 1981). Alpha-adrenergic antagonists have an opposite, facilitatory presynaptic effect on noradrenergic function to that of the opioids.

The mnemonic actions of opioids raise in an acute form the question of how direct their action on memory actually is. It is known that opioids usually diminish the sensorimotor and emotional impact of pain, and it is also known that the amygdala is involved in mediating emotions. Opioids not only reduce emotions like fear but they also sometimes impair attention (see Squire & Davis, 1981). Although these peptides could be modulating consolidation processes through their effects on the non-specific emotional consequences of learning, it is difficult to explain on this view why they should have opposite effects on appetitive and aversive task retention. An alternative possibility is that they change the reinforcement significance of a task so actually altering what is learned, and that this altered memory *content* is often further clouded by attentional confusion. This view is supported by lack of evidence for clear effects of opioids on human memory, but has difficulty in explaining why opioids influence retention when given up to 30 min after training. Current evidence is insufficient to resolve the issue or to distinguish the above views from a more general possibility raised by Squire and Davis (1981). They argue that memory formation requires the interaction of many neural structures in the post-learning period and that this interaction might be affected by *any* important brain activity. Such an activity might of itself have nothing directly to do with memory.

A growing body of evidence suggests that peptide effects on memory may be mediated by central catecholaminergic neurons. These, together with the peripheral endocrinal catecholamines, noradrenaline and adrenaline, are activated when events are perceived as significant, and could therefore serve a mnemonic modulatory function. Squire and Davis (1981) discuss evidence that the facilitatory effects on retention of post-training amphetamine depends on the drug's action on the adrenal medulla. The amnesic action of reserpine also appears to depend on an opposite kind of action on this endocrine gland. It does seem likely that many mnemonic effects depend on both peripheral and central catecholaminergic disturbances. Thus, combining lesions of the dorsal noradrenergic bundle and adrenalectomy has been reported to impair active and passive avoidance retention whereas the separate treatments were without effect (Mason et al., 1979). This suggests that memory may be modulated by related systems in a redundant fashion. Peripheral catecholamine activity satisfies one requirement for a modulatory system. Post-training treatments of amphetamine and adrenaline affect retention not only in a dose-dependent way, but also depending on the level of motivation used in training. Treatment, following highly motivated learning tends to disrupt (Gold & Van Buskirk, 1976a). Effects of the drugs on human memory are consistent with this. Improvements in learning tend to be seen in underaroused or depressed individuals. In the human studies, however, the treatments have only been given at the time of learning so must affect processing efficiency at that stage.

Haycock et al. (1977b) found that intracerebroventricular administration of low levels of catecholamines, such as noradrenaline, dopamine and catecholamine agonists, in the immediate post-learning period, can improve retention in mice. Conversely, similar application of diethyldithiocarbamate (DDC) and other catecholamine antagonists has been found to impair retention of a passive avoidance (Jensen et al., 1977). This DDC-induced amnesia can be reversed either by central administration of minute quantities of noradrenaline or by peripheral injections of much larger concentrations of adrenaline (McGaugh et al., 1979). It remains open as to whether these central and peripheral effects have different mechanisms. There are also reports that alpha-adrenergic antagonists (which may increase central noradrenaline activity by stimulating its release) and adrenergic agonists can attenuate amnesia induced by other treatments, such as CXM or electrical stimulation of the frontal cortex or amygdala (Gold & Sternberg, 1978; Barondes & Cohen, 1968). The claim that these are central catecholaminergic effects is consistent with Gallagher and Kapp's (1981) finding of improved passive avoidance retention following post-training administration of an alpha-adrenergic antagonist to the amygdala complex. Treatments may non-specifically influence retention or amnesia by affecting the activity of catecholaminergic neural systems in the amygdala and other limbic structures.

Sternberg and Gold (1980) have reported that pre-treatment with both alpha- and beta-adrenergic antagonists can attenuate the amnesia induced by frontal cortex stimulation. This is puzzling as these agents act in an opposite way on catecholaminergic neurons. The effects are not fully understood, however, and may be explained in terms of observations by Gold et al., (1977). These workers reported that passive avoidance retention was good when forebrain noradrenaline levels fell to around 80% of their normal level within 10 min of training. Smaller or larger falls correlated with poor retention. These correlations, it is claimed, hold whether the levels are functions of degree of training, motivation or the action of a variety of amnesic agents.

Squire and Davis (1981) have recently indicated that the evidence relating central catecholaminergic activity to memory is equivocal. There have been negative findings. For example, Haycock et al., (1977a) gave rats post-training treatments with 12 different catecholamine antagonists. Only DDC disturbed passive avoidance retention although three of the other agents had similar effects on brain noradrenergic function. Perhaps more seriously, when brain catecholamine levels are reduced to very low levels over a long period of time, by agents like reserpine, retention and learning may not be impaired (Palfai *et al.*, 1978). It is likely that the relationship between forebrain noradrenaline levels and memory involves relative shifts rather than absolute levels. The relationship may also only apply to some aversively motivated tasks, and the reserpine data make it probable that intact catecholamine function is not essential for normal memory.

4.3.2 Some More Exotic Data Concerning Catecholamine Modulation

There have been a number of studies which have reported that catecholamine function can be associated with prolonged susceptibility to amnesia. The effects are superficially similar to cue-dependent amnesia except that they show a long, but clear temporal gradient. They have been found in three kinds of study. First, it has been reported that PS deprivation extends the period of susceptibility to amnesic agents like ECS for up to a week (Fishbein & Gutwein 1977; Fishbein *et al.*, 1971). Second, unilateral lesions of the locus coeruleus made before or up to 6 h after training prolonged susceptibility to amnesia for up to 14 days after training (Zornetzer *et al.*, 1978; Zornetzer & Gold, 1976; De Carvalho & Zornetzer, 1981). Handwerker (1976) found similar effects when bilateral locus coeruleus lesions were made before training although amnesia susceptibility was only extended for 6 h after training. De Carvalho and Zornetzer (1981) have shown, however, that such bilateral lesions may actually increase forgetting over 14 days without apparently affecting learning. These bilaterally lesioned animals actually showed memory facilitation when ECS was given 14 days post-training. They related the different effects of unilateral and bilateral lesions to the differential effects on forebrain noradrenergic activity which unilateral and bilateral disruptions are known to have. Third, Gold and Reigel (1980) have reported that rats injected with adrenaline as long as 1 week after training, and then given disruptive frontal cortex stimulation, showed amnesia for a passive avoidance task. Although similar to the first two effects, this third effect also resembles cue-dependent amnesia in that the catecholamine treatment did not have to be given immediately after learning. This difference may be one between peripheral and central catecholamine mechanisms. Nevertheless, all three effects show time dependency in a way that cue-dependent amnesia does not.

If these effects are mediated by the noradrenergic modulations of the locus coeruleus, it becomes important to consider what influence manipulations of the structure have on learning and retention. Although it has been reported that lesions of it have no effect on retention De Carvalho and Zornetzer's data suggest otherwise, as does the interesting evidence of Pettigrew (1978). Pettigrew examined an unusual form of memory: that involved in the development of visual sensitivities in kittens, which occurs within a critical period. He found that the development of monocular driving in visual cortex neurons did not occur, if the forebrain noradrenergic projections were destroyed by 5-hydroxydopamine, injected into the kittens' lateral ventricles. The ability to develop this plastic visual change could be restored by infusing small areas of visual cortex with noradrenaline. Adjacent areas which were not perfused did not show plasticity.

As the noradrenergic neurons of the locus coeruleus project in a diffuse and non-specific way to visual cortex neurons, Pettigrew's results provide a probable case of consolidation process modulation. Whether such modulation occurs with other kinds of learning is less clear. The cases described of prolonged amnesic susceptibility could mean that catecholamine abnormalities slow down consolidation, but it is more likely that they make later memory expression more labile. The effect could be a temporary one on retrieval or it might even be affecting some non-memory aspect of performance (the locus coeruleus is, for example, thought to exert a modulatory effect on sensory processing). The time dependency of the effects nevertheless is interesting as other long-term changes in memory have been described (see Section 4.6.1).

If modulatory effects on memory exist they should be relatively non-specific with respect to learning tasks, and depending on their degree of intensity may either impair or enhance retention. The studies described in this and the last section suggest that modulations may not only be of consolidation, but also of post-learning encoding and retrieval, and perhaps of memory processes as yet unspecified. Researchers have, however, underestimated problems of control and many experimental effects may not be on memory at all, but on perceptual, motivational and motor factors which influence memory performance. It is not always possible or appropriate to see whether putative memory effects can be found in humans.

Certainly several apparent effects on memory involve structures involved in mediating emotional behaviours. For example, Bresnahan and Routtenberg (1980) reported that low level stimulation of the amygdala, substantia nigra and medial frontal cortex all cause amnesia in rats for passive avoidance. Similar effects followed stimulation of the medial forebrain bundle, which is not only intimately linked to the other structures but like them is associated with motivational and self-stimulational behaviours. Here, stimulation is as likely to affect what is learned as it is to affect memory processes *per se*. Another example of an effect on performance factors rather than on memory as such is provided by Tapp and Holloway (1981). They found that phase shifting the circadian rhythm of rats causes a striking retrograde amnesia for passive avoidance — an effect which was not simply due to 'jet-lag. It seems improbable that similar effects would occur in phase-shifted humans. In the face of these great difficulties of interpretation it seems wise to add further constraints to the search for consolidation and modulatory processes by considering on other grounds what changes are likely to underlie stable memory and short-term memory, if they exist.

4.4   Possible Bases for Long-Term Memory

4.4.1   The Effects of Protein Synthesis Blockers

The view that long-term memory requires macromolecular changes is nearly universal. Doty (1979) provides a popular variant of this view in arguing that memory depends on ionic and macromolecular processes. He regards the former process as effectively a property of all neurons and the basis of short-term memories whereas the latter process is seen as necessary for stable memory, particularly in more complex systems, and possibly only prominent in specialized neural groups. Although it is no longer believed that memories are uniquely coded by neural macromolecules (particularly proteins), such macro-molecules may be implicated in memory either via their pivotal enzymic functions or because their synthesis may be associated with structural changes within and between neurons. The formation of stable memory requires the potential for an altered pattern of neural activity and this, in turn, could involve the selective facilitation of neurotransmission or selective synaptic changes. Quite possibly such changes are not distinct, i.e. synaptic changes may alter neurotransmission efficiency.

It is well established that neuronal structure is susceptible to plastic changes consequent upon natural and pathological conditions. For example, when unilateral lesions of the entorhinal cortex cause the projection to the dentate gyrus to degenerate, then other inputs produce collateral sprouts which inner-vate the vacated site (Lynch & Wells, 1978). This collateral growth only becomes apparent 5 days post-lesion and takes 2 days to reach completion (Lynch et al., 1977). Other similar changes have been reported in the damaged brain and are found to be greater in younger systems (Schneider, 1979). It is also apparent that some of these changes have behavioural consequences even if they are maladaptive (Schneider, 1979). Less drastic manipulations are also known to cause structural alterations in neurons. Thus, monocular visual deprivation in kittens produces adults in which cortical cells are driven exclu-sively by the experienced eye (Wiesel & Hubel, 1965). This effect depends on the subtle interplay of inputs from the two eyes and occurs at a time when synapse formation is occurring at its greatest rate in the visual cortex. Although the precise synaptic changes involved are unknown, dark-rearing has been reported to lead to a reduced frequency of spines (postsynaptic structures), and to alter the orientation and possibly the number of dendritic branches on visual cortex neurons (see Greenough et al., 1979). It is also reported that visual cortex neurons are smaller and that there are a smaller number of synapses per neuron (Cragg, 1975). Both the lesion data and the monocular deprivation data show that one kind of plasticity depends on the interaction between competing inputs upon a common target — the decrease in one input increases the influence of the other. A similar form of competitive interaction may underlie the synapse elimination and reorganization which is one feature of neural development.

More naturalistic stimuli have also been shown to influence neuronal plasticity. Best known is Rosenzweig et al.'s (1972) work on the effects of rearing in an enriched environment. Rats, so treated, have thicker cortices (particularly visual cortices), larger cortical neurons and more glial cells. More detailed study shows these animals to have increased dendritic branching in several layers of their visual cortices and small increases of synaptic length in the same region — clear effects of experience (Volkmar & Greenough, 1972). The effects described so far have been observed largely in the growing brain, smaller increases in dendritic branching have been found in adult rats after 25 days' experience of an enriched environment. It has even been reported that 'elderly' rats show increased cortical dimensions following extended maze training (Cummins et al., 1973). More recently, Greenough et al. (1979) found that similar training in adult animals led to increased branching of the more distal apical dendrites of layers IV and V pyramidal neurons in the visual cortex. They noted no changes in layer IV stellate neurons or in the basal dendritic branching of the pyramidal cells. These latter changes have been reported after enriched environment rearing and this raises the interesting possibility that maze training initiates

149

different structural changes from those associated with environmental enrichment.

Current evidence, therefore, suggests that the after-effects of lesions and of experience may be mediated by several kinds of structural change, including alterations in synaptic size, changes in dendritic branching and the concomitant changes in synaptic number and disposition. To these potential mediators of memory might be added changes affecting neuronal excitability, patterns of action potential generation and neurotransmitter efficiency. It seems probable that many of these processes depend critically on the synthesis of appropriate proteins. In the last decade, it has become clearer how electrochemical activity in neurons might trigger protein synthesis. Many neurotransmitters act on the postsynaptic neuron by catalysing the release of second messenger molecules of cAMP or cGMP. These molecules activate protein kinases which phosphorylate specific proteins. This enables the functions of the cell membrane to be modified. Protein kinases, which are dependent on cAMP, can also phosphorylate histones, associated with DNA, in the nucleus — a chain which may trigger the synthesis of specific proteins. Such a relatively delayed effect of neural input may be critical for the structural modifications which underlie stable memory.

If protein synthesis is essential for stable memory then preventing its occurrence during and after learning should be an effective means of causing amnesia. It is impossible totally to inhibit brain protein synthesis without fatal results, but many antibiotic blockers can achieve 95% suppression, and amnesic-like effects with this degree of suppression are well documented. Unfortunately, the use of protein synthesis blockers is heir to the problems of the retrograde amnesia paradigm and introduces others as well. First, the major groups of protein-synthesis-inhibiting drugs do not appear to have equivalent effects on memory. Thus, the actinomycins have inconsistent effects, the glutaramides are usually only effective when injected before training whereas, under some conditions of administration, puromycin causes amnesia even when given days after initial training (see Mayes, 1981). Second, the amnesias do not develop immediately. For example, Squire and Barondes (1972) found that CXM-induced amnesia took 3 h to develop, when mice had received 15 trials on a discrimination habit under the drug's influence. If 21 trials were given, complete amnesia took 12 h to develop. Third, recovery from amnesia occurs, either spontaneously (as has been reported with the glutaramides) or following treatments such as behavioural reminders or pharmacological manipulations. For example, although memory does not return spontaneously after injections of puromycin, intracranial injections of saline do have this effect (Flexner & Flexner, 1967). Recovery, it is claimed only occurs when the drug is injected at least 1 day post-training and does not occur with injections given before or immediately after training (Flexner & Flexner, 1970). In contrast, CXM-induced amnesia is prevented by rearing chicks in isolation even though the drug is given close to the time of training. Fourth, there is some evidence that cue-dependent amnesia may be produced by protein inhibitors. Thus, Davis and Klinger (1969) were able to extend the time over which puromycin and acetoxycycloheximide could cause amnesia in goldfish by keeping the subjects in the conditioning chamber (which could act as a continuous reminder cue). Nevertheless, the effect needs to be demonstrated more rigorously in mammals.

150

The above points must raise some doubt about whether the protein-blocker drug are disturbing consolidation processes. Even if they are there is considerable uncertainty about whether such a disturbance is a consequence of the protein synthesis blockade. Not only do the drugs have variable effects on memory, they also affect many processes apart from protein synthesis. Indeed, although ECS and the protein synthesis blockers have many dissimilar effects, it has even been argued that their amnesic effects are mediated by a common mode of action (see Miller, 1978). Against this possibility, Andry and Luttges (1972) reported that the amnesic effects of CXM and ECS are additive. They found that ECS caused amnesia for a passive avoidance task at extended intervals when neither treatment alone was effective, if mice were treated with CXM before training. Flood et al. (1978) have extended this finding using anisomycin and ECS. They interpreted their results as showing that ECS causes amnesia when little or no protein synthesis has occurred, and that to the extent that synthesis has occurred, amnesia is diminished, ECS itself has a small and somewhat inconsistent effect on protein synthesis, which these workers discounted preferring instead the suggestion that ECS produces amnesia via the production of conformational changes in the synaptic membrane.

Although ECS and protein blockers may cause amnesia through different mechanisms, many believe that the latter agents do not produce their effects via their action on protein synthesis. Alternative suggestions for mediating effects include sickness, occult or manifest seizure activity in brain regions like the hippocampus, disturbance of adrenal steroidogenesis, and most polemically, impairment of catecholamine activity. These possibilities are lucidly discussed by Dunn (1980). In brief, the emetic effects of protein blockers are insufficient to account for their amnesic action, as other emetics such as lithium chloride are ineffective amnesic agents. Nor can the amnesic action of the agents be explained as a state-dependent effect. Seizure effects cannot be so readily discounted although the main problems seem to arise with puromycin. The observations that puromycin and CXM-induced amnesias are prevented by adrenalectomy, led Nakajima (1975) to propose that their effects were mediated via an inhibition of adrenocortical activity. Squire et al. (1976b), however, did not find amnesia when they selectively blocked steroidogenesis, leaving protein synthesis intact. Nor did they reverse CXM-induced amnesia by administering doses of corticosterone at a level mimicking those produced by the training procedure. It is also hard to reconcile the significance of the peripheral effects of protein blocking drugs with the observation that their topical application in the brain still causes amnesia. For example, Grecksch et al. (1980) found that intrahippocampal injections of anisomycin, which lowered protein synthesis in that structure by over 90%, were sufficient to cause amnesia for a brightness discrimination task.

It has become very popular to argue that protein blocking drugs produce amnesia by the secondary effect of inhibiting catecholamine function. This view derives support from evidence that the drugs typically used do impair catecholamine metabolism and from the work previously described, which shows that their amnesic effect is reversed by catecholamine manipulations. Barraco and Stettner (1976) have proposed a version of this position which postulates three modes of action for protein synthesis blocking drugs. First, they argue that puromycin disrupts the operation of a widely distributed catecholamine system essential for long-term memory, when it is injected a day or more following training. Second, they argue that the glutaramides, such as CXM, disrupt another catecholamine system which is active during and shortly after learning. Both of these actions are thought to be on neurotransmitter efficiency. They do not interfere with consolidation and are reversible by behavioural or biochemical means, as they disrupt modulatory, activational processes, which serve to organize established memories. The degree of amnesia produced by these actions is, not surprisingly, a function of task preparedness and level of training. The third mode of action proposed by Barraco and Stettner is, however on consolidation. They argue that when puromycin is given before or immediately following training then it disrupts a cholinergic system involved in consolidation. Their suggestion is based on observations showing that under these conditions amnesia is marked, not readily reduced by increased training and not reversible by behavioural or pharmacological means. This contrasts with the effects of glutaramides given under similar conditions. It should be noted that the claim of no recovery, following intracranial saline injections, when puromycin is given around the time of learning (Flexner & Flexner, 1970), has been questioned by Deutsch (1969), who asserts that the effect is marginal and that some recovery of memory does occur after saline treatment.

Although puromycin and the glutaramides do have anticatecholaminergic effects, it has been argued that the time-course of these effects is inconsistent with their having a central amnesia-inducing role (Dunn, 1980). Thus, CXM has its greatest effect on catecholamine activity at a time when it does not cause amnesia. Squire *et al.* (1974) reported that the amnesic effects of CXM and anisomycin were not mimicked by treatments, which did not affect protein synthesis but did purportedly match the drugs' action on catecholamine metabolism. Further evidence suggests that CXM and the catecholamine inhibitor DDC produce amnesia in different ways. Reversal of the amnesia induced by protein blockers does not, of course, mean that these agents and the stimulants responsible for the reversal have a common mechanism of action. It should also be reiterated that although many catecholamine manipulations alleviate amnesia, the evidence is far from clear in indicating these manipulations always facilitate the efficiency of the transmitter system. Flood *et al.* (1978) have proposed that stimulants and depressants determine the period of time over which the protein synthesis stage of memory lasts. This accords with the view that catecholamine activity modulates basic consolidation processes such as protein synthesis or cholinergic activation.

It would be wrong to imply that the issues briefly reviewed here have been clearly resolved. They have not, as the exchange between Squire *et al.* (1980) and Gold and Sternberg (1980) over the reversal of CXM-induced amnesia by the alpha-adrenergic antagonist PBZ, indicates. Attempts to develop different or more specific interventive agents may facilitate resolution. For example, L-proline is amnesic for passive avoidance in chicks (Cherkin *et al.*, 1976) — an action which may depend on the inhibition of amino acid uptake into critical neurons. Antisera specific against given proteins have also been found to be amnesic. For example, Hyden (1976), reported that antiserum to protein S-100 causes amnesia when it is given intracerebrally. If protein synthesis is necessary for stable memory, one might expect that its transport within cells would be essential. Such transport involves the microtubules, so agents, such as colchicine, which impair microtubule function should cause amnesia. This has indeed been reported by Cronly-Dillon *et al.* (1974) with active avoidance in goldfish. Possibly colchicine prevents transport from the perikaryon or destabilizes recent changes on the postsynaptic membrane. Further work with this and similar agents may help give focus to the protein synthesis hypothesis.

Even if the primary action of protein blockers can be shown to cause amnesia it is far from sure that this is achieved by a disruption of consolidation. Their many other physiological effects cloud interpretation and the subtlety of the amnesic effects preclude the confident acceptance of a simple consolidation view, with a central role for protein synthesis. The interventive approach is, however complemented by a range of correlational studies. As these may be heuristically of value in suggesting what kinds of protein activity (if any) are likely to underlie the development of stable memory, they will be briefly reviewed.

4.4.2 Learning and Correlated Protein Synthesis

The usual method of studying the macromolecular concomitants of learning involves measuring the extent of incorporation of their radiolabelled precursors, i.e. amino acids in the case of proteins and nucleotides with RNA. Such measurements are affected by changes of blood flow and precursor metabolism so must be interpreted with care as estimates of macromolecular synthesis. More seriously it is a perennial problem whether this synthesis, if it is increased, is directly related to the formation of stable memory rather than some concomitant of learning, such as stress, activity, arousal or sensory stimulation. Bearing these points in mind, increased incorporation of amino acids into proteins and nucleotides into RNA, has been reported following learning in rats, chicks and fish. In chicks, Rose *et al.* (1976) imprinted their subjects to a flashing light and observed a sequence of biochemical changes which occurred selectively in the forebrain roof. The synthesis of RNA polymerase was followed by that of RNA, and this finally led to protein synthesis. The changes were observed at learning but not at later retrieval, did not occur in older chicks which failed to imprint, and were absent from the untrained hemisphere of split-brain subjects.

In fish, Shashoua (1976) adopted a task in which his subjects were fitted with a float and had to learn to swim upright. Increased incorporation of precursors into RNA and protein was only found at the time of learning and was not found in fish given a similar, but insoluble task to learn. More significantly, Shashoua (1976, 1977) found that the increased synthesis was selective. Three cytoplasmic proteins were isolated, and further work indicated that one of these was localized within about 15 000 periventricular cells. These cells were believed to be glia, not neurons, and perhaps to secrete the proteinous material synthesized during training in order to alter synaptic connectivity elsewhere in the brain.

The importance of demonstrating selective changes in protein synthesis in localized brain regions should not be underestimated. Greater specificity makes less attractive the possibility that the effects are non-specific concomitants of training, especially if independent evidence links the brain regions involved with adequate performance in the relevant task. The work of Routtenberg (1979) provides a neat illustration of an attempt to obtain specificity of this kind. Routtenberg and his co-workers trained rats on a passive avoidance task and examined the incorporation of radiolabelled fucose into the synaptosomal fractions of four brain regions, including the hippocampus and substantia nigra, pars compacta. Previous work had shown that electrical or chemical (angiotensin II) treatment of the second, but not the first structure impaired passive avoidance memory (although lesions do not impair passive avoidance learning — an embarrassment for Routtenberg). A selective increase in some glycoprotein fractions was found only in the substantia nigra. Routtenberg speculated that these glycoproteins which are long-lasting may subserve stable memory by altering the fine tuning characteristics of synaptic connections. He has also observed increases in the band F phosphoproteins as a consequence of training, and suggested that this may be important in the earlier stages of memory formation, as these proteins are less long-lasting than glycoproteins. Interestingly, the F phosphoprotein band does not seem to be dependent on cAMP for its activation, but unlike the other phosphoproteins studied is most responsive to environmental stimuli.

Learning-related changes in phosphoprotein synthesis, corroborating those of Routtenberg, have also been reported by Perumal et al. (1977). These workers found an increase in the phosphorylation of synaptosomal proteins in mice, trained in a shock avoidance task. The changes were not seen in control animals whether these were quiet controls or were performing the task, having been previously trained to criterion. Mice, which had undergone extinction of the avoidance did show increased phosphorylation. Gispen et al. (1977) argued that these results provided a strong case for the change being specifically related to memory.

Routtenberg argued that most protein synthesis in the brain is highly regulated and does not respond appreciably to electrochemical activity. If only a small subset of proteins respond to training and these only in brain regions, independently implicated with a specific kind of memory, then the results become interesting. Unfortunately, current techniques are not adequate to determine whether these changes persist over time and correlate closely with memory strength. Nevertheless, if these changes do underlie stable memory, then selective disruptive treatments given in localized brain regions should cause amnesia. Such treatments in other brain regions or treatments which affect synthesis of irrelevant protein groups should be ineffective. Pilcher and Booth (1975) have made an opening foray into this kind of investigation, in a study where they show that CXM prevents a long-term change in paw preference when intracranially given so as to produce maximal protein synthesis inhibition in a region of sensorimotor cortex, critical in mediating the preference shift.

Similarly, it has been shown with imprinting in chicks that destruction of the region, which selectively displays post-learning increases in RNA and protein, causes a loss of the imprinted response (Bateson et al., 1978; Horn et al., 1979). Specifically, destruction of the medial hyperstriatum ventrale not only causes the imprinted response to be lost but prevents its reacquisition. This finding is consistent with the view that the chick hyperstriatum contains part of the system which processes and stores information relevant to imprinting. The proteins whose synthesis follows successful imprinting may mediate such storage. In contrast, Squire and Davis (1981) have argued that the proteins, synthesized when float-wearing fish learn to swim upright, are more likely to modulate another system in which storage occurs. These proteins seem to modulate performance by diffusing into the ventricles (Shashoua, 1981). The distinction between changes directly related to the intrinsic storage system, and others which reflect the less specific activities of an extrinsic modulatory system, is an important but difficult one to make. Apart from showing a perhaps more limited anatomical distribution intrinsic system changes should be more specific to the learning task. Extrinsic system changes should be common to all those learning tasks which the system modulates (see Squire & Davis, 1981). Their view leaves too many loose ends and until the two kinds of test adumbrated above can be more completely achieved advances in understanding the role in memory of protein synthesis are likely to remain very limited. Only when further advances are made will it be possible to assess whether, for example, training-related changes in protein synthesis alter connectivity in neurons which store memory, or whether they reflect the activity of a 'booster' system, which acts on another system where connectivity can be modified.

Many of the frustrations associated with the work described above are inherent in the study of very complex systems. For this reason, in the past decade there has been a growing interest in the study of simple systems, in which the physiology of a given behaviour can be completely specified. These systems have provided models of relatively short-term memory which, as they occur at a cellular level, may be applicable to mammalian memory. Such short-term memory stores may hold information before macromolecular storage is effected.

4.5   Short-Term Storage

4.5.1   Simple Systems and Short-Term Storage

Numerous experiments have shown that neuronal stimulation often causes depressed or increased excitability which outlasts the stimulation. Some neurons display both effects with different time-courses and are responsive to different patterns of stimulation. Post-tetanic potentiation effects can persist for hours and seem to depend on increases in neurotransmitter release, which are in turn functions of increased availability or the greater efficiency of the release mechanism (see Squire & Schlapfer, 1981). Analysis of these post-tetanic changes has been pursued in the crayfish and *Aplysia californica* (Krasne, 1978; Kandel, 1976, respectively).

The tail flip escape response of the crayfish habituates to repeated tactile stimulation. Behavioural habituation is associated with a decrease in synaptic potential with repeated stimulation for synapses between certain sensory neurons and interneurons. These neurons form part of the reflex circuit which controls escape. A similar form of habituation occurs with the gill withdrawal response of *Aplysia*. In this species, repeated stimulation of the siphon with jets of water eventually causes a decrease in the gill withdrawal response. Prolonged training (over 5 days) can cause some degree of habituation to persist for up to 26 days. Behavioural habituation causes the synapses, between the sensory and motor neurons which control the behaviour, to undergo depression. In both the above cases, depression was based on a reduction in transmitter release.

It is clear that in the above cases the synaptic changes occur in th already existing pathways, which reflexly control the habituated response. Further work has shown that synaptic efficiency can also be influenced heterosynaptically, that is to say by changes occurring outside the controlling (and plastic) pathway. For example, in *Aplysia*, habituation of the gill withdrawal reflex can be dishabituated by a strong stimulus to the neck. Kandel (1976) has shown that

155

the synapses between sensory neurons and interneurons received a facilitatory heterosynaptic input under these circumstances. Their functioning is, therefore, being influenced by external controlling pathways, which increase transmitter release between sensory neurons and the motor neurons controlling gill withdrawal.

Low-frequency depression and heterosynaptic facilitation have not only been demonstrated and studied electrophysiologically, but have been shown to mediate simple learned behaviours in animals like *Aplysia*. These processes probably depend upon presynaptic changes and do not seem to require the synthesis of new proteins. Thus, Schwartz *et al.* (1971) found that prolonged inhibition of protein synthesis did not affect the development and persistence of habituation, dishabituation and post-tetanic potentiation in *Aplysia*. It remains uncertain whether the longer-term habituation of *Aplysia* is independent of protein synthesis. Peterson and Squire (1977) have reported, however, that pre- or post-training treatment with anisomycin blocks long-term habituation to conspecific distress calls in mice. A similar question should be asked of the long-term potentiation of the hippocampus produced by intermittent stimulation of the perforant pathway in mammals, which may persist for a week. *Aplysia* provides an excellent model system for determining whether transient and more enduring learned changes involve basically different processes and occur at the same neuronal sites. As the mechanisms of short-term storage found in animals like crayfish and *Aplysia* have similarities to the 'ionic' short-term processes postulated to occur in vertebrates by some workers, the interventive studies on which such views are based will be discussed briefly.

4.5.2 Short-Term Storage and the Use of Interventive Agents

Despite the problems of the interventive approach, already described, Gibbs and Ng (1977) and Mark (1979) have formulated an attractive system for consolidation and short-term storage, which relies on this approach. Their views are summarily outlined in Section 4.2.2. They have disrupted memory in chicks for several tasks, using three kinds of agent — those such as lithium and potassium chloride; sodium pump inhibitors such as ouabain; and protein synthesis inhibitors such as CXM. Although each of these three kinds of agent causes amnesia which is usually permanent, they all differ with respect to how close in time to training they must be given, and with respect to how rapidly the amnesia they produce develops. Agents like lithium chloride must be given within 5 min of training and cause amnesia which is complete shortly after this delay. The sodium pump inhibitors must be given within about 10 or 15 min of training and cause amnesia which begins then and is complete about 90 min following training. Finally, protein blockers are effective when given up to about 30 min following training with complete amnesia developing some time later.

The different action of the three groups of agent receives further support from the effects of counteractive agents. Thus, drugs such as amphetamine which counteract ouabain's inhibition of sodium pump activity, alleviate ouabain-induced amnesia, but have no effect on that produced by agents such as lithium chloride. Furthermore, the recovery agent is only effective when given within the same time period that shows ouabain-induced amnesia. Amphetamine can also reverse CXM-induced amnesia, but only if it is given within the period during which ouabain causes amnesia. This suggests that it prolongs the phase of memory which ouabain counteracts until the protein synthesis level has returned to near normal levels.

Marks (1979) interprets these data as showing that the reverberatory activity caused by training causes neurons to lose potassium and accumulate sodium (a process sensitive to lithium chloride). This change, independent of sodium pump activity, stimulates a prolonged phase of pump activity to restore the ionic balance. One of the effects of such activity is to stimulate the preferential uptake of amino acids, which then act as building blocks in the stage of protein synthesis. The newly synthesized proteins are transported to pre- or post-synaptic membranes where they alter the efficiency of local transmission. If sodium pump activity does stimulate the necessary initial step of amino acid uptake, essential to protein synthesis, then it should be possible to block long-term storage, leaving short-term storage intact, but only if treatment is given when the pump is active. The non-metabolizable amino acid aminoisobutyrate (AIB) competes with functional amino acids for membrane uptake, and so disrupts the uptake stage in Marks's theory. It causes amnesia which develops with the same time-course as that induced by CXM. It is only effective, however, when given within about 10 min of training, which is also the effective period for ouabain. Marks also cites the unpublished study of Bell and Hambley, which found that blocking the neuronal transport system with colchicine, produced an amnesia whose onset was similarly delayed. He argues that this supports his view that the newly synthesized proteins must be actively transported to the membrane sites which they will modify.

Both Marks (1979) and Gibbs and Ng (1977) postulate protracted consolidation and, therefore, need to posit the existence of one or more short-term stores. Marks at least, also regards the stages identified by the interventive approach, as constituting a causally linked sequence. This view is supported by data derived from a one-trial passive avoidance task, commonly used with chicks. Ouabain can produce a permanent amnesia with this task. Marks has also used a multi-trial task in which chicks must learn to confine their pecks to food grains and ignore immovable pebbles, which are initially favoured. CXM, given before training does not impair the learning of a preference, but does cause a delayed onset amnesia. In contrast, when ouabain is given before training, chicks show no tendency to acquire a preference. Presumably, such chicks cannot use information in short-term memory. Surprisingly, when the same animals are tested after a delay of 30 to 60 min, they reveal an increasing preference for grain. It would seem then that with this kind of task sodium pump activity is not required for the development of stable memory.

It is implicit in Marks's thinking that ouabain is not only a usually effective consolidation disrupter, but that it also blocks a short-term storage system. In both cases the critical process involves sodium pump activity. Gibbs and Ng (1977) have argued that although ouabain disrupts the formation of a short-term store it cannot disturb the store's maintenance, which must depend on a process different from sodium pump activity. Their conclusion is based on the observation that ouabain is ineffective in producing amnesia when given at a time after training at which memory must be based on short-term storage, because CXM-induced amnesia does not start to appear until after a greater delay. A similar argument is used to support the view that agents like lithium chloride disrupt a process which initiates but does not maintain an even briefer kind of memory storage.

Despite the currently high level of internal consistency in the evidence related to the multi-stage model it can be seen that all is perhaps not so straightforward. To extrapolate pessimistically from other interventive studies, it is likely that when other groups begin to use the chick paradigm more conflicts will emerge — there are hints of this already (see Gibbs & Ng, 1977). Further, there have been few attempts to see whether these amnesias can be reversed by behavioural or pharmacological means, and none to see whether the agents used can cause cue-dependent amnesia with the chick paradgim. The effects of raising chicks in isolation on ouabain and CXM-induced amnesia have already been described (delayed onset in the former case and prevention of amnesia in the latter). These can be plausibly explained by supposing that isolation causes stress, which prolongs the ouabain-dependent phase of memory beyond the time when protein synthesis is inhibited. This claim is testable. It may be that other 'modulatory' effects will be found which cannot be explained so readily. It is particularly disturbing that the effects of ouabain depend so critically on the kind of learning task involved. What then are the chances that these effects will apply to mammalian species?

Work reviewed in the last two sections nevertheless makes it seem possible that there may be one or more short-term storage processes independent of the need for protein synthesis, subserving memory in the period of minutes or perhaps longer, during which stable storage involving structural modification is developing. Some further research on mammals suggests such short-term storage may sometimes be expressed through a specialized neuronal system. This case has been argued by Alpern and Jackson (1978). They noted that whereas drugs which interfere with cholinergic, dopaminergic, noradrenergic and serotonergic activity can disturb long-term memory in mice, that only anti-cholinergic drugs disrupted a delayed response task, putatively dependent on short-term memory. Specifically, they establishd a learning set for a position reversal habit such that a single reversal trial ensured accurate performance which was retained for delays of up to 30 min. This retention period was extended by pre-trial injections of the anticholinesterase physostigmine.

Rose et al. (1980) have reported that passive avoidance in chicks learning is accompanied by a transient rise in muscarinic cholinergic receptor binding in the forebrain. Rose (1979) has described a similar transient increase, confined to rats' visual cortices following first exposure to light of dark-reared animals. The increase was in choline acetyltransferase and acetyl cholinesterase as well as in binding activity. These changes are suggestive of a cholinergic role in short-term storage although the observation that the change is prevented by protein synthesis blockers in the chicks at least, suggests caution.

Although this evidence is weak, it is congruent with Deutsch's (1971) finding that cholinesterase inhibitors affect memory in a biphasic fashion. Such drugs produce amnesia in rodents when given within 30 min of training and also when given at 1 week. They do not cause amnesia when given at 1 day. These effects seem to be on the expression of memory as they are not permanent. They are, however, unlikely to be due to emotional or other performance factors, as animals acquire the reverse habit faster than controls when they are made amnesia for the learned habit. Cholinergic drugs also affect human memory in ways which preclude obvious performance factors. The finding can be interpreted then as indicating that a short-term system dependent on cholinergic activity comes into operation rapidly after training, and that as it decays away (perhaps over an hour) a long-term system gradually develops over a period of days. The notion that memories can continue to change and indeed strengthen physiologically over a period of days or longer, suggests that they are still developing long after their initial consolidation is achieved.

4.6 Longer-Term Changes in Memory

4.6.1 Possible Longer-Term Physiological Changes in the Memory Trace

The cholinergic intervention paradigm used by Deutsch is particularly significant for two main reasons. First, a wide variety of control procedures have been deployed to eliminate easy explanations in terms of performance effects, and the basic effects have been independently replicated by several groups (see Deutsch, 1979). Second, the treatments affect the expression of memory rather than its consolidation and can be used to measure changes in the memory both over time and in response to varying the degree of training. Anticholinergic agents, applied immediately after training may sometimes disrupt consolidation. For example, Flood et al. (1981) found that retention of discriminated avoidance was disrupted for at least 1 week when anticholinergic agents were applied to the third ventricle immediately after training.

On the first point, rats have been trained on a number of discrimination tasks and given post-training treatments with both anticholinesterase drugs such as physostigmine and DFP, and anticholinergic drugs such as scopolamine. Whereas scopolamine produces amnesia for habits 1 to 3 days old and none for habits 7 to 10 days old, anticholinesterase agents have the opposite effects (memory testing was carried out 20 min after drug injections). This pattern of results makes sense if it is assumed that the level of memory expression is a simple function of the efficiency of one or more cholinergic systems of neurons. There is evidence that anticholinesterase agents increase the efficiency of the cholinergic synapse when it is in a state of poor conductivity, but increasingly interfere when efficiency improves. Flood et al.'s (1981) finding that the post-training application of several cholinergic drugs influences retention according to a U-shaped dose–response function (low doses improving and high ones impairing memory) is also consistent with this interpretation. In contrast, the anticholinergic agents are less disruptive when conductivity at the synapses is good.

Deutsch and his co-workers have shown (see Deutsch, 1979) that when habit strength is increased by varying the number of training trials or task difficulty, then anticholinesterases become more disruptive. Similarly these agents disrupt recall in massed trial learning much more than with spaced trial learning. Spaced trials enable accumulated acetylcholine to be destroyed so that cholinergic conductivity is lower than with massed learning on any given trial. This interpretation received support from the finding that reversal learning is quicker under massed trial training when anticholinesterases are given. The rats must genuinely have forgotten the initially learned habit to show this effect. Given this background, the effect of the drugs on memory as a function of delay is most interesting. Not only are they more disruptive between 7 and 10 days than they are between 1 and 3 days, but at delays of between 3 and 4 weeks they actually facilitate memory. These pharmacological effects seem to correspond quite closely with the strength of the memories as measured behaviourally. Thus memory performance tends to be better at 7 days than it is at 3 days (i.e. reminiscence sometimes occurs) and after 1 month a considerable amount of forgetting has usually occurred. Deutsch argues that the efficiency of recall depends on the conductivity of critical cholinergic neurons. Learning initiates an increase in this conductivity, which builds up slowly over many days before eventually declining. These ideas are congruent with demonstrations (for example, see Schulman & Wright, 1976) of the potentiation of cholinergic afferents by electrical stimulation of other pathways, which persists for at least several hours. These models may correspond to Deutsch's short-term cholinergic system rather than the one which evolves over days. As the consolidation processes underlying cholinergic activation are unknown the models may provide a powerful inroad into their elucidation.

Whereas Deutsch has argued that memory performance over time is determined by conductivity within a given cholinergic system, other workers have speculated that as memories age and become generally less vulnerable to physiological insults they are more widely represented in the brain. Flexner and Flexner (1976) have espoused this position on the basis of their findings with intracranial administration of puromycin. They have reported that this drug impairs discrimination memory in mice when injected bitemporally up to 3 days following training. Beyond that delay it is ineffective although it can still produce amnesia with much longer delays if it is applied to additional cortical sites. They also found that treating mice for 7 days with dopamine-β-hydroxylase inhibitors extended the period of amnesia susceptibility, to bitemporal puromycin applications, to 9 days. In their view, a memory trace localized to the hippocampal entorhinal region spreads to other cortical regions over a period of several days, at a rate which is modulated by catecholaminergic activity.

The Flexners' speculation relates the distribution over time of the memory trace to its decreasing vulnerability to disruption rather than to its ease of retrieval. In contrast, Deutsch's postulation of conductivity changes within a critical cholinergic system is related mainly to variations in ease of retrieval. The two processes may, therefore, correspond to Wickelgren's notions of memory strength (measured by recall and recognition, i.e. retrieval efficiency) and the independent trace fragility (measured as a reciprocal of memory's vulnerability to physiological insult). The Flexners' position is compatible with a view, sometimes advanced, about the functions of the limbic structures damaged in human amnesia. On this view, memories are stored temporarily in the hippocampus and related structures for a short period before being distributed to a wider set of brain structures. The idea that the hippocampus acts as a temporary store for a large variety of memories is speculative and based, as yet, on little evidence. Rather than acting as a temporary home for memory, it is more likely that this structure plays a role in the establishment and subsequent retrieval of memories from those brain regions in which they are stored.

This last position is strongly supported by some evidence from Kesner (1977). He reported that rats trained on a conditioned suppression task could be made temporarily amnesic by hippocampal stimulation which caused after discharges, when this was administered 1 day but not 7 days after training. Memory in untreated controls was equivalent at these two retention intervals so the effect was unlikely to be on performance. Rather, the occurrence of spontaneous recovery suggested that the hippocampus is involved in the retrieval of relatively young memories but not of older ones.

The extent to which conductivity in critical memory systems changes over time and whether memory traces become more distributed as the memory ages remain fascinating and largely unresolved issues. There is no doubt that memory does change with time, both with respect to retrievability and fragility. These changes are considered further in the next section.

4.6.2   Forgetting, Fragility and Interference

In general, the older a memory is the harder it is to recall or recognize. Many memories seem eventually to be lost completely. Prima facie, the existence of this kind of forgetting function is strong evidence against the view that memories, once properly consolidated, are permanent and relatively static in nature. They seem, in contrast, to decay at an ever-decreasing rate until they become vanishingly weak. The rate of decay is determined by their initial strength at input. Speculatively, initial strength at input may be thought of as a function of how richly the memory is encoded (i.e. how distinct it is from other memories) and how well consolidated each of its encoded features is. As the physiological basis of memory has not been identified, however, many theorists have been reluctant to acknowledge that decay may play a central role in memory dynamics. Instead, they have appeared to believe that forgetting is a direct consequence of interference operating between memories in store. In its extreme form, this view is that although consolidated memories remain static and undecayed, they become increasingly less recallable or recognizable, because there are more and more other and similar memories which competitively interfere with them. Hence, memories are lost in the store rather than from it. To assess these contrasting positions more fully, it may be useful briefly to consider exceptions to the normal forgetting function, normal forgetting in relation to interference, and the view that consolidation processes are not all complete by the time forgetting begins.

In reminiscence, retention is better after long than short intervals. Humans may display this effect following the learning of a motor skill by massed practice. The effect has typically been explained in terms of the dissipation of some hypothetical inhibitory factor, which enables the memory to be expressed more readily. No one has argued that the memory trace itself automatically gains strength in the first day or so following learning. This theoretical bias is probably supported by the extreme difficulty of demonstrating reminiscence for other kinds of human memory. Reminiscence for verbal material may nearly always be a result of rehearsal, occurring in longer delays, or of the cueing effect provided by repeated testing. For example, Howarth and Eysenck (1968) reported that introverts actually recalled more paired associates at 24 h delay than they did after fairly immediate testing. Extroverts showed a diametrically opposite pattern of performance. Although it is possible that this pattern results from chronic differences in arousal between extroverts and introverts, it seems more likely that introverts engage in considerably greater amounts of rehearsal during the 1 day retention interval. According to Spear (1978) there are only three clear demonstrations of verbal reminiscence in humans and these all apply to short intervals, ranging from seconds to minutes, typically using a

Brown–Peterson paradigm. Humans do not seem to display 'automatic' verbal reminiscence beyond the intervals traditionally required for consolidation (minutes to hours).

Whereas humans usually forget at a rate which decreases monotonically over time, many animal learning paradigms display far more exotic patterns of retention. For example, it has been reported in the octopus, cuttlefish and the rat that the retention function for certain passive avoidance tasks has a multiphasic form (see Spear, 1978, p. 160). Wansley and Holloway (1975) have noted a retention function in which performance fluctuates from maximum to minimum every 6 h, and find this not only with passive avoidance but also with a one-trial appetitive task. This may be an example of state-dependent retention where the state is determined by some aspect of circadian rhythmicity. The most studied examples of atypical retention in animals have been the incubation phenomenon and the Kamin effect. These are both associated with fear conditioning. Incubation represents a case of reminiscence as it involves an apparent improvement over time in retention of fear-related behaviours. There is evidence that autonomic indices of fear may also incubate in humans. In the Kamin effect there is a decline in the apparent retention of fear-related behaviours between 1 and 6 h after learning and a subsequent improvement noticeable at 24 h delay. It is found robustly after multiple training trials with a variety of passive and active avoidance tasks. These performance changes (particularly those of the Kamin effect) have been correlated with temporal fluctuations of stress-related responses, such as those of the pituitary adrenal system. Spear (1978) has argued that the retention functions may arise as state-dependent retrieval deficits, as performance factors, such as activity, do not vary in accordance with memory efficiency. In other words, the normal forgetting function is caused by either decay, or interference, or both, but memory retrieval also depends on factors which affect retrieval efficiency such as state-or context-similarity between learning and testing. These latter factors may sometimes dominate and determine the function's form.

The fundamental problem with tests of animal memory, however, is that one cannot instruct an animal about what precisely one wants it to retrieve. To a considerable extent state- and context-cues act as indicators as to what memory is appropriate. When these are changed then an animal may no longer treat the target memory as relevant. This would be like instructing a human that a particular memory was not the one being requested. In this situation, therefore, an animal's failure to show evidence of adequate retrieval may not reflect retrieval failure in the sense understood for human memory, but rather a misunderstanding of what is wanted. Crudely, the animal is confused. This point may not only apply to the Kamin effect, but also to some apparent cases of amnesia produced by variations of the retrograde amnesia paradigm, and perhaps to some of the phenomena of interference shown in animal memory. To resolve whether poor performance results from retrieval failure or 'confusion' it would be necessary to know precisely what an animal has learned. But this is hard to achieve without circularity, given an animal's lack of verbal ability. It should be further noted that contextual and state-dependent cues may not only instruct animals as to the relevant task, but they may also act as retrieval cues for both humans and animals. Just how important contextual and state changes are for long-term forgetting remains polemical although some workers like Spear (1978) regard such changes as playing a major role.

Wickelgren (1974) has suggested that retention, over a period ranging from seconds to at least 2 years, satisfies the equation:

$$m = Lt^{-D}e^{-It}$$

where m is the memory trace's strength (measured by recognition), L is initial strength at the end of learning, t is the retention interval, D is the time decay rate, and I is a measure of the degree of similarity between original and interpolated learning (and hence a measure of the degree of interference). This equation indicates that the rate of forgetting and the shape of the forgetting curve are functions both of the extent to which decay has occurred and of the degree of similarity of interpolated material. Wickelgren argued that in short-term memory paradigms, where information is superficially encoded, then the value of I is high (because similarity is high) and consequently the retention function is dominated by the exponential component (e^{-It}). In long-term memory paradigms encoding is much richer so that the similarity of interpolated material is very low, so the retention function is dominated by the power component (t^{-D}). So, it is claimed that short- and long-term forgetting curves have differing forms because the former are largely determined by interference whereas the latter depend on autonomous decay. Wickelgren's view is superficially similar to that of Baddeley (1976). Baddeley also believes that forgetting is largely determined by spontaneous decay, which occurs at a decreasing rate over time, and that interference causes further forgetting in a manner which depends on the strengths of the competing memories. He also seems to ascribe to interference only a minor role in long-term forgetting.

If Wickelgren is to make a clear separation between the factors of interference and decay it is important for him to show that the former has an effect which is independent of the delay following original learning. In contrast, to fit the form of empirically derived forgetting curves, a monolithic interference view requires that the effects of interference should decrease as the target memories become older. Wickelgren (1974) has tested these alternatives, using a verbal running recognition task in which he kept the retention interval constant but varied the delay between the target items and the later interfering items. A yes/no recognition procedure enabled a signal detection analysis to be used, which showed that delaying interference had no effect on d'm. He found no effect of delay. Implicit in Wickelgren's thinking seems to be the preconception that yes/no recognition-derived measures of d'm directly tap the strength of the memory trace (a physiological notion) whereas measures like free recall or modified modified free recall (MMFR) are likely to be contaminated with retrieval-interference factors.

Two points should be made here. First, traditional associative interference theory claims just what Wickelgren appears to want to deny, viz. interference is basically a phenomenon of retrieval disturbance — it does not in any sense act as an acid bath on the memory trace itself. Second, *pace* Wickelgren, the evidence indicates that interference, measured by free recall or MMFR, does decrease the greater the delay between original learning and interference, when the delay between interference and testing is kept constant across conditions (Underwood & Freund, 1968). This evidence is also consistent with that which shows that proactive interference is reduced when the first learning is spaced out over a long period of time (see Baddeley, 1976), an effect which suggests that interference plays an insignificant role in everyday forgetting. Indeed, these time-dependent phenomena support the view that interference (measured by free recall, MMFR or recognition tests which vie competing items against each other) is a function of item or list discriminability, and that such discriminability is mainly based on temporal separation and distinctiveness (see Crowder, 1976, for a discussion).

There is no space to consider contemporary interference theory properly. The complex edifice has been built on some fairly simple observations, however, and these are enumerated by Baddeley (1976). First, retroactive interference depends on the amount and similarity of interpolated material, and decreases with delay between interpolated learning and recall. Second, proactive interference also depends on the amount and similarity of interpolated material, but increases with delay between interpolated learning and recall. It was this difference between retroactive (RI) and proactive (PI) interference which led to two-factor associative interference theory, in which RI caused response competition and unlearning whereas PI only caused response competition. The recovery from unlearning of the material acquired first explained why RI effects diminished with time whereas those of PI tended to increase. The postulation of unlearning, always strange, has failed to achieve support. MMFR, in which subjects are free to recall target and interfering items at their leisure, was supposed to eliminate response competition. Unfortunately, it revealed interference not only with RI but also with PI, where there should have been none. The technique did not eliminate response competition. Instead its use should have prompted questions about the nature of response competition. For example, need the degree of interference be closely related to the number of response intrusions from competing items? This seems to have been the traditional assumption, so that when Melton and Irwin (1940) discovered that response intrusions decreased while interference was still increasing, they felt bound to postulate an extra factor X.

The model of response competition apparently adopted by Melton and Irwin is illustrated by automatic recall of words in normal speech. People often produce a wrong word, which is more dominant in the sentential context than the appropriate word. This is a form of interference in which the degree of competition correlates perfectly with intrusions from the competing items. The speaker is, however, usually rapidly aware of his error, which would not have been made if more attentional resources had been devoted to the task. When attention is paid to retrieval and interference still occurs, the retriever may identify the competing item but not produce it overtly as it is recognized as wrong. The strong associative habit is inappropriate for the situation and prevents retrieval of the target material. In this situation, however, there will be a poor correlation between degree of interference and overt response intrusions. It seems that response competition may produce forgetting by preventing location of the target trace at retrieval. This kind of interference may be associated with few overt intrusion errors, because the rememberer can correctly identify from which list response items are drawn. A rememberer may suffer from retrieval-block interference, therefore, while showing little evidence of 'list or item discrimination-loss' interference as shown by forced-choice recognition tests, which vie competing items against each other. To judge by Melton and Irwin's (1940) results 'discrimination-loss' interference is prevalent with low levels of learning competing material, thereafter rapidly diminishing, whereas retrieval-block interference continues to increase with higher levels of acquisition of the interfering material. It remains an open question whether both kinds of interference diminish as the temporal gap between target and competing material is increased, or whether this effect is only found with 'discrimination-loss' interference. The three kinds of interference delineated in this paragraph may all arise from forms of response competition, which operate at different levels in the memory system. It seems otiose to account for them by postulating nebulous hypothetical processes such as unlearning.

Wickelgren's observation that interference, as measured by recognition tests (which do not vie competing items against each other) does not diminish when the delay between learning and interference increases, suggests that another kind of interference may operate. Baddeley (1976) argues that interference may make trace discrimination harder, comparing recognition to the visual identification of superimposed stimuli of different strengths. This analogy still allows for no 'acid bath' interaction between memory traces and should predict diminishing interfering effects with delay. Wickelgren, on the other hand, seems to be asserting that the target trace may actually deteriorate as a result of interference. The matter is unresolved and resolution will be hard although, as a first step, examination of the effect of varying learning-interference, learning-test and interference-test intervals on interference, as assessed by cued and free recall, and several kinds of recognition test, may prove helpful.

One feature of Wickelgren's model which warrants emphasis is that decay of memory is coupled to consolidation, which is consequently seen as a very extended process. As the memory decays so does memory strength, but at the same time, the resistance of the trace to physiological disruption (the inverse of fragility) increases. Consolidation is the process which diminishes fragility. So the degree of forgetting and the degree of consolidation are very closely related with decreasing delay. Wickelgren (1974) and Squire and Schlapfer (1981) have argued that consolidation changes may continue for years on the basis of evidence which shows that organic amnesics may show graded retrograde amnesias of several years' duration. Squire and Schlapfer (1981) have speculated that this increased resistance associated with forgetting may be explained in terms of the competitive principles which apply in simpler cases of plasticity. For example, the neural influence of the experienced eye increases following a reduction of input from the other eye. Similarly, memories may be represented as a system of competing connections, some of which are strengthened as others weaken.

Even if Wickelgren is correct in supposing that there is a prolonged autonomous consolidation process, in which there is an interaction between forgetting and increased resistance, he does not specify what causes decay. For him, resistance is not only against physiological disruptive agents such as ECT, but also resistance to the unspecified factors which cause normal decay. The factors are presumably to be isolated at the neuronal and biochemical level.

The analysis so far has paid little attention to the role of psychological processes or to the complexity of memories — particularly human memories. Both these factors may be critical in explaining apparently qualitative changes which occur as memories age. As memory for complex material such as pictures, stories or even words, gets older, forgetting almost certainly occurs in a fragmented fashion (see Jones, 1979) rather than uniformly reducing access to all aspects of the memory. In addition, most memories are likely to be rehearsed either voluntarily in the waking state or more automatically during sleep. Such repeated rehearsals may protect against forgetting but may also produce gradually increasing distortion of the original memory. This latter effect occurs because schematic knowledge is constantly being changed by updating, and active rehearsal involves interpreting what is remembered of the target material in the light of current schemata. Qualitative changes are most unlikely to arise from autonomous changes in the memory trace. Rather, they probably are results of an active rehearsal process interacting periodically with a complex memory whose components are becoming increasingly inaccessible. The decreased accessibility of the components arises, largely, no doubt, from autonomous decay.

4.7 Some Final Comments

The main problem of reviewing studies on consolidation and memory change over time is that there are too many conflicting data and the gap between evidence and theory is uncomfortably large. No confident conclusions can be justified so one can only make hopeful guesses. This section will contain some of these concerning general theories, some methodological problems and some specific possibilities for clarifying issues.

Consolidation should primarily be regarded as a linked series of physiological and biochemical processes necessary for the formation of relatively stable memory. If it occurs very rapidly there is no need to postulate the existence of short-term stores which can subserve memory until the stable system becomes operative. Even when stable memory has become operative consolidation-like processes continue to change it, possibly over many years. These processes may well be linked to those underlying decay and forgetting. Active psychological processes, such as rehearsal and elaborative encoding, also modify the memory from the time of learning for a period which can extend to decades in humans. Animals will display these psychological processes, but to a smaller extent. Psychological processes and arousal will activate physiological and hormonal processes which will modulate consolidation in a time-dependent fashion. This modulation will affect how rapidly consolidation occurs and also the intensity with which it occurs. Intensity of consolidation will determine the strength of the stable memory and the rate at which it develops. The limbic structures disturbed in organic amnesia may well constitute a critical component of this modulatory system, influencing consolidation in cortical and perhaps other regions. The durability of complex material in memory will depend both on how elaborately and distinctively that material is encoded and on how well the encoded features are consolidated. These two activities may be mediated by an interaction between the frontal cortex and the limbic 'amnesia' structures (see Chapter 6).

Empirically, it remains unclear whether stable memory becomes operative very rapidly (in a few seconds) or whether it is necessary to postulate short-term holding mechanisms. The answer may even vary with species and learning task. Squire (1975) has argued that a minimal period of about 1 min is required for stable memory to become operative if this depends on protein synthesis. If the estimates of Gibbs and Ng (1977) are correct, then the actual period is considerably longer. On the whole, the picture these workers give of consolidation seems to be the most attractive. It is built on the retrograde amnesia paradigm. This paradigm has generated more confusion than illumination. Although delayed onset of amnesia and recovery of memory are found in both animal and human amnesia, manipulations which greatly extend the period over which animals are susceptible to amnesia raise the question about whether the effects are directly on memory at all. A minimal requirement in such cases should be that the phenomena also appear in humans, and this has not yet been shown. If the paradigm is to be heuristically valuable disruptive agents with far more specific actions need to be developed. For example, agents like antibodies to specific proteins or gangliosides could be applied to small, rationally selected brain regions. In this connection, Karpiak and Rapport (1979) have noted that passive avoidance retention may be disrupted in a time-dependent way by antibodies to gangliosides, S-100 protein and synaptic membranes, but not those to 14–3–2 protein, galactocerebroside and myelin. Huston and Staubli (1979) have also reported that the same task is facilitated by injections of substance P into the lateral hypothalamus, but impaired by similar injections into the amygdala. This last study, however, also illustrates the danger of using a poorly understood task. The effects may be related to those found with opioids and could well be acting on motivational or modulatory systems. Learning tasks, used in the retrograde amnesia paradigm must be understood better than is passive avoidance. Understanding should take the form of knowing as well as possible what is being learned and which brain regions and processes are activated by the learning. This, in turn, involves the parallel use of the correlational and interventive approaches.

Learning physiology is more accessible in simple systems such as *Aplysia*. The physiological and biochemical changes mediating learnt changes, such as habituation, can be revealed by research. *Aplysia* displays both short- and long-term habituation (and may also be conditionable). Therefore, it provides a model for determining whether there are qualitiatively distinct short- and long-term storage systems. For this species, short-term habituation seems to be based on a system independent of protein synthesis, and as long-term habituation in mice has been reported to depend on protein synthesis, it becomes an important issue whether the same applies to *Aplysia*. The use of *Aplysia* as a model of how nervous tissue is reorganized to represent learnt information is more limited. *Aplysia* does illustrate the principles that engram changes occur in those brain regions which normally process the relevant information, although the learnt changes can be initiated or augmented by an external control system. The leap to mammalian learning is nevertheless considerable.

The possible value of hippocampal long-term potentiation (LTP) in mammals should not be ignored, therefore. This plastic change is found in a structure which has been repeatedly associated with memory. The change may persist for several days and is supported by several hippocampal pathways as well as the perforant path. Input patterns which cause LTP have been explored in detail. It has different dynamics from those which underlie post-tetanic potentiation and so may not rely on the same presynaptic changes which mediate the latter. On the other hand, the initial development of LTP does not depend on protein synthesis, but requires an accumulation of intraterminal Ca^{2+}, and is blocked by following seizure activity and is prevented when commissural stimulation precedes that of the perforant path. Bliss (1979) suggests a possible presynaptic mechanism for the change in which only those activated fibres with sufficient accumulated Ca^{2+} would show LTP, and then only if sufficient neighbouring fibres were active to concentrate enough of another unidentified substance, in the extracellular space, to cause presynaptic changes. An alternative postsynaptic mechanism would require the convergence of afferents on postsynaptic cells, in which LTP would be activated when there was sufficient accumulation of a second messenger. Speculations apart, there is some evidence that LTP is associated with an increase in the diameter of synaptic spines in dendate gyrus cells after perforant pathway stimulation. This increase should mediate a more efficient distribution of synaptically induced current in the postsynaptic cell's soma.

Despite its intrinsic interest the LTP phenomenon is little more than a curio unless it can be related to memory. It is, therefore, important that Barnes (1979) has reported an association between learning and LTP in the rat. Specifically, Barnes compared young adult controls with senescent animals on the learning of a spatial task as well as on their ability to maintain LTP in the perforant path. The senescent rats not only showed poor memory for the spatial task but deficient maintenance of the LTP response. Whereas three repetitions of brief high frequency stimulation produced a change lasting at least 14 days in the younger rats, this was not so for the senescent. Although the synapses of ageing rats were found to be less capable of long-lasting enhancement they did not differ from the young on measures such as recurrent inhibition and excitation. It was also found that the correlation between spatial memory and LTP durability held up within the young group itself. Further, Bliss cites evidence that the perforant path in rats is activated by auditory stimuli and argues that the conditions underlying LTP may well occur naturally in some conditioning paradigms.

One line of thought that has emerged largely from the retrograde amnesia paradigm is that consolidation processes and perhaps stable memory itself are modulated in a time-dependent manner by one or more external control systems, whose activation and actions are relatively non-specific. This modulation may be of physiological processes directly or indirectly through eliciting psychological processes such as rehearsal or elaborative encoding. Prominent as a candidate modulator system is the dorsal noradrenergic bundle arising in the locus coeruleus. This system may itself be subject to modulation by hormones such as vasopressin and ACTH (and also opioid agents as mentioned in Section 4.2.1), which are known to affect noradrenergic function. As the locus coeruleus projects to many forebrain structures diffusely, the LTP model may offer a means of exploring the modulatory effect precisely on a well understood plastic phenomenon. The model may succeed in showing why ACTH and many other agents which influence catecholaminergic metabolism sometimes impair and sometimes facilitate retention. More centrally, this model and others like it which may be discovered, should help researchers to make a clearer separation between consolidation and modulatory processes. As normally used, the retrograde amnesia paradigm seems too blunt an instrument for this purpose. For example, Hall (1977) reported that both the protein synthesis blocker CXM and the catecholamine antimetabolite DDC may actually enhance retention of a discriminated escape task if the degree of learning was minimal. Although this particular finding may not be replicable, it serves to show that the paradigm, used with ill-understood learning tasks, confounded with non-learning factors, and with relatively non-specific agents, is unlikely to yield interpretable results. The paradigm may reveal apparent time-dependent amnesia for many reasons, several of which may operate at any one time. Early consolidation theorists ignored the possibility that agents may disturb post-training rehearsal or even act similarly to retroactive interference. Later critics of prolonged consolidation have shown a marked predilection for overinterpreting their data and studiously neglecting other evidence (such as that from correlational studies) which is difficult for them to accommodate.

Squire and Davies (1981) have proposed a number of criteria which should apply whenever either consolidational or modulatory systems are affected. These include: (a) the agent should affect memory in a time- and dose-dependent manner; (b) appropriate manipulations should respectively improve or impair memory; (c) removal of the involved brain system should have an effect on memory; (d) there should be a correlation between learning and the appropriately determined biochemical and/or physiological changes. If a modulatory system is being affected then a wide range of tasks will be influenced by the manipulation whereas effects on consolidation will be more selective. One would also expect manipulations of consolidation to have more drastic effects on memory. The convergent methods approach, implicit in these criteria, provides the main hope for obtaining reliable, interpretable data in the future.

To summarize: the mania for crude studies within the retrograde amnesia paradigm has been prodigal of effort and deficient in yielding firmly grounded theoretical generalizations. The problem has been exacerbated by the willingness of workers confidently and dogmatically to overinterpret their data. Learning tasks and disruptive/facilitative agents have been used with little understanding. There has also been a tendency to underestimate the difficulty of relating animal behaviour to the underlying hypothetical processes involved in memory. Future research might more fruitfully be concerned with understanding simple model systems by using interventive and correlational approaches in tandem. Appropriate models will become more abundant as analytic techniques advance, and they will be explored more effectively as more specific agents are developed. These models should help illuminate not only the changes required for stable memory but eventually those changes which this memory undergoes over a long time period and which lead to forgetting.

References

ALPERN, H.P. and JACKSON, S.J. (1978) Short-term memory: A neuropharmacologically distinct process, *Behavioural Biology*, **22**, 133–146.

ANDRY D.K. and LUTTGES, M.W. (1972) Memory traces: Experimental separation by cycloheximide and electroconvulsive shock. *Science*, **178**, 518–520.

AZMITIA, E.C. MCEWEN, B.S. and QUARTERMAIN, D. (1972) Prevention of ECS-induced amnesia by re-establishing continuity with the training situation. *Physiology and Behaviour*, **8**, 853–855.

BADDELEY, A.D. (1976) *The Psychology of Memory*, Harper and Row, New York.

BARNES, C.A. (1979) Memory deficits associated with senescence: A neurophysiological and behavioural study in the rat. *Journal of Comparative and Physiological Psychology*, **93**, 74–104.

BARONDES, S.H. and COHEN, H.D. (1968) Memory impairment after subcutaneous injection of acetoxycycloheximide. *Science*, **160**, 556–557.

BARRACO, R.A. and STETTNER, L.H. (1976) Antibiotics and memory. *Psychological Bulletin*, **83**, 242-302.

BARTLETT, F.C. (1932) *Remembering: A Study in Experimental and Social Psychology*. Cambridge University Press, Cambridge.

BATESON, P.P.G., HORN, G. and McGABE, B.J. (1978) Imprinting: The effect of partial ablation of the medial hyper-striatum ventrale of the chick. *Journal of Physiology*, **285**, 23 pp.

BLISS, T.V.P. (1979) Synaptic plasticity in the hippocampus. *Trends in Neurosciences*, **2**, 42-45.

BLOCH, V. (1970) Facts and hypotheses concerning memory consolidation processes. *Brain Research*, **24**, 561-575.

BLOCH, V. (1976) Brain activation and memory consolidation. In: M.R. ROSENZWEIG and E.L. BENNETT (Eds.) *Neural Mechanisms of Learning and Memory*, pp. 583-590. MIT Press, Cambridge, Mass.

BLOCH V., DEWEER, B. and HENNEWIN, E. (1970) Suppression de l'amnesie retrograde et consolidation d'un apprentissage a' essai unique par stimulation reticulaire. *Physiology and Behaviour*, **5**, 1235-1241.

BRESNAHAN, E.L. and ROUTTENBERG, A. (1980) Medial forebrain bundle stimulation during learning and subsequent retention disruption. *Physiological Psychology*, **8**, 112-119.

CHERKIN, A., ECKHARDT, M.J. and GARMAN, M.W. (1976) Memory: proline induces retrograde amnesia in chicks. *Science*, **193**, 242-244.

CHOROVER, S.L. and SCHILLER, P.H. (1965) Short-term retrograde amnesia in rats. *Journal of Comparative and Physiological Psychology*, **59**, 73-78.

CRAGG, B.G. (1975) The development of synapses in the visual system of the cat. *Journal of Comparative Neurology*, **160**, 147-166.

CRONLY-DILLON, J., CARDEN, D. and BIRKS, C. (1974) The possible involvement of microtubules in memory fixation. *Journal of Experimental Biology*, **61**, 443-454.

CROWDER, R.G. (1976) *The Principles of Learning and Memory*. Lawrence Erlbaum Associates, Hillsdale, New Jersey.

CUMMINS, R.A., WALSH, R.N., BUDTZ-OLSEN, O.E., KONSTANTINOS, T. and HORSFALL, C.R. (1973) Environmentally induced brain changes in elderly rats. *Nature (London)*, **243**, 516-518.

DAVIS, R.E. and KLINGER, P.D. (1969) Environmental control of amnesic effects of various agents in goldfish. *Physiology and Behaviour*, **4**, 269-271.

DAWSON, R.G. and McGAUGH, J.L. (1969) Electroconvulsive shock effects on a reactivated memory trace: further examination. *Science*, **166**, 525-527.

DeCARVALHO, L.P. and ZORNETZER, S.F. (1981) The involvement of the locus coeruleus in memory. *Behavioral and Neural Biology*, **31**, 173-186.

DEUTSCH, J.A. (1969) The physiology of memory. *Annual Review of Psychology*, **20**, 85-104.

DEUTSCH, J.A. (1971) The cholinergic synapse and the site of memory. *Science*, **174**, 788-794.

DEUTSCH, J.A. (1979) Physiology of acetylcholine in learning and memory. In: A. BARBEAU, J.H. GROWDON, and R.J. WURTMAN (Eds.) *Nutrition and the Brain. Volume 5*, pp. 343-350. Raven Press. New York.

DE VAUS, J.E. GIBBS, M.E. and NG, K.T. (1980) Effects of social isolation on memory formation. *Behavioural and Neural Biology*, **29**, 473-480.

DE WIED, D. (1967) Opposite effects of ACTH and glucocorticosteroids on extinction of conditioned avoidance behavior. *Proceedings of the International Congress on Hormonal Steroids, Milan, 1966* (Eds. L. MARTINI *et al.*). Internationl Congress Series, No. 32, Amsterdam. Excerpta Medica Foundation, New York.

DE WIED, D. and BOHUS, B. (1979) Modulation of memory processes by neuropeptides of hypothalamic-neuro-hypophyseal origin. In: M.A.B. BRAZIER (Ed.) *Brain Mechanisms in Memory and Learning: From the Single Neuron to Man*, pp. 139-150. Raven Press, New York.

DOTY, R.W. (1979) Neurons and memory: Some clues: In: M.A.B. BRAZIER (Ed.) *Brain Mechanisms in Memory and Learning: From the Single Neuron to Man*, pp. 53-63. Raven Press, New York.

DUNN, A.H. (1980) Neurochemistry of learning and memory: An evaluation of recent data. *Annual Review of Psychology*, **31**, 343-390.

FISHBEIN, W. (1981) *Sleep, Dreams and Memory*. MTP Press, Lancaster.

FISHBEIN, W. and GUTWEIN, B.M. (1977) Paradoxical sleep and memory storage processes. *Behavioral Biology*, **19**, 425-464.

FISHBEIN, W., MCGAUGH, J.L. and SWARZ, J.R. (1971) Retrograde amnesia: Electro-convulsive shock effects after termination of rapid eye movement sleep deprivation. *Science*, **172**, 80-82.

FLEXNER, J.B. and FLEXNER, L.B. (1967) Restoration of expression of memory lost after treatment with puromycin. *Proceedings of the National Academy of Sciences of the USA*, **66**, 48-52.

FLEXNER, J.B. and FLEXNER, L.B. (1970) Further observations on restoration of memory lost after treatment with puromycin. *Yale Journal of Biology and Medicine*, **42**, 235-240.

FLEXNER, J.B. and FLEXNER, L.B. (1976) Effect of two inhibitors of dopamine β-hydroxylase on maturation of memory in mice. *Pharmacology, Biochemistry and Behavior*, **5**, 117-121.

FLOOD, J.F. Bennett, E.L. ORME, A.E. and JARVIK, M.E. (1977) Protein synthesis dependent gradient of ECS retrograde amnesia. *Behavioral Biology*, **21**, 307-328.

FLOOD, J.F., BENNETT, E.L., ORME, A.E., ROSENSWEIG, M.K. and JARVIK, M.E., (1978) Memory: Modification of anisomycin-induced amnesia by stimulants and depressants. *Science*, **199**, 324-326.

FLOOD, J.F., LANDRY, D.W. and JARVIK, M.E. (1981) Cholinergic receptor interactions and their effects on long-term memory processing. *Brain Research*, **215**, 177-185.

GALLAGHER, M. and KAPP, B.S. (1981) Effect of phentolamine administration into the amygdala complex of rats on time-dependent memory processes. *Behavioral and Neural Biology*, **31**, 90-95.

GELLER, A. and JARVIK, M.E. (1968) The time relations of ECS induced amnesia *Psychonomic Science*, **12**, 169-170.

GIBBS, M.E. and NG, K.T. (1977) Psychobiology of memory: Towards a model of memory formation. *Biobehavioral Reviews*, **1**, 113-136.

GISPEN, W.H., PERAMAL, R., WILSON, J.E. and GLASSMAN, E. (1977) Phosphorylation of proteins of synaptosome-enriched fractions of brain during short-term training experience. The effects of various behavioral treatments. *Behavioral Biology*, **21**, 358-363.

GOLD P.E. and KING, R.A. (1974) Retrograde amnesia: storage failure versus retrieval failure. *Psychological Review*, **81**, 456-469.

GOLD, P.E. and MCGAUGH, J.L. (1975) A single-trace, dual process view of memory storage processes. In: D. DEUTSCH and J.A. DEUTSCH (Eds.) *Short-Term Memory*, pp. 355-378. Academic Press. New York.

GOLD P.E., MACRI, J. and MCGAUGH, J.L. (1973) Retrograde amnesic gradients: Effects of direct cortical stimulation. *Science*, **179**, 1343-1345.

GOLD, P.E. and REIGEL, J.A. (1980) Extended retrograde amnesia gradients: Peripheral epinephrine and frontal cortex stimulation. *Physiology and Behavior*, **24**, 1101-1106.

GOLD, P.E. and STERNBERG, D.B. (1978) Retrograde amnesia produced by several treatments: Evidence for a common neurobiological mechanism. *Science*, **201**, 367-369.

GOLD, P.E. and STERNBERG, D.B. (1980) Neurobiology of Memory. *Science*, **209**, 837.

GOLD, P.E. and VAN BUSKIRK, R. (1976a) Effects of post-trial hormone injections on memory processes. *Hormones and Behavior*, **7**, 509-517.

GOLD, P.E. and VAN BUSKIRK, R.B. (1976b) Enhancement and impairment of memory processes with post-trial injections of adrenocorticotrophic hormone. *Behavioral Biology*, **16**, 387-400.

GOLD, P.E., VAN BUSKIRK, R. and HAYCOCK, J.W. (1977) Effects of post-training epinephrine injections on retention of avoidance training in mice. *Behavioral Biology*, **20**, 197–204.

GORDON, W.C. (1977a) Similarities between recently acquired and reactivated memories with production of memory interference. *American Journal of Psychology*, **90**, 231–242.

GORDON, W.C. (1977b) Susceptibility of a reactivated memory to the effects of strychnine: A time-dependent phenomenon. *Physiology and Behavior*, **18**, 95–99.

GORDON, W.C. and FELDMAN, D.T. (1978) Reaction induced interference in a short-term retention paradigm. *Learning and Motivation*, **9**, 164–178.

GORDON, W.C. and SPEAR, N.E. (1973) Effect of reactivation of a previously acquired memory on the interaction between memories in the rat. *Journal of Experimental Psychology*, **99**, 349–355.

GRECKSCH, G., OTT, T. and MATHIES, H. (1980) The effect of intrahippocampally applied anisomycin on the retention of brightness discrimination in rats. *Behavioral and Neural Biology*, **29**, 281–288.

GREENOUGH, W.T., JURASKA, J.M. and VOLKMAR, F.R. (1979) Maze training effects on dendritic branching in occipital cortex of adult rats. *Behavioral and Neural Biology*, **26**, 287–297.

HALL, M.E. (1977) Enhancement of learning by cycloheximide and DDC: A function of response strength. *Behavioral Biology*, **21**, 41–51.

HANDWERKER, M.J. (1976) The role of the nucleus locus coeruleus in avoidance learning and retention stability in rats. Doctoral Dissertation, University of California, Irvine.

HAYCOCK, J.W., VAN BUSKIRK, R. and MCGAUGH, J.L. (1977a) Effects of catecholaminergic drugs upon memory storage processes in mice. *Behavioral Biology*, **20**, 281–310.

HAYCOCK, J.W., VAN BUSKIRK, R., RYAN, J.R. and MCGAUGH, J.L. (1977b) Enhancement of retention with centrally administered catecholamines. *Experimental Neurology*, **54**, 199–204.

HEBB, D.O. (1949) *Organization of Behavior*. Wiley. New York.

HORN, G., MCGABE, B.J. and BATESON, P.P.G. (1979) An autoradiographic study of the chick brain after imprinting. *Brain Research*, **168**, 361–373.

HOWARTH, E. and EYSENCK, H.J. (1968) Extraversion, arousal and paired-associate recall. *Journal of Experimental Research into Personality*, **3**, 114–116.

HUGHES, R.A., BARRETT, R.J. and RAY, O.S. (1970) Retrograde amnesia in rats increases as a function of ECS-test interval and ECS intensity. *Physiology and Behaviour*, **5**, 27–30.

HUSTON, J.P. and STAUBLI, U. (1979) Post-trial injection of substance P into lateral hypothalamus and amygdala, respectively, facilitates and impairs learning. *Behavioral and Neural Biology*, **27**, 244–248.

HYDEN, H. (1976) Plastic changes of neurons during acquisition of new behavior as a problem of protein differentiation. *Progress in Brain Research*, **45**, 83–100.

JENSEN, R.A., MARTINEZ, Jr., J.L. VASQUEZ, B., MCGAUGH, J.L. MCGUINESS, T., MARRIJO, D. and HEMESS, S. (1977) Amnesia produced by intraventricular administration of diethyldithiocarbarmate. *Neuroscience Abstracts*, **3**, 235.

JONES, G.V. (1979) Analyzing memory by cuing: intrinsic and extrinsic knowledge. In: N.S. SUTHERLAND (Ed.) *Tutorial Essays in Psychology: A Guide to Recent Advances*, pp. 119–147 Lawrence Erlbaum Ass, Hillsdale, NJ.

JOUVET, M. (1972) The role of monoamines and acetylcholine in the regulation of the sleep–wake cycle. *Ergebnisse der Physiologie, Biologischen Chemie, und Experimentallen Pharmakologie*, **64**, 166–308.

KANDEL, E.R. (1976) *Cellular Basis of Behavior*. Freeman, New York.

KAPP, B.S. and GALLAGHER, M. (1979) Opiates and memory. *Trends in Neurosciences*, **2**, 177–180.

172

KARPIAK, S.E. and RAPPORT, M.M. (1979) Inhibition of consolidation and retrieval stages of passive-avoidance learning by antibodies to gangliosides. *Behavioral and Neural Biology*, **27**, 146–156.

KESNER, R.P. (1977) A neural system approach to the study of memory storage and retrieval. In: R.R. DRUCKER-COLIN and J.L. MCGAUGH (Eds.) *Neurobiology of Sleep and Memory*, pp. 277–254. Academic Press, New York.

KOVACS, G.L., BOHUS, B. and VERSTEEG, D.H.F. (1979) The effects of vasopressin on memory processes: The role of noradrenergic neurotransmission. *Neuroscience*, **4**, 1529–1537.

KRASNE, F.B. (1978) Extrinsic control of intrinsic neuronal plasticity: An hypothesis from work on simple systems. *Brain Research*, **14**, 197–216.

LEWIS, D.J. (1979) Psychobiology of active and inactive memory. *Psychological Bulletin*, **86**, 1054–1083.

LEWIS, D.J., MILLER, R.R. and MISANIN, J.R. (1969) Selective amnesia in rats produced by electroconvulsive shock. *Journal of Comparative and Physiological Psychology*, **69**, 136–140.

LYNCH, G., GALL, C. and COTMAN, C.W. (1977) Temporal parameters of axon sprouting in the adult brain. *Experimental Neurology*, **54**, 179–183.

LYNCH, G. and WELLS, J. (1978) Neural anatomical plasticity and behavioral adaptability. In: *Brain and Learning*, pp. 105–124. Greylock, New York.

MCGAUGH, J.L. (1966) Time-dependent processes in memory storage. *Science*, **153**, 1351–1358.

MCGAUGH, J.L., GOLD, P.E., HANDWERKER, M.J., JENSEN, R.A., MARTINEZ, J.L. MELIGENI, J.A. and VASQUEZ, B.J. (1979) Altering memory by electrical and chemical stimulation of the brain. In: M.A.B. BRAZIER (Ed.) *Brain Mechanisms in Memory and Learning: From the Single Neuron to Man*, pp. 151–164. Raven Press, New York.

MACTUTUS, C.F., SMITH, R.L. and RICCIS, D.C. (1980) Extending the duration of ACTH-induced memory reactivation in an amnesic paradigm. *Physiology and Behavior*, **24**, 541–546.

MAH, C.J., ALBERT, D.J. and JAMIESON, J.L. (1972) Memory storage: Evidence that consolidation continues following electroconvulsive shock. *Physiology and Behavior*, **8**, 283–286.

MARKS, R. (1979) Concluding comments. In: M.A.B. BRAZIER (Ed.) *Brain Mechanisms in Memory and Learning: From the Single Neuron to Man*, pp. 375–381. Raven Press, New York.

MASON, S.T., ROBERTS, D.C.S. and FIBIGER, H.C. (1979) Interaction of brain noradrenaline and pituitary–adrenal axis in learning and extinction. *Pharmacology, Biochemistry and Behavior*, **10**, 11–16.

MAYES, A.R. (1973) Disruption of the interhemispheric transfer of active avoidance learnt during unilateral cortical spreading depression. *Behavioral Biology*, **8**, 207–217.

MAYES, A. (1981) The physiology of memory. In: G. UNDERWOOD and R. STEVENS (Eds.) Aspects of *Consciousness*, pp. 1–38. Academic Press, London.

MELTON, A.W. and IRWIN, J.M. (1940) The influence of degree of interpolated learning on retroactive inhibition and the overt transfer of specific responses. *American Journal of Psychology*, **53**, 173–203.

MICHEAU, J., DESTRADE C. and SOUMIREU-MOURAT, B. (1981) Intraventricular corticosterone injection facilitates memory of an appetitive discriminative task in mice. *Behavioral and Neural Biology*, **31**, 100–104.

MILLER, R.R. (1978) Some physiological aspects of memory. In: M.M. GRUNEBERG and P. MORRIS (Eds.) *Aspects of Memory*, pp. 104–131. Methuen, London.

MISANIN, J.R., MILLER, R.R. and LEWIS, D.J. (1968) Retrograde amnesia produced by electroconvulsive shock after reactivation of a consolidated memory trace. *Science*, **160**, 554–555.

MULLER, G.E. and PILZECKER, A. (1900) Experimental beitrage zue lehre bom gedactnesses. *Zeitschrift fur psycholoie*, **1**, 1–288.

NAKAJIMA, S. (1975) Amnesic effect of cycloheximide in the mouse mediated by adrenocortical hormones. *Journal of Comparative and Physiological Psychology*, **83**, 378–385.

173

PALFAI, T., BROWN, O.M. and WALSH, T.J. (1978) Catecholamine levels in whole brain and the probability of memory formation are not related. *Pharmacology, Biochemistry and Behavior*, **8**, 717–721.

PERUMAL, R., GISPEN, W.H., GLASSMAN, E. and WILSON, J.E. (1977) Phosphorylation of proteins of synaptosome-enriched fractions of brain during short-term training experience: Biochemical characterisation. *Behavioral Biology*, **21**, 341–357.

PETERSON, G.M. and SQUIRE, L.R. (1977) Cerebral protein synthesis and long-term habituation. *Behavioural Biology*, **21**, 443–339.

PETTIGREW, J.D. (1978). The locus coeruleus and cortical plasticity. *Trends in Neurosciences*, **1**, 73–74.

PILCHER, C.W.T. and BOOTH, D.A. (1975) Effect of cycloheximide on the long-term retention of reversed paw-preference in the rat. *Experimental Brain Research*, **23**, (Supplement), 161.

POSNER, M.I. and KONICK, A.F. (1966) Short-term retention of visual and kinaesthetic information. *Organizational Behavior and Human Performance*, **1**, 71–86.

QUARTERMAIN, D. (1976) The influence of drugs on learning and memory. In: M.R. ROSENZWEIG and E.L. BENNETT (Eds.) *Neural Mechanisms of Learning and Memory*. MIT Press, Cambridge, Mass.

RIGTER, H. and VAN RIEZEN, H. (1975) Anti-amnestic effect of $ACTH_{4-10}$: Its independence of the nature of the amnestic agent and the behavioral test. *Physiology and Behavior*, **14**, 563–566.

RIGTER, H., VAN RIEZEN, H. and DE WIED, D. (1974) The effects of ACTH and vasopressin analogues on CO_2-induced retrograde amnesia in rats. *Physiology and Behavior*, **13**, 381–388.

ROBBINS, M.J. and MEYER, D.R. (1970) Motivational control of retrograde amnesia. *Journal of Experimental Psychology*, **84**, 220–225.

ROSE, S.P.R. (1979) Transient and lasting biochemical reponses to visual deprivation and experience in the rat visual cortex. In: M.A.B. BRAZIER (Ed.) *Brain Mechanisms in Memory and Learning: From the Single Neuron to Man*, pp. 165–178. Raven Press, New York.

ROSE, S.P.R., GIBBS, M.E. and HAMBLEY, J. (1980) Transient increase in forebrain muscarinic cholinergic receptor binding following passive avoidance learning in the young chick. *Neuroscience*, **5**, 169–172.

ROSE, S.P.R. HAMBLEY, J. and HAYWOOD, J. (1976) Neurochemical approaches to developmental plasticity and learning. In: M.R. ROSENZWEIG and E.L. BENNETT (Eds.) Neural Mechanisms of Learning and Memory, pp. 293–310. MIT Press, Cambridge, Mass.

ROSENZWEIG, M.R., BENNETT, E.L. and DIAMOND, M.C. (1972) Brain changes in response to experience. *Scientific American*, **226**, 22–29.

ROSSOR, M.N., IVERSON, L.L., HAWTHORN, J., ANG, V.T.Y. and JENKINS, J.S. (1981) Extrahypothalamic vasopressin in human brain. *Brain Research*, **214**, 349–355.

ROUTTENBERG, A. (1979) Anatomical localization of phosphoprotein and glycoprotein substrates of memory. *Progress in Neurobiology*, **12**, 85–113.

SCHNEIDER, A.M. (1975) Two faces of memory consolidation: storage of instrumental and classical conditioning: In: D.D. DEUTSCH and J.A. DEUTSCH (Eds.) *Short-Term Memory*, pp. 340–355, Academic Press, London.

SCHNEIDER, G.E. (1979) Is it really better to have your brain lesion early? A revision of the 'Kennard Principle'. *Neuropsychologia*, **17**, 557–584.

SCHULMAN, J. and WRIGHT, F.F. (1976) Synaptic transmission: long-lasting potentiation by a post-synaptic mechanism. *Science*, **194**, 1437–1439.

SCHWARTZ, J.G., CASTELLUCCI, V.F. and KANDEL, E.R. (1971) The functioning of identified neurons and synapses in the absence of protein synthesis. *Journal of Neurophysiology*, **34**, 939–953.

SHASHOUA, V.E. (1976) Identification of specific changes in the pattern of brain protein synthesis after training. *Science*, **193**, 1264–1266.

SHASHOUA, V. (1977) Brain protein metabolism and the acquisition of new behaviors. II. Immunological studies of the proteins of goldfish brain. *Brain Research*, **122**, 113–124.

SHASHOUA, V.E. (1981) Biochemical changes in the CNS during learning. In: A. BECKMAN (Ed.) *Neural Basis of Behavior*. Spectrum, New York. In Press.

SKINNER, D.M., OVERSTREET, D.H. and ORBACH, J. (1979) Reversal of the memory-disruptive effect of REM sleep deprivation by physostigmine. *Behavioral and Neural Biology*, **25**, 189–198.

SMITH, C. and YOUNG, J. (1980) Reversal of paradoxical sleep deprivation by amygdaloid stimulation during learning. *Physiology and Behavior*, **24**, 1035–1039.

SPEAR, N.E. (1978) *The Processing of Memories: Forgetting and Retention*. Lawrence Erlbaum Ass, Hillsdale, New Jersey.

SQUIRE, L.R. (1975) Short-term memory as a biological entity. In: D. DEUTSCH and J.A. DEUTSCH (Eds.) *Short-Term Memory*. Academic Press, London.

SQUIRE, L.R. and BARONDES, S.H. (1972) Variable decay of memory and its recovery in cycloheximide-treated mice. *Proceedings of the National Academy of Sciences, USA*, **69**, 1416–1420.

SQUIRE, L.R. and DAVIS, H.P. (1981) The pharmacology of memory: A neurobiological perspective. *Annual Review of Pharmacology and Toxicology*, **21**, 323–356.

SQUIRE, L.R., DAVIS, H.P. and SPANIS, C.W. (1980) Neurobiology of amnesia. *Science*, **209**, 836–837.

SQUIRE, L.R., KURZENSKI, R. and BARONDES, S.H. (1974) Tyrosine hydroxylase inhibition by cycloheximide and anisomycin is not responsible for their amnesic effects. *Brain Research*, **82**, 241–248.

SQUIRE, L.R. and SCHLAPFER, W.T. (1981) Biochemical aspects of learning, memory and its disorders. In: H.M. VAN PRAAG, M.H. LADER, O.H. RFAELSON and E.J. SACHAR (Eds.) *Handbook of Biological Psychiatry, Vol. ll, Brain Mechanisms and Abnormal Behavior*, pp. 309–341. Dekker, New York.

SQUIRE, L.R., SLATER, P.C. and CHASE, P.M. (1976a) Reactivation of recent and remote memory before electroconvulsive therapy does not produce retrograde amnesia. *Behavioural Biology*, **18**, 335–344.

SQUIRE, L.R., ST. JOHN, S. and DAVIS, H.P. (1976b) Inhibitors of protein synthesis and memory: Dissociation of amnesic effects and effects of adrenal steroidogenesis. *Brain Research*, **112**, 200–206.

STERN, W.C. and MORGANE, P.J. (1974) Theoretical view of REM sleep function: Maintenance of catecholamine systems in the central nervous system. *Behavioral Biology*, **11**, 1–32.

STERNBERG, D.B. and GOLD, P.E. (1980) Effects of α- and β-adrenergic receptor antagonists on retrograde amnesia produced by frontal stimulation. *Behavioral and Neural Biology*, **29**, 289–302.

TAPP, W.N. and HOLLOWAY, F.A. (1981) Phase shifting circadian rhythms produces retrograde amnesia. *Science*, **211**, 1056–1058.

TELEGDY, G. and KOVACS, G.L. (1979) Role of monoamines in mediating the action of hormones on learning and memory. In: M.A.B. BRAZIER (Ed.) *Brain Mechanisms in Memory and Learning: From the Single Neuron to Man*, pp. 249–268. Raven Press, New York.

UNDERWOOD, B.J. and FREUND, J.S. (1968) Effect of temporal separation of two tasks on proactive inhibition. *Journal of Experimental Psychology*, **78**, 50–54.

VAN WIMERSMA GREIDANUS, T.B. and DE WIED, D. (1969) Effects of intracerebral implantation of corticosteroids on extinction of an avoidance response in rats. *Physiology and Behavior*, **4**, 365–370.

VAN WIMERSMA GREIDANUS, T.B. and DE WIED, D. (1971) Effects of systemic and intracerebral administration of two opposite acting ACTH-related peptides on extinction of conditioned avoidance behavior. *Neuroendocrinology*, **7**, 291–301.

VAN WIMERSMA GREIDANUS, T.B. and DE WIED, D. (1976) Modulation of passive-avoidance behavior of rats by intracerebroventricular administration of antivaso-pressin serum. *Behavioral Biology*, **18**, 325–333.

VOLKMAR, F.R. and GREENOUGH, W.T. (1972) Rearing complexity affects branching of dendrites in the visual cortex of the rat. *Science*, **176**, 1445–1447.

WANSLEY, R.A. and HOLLOWAY, F.A. (1975) Multiple retention deficits following one-trial appetitive training. *Behavioral Biology*, **14**, 135–149.

WEINGARTNER, H., GOLD, P., BALLENGER, J.C., SMALLBERG, S.A., SUMMERS, R., RUBINOW, D.R., POST, R.M. and GOODWIN, F.K. (1981) Effects of vasopressin on human memory functions. *Science*, **211**, 601–603.

WICKELGREN, W.A. (1974). Single trace fragility theory of memory dynamics. *Memory and Cognition*, **2**, 775–780.

WICKELGREN, W.A. (1977). *Learning and Memory*. Prentice-Hall, New Jersey.

WICKELGREN, W.A. (1979). Chunking and consolidation: a theoretical synthesis of semantic networks, configuring in conditioning, S–R versus cognitive learning, normal forgetting, the amnesic syndrome, and the hippocampal arousal system. *Psychological Review*, **86**, 44–60.

WIESEL, T.N. and HUBEL, D.H. (1965). Extent of recovery from the effects of visual deprivation in kittens. *Journal of Neurophysiology*, **29**, 1029–1040.

WITTMAN, T.K. and DEVIETTI, T.L. (1980). Heart-rate reactivity to reminder treatment predicts test performance in rats given ECS following training. *Physiological Psychology*, **8**, 515–521.

ZINKIN, S. and MILLER, A.J. (1967). Recovery of memory after amnesia induced by electroconvulsive shock. *Science*, **155**, 102–104.

ZORNETZER, S.F. ABRAHAM, W.C. and APPLETON, R. (1978). The locus coeruleus and labile memory. *Pharmacology, Biochemistry and Behavior*, **9**, 227–234.

ZORNETZER, S.F. and GOLD, P.E. (1976). The locus coeruleus: Its possible role in memory consolidation. *Physiology and Behavior*, **16**, 331–337.

CHAPTER 5

Short-Term Memory Processes in Humans and Animals

Graham J. Hitch

5.1 Introduction

The study of human short-term memory is a well-established field of interest with an extensive research literature. There is broad agreement about many of the basic phenomena, even though there is equally broad disagreement about their interpretation. Furthermore, theoretical approaches to human short-term memory typically treat it not as an isolated topic, but one that is related to more general issues of learning and cognition. In contrast, the study of animal short-term memory has received much less attention, even though the position is now changing very rapidly. Many of the basic phenomena of animal short-term memory have yet to be fully explored or even discovered. Apart from a few isolated examples theories of animal short-term memory have yet to be developed, and certainly none has been subjected to thorough and extensive testing. In discussing animal and human short-term memory together, therefore, it would be difficult and indeed inappropriate to adopt a similar approach to the topic in each case. Accordingly the discussion of human short-term memory is mainly concerned with the broad theoretical issue of its general structure, whereas the discussion of animal short-term memory is more concerned with exploring a series of narrower questions that are essential preliminaries to establishing a more general theoretical viewpoint. In both cases the discussion is centred on information processing analyses of behavioural evidence from normal individuals, with the exception that evidence from human neuropsychological disorders of memory is also briefly discussed. Section 5.4 considers aspects of animal short-term memory in relation to human memory and reviews some of the problems of relating these two areas of research.

In what follows, the phrase short-term memory will be used in two ways. Its main use will be to refer to experimental situations in which materials are typically presented fairly briefly and retention is tested within at most a minute after presentation. A second use will be to indicate in a general way the processes underlying performance in such tasks, without commitment to any particular theoretical interpretation.

5.2 Short-Term Memory in Humans

Although models of human memory which distinguished separate short- and long-term memory stores (e.g. Atkinson & Shiffrin, 1968) were exceedingly successful for a short period, they attracted growing criticism in the form of both empirical challenges and alternative frameworks for interpreting the known phenomena. Wickelgren (1974), for example, proposed that trace-strength dynamics within a unitary system can account for effects normally cited as evidence for separate stores, and Craik and Lockhart (1972) suggested that the concept of separate stores should be replaced by a continuum of levels of stimulus processing. Others have argued that short-term memory consists of currently active long-term memory rather than a separate store (e.g. Shiffrin, 1975). Nevertheless, it is interesting that the idea of some kind of distinction between short- and long-term memory processes still seems to persist. Thus although Wickelgren (1981) rejected the notion of a separate 'short-term memory buffer', he maintained a commitment to a separate attentional 'active memory'. Similarly Craik and Lockhart (1972) proposed a distinct primary memory as a limited capacity attentional system within the levels of processing framework.

In the present chapter the issue of the distinction between human short-term memory and other types of memory such as sensory and long-term memory is not the main focus of interest. Such a distinction will be assumed without detailed supporting arguments (for which see, e.g. Baddeley, 1976). The emphasis is instead on charting the experimental evidence which suggests that human short-term memory is not a unitary resource but a collection of separate systems, each with different properties and functions. This approach stems from evidence that human short-term memory acts as a working memory system in which different patterns of memory resources are deployed in different cognitive tasks (e.g. Baddeley & Hitch, 1974; Hitch & Baddeley, 1978). The types of short-term memory outlined in this section correspond to possible subsystems of the working memory system. Since the present aim is to bring animal and human short-term memory into a common focus, the emphasis will be on identifying major subsystems of human short-term memory rather than elaborating a particular theory of how they are combined to form an integrated working memory system. The treatment will be illustrative rather than exhaustive and will attempt to deal with aspects of human short-term memory where there is, or could be, a fruitful interchange of ideas and results with research on animal short-term memory.

5.2.1   Verbal Short-Term Memory

One of the most striking aspects of verbal STM is the sharp limitation on how much material can be recalled immediately after a single presentation. In short-term serial recall, where a random sequence of letters, digits or words must be reported in their correct order, most people make errors if the sequence is more than a few items long (e.g. Miller, 1956.) The span of immediate memory corresponds to the maximum length of sequence that can be recalled, and was found by Miller to be roughly constant across different types of verbal materials. This suggested the idea of a limited capacity slot-like storage system, each slot capable of being occupied by a single 'chunk' of information, defined loosely as a meaningful unit (Miller, 1956). A separate source of evidence for this view came from experimental investigations of single-trial free recall (see, e.g. Glanzer, 1972 for a summary). In this task a *supra*-span list of words is presented for subsequent recall of the items regardless of their order. When recall follows immediately after list presentation there is very marked tendency for the most recently presented items to be recalled better than items earlier in the list. However, this 'recency effect' is selectively removed if recall is delayed for a few seconds spent performing an irrelevant, attention-demanding task (Postman & Phillips, 1965). Moreover, a number of other factors, such as list length and presentation rate, affect recall of pre-recency items but not the size of the recency component of recall (Postman & Phillips, 1965; Glanzer & Cunitz, 1966). Further evidence of this sort from free recall adds support for a clear double dissociation between two separate components of performance. These components were typically interpreted in terms of short-term memory, responsible for the recency effect, and long-term memory, underlying retention of earlier items. The restriction of the recency component in free recall to just a few items corresponded nicely with the limit on memory span (though in fact the latter is typically slightly higher), suggesting that both phenomena reflect the same short-term store (cf. the Atkinson–Shiffrin model) However, subsequent evidence has now made it clear that memory span and the recency component in free recall must be given separate explanations, and that it is useful to identify them with different mechanisms rather than a single short-term store (Baddeley & Hitch, 1974; Hitch, 1980). The evidence concerns differences in coding, effects of performing a concurrent task during free recall learning and studies of individual differences.

Although it is customarily claimed that verbal short-term memory typically involves the retention of speech-based codes, most of the evidence comes from studies of short-term serial recall rather than immediate free recall. Performance in short-term serial recall is markedly disrupted by increasing the phonemic similarity among the items (Baddeley, 1966; Conrad & Hull, 1964) or their spoken durations (Baddeley et al., 1975b). These effects are very clear and have been repeatedly observed over a wide variety of conditions. On the other hand the recency component of free recall is not sensitive to word length (Craik 1968a; Watkins, 1972) and the effects of phonemic similarity do not appear to be at all comparable with those in short-term serial recall. A weak tendency has been observed for intrusion errors in free recall to be phonemically related to the most recently presented items (Craik, 1968b; Shallice, 1975). However, other studies have found either no effect of phonemic similarity on the recency component (Glanzer et al., 1972) or a facilitative effect common to both recency and pre-recency items (Craik & Levy, 1970).

Studies of the mutual interference between two concurrent memory tasks provide perhaps the clearest evidence against the idea of a unitary verbal short-term memory system. Baddeley and Hitch (1974, 1977) investigated the effect of performing a task involving the immediate serial recall of sequences of up to six digits during presentation of a list of words for subsequent free recall. One set of materials was presented auditorily and the other visually, and the digit recall task was terminated when presentation of the words for free recall was completed. Regardless of the way presentation modality was assigned to the two tasks it was found that concurrent short-term serial recall of sequences of six digits had only a general interfering effect on free recall. There was no tendency for the recency component to be particularly disrupted. If the recency component had depended on the same underlying limited capacity mechanism as serial recall it would have been expected to suffer massive interference under these conditions, since six items is close to its presumed capacity. A related finding is the observation that irrelevant concurrent articulation during the presentation phase of free recall also has only a general interfering effect, rather than an effect specific to the most recent items (Richardson & Baddeley, 1975). By comparison, immediate serial recall is particularly sensitive to this type of interference (see below).

Finally, individual differences in the size of the recency component in free recall do not correlate with measurements of digit span (Martin, 1978), and the difference in digit span performance between groups of 'good' and 'poor' beginning readers is not reflected in measures of recency in free recall (Byrne & Arnold, 1981). Again, one would not expect this if the two phenomena reflect a single, common resource.

Although when taken together this evidence provides a reasonably strong case for distinguishing between the memory processes responsible for recency and immediate ordered recall, most of it says little about the *nature* of the two processes. According to one class of interpretation (Baddeley & Hitch, 1974, 1977; Tulving, 1968), recency reflects the use of an ordinal retrieval strategy, which utilizes the ordinal positions of items in a sequence as retrieval cues, and in which the discriminability of the cues declines with distance from the end of the list. Baddeley and Hitch (1977) proposed that such a strategy may be used in remembering any sequence of events of a particular class, not just lists of words for free recall. They reported a long-term recency effect in rugby players' memory for details of matches they had played, and there is further evidence for long-term recency in other situations (Bjork & Whitten, 1974; Tzeng, 1973). According to Baddeley and Hitch (1977) a general-purpose ordinal retrieval strategy might serve the important function of 'keeping track' of events of different types over different time-spans. However, it remains to be established whether long-term and short-term recency effects reflect such a common retrieval strategy applied to different types of store. Close examination suggests that there are indeed distinguishing characteristics of short-term recency, which are consistent with the suggestion that it may reflect retrieval from a limited capacity input buffer (Hitch, 1980). Moreover, independent grounds for postulating an input buffer store arise from considering speech comprehension processes in which it seems necessary to suppose that there is temporary storage of sentence constituents (Jarvella, 1978).

In contrast, experiments on short-term serial recall suggest that it involves an articulatory memory system whose normal function is connected with the production of fluent speech. In most of their experiments demonstrating the effect of word length on short-term serial recall Baddeley et al. (1975b) manipulated word length by varying the number of syllables in each word, a relatively crude technique which leaves open the question of what aspect of word length is crucial for its effect. However, two further findings suggested that the spoken duration of the words was important. In one, Baddeley et al. compared short-term serial recall for lists of short- and long-duration words while holding number of syllables constant and found an effect of temporal duration such that the longer words were remembered less well. In a second experiment a quantitative linear relationship was found between the numbers of items of different lengths that could be recalled and their mean articulation rates. Across a range of materials, subjects' memory performance corresponded to the number of items they could articulate within 1.5–2.0 s. Baddeley et al.

interpreted their results in terms of the concept of an 'articulatory loop', a special-purpose store containing articulatorily coded traces which decay in about 2 s unless refreshed by rehearsal. Since long words take longer to rehearse, less of them can be simultaneously maintained within the loop. Further experiments by Baddeley *et al.* studied the effects of requiring subjects to engage in irrelevant vocalization such as repeating the redundant word 'the' during presentation of the word sequences, a technique often referred to as articulatory suppression. The results showed that articulatory suppression removed the effect of word length in the recall of visually presented lists, but had only a small, non-specific interfering effect on recall of auditorily presented lists. The first of these results is exactly what would be predicted if irrelevant vocalization interferes with use of the articulatory buffer. The second result is more problematic since it is not clear why modality of presentation should make a difference. However, more recent findings show that irrelevant vocalization does remove the word-length effect in auditory lists if it is present during both input and recall (Baddeley, Lewis & Vallar, personal communication). Interestingly, suppression during input also abolishes the effect of phonemic similarity on short-term serial recall of visual, but not auditory, sequences (Murray, 1968). The total pattern of results, therefore, seems to be captured quite simply by assuming that short-term serial recall is mediated by a temporally decaying articulatory buffer capable of being refreshed by subvocal rehearsal. The sensitivity of the buffer to articulatory suppression favours the idea that it is normally involved in the processes of speech production. Furthermore, the occurrence of transpositions involving pairs of elements of an utterance in certain kinds of speech error is consistent with this idea. Yet more support comes from detailed study of the patterns of occurrence of phonemic transpositions in short-term serial recall which suggests a number of close correspondences with their patterns of occurrence in errors of normal speech (Ellis, 1980).

Verbal short-term memory, therefore, seems to be mediated by separate stores for verbal output and verbal input rather than a single system. A general ordinal retrieval strategy may also be involved in recency in verbal short-term recall.

5.2.2 Visual Short-Term Memory

Although less intensively investigated than verbal short-term memory, two independent lines of evidence suggest that an active process of 'visualization' can be used to maintain visuo-spatial information over periods of several seconds, a time-course much longer than iconic memory, the sensory store investigated by Sperling (1960).

The first type of evidence comes from a letter-matching task developed by Posner and Keele (1967). In this task subjects are visually presented with a single letter to remember, then after a variable interstimulus interval (ISI) they are shown a second comparison letter. The subjects' task is to indicate as rapidly as possible whether or not the two letters share the same name. Posner and Keele found that 'same' judgements were faster for visually identical pairs (e.g. AA, aa) than for visually different pairs (e.g. Aa, aA), a difference that was maximal at short ISIs but declined with increasing ISI, being effectively absent for an ISI of 2 s. Posner and Keele (1967) interpreted their results by assuming that comparisons between the stimuli were based on a decaying visual representation of the first stimulus at shorter ISIs but that at longer ISIs they were based on more abstract name codes.

In subsequent experiments, Posner *et al.* (1969) found that presenting a visual pattern mask after the first stimulus did not affect the superiority of physical matches over name matches thus enabling the short-term visual trace to be clearly distinguished from iconic memory, which is sensitive to masking. However, the superiority of physical matches was disrupted by interpolating mental arithmetic between the two stimuli, suggesting the possibility that general attentional resources are involved in maintaining the visual trace. Active maintenance of the visual trace is also suggested in another experiment by Posner *et al.* (1969) where subjects' expectancies were manipulated. When the original procedure was modified and stimuli were arranged so that matches could always be made on the basis of physical identity there was no suggestion of decay of the visual trace over a 1 s period. Presumably, rehearsal of the visual trace is increased when there is no need to generate the corresponding name code.

Further studies of the matching task suggest that Posner's original estimate of the duration of visual short-term memory was unduly conservative. Parks *et al.* (1972) found that when an auditory shadowing task was interpolated between the memory and test stimuli, physically identical pairs were judged 'same' faster than physically different pairs at ISIs as long as 8 s. Presumably shadowing interferes with the generation of name codes, giving subjects an incentive to maintain a visual trace of the memory letter. However, such an interpretation draws attention to a commonly recognized problem of inference in the letter-matching paradigm which arises because there are essentially two unknowns, the rate of loss of the visual trace of the test stimulus and the rate at which a verbal trace is generated. Alternative measures of short-term visual memory can be obtained by using visual nonsense patterns which cannot readily be given verbal descriptions.

In one such study Phillips (1974) investigated recognition memory for briefly exposed random chequerboard patterns. Subjects were presented with a single pattern followed by a variable dark retention interval, after which they were presented with a test pattern which was either identical to the initial sample or minimally changed by randomly altering one cell of the chequerboard. When examined as a function of the length of the retention interval recognition performance declined rapidly over the first 100 ms or so but thereafter fell more slowly and was still above chance at 9 s. Phillips was able to demonstrate that different memory processes underly these two phases of forgetting by producing a double dissociation. Varying pattern complexity by changing the number of cells in the matrix affected performance at longer retention intervals but not during the initial phase of very rapid forgetting. On the other hand, presenting the test stimulus at a slightly different location from the original stimulus completely removed the early phase but did not affect performance at the longer intervals. This pattern of results is consistent with the suggestion that memory at very short intervals is based on iconic storage, with a large instantaneous capacity and localization in space, but that a separate, limited-capacity short-term visual memory operates at slightly longer intervals. It is interesting to note that the durability of short-term visual memory for unnameable patterns is comparable with Parks *et al.*'s (1972) results using letters but with verbal interference during the retention interval.

In further experiments, Phillips and Christie (1977a) found that recognition memory for sequences of random chequerboard patterns showed a pronounced recency effect for the last item presented and a lower asymptotic level for earlier items. The recency effect was still present if a pattern mask was presented after the final list item, suggesting that it was not attributable to iconic memory. Furthermore, performing mental arithmetic for a few seconds in between presentation and test removed the recency effect but left recall of earlier items unaffected, while changing the presentation rate affected recall of earlier items without affecting recency. Once again, therefore, the evidence amounts to a double dissociation, which Phillips and Christie (1977a) interpreted in terms of a distinction between short-term and long-term visual memory. In subsequent experiments with similar materials Phillips and Christie (1977b) showed that short-term visual memory is not disrupted by unattended visual input, but is affected by auditory events requiring active processing. Hines (1975) also found a single-item recency effect in visual recognition memory for sequences of random shapes, but the recency effect was not sensitive to a 30 s delay filled by a task of copying triangles, or copying combined with oral counting. Thus it is not yet fully clear how to characterize the conditions under which interpolated activity removes recency in visual memory. Despite this, however, there does appear to be a reasonable amount of convergence between the results of studies of the visual trace using the Posner–Keele matching task and findings obtained in recognition memory for nonsense patterns.

With more meaningful pictorial stimulus materials such as scenes on the other hand it seems that rather different results are observed. Serial position curves in recognition memory for sequences of complex pictures typically show no recency effect (Shaffer & Shiffrin, 1972; see also Weaver & Stanny, 1978), and when recency occurs it is under conditions of very rapid presentation (Potter & Levy, 1969), where it can be attributed to backward masking of earlier list items. Given such a radical shift in type of materials, the discrepancy raised by these results may be resolvable without challenging the hypothesis of a short-term visual store. One possibility is that the difference is attributable merely to the visual complexity of pictures, since it is already known that short-term visual memory is highly sensitive to complexity (Phillips, 1974). The suggestion would have to be that with sufficiently complex pictures there is effectively no short-term visual memory at all. However, this is a speculation which has yet to be directly investigated.

A further aspect of short-term visual memory is related to the suggestion that it corresponds to an active process of visualization rather than a passive store (Phillips & Christie, 1977a). Avons and Phillips (1980) studied the effect of manipulating display time and post-stimulus processing time on long-term visual memory for matrix patterns. They introduced interference prior to the test pattern sufficient to remove the short-term component of performance. In one experiment they found that long-term visual memory improved as a function of stimulus display time but was not affected by increasing post-stimulus processing time, even though occasional probe trials without interference showed that short-term visual memory was maintained throughout the post-stimulus interval. Avons and Phillips interpreted visualization as a maintenance process which holds material in short-term visual memory but does not necessarily result in transfer to long-term memory. Such an interpretation implies that the duration of short-term visual memory will depend on the costs and benefits of the process of visualization rather than having a fixed absolute value.

Visual memory also has been studied using the dual task technique in which one of the tasks is designed to disrupt the use of spatial coding. Baddeley *et al.* (1975a) showed that a concurrent spatial tracking task interfered with short-term memory for a spatial matrix of digits but had no effect on retention of purely verbal sequences. Further experiments explored the nature of the interference by contrasting the effects of purely spatial and purely visual secondary tasks (Baddeley & Lieberman, 1980). Spatial interference consisted of tracking a moving sound source while blindfold whereas visual interference consisted of tracking changes in the brightness of a large visual field. The spatial short-term memory task was found to be sensitive to spatial rather than visual interference, a result which was interpreted in terms of the concept of a 'visuo-spatial scratchpad', a spatially coded temporary storage device involved in visual imagery. Because of the large differences in materials and techniques, it is not yet clear whether the visuo-spatial scratchpad can be directly equated with the idea of short-term visual memory. Nevertheless, the close relation between the two concepts is evident. For the present, therefore, it is sufficient to point out that several independent sources of evidence suggest the need to distinguish some form of purely visuo-spatial storage in human short-term memory.

5.2.3 Summary

Research on human short-term memory suggests a number of dissociations and the concept of a unitary short-term memory system, therefore, cannot be maintained. Instead, it seems more profitable to assume a working memory system consisting of a set of interacting special-purpose subsystems distinguished by their properties, such as coding, capacity and control processes, and by their function in normal cognition. This approach leads to a broad distinction between visual and verbal short-term memory subsystems and to a distinction within the verbal domain between an articulatory buffer used in speech production and a recency-based system which is probably involved in language comprehension.

5.2.4 Neuropsychological Aspects of Short-Term Memory

Neuropsychological research into disorders of memory has shown a double dissociation between verbal memory tasks involving long-term retention and those involving short-term memory (see, e.g. Shallice, 1979). Amnesic patients typically perform badly in long-term tasks such as delayed free recall and serial learning, but show a normal recency effect in immediate free recall and a normal verbal memory span (Baddeley & Warrington, 1970; Drachman & Arbit, 1966). In contrast, there are patients with conduction aphasia who show a normal long-term component in free recall, and who perform normally on other tests of long-term memory, yet have very poor digit span and a sharply reduced recency effect in immediate free recall (Shallice & Warrington, 1970; Warrington *et al.*, 1971). This neuropsychological double dissociation is powerful evidence for the separation of memory systems underlying short- and long-term retention, and parallels the separation in normal subjects. Of more importance here, however, is the further question of whether the neuropsychological evidence has implications for the fractionation of short-term memory into separate subsystems.

Perhaps the most striking aspect of the poor short-term memory of conduction aphasics is that it is specific to auditorily presented verbal materials (Shallice & Warrington, 1974; Saffran & Marin, 1975). Saffran and Marin reported a patient whose auditory digit span was less than three items, but whose visual digit span was about six. Normal subjects typically show an auditory advantage in this comparison. In addition, Shallice and Warrington (1974) found that short-term memory for sequences of non-speech noises was essentially normal in conduction aphasia. Baddeley and Hitch (1974) put forward the suggestion that the damaged store should be equated with the articulatory loop of working memory, the subsystem implicated in memory span and in speech production. However, strong evidence against this idea comes from a study of the spontaneous speech of a conduction aphasic with a digit span of less than four, which found no abnormality in pauses or errors (Shallice & Butterworth, 1977). Interestingly, this patient did have difficulty comprehending complex sentences of the type used in the Token test (De Renzi & Vignolo, 1962), and a similar comprehension deficit in conduction aphasia has also been reported by Saffran and Marin (1975). This pattern of results can be interpreted in terms of damage to a store for verbal input, used to hold surface structure in speech comprehension, rather than to an output store (Hitch, 1980; Shallice, 1979). Shallice assumes that the store is specific to auditory presentation, but it is not yet clear that this is a necessary assumption. In any event it seems clear that a satisfactory interpretation of the short-term memory deficit in conduction aphasia will involve the assumption of separate subsystems in verbal STM.

An interesting further question is whether there is any neuropsychological support for the concept of a separate visual STM. One claim that has been made is that the relatively normal performance of conduction aphasics on visual STM tasks is evidence for a separate visual store. Warrington and Shallice (1972) found that one such patient showed much slower forgetting of visually presented letters in the Brown–Peterson task, and produced some sign of making visual confusion errors in short-term serial recall of visually presented letters. Studies of other types of patient suggest that visual short-term retention can be selectively impaired. De Renzi and Nichelli (1975) reported reduced memory span for spatial locations but normal verbal span in a group of patients with right posterior lesions. Unfortunately, the evidence on this issue is at present too sparse to support any really firm conclusions. There is a particular need for neuropsychological research to make use of experimental methods which have been shown to be useful in separating visual short-term memory from other forms of memory in the normal population.

To sum up, therefore, the general conclusion to be drawn is that disorders of short-term memory do not appear to be interpretable in terms of damage to a single, undifferentiated memory resource. Instead, they imply a more complex system. However, the extent to which observed patterns of disorder reflect damage to the separate subsystems hypothesized to account for normal short-term memory remains to be more fully established.

185

5.3 Short-Term Memory in Animals

Rather like much research into human short-term memory, the investigation of animal short-term memory has been dominated by a small set of experimental paradigms. However, because interest in the problem has flourished only relatively recently, even the established paradigms are not yet particularly well understood. One particularly widely used task which illustrates some of the general phenomena is that of delayed matching to sample (DMTS). On each trial of this task the animal is typically presented with one of two 'sample' stimuli followed after some variable delay by the presentation of two 'comparison' stimuli. The animal is rewarded for choosing the comparison stimulus that is identical to the initial sample.

In pigeons, matching performance declines from a high level to chance as the retention interval is extended to a few seconds (Roberts, 1972; Roberts & Grant, 1976), and is improved by increasing the presentation duration of the sample (Roberts & Grant, 1974). There is also an effect of proactive interference from prior trials, provided that the temporal separation between trials is not more than a few seconds (Grant, 1975; Maki *et al.*, 1977). Finally, there is evidence of retroactive interference from events occurring during the retention interval, in particular from the presence of general illumination as opposed to darkness (Grant & Roberts, 1976; Maki *et al.*, 1977). D'Amato (1973) observed a broadly similar pattern of results with capuchin monkeys, with the major exception that they were still able to match at above chance levels at delays of minutes rather than seconds. Like pigeons, the presence of general illumination during the retention interval produced retroactive interference, but unlike pigeons, monkeys were not sensitive to the exposure duration of the sample stimulus. Indirect evidence for proactive interference in DMTS in primates is provided by Jarrard and Moise (1973), who found that decreasing the inter-trial interval led to poorer performance in stump-tail macaques.

From this brief summary of DMTS in animals it is clear that they have the capacity to remember a stimulus over short delays, that forgetting is fairly rapid and that interference effects can be observed. The remainder of this section considers particular questions about rehearsal, recency effects, capacity and coding in animal short-term memory, and examines them in the light of human STM. Such an approach is necessarily selective, and omits questions such as effects of general illumination on animal STM which have not been extensively studied in the human case.

5.3.1 Rehearsal Processes

Atkinson and Shiffrin's (1968) distinction between the structure of the human memory system and control processes relating to the flow of information within it was an important aspect of their model, and the distinction has been retained in subsequent theoretical alternatives (see, e.g. Baddeley & Hitch 1974; Craik & Lockhart 1972). The most fully investigated control process in humans has been verbal rehearsal, but non-verbal rehearsal in the form of visualization is also clearly possible (see Section 5.2.2). In animals, the emphasis so far has been on establishing whether active rehearsal takes place at all, with much less interest being shown in the subsequent issue of what (if anything) is rehearsed. In examining the evidence for rehearsal processes in animals it will be useful to begin with an operational definition. Such a definition is most easily applied to overt rehearsal, which can be defined as any behaviour during a retention interval which alleviates the forgetting that would otherwise occur. By analogy with some types of rehearsal in humans, such behaviour may be expected to involve the repetition of responses related to the memory task.

In an early study of DMTS in pigeons Blough (1959) observed a tendency for some animals to exhibit superstitious sample-specific behaviour patterns during the retention interval. Such behaviour was associated with reduced forgetting. More recently, Zentall et al. (1978) attempted to encourage sample-specific behaviours in DMTS. During initial training on zero-delay matching pigeons learned to make either identical or different observing responses to the two possible sample stimuli. When subsequently shifted to 1 s DMTS, the animals trained to make sample-specific observing responses performed better. In a second experiment, investigating DMTS at delays of up to 28 s, it was found that retention was directly related to the observed presence or absence of sample-specific behaviour during the retention intervals though the presence of such behaviour was not strongly related to type of initial training. This evidence is strongly suggestive of rehearsal processes in the pigeon, although the design of the task was clearly not particularly successful in bringing such processes under experimental control.

Grant (1981) attempted to bring active maintenance in pigeon DMTS under control by following each sample with either a 'remember' cue signalling that memory would be subsequently tested, or a 'forget' cue signalling that it would not. Memory was occasionally tested on 'forget' trials to allow the differential effectiveness of the cues to be determined. The experiment showed that a 'remember' cue resulted in less forgetting between 3 and 6 s after sample pre-sentation and that the effect of differential cueing was greatest when the cue came early in the retention interval. Such results are consistent with the control of active maintenance rehearsal by the cue. However, it is interesting that a remember cue did not lead to better retention than the absence of any cue at all, and that the effect of cue delay was to improve retention on forget trials leaving performance on remember trials unaffected. These aspects of the results imply that rehearsal is a process that always takes place unless it is specifically inhibited. If generally confirmed, this would be a surprising conclusion. Unfortunately Grant supplied no observations of behaviour during the retention interval, so it is not clear whether overt rehearsal was occurring. Of particular interest is whether overt rehearsal was present in the absence of any cue. Maki and Hegvik (1980) have also shown that a post-sample forget cue decreases DMTS in pigeons, but they too do not report on the animals' retention interval behaviour.

· More recently a detailed study of directed forgetting by Kendrick et al. (1981) has shown that the effect of a forget cue is not contingent upon it controlling differential overt behaviour during the retention interval, a result which the authors interpret as being inconsistent with a rehearsal-based explanation of the phenomenon. However, rather stronger evidence than this would be necessary to rule out rehearsal altogether, and the effects of varying the delay of the forget cue remain a problem for alternative explanations of the phenomenon.

Jans and Catania (1980) claim to have demonstrated overt rehearsal in the pigeon in a delayed response paradigm. Each trial of this task began with the presentation of one of two sample stimuli. There was then a variable delay after which a peck to either a left or a right-hand illuminated key was reinforced, depending on which sample had been presented. In an 'activity' condition a feeder hopper was available during the retention interval and animals operated it for food. In another 'rehearsal' condition the response keys were illuminated during the retention interval but responses to them brought no consequences until the interval was terminated. The results showed slower forgetting in the rehearsal condition. It was also observed that in this condition birds typically pecked at the appropriate illuminated response keys during the delay. In the activity condition, feeding responses appear to have disrupted such mediating behaviour. Although some controls are missing from this study it strongly suggests the occurrence of overt rehearsal during a retention interval and its association with slower forgetting. In early experiments on delayed response, Hunter (1913) observed that rats required to remember which of a spatially arranged set of responses would subsequently be rewarded, oriented their bodies towards the critical location during the retention interval. Such behaviour has been generally regarded by psychologists as an uninteresting way for the animal to solve the problem by avoiding the use of memory. However, the contrast between such behaviour and the rehearsal behaviour observed by Jans and Catania may be more apparent than real, since in order to maintain an oriented posture during a retention interval the animal may have to repeat the appropriate postural response, in some covert form.

It is interesting to note that in so far as rehearsal can be said to occur in the delayed response paradigm, what is being rehearsed appears to correspond to response information. In DMTS on the other hand, the animal's response is determined only at the end of the retention interval, so that any rehearsal that takes place must involve information related to which stimulus was presented initially. Another aspect of the work on overt rehearsal in animals is that all the tasks have required rehearsal of only a single stimulus or response alternative, and that there appear to have been no demonstrations that such rehearsal is sufficient to prevent forgetting altogether. Given such low effectiveness it seems highly unlikely that animals such as pigeons would be able to rehearse much more than a single item of information at a time. Animal rehearsal processes are, therefore, sharply distinguishable from verbal rehearsal in humans in terms of their presumed low capacity and observed ineffectiveness.

Animals may also be able to perform covert rehearsal operations, and there have been claims that such processes can be inferred from performance in some circumstances. Two sources of such evidence are often cited, the more well known being studies of the effect of 'surprise' on learning (see, e.g. Wagner, 1978).

In one study, Wagner et al. (1973) observed that the speed of acquisition of eyeblink conditioning in the rabbit is dependent upon the nature and temporal proximity of additional post-trial events (PTEs). They investigated PTEs which were pairings of each of two previously trained conditioned stimuli (CSs) and either the presence or absence of an unconditioned stimulus (US). These pairings were either 'congruent' with previous training, in which case the CS was followed by the event it had predicted during initial learning, or 'incongruent', in which case it was not. It was found that incongruent or 'surprising' PTEs disrupted acquisition of eyeblink conditioning, the amount of disruption being greater the shorter the interval prior to the PTE. Unsurprising PTEs had no effect on learning. Wagner interpreted these results in terms of a model of animal memory similar to the Atkinson and Shiffrin (1968) model of human memory. The model assumes separate short- and long-term memory stores, with information in STM being rapidly forgotten unless subjected to a limited capacity rehearsal process which also results in long-term learning. Added to this theoretical framework is the further supposition that animals are predisposed to rehearse information about surprising events. Because of the limited capacity of the rehearsal process any such rehearsal is likely to deprive an earlier, temporally adjacent event of rehearsal. Hence the disruptive effect of a surprising PTE on conditioning and its dependence on temporal proximity to the learning trial is explained.

In a further set of studies of eyeblink conditioning in rabbits, Terry and Wagner (1975) attempted to assess memory for a surprising event directly rather than via its effect on temporally adjacent learning. In preliminary training on a 'preparatory-releaser' task, animals learned to respond to a CS whenever it was preceded by a preparatory US. Performance declined with increasing delay of the CS, a trend which Terry and Wagner ascribed to forgetting the presentation of the US. In an interim phase, animals were given training on two new CSs, each of which reliably signalled the ensuing presence or absence of the US. Finally, animals were returned to the original preparatory releaser paradigm with the US made either surprising or expected according to whether it was preceded by the positive or negative CS of the interim phase. The results showed a more gradual decline in performance as a function of delay of the releaser CS for surprising preparatory USs, a result consistent with Wagner's suggestion that surprising stimuli receive preferential rehearsal. Extending this result, Maki (1979) manipulated the surprisingness of the sample stimulus using a similar technique in a DMTS task involving pigeons and found more accurate matching performance following surprising samples. However, more recent work has suggested that surprise may not be the critical factor determining performance in these situations.

Colwill and Dickinson (1980a) gave pigeons initial training in a preparatory-releaser task using a preparatory US that was always signalled by a preceding stimulus. In a second group of animals the US was never signalled, following Terry and Wagner. When the surprisingness of the preparatory US was subsequently manipulated, responding to the releaser was affected only in the group initially trained with an unsignalled US. The signalled group showed no effect of surprise. In another study, Colwill and Dickinson (1980b) obtained the effect of surprise on DMTS observed by Maki but showed that it too disappeared if the sample stimulus was always preceded by a signal in initial training. Such results present problems for Wagner's rehearsal hypothesis and Colwill and Dickinson advance an alternative explanation of their results in terms of stimulus generalization decrement. Thus, although Wagner's theory of rehearsal in animal short-term memory remains one of the most comprehensive attempts to relate ideas about animal and human memory processes, there are at present no compelling reasons for accepting it.

Another source of evidence that has been linked with rehearsal processes is the existence of primacy in memory for a list of items: the tendency for items early in the list to be remembered better than items from middle positions. Human memory for lists of verbal items typically shows such an effect and Rundus (1971) has shown that in free recall primacy is correlated with the amount of overt rehearsal allocated to individual items. Given that human rehearsal capacity for verbal materials appears to be rather greater than for visual materials (see Sections 5.2.1 and 5.2.2), it is interesting to note that primacy is typically absent in human memory for sequences of visual items that cannot be readily recoded verbally (Broadbent & Broadbent, 1981; Hines, 1975; Phillips & Christie 1977a; Potter & Levy, 1969; Shaffer & Shiffrin, 1972; Weaver & Stanny, 1978).

In species such as pigeons, rats and dolphins, memory for lists of items shows recency but no sign of primacy (Macphail, 1980; Roberts & Smythe, 1979; Thompson & Herman, 1977). However, primacy has been observed in the rhesus monkey. Sands and Wright (1980) presented a single monkey with lists of photographs of familiar objects, each list being followed immediately by a single probe item which was either 'old', an item from the list, or 'new'. The animal was differentially rewarded for correctly discriminating the two types of recognition probe. Performance was extremely good on this task, averaging 80% correct on 10-item lists. A significant one-item primacy effect was observed, in addition to the expected recency effect. Sands and Wright also presented similar data for a single human control subject. While they present us with an intriguing comparison between man and ape, an interpretation in terms of rehearsal processes is not a necessary conclusion, as Sands and Wright themselves point out. In human memory, primacy has been attributed to the use of distinctive retrieval cues (Tulving, 1968) or the build-up of within-list proactive interference (Postman & Phillips, 1965), as alternatives to the idea of differential rehearsal. In the absence of evidence ruling out such possible interpretations, or direct evidence in favour of rehearsal, the existence of primacy in animal memory can probably tell us very little. Furthermore, it is not clear how replicable the phenomenon of primacy will prove to be since Gaffan and Weiskranz (1980) failed to observe it in rhesus monkeys using a slightly different procedure from Sands and Wright.

In conclusion, studies of behaviour during the retention interval of DMTS and delay of reinforcement tasks provide the clearest support for the suggestion that overt rehearsal associated with improved memory does occur in animals. Other sources of evidence such as the shape of serial position curves in list memory and effects of surprise on learning are less direct and can be given alternative explanations.

5.3.2 Recency Effects

The empirical evidence for two separate components in verbal free recall formed an important part of the evidence for a two-store theory of human memory. Current interpretations of the recency effect in man distinguish it from other short-term memory phenomena such as memory span and suggest that it reflects either a separate input store playing a role in language comprehension, or the application of a general, non-linguistic ordinal retrieval strategy (see Section 5.2).

One common technique for assessing recency effects in animals is to present the animal with a list of stimuli followed by a single probe to which it must make a discriminative response according to whether the probe item was included in the list. This method shows there is a recency effect in rhesus monkeys' memories for lists of photographs of familiar objects (Sands & Wright, 1980), and sequences of spatial locations and colours (Gaffan, 1977). Gaffan and

Weiskranz (1980) also obtained a recency effect in rhesus monkeys when memory for each item in a list of junk objects was tested by a two-alternative simultaneous dicrimination. In the dolphin, the more usual single probe technique reveals a recency effect in memory for lists of sounds which extends over the final four items (Thompson & Herman, 1977). In pigeons, performance is typically poor, but the probe technique shows a shallow recency effect extending throughout the list in memory for sequences of from three to five colours (Macphail, 1980). Another method is to present the animal with a list of S–R pairs followed by a single probe stimulus drawn from one of the pairs. The animal's task is to produce the previously paired response, a procedure more analogous to recall than recognition. It reveals a recency effect when pigeons are required to remember lists of three S–R pairs (Shimp & Moffit, 1977). In a modification of the technique in which all the S–R pairs are tested on any given trial, Roberts and Smythe (1979) found a recency effect extending over up to seven items in memory in rats.

There is thus ample evidence that recency occurs in memory for lists of items or associations in animals across a range of species and testing conditions. Unfortunately, most studies have taken the form of simple demonstrations of the phenomenon. Some have attempted to explore the role of factors such as decay and interference in determining it but as yet there is too little work to support firm conclusions. There appear to have been virtually no attempts to establish whether the recency effect reflects a separable component of animal memory, distinguishable from memory for pre-recency items in a list. If there is any parallel to be drawn with recency in human memory, it should be possible to find experimental variables which affect memory for recency items but not for earlier items. There are numerous methodological problems in performing such studies with animals because the range of list lengths which avoid floor effects may well be such as to show recency extending throughout the whole list. Nevertheless Gaffan and Weiskranz (1980) have shown that in the rhesus monkey, enhanced recognition memory for the final item in a five-item list is contingent upon testing memory after a short delay (an unfilled post-list delay of 10 s). A longer unfilled delay of 70 s, or a 20 s delay filled by testing items from earlier in the list abolishes the recency advantage for the final item but leaves recall of earlier items unaffected. This points to a separable one-item recency component in the rhesus monkey. However, the dissociation would only be fully convincing if some other variable (for example, rate of presentation) could be shown to affect recall of all list items except the last. Other incomplete and only suggestive evidence comes from the observation that the recency effect is independent of list length in dolphins (Thompson & Herman, 1977) and in rats (Roberts & Smythe, 1979). Though this parallels the evidence from human short-term retention of lists of either verbal or visual materials (Postman & Phillips, 1965; Phillips & Christie, 1977a), there is as yet no complementary evidence to show that list length affects recall of pre-recency items. Thus the absence of appropriate experimentation, rather than any evidence pointing to the contrary, means that it is unclear whether recency in animal memory should be taken as reflecting a separate storage component.

5.3.3 Capacity Limitations

In human short-term memory the 'classic' capacity limitation is that of verbal memory span, the inability to repeat back sequences of more than a small number of items immediately after presentation. However, there are in addition other short-term memory capacities which can be usefully distinguished from the span, such as the limited extent of the recency component in immediate free recall of lists of verbal items and the recency component in visual short-term memory. These empirically separable capacities may be accounted for by a range of alternative theoretical assumptions some of which have been described earlier in this chapter.

In the case of animal short-term retention, there is not yet a sufficiently large body of evidence to indicate clearly even the empirical limitations on performance, let alone give support to particular theoretical interpretations. For instance, in the previous section it was concluded that more evidence is needed in order to ascertain whether or not the recency effect in animal memory for lists of items reflects a separable short-term memory process. It would, therefore, be premature to select any one particular measure, such as the number of items contributing to the recency effect as an indicator of the capacity of such a process. The Gaffan and Weiskranz (1980) results on recency in the rhesus monkey nicely illustrates this point since recency was found to extend through all five items in a five-item list, and yet the effect of a post-list delay was apparently to lower recall of only the final item. Nevertheless it is perhaps plausible to take the extent of the recency effect as setting an upper bound on the capacity of any underlying short-term holding mechanism associated with it, in which case the evidence from all species studied suggests a capacity of at most a few items. Interestingly, such a limitation is of roughly the same order of magnitude as the various alternative human short-term memory capacities when these are also estimated in terms of numbers of items. The difference between humans and the animals studied is not so great in this respect.

The delayed matching to sample task may also have implications concerning the capacity of rehearsal processes and seems to suggest that pigeons' rehearsal capacity is sharply limited (see Section 5.3.1). However, it remains to be seen whether this conclusion holds up in the light of further evidence, and whether animal rehearsal capacity is empirically distinguishable from any capacity that may be found to underlie recency effects.

Before closing the discussion of capacity limitations in animal short-term memory it is necessary to consider Olton's (1978) claim that rats have an exceptionally high span for spatial information, corresponding to as many as 'at least 17 items and probably 25'. This claim stands in complete contrast to the picture so far presented. How may the discrepancy be resolved?

It appears that methodological factors may be important. Olton's technique is to allow a rat to explore a radial maze, each arm of which is baited with a hidden food pellet. The measure of memory is the degree to which the animal optimizes his search of the maze, as given by the probability of choosing a previously unentered arm on each successive choice. Olton *et al.* (1977) found a smooth decline in this measure across successive choices in a 17-arm maze but performance was very high and was still above chance even on the seventeenth choice. Unfortunately, it is far from clear how chance levels of performance should be calculated for this situation, in view of the observation (Olton, 1978) that after leaving an arm, rats display a strong tendency to turn in a consistent direction and enter an arm that is near to them. Such a simple response strategy alone could lead to remarkably high levels of performance, and the exceptional difficulty of allowing for such complexities mars any unambiguous interpretation of the maze exploration paradigm in terms of memory processes. This difficulty is illustrated by studies of the effect of a forced interruption between the fourth and fifth choices in the exploration of an eight-arm maze. Maki *et al.* (1979) found that interruptions lasting between 15 s and 2 min filled with a variety of activities had no effect on performance even if the activity was exploration of another radial maze. Even more striking is Beatty and Shavalia's (1980) observation that a 4 h delay during which the rat ran a second identical maze in another room produced no interference. If such evidence is taken to imply an extraordinary spatial memory capacity in rats then the system involved is clearly not a short-term memory system. On the other hand, the extreme resistance of performance to interference could be taken to confirm the suspicion that non-memory factors are heavily involved in performance in this task. Either way, the results of maze exploration studies in rats seem to have no very clear implications for the capacity of specifically short-term memory systems.

5.3.4   Coding

The question of the coding of information in human memory has played an important role in distinguishing between subsystems whereas techniques for investigating coding in animal memory are only just beginning to emerge. Thus there appear to have been no systematic attempts to investigate whether short-term retention by animals is characterized by use of a particular type of coding which differentiates it from long-term retention. It is not even clear whether some delayed matching tasks are tests of sensory memory or representational memory. For example, the recency effect found in the bottle-nosed dolphin's recognition memory for lists of sounds (Thompson & Herman, 1977) might reflect auditory sensory memory, and recency in the rhesus monkey's recognition memory for lists of junk objects (Gaffan & Weiskranz, 1980) could reflect visual sensory storage. In a study of the effect of stimulus modality in short-term memory in the rat, Wallace *et al.* (1980) found that auditory and visual stimuli gave equally good performance at zero delay, but there was an auditory advantage after a delay of a few seconds. This result parallels a difference which is normally found in human short-term memory and commonly interpreted in terms of the relative durability of auditory and visual sensory storage. However, Wallace *et al.* observed the modality effect in a conditional DMTS task, in which a symbolic rule rather than physical identity determines which matching stimulus will be reinforced. Reliance upon sensory memory under these circumstances, while logically possible, would appear to be unlikely. Honig (1978) has investigated this issue in a related paradigm in which a pigeon is presented with one of two differentially reinforced sample stimuli and is then required to make a delayed conditional response after a variable retention interval. In general, performance in this task was quite good and showed rather slower forgetting than that typical of the conventional DMTS procedure. In one of Honig's investigations, he found that pigeons showed good transfer when the sample stimuli were changed to a new pair which had been differentially reinforced during initial pre-training, but poor transfer if previous reinforcement had not been differential. Honig concluded that pigeons were encoding the associative value of the sample stimulus or responses made to it during presentation, rather than its physical appearance. To account for this and other findings he suggested that the pigeon was remembering an 'instruction' to respond subsequently in a particular way.

Support for this idea comes from an elaborate study of conditional DMTS in pigeons in which there were three sample and three comparison stimuli and where following an incorrect first matching response, the animal was allowed to make a second choice between the two remaining comparison stimuli (Roitblatt, 1980). Similarity among the set of sample stimuli (e.g. colours) was made orthogonal to similarity among the comparison stimuli (e.g. line orientations), so that second choices could be analysed separately in terms of effects of similarity along each dimension. The results showed that animals were more sensitive to similarity among the comparison stimuli than among the sample stimuli, particularly at long retention intervals. This result suggests that animals were remembering a representation of the physical appearance of the comparison stimulus rather than the sample, consistent with Honig's general notion of instructional memory. However, it remains to be seen whether this particularly interesting finding can be replicated.

What further evidence there is on coding in animal short-term memory suggests that Honig's concept of an instruction may need to be elaborated in greater detail in order to cope with differences across tasks. For example, it will be recalled that in tasks where a discriminative stimulus signals that reinforcement will be given for a particular response after a delay, pigeons tend to repeat the appropriate response during the delay (Jans & Catania, 1980). In this case the 'instruction' is presumably a tendency to respond in a particular way, rather than a stimulus that must subsequently be chosen. In conventional DMTS it is interesting to note that where overt rehearsal has been observed it has consisted of sample-specific orienting responses (Zentall *et al.*, 1978). Unfortunately, because of the nature of the paradigm it is not possible to say whether this corresponds to an instruction to orient to the appropriate comparison stimulus subsequently or whether it reflects maintenance of a physical representation of the initial stimulus.

In general, the question of 'what is remembered' in animal short-term memory is clearly only just beginning to be investigated. Empirical techniques which will distinguish between sensory, symbolic and motor representations in memory are in urgent need of development, and are yet to be applied to the question of distinguishing between short- and long-term memory systems in animals.

5.4 Convergence or Divergence between Short-Term Memory in Animals and Humans?

Although it should be borne in mind that only selected aspects of research into human and animal short-term memory have been discussed here, it is clear that, at least to some extent, the two domains share the use of common information processing concepts such as capacity, coding and rehearsal. However, despite this, the human and animal researchers seem to have been concerned with rather different sorts of question. Thus the present chapter has emphasized attempts to specify separate subsystems in human short-term memory in terms of such properties as their capacity, coding and control processes. This approach stems from the more general view that these subsystems perform a range of specific temporary storage functions in a common working memory system occupying a central role in human cognition (Hitch, 1980). One implication of this view is that subsystems can be distinguished in terms of what purpose they serve in normal cognition as well as by their basic structure. In contrast, the animal research reported here has not been concerned with the structure of short-term memory, which is typically treated either as an operationally defined concept tied to particular experimental procedures such as delayed matching, or as a unitary storage resource associated with a single type of rehearsal process (e.g. Wagner, 1978). Another distinction is that the question of the function of short-term memory in animals has yet to be systematically explored. The most common assumption is that short-term memory is essential for long-term learning (e.g. Shimp, 1978; Wagner, 1978), a view which relates directly to the Atkinson and Shiffrin (1968) model of human memory. This idea is narrow in comparison with the range of functions suggested for human working memory, and has in any case been somewhat discredited by human neuropsychological evidence (Shallice & Warrington, 1970). Honig (1978) has suggested that animals use short-term memory to maintain instructions for action over short intervals without the implication of transfer to long-term storage, an idea which comes closer to the concept of human working memory but which has yet to be fully developed.

The lack of attention to questions of structure and function within animal short-term memory is most probably merely a reflection of the relatively short time for which the topic has been studied when compared with human short-term memory. Indeed it has already been observed that there appears to be no body of evidence comparable to that for humans on the broader issue of establishing criteria for distinguishing short-term memory from various other forms of memory in animals such as sensory memory or long-term memory. Such distinctions are of course logically prior to any attempt to fractionate short-term memory into separate subsystems. Yet another contributor to the divergence between the animal and human research may be differences in techniques and methodological problems. However, this has not been clearly demonstrated and indeed it can be argued that many techniques are actually common to both fields. Regardless of their origins, the different emphases in animal and human short-term memory research make it at best difficult, and at worst inappropriate, to try to make detailed comparisons. The remainder of this section is therefore a discussion of selected aspects of animal short-term memory in the light of what is known about humans, with particular emphasis on their possible functional significance. Some human short-term memory subsystems are assumed to have their primary roles in the comprehension and production of spoken language, a means of communication not available to animals. Should one therefore expect such systems to be absent altogether in animals, or present in a more primitive, emergent form serving a related function? Might they perhaps even be present in primitive form and serving some quite different species-specific function? On the other hand, should one expect at least some animals to possess direct analogues of human visual short-term memory, a non-linguistic system? More generally, given the relationship between short-term memory performance and general intelligence in humans should one expect a similar relationship to hold across species? Such questions seem to provide an interesting and meaningful framework within which to discuss human and animal short-term memory. Unfortunately, at present we know very little about how they should be answered, as will be evident in what follows.

5.4.1 Rehearsal

As has been seen, human rehearsal processes are not all of one type. In particular, visual and verbal rehearsal appear to be mediated by different systems. Thus, human visualization appears to be limited to one or perhaps two visual patterns whereas verbal rehearsal is limited to the longer number of verbal responses that can be articulated within about 2 s. It has been suggested that visualization does not involve transfer to long-term memory (Avons & Phillips, 1980) and that verbal rehearsal can serve both an elaborative and a pure maintenance role (Craik & Watkins, 1973) though the evidence on these points is not decisive. Research on animal memory has been mainly concerned with demonstrating that animals such as pigeons can and do rehearse, for which there appears to be reasonably good evidence. It seems likely that animals can rehearse different types of experimenter-defined information, such as sample-specific behaviour in delayed matching to sample and response-specific behaviour in delayed response. However, it is not clear whether different rehearsal systems are implicated in these cases. Animal rehearsal seems to serve a maintenance function, and even with only a single item performance it is not associated with perfect memory, suggesting a low capacity. Empirically, therefore, animal rehearsal is more comparable with human visualization than with human articulatory rehearsal. This is, of course, compatible with the general consideration that animals are in any case not expected to have language production mechanisms. However, a counter-argument is that human visualization should not be linked with response processes. It does not involve response repetition whereas overt animal rehearsal and human articulatory rehearsal both clearly do. In this case one might be led to conclude that animal rehearsal involves a motoric system which appears in a more highly developed form specific to speech production in humans. These two alternatives are radically different, yet there seem to be no good grounds at present for deciding between them. In accordance with the general theme of this discussion, a clearer idea of the functions of animal rehearsal in general and of human visualization processes seems called for before meaningful and detailed comparisons can be made between animals and humans.

5.4.2 Recency

The phenomenon of recency in memory for sequences of items or events is common to a range of animal species including humans. Although this might be taken as suggesting that recency may reflect a single very general underlying process, the phenomenon in humans seems to be multiply determined, in which case it may also involve different processes in different species. Work on the rhesus monkey suggests that memory for the most recent item in a visual list is sensitive to a post-list delay. Such an effect is comparable with recency attributable to visualization in human short-term memory, but more convergent evidence would be required to establish the visual nature of the effect in the rhesus monkey. Indeed a major problem in interpreting recency effects in animal memory in relation to human memory is the general absence of evidence about the nature of such effects in animals. In some instances, even a sensory storage locus of the effect cannot be confidently ruled out. However, it is perhaps worth stating that one might expect recency based on the use of ordinal or temporal retrieval cues to be common to animals and humans. Such a retrieval strategy gives access to the last event, or few events, of a particular class and would seem to be well suited to the need for any animal to keep track of recent events. On the other hand short-term recency of the type found in verbal free recall in humans presents a different case. It would not be expected to have a direct analogue in animals on the grounds that its function is specific to language comprehension. However, as in the case of the articulatory system, one might expect to find evidence of an emergent analogue of a verbal input store in animal species with highly developed forms of communication. The existence of an auditory recency effect in dolphins is particularly interesting in this respect, though it is not yet possible to distinguish sensory and post-categorical explanations of the effect.

5.4.3 Coding

There appear to have been few attempts to investigate the question of coding of information in animal short-term memory. Work on humans has made extensive use of distinctions between auditory, phonological, articulatory and visuospatial codes in short-term memory, some of which have been linked with particular subsystems. The most sophisticated of these distinctions apply to the coding of linguistic information and are not directly applicable to animals. Indeed, ideas about ways in which an animal might encode information are notable for their general absence. The general assumption of coding in terms of stimulus-response associations fails to help since it does not distinguish between alternative ways in which stimuli, responses and their associations might be represented. A distinction between sensory and symbolic representations of stimulus information is obviously necessary in making any comparisons between human and animal short-term memory. Though this distinction is unfortunately only rarely made in research on animals, Honig (1978) used it in his studies of delayed conditional matching in the pigeons and showed that animals remembered the more abstract representation of an 'instruction' rather than a physical trace of the sample stimulus. Other studies of delayed conditional matching suggest that such an instruction may consist of a representation of the correct comparison stimulus. On the other hand studies of overt rehearsal in simpler tasks such as delayed matching to sample and delayed response suggest that animals encode and remember response information. Thus, at this stage it is not yet clear whether animal short-term memory can be characterized by the use of any particular form of coding, or indeed precisely what are the coding options. One might expect sensory and motor codes to share some properties across species, since many problems of perception and action are in common. In contrast, large differences would be expected in terms of symbolic coding since it is presumably just here that human linguistic and intellectual achievement becomes relevant. Errors and confusions in memory in the human case have provided a particularly rich source of evidence about the nature of coding. It seems likely that the study of errors could provide equally interesting information about coding in animal short-term memory.

5.4.4 Conclusion

The evidence reviewed in this chapter suggests that animal short-term memory exhibits some of the phenomena of human short-term memory including rapid forgetting, recency effects and the use of rehearsal to alleviate forgetting. However, an important problem for comparing animal and human short-term memory is that short-term memory in animals has yet to be clearly distinguished from other forms of memory. Research on humans typically accepts this point and is exploring subsequent issues. For example, the concept of working memory in humans involves the fractionation of short-term memory systems, and the identification of their roles in different aspects of cognition. It is suggested that the question of the purpose of short-term memory, *what is it for?*, is just as important in animals as in humans and may indeed be crucial in establishing intelligible relationships between human and animal short-term memory.

Acknowledgements

I am very grateful to Dr. Euan Macphail for making available the manuscript of his forthcoming book, *Brain and Intelligence in Vertebrates* (Clarendon Press, Oxford, 1982), which stimulated some of the ideas in this chapter. I also thank Dr. Andrew Mayes for many hours of useful discussion.

References

ATKINSON, R.C. and SHIFFRIN, R.M. (1968) Human memory: a proposed system and its control processes. In: K.W. SPENCE and J.T. SPENCE (Eds.) *The Psychology of Learning and Motivation: Advances in Research and Theory, Vol. 2.* Academic Press, New York.

AVONS, S.E. and PHILLIPS, W.A. (1980) Visualization and memorization as a function of display time and poststimulus processing time. *Journal of Experimental Psychology: Human Learning and Memory,* **6**, 407–420.

BADDELEY, A.D. (1966) Short-term memory for word sequences as a function of acoustic, semantic and formal similarity. *Quarterly Journal of Experimental Psychology,* **18**, 362–365.

BADDELEY, A.D. (1976) *The Psychology of Memory.* Basic Books, New York.

BADDELEY, A.D. GRANT, S. WIGHT, E. and THOMSON, N. (1975a) Imagery and visual working memory. In: P.M. RABBITT and S. DORNIC (Eds.) *Attention and Performance, V.* Academic Press, London.

BADDELEY, A.D. and HITCH, G.J. (1974) Working memory. In: G.H. BOWER (Ed.) *The Psychology of Learning and Motivation: Advances in Research and Theory, Vol. 8.* Academic Press, New York.

BADDELEY, A.D. and HITCH, G.J. (1977) Recency re-examined. In: S. DORNIC (Ed.) *Attention and Performance, IV.* Academic Press, New York.

BADDELEY, A.D. and LIEBERMAN, K. (1980) Spatial working memory. In: R. NICKERSON (Ed.) *Attention and Performance, VIII.* Erlbaum, Hillsdale, New Jersey.

BADDELEY, A.D. THOMSON, N. and BUCHANAN, M. (1975b) Word-length and the structure of short-term memory. *Journal of Verbal Learning and Verbal Behavior,* **14**, 575–589.

BADDELEY, A.D. and WARRINGTON, E.K. (1970) Amnesia and the distinction between long- and short-term memory. *Journal of Verbal Learning and Verbal Behavior*, **9**, 176–189.

BEATTY, W.W. and SHAVALIA, D.A. (1980) Rat spatial memory: Resistance to retroactive interference at long retention intervals. *Animal Learning and Behavior*, **8**, 550–552.

BJORK, R.A. and WHITTEN, W.B. (1974) Recency-sensitive retrieval processes in long-term free recall. *Cognitive Psychology*, **2**, 99–116.

BLOUGH, D.S. (1959) Delayed matching in the pigeon. *Journal of the Experimental Analysis of Behavior*, **2**, 151–160.

BROADBENT, D.E. and BROADBENT, M.H.P. (1981) Recency effects in visual memory. *Quarterly Journal of Experimental Psychology*, **33A**. 1–15.

BYRNE, B. and ARNOLD, L. (1981) Dissociation of the recency effect and immediate memory span: Evidence from beginning readers. *British Journal of Psychology*, **4**, 161–169.

COLWILL, R.M. and DICKINSON, A. (1980a) Short-term retention of 'surprising' events by pigeons. *Quarterly Journal of Experimental Psychology*, **32**, 539–556.

COLWILL, R.M. and DICKINSON, A. (1980b) Short-term retention of 'surprising' events following different training conditions. *Animal Learning and Behavior*, **8**, 561–566.

CONRAD, R. and HULL, A.J. (1964) Information, acoustic confusion and memory span. *British Journal of Psychology*, **55**, 429–432.

CRAIK, F.I.M. (1968a) Two components in free recall. *Journal of Verbal Learning and Verbal Behavior*, **7**, 996–1004.

CRAIK, F.I.M. (1968b) Types of error in free recall. *Psychonomic Science*, **10**, 353–354.

CRAIK, F.I.M. and LEVY, B.A. (1970) Semantic and acoustic confusion in primary memory. *Journal of Experimental Psychology*, **86**, 77–82.

CRAIK, F.I.M. and LOCKHART, R.S. (1972) Levels of processing: a framework for memory research. *Journal of Verbal Learning and Verbal Behavior*, **11**, 671–684.

CRAIK, F.I.M. and WATKINS, M.J. (1973) The role of rehearsal in short-term memory. *Journal of Verbal Learning and Verbal Behavior*, **12**, 599–607.

D'AMATO, M.R. (1973) Delayed matching and short-term memory in monkeys. In: G.H. BOWER (Ed.) *The Psychology of Learning and Motivation: Advances in Research and Theory, Vol. 7.* Academic Press, New York.

DE RENZI, E. and NICHELLI, P. (1975) Verbal and non-verbal short-term memory impairment following hemispheric damage. *Cortex*, **11**, 341–354.

DE RENZI, E. and VIGNOLO, L.A. (1962) The Token Test: A sensitive test to detect receptive disturbances in aphasics. *Brain*, **85**, 665–678.

DRACHMAN, D.A. and ARBIT, J. (1966) Memory and the hippocampal complex, II. *Archives of Neurology*, **15**, 52–61.

ELLIS, A.W. (1980) Errors in speech and short-term memory: The effects of phonemic similarity and syllable position. *Journal of Verbal Learning and Verbal Behavior*, **19**, 624–634.

GAFFAN, D. (1977) Recognition memory after short retention intervals in fornix-transected monkeys. *Quarterly Journal of Experimental Psychology*, **29**, 577–588.

GAFFAN, D. and WEISKRANZ, L. (1980) Recency effects and lesion effects in delayed non-matching to randomly baited samples by monkeys. *Brain Research*, **196**, 373–386.

GLANZER, M. (1972) Storage mechanisms in recall. In: G.H. BOWER (Ed.) *The Psychology of Learning and Motivation: Advances in Research and Theory, Vol. 5.* Academic Press, New York.

GLANZER, M. and CUNITZ, A.R. (1966) Two storage mechanisms in free recall. *Journal of Verbal Learning and Verbal Behavior*, **5**, 351–360.

GLANZER, M., GIANUTSOS, R. and DUBIN, S. (1969) The removal of items from short-term storage. *Journal of Verbal Learning and Verbal Behavior*, **8**, 435–437.

GLANZER, M., KOPENAAL, L. and NELSON, R. (1972) Effects of relations between words on short-term storage and long-term storage. *Journal of Verbal Learning and Verbal Behavior*, **11**, 403–416.

GRANT, D.S. (1975) Proactive interference in pigeon short-term memory. *Journal of Experimental Psychology: Animal Behavior Processes*, **1**, 207–220.

GRANT, D.S. (1981) Stimulus control of information processing in pigeon short-term memory. *Learning and Motivation*, **12**, 19–39.

GRANT, D.S. and ROBERTS, W.A. (1976) Sources of retroactive inhibition in pigeon short-term memory. *Journal of Experimental Psychology: Animal Behavior Processes*, **2**, 1–16.

HINES, D. (1975) Immediate and delayed recognition of sequentially presented random shapes. *Journal of Experimental Psychology: Human Learning and Memory*, **1**, 634–639.

HITCH, G.J. (1980) Developing the concept of working memory. In: G. CLAXTON (Ed.) *Cognitive Psychology: New Directions*. Routledge & Kegan Paul, London.

HITCH, G.J. and BADDELEY, A.D. (1978) Working memory and information processing. In: *Cognitive Psychology, Course No. D303*. Open University Press, Milton Keynes.

HONIG, W.K. (1978) Studies of working memory in the pigeon. In: S.H. HULSE, H. FOWLER and W.K. HONIG (Eds.) *Cognitive Processes in Animal Behavior*. Erlbaum, Hillsdale, New Jersey.

HUNTER, W.S. (1913) The delayed reaction in animals and children. *Behavior Monographs, 2, No. 6*.

JANS, J.E. and CATANIA, A.C. (1980) Short-term remembering of discriminative stimuli in pigeons. *Journal of the Experimental Analysis of Behavior*, **34**, 177–183.

JARRARD, L.E. and MOISE, S.L. (1973) Short-term memory in the monkey. In: L.E. JARRARD (Ed.) *Cognitive Processes of Nonhuman Primates*. Academic Press, New York.

JARVELLA, R.J. (1978) Immediate memory in discourse processing. In: G.H. BOWER (Ed.) *The Psychology of Learning and Motivation: Advances in Research and Theory, Vol. 12*. Academic Press, New York.

KENDRICK, D.F., RILLING, M. and STONEBRAKER, T.B. (1981) Stimulus control of delayed matching in pigeons: directed forgetting. *Journal of the Experimental Analysis of Behavior*, **36**, 241–251.

MACPHAIL, E.M. (1980) Short-term visual recognition memory in pigeons. *Quarterly Journal of Experimental Psychology*, **32**, 521–538.

MAKI, W.S. (1979) Pigeons' short-term memories for surprising vs. expected reinforcement and nonreinforcement. *Animal Learning and Behavior*, **7**, 31–37.

MAKI, W.S.. BROKOFSKY, S. and BERG, B. (1979) Spatial memory in rats: Resistance to retroactive interference. *Animal Learning and Behavior*, **7**, 25–30.

MAKI, W.S. and HEGVIK, D.K. (1980) Directed forgetting in pigeons. *Animal Learning and Behavior*, **8**, 567–574.

MAKI, W.S., MOE, J.C. and BIERLEY, C.M. (1977) Short-term memory for stimuli, responses and reinforcers. *Journal of Experimental Psychology: Animal Behavior Processes*. **3**, 156–177.

MARTIN, M. (1978) Assessment of individual variation in memory ability. In: M.M. GRUNEBERG, P.E. MORRIS and R.N. SYKES (Eds.) *Practical Aspects of Memory*. Academic Press, New York.

MILLER, G.A. (1956) The magical number seven plus or minus two. *Psychological Review*, **63**, 81–97.

MURRAY, D.J. (1968) Articulation and acoustic confusability in short-term memory. *Journal of Experimental Psychology*, **78**, 679–684.

OLTON, D.S. (1978) Characteristics of spatial memory. In: S.H. HULSE, H. FOWLER, and W.K. HONIG, (Eds.) *Cognitive Processes in Animal Behavior*. Erlbaum, Hillsdale, New Jersey.

OLTON, D.S., COLLISON, C. and WERZ, M. (1977) Spatial memory and radial arm maze performance of rats. *Learning and Motivation*, **8**, 289–314.

PARKS, T.E., KROLL, N.E.A., SALZBERG, P.M. and PARKINSON, S.R. (1972) Persistence of visual memory as indicated by decision time in a matching task. *Journal of Experimental Psychology*, **92**, 437–438.

PHILLIPS, W.A. (1974) On the distinction between sensory storage and short-term visual memory. *Perception and Psychophysics*, **16**, 283–290.

PHILLIPS, W.A. and CHRISTIE, D.F.M. (1977a) Components of visual memory. *Quarterly Journal of Experimental Psychology*, **29**, 117–133.

PHILLIPS, W.A. and CHRISTIE, D.F.M. (1977b) Interference with visualization. *Quarterly Journal of Experimental Psychology*, **29**, 637–650.

POSNER, M.I., BOIES, S.J., EICHELMAN, W.H. and TAYLOR, R.L. (1969) Retention of visual and name codes of single letters. *Journal of Experimental Psychology Monograph*, **79** (1, Pt. 2).

POSNER, M.I. and KEELE, S.W. (1967) Decay of information from a single letter. *Science*, **158**, 137–139.

POSTMAN, L. and PHILLIPS, L.W. (1965) Short-term temporal changes in free recall. *Quarterly Journal of Experimental Psychology*, **17**, 132–138.

POTTER, M.C. and LEVY, E.I. (1969) Recognition memory for a rapid sequence of pictures. *Journal of Experimental Psychology*, **81**, 10–15.

RICHARDSON, J.T.E. and BADDELEY, A.D. (1975) The effect of articulatory suppression in free recall. *Journal of Verbal Learning and Verbal Behavior*, **14**, 623–629.

ROBERTS, W.A. (1972) Short-term memory in the pigeon: Effects of repetition and spacing. *Journal of Experimental Psychology*, **94**, 74–83.

ROBERTS, W.A. and GRANT, D.S. (1974) Short-term memory in the pigeon with presentation time precisely controlled. *Learning and Motivation*, **5**, 393–408.

ROBERTS, W.A. and GRANT, D.S. (1976) Studies in short-term memory in the pigeon using the delayed matching-to-sample procedure. In: D.L. MEDIN, W.A. ROBERTS and R.T. DAVIS, (Eds.) *Processes of Animal Memory*. Erlbaum, Hillsdale, New Jersey.

ROBERTS, W.A. and SMYTHE, W.E. (1979) Memory for lists of spatial events in the rat. *Learning and Motivation*, **10**, 313–336.

ROITBLATT, H.L. (1980) Codes and coding processes in pigeon short-term memory. *Animal Learning and Behavior*, **8**, 341–351.

RUNDUS, D. (1971) Analysis of rehearsal effects in free recall. *Journal of Experimental Psychology*, **89**, 63–67.

SAFFRAN, E.M. and MARIN, O.S.M. (1975) Immediate memory for word lists and sentences in a patient with deficient auditory short-term memory. *Brain and Language*, **2**, 420–433.

SANDS, S.F. and WRIGHT, A.A. (1980) Primate memory: Retention of serial list items by a rhesus monkey. *Science*, **209**, 238–240.

SHAFFER, W.O. and SHIFFRIN, R.M. (1972) Rehearsal and storage of visual information. *Journal of Experimental Psychology*, **92**, 292–296.

SHALLICE, T. (1975) On the contents of primary memory. In: P.M.A. RABBITT and S. DORNIC (Eds.) *Attention and Performance V*. Academic Press, London.

SHALLICE, T. (1979) Neuropsychological research and the fractionation of memory systems. In: L. NILSSON (Ed.) *Perspectives in Memory Research*. Erlbaum, Hillsdale, New Jersey.

SHALLICE, T. and BUTTERWORTH, B.B. (1977) Short-term memory impairment and spontaneous speech. *Neuropsychologia*, **13**, 729–736.

SHALLICE, T. and WARRINGTON, E.K. (1970) Independent functioning of the verbal memory stores: A neuropsychological study. *Quarterly Journal of Experimental Psychology*, **22**, 261–273.

SHALLICE, T. and WARRINGTON, E.K. (1974) The dissociation between short-term retention of meaningful sounds and verbal material. *Neuropsychologia*, **12**, 553–555.

SHALLICE, T. and WARRINGTON, E.K. (1977) Auditory–verbal short-term memory impairment and conduction aphasia. *Brain and Language*, **4**, 479–491.

SHIFFRIN, R.M. (1975) Short-term store: The basis for a memory system. In: F. RESTLE, R.M. SHIFFRIN, N.J. CASTELLAN, H.R. LINDMAN and D.B. PISONI (Eds.) *Cognitive Theory*. Erlbaum, Hillsdale, New Jersey.

SHIMP, C.P. (1978) Memory, temporal discrimination, and learned structure in behaviour. In: G.H. BOWER (Ed.) *The Psychology of Learning and Motivation: Advances in Research and Theory, Vol. 12.* Academic Press, New York.

SHIMP, C.P. and MOFFITT, M. (1977) Short-term memory in the pigeon: Delayed-pair-comparison procedures and some results. *Journal of the Experimental Analysis of Behavior*, **28**, 13–25.

SPERLING, G. (1960) The information available in brief visual presentations. *Psychological Monographs*, **74** (Whole No. 11).

TERRY, W.S. and WAGNER, A.R. (1975) Short-term memory for 'surprising' vs. 'expected' unconditioned stimuli in Pavlovian conditioning. *Journal of Experimental Psychology: Animal Behavior Processes*, **1**, 122–133.

THOMPSON, R.K.R. and HERMAN, L.M. (1977) Memory for lists of sounds by the bottle-nosed dolphin: Convergence of memory processes with humans? *Science*, **195**, 501–503.

TULVING, E. (1968) Theoretical issues in free recall. In: T.R. DIXON and D. HORTON (Eds.) *Verbal Behavior and General Behavior Theory.* Prentice-Hall, New Jersey.

TZENG, O.J.L. (1973) Positive recency effect in delayed free recall. *Journal of Verbal Learning and Verbal Behavior*, **12**, 436–439.

WAGNER, A.R. (1978) Priming in STM: An information processing mechanism for self-generated or retrieval-generated depression in performance. In: S.H. HULSE, H. FOWLER and W.K. HONIG (Eds.) *Cognitive Processes in Animal Behavior.* Erlbaum, Hillsdale, New Jersey.

WAGNER, A.R., RUDY, J.W. and WHITLOW, J.W. (1973) Rehearsal in animal conditioning. *Journal of Experimental Psychology Monograph*, **97**, 407–426.

WALLACE, J., STEINERT, P.A., SCOBIE, S.R. and SPEAR, N.E. (1980) Stimulus modality and short-term memory in rats. *Animal Learning and Behavior*, **8**, 10–16.

WARRINGTON, E.K., LOGUE, V. and PRATT, R.T.C. (1971) The anatomical localisation of auditory–verbal short-term memory. *Neuropsychologia*, **9**, 377–387.

WARRINGTON, E.K. and SHALLICE, T. (1972) Neuropsychological evidence of visual storage in short-term memory tasks. *Quarterly Journal of Experimental Psychology*, **24**, 30–40.

WATKINS, M.J. (1972) Locus of the modality effect in free recall. *Journal of Verbal Learning and Behavior*, **11**, 644–648.

WEAVER, G.E. and STANNY, C.J. (1978) Short-term retention of pictorial stimuli as assessed by a probe recognition technique. *Journal of Experimental Psychology: Human Learning and Memory*, **4**, 55–65.

WICKELGREN, W.A. (1973) The long and the short of memory. *Psychological Bulletin*, **80**, 425–438.

WICKELGREN, W.A. (1974) Single-trace fragility theory of memory dynamics. *Memory and Cognition*, **2**, 775–780.

WICKELGREN, W.A. (1981) Human learning and memory. *Annual Review of Psychology*, **32**, 21–52.

ZENTALL, T.R., HOGAN, D.E., HOWARD, M.M. and MOORE, B.S. (1978) Delayed matching in the pigeon: Effect on performance of sample-specific observing responses and differential delay behavior. *Learning and Motivation*, **9**, 202–218.

CHAPTER 6

Amnesia in Humans and Other Animals

Andrew Mayes and Peter Meudell

6.1 Introduction

The focus of this chapter is the organic amnesia syndrome. In humans, this syndrome is characterized by severe impairment in learning and remembering of a very large variety of tasks and materials (anterograde amnesia) and poor memory for pretraumatic events (retrograde amnesia) which may extend for years or decades (Marslen-Wilson & Teuber, 1975; Meudell *et al.* 1980c). Although they display dramatic anterograde and retrograde amnesia, many amnesics are reported to perform within the normal range in short-term memory, as assessed by digit span performance, the recency effect in free recall and even the Brown–Peterson task (see Piercy, 1977, for a discussion). It is claimed that many of them have relatively intact cognitive functions as evinced by performance on tests such as the WAIS. The minimal lesion which causes the above pattern of breakdown is currently controversial, but recent candidates have included one or more of the following: the hippocampus, the mammillary bodies, their fornical connection, the dorsomedial nucleus of the thalamus, and the amygdala and the temporal stem (see Mair *et al.*, 1979, for a recent discussion). These candidates are all limbic or limbic-related structures and share the property of interfacing neocortex with brain stem and diencephalic systems.

In studying the pattern of memory breakdown in amnesia, psychologists have usually tried to select patients with minimal cognitive disturbances, in order to simplify the task of distinguishing the core amnesic features from the memory deficits secondary to any additional cognitive problems. Unfortunately, appropriate cognitive assessment is difficult and amnesia, which is associated with several different aetiologies, is rarely (if ever) 'pure'. Normal ageing and the dementias of Huntington's chorea (Meudell *et al.*, 1978) and Alzheimer's disease (Miller, 1977) involve not only amnesia-like memory problems but also cognitive failures of varying degrees of severity. More critically, the well known amnesic aetiologies of chronic alcoholism, encephalitis, medial temporal lobe surgery, head injury, carbon monoxide poisoning and occlusion of the posterior cerebral artery (Whitty & Zangwill, 1966), are all frequently linked with detectable cognitive impairments, and, in common with the senile and presenile dementias, with damage of many non-limbic structures, including association cortex. As a result it has proved very difficult to determine what pattern of memory symptoms constitutes the core amnesic syndrome. Worse, it is extremely hard to determine whether the claim, sometimes made, that the core syndrome can be dissociated into more than one kind of memory impairment (Lhermitte & Signoret, 1976; Huppert & Piercy,

1979; Squire, 1980a) is true. Indeed, it remains plausible to argue that different amnesic aetiologies are related to distinct core memory symptoms, whose interpretation is confounded by varying degrees of cognitive loss.

One strategy which has been used, that may circumvent such problems, is the investigation of amnesic disturbances in mammals. Mammals, unlike humans, can be given selective and precisely localized lesions. Early work with hippocampally lesioned rats and monkeys did not, however, reveal the expected global amnesia. The picture is now less bleak but still confused and will be discussed in detail later in the chapter. Briefly, three kinds of explanation have been advanced to account for the animal/human discrepancy apparent in early work. First, there may have been an evolutionary change with the result that the hippocampus or allied systems subserve unique functions in humans. In support of this claim, Lhermitte and Signoret (1976) have, for example, pointed out that, in man, the mammillary bodies contain about 400 000 neurons, six to seven times the number found in monkeys, and that this represents a much greater proportional increase of cells than that found in parieto-occipital cortex. Second, the animal lesion does not match the human one in some critical respect. Thus, it has been argued that hippocampal lesions only cause global amnesia if complicated by pre-existent epilepsy (Isaacson, 1972), that damage must be to the temporal stem and not the hippocampus (Horel, 1978), or that damage must be to two structures such as the hippocampus and the amygdala if severe permanent amnesia is to be seen (Mishkin, 1978). Third, the hippocampus and its related structures may cause amnesia in animals and man, but until recently animals have been given inappropriate memory tests on which even human amnesics would perform well (Gaffan, 1976). Clearly, more than one of these kinds of explanation may contain a measure of truth.

At present, there is no conclusive resolution of how a rapprochement between animal and human amnesias may be achieved. Each position has its able and active protagonist. Evidence from animal amnesias should inform our knowledge of human amnesia, however, our uncertainty about the functional breakdown and locus of the critical lesion(s) in human amnesia must qualify our interpretation of the animal data. Thus, if, for example, hippocampal damage is not the critical lesion in human amnesia, then any inferences, drawn from the effects on memory of such lesions in animals, are liable to be wrong. In order to achieve a better position for assessing the mutual implications of the human and animal literatures, the main sections of the chapter will treat, in turn, the functional breakdown in human amnesia, the evidence concerning the critical lesion which produces this, and the effect of 'relevant' amnesic lesions in animals before drawing tentative conclusions.

Before beginning the main sections it is worth noting the two major reasons why psychologists are interested in organic amnesia. Their first and more modest aim is to discover which features of memory can be dissociated from each other through lesion studies and hence determine the number of independent memory systems. Warrington's (1975) report of a double dissociation between semantic and episodic memory impairments in certain visual object agnosics and in organic amnesics provides a good illustration of this approach. Shallice and Warrington's (1970) demonstration of a double dissociation between short- and long-term memory (discussed by Graham Hitch Chapter 5) provides another. Comparisons are made either between amnesics and subjects with different kinds of memory problem in order to find double dissociations, or between amnesics and controls in order to find single dissociations. Attempts to demonstrate the heterogeneity of the core syndrome must, of course, compare the putatively different groups. The advantage of the first aim is that it largely avoids the problem of how lesions impair normal functioning and its disadvantage is that it tells us very little about why identified dissociations occur. The second and more basic source of psychological interest is that organic amnesia may illuminate our understanding of how the brain mediates memory processes. Fulfilment of this ambition minimally requires accurate location of the critical lesion and of the pattern of the functional memory disturbance in amnesia. To assist the interpretation of lesion effects this knowledge needs to be supplemented by electrophysiological, neurochemical and neuroanatomical data. These data are most readily obtained from animal studies.

There are further and related points about the above reasons for psychologists' interest in amnesia. The first is a sceptical one. Attempts to demonstrate dissociations or find functional correlates of lesions have been parasitic on functional categories derived either from our common heritage of pre-theoretical psychological knowledge, or, particularly in recent years, from theoretical ideas, based on the experiments of cognitive psychologists with intact humans. There has, for example, been much work relating Craik and Lockhart's (1972) 'levels of processing' concept, and the short- and long-term distinction to the disruptive effects of lesions. Disquiet with this scenario should arise because of the strong suspicion that cognitive psychology is not a good source of powerful functional explanatory ideas (see Allport, 1975). The risk is that weak functional concepts are apparently buttressed by lesion studies which, at the same time, provide no valuable new insight into how those functions are mediated. There is little reason to believe that the brain's basic processes are going to be isomorphic with our preconceived functional categories. Two possible routes out of this impasse constitute the second and third points. The first route is to give a role for *ad hoc* theorizing, founded on the pattern of memory breakdown seen in humans and animals. How, for example, can we explain the sparing of old memories often reported in retrograde amnesia? An actual example of this approach is provided in Gaffan's (1976) proposal that amnesics' memory problems arise from a deficit in their sense of familiarity (an extrapolation from lesion effects in rats and monkeys). The view that familiarity may be required for successful remembering in some kinds of task but not others is not one which has achieved much prominence in the study of intact human memory (but see Mandler, 1980). The study of amnesia has served to highlight this previously neglected process. The second route is still in its infancy and involves the the derivation of functional models from the known 'wiring plan' and suspected physiological mode of activity of those brain regions believed to be damaged in amnesia. To take a simple, programmatic example, the view that the structures implicated in amnesia act as 'interfaces' between cortical analysers of the external world and brain stem and diencephalic structures, concerned with internal states of reinforcement and non-specific activation, already provides certain constraints on their role(s) in memory.

6.2 The Varieties of Amnesia

The varieties of memory disorder are discussed in Chapters 1, 2, 5 and 9.

Briefly, however, two kinds of fractionation have been reported. The first kind, clearly distinct from the core amnesic syndrome and associated with cortical lesions, includes claims for selective deficits in semantic memory (Warrington, 1975), in auditory verbal short-term memory (Warrington & Rabin, 1971; Butters et al., 1970; Samuels et al., 1972). An interesting example of this group is provided by recent case reports of patients who have relatively selective topographical memory problems (De Renzi et al., 1977; Whiteley & Warrington, 1978, 1979). Although these deficits are probably cortical in origin the symptoms seem similar to the topographical memory failure of the core amnesic syndrome. The syndrome(s) may represent a specific cortical–limbic/diencephalic disconnection which prevents cortically processed topographical information from being remembered. Speculatively, a similar disconnection may explain the specific semantic amnesia proposed by Warrington (1975). The second kind of fractionation involves attempts to subdivide the core amnesic syndrome itself. Such attempts have themselves taken two forms. Thus, it has been shown convincingly that left medial temporal lobectomy causes selective memory problems with verbal material whereas right temporal lobectomy causes selective problems with material that is difficult to verbalize (see Milner, 1971). Such material-specific memory deficits have also been reported for lateralized lesion of the thalamus and amygdala (see Squire, 1980a; Vilkki, 1978; Jurko, 1978). Patten (1972) has further suggested that left hemisphere lesions are associated with a modality-specific impairment of gustatory memory and that right hemisphere lesions are associated with an impairment of olfactory memory.

More controversial than the above reports of the selective effects on amnesia of lateralized lesions, are the claims that bilateral lesions to different limbic–diencephalic structures cause dissociable memory deficits, i.e. the core global amnesic syndrome is heterogeneous. For example, it has been reported that amnesics with an alcoholic aetiology forget at a normal rate, when initial degree of learning is equated (Huppert & Piercy, 1979; Squire, 1980b). Squire (1980a) has reported the same effect in patient N.A. As recent CT scan evidence indicates there is a selective left lesion in the left dorsomedial thalamic nucleus of this patient, (Squire & Moore, 1979) and Victor et al. (1971) have implicated this nucleus in alcoholic amnesia, the suggestion is that damage here causes an amnesia with poor learning but in which the forgetting rate is normal for the level of acquisition achieved. In contrast, patient H.M. who has had a bilateral ablation of the medial temporal lobes and ECT patients, who may suffer reversible disruption of temporal lobe activity, forget at an accelerated rate even when matched for learning level with controls (Huppert & Piercy, 1979; Squire, 1980b). If corroborated these findings imply that temporal/hippocampal lesions cause both poor learning and faster forgetting. Before accepting these conclusions, however, we need to be convinced, not only about the effect's reliability, but also that the two hypothetical amnesic groups are processing the to-be-learnt material in the same way in the extra time allowed to bring their initial performance up to the level of control subjects. This is important because evidence to be discussed indicates that some alcoholic amnesics have information processing problems which are incidental and additional confounding factors for the core amnesic symptoms. In other words, alcoholic amnesics may only differ from temporal lobe cases in that the features of their memory breakdown are clouded by further cognitive problems. We will now

206

consider, in more detail, the interpretive problems which arise from (a) the incidental cognitive deficits and motivational disturbances found in many amnesics, and (b) the comparison of amnesics' very poor memory with the much better memory of control subjects. Only then can we assess the data bearing on the functional breakdown in the core amnesic syndrome or syndromes.

6.3 Methodological Problems

6.3.1 Incidental Cognitive and Motivational Disturbances in Amnesics

The functional deficit in amnesia is isolated by comparing the pattern of amnesic memory performance with that of control subjects. It has been reported that amnesic remembering is not only poor but differs qualitatively from that of controls. For example, amnesics show good cued recall, but poor free recall and recognition (see Meudell & Mayes, 1981c, for a discussion). If the amnesics studied have cognitive and/or motivational disturbances which are incidental to their poor memory, these may produce characteristic patterns of performance in remembering or conceal patterns which would otherwise be apparent. For example, some amnesics confabulate although this is actually an unusual concomitant of the chronic condition. In contrast very demented amnesics are likely to have difficulty in following instructions and might fail to show the usual amnesic effect of good cueing, although amnesics with less severe dementias do show this effect (Miller, 1975; Rozin, 1976). To resolve this kind of problem it is necessary to determine whether chosen amnesics have incidental disturbances, and if so, whether these are affecting their pattern of memory performance and also adding to their memory problems. For example, confabulation is often not found in chronic amnesics, whatever their aetiology, so it represents an incidental impairment, which may form part of the amnesic pattern of memory performance but is unlikely to worsen the overall level of their remembering.

A number of incidental disturbances of alcoholic amnesics, which impair memory and affect the pattern of performance, have been detailed recently by Meudell and Mayes (1981c). They are considered in the section on the nature of the functional disorder in amnesics, where it will be suggested that some alcoholic amnesics have direct or indirect damage to their frontal cortices. Such damage, which is common but not invariable in this aetiological group, is associated with apathy and other cognitive changes, which lead patients to adopt impoverished encoding and retrieval strategies. It is interesting to note that fantastic confabulation, in which the patient generates false memories spontaneously and acts as if they were true, has been related directly to frontal lobe lesions (Kapur & Coughlan, 1980). It has been shown that as performance on other 'frontal tests', such as the Wisconsin Card Sort test, improved so the tendency to confabulate fantastically decreased. Frontal lobe disturbances may, therefore, influence the manner in which patients remember, and often produce a mild memory problem, which is secondary to the 'core' amnesia. Similar information processing disturbances have been reported in depressive and schizophrenic patients and may cause memory impairments, which are so minor that some tests show apparently normal levels of remembering (Hasher & Zachs, 1979).

The problem of identifying the contaminating effects of disturbances incidental to the amnesic syndrome merges with the one of determining whether the apparently more central features of the syndrome are dissociable. If they are there is no single core syndrome and views about the functional break-down(s) must change radically. For example, anterograde amnesia seems to be invariably accompanied by retrograde amnesia. Indeed in closed head injury cases a good correlation is found between the two (Russell, 1971). It may be, however, that damage to functionally distinct, but physically juxtaposed or even intermeshing structures, causes the two memory impairments. Lesions in humans are unlikely to correspond to such nice functional differentiation. Experimental lesions in animals may. Thus, Jarrard (1980) found that CAI lesions in rats disturbed the acquisition of a spatial task, but left its retention unaffected provided learning was achieved pre-operatively. Fimbrial lesions, in contrast, impaired both acquisition and retention. Even in humans, Penfield and Mathieson (1974) have argued that retrograde amnesia is more severe the further hippocampal damage extends posteriorly. This proposal is concordant with the finding of Fedio and Van Buren (1974) that electrical stimulation of the temporal cortex in epileptics produced retrograde amnesia when posterior and anterograde amnesia when anterior. Unfortunately these observations, despite their fundamental importance, are as yet straws in the wind.

As well as the flamboyant variety of confabulation just discussed, several researchers have identified another termed 'momentary confabulation' (Kapur & Coughlan, 1980), in which a patient fabricates a false memory in response to a direct question. Typically, the fabrication is of a real event, located in the wrong place or time. Many amnesics do not show this kind of behaviour any more than normal people. They simply deny remembering and refuse to respond. Although this kind of confabulation may be aggravated (like the other kind) by frontal lesions, normal people confabulate in this way, especially when the passage of time has caused their memories to deteriorate (Bartlett, 1932). Momentary confabulation may well be a result of trying to recall faint memories under pressure. In other words, this type of fabrication could under certain conditions be a consequence of amnesia, rather than a contributory cause or an incidental concomitant. This opens the possibility that other peculiarities of amnesic remembering may be effects found when retrieving very faint memories rather than reflective of the cause(s) of amnesia. The next section examines how this possibility may be assessed.

6.3.2 Problems of Comparing Poor with Good Memory

Amnesics, compared to control subject tested under similar circumstances, show very good cued recall of words in contrast to their very poor recognition (for example, see Warrington & Weiskrantz, 1974). This observation has been interpreted as critical evidence for the view that amnesics' memory problems are caused by an excessive susceptibility to interference at the time of retrieval from irrelevant items in memory (see Weiskrantz & Warrington, 1975). Cues are said to aid amnesics more than controls because they eliminate most com-peting items as candidate memories — and amnesics have more such competi-tion to reduce. Miller (1977) also interprets a study of his on memory in relatively intact, but dementing amnesics, in terms of the interference hypo-thesis. He found that dements, in comparison to similarly tested controls, did differentially worse in terms of percentage correct, when the number of 'foil' words was increased in a test of recognition memory. The introduction of more 'foil' words was said to increase interference to which the dements were more prone. In both these examples a pattern of amnesic performance is taken to be reflective of the cause of the memory problem. It is possible, however, that the pattern is, instead, a consequence of amnesics' memory being poor, or even an artefact, arising from the way the tests were given. Interpretation of the cueing and recognition effects, as well as further similar phenomena, requires four broad types of possibility to be considered.

First, the appearance of a differential deficit in amnesics may be a consequence of tests being used, which are not matched for reliability and difficulty. The more reliability a test has, other things being equal, the more likely it is to discriminate between two subject groups, and the greater will be observed test score differences (Chapman & Chapman, 1973). Task difficulty is clearly a vital factor when ceiling or floor effects are present, and the amnesia literature has been bedevilled by just such effects. When amnesics score better than chance, controls often gain perfect scores. Unfortunately, less extreme differences in difficulty level also affect the degree of group separation achieved by tests. Thus, for tests comprising dichotomously scored items, maximum discrimination is attained for item error rates of about 50% (Lord & Novik, 1968). So even when obvious floor and ceiling effects are avoided, tests differing in difficulty level may have very different powers of discrimination between groups such as amnesics and controls. If differences in test reliability and/or difficulty artefactually produce qualitative differences in amnesic performance, then the same pattern should emerge in the memory performance of control subjects when their overall level of remembering is made as poor as that of amnesics. Furthermore, the pattern should emerge regardless of whether memory is attenuated by increasing the retention interval or reducing the opportunity to learn to retrieve. Such complete control procedures have not yet been used. Worse, no attempts have been made to ascertain tests' reliability or even to devise a difficulty level so that normal controls achieve equivalent performance across tests. For example, in Warrington and Weiskrantz's (1974) study the controls scored just under 75% correct on the word recognition test and at some indeterminate figure (there was no guessing control) under 25% on a cued recall test. This difference in difficulty level of the two tests could explain why their amnesics were inferior to controls on recognition but not cued recall. The possibility receives support from one study, where the controls' cued recall was around 50% correct and the amnesics were clearly inferior (Mayes *et al.*, 1978).

A second possible explanation for a qualitatively different pattern of amnesic performance on memory tests is that the observed pattern is a consequence of examining weak memory. If this possibility obtains, then the given pattern of performance should appear whether the poor memory is found in amnesics tested at short retention intervals, normal subjects tested at long intervals, or normal subjects tested when given an inadequate chance to learn or retrieve target material. The pattern should still appear when test difficulty and reliability are controlled because it is a result of trying to retrieve a relatively inaccessible trace. Even so the pattern may sometimes be a trivial result of testing poor memory. For example, Meudell and Mayes (1981c) have found that normal people tested after a long delay show a differential impairment on

209

harder recognition tasks compared to those tested immediately after learning. Thus, normal subjects, tested after a delay, behave like the amnesics in Miller's (1977) study who were tested immediately. Furthermore, this effect only occurs (certainly in normal subjects) if recognition is scored in terms of per cent correct. If signal detection theory is applied, then there is no effect with d' As d' is probably the appropriate measure of memory strengths here, Miller's effect can be seen as an artefact arising from the method of measurement. There may, however, be more significant effects which are consequences of testing poor memory. For example, amnesics have often been described as having a deficient sense of familiarity even when they accurately remember, i.e. they show evidence of memory but believe they are guessing (see Meudell & Mayes, 1981c, for a review). This effect is also found in the delayed cued recall of normal subjects (Mayes & Meudell, in press), where the words can be cued correctly but subjects think they are guessing. A similar phenomenon has been reported by Kunst-Wilson and Zajonc (1980), who found that subjects, very briefly exposed to a series of polygons, showed changed aesthetic preferences for these shapes although they completely failed to recognize them. There is then a case for arguing that a deficient familiarity sense is less likely to be a selective cause of amnesia than a general consequence of trying to access feeble memories of whatever provenance.

The third possibility arises when the immediate pattern of amnesic memory performance is matched by that of normal subjects tested at a long delay, but not the performance of normals whose memory is made poor in other ways. In this case there seem to be two broad explanations. Amnesics may show accelerated but qualitatively normal forgetting so that the structure of their relatively immediate memory closely resembles that of a normal subject after prolonged forgetting. If memories are multiattribute structures then, following deterioration, certain features may have become differentially unavailable in both amnesics and normals. Alternatively, the similarity between immediate amnesic and delayed normal memory may be a coincidence. For example, in amnesics poor encoding of certain features could lead to a pattern of performance, which appears in delayed normal memory not because of encoding failures but because the same features become unavailable particularly fast. The latter interpretation would be supported by evidence which suggests that alcoholic amnesics forget at a normal rate when matched on initial learning (Huppert & Piercy, 1978a). There are now several studies which show that normal subjects, tested after a delay, cue differentially well in the fashion of immediately tested amnesics (Woods & Piercy, 1974; Squire et al., 1978; Mayes & Meudell, in press). This effect has not yet been demonstrated in poor normal memory arising from inadequate learning so it may be an example of the possibility now being considered. If so, the determination of whether the cueing effect is the same size in immediate amnesic and delayed normal memory, and of how increasing delay affects amnesics' ability to cue, may point to the correct explanation of its occurrence.

One interesting variant of the third possibility, not so far considered, is that an amnesic pattern of memory performance can *only* be reproduced in normal subjects whose memory has been made poor by inadequate exposure for learning or retrieval, or by introducing extra tasks which interfere with learning and/or retrieval. With this possibility, amnesic pattern effects are *not* found in delayed normal memory, so it represents the complementary case to the possibility just discussed. The possibility is important because if it is realized the amnesic condition may have been simulated. That is to say, the functions disturbed by brain damage in amnesics may have been impeded experimentally in the normal controls. Investigation of such artificial impediments provides a royal road to understanding the cause of amnesia.

The final possibility arises if a pattern of memory performance is found in amnesics which cannot be duplicated in normal subjects, matched for level of memory performance, however this levelling is achieved. In this case, the amnesic performance may well be reflective of a contributory cause of their memory failure. An instance of this final possibility may be provided by the observations of Huppert and Piercy (1978b). Unlike alcoholic controls, their amnesic subjects made judgements about the frequency and recency of exposure of a series of pictures on the basis of overall memory strength rather than specific information. This pattern of results did not appear in normals, matched for overall level of memory performance whether it was achieved by brief initial exposures or prolonged testing delays (Meudell & Mayes, in preparation). Some or all amnesics may then have problems encoding or consolidating frequency and recency information which contribute to their memory failure (although this latter point still needs to be demonstrated).

In summary, even if immediate amnesic memory performance differs qualitatively from that of immediately tested controls, it should not be concluded that their performance is reflective of a specific cause of their memory failure. The effect could have several other explanations, which can only be eliminated with confidence if the same pattern is not reproduced by control subjects whose overall level of performance has been reduced in a number of ways to that of the amnesics. To date these control procedures have only been applied to a limited extent. Even so, when they have been applied (with the exception just considered), poor normal memory seems qualitatively similar to that of amnesics (see Meudell & Mayes, 1981c, for a review). The alternative explanations must then be considered as serious contenders.

6.4 Theories about the Functional Deficit in Human Amnesia

6.4.1 Encoding Deficit Theories

(a) Anterograde amnesia. In recent years, theorists have ascribed amnesic breakdown to selective encoding failure, selective consolidation failure, or selective retrieval failure (see Meudell & Mayes, 1981c, for a review). Some theorists have suggested that several selective deficits may coexist (Rozin, 1976). This section considers the status of encoding failure views, first in relation to the pattern of anterograde amnesia and then in relation to retrograde amnesia.

Butters and Cermak (1975) have formulated the most influential contemporary encoding failure hypothesis. This view is based on observations of alcoholic amnesics and, in its generalized form, states that amnesics' memory problems arise from their habitual tendency of ignoring meaningful features of stimuli the encoding of which would lead to good memory. Instead they focus on superficial features of stimuli the encoding of which leads to poor memory. It is argued that this impoverished encoding strategy is spontaneously adopted but does not represent an absolute cognitive limitation. When appropriately encouraged amnesics encode information like normal people. The origins of their spontaneous tendency will be discussed later in this section.

Evidence for this view largely takes the form of correlational studies. For example, in a recognition study, Butters and Cermak (1975) reported that alcoholic amnesics chose more homonym and associate 'foil' words than did controls. This was interpreted as showing that amnesics attend disproportionately to superficial features of words, such as their sound. A more dramatic kind of support derives from the failure of the Boston alcoholic amnesics to show release from proactive interference (PI) in the Wickens' paradigm with shifts of semantic category (Cermak et al., 1974). This support is more striking still as these amnesics do show release with alphanumeric shifts. The Boston workers argued that release, following a semantic shift did not occur because the amnesics were not properly encoding semantic features, whereas alphanumeric shift occurred because the patients were normally encoding physical or lower-level features. Amnesics were not carrying out more effortful kinds of processing at a normal level.

We decided to test the hypothesis more directly by manipulating encoding strategies with amnesics and controls. If the view is correct, then forcing amnesics to encode the deeper (i.e. more meaningful and more mnemonically valuable) features of stimuli (by choosing appropriate orienting tasks) should differentially improve their memory, relative to a spontaneous learning condition, in comparison to controls. Controls will improve less because their spontaneous encoding is optimal or more nearly so, than that of amnesics. Conversely, the memory of amnesics should be largely unimpaired by an orienting task which prevents the efficient extraction of meaning from stimuli. Amnesics do not spontaneously extract meaning from stimuli so preventing them from doing this has little detrimental effect. In contrast, normal people do spontaneously extract meaning so a low-level orienting task may drastically impede their memory. Normal subjects should then show a differential decrement relative to amnesics.

These predictions have been tested by us on a group of alcoholic amnesics, using a wide range of stimuli including words, faces, nonsense shapes, and neutral or funny cartoon pictures (Mayes et al., 1978, 1980b; Meudell et al., 1980b). Except with the verbal stimuli, the level of memory performance of amnesics and controls was equated by testing the controls at a longer retention interval. This procedure avoided floor and ceiling effects and minimized the problems considered in the last section. Contrary to the expectations on the encoding deficit hypothesis, the high- and low-level orienting tasks affected amnesic and control memory in the same way. For example, although being asked to make judgements about the pleasantness of faces improved amnesics' memory, it also improved controls' memory and to the same degree. Conversely, although the 'low-level' tasks of making judgements about hair straightness or curliness, impaired controls' memory, it also impaired amnesics' memory and to the same degree. These results were unlikely to be a result of differences in efficiency of performance on the orienting tasks, as the two groups of subjects showed closely equivalent judgements or levels of accuracy on the tasks.

These findings indicate that a failure to encode stimuli spontaneously in terms of meaningful, mnemonically useful features is unlikely to be the cause of the Manchester amnesics' memory problems. Do the Boston and Manchester alcoholic amnesics differ in important ways? This question is hard to answer in the absence of tests given to both groups. There are, however, some relevant observations. First, it could be that the amnesic deficit is one of impoverished encoding *and* retrieval. If so, a high-level orienting task applied only at encoding might not differentially assist amnesics. In our experiments, however, subjects were reminded repeatedly about the conditions of learning, at the time of memory testing. Despite this re-evocation of the meaningful processing initially activated at learning, amnesics did not benefit differentially from the 'high-level' tasks. So the Manchester amnesics do not seem to have a generalized tendency toward impoverished processing. Second, there are suggestions of differences between the Manchester and Boston patients. The cognitive processing speed of the former group is relatively normal when assessed by reaction time to make judgements about semantic category membership or even 'divided attention', i.e. multiple judgements (Meudell *et al.*, 1980b). In contrast, there is some evidence that the Boston patients are cognitively slow (Cermak *et al.*, 1974). The Boston amnesics have frequently been described as emotionally bland, unspontaneous and apathetic (Victor *et al.*, 1971) whereas this is not the impression given by the Manchester patients. This impression is concordant with the results of an electrophysiological study (Mayes *et al.*, 1980a). In this we showed that the $N_1 - P_2$ and P_3 components of the visual evoked potential are of normal or above normal amplitude in the Manchester amnesics. Such results support the feeling that they are not apathetic (if anything concentrating more than controls), given that these measures index the efficiency of various aspects of attention. Furthermore, this conclusion is corroborated by the finding that, although our patients' recognition of cartoons which they found very funny was better than their recognition of less funny cartoons, the same effect applied to normal subjects. Good memory here probably depended on the arousing effects of perceived funniness, which was equal in the two groups.

Alcoholic amnesics seem to constitute a heterogeneous group with respect to functional deficits. Some of these deficits may be incidental to the basic amnesia, but worsen and distort the appearance of the primary memory problem. For example, McDowall (1979) has found that a group of New Zealand alcoholic amnesics did show differential improvement when given semantic encoding instructions, in comparison to alcoholic controls. This differential effect was not found, however, when subjects were given semantic cues at recall. Mayes *et al.* (1978) found no such differential improvements in their patients, using a semantic orienting task, with or without semantic cues at retrieval. McDowall's amnesics had lower WAIS 'Similarities' scores than their controls whereas this was not the case for the Manchester patients. Stoff and Eagle (1971) have shown that there is a positive relationship between performance on this test and the reported use of elaborative processing strategies. If the New Zealand patients did not use these strategies normally they would suffer memory problems additional to their primary one.

Many alcoholic amnesics have extensive damage either directly to the prefrontal cortex or to its major projection nucleus, the dorsomedial nucleus of the thalamus (Victor *et al.*, 1971). Many of the functional deficits reported in the Boston patients are 'frontal' in nature. Amnesics' apathy corresponds to the pseudodepression found in many frontal patients. Oscar-Berman has extensively delineated the attentional difficulties of these patients which are not dissimilar to those seen in frontal patients (see Oscar-Berman & Samuels, 1977). These include abnormally strong perseverative tendencies (Oscar-Berman, 1978) of a kind revealed, for example, by the Wisconsin Card Sort test. Interestingly, this task is difficult even for non-amnesic alcoholics, who have frontal atrophy (Tarter, 1973), whereas the temporal lobectomy amnesic HM experiences no unusual difficulty (Milner, 1963). Very small orienting responses (as measured by electrodermal activity) have also been reported, in conjunction with an abnormally slow rate of habituation (Oscar-Berman & Gade, 1978). Several studies have found slow habituation in frontally lesioned animals (see Kolb & Whishaw, 1980). Alcoholic amnesics have further been shown to have impairments not only in delayed alternation and DRL, which in monkeys can be caused by limbic system or frontal cortex lesions, but also on direct-method delayed-response tasks, which are selectively sensitive to pre-frontal cortex lesions in monkeys (Oscar-Berman, Oberg & Zola-Morgan cited by Oscar-Berman & Zola-Morgan, 1980b). Talland's (1965) original proposal about the cause of amnesia in these patients was that it arose from 'reduced activation and premature closure of function'. This sounds very like a symptom of some kinds of frontal damage. Amnesics with this kind of frontal activation problem may well show the pattern of impoverished encoding (and possibly retrieval) postulated by Butters and Cermak, particularly in rather tedious laboratory experiments.

It is interesting that Winocur and Kinsbourne (1978) have reported that alcoholic amnesics' retention of related paired associates is much better if learning and retrieval take place in a strikingly distinctive environment. As normals, tested at much longer retention intervals, do not appear to benefit from being similarly exposed to a distinctive environment (Mayes *et al.*, 1981), this effect is probably not a non-specific result of testing deteriorated memory. In alcoholic amnesics, the distinctive context may act to focus and maintain attention to the task. This possibility should be tested in other amnesic groups and patients with selective frontal lesions.

The view that impoverished processing in alcoholic amnesics (when it occurs) has its origin in 'incidental' frontal dysfunction, receives support from observations of Signoret and Lhermitte (1976). They studied two patients with frontal vascular lesions, who showed no major cognitive problems, but complained about their memories despite retaining everyday events. These patients were very poor at unguided learning of paired associate words. When the experimenters showed them how to use sentential mediators, however, their performance was greatly improved. The same effect was noted with imaginal mediators which improved their performance to nearly normal levels. The lesions prevented them from taking the initiative in adopting an appropriate mnemonic strategy although their encoding abilities remained intact. Signoret and Lhermitte's frontal patients sound very like the amnesics of Butters and Cermak's hypothesis.

The 'frontal' interpretation of Butters and Cermak's hypothesis also received support from more recent data relevant to the failure of the Boston patients to show release from PI following a shift of semantic category in Wickens' paradigm. A similar failure to show release has been reported in frontally lesioned patients with minor memory difficulties, although unilateral temporal lobectomy patients, who display material-specific amnesias, do show release

(Moscovitch, 1976). Cermak (1976) also reported that a densely amnesic post-encephalitic patient showed normal release from PI following a semantic shift. The effect is not then confined to amnesics nor is it seen in all types of amnesic.

Recently, Winocur *et al.* (in press) have reported that Canadian and Bostonian alcoholic amnesics do show release from PI but only when there is a second shift of semantic category in a sequence of nine trials, or on the first shift when they are told to expect one. Even when amnesics did not show release (on first shifts about which they were not told), they produced virtually no intrusion errors from the previous and now inappropriate semantic category. The amnesics seemed to be aware of the new category but were unable to make use of this knowledge in retrieving responses. Luria (1973) describes many cases in which frontally lesioned patients display similar failures to use available information to direct their cognitive activities. Independent evidence suggests, that with failure to obtain release from PI following category shifts, the cognitive failure is as likely to involve retrieval as it is encoding (Jones, 1979). It is also interesting that institutionalized elderly people, with minor memory problems, show similar failures to obtain PI release following shifts (Mistler-Lachman, 1977). This failure may be associated with apathy, whether or not the apathy is caused by frontal cortex atrophy. As release following shift in normals is accompanied by arousal, indexed by heart rate deceleration (Yuille & Hare, 1980), it would be interesting to see if amnesics showed similar arousal after the first shift.

The occurrence of incidental frontal cortex damage, in some but not all amnesics, may help explain a much discussed discrepancy in the literature. Whereas the short-term memory of Boston alcoholic amnesics, as assessed in the Peterson task, is defective (see Butters & Cermak, 1975, for a discussion), Baddeley and Warrington (1970) found normal performance in a carefully selected group of amnesics with a mixed aetiology. In this task, items are partly maintained in memory by occasional subvocal rehearsals which are interspersed with performance of the distracting task during the retention interval (see Baddeley, 1982). More recently, Yuille and Hare (1980) have shown that memory in the Peterson task is correlated with the level of physiological arousal (e.g. heart rate acceleration) observed in the distraction–retention interval. Success at the task seems to require the deployment of attention between the distracting operation and covert rehearsal, which involves effort and arousal. It is just the kind of task at which frontally lesioned patients are deficient and indeed they are known to do poorly at it (Stuss, personal communication).

It has been argued that many amnesics, particularly those with an alcoholic aetiology, have incidental damage to the frontal cortex which causes processing problems of the kind described but Butters and Cermak (1975). These processing problems originate in the apathy of some frontal patients which is associated with failures in modulating attention and cognitive activity. Not only are these symptoms absent in some amnesics with a non-alcoholic aetiology, they are less apparent in some alcoholic amnesics. For example, whereas the Bostonian patients seem to use passive, repetitive rehearsal strategies (Cermak *et al.*, 1976), an orienting task study of the Manchester amnesics suggests that they, like controls, use active, elaborative rehearsal strategies (Meudell & Mayes, 1980). Also, whereas the face recognition memory of the Manchester patients does not benefit differentially from 'deep' level orienting tasks (Mayes *et al.*, 1980b), that of the Bostonian patients does (Biber *et al.*, 1981), which suggests that only the latter group has a problem encoding facial stimuli.

Under some circumstances, however, all alcoholic amnesic groups appear to show no benefit from 'deep' orienting instructions (Cermak & Reale, 1978; Mayes et al., 1978; Wetzel & Squire, 1980; McDowall, 1979). All these studies involved either 'difficult' tasks or some kind of overload, the nature and origin of which may prove to be a 'frontal' dysfunction. There is an urgent need, therefore, to see whether alcoholic amnesics have different degrees of frontal involvement by applying common test procedures to amnesic patients from different laboratories, as well as to patients with localized frontal damage. Only in this way can memory failures incidental to the core amnesia(s) be identified. It could be that all alcoholic amnesics have some frontal impairment, but that this varies across patients in a way which is reflected more sensitively by some tests than others. Further, not all incidental failures need be caused by 'frontal' damage. For example, the processing deficit of McDowall's alcoholic amnesics may have been associated with their poor WAIS similarities score and this may well have been caused by parietal cortex dysfunction. It may also be that the extent of dorsomedial thalamic damage varies considerably in alcoholic amnesics (see Mair et al., 1979).

Whereas Butters and Cermak have identified a failure of effortful processing as the cause of amnesia, Huppert and Piercy, (1978a) attribute the memory problem to a deficit in the automatic encoding of features, such as item frequency and recency. Hasher and Zachs (1979) distinguish between automatic and effortful encoding processes, regarding the former as involving minimal attentional capacity (so they do not interfere with other activities and need minimal intentional guidance) and being subject to very small developmental changes. Huppert and Piercy's view requires the assumption that the automatic encoding of background contextual features (such as an event's spatio-temporal features) at learning, and their reactivation at retrieval, is essential for good recall and recognition. After showing that alcoholic amnesics did relatively well at making 'familiarity' judgements but very poorly at judging item recency (Huppert & Piercy, 1976), they showed that amnesics seemed to make recency and frequency judgements differently from controls (Huppert & Piercy, 1978a). Thus, amnesics judged recent items as having occurred frequently and frequent items as having occurred recently. Huppert and Piercy interpreted this discrimination failure as indicating that amnesics' frequency and recency judgements were based solely on the perceived strength of their memories, whereas the judgements of controls were also based on specific frequency and recency information.

Amnesics and controls were tested at the same retention interval in Huppert and Piercy's 1978 experiment so it is feasible to argue that their pattern of performance is a consequence of their poor memory rather than reflective of its cause. To test the possibility we have repeated their study, operationally lowering normal memory performance to that of their amnesics, both by reducing exposure time of items and by increasing the retention intervals (Meudell & Mayes, in preparation). Despite the success of these manipulations in worsening normals' memory, they still continued to base their judgements on strength and specific feature information. The encoding problem, identified by Huppert and Piercy, is not then likely to be an artefact of comparing poor and good memory.

It has been reported, however, that frontal patients are very poor at judging the temporal order of recently presented words or abstract pictures, although they recognize the items very well (Corsi, see Milner, 1971). Some amnesics with incidental frontal damage may have a problem with temporal judgements (and perhaps frequency judgements) which is disproportionate to their memory loss. There is also some evidence that stereotaxic lesions of the dorsomedial nucleus of the thalamus may cause temporal disorientation (Spiegel *et al.*, 1955) and it has been reported that cingulectomy causes a transient memory disorder in which recent events may be accurately remembered but attributed to the wrong time (Whitty & Lewin, 1960). Damage to these structures is likely to disturb the functioning of the frontal cortex and it should be noted that Huppert and Piercy tested Boston amnesics, most of whom would have had frontal cortex and dorsomedial thalamic damage. Whether a specific deficit in temporal memory judgements is associated with damage to a frontal system, and occurs incidentally in 'limbic system' amnesia, remains to be determined. A preliminary step would be to see if Huppert and Piercy's pattern of results occur in all amnesics and if they occur in some patients with focal frontal lesions. It is of interest, therefore, that Squire *et al.* (1981) have reported that recency and recognition judgements are qualitatively similar in ECT patients and NA, and in normal subjects, tested at a longer delay. There does not seem to be a special problem of temporal memory in these amnesic patients.

(b) *Encoding deficit theories and retrograde amnesia.* If organic amnesia is caused solely by encoding deficits then retrograde amnesia should not occur. The existence of retrograde amnesia might be accommodated by encoding deficit theories in a number of ways. First, the theories may be generalized to become processing deficit explanations which postulate deficiencies at retrieval as well as encoding. Second, if the onset of brain damage is gradual then the retrograde amnesia may be caused by a progressively worsening acquisition deficit. Third, retrograde and anterograde amnesia may be dissociable deficits caused by damage to closely related brain systems. If so, then anterograde amnesia could still be caused by an encoding problem whereas retrograde amnesia would be associated with a different functional defect.

If amnesics are deficient at those kinds of effortful processing which involve accessing meaningful aspects of information, then some kind of retrograde problem would be expected. Although the Manchester alcoholic amnesics did not benefit differentially from the combined use of semantic orienting tasks at learning and semantic cueing at retrieval (Mayes *et al.*, 1978), Cermak *et al.* (1980) have recently suggested that the Boston alcoholic amnesics may benefit from this kind of semantic processing guidance. Some amnesics may then have generalized problems of effortful processing although, as has been argued, these problems probably arise from frontal lesions incidental to the central limbic system damage. Two predictions can be made from this hypothesis. First, semantic cues should lead to differential improvement in memory for pre-traumatic events when amnesics are compared with controls. Second, the retrograde amnesia should extend back uniformly into the pretraumatic period, with no sparing of distant memories. Neither of these predictions is upheld. Thus Albert *et al.* (1979a) reported that although the retrograde amnesia of Boston amnesics extended over many decades, there were savings for the most distant memories. Furthermore, although their patients benefited from phonemic and semantic cues, controls did as well and to the same extent.

217

The relative sparing of distant memories in retrograde amnesia might be explained, however, if the problem was caused by a progressively worsening failure of effortful processing. More recent memories would not only be retrieved inefficiently, but they would also be encoded less adequately than older memories. Although this explanation may apply to some amnesics, it is difficult to test, and it is clear that there are amnesics with acute onset of brain dysfunction, either from bilateral temporal lobectomy or from a series of electroconvulsive shock treatments (ECT) who show steeply graded retrograde amnesia (Marslen-Wilson & Teuber, 1975: Squire & Chace, 1975). If effortful processing failures do arise from incidental frontal cortex damage then the prediction could be tested by seeing whether patients with acute onset, focal frontal lesions show mild retrograde amnesias with no sparing of distant memories.

It has often been reported that some amnesics, particularly those with an alcoholic aetiology, often jumble the temporal order of distant memories. These observations are compatible with an extension of the views of Huppert and Piercy viz. some amnesics may be poor at encoding and retrieving those automatically processed contextual features of information, which *inter alia* may be important for making temporal judgements. If this processing problem occurs and is a consequence of incidental 'frontal involvement', then temporal disorientation should be disproportionately severe in amnesics with such involvement, compared to other amnesics matched for overall severity of retrograde amnesia. It is clear, however, that tests of the temporal order of past events are more difficult than tests which simply require familiarity for the events. Thus, Squire *et al.* (1976) found that ECT patients had a retrograde amnesia of 7 years' duration for temporal order information whereas their amnesia for the events only extended back 3 years (Squire *et al.*, 1975). This 'difficulty effect' may explain the apparently disproportionate difficulty which the Manchester amnesics show in placing correctly identified well-known voices into their 'correct' decades (Meudell *et al.*, 1980c). The interaction may well have been an artefact of difficulty level. Two people can both identify a voice but one may retain much more detailed information about it than the other. Temporal information would merely be an instance of this more detailed information.

The possibility that anterograde and retrograde amnesia dissociate has already been considered in Section 6.3.1. Despite the fact that the severity of the two forms of amnesia is usually correlated, Roman-Campos *et al.* (1980) have described an unusual case of transient global amnesia, in which the recent memory deficit completely recovered after 10 days, leaving the patient totally amnesic for the acute episode and with a persistent, patchy retrograde amnesia for a 5- to 10-year period, (only slightly less severe than during the attack itself). Similar cases have been described by Williams and Smith (1954) as sequelae of tubercular meningitis and by Symonds (1966), following head injury.

No cases of anterograde without retrograde amnesia have been reported in humans although Jarrard's (1978) study provides an analogue for this syndrome in rats. An analogous effect has been reported, however, in patients recovered from transient global amnesia (Fredericks, 1979; Fogelholm *et al.*, 1975), or from having an injection of sodium amytal to the hemisphere contralateral to pre-existing temporal lobe pathology. Milner's (1966) results show persistent amnesia for the period of dysfunction itself but patients recover their (previously lost) memory for the pretrauma or pre-anaesthetic period. This permanent loss of memory for the transient anterograde amnesia episode can be interpreted in two ways. It could be caused by state-dependent forgetting as the brain may well be in a highly abnormal 'sensory' condition during the episode. State- and context-dependent forgetting, however, probably apply to free recall but not to recognition (Godden & Baddeley, 1980), whereas the forgetting in the transient amnesic states is supposed to apply to both recall and recognition. It is therefore possible that the episode is permanently forgotten because the events in it are not acquired normally whereas events occurring before the episode are only temporarily lost owing to some kind of retrieval difficulty. If these transient amnesias are similar to chronic amnesia this interpretation suggests that at least some chronic amnesias arise from both acquisitional and retrieval deficits.

In summary, there is no compelling evidence for the view that 'limbic system' amnesia is caused by deficits in effortful processing at encoding, or at both encoding and retrieval. If such deficits are present they may distort the pattern of memory performance and add to the severity of the amnesia. These deficits are, however, probably secondary to incidental damage of, for example, the frontal cortex. The same points can be made about the view that amnesia arises from a failure of automatic processing. The impact of selective frontal lesions on the postulated kinds of processing and on memory for pretraumatic events warrants investigation, as does the plausible suggestion that retrograde and anterograde amnesia are dissociable.

6.4.2   Retrieval Deficit Theories of Human Amnesia

(a) Anterograde amnesia.   In recent years retrieval deficit theories of amnesia have become somewhat protean, but in its original form, the best known of these theories claimed that amnesics encode and consolidate information normally, but at retrieval suffer excessively the competitive interference of other information in memory (Weiskrantz & Warrington, 1975). Most of this theory's problems have arisen in trying to describe the nature of the interference and explain its origins.

The theory receives support from three, probably related areas. First, amnesics show very poor free recall and recognition for words, but relatively normal cued recall (Warrington & Weiskrantz, 1970, 1974). Provision of a degraded version of a target word, or its initial letters, helped amnesics differentially with respect to controls. Similarly, Winocur and Weiskrantz (1976) have shown differentially good amnesic learning of paired associates, which are either related by a rhyme rule or a semantic one. It was argued that all these cues are effective because they constrain the number of alternatives which can compete with the target word. Second, although amnesics show good cued recall under the circumstances described, they show very poor learning and cued recall of a second similar list, presented a few minutes after the first (Warrington & Weiskrantz, 1974, 1978; Winocur & Weiskrantz, 1976). The second list, in these reversal learning studies, consists either of words beginning with the same initial three letters as those of list one, or of word pairs, linked by the same rule, but in which the response differs from that of list one. These studies suggested that amnesics are very sensitive to PI, especially as it is claimed that they showed many intrusion errors. Third, amnesics show good learning and retention of tasks which seem resistant to PI in normal people. For example, Brooks and Baddeley (1976) have found good amnesic performance with the Porteus Maze, jig-saw puzzles and pursuit rotor tracking, and Starr and Phillips (1970) found a musical amnesic who learned to play new piano tunes.

Difficulties appear when detailed predictions of the theory are tested. First, there is a problem about the way cues operate. If they help amnesics by constraining the number of competing alternatives at retrieval, then this help should be increased differentially when the constraint is more extreme. Some three-letter cues begin 10 or more English words, whereas others begin only one or two. Amnesics, relative to controls, should gain more assistance from cues of the latter kind. Tests of this prediction have yielded equivocal results, and Warrington and Weiskrantz (1978) have now suggested that the cues probably do not work by limiting response alternatives. The original position nevertheless may be retained on an *ad hoc* basis, if it is argued that initial letter cues activate fewer words than they begin in the dictionary, because recently shown words are 'primed' for cueing. The postulation of priming and its intactness introduces new unproved assumptions, however.

A second difficulty is associated with the role of prior list intrusions and response competition in producing interference effects. Kinsbourne and Winocur (1980) have recently extended the reversal learning paradigm with a group of Boston alcoholic amnesics. Subjects learned two lists of paired associates in succession. The stimulus terms and type of semantic linking rule were the same for both lists, but the response terms differed. In a first experiment, they found that minor changes in the context of second list learning led to a marked reduction in prior list intrusion errors but that list was still just as disrupted by interference from the first list. Subsequent recognition tests, given when subjects failed to recall words, showed that amnesics still frequently failed to identify word targets. In a second experiment, the possibility of prior list response intrusions was abolished by making the response terms of list one, part of the stimulus term for list two. For example, if a list one pair was milk–butter, then the list two pair became milk + butter–cheese. Under these conditions, the amnesics learning of list two improved but they were still worse than controls.

Kinsbourne and Winocur argued their amnesics' poor learning of the second list could not be caused from response competition deriving from the first list. Rather, they proposed that amnesics are abnormally dominated by prevailing thought patterns and impressions, which cause them to encode current conflicting material inadequately. They also proposed that a similar problem might apply at retrieval. Their study and interpretation warrant two comments. First, their interpretation is feasible but not compelling as it seems to be based on an outmoded view of how associative interference works. A recent review (Baddeley, 1976) makes clear that response competition may operate in a way uncorrelated with response intrusions and that such interference can cause recognition as well as recall failures.

Second, if the interpretation is correct then the description of the deficit sounds very like the kind of frontal lobe impairment documented by Luria (1973). This does not of course prove the deficit is a frontal one, but at least it speaks to the importance of determining whether selective frontal lesions can cause this type of difficulty, also whether there are cases of selective limbic system amnesia in which this difficulty is not apparent. Some light is thrown on this issue by Oscar-Berman and Zola-Morgan's (1980b) finding that alcoholic amnesics are severely impaired not only on learning novel concurrent discrimination tasks but also equally impaired at such tasks even when the discriminations have already been learned individually. Huntington's chorea patients were not impaired on the latter tasks. They argued that the high error scores for both tasks may have been caused by an inherent procedural feature such as high interference resultant on facing multiple problems. Frontal lesions in monkeys can cause similar deficits, as can hippocampal lesions. It remains open whether amnesic susceptibility to interference is causally related to the memory problem, or incidental to it. There may well be several kinds of interference processes, differentially affected by limbic system and frontal lesions.

Even if amnesia does arise from excessive response competition at the stage of retrieval, the origin of this interference has to be explained. Warrington and Weiskrantz (1978) have suggested that learned information is extinguished, or decays more slowly in amnesics, so that more competing information is available at the time of retrieval. In support of this view, they cite a study in which amnesic cued recall at 1 day was superior to that of controls, when the cues comprised the initial letters of words they began uniquely (e.g. ONI — for onion). Their amnesics were, however, better than controls at generating words from cues even without a memory component, so this evidence is not convincing.

A more plausible explanation of amnesics' excessive susceptibility to interference can be drawn from Gaffan's (1972) suggestion that they have difficulty in judging the familiarity of items in memory. In the free recall recognition of words, both targets and non-targets would seem equally familiar or unfamiliar, so the choice of any one would be arbitrary. On the other hand, when cues are provided, most of the competing items would be seen to be inappropriate, and performance would improve. In support of this view, Mayes and Meudell (1981b) have shown that amnesics do not recognize their cued responses as memories even when their cued recall is as good as controls' tested at the same retention interval. They feel they are guessing most of their correctly cued responses. Relative loss of the sense of familiarity should explain amnesics' pattern of memory performance. Free recall and recognition presumably require this feeling whereas the learning and retention of classical conditioning (Weiskrantz & Warrington, 1979) and a range of perceptuomotor skills do not (see Meudell & Mayes, 1981c, for a review). The so-called Claparède effect (Claparède, 1911) arises, on this view, when a memory skill requiring the familiarity sense is contrasted with another which does not. Thus, an amnesic may display a skill without recognizing the stimuli involved in the skill, or he may display the skill without recognizing where it was learned. This is called source amnesia. For example, a patient may retain the ability to play a new piano tune but have no recognition or recall for the circumstances of its acquisition.

Mandler (1980) has proposed that the sense of knowing or familiarity depends on the conjoint operation of two processes. Recognition by familiarity, which is a function of intra-event organizational integrative processes, and retrieval, particularly contextual retrieval, which is a function of inter-event elaborative processes. If either of these processes is disturbed then the ability to make judgements about prior event occurrence (i.e. has this been experienced before?) should be impaired. On Gaffan's view, amnesics have an impairment in the first kind of process. He argues that the limbic memory structures form part of a system which increases item familiarity, in a context-free way, each time that item is presented. This system is not only important for context-free memory but also for the more typical episodic memory, tested experimentally. For example a Yes/No recognition test, for recently presented words, tests episodic memory, and yet it can be answered by assessing the directly perceived familiarity of words.

There is also evidence that the contextual retrieval system is impaired in amnesics. Thus, Winocur and Kinsbourne (1978), using their interference paradigm for related paired associate lists, found that amnesic learning of the second list was markedly improved, i.e. interference was reduced, when this list was acquired in radically different contextual surroundings. Controls did not show this improved performance. Winocur *et al.* (in press) have also shown that only amnesics benefit from a contextual shift in the Wickens' paradigm. They argued that amnesics cannot make spontaneous use of contextual information at retrieval, although they can use it when the original circumstances are re-presented. Their hypothesis is similar to that of Huppert and Piercy and indeed it seems likely that the retrieval deficit is a partial consequence of the initially inadequate encoding of contextual information. Mandler has argued that this process, putatively impaired in amnesics, is involved not only in context-bound recognition (e.g. did I see this face in the supermarket yesterday), but also in context-free recognition (e.g. have I ever seen this face before?). If impaired, it may also cause free recall failures, where the item to be remembered is not successfully accessed, so failure occurs *before* the stage of identification (which, in turn, depends on familiarity *and* retrieval processes).

The foregoing argument suggests that amnesics' poor memory arises from two deficits which may be independent. The first is an impairment in the familiarity sense, which is a function of intra-event organization, and the second is contextual retrieval, which is a function of inter-event organization. In both cases, it is plausible to argue that the deficits lie at the stages of encoding and consolidation as much as retrieval. There is, however, a fundamental difficulty, which may undermine this whole position and earlier versions of the retrieval deficit hypothesis. These views depend on showing that, when amnesic and control subjects are tested shortly after learning, amnesics display good cued recall (e.g. Warrington & Weiskrantz, 1974), good memory for highly associated word pairs (e.g. Winocur & Weiskrantz, 1976), loss of familiarity for correctly cued words (Mayes & Meudell, 1981b), sensitivity to contextual shifts (Winocur & Kinsbourne, 1978), and dissociations of the Claperède type where memory is evinced in the absence of recognition (e.g. Weiskrantz & Warrington, 1979). All these effects have been reported, however, in normal subjects, at longer retention intervals, when their memories have deteriorated to amnesic levels. Thus, delayed normal memory shows good cued recall (Woods & Piercy, 1974; Squire, *et al.*, 1978; Mortensen, 1980; Mayes & Meudell, 1981a), good retention of highly (but not weakly) associated word pairs (Mayes *et al.*, 1981), loss of familiarity for correctly cued words (Mayes & Meudell, 1981a), sensitivity to contextual shifts (Mayes *et al.*, 1981c), and a Claperède dissociation between recognition and performance on a perceptual skill task (Meudell & Mayes, 1981). The phenomena of excessive susceptibility to interference and associated prior list intrusions, reported in amnesics, may also occur in normal subjects whose memory has been weakened experimentally (see Meudell & Mayes, 1981c, for a discussion). Preliminary data from our laboratory suggest that this is the case for paired associate lists.

222

It needs to be determined whether these effects also occur when normal memory is weakened by reducing exposure at learning (as in Kunst-Wilson and Zajonc's study of recognition) and also whether they are of the same size in amnesics and normals. Nevertheless, there is a strong prima facie case for the view that effects, traditionally interpreted in favour of the retrieval deficit hypothesis of amnesia, can with equal plausibility be interpreted as a consequence of testing poor memory, regardless of why it is poor. If so, then the current evidence leaves the retrieval deficit view without specific support. Such specific support would comprise amnesic memory effects not found in attenuated normal memory. Cohen and Squire's (1980) claim that amnesics learn and retain rule-governed skills for reading mirror-reversed words as well as normals, may provide this kind of evidence. In their study, memory for the rule-governed skills showed no apparent forgetting over 13 weeks, however, so the test conditions may not have been sufficiently sensitive to discriminate group differences. Although there are undoubtedly many kinds of memory independent of the limbic memory system, it remains an open question whether the class of rule-governed skills is among them.

(b) Retrieval deficit theories and retrograde amnesia. If amnesia is caused by a general failure of memory retrieval, then there should be a retrograde amnesia in which recall and recognition of recent and distant pretraumatic events should be equally impaired. The majority of the evidence, however, supports the view that there is sparing of the more remote pretraumatic memories. This evidence makes it difficult to maintain a simple retrieval hypothesis unless the majority evidence can be shown to founder on artefacts. This evidence is no longer solely anecdotal but has recently been derived from objective tests of knowledge about past events, famous faces and television programmes (see Cohen & Squire, 1981). It is important that these tests contain items which were learned within a particular period, and which were learned to the same extent and forgotten at similar rates. These criteria are hard to fulfil because prominent past events are frequently rehearsed after their initial exposure, and anyway it is difficult to equate for degree of learning. 'Remote' memories, therefore, may be spared because they are rehearsed later and overlearned relative to more 'recent' memories. In an extreme form this can be seen to happen with semantic memories, which undemented amnesics recall effectively. These memories, although often acquired initially in the remote past have subsequently been drastically overlearned.

Sanders and Warrington (1971, 1975) tried to minimize the confounding factors by selecting very difficult test items. They found no sparing of remote memories in amnesics. The patients performed at chance, however, so interpretation is impossible. In their later study, amnesic performance was improved by cueing but again the interpretation is uncertain as cues were not given to the controls. In an excellent study, Cohen and Squire (1981) have provided convincing evidence that the sparing of remote memory in retrograde amnesia is not an artefact. They have identified two forms of retrograde amnesia. In one, typifying alcoholic and many encephalitic amnesics, there is extensive remote memory impairment. In the other, typifying ECT patients, temporal lobectomy cases like HM (Marslen-Wilson & Teuber, 1975), and the case with the midline epee wound, NA, the retrograde amnesia is steeply graded.

223

Even the prolonged retrograde amnesia of alcoholic amnesics is characterized by some sparing of memory for the most remote events, despite the fact that the memory loss extends back for decades into all periods tested. Careful analysis showed that amnesics remembered the hardest items from the 1930s better than the easiest from the 1970s, whereas controls showed the opposite pattern of performance (difficulty was assessed in terms of normal performance). Similarly, patients with Huntington's chorea remember 1970s items better and 1930s items worse than amnesics showing that recall was not a simple function of item difficulty (Butters *et al.*, 1980).

Steeply graded retrograde amnesia seems to support Ribot's hypothesis (Ribot, 1882) that resistance to disruption increases with a memory's age (separately from degree of learning). Squire and Cohen (1979) have considered the alternative possibility that ECT disrupts memory for recent events only, because its effects are restricted to detailed information (rather than salient features) which is lost rapidly anyway. Recent memories would comprise detailed and salient information whereas older memories mainly comprise salient information. A qualitative analysis of detailed and salient facts, recalled from different periods, clearly showed, however, that ECT affected memory for both kinds of fact in recent periods, but did not even affect recall of detailed factual material from more distant periods. This analysis was corroborated by a quantitative one which showed that, after ECT, patients' memory was worse for recent than distant memories, whereas before ECT it had been the other way round. Assuming that ECT selectively affects memory for detailed information and that salient information is at least as abundant in recent memories as it is in older ones, then this pattern of results should be impossible. Therefore, steeply graded retrograde amnesia is unlikely to be an artefact.

Squire and Cohen (1982) reported one strange feature of this kind of retrograde amnesia. They found it, if and only if, their objective tests produced a forgetting gradient in normal memory. When normal performance revealed equivalent performance across all time periods, then NA and ECT patients showed extensive retrograde amnesias. In other words and paradoxically, the resistance of a memory to the disruptive effects of limbic lesions or ECT seems to increase if that memory has been partially forgotten.

It has been fashionable to propose that amnesia is a disorder of episodic memory in which semantic memory is preserved (see Kinsbourne & Wood, 1975). As Cohen and Squire point out, however, this view only gains plausibility from the inappropriate comparison of memory for overlearned, premorbid semantic knowledge, which is good, and of post-traumatic learning of episodic information which is poor. The post-traumatic acquisition of semantic information is also poor, however, and objective tests indicate that retrograde amnesia applies to semantic as well as episodic information. Kinsbourne and Wood's (1975) finding that alcoholic amnesics have difficulty in generating episodic memories in response to trigger words like 'flag' also involves an unfair comparison with normal people. The alcoholic amnesics, with their extended retrograde amnesias, have a far smaller pool of episodic memories on which they can draw. Even so, this category of amnesics can retrieve episodic memories when given more natural probes (Piercy, personal communication).

Two explanations of the extended retrograde gradient of alcoholic amnesics have been considered by Cohen and Squire (1981) and others. The first explanation ascribes the disturbance of remote memories to a progressive acquisitional failure. This view gains support from their observation that chronic alcoholics (with minimal memory problems) recall fewer items from the 1970s than non-alcoholic controls, and the fact that alcoholic amnesia often has an insidious onset. Some encephalitic amnesics whose illness has an acute onset have, however, also been reported to show prolonged retrograde amnesias (Albert et al., 1979b). Cohen and Squire, therefore, suggested that in some cases additional brain damage causes this pattern of impairment. For example, incidental damage to the frontal cortex may be responsible for the remote memory impairment. This view is supported by the observation that patients with advanced Huntington's chorea show severe retrograde amnesia with equal loss for all decades (Butters & Albert, 1982). A qualitatively similar pattern has been reported in recently diagnosed cases with minimal cognitive loss (Butters et al., 1980). These patients have 'frontal' disturbances. Alternatively, the additional damage might extend into posterior tempero-limbic regions which Penfield and Mathieson (1974) implicated in the retrieval of remote memories. Incidental damage is less extensive in some encephalitic and alcoholic amnesics than it is in others. Rose and Symonds (1960), for example, described some encephalitic amnesics who appear to have had fairly steeply graded retrograde amnesias. Two alcoholic amnesics with fairly local damage, described by Mair et al. (1979), showed extensive forgetting of remote events, however, although interpretation is uncertain because the test produced floor effects. Even so, the patient with most brain damage showed the more prolonged retrograde amnesia.

Theories of amnesia must explain both short- and long-gradient retrograde amnesias and allow for the possibility that in rare cases retrograde and antero-grade amnesia may dissociate. These factors suggest that several independent functional deficits may underlie amnesia. If graded retrograde amnesia can occur without anterograde amnesia (as has been reported), then at least two deficits seem likely. One would explain retrograde amnesia as an isolated complaint, and this deficit with another would explain anterograde amnesia in association with steeply graded retrograde amnesia. The isolated syndrome has not been seriously considered, but it is clear that Cohen and Squire believe that the combined syndrome arises from a storage deficit. In cases with extensive retrograde amnesia, they argue that this storage deficit (caused by limbic lesions) is complicated by a general retrieval deficit, which is probably caused by damage to extra-limbic sites such as the frontal cortex. A third deficit might be added to explain why graded retrograde amnesia is nearly always accompanied by anterograde amnesia. If anterograde amnesia can be found in isolation, then this deficit is almost certainly in storage, but if not, then some unusual kind of retrieval failure would remain possible as an explanation. This third deficit remains speculative, however, and one of the issues which needs to be discussed in the next section is whether a storage deficit can explain Cohen and Squire's steeply graded retrograde amnesias.

6.4.3 Some Comments on Storage Deficit Theories of Amnesia

Although the preservation of many pretraumatic memories makes it unlikely that the limbic memory structures are sites of memory storage, these structures may well be important in the consolidation and preservation of memories. Limbic system damage might disturb these physiological processes, activated

225

by learning, which establish stable memories, and/or they may cause more rapid forgetting of learned information. Such impairments are likely to be partial so, for example, the acquisition of some enduring memories in amnesics should not be surprising.

If some limbic system lesions impair aspects of consolidation, then it should be possible to detect physiological abnormalities at, and shortly after learning even when encoding problems can be partialled out. Mayes *et al.* (1980a) have reported EEG abnormalities of this kind in the Manchester group of alcoholic amnesics, which has not yet been found to show encoding deficiencies. These patients displayed reduced overall EEG power in the first second after the offset of words, which they had been attending to under either intentional or inciden-tal learning instructions. As their EEG power was normal in the subsequent 2 s, these amnesics may have an activational deficit confined to the immediate post-stimulus interval. Wood *et al.* (1980) have, however, also described an abnormal pattern of activation in regional cerebral blood flow during recognition testing of a densely amnesic patient with, putatively, a large medial thalamic infarct. Amnesics may, therefore have abnormal 'activation' during both learning and retrieval. The relationship of these disturbances to memory must be regarded with caution, especially as Wood *et al*'s patient was clinically underaroused.

The evidence about whether amnesics forget faster than controls is equivocal (see Meudell & Mayes, 1981a, for a discussion). Comparisons should only be made when degree of initial learning is equated. Huppert and Piercy (1978b) equated for immediate picture recognition memory by allowing alcoholic amnesics four to eight times as long to inspect the pictures as controls. Squire (1980b) has recently found a similar result in another group of alcoholic amnesics and in patient NA (who may like the alcoholics have damage to the dorsomedial nucleus of the thalamus). In contrast, it has been reported that, under conditions where initial learning is equated, HM and ECT patients forget more rapidly than controls (Huppert & Piercy, 1979; Squire, 1980b). These results need confirmation but once again suggest that memory processes are mediated by several independent limbic structures. In this case the dissociation may be between diencephalic and medial temporal systems. If genuine, faster forgetting following temporal lesions is compatible with the operation of excessive PI (see Kinsbourne & Wood, 1975) and possibly retroactive interference as well. This might occur if the lesions blocked the activity of prolonged consolidation necessary for maintaining memories. Further implications of such activity and its prevention are now con-sidered.

If there is a system which modulates these activational processes, influencing consolidation in the few seconds after stimulus exposure, then damage to it will cause poor learning and memory. Such a deficit would appear shortly after stimulus exposure (following distraction) and can clearly explain anterograde amnesia if that should appear in isolation. Can it explain the normal syndrome in which anterograde amnesia is associated with a steeply graded retrograde amnesia? The problem is to explain how memories, laid down months or even years before the disease's onset, can be disturbed by a deficit which only influenced them for a few seconds after learning. Both Wickelgren (1979) and Cohen and Squire (1981) have tried to solve this problem by suggesting that there are some consolidation-type processes which continue for months and indeed years. They then argue that limbic system lesions disturb these processes.

In Wickelgren's view, the limbic memory system is involved in creating new 'chunks' or groupings of information by differentially activating 'free' as opposed to 'bound' (i.e. ones already involved in storing 'chunks') neocortical neurons. This activation stimulates the consolidation of these informational groupings. Once they are involved in the storage of a 'chunk', 'free' neurons become progressively bound. This means that their links with the limbic memory system are progressively suppressed so that they become increasingly unlikely to take part in the formation of new 'chunks', which would disrupt their ability to retain the 'chunks' they already are storing. The negatively accelerated disconnection is a kind of extended consolidation process. Cohen and Squire consider a somewhat different sort of prolonged consolidation. In fact, they consider two activities which may not be the same. First, there appears to be a proposal that as memories age they receive periodic rehearsals, which cause them to be gradually restructured and fitted into new schemata. Second, they suggest a physiological principle of competition, supported by observations of primitive animals, in which the weakening of one set of neural links through forgetting is associated with the strengthening of others (Squire and Schlapfer, 1981). These activities of prolonged reorganization or strengthening are seen as consolidatory, and they are thought to be mediated by the limbic structures, lesioned in amnesia.

To assess the success of these theories as accounts of consolidation deficits it is necessary to consider two kinds of effect limbic system lesions may have. Such lesions may prevent the affected region's normal function (e.g. prolonged consolidation), or influences from the damaged region may disturb the functioning of intact, related regions (i.e. produce 'noise'). If only the former kind of effect occurs, then no retrograde amnesia should be present immediately after the trauma. At that stage, amnesic memories of the recent past should be as well consolidated as those of intact subjects. As time passes, following the trauma, a retrograde amnesia should gradually develop for the events which occurred shortly (weeks and months) before it. After a few years this deterioration will cease. Both effects should occur because amnesics lack prolonged consolidation processes which operate for several years (in a diminishing fashion) to maintain memory in intact people. No one has reported how retrograde amnesia evolves over time in stable chronic amnesics, but retrograde amnesia is known to be present immediately post-trauma. So, a simple 'loss of function' view cannot explain the pattern of amnesia. If lesioning a limbic consolidation system causes it to send 'noisy' signals to related systems, however, then such immediate retrograde amnesia could be explained. Retrieval of recent memories should not be possible if the consolidation system, linked to them, is producing noisy signals. This appears to be Wickelgren's view although he does not explicitly state it. Cohen and Squire could argue similarly. According to Wickelgren, 'bound' cortical neurons eventually become disengaged by an automatic process from their 'noisy' limbic input. When this 'noisy' input decreases so should the severity of the retrograde amnesia. Wickelgren must, therefore, predict that retrograde amnesia should diminish over time in stable chronic amnesics. His theory only allocates the limbic system an indirect role in the prolonged process of disconnecting 'bound' neocortical neurons. There should, therefore, be little or no countervailing effect of worsening retrograde amnesia, caused by the continued deficit of consolidation. In Cohen and Squire's theory, however, limbic lesions must both block extended consolidation, and disrupt retrieval of more recent memories by creating 'noise'. The relative contribution of these two influences would determine whether memory for recent pretraumatic events improved or worsened with time (in otherwise stable amnesics).

The suggestion that some of the memory impairment in retrograde amnesia is caused by a retrieval failure gains some support from work of Kesner (1977). He conditioned rats to suppress a bar-pressing response and then administered hippocampal stimulation either 1 or 7 days after training. The stimulation was strong enough to produce after-discharges. Retention was tested between 2 and 180 min after the stimulation. Kesner found that a temporary amnesia was produced in the 1 day delay animals but not the 7 day delay ones. Without treatment, retention at those two intervals was similar. These results suggest that disturbing normal hippocampal function can make retrieval difficult for memories which would normally be thought of as consolidated, provided they are as yet relatively young. Similar results have been reported with spreading depression (see Mayes, 1981). Although these tasks are very different from those found in human amnesia, electrical stimulation of the hippocampus in humans has been found to cause reversible retrograde amnesias, whose extent depends on stimulation duration (see Bickford et al., 1958).

It seems that consolidation deficit explanations of steeply graded retrograde amnesia must posit both prolongated consolidation and retrieval disturbance from lesion-induced 'noise'. Such theories predict that the retrograde amnesia will change in complex ways after the initial trauma. The transience of post-traumatic and ECT-induced retrograde amnesia strongly suggests recovery of limbic function and that at least for these groups, there is a retrieval problem for more recent memories. Such observations have led Squire (1979) to propose that the 'limbic memory system' is involved both in the prolonged consolidation of memories and the retrieval of the same memories during this period. A variant of this proposal might require the initial storage of memories in the system and their gradual 'reading out' into other structures. If this combined deficit causes retrograde amnesia, then even when gradual recovery ends in completely normal limbic function, there should never be complete restoration of pretraumatic memories (because of their lack of prolonged consolidation). Complete restoration would be predicted if another brain system was responsible for prolonged consolidation, and the retrograde amnesia arose from direct or 'noise'-induced disturbance of a special retrieval process, somehow intermeshed with the consolidation activity (as Wickelgren suggests).

In summary, the evidence is sketchy, but amnesia probably comprises several independent functional deficits, arising from different limbic–diencephalic lesions and loosely associated with aetiological categories. There is no strong evidence that limbic lesions cause encoding problems although such deficits probably arise from frontal or other damage. Finally, available evidence is consistent with the presence of several storage and retrieval deficits in amnesia, but their possible nature has only been loosely adumbrated.

6.5 The Critical Lesions in Human Organic Amnesia

6.5.1 Anatomy

Evidence about the minimal critical lesion(s) is poor for several reasons. First, there is incidental damage in most, if not all cases, which does not relate to core amnesic symptoms. Second, lesion location in living subjects, despite modern methods, still lacks precision. Third, post-mortem analyses may be precise but are rare and may describe lesions which evolved further in the period before death. Fourth, assessment of amnesia has been inadequate in many cases. Not surprisingly, therefore, the literature is not internally consistent. Even so, until recently the consensual view was undoubtably that amnesia arose from lesions of the hippocampus and/or of serially connected structures in Papez circuit. These latter structures notably included the mammillary bodies and their fornical link to the hippocampus with less emphasis being placed on the anterior thalamus and the cingulate cortex.

The critical evidence involves the effects of temporal lobectomy on memory. This surgical work showed that even after bilateral removal of the anterior temporal cortex, uncus and amygdala, only minor memory problems resulted unless the hippocampus was also invaded. Unilateral lesions, which caused material-specific memory deficits, confirmed this impression as the defects correlated with the amount of hippocampus removed (Milner, 1971). These data do not unequivocally support the hippocampal hypothesis. One alternative interpretation, provided by Mishkin (1978) is that amnesia depends on combined hippocampal and amygdala lesions. All the surgical cases involve damage to both structures. A second alternative interpretation, provided by Horel (1978) is that amnesia is caused by damage to the temporal stem or albal stalk. He argues that all the surgical lesions damage this white matter which links the temporal cortex and amygdala to diencephalic structures, such as the dorsomedial nucleus of the thalamus. Further, more posterior and extensive hippocampal removal is associated with more temporal stem damage.

Evidence that fornix lesions cause amnesia in humans is weak. Squire and Moore (1979) reviewed 50 cases of putative fornical damage and found evidence of amnesia in only three. Heilman and Sypert (1977) have argued that in the negative cases damage was confined to the post-commissural fornix whereas their case and the other two positive ones, involved damage to both pre- and post-commissural fornix. It remains open whether their interpretation is correct, or whether the lesions extended into the closely adjacent medial thalamus or mammillary bodies. (Heilman and Sypert did describe additional damage to the hippocampal commissure in their case.) Even if their interpretation is correct, the amnesic effect of the more radical fornix section may depend on projections to the thalamus.

Most cases of amnesia, putatively caused by mammillary body lesions, have been associated with an aetiology of chronic alcoholism. Such cases probably always suffer other lesions. Furthermore, Victor *et al.* (1971), in the classic study of Korsakoff pathology, identified five cases with the mammillary body abnormalities who had not shown an amnesic syndrome in life. These cases did not have identifiable damage to the dorsomedial thalamic nucleus. It was probably that 38 other cases, with damage to both structures, showed amnesia (although this was not clearly established). Other evidence apparently contradicts these data. Thus, Brion and Mikol (1978) described 11 amnesics, 4 of whom had mammillary body damage uncomplicated by lesions of the dorsomedial thalamic nucleus. There may, however, have been destruction of other structures. This possibility is supported by the finding of Mair *et al.* (1979) that, at post-mortem, two severely amnesic patients had severe atrophy of the medial nuclei of the mammillary bodies together with damage to the little known paratenial nucleus, lying slightly medial and running anterior to the dorsomedial thalamic nucleus. The thalamic lesions described probably overlap with those in Victor *et al.*'s series, but do not extend so far laterally into the dorsomedial nucleus. It remains unclear, therefore, whether mammillary body lesions are sufficient to cause amnesia or whether they must be combined with medial thalamic or possibly other lesions.

In contrast to the 'hippocampal hypothesis', another possibility is that dorsomedial thalamic lesions are sufficient to cause amnesia, and that this is the explanation of alcoholic amnesia. Damage is, however, too widespread in alcoholic amnesics for them to provide a useful testing ground. Tumours may be more focal and McEntee *et al.* (1976) have described amnesia in a bilateral tumour case where the medial and posterior thalamus were invaded, but not the mammillary bodies. Psychological assessment of this case was minimal as the patient was drowsy and soon lapsed into coma, so caution is warranted. Squire and Moore (1979) have described CAT scans of patient NA (fencing foil accident case), which they argued are consistent with a lesion to the left dorsal thalamus, in the region of the dorsomedial thalamus. This technique's use cannot exclude convincingly the possibility of other more subtle lesions, however, so it remains unproved that this thalamic lesion is sufficient for amnesia. Indeed, two pieces of evidence argue for a different conclusion. First, Spiegel *et al.*'s (1955) report on the effects of stereotaxic dorsomedial thalamotomy, suggests that patients experienced only a transient amnesia compounded with disproportionate temporal confusion. The description which is tantalizingly inadequate does indicate emotional changes occur, e.g. apathy. Second, Jurko (1978) has shown that neither amygdala nor thalamic centre median lesions alone impair paired-associate learning whereas combined lesions of the left amygdala and centre median do. Jurko suggested that the amygdala–centre median perform complementary alerting and attentional roles, critical for learning.

If the case for hippocampal, fornical or mammillary body lesions alone causing permanent amnesia is unconvincing, then that for a role of anterior thalamic or cingulate lesions is extremely fragmentary. Whitty and Lewin (1960) described a mild transient amnesia, associated with surprisingly poor memory for temporal order, in 14 cingulectomy patients. More recently, Lhermitte and Signoret (1976) reported a case of amnesia following bilateral cingulectomy in the treatment of an aneurysm of the anterior communicating artery. The amnesia was, however, unusual as the patient would learn normally, but showed poor free recall with confabulation, unless he was helped by cues in which event his memory was normal. They interpreted the case as one with an isolated retrieval deficit. Hassler (1962) has described an isolated case in which bilateral coagulation of the anterior thalamus appeared to alleviate hallucinatory schizophrenia while causing severe amnesia. This case is obviously hard to assess. It should perhaps be pointed out here that there is a growing body of evidence which suggests that lesions or stimulation of a variety of thalamic nuclei can cause short-term memory deficits, e.g. in digit span (see Dimond, 1980, for a review). Most of these deficits are not found in 'pure' amnesics.

The 'hippocampal hypothesis' is currently competing for acceptance with Horel's temporal stem hypothesis of amnesia and the view, inspired by Mishkin (1978) that a combined hippocampal and amygdala lesion is necessary for amnesia. Both these proponents claim to find support from animal lesion studies. More recent evidence, however, strongly supports Mishkin's as against Horel's view (see Squire and Zola-Morgan, 1982; Zola-Morgan *et al.*, 1981). This is discussed in the final section. The human data are weakly consistent with Horel's view, in that cases of temporal damage have lesions of the temporal stem, and alcoholic and other cases may be seen to have damage to the principal projection sites of the stem, such as the dorsomedial nucleus. The data are also weakly consistent with a generalized version of Mishkin's (lesions to hippocampus or directly connected structures plus lesions to amygdala or directly connected structures such as centre median or dorsomedial thalamic nuclei). Both hypotheses are compatible with the notion that amnesia involves damage to several independent, but overlapping, functional–anatomical systems whereas such a notion is hard to accommodate within the 'hippocampal hypothesis'.

Oscar-Berman and Zola-Morgan (1980a, 1980b) have recently described an alternative means of locating the critical lesions in amnesics which, given the great problem in directly and accurately identifying lesion sites in humans, may have some value. They have tested alcoholic amnesics on a variety of tasks, whose sensitivity to disruption by a variety of lesions in monkeys is already reasonably well known. Thus, they have found that alcoholic amnesics are impaired on some reversal trials, but not original learning, of both spatial and visual reversal learning paradigms. This exact pattern of impairment is not seen in monkeys following lesions of either orbital or dorsolateral frontal cortices, the amygdala, the hippocampus or the fornix, or the anterior inferotemporal zone. More similar patterns of breakdown are seen, however, following combined lesions such as those of different parts of the frontal cortex, or large lesions of the medial temporal lobe, which affect both hippocampus and amygdala (see Oscar-Berman & Zola-Morgan, 1980a). They also reported that alcoholic amnesics are mildly impaired at learning two-choice visual discrimination problems, but severely impaired at learning such problems when presented concurrently (Oscar-Berman and Zola-Morgan, 1980b). They argued that these impairments, like those on reversal learning, represented deficits in the ability to form and modify stimulus–reinforcement associations, which studies of monkeys suggest may involve lesions of the amygdala and anterior inferotemporal cortex or of structures linked to these. Clearly, the power of this approach depends on both the precision with which monkey lesion effects can be identified and on the degree of similarity between humans and monkeys. Nevertheless the approach provides a useful adjunct to traditional ones. The next section considers another way of revealing the complexity of the disturbances underlying amnesia.

6.5.2 *Biochemistry*

Both noradrenergic and cholinergic deficits have been associated with human amnesia. The association has plausibility as both neurotransmitters are involved in hippocampal and other limbic system circuits. McEntee and Mair (1978, 1980) have provided the most direct evidence, which implicates a noradrenergic deficit in amnesia. Their initial study involved measuring the concentration of 3-methoxy-4-hydroxy-phenyl glycol (MHPG), which is a primary metabolite of noradrenaline. This chemical was assayed in the lumbar spinal fluid of patients with alcoholic amnesia. The concentrations were reduced in the amnesics and the reduction correlated with the size of the patients' WAIS–Wechsler Memory Scale (WMS) score difference. No significant deficits were observed in the metabolites of dopamine and serotonin. Victor *et al*. (1971) found many alcoholic amnesics had symmetrical lesions about the third and fourth ventricles, which would interrupt noradrenaline pathways. In some cases there was also damage to the locus coeruleus.

McEntee and Mair (1980) have subsequently administered drugs to eight alcoholic amnesics in an attempt to boost central noradrenergic function and so improve their memory. Only clonidine, which is a putative alpha-adrenergic agonist, significantly improved memory. They found that D-amphetamine was ineffective although patients with evidence of higher central dopaminergic activity seemed to show more response. The pattern of the pharmacological data led the experimenters to conclude that clonidine's action was post- and not presynaptic. Inspection of the memory data, however, reveals clonidine only improves memory for a consonant trigram version of the Peterson task and some tests on the WMS. These latter tests included the digit span which improved but not significantly, and the memory passages and visual reproduction which improved significantly. All these tests contain a considerable short-term memory component which should be normal in amnesics. It has been argued that poor performance on the Peterson task is an effect of incidental frontal damage and the same argument may apply to the other tasks from the WMS. The fact that clonidine still improved memory passage and visual reproduction performance at 10 min probably reflected the maintenance of initially better performance (which may depend on processing efficiency). It is unfortunate that the WMS contains subtests, tapping functions, which should be relatively normal after limbic lesions. It is also notable that clonidine failed to improve paired associate learning, which is known to be deficient in amnesics.

The evidence relating a cholinergic deficit to amnesia is less direct. It has been shown that senile and presenile dements of the Alzheimer type (who initially present with fairly isolated memory problems) have low levels of the enzymes choline acetyltransferase (CAT) and acetyl cholinesterase. These deficits are particularly apparent in the hippocampus (Davies & Maloney, 1976). Drachman (1977) complemented these observations, by showing that the anticholinergic drug scopolamine produced a 'model dementia' in humans in which memory deficits were accompanied by a lowering of performance IQ. This 'dementia' was not reversed by amphetamine although this increased subjects' alertness, but was reversed by the anticholinesterase physostigmine. Cholinergic agonists (or other facilitatory drugs) such as choline, lecithin, arecoline and physostigmine have been given to young, elderly and dementing people with varying effects on memory (see Christie *et al*., 1981, and Drachman & Sahakian, 1979, for reviews). Effects are very sensitive to dose and may vary with subject age and mental efficiency, but positive results have been reported for young, old and dementing patients of the Alzheimer type. Peters and Lewin

(1977) have also reported that a patient with post-encephalitic amnesia showed an improvement in memory after receiving 0.8 mg of physostigmine subcutaneously. Drachman and Sahakian (1979), however, have criticized the memory scoring methods used in this study, which casts doubts upon the effect's reliability. Even so, Goldberg *et al.* (1980) have more recently reported improvement in verbal recall in post traumatic amnesics during combined treatment with physostigmine and lecithin. They thought the effect was on 'rote storage and/or retrieval' rather than on encoding strategies.

There is some evidence that scopolamine impairs learning and subsequent memory while leaving short-term memory (digit span) intact and pre-drug memory relatively intact (Drachman & Sahakian, 1979; Petersen, 1977). This apparent absence of retrograde amnesia following the administration of anticholinergic drugs contrasts with the effects of medial temporal lobe amnesia. The claim clearly needs confirmation through the use of objective tests for retrograde amnesia. If supported, then there may be a cholinergic circuit important in memory consolidation. The septohippocampal system could well constitute such a circuit. Scopolamine might also disturb cortical cholinergic neurons to cause the deficit in performance IQ. No study has yet examined whether 'limbic' amnesics have a cholinergic deficit but this seems likely.

In summary, amnesics may suffer from one or more neurotransmitter dysfunctions. Noradrenergic impairment may be incidental to the core amnesic syndrome(s). It may resemble frontal impairment in this respect — indeed, the two impairments may be related. Cholinergic disturbances of limbic structures may be more central to the syndrome. Drugs which affect this transmitter may provide a powerful tool in fractionating the functional deficits of amnesia. In humans, they can be used in normal volunteers or amnesic patients. Their use is limited, however, by ethical consideration, so animal models are essential. Such models are also vital for studying the effects of limbic lesions on memory. These will now be reviewed.

6.6 Amnesia in Animals

6.6.1 Animal Models of Chronic Alcoholism

Alcoholic amnesics are not a homogeneous group with respect to both lesion extent and functional deficits. This heterogeneity may reflect the complex aetiology of chronic alcoholism. Thiamine deficiency, secondary to alcoholism, has generally been seen as the cause of the subcortical damage underlying amnesia. This view gains support from Blass and Gibson's (1977) report that cells, cultured from alcoholic amnesics, have a deficit in the thiamine-dependent enzyme transketolase. Further, thiamine deficiency almost certainly caused 52 cases of Wernicke–Korsakoff disease in a Singapore prisoner of war camp (de Wardener & Lennox, 1947). Whereas the memory problems of these cases responded well to thiamine therapy, however, those of alcoholic amnesics do not (Victor *et al.*, 1971). The possibility that other agents may cause amnesia in the alcoholic syndrome is supported by reports that nicotinic acid deficiency can also lead to memory problems (Jolliffe *et al.*, 1940) but more importantly there is considerable evidence that chronic alcoholism can lead to cortical atrophy with associated mental deterioration and memory problems (Lishman *et al.*, 1980). This damage may be a direct effect of alcohol's toxicity.

The effect of chronic alcoholism *per se* has been explored in rats fed a vitamin-fortified diet in conjunction with a regular intake of alcohol over periods of 3 to 7 months. Animals kept on this regimen and then allowed to 'dry out', have displayed residual impairments of learning with several tasks (e.g. Walker *et al.*, 1982). Such animals also show a loss of hippocampal pyramidal and dentate gyrus granule cells, together with a decrease of 50–60% in dendritic spines for surviving cells of these kinds (Walker *et al.*, 1980; Riley & Walker, 1978). These workers found no changes in the dorsomedial nucleus of the thalamus. Cortical atrophy was apparently not looked for, but might have been expected on the basis of human cases. There is then a strong suggestion that the direct effects of alcoholic toxicity include hippocampal atrophy (possibly related to learning deficits) as well perhaps as cortical atrophy (related to deterioration in cognition and perhaps memory).

Early work on thiamine-deficient animals demonstrated the neurological defects associated with Wernicke's encephalopathy but only equivocally showed learning deficits (see Vorhees, 1979). Vorhees (1979) has shown that rats, recovered from even mild thiamine deficiency, are poor at learning a Y-maze avoidance task, and those recovered from a severe deficiency are also poor at brightness discrimination acquisition (Vorhees *et al.*, 1975). Interestingly, Vorhees relates these learning failures to regionally specific reductions in acetylcholine turnover which are effects of thiamine deficiency (Vorhees, *et al.*, 1977).

An attractive interpretation of available data is that a combination of thiamine deficiency and direct alcoholic toxicity causes brain damage in amnesics with the relative contribution determined by intake pattern and hereditary factors. Other agents may also play a role. Thiamine deficiency causes Wernicke symptoms and perhaps through damaging limbic system cholinergic neurons, it causes amnesia. Alcoholic toxicity may cause amnesia for other reasons via hippocampal damage (the two alcoholic amnesics described by Mair *et al.*, 1979, did not show hippocampal damage, perhaps indicating an aetiology of thiamine deficiency or another agency) and its effects on the cortex (particularly frontal regions) will cause mild dementia and encoding perseverative problems with memory. This hypothesis can be usefully explored through animal models. So can the relationship between the pattern of alcohol intake and the extent of dorsomedial thalamic damage (an important issue as the extent of this damage seems to differ across alcoholic amnesics).

6.6.2 *Effects of Frontal Cortex Lesions in Animals*

It has been argued consistently here that frontal lesions and those to the 'limbic memory system' have different effects on cognition and memory. Iversen (1976), however, has argued that hippocampal and frontal lesions have similar effects on memory and other functions in rats, cats and monkeys. For example, in monkeys, lesions of the hippocampus or dorsolateral frontal cortex impair delayed response and delayed alternation performance. In addition, both frontal and hippocampal lesions have been associated with problems on spatial reversal learning and tasks requiring the ordering of a sequence of responses (see Kolb & Whishaw, 1980). In further support of her view, Iversen has pointed out that frontal and hippocampal systems receive similar combinations of intero- and exteroceptive inputs. For example, visual information passes from modality-specific association cortex to the frontal region, and via area TH and entorhinal cortex to the hippocampus. Similarly, olfactory information projects to frontal cortex via the dorsomedial thalamus and to the hippocampus via the entorhinal cortex. Some interoceptive information may reach both structures from the tegmentum via the septum (to the hippocampus) and dorsomedial thalamus (to frontal cortex).

Similarities may be exaggerated and may in this case partly reflect the insensitivity of available behavioural tests. The anatomical data show that there may be some degree of parallel processing with frontal cortex and temporal limbic structures such as the hippocampus. The two systems may be operating on the inputs in very different ways. A precedent for this possibility is provided by the 'secondary' visual areas of the rhesus monkey, which receive similar inputs but are individually concerned with analysing different features such as retinal disparity and colour (see Ratcliff & Cowey, 1979). Clearly, the nature of the inputs differs in detail, and the same point applies to the hippocampus and frontal cortex, both of which are probably functionally heterogeneous. For example, Rosenkilde (1979) has identified five frontal subregions, on the basis of differential lesion effects. Thus, sulcus principalis lesions impair spatial delayed response and alternation performance whereas inferior prefrontal convexity lesions impair performance on delayed matching to sample, go/no-go differentiation and delayed alternation. The anatomical connections of such areas differ on fine analysis. Whether the different subregions mediate related functions (e.g. concerned with performance of various kinds of delay tasks) remains an open question.

Alcoholic (and other) amnesias are unlikely to be accompanied with just one subgroup of frontal impairments. Animal lesion studies can clearly play a role in pinpointing which frontal subregions may be responsible for specific amnesic symptoms. Finer behavioural analyses and other techniques will be essential for this purpose and that of distinguishing between frontal and limbic system function. For example, the spatial delayed response impairments, associated with sulcus principalis lesions, have been investigated by Stamm (1969), using electrical stimulation. Application of this stimulation to the sulcus impairs performance only when given during cue presentation and shortly afterwards, whereas ventrolateral caudate stimulation disturbs performance when given at any stage during the retention interval but not during cue presentation. Lesions in both structures impair performance. In contrast, Fuster (1973) and Fuster and Alexander (1973) have shown that there are activity changes for single neurons during cue presentation and shortly afterwards, in both sulcal and dorsomedial thalamus neurons. Lesions in the thalamic nucleus also disturb delayed response performance (Schulman, 1964). Clearly, the processes required in delayed responding are complex and involve many structures, mediating separable subfunctions. Some of these subfunctions may involve memory and others not. It is uncertain, for example, whether sulcal lesions cause direct memory problems because the delayed response impairment is reversed if darkness is maintained in the delay period or if trials are spaced. Similarly, Correll and Scoville (1967) have argued that the deficit in delayed alternation caused by medial temporal lesions, depends on the task not the delay, i.e. it is as great with no delay as it is after one of 10 s.

235

Two final points are warranted. First, the frontal lobes may stand in a super-ordinate relation to the 'limbic memory' structures. The latter may subserve more 'basic' memory functions while the frontal system 'pulls the strings' by coordinating these functions in accord with plans of action which it generates. Second, frontal lesions in animals cause delayed response impairments. In humans, these lesions do not impair delayed response in this way, although they impair delayed matching to sample (Prisko, cited by Milner, 1971) and recency judgements. It is unclear whether these animal and human deficits have a common origin, and whether they represent a kind of sensitivity to interference not found after limbic system lesions.

6.6.3 Amnesic Effects of Limbic System Lesions in Animals

The use of limbic system lesions in animals is currently limited by our inadequate knowledge of the critical lesion in humans and disagreement about the pattern of memory breakdown characteristic of human amnesics. One strategy is to compare the effects of lesions to the hippocampus, mammillary bodies, dorsomedial thalamus, temporal stem, amygdala or some combination of these, on those aspects of memory most similar to those disturbed in human amnesics. Alternatively, some patterns of breakdown may be found first in lesioned animals and then looked for in human amnesics.

The most explored structure has been the hippocampus. Even if hippocampal lesions cause the loss of a single coherent function, however, it has proved difficult to identify a functional deficit of this kind, which can encompass the range of lesion effects. The effects include perseverative tendencies, difficulty in ordering long chains of behaviour, spatial mapping problems, memory deficits in high interference situations and attentional disturbances. Early lesion work did, however, fail to reveal the kind of global memory loss which had been expected and gave rise to much theorizing about the role of the hippocampus in inhibiting responding or modulating attention when circumstances changed (see Douglas, 1972). These theories came to be seen as plausible accounts of human amnesia only when Weiskrantz and Warrington (1975) formulated their retrieval deficit hypothesis, in which memory failure is caused by excessive interfering competition from irrelevant memories. In other words, animals with hippocampal lesions, fail to shift their response patterns when new or altered circumstances demand, and human amnesics fail to change their patterns of retrieval when the circumstances of memory change. Lesioned animals failed to show learning problems in simple associative tasks because these involved no interfering shifts of environmental contingencies. In tasks where contingencies change, such as with some types of reversal learning and extinction, then hippo-campally lesioned animals had learning impairments. Similarly, human amnesics' memory problems were most apparent in tests where requirements changed and the level of interference was very high. In tasks such as classical conditioning and perceptuomotor skills, where putative levels of interference were low, then their performance was relatively good. In outline, a disturbance of attentional modulation seemed capable of comprehending human amnesic interference phenomena and the problems of hippocampal animals in situations of changing significance. Certainly, such unification was more likely to be achieved, by postulating the disruption of attentional rather than motor control, as suggested by some theorists (see Vanderwolf et al., 1975).

One major criticism of the equation of animal and human hippocampal lesions with the amnesic syndrome, has been that the human syndrome is associated with disturbances not found in the case of hippocampal lesions in animals. Horel (1978) has argued that monkeys perform normally on delayed matching to sample unless their lesions extend beyond the hippocampus to include the rest of the ventromedial quadrant of the temporal lobe. Further, he has claimed that the deficit in this task correlates best with the extent of temporal stem damage. Also, hippocampal animals have been found to perform go/no-go alternation and object reversal tasks normally despite showing the usual impairments on left/right alternation and spatial reversal tasks (Pribram & Isaacson, 1975). One interpretation of these data is in terms of the currently pre-eminent view of hippocampal function, viz. that the structure is the centre of a system which creates an absolute, non-egocentric, spatial framework (see O'Keefe & Nadel, 1978). Specifically, it is proposed that an animal or human gets around the environment either by using taxon systems or a locale system, of which only the latter depends on the hippocampus. Taxon systems guide or orient behaviour in relation to egocentric cues, e.g. 'Go to the light', whereas the locale system involves the use of environmental maps, comprising place representations linked by rules specifying distance and direction. The hypothesis is supported by the fact that most behaviours disturbed by hippocampal lesions have a clear spatial component, and by the evidence suggesting that some hippocampal units respond selectively to spatial location (see O'Keefe & Nadel, 1979, for a discussion).

The hypothesis has received support from two other sources. The first involves hippocampal theta activity. Some research suggests that the electrical stimulation of this activity in the short period after learning improves later memory (Landfield, 1976; Wetzel et al., 1977). Winson (1978) reported that medial septal lesions, which eliminated hippocampal theta activity, impaired performance on a spatial task learnt before lesioning. Two types of theta have been postulated (Robinson, 1980), one of which is driven by a cholinergic medial septum–hippocampal system. It is, therefore, interesting that the anti-cholinergic scopolamine has been found to impair acquisition and retention of a spatial habit (Watts et al., in press). Furthermore, this drug-induced deficit was only seen in animals using spatial strategies. There are two problems with this evidence. First, Winson's animals do relearn the spatial task which suggests that the theta system is only part of a larger hippocampal mapping process. Second, O'Keefe and Nadel (1978) believe that scopolamine-resistant theta reflects spatial mapping, because it is correlated with translation in space and its frequency is proportional to velocity (but see Vanderwolf, 1979). The correlates of scopolamine-sensitive theta are less well defined although some think they include activation and learning (see Robinson, 1980).

If the spatial hypothesis is correct, then the 'hippocampal hypothesis' cannot be an adequate account of human amnesia, unless extraordinary ad hoc assumptions are made (see O'Keefe & Nadel, 1978). The position has been challenged however, by Olton et al. (1979) who think the hippocampus mediates, what they call, working as opposed to reference memory, even when the locale system is not involved. In reference memory, information remains relevant for many trials and usually a whole task, whereas in working memory stimulus information is useful for one trial only. Two crucial experiments were performed involving radial mazes, in which extra-maze cues could play a prominent part in guiding behaviour. In the first experiment, 8 of 17 arms were baited with food and the choice behaviour of rats was recorded over a number of 'trials'. The same arms were rebaited after each trial and the ability to choose them was the test of reference memory. Within each trial, however, the optimal strategy involves visiting each baited arm in turn and not revisiting previously baited arms — this was the test of working memory. Rats with fimbria–fornix lesions were able to relearn the spatial reference memory component of the task but not the working memory component. The second experiment showed that these lesions disturbed working memory even when performance was not based on the locale system. This was achieved by making each arm of a four arm maze distinctive, and moving the arms relative to each other, each time the rat made a choice. Behaviour was based on intra-maze cues.

Working memory is peculiarly susceptible to interference and the similarity between this view of hippocampal function and earlier views, such as that of Douglas (1972) is apparent. According to Douglas (1979) 'the hippocampus acts to suppress orienting or attention to a stimulus or its central representation (the idea)'. If a reference memory task is modified to include a high level of interference, then animals with hippocampal dysfunction should do very poorly. Douglas has shown this, using a T-maze in which rats must learn sequences like left, left, or right, right, left, where much interference operates. Scopolamine blocks the learning or retention of this task. Similarly, Winocur and Breckenridge (1973) found that small hippocampal lesions impaired learning of a left, right, left, right, right, left sequence. Three brief comments are warranted here. First, these data corroborate others which show a striking overlap between the effects of hippocampal lesions and anticholinergic drugs. This overlap is relevant to the human data discussed in Section 6.5.1. Second, Douglas (1979) has argued that rats can solve the above tasks with strategies which make little use of the locale system. This reaffirms his original view that hippocampal lesions disturb the ability to cope with high interference situations rather than those requiring spatial mapping. Third, the role of the hippocampus in spatial mapping must remain open. O'Keefe (1979) believes that Olton *et al.*'s four arm maze may have needed the locale system for its solution, and that relearning of the reference component of the 17 arm maze may have been based on a guidance hypothesis (dependent on taxon systems). His arguments raise doubts about the testability of the spatial hypothesis, but be that as it may, Nadel and MacDonald (1980) have reported data that conflict with those of Olton *et al.* They found that hippocampally lesioned rats could not relearn a maze task, dependent on extra-maze place cues, but could relearn a similar task, of comparable difficulty for intact rats, which was based on 'non-spatial' intra-maze cues. Only further experiments can resolve this particular discrepancy.

Although spatial mapping may be an important hippocampal function, there are hippocampal lesion effects not readily explained as spatial deficits. For example, Moss *et al.* (1979) found that such lesions impaired the ability of monkeys to learn a concurrent object discrimination task, despite being able to learn the discriminations one at a time quite normally. Not only is the hippocampus involved in this high interference non-spatial task, but there is also evidence implicating it in temporal processing. Thus, it has been shown that during the simple classical conditioning of the rabbit nictitating membrane response (NMR), hippocampal neurons increase their firing rate so as to create a kind of temporal model of the intensity of the conditioned response (Berger & Thompson, 1978). The learned increase in hippocampal neural activity alternates according to whether trials are reinforced or unreinforced (even though the overt conditioned response does not), which could only occur if stimulus information from the preceding trial was monitored (Thompson, 1976). The fact that the hippocampal lesions do not impair the simple acquisition of this task, suggests that the structure does not necessarily use the information about the fine temporal structure of the learning which it is monitoring. Moore (1979) has suggested that the hippocampus receives a 'copy' of the associative information from the brainstem reticular formation (where it is stored) and uses it when a complex stimulus array contains irrelevant or non-salient components which the animal must learn to ignore. This view is supported by the disruptive effects of hippocampal lesions on latent inhibition (where pre-exposure weakens the conditionability of a stimulus) and blocking (in which pretraining one component of a compound CS inhibits conditioning of the other component) in NMR conditioning (see Solomon, 1979).

The hippocampus probably monitors spatiotemporal and other complex kinds of information and damaging it makes an animal very susceptible to high interference tasks because it cannot use this information to modulate attention, and particularly to show flexible, strategy shifting. Even tasks which hippocampal animals can learn normally show impairments under conditions of high interference. Thus, Winocur (1979) found lesioned rats learned and retained a visual discrimination normally unless an unsolvable problem using similar stimuli was interposed in the retention interval. When the unsolvable problem was presented before learning then the lesioned rats had difficulty acquiring the normally simple discrimination skill. Interference seemed particularly disruptive of either learning or retrieval in hippocampal animals. Similar interference effects have been shown by Oulton (1979), who used a paradigm in which memory for two tasks was concurrently tested. He found excessive interference in hippocampal rats, in proportion to the similarity of the tasks. The tasks had been originally learned as well by hippocampal animals as by normal ones. The effects occurred even with overtraining. When concurrent retention testing was given in different apparatuses, however, the interference effects were markedly reduced. A related context effect has been found by Winocur and Olds (1978). They trained lesioned and control rats in a simultaneous pattern discrimination and tested retention — either in the same context or a very different one. Under the context shift condition alone, the hippocampal rats showed a retrieval impairment.

These data may indicate that lesioned animals fail to use spatial, temporal and possibly other information to discriminate between different situations. Their 'soft focus' discrimination makes them vulnerable whenever two or more contexts are similar but demand different responses. Depending on the contextual demands, they may show either learning or retrieval problems. These failures of conditional learning and retrieval are minimal for simple associative tasks, performed in distinctive contexts where one response is clearly dominant (Hirsh, 1980). Sensitivity to interference is, therefore, secondary to a contextual discrimination deficit. It can be argued that this deficit occurs in hippocampal animals that cannot properly encode and/or retrieve stimuli which have no direct motivational significance. Thus, they show deficits not only in blocking and latent inhibition, but also in latent learning (Owen & Butler, 1980). Lesioned animals have a selective problem with these contextual stimuli and fail to appreciate their true significance, although similar stimuli, when of clear motivational significance can form the basis of normally learned associative habits.

The above account of the effects of hippocampal lesions in animals is very similar to the theory of human anterograde amnesia given in Section 6.4.2. It was pointed out there that the effects on which the human theorizing is based are also found in attenuated human memory, which suggests that they may be effects of poor memory rather than reflective of its cause. Similar arguments do not seem applicable to the animal data as more care has been taken to equate the initial learning of hippocampal and control animals. There is, therefore, a tension between the two literatures. The human memory strength criticism may turn out to be a red herring, or the hippocampal animals may turn out not to be properly matched on learning. Matching hippocampal and control animals on learning may, however, not be sufficient to ensure matching after a delay at retention. If like HM they forget faster than controls (Huppert & Piercy, 1979), then their memories will be poorer at retention even without a contextual change. A third possibility is that the human and animal data may not be so closely related as they seem to be at first sight. This would be so if the significance of context, and nature of the failure to use it, was different in humans and animals. Human and animal task paradigms are after all radically different in most studies and animals cannot be instructed as humans can. Hippocampally lesioned animals may genuinely fail to discriminate between contexts and hence show some memory problems whereas human amnesics may show pecularities in contextual discrimination because of their poor memory, which is caused by other factors.

The lack of a close similarity between hippocampally lesioned animals and at least some groups of human amnesics might also be expected as the human cases often have lesions of the mammillary bodies and/or dorsomedial nucleus of the thalamus rather than the hippocampus. Although the mammillary bodies are linked by the fornix to the hippocampus it does not follow that the functions of the two structures are identical. The hippocampus also projects to other cortical and subcortical sites, such as entorhinal and medial frontal cortex, and the amygdala. Furthermore, lesions of the fornix do not have identical effects to those of the hippocampus. The degree of similarity may depend on the tests used. Thus, Gaffan, (1974) has found that monkeys with fornix transection show good associative but poor recognition memory. If some objects are presented with reward and others not, such monkeys can discriminate rewarded from non-rewarded objects, but cannot distinguish presented from novel objects. Although Gaffan would argue for a similar deficit following hippocampal lesions, Mahut et al. (1981) have reported deficits on tasks which require not only object recognition but also the ability to form and retain stimulus–reinforcement associations in more than one modality. Their animals were tested entirely post-operatively on the learning, retention and reversal of object discriminations.

Unlike those with hippocampal lesions, fornix-sectioned monkeys, improve performance in object reversal tasks, retain discriminations well when the retention tests are alternated with reversal testing and perform slightly better than controls on concurrent discrimination tasks (see Mahut *et al.*, 1981). Fornix-sectioned monkeys do well on tasks which require frequent response shifts and the concurrent handling of several objects whereas they are very poor at maintaining consistent choices for a long time. Zola-Morgan (in Mahut *et al.*, 1981) speculated that these animals have an exaggerated need for perceptual novelty based possibly on pathologically rapid satiation. This view would be compatible with the claim that the lesion does *not* cause amnesia in humans.

Not only do lesions in different limbic structures appear to have different effects, but the hippocampus itself also seems to be a functionally diverse structure. Thus, Jarrard (1980) has argued that whereas fimbrial or extensive hippocampal lesions increase activity and susceptibility to interference, lesions confined to the CAI field do not increase activity, have less influence on sensitivity to interference and only impair *acquisition* of complex tasks. This suggests that CAI lesions cause a selective anterograde amnesia in which there is little increase in susceptibility to interference. Also, Stevens and Cowey (1973) have interpreted the effects of ventral hippocampal lesions as results of impoverished hypothesis behaviour in contrast to the effects of dorsal hippocampal lesions which they viewed as results of a failure to ignore repeated or irrelevant stimuli. Neither the CAI deficit proposed by Jarrard nor those proposed by Stevens and Cowey can be readily equated with the view that hippocampal lesions impair the processing of contextual stimuli. Indeed, Stevens and Cowey (1972) reported that hippocampally lesioned rats actually learned a two-lever alternation task faster than controls when a remote visual cue was present. This finding is not obviously compatible with a failure to process properly those stimuli which form the background of a task. It may prove of value to follow the example of Oscar-Berman and Zola-Morgan (1980a, 1980b) and see whether effects such as this are seen in human amnesics.

Unfortunately, too few animal studies have been performed as yet to show whether the effects of mammillary body lesions differ from hippocampal ones. The evidence cited concerning fornix lesions and the recording work of Vinogradova (1975) is certainly consistent with somewhat different functions for the structures in Papez circuit. In a suggestive study, Rosenstock *et al.* (1977) reported that mammillary body lesions impaired the acquisition of a simple alternation habit and that inter-trial delay adds to the severity of the deficit. The retention of this spatial habit was found not to be impaired if it was learned pre-operatively. This indicates that the lesion may cause anterograde but not retrograde amnesia for spatial and possibly other kinds of tasks. Further work is clearly needed to ascertain the degree of similarity between hippocampal and mammillary body lesions.

There is a similar paucity of studies on lesions of the dorsomedial nucleus of the thalamus, Waring and Means (1976) have, however, shown that lesions of this nucleus in rats impaired performance on associative tasks, spatial and non-spatial go/no-go tasks as well as reducing the display of emotionality. In monkeys with similar lesions, Schulman (1964) found delayed response and associative visual task impairments but noted that even a small remnant of the lesioned structure was sufficient for performance. As magnocellular and parvocellular divisions of the lesioned nucleus have different frontal projections, the large lesions may have disturbed two or more functional systems. Furthermore, Weiss and Means (1980) have found that only bilateral dorsomedial thalamic lesions cause spontaneous alternation and visual–tactile discrimination deficits whereas medial frontal and combined frontal–thalamic unilateral lesions do not. This suggests that thalamic and frontal functions may be complementary rather than identical. A basic and still unsolved problem in these lesion studies is how to select tasks which are both differentially sensitive to different lesions and correspond to those measures which are disturbed in human amnesics.

This difficulty is apparent in the work of Horel and Misantone (1976) which seems to support the view that temporal stem lesions, or lesions of the stem's projection sites, play a critical role in human amnesia. They found that temporal stem lesions drastically impaired the ability of monkeys to relearn an associative visual discrimination task. The view that this reflects a severe amnesia seems compatible with the observation that dramatic cases of human amnesia have been reported with combined temporal cortex and subcortical damage (see Kolb & Whishaw, 1980). A study by Zola-Morgan et al. (1981), however, raises the question whether the effects of temporal stem lesions on discrimination learning involve memory per se. They compared the performance of monkeys with temporal stem lesions and those with combined amygdala–hippocampal lesions on a delayed non-matching to sample task as well as a two-choice pattern discrimination. Although histological confirmation is as yet incomplete, animals putatively with the combined lesions were severely impaired in their retention across a delay but showed only a mild deficit on the discrimination task. It contrast, animals putatively with the temporal stem lesions performed normally on the retention task but were severely impaired on the discrimination task. It seems plausible that the stem lesion, as it does not affect retention, impairs learning of the visual discrimination because it disturbs the processing of visual stimuli. The lesion's proximity to the visually important temporal lobe structures certainly supports this interpretation.

The results of Zola-Morgan et al. (1981) are consistent with those of Mishkin (1978) in arguing for the importance of combined amygdala–hippocampal lesions in human amnesia. Mishkin reported that the combined lesion had a disproportionate effect (relative to single structure lesions) on one-trial recognition — an effect which increased with delay and number of objects. Spiegler and Mishkin (1978) also found that the combined lesion had a dramatic effect on an associative version of this task (with isolated amygdala lesions having more effect than hippocampal ones). Combined lesions do not always have different, or more severe effects than individual structure lesions. In a recent study, Mahut et al. (1981) point out that although the combined lesion is necessary for impairment in matching to sample, object reversal and trial-unique non-matching to sample tasks, there are other tasks on which hippocampal lesions have very similar effects. Thus, they found that both hippocampal and combined lesion monkeys were impaired on tasks requiring both the recognition of objects and retention of their reward value. How good a model of human amnesia the combined lesion provides and the nature of the interaction between the two structures remains to be established. Even so, Squire and Zola-Morgan (in press) have claimed that monkeys with the combined lesion do not appear to be impaired on what they term 'procedural' memory, whereas tasks which require what they term 'declarative' memory are poorly performed. Cohen and Squire (1980) have previously argued that human amnesics learn and retain normally 'procedural' tasks where knowledge can only be shown by performing a task whereas they are severely impaired at 'declarative' memory tasks, which require the explicit declaration of acquired knowledge.

6.7 Conclusion

The animal data are compatible with the view that lesions of several limbic structures contribute to the human amnesic syndrome. The separate contribution of these lesions is far easier to determine in animal models than it is in humans, in whom damage usually involves more than one limbic–diencephalic structure as well as neocortex (particularly frontal cortex). Lesion studies need to be focused on potential differences between structures. For example, are frontal lesion interference effects different from those seen after hippocampal damage? Are lesions of the thalamic dorsomedial nucleus more similar in their effects to those of the amygdala or the hippocampus? Animal lesion models should also be used to examine closely dissociations between anterograde and retrograde amnesias (Jarrard, 1978; Rosenstock et al., 1977), as well as determining the form these take.

There is a suggestion that hippocampal lesions in animals cause memory failure as a secondary consequence of an information processing failure. If so, some non-memory deficits (perceptual ones?) should *always* be found in human amnesics. This cross-fertilization is valuable but must be tempered with the caution that it is difficult to establish isomorphism between inferred processes in animals and humans (for example, those involved in contextual processing). Even so, animal lesions can certainly help identify the role of limbic and frontal structures in information processing and memory. They can also clarify the role of different transmitter systems. Future human studies need to compare a wider variety of lesions on a broader set of cognitive and memory tests, including those impaired by specified limbic system lesions in animals.

Current uncertainties about the essential pattern of human amnesia and the minimal critical lesions which produce it, together with similar uncertainties in the animal literature and the problem of comparability, make dogmatic conclusions unwise. Nevertheless, it is likely that the limbic system structures, implicated in amnesia, constitute a kind of 'extrinsic memory system' (See Squire & Schlapfer, 1981) which modulates memories which are stored eventually in other regions of the brain ('the intrinsic memory system') — probably the neocortex as well as other structures. It is also probable that the limbic extrinsic system only modulates some kinds of memory. Although attempts to specify these are still controversial, any kind of memory not so modulated should be unaffected by limbic–diencephalic lesions. The extrinsic system is probably a complex, and different structures in it are likely to exercise different modulating functions. It is the specification of these in terms of specific registration, storage and retrieval processes which has engendered perhaps the most research, but the least resolution. This is partly because functional interpretations of lesion studies are always perilous, partly because many amnesics have incidental processing failures caused by cortical lesions which confound interpretation, but also because in amnesia research there is an extra chicken and egg conundrum. Are 'selective' failures the cause of general memory failures, or are these 'selective' failures consequences of unspecified and more general memory or cognitive losses? Future prospects for unravelling the complexities of memory are exciting, provided the temptation to show 'premature closure of search' is avoided.

References

ALBERT, M.S., BUTTERS, N. and LEVIN, J. (1979a) Temporal gradients in the retrograde amnesia of patients with alcoholic Korsakoff's disease. *Archives of Neurology*, **36**, 211–216.

ALBERT, M.S., BUTTERS, N. and LEVIN, J. (1979b) Memory for remote events in chronic alcoholics and alcoholic Korsakoff patients. In: H. BEGLEITER and B. KISSEN (Eds.) *Alcohol Intoxication and Withdrawal*, Plenum Press, New York.

ALLPORT, D.A. (1975) The state of cognitive psychology. *Quarterly Journal of Experimental Psychology*, **27**, 141–152.

BADDELEY, A.D. (1976) *The Psychology of Memory*. Harper and Row, New York.

BADDELEY, A. (1982) Amnesia: A minimal model and an interpretation. In: L.S. CERMAK, *Memory and Amnesia*. Lawrence Erlbaum, Hillsdale, NJ.

BADDELEY, A.D. and WARRINGTON, E.K. (1970) Amnesia and the distinction between long- and short-term memory. Journal of Verbal Learning and Verbal Behaviour, **9**, 176–189.

BARTLETT, F.C. (1932) *Remembering: A Study in Experimental and Social Psychology*. Cambridge University Press, Cambridge.

BERGER, T.W. and THOMPSON, R.F. (1978) Neuronal plasticity in the limbic system during classical conditioning of the rabbit nictitating membrane response. 1. The hippocampus. *Brain Research*, **145**, 323–346.

BIBER, C., BUTTERS, N., ROSEN, J. and GERSTMAN, L. (1981) Encoding strategies and recognition of faces by alcoholic Korsakoffs and other brain-damaged patients. *Journal of Clinical Neuropsychology*, **3**, 315–330.

BICKFORD, R.G., MULDER, D.W., DODGE, H.W., SVIEN, H.J. and ROME, H.P. (1958) Changes in memory function produced by electrical stimulation of the temporal lobe in man. *Research Publications Association for Research in Nervous and Mental Disease*, **36**, 227–243.

BLASS, J.P. and GIBSON, G.E. (1977) Abnormality of a thiamine-requiring enzyme in patients with Wernicke–Korsakoff syndrome. *New England J. of Medicine*, **297**, 1367–1370.

BRION, S. and MIKOL, J. (1978) Atteinte du noyau lateral dorsal du thalamus et syndrome de Korsakoff alcoolique. *Journal Neurological Science*, **38**, 249–261.

BROOKS, D.N. and BADDELEY, A.D. (1976) What can amnesic patients learn? *Neuropsychologia*, **14**, 111–122.

BUTTERS, N. and ALBERT, M.S. (1982) In: L.S. CERMAK (Ed.) *Memory and Amnesia*. Lawrence Erlbaum, Hillsdale, NJ.

BUTTERS, N., ALBERT, M. and BRANDT, J. (1980) The development of memory deficits in Huntington's disease: A comparison of retrograde amnesia during the early and advanced stages of the disorder. *The INS Bulletin*, December, 20.

BUTTERS, N. and CERMAK, L. (1975) Some analyses of amnesic syndromes in brain-damaged patients. In: R. ISAACSON and K. PRIBRAM (Eds.) *The Hippocampus Vol. 2*, pp. 377–409. Plenum. New York.

BUTTERS, N. SAMUELS, I. GOODGLASS, H. and BRODY, B. (1970) Short-term visual and auditory memory disorders after parietal and frontal lobe damage. *Cortex*, **6**, 440–459.

CERMAK, L.S. (1976) The encoding capacity of a patient with amnesia due to encephalitis. *Neuropsychologia*, **14**, 311–326.

CERMAK, L.S., BUTTERS, N. and MOREINES, J. (1974) Some analyses of the verbal encoding deficit of alcoholic Korsakoff patients. *Brain and Language*, **1**, 141–150.

CERMAK, L.S., NAUS, M.J. and REALE, L. (1976) Rehearsal strategies of alcoholic Korsakoff patients. *Brain and Language*, **3**, 375–385.

CERMAK, L.S. and REALE, L. (1978) Depth of processing and retention of words by alcoholic Korsakoff patients. *Journal of Experimental Psychology: Human Learning and Memory*, **4**, 165–174.

CERMAK, L.S., UHLY, B. and REALE, L. (1980) Encoding specificity in the alcoholic Korsakoff patient. *Brain and Language*, **11**, 119–127.

CHAPMAN, L.J. and CHAPMAN, J.P. (1973) Problems in the measurement of cognitive deficit. *Psychological Bulletin*, **79**, 180–185.

CHRISTIE, J.E., SHERING, A., FERGUSON, J. and GLEN, A.I.M. (1981) Physostigmine and arecoline: effects of intravenous infusions in Alzheimer presenile dementia. *British Journal of Psychiatry*, **138**, 46–50.

CLAPARÈDE, E. (1911) Recognition et moiite. *Archives of Psychology Geneve*, **11**, 79–90.

COHEN, N.J. and SQUIRE, L.R. (1980) Preserved learning and retention of pattern-analyzing skill in amnesia: Dissociation of knowing how and knowing that. *Science*, **210**, 207–210.

COHEN, N.J. and SQUIRE, L.R. (1981) Retrograde amnesia and remote memory impairment. *Neuropsychologia*, **19**, 337–356.

CORRELL, R.E. and SCOVILLE, W.B. (1967) Significance of delay in the performance of monkeys with medial temporal lobe resections. *Experimental Brain Research*, **4**, 85–96.

CRAIK, F.I.M. and LOCKHART, R.S. (1972) Levels of processing: a framework for memory research. *Journal of Verbal Learning and Verbal Behaviour*, **11**, 671–684.

DAVIES, P. and MALONEY, A.J.F. (1976) Selective loss of central cholinergic neurons in Alzheimer's disease. *The Lancet*, **ii**, 1403.

DE RENZI, E., FAGLIONI, P. and VILLA, P. (1977) Topographical amnesia. *Journal of Neurology, Neurosurgery and Psychiatry*, **40**, 498–505.

DIMOND, S.J. (1980) *Neuropsychology*. Butterworths, London.

DOUGLAS, R.J. (1972) Pavlovian conditioning and the brain. In: R. BOAKES and M. HALLIDAY (Eds.) *Inhibition and Learning*, pp. 529–553. Academic Press, London.

DOUGLAS, R.J. (1979) Working memory, interference and inhibition. *Behavioural and Brain Sciences*, **2**, 327–328.

DRACHMAN, D. (1977) Memory and cognitive function in man: Does the cholinergic system have a specific role? *Neurology*, **27**, 783–790.

DRACHMAN, D. and SAHAKIAN, B.J. (1979) Effect of cholinergic agents on human learning and memory. In: A. BARBEAU, J.H. CROWDON and R.J. WURTMAN (Eds.) *Nutrition and the Brain, Volume 5*, pp. 351–366. Raven Press, New York.

FEDIO, P. and VAN BUREN, J.M. (1974) Memory deficits during electrical stimulation of the speech cortex in conscious man. *Brain and Language*, **1**, 29–42.

FOGELHOLM, R., KIRALS, E. and BERGSTROM, L. (1975) The transient global amnesia syndrome. An analysis of 35 cases. *European Neurology*, **13**, 72–84.

FREDERIKS, J.A.M. (1979) Transient global amnesia. *The INS Bulletin*, June, 18.

FUSTER, J.M. (1973) Unit activity in prefrontal cortex during delayed response performance: Neuronal correlates of transient memory. *Journal of Neurophysiology*, **36**, 61–78.

FUSTER, J.M. and ALEXANDER, G.E. (1973) Firing changes in cells of the nucleus medialis dorsalis associated with delayed response behavior. *Brain Research*, **20**, 85–90.

GAFFAN, D. (1972) Loss of recognition memory in rats with lesions of the fornix. *Neuropsychologia*, **10**, 327–341.

GAFFAN, D. (1974) Recognition impaired and association intact in the memory of monkeys after transection of the fornix. *Journal of Comparative and Physiological Psychology*, **86**, 1100–1109.

GAFFAN, D. (1976) Recognition memory in animals. In: J. BROWN (Ed.), *Recall and Recognition*, pp. 229–242 John Wiley, London.

GODDEN, D. and BADDELEY, A. (1980) When does context influence recognition memory? *British Journal of Psychology*, **71**, 99–104.

GOLDBERG, E., MATTIS, S., HUGHES, J., SIRIO, C. and BILDER, R. (1980) Physostigmine and lecithin treatment in a case of post traumatic amnesia. *The INS Bulletin*, December, 20.

HASHER, L. and ZACHS, R.T. (1979) Automatic and effortful processes in memory. *Journal of Experimental Psychology (General)*, **108**, 356–388.

HASSLER, F. (1962) In: J.D. FRENCH (Ed.) *Frontiers in Brain Research*. Columbia University Press, New York.

HEILMAN, K. and SYPERT, G. (1977) Korsakoff's syndrome resulting from bilateral fornix lesions. *Neurology (Minneap.)*, **27**, 490–493.

HIRSH, R. (1980) The hippocampus, conditional operations and cognition. *Physiological Psychology*, **8**, 175–182.

HOREL, J.A. (1978) The neuroanatomy of amnesia: A critique of the hippocampal memory hypothesis. *Brain*, **101**, 403–445.

HOREL, J.A. and MISANTONE, L.G. (1976) Visual discrimination impaired by cutting temporal lobe connections. *Science*, **193**, 336–338.

HUPPERT, F.A. and PIERCY, M. (1976) Recognition memory in amnesic patients: effect of temporal context and familiarity of material. *Cortex*, **12**, 3–20.

HUPPERT, F.A. and PIERCY, M. (1978a) The role of trace strength in recency and frequency judgements by amnesic and control subjects. *Quarterly Journal of Experimental Psychology*, **30**, 346–354.

HUPPERT, F.A. and PIERCY, M. (1978b) Dissociation between learning and remembering in organic amnesia. *Nature*, **275**, 317–318.

HUPPERT, F.A. and PIERCY, M. (1979) Normal and abnormal forgetting in organic amnesia: effect of locus of lesion. *Cortex*, **15**, 385–390.

ISAACSON, R.L. (1972) Hippocampal destruction in man and other animals. *Neuropsychologia*, **10**, 47–64.

IVERSEN, S.D. (1976) Do hippocampal lesions produce amnesia in animals? *International Review of Neurobiology*, **19**, 1–49.

JARRARD, L.E. (1978) Selective hippocampal lesions: Differential effects on performance by rats of a spatial task with pre-operative versus post-operative training. *Journal of Comparative and Physiological Psychology*, **92**, 1119–1127.

JARRARD, L.E. (1980) Selective hippocampal lesions and behavior. *Physiological Psychology*, **8**, 198–206.

JOLLIFFE, N., BOWMAN, K.M., ROSENBLUM, L.A. and FEIN, H.D. (1940) Nicotinic acid deficiencies encephalopathy. *Journal of the American Medical Association*, **114**, 307–312.

JONES, G.V. (1979) Analyzing memory by cueing: intrinsic and extrinsic knowledge. In: N.S. SUTHERLAND (Ed.) *Tutorial Essays in Psychology: A Guide to Recent Advances*, pp. 119–147. Lawrence Erlbaum Ass., Hillsdale, NJ.

JURKO, M.F. (1978) Center median 'alerting' and verbal learning dysfunction. *Brain and Language*, **5**, 98–102.

KAPUR, N. and C OUGHLAN, A.K. (1980) Confabulation and frontal lobe dysfunction. *Journal of Neurology, Neurosurgery and Psychiatry*, **43**, 461–463.

KESNER, R.P. (1977) A neural system approach to the study of memory storage and retrieval. In: R.R. DRUCKER-COLIN and J.L. MCGAUGH (Eds.) *Neurobiology of Sleep and Memory*. pp. 227–254 Academic Press, New York.

KINSBOURNE, M. and WINOCUR, G. (1980) Response competition and interference effects in paired-associate learning by Korsakoff amnesics. *Neuropsychologia*, **18**, 541–548.

KINSBOURNE, M. and WOOD, F. (1975) Short-term memory processes and the amnesic syndrome. In: D. DEUTSCH and J.A. DEUTSCH, (Eds.) *Short Term Memory*, Academic Press, New York.

KOLB, B. and WHISHAW, I.Q. (1980) *Fundamentals of Human Neuropsychology*. Freeman, San Francisco.

KUNST-WILSON, W.R. and ZAJONC, R.B. (1980) Affective discrimination of stimuli that cannot be recognised. *Science*, **207**, 557–558.

LANDFIELD, P.W. (1976) Synchronous EEG rhythms: their nature, and their possible functions in memory, information transmission and behavior. In: W.H. GISPEN (Ed.) *Molecular and Functional Neurobiology*, pp. 389–424. Elsevier, New York.

LHERMITTE, F. and SIGNORET, J.L. (1976) The amnesic syndromes and the hippocampal–mammillary system. In: M.R. ROSENZWEIG and E.L. BENNETT (Eds.) *Neural Mechanisms of Learning and Memory*, pp. 49–56. MIT Press, Cambridge, Mass.

LISHMAN, W.A., RON, M.A. and ACKER, W. (1981) Computed tomography and psychometric assessment of alcoholic patients. In: D. RICHTER (Ed.) *Addiction and Brain Damage*. Croom Helm, London.

LORD, F.M. and NOVIK, M.R. (1968) *Statistical Theory of Mental Test Scores*. Addison-Wesley. Reading, Mass.

LURIA, A.R. (1973) *The Working Brain*. Penguin, Harmondsworth.

McDOWALL, J. (1979) Effects of encoding instructions and retrieval cueing on recall in Korsakoff patients. *Memory and Cognition*, **7**, 232–239.

McENTEE, W.J., BIBER, M.P., PERL, D.P. and BENSON, D.F. (1976) Diencephalic amnesia: a reappraisal. *Journal of Neurology, Neurosurgery and Psychiatry*, **39**, 436–441.

McENTEE, W.J. and MAIR, R.G. (1978) Memory impairment in Korsakoff's psychosis: a correlation with brain noradrenergic activity. *Science*, **202**, 905–907.

McENTEE, W.J. and MAIR, R.G. (1980) Memory enhancement in Korsakoff's psychosis by clonidine: Further evidence for a noradrenergic deficit. *Annals of Neurology*, **7**, 466–470.

MAHUT, H., MOSS, M. and ZOLA-MORGAN, S. (1981) Retention deficits after combined amygdala–hippocampus and selective hippocampal resections in the monkey. *Neuropsychologia*, **19**, 201–226.

MAIR, W.G.P., WARRINGTON, E.K. and WEISKRANTZ, L. (1979) Memory disorders in Korsakoff's psychosis: a neuropathological and neuropsychological investigation of two cases. *Brain*, **102**, 749–783.

MANDLER, G. (1980) Recognizing: the judgement of previous occurrence. *Psychological Review*, **87**, 252–271.

MARSLEN-WILSON, W.D. and TEUBER, H.L. (1975). Memory for remote events in anterograde amnesia: recognition of public figures from newsphotographs. *Neuropsychologia*, **13**, 353–364.

MAYES, A.R. (1981) The physiology of memory. In: G. UNDERWOOD and R. STEVENS (Eds.) *Aspects of Consciousness, Vol. 2*. Academic Press, London.

MAYES, A., BODDY, J. and MEUDELL, P. (1980a) Is amnesia caused by an activational deficit? *Neuroscience Letters*, **18**, 347–352.

MAYES, A. and MEUDELL, P. (1981a). How similar is the effect of cueing in amnesics and in normal subjects following forgetting? *Cortex*, **17**, 113–124.

MAYES, A. and MEUDELL, P. (1981b). How similar is immediate memory in amnesic patients to delayed memory in normal subjects? A replication, extension and reassessment of the amnesic cueing effect. *Neuropsychologia*, **19**, 647–654.

MAYES, A.R., MEUDELL, P.R. and NEARY, D. (1978) Must amnesia be caused by either coding or retrieval disorders? In: M.M. GRUNEBERG, P.E. MORRIS and R.N. SYKES (Eds.) *Practical Aspects of Memory*, pp. 712–719. Academic Press, London.

MAYES, A., MEUDELL, P. and NEARY, D. (1980b). Do amnesics adopt inefficient encoding strategies with faces and random shapes? *Neuropsychologia*, **18**, 527–540.

MAYES, A.R., MEUDELL, P.R., and SOM, S. (1981). Further similarities between amnesia and normal attenuated memory: Effects with paired-associate learning and contextual shifts. *Neuropsychologia*, **19**, 655–664.

MEUDELL, P., BUTTERS, N. and MONTGOMERY, K. (1978). The role of rehearsal in the short-term memory performance of patients with Korsakoff's and Huntington's disease. *Neuropsychologia*, **16**, 507–510.

MEUDELL, P. and MAYES, A. (1980) Do alcoholic amnesics passively rehearse verbal information? *Brain and Language*, **10**, 189–204.

MEUDELL, P. and MAYES, A. (1981a) A similarity between weak normal memory and amnesia with two and eight choice word recognition: a signal detection analysis. *Cortex*, **17**, 19–30.

MEUDELL, P. and MAYES, A. (1981b) The Claparède phenomenon: a further example in amnesics, a demonstration of a similar effect in normal people with attenuated memory and a reinterpretation. *Current Psychological Research* (in press).

MEUDELL, P. and MAYES, A. (1981c) Normal and abnormal forgetting: Some comments on the human amnesic syndrome. In: L.A. ELLIS (Ed.) *Normality and Pathology in Cognitive Function*. Academic Press, London (in press).

MEUDELL, P., MAYES, A. and NEARY, D. (1980a) Orienting task effects on the recognition of humorous pictures in amnesic and normal subjects. *Journal of Clinical Neuropsychology*, **2**, 75–88.

MEUDELL, P., MAYES, A. and NEARY, D. (1980b) Amnesia is not caused by cognitive slowness, *Cortex*, **16**, 413–420.

MEUDELL, P.R., NORTHEN, B., SNOWDEN, J.S. and NEARY, D. (1980c) Long term memory for famous voices in amnesic and normal subjects. *Neuropsychologia*, **18**, 133–139.

MILLER, E. (1975) Impaired recall and memory disturbance in presenile dementia. *British Journal of Social and Clinical Psychology*, **14**, 73–79.

MILLER, E. (1977) *Abnormal Ageing: The Psychology of Senile and Presenile Dementia.* Wiley, London.

MILNER, B. (1963) Effects of different brain lesions on card sorting. *Archives of Neurology*, **9**, 100–110.

MILNER, B. (1966) Amnesia following operation on the temporal lobes. In: C.W.M. WHITTY and O.L. ZANGWILL (Eds.) *Amnesia*, First Edition, Butterworths, London.

MILNOR, B. (1971) Interhemispheric differences in the localisation of psychological processes in man. *British Medical Bulletin*, **27**, 272–277.

MISHKIN, M. (1978) Memory in monkeys severely impaired by combined but not by separate removal of amygdala and hippocampus. *Nature*, **273**, 297–298.

MISTLER-LACHMAN, J.L. (1977) Spontaneous shift in encoding dimensions among elderly subjects. *Journal of Gerontology*, **32**, 68–72.

MOORE, J.W. (1979) Information processing in space–time by the hippocampus. *Physiological Psychology*, **7**, 224–232.

MORTENSEN, E.L. (1980) The effects of partial information in amnesic and normal subjects. *Scandinavian Journal of Psychology*, **21**, 75–82.

MOSCOVITCH, M. (1976) Differential effects of unilateral temporal and frontal lobe damage on memory performance. Paper presented at the International Neuropsychological Society Meeting, Toronto.

MOSS, M., ZOLA, S. and MAHUT, H. (1979, in preparation) Concurrent discrimination learning of monkeys after hippocampal, entorhinal or fornix lesions.

NADEL, L. and MACDONALD, L. (1980) Hippocampus: Cognitive map or working memory? *Behavioral and Neural Biology*, **29**, 405–409.

O'KEEFE, J. (1979) Hippocampal function: does the working memory hypothesis work? Should we retire the cognitive map theory? *Behavioral and Brain Sciences*, **2**, 339–343.

O'KEEFE, J. and NADEL, L. (1978) *The Hippocampus as a Cognitive Map*. Clarendon Press, Oxford.

O'KEEFE, J. and NADEL, L. (1979) Precis of O'Keefe and Nadel's. *The Hippocampus as a Cognitive Map. Behavioral and Brain Sciences*, **2**, 487–533.

OLTON, D.S., BECKER, J.T. and HANDELMAN, G.E. (1979) Hippocampus, space and memory. *Behavioural and Brain Sciences*, **2**, 313–365.

OSCAR-BERMAN, M. (1978) Commentary. In: E. CALLAWAY and S.H. KOSTOW (Eds.) *Event Related Brain Potentials in Man*. Academic Press, New York (in press).

OSCAR-BERMAN, M. and GADE, A. (1978) Electrodermal measures of arousal after cortical or subcortical human brain damage. In: K.D. KUMMEL, E.H. VAN OLST and J.F. ORLEBEKE (Eds.) Lawrence Erlbaum Assoc., Hillsdale, NJ (in press).

OSCAR-BERMAN, M. and SAMUELS, I. (1977) Stimulus-preference and memory factors in Korsakoff's syndrome. *Neuropsychologia*, **15**, 99–106.

OSCAR-BERMAN, M. and ZOLA-MORGAN, S. (1980a) Comparative neuropsychology and Korsakoff's syndrome I-Spatial and visual reversal learning. *Neuropsychologia*, **18**, 499–512.

OSCAR-BERMAN, M. and ZOLA-MORGAN, S. (1980b) Comparative neuropsychology and Korsakoff's syndrome II-Two choice visual discrimination learning. *Neuropsychologia*, **18**, 513–528.

OULTON, A. (1979) The role of the hippocampus and memory processes. Unpublished Ph.D. thesis, University of Nottingham.

OWEN, M.J. and BUTLER, S.R. (1980) The effects of fornix on latent learning in the rat. *Physiology and Behavior*, **24**, 817–822.

PATTEN, B.M. (1972) Modality specific memory disorders in man. *Acta Neurol. Scandinav.*, **48**, 69–86.

PENFIELD, W. and MATHIESON, G. (1974) Memory: autopsy findings and comments on the role of hippocampus in experiential recall. *Archives of Neurology, Chicago*, **31**, 145–154.

PETERS, B. and LEVIN, S. (1977) Memory enhancement after physostigmine treatment in the amnesic syndrome. *Archives of Neurology*, **34**, 215–219.

PETERSEN, R. (1977) Scopolamine induced learning failures in man. *Psychopharmacology*, **52**, 283–289.

PIERCY, M.F. (1977) Experimental studies of the organic amnesic syndrome. In: C.W.M. WHITTY and O.L. ZANGWILL (Eds.) *Amnesia*. Second Edition, Butterworths, London.

PRIBRAM, K.H. and ISAACSON, R.L. (1975) Summary. In: R.L. ISAACSON and K.H. PRIBRAM (Eds.) *The Hippocampus Volume 2*, pp. 429–441. Plenum, New York.

RATCLIFF, G. and COWEY, A. (1979) Disturbances of visual perception following cerebral lesions. In: D.J. OBORNE, M.M. GRUNEBERG, J.R. EISER (Eds.) *Research in Psychology and Medicine*, pp. 307–314. Academic Press, London.

RIBOT, T. (1882) *Diseases of Memory*. Appleton, New York.

RILEY, J.N. and WALKER, D.W. (1978) Morphological alterations in hippocampus after long-term alcohol consumption in mice. *Science*, **201**, 646–648.

ROBINSON, T.E. (1980) Hippocampal rhythmic slow activity (RSA: theta): A critical analysis of selected studies and discussion of possible species-differences. *Brain Research Reviews*, **2**, 69–101.

ROMAN-CAMPOS, G., POSER, C.M. and WOOD, F.B. (1980) Persistent retrograde memory deficit after transient global amnesia. *Cortex*, **16**, 509–516.

ROSE, F.C. and SYMONDS, C.P. (1960) Persistent memory defect following encephalitis. *Brain*, **83**, 195–212.

ROSENKILDE, C.E. (1979) Functional heterogeneity of the prefrontal cortex in the monkey: A review. *Behavioral and Neural Biology*, **25**, 301–345.

ROSENSTOCK, J., FIELD, T.D. and GREENE, E. (1977) The role of mammillary bodies in spatial memory. *Experimental Neurology*, **55**, 340–352.

ROZIN, P. (1976) The psychobiological approach to human memory. In: M.R. ROSENZWEIG and E.L. BENNETT (Eds.) *Neural Mechanisms of Learning and Memory*, pp. 3–48. MIT Press, Cambridge, Mass.

RUSSELL, W.R. (1971) *Traumatic Amnesia*, p. 48. Oxford University Press, London.

SAMUELS, I., BUTTERS, N. and FEDIO, P. (1972). Short-term memory disorders following temporal lobe removals in humans. *Cortex*, **8**, 283–298.

SANDERS, H.I. and WARRINGTON, E.K. (1971) Memory for remote events in amnesic patients. *Brain*, **94**, 661–668.

SANDERS, H.I. and WARRINGTON, E.K. (1975) Retrograde amnesia in organic amnesic patients. *Cortex*, **11**, 397–400.

SCHULMAN, S. (1964) Impaired delayed response from thalamic lesions. *Archives of Neurology (Chicago)*, **11**, 477–499.

SHALLICE, T. and WARRINGTON, E.K. (1970) Independent functioning of verbal memory stores: a neuropsychological study. *Quarterly Journal of Experimental Psychology*, **22**, 261–273.

SIGNORET, J.L. and LHERMITTE, F. (1976) The amnesic syndromes and the encoding process. In: M.R. ROSENZWEIG and E.L. BENNETT (Eds.) *Neural Mechanisms of*

Learning and Memory, pp. 67–75. MIT Press, Cambridge, Mass.

SOLOMON, P.R. (1979) Temporal versus spatial information processing theories of hippocampal function. *Psychological Bulletin*, **86**, 1272–1279.

SPIEGEL, E.A., WYCIS, H.T., ORCHNIK, C.W. and FREED, H. (1955) The thalamus and temporal orientation. *Science*, **121**, 771–772.

SPIEGLER, B.J. and MISHKIN, M. (1978) Evidence for the sequential participation of inferior temporal cortex and amygdala in stimulus-reward learning. *Neuroscience Abstracts*, **4**, 821.

SQUIRE, L.R. (1979) The hippocampus, space, and human amnesia. *Behavioral and Brain Sciences*, **2**, 514–515.

SQUIRE, L.R. (1980a) The anatomy of amnesia. *Trends in Neurosciences*, March, 52–54.

SQUIRE, L.R. (1980b) Two forms of amnesia identified through an analysis of forgetting. *Society for Neuroscience Abstracts* (in press).

SQUIRE, L.R. and CHACE, P.M. (1975) Memory functions six to nine months after electroconvulsive therapy. *Archives of General Psychiatry*, **32**, 1557–1564.

SQUIRE, L.R., CHACE, P.M. and SLATER, P.C. (1976) Retrograde amnesia following electroconvulsive therapy. *Nature (London)*, **260**, 775–777.

SQUIRE, L.R. and COHEN, N. (1979) Memory and amnesia: Resistance to disruption develops for years after learning. *Behavioral and Neural Biology*, **25**, 115–125.

SQUIRE, L.R. and COHEN, N.J. (1981) Remote memory, retrograde amnesia and the neuropsychology of memory. In: L. CERMAK (Ed.) *Memory and Amnesia*. Lawrence Erlbaum, Hillsdale, NJ (in press).

SQUIRE, L.R. and MOORE, R.Y. (1979) Dorsal thalamic lesion in a noted case of chronic amnesic dysfunction. *Annals of Neurology*, **6**, 503–506.

SQUIRE, L.R., NADEL, L. and SLATER, P.C. (1981) Anterograde amnesia and memory for temporal order. *Neuropsychologia*, **19**, 141–146.

SQUIRE, L.R. and SCHLAPFER, W.T. (1981) Biochemical aspects of learning, memory and its disorders. In: H.M. VAN PRAAG, M.H. LADER, O.J. RAFAELSON and E.J. SACHAR (Eds.) *Handbook of Biological Psychiatry*, IV, 309–341. *Brain Mechanisms and Abnormal Behavior*. Dekker, New York.

SQUIRE, L.R., SLATER, P.C. and CHACE, P.M. (1975) Retrograde amnesia: temporal gradient in very long term memory following electroconvulsive therapy. *Science*, **187**, 77–79.

SQUIRE, L.R., WETZEL, C.D. and SLATER, P.C. (1978) Anterograde amnesia following ECT: An analysis of the beneficial effects of partial information. *Neuropsychologia*, **16**, 339–348.

SQUIRE, L.R. and ZOLA-MORGAN, S. (in press) Neuropsychology of memory: Studies in man and sub-human primates. In: J.A. DEUTCSH (Ed.) The *Physiological Basis of Memory, 2nd Edition*. Academic Press NY.

STAMM, J.S. (1969) Electrical stimulation of monkeys' prefrontal cortex during delayed-response performance. *Journal of Comparative and Physiological Psychology*, **67**, 535–546.

STARR, A. and PHILLIPS, L. (1970) Verbal and motor memory in the amnesic syndrome. *Neuropsychologia*, **8**, 75–88.

STEVENS, R. and COWEY, A. (1972) Enhanced alternation learning in hippocampectomized rats by means of added light cues. *Brain Research*, **46**, 1–22.

STEVENS, R. and COWEY, A. (1973) Effects of dorsal and ventral hippocampal lesions on spontaneous alternation, learned alternation and probability learning in rats. *Brain Research*, **52**, 203–224.

STOFF, D.M. and EAGLE, M.N. (1971) The relationship among reported strategies, presentation rate, and verbal ability and their effects on free recall learning. *Journal of Experimental Psychology*, **87**, 423–428.

SYMONDS, C.P. (1966) Disorders of memory. *Brain*, **89**, 625–644.

TALLAND, G.A. (1965) *Deranged Memory: A Psychonomic Study of the Amnesic Syndrome*. Academic Press, New York.

TARTER, R.E. (1973) An analysis of cognitive deficits in chronic alcoholics. *Journal of Nervous and Mental Disease*, **157**, 138–147.

THOMPSON, R.F. (1976) The search for the engram. *American Psychologist*, **31**, 209–227.

VANDERWOLF, C.H. (1979) Is hippocampal rhythmical slow activity specifically related to movement through space? *Behavioral and Brain Sciences*, **2**, 518–519.

VANDERWOLF, C.H., KRAMIS, R., GILLESPIE, L.A. and BLAND, B.H. (1975) Hippocampal rhythmic slow activity and neocortical low voltage fast activity: Relations to behavior. In: R.L. ISAACSON and K.H. PRIBRAM (Eds.) *The Hippocampus, Vol. 2*, pp. 101–128. Plenum, New York.

VICTOR, M., ADAMS, R.D. and COLLINS, G.H. (1971) *The Wernicke-Korsakoff Syndrome. A Clinical and Pathological Study of 245 Patients, 82 with Post-mortem Examinations*. Blackwell. Oxford.

VILKKI, J. (1978) Effects of thalamic lesions on complex perception and memory. *Neuropsychologia*, **16**, 427–437.

VINOGRADOVA, O.S. (1975) Functional organization of the limbic system in the process of registration of information: Facts and hypotheses. In: R.L. ISAACSON and K.H. PRIBRAM (Eds.) *The Hippocampus, Volume 2* pp. 3–69. Plenum, New York.

VORHEES, C.V. (1979) Avoidance deficits in rats after recovery from mild to moderate thiamine deficiency. *Behavioral and Neural Biology*, **25**, 398–405.

VORHEES, C.V., BARRETT, R.J. and SCHENKER, S. (1975) Increased muricide and decreased avoidance and discrimination learning in thiamine deficient rats. *Life Sciences*, **16**, 1187–1200.

VORHEES, C.V., SCHMIDT, D.E., BARRETT, R.J. and SCHENKER, S. (1977) Effects of thiamine deficiency on acetylcholine levels and utilization *in vivo* in rat brain. *Journal of Nutrition*, **107**, 1902–1908.

WALKER, D.W., BARNES, D.E., ZORNETZER, S.F., HUNTER, B.E. and KUBANIS, P. (1980) Neuronal loss in hippocampus induced by prolonged ethanol consumption in rats. *Science,* **209**, 711–713.

WALKER, D.W., HUNTER, B. and ABRAHAM, W. (1982) Neuroanatomical and functional deficits subsequent to chronic ethanol administration in animals. *Alcoholism: Clinical and Experimental Research*, **5**, 267–282.

DE WARDENER, H.E. and LENNOX, B. (1947) Cerebral beri-beri. *The Lancet*, **1**, 11.

WARING, A.E. and MEANS, L.W. (1976) The effect of medial thalamic lesions on emotionality, activity, and discrimination learning in the rat. *Physiology and Behavior*, **17**, 181–186.

WARRINGTON, E.K. (1975) The selective impairment of semantic memory. *Quarterly Journal of Experimental Psychology*, **27**, 635–657.

WARRINGTON, E.K. and RABIN, P. (1971) Visual span of apprehension in patients with unilateral cerebral lesions. *Quarterly Journal of Experimental Psychology*, **23**, 423–431.

WARRINGTON, E.K. and WEISKRANTZ, L. (1970) Amnesic syndrome: consolidation or retrieval? *Nature*, **228**, 628–630.

WARRINGTON, E.K. and WEISKRANTZ, L. (1974) The effect of prior learning on subsequent retention in amnesic patients. *Neuropsychologia*, **12**, 419–428.

WARRINGTON, E.K. and WEISKRANTZ, L. (1978) Further analysis of the prior learning effect in amnesic patients. *Neuropsychologia*, **16**, 169–177.

WATTS, J., STEVENS, R. and ROBINSON, C. (in press). Effects of scopolamine on radial maze performance in rats. *Physiology and Behavior*.

WEISKRANTZ, L. and WARRINGTON, E.K. (1975) The problem of the amnesic syndrome in man and animals. In: R.L. ISAACSON and K.H. PRIBRAM (Eds.) *The Hippocampus, Volume 2*. Plenum Press, New York.

WEISKRANTZ, L. and WARRINGTON, E.K. (1979) Conditioning in amnesic patients. *Neuropsychologia*, **17**, 187–194.

WEISS, B.J. and MEANS, L.W. (1980) A comparison of the effects of medial frontal, dorsomedial thalamic, and combination lesions on discrimination and spontaneous alternation in the rat. *Physiological Psychology*, **8**, 325–329.

WETZEL, C. and SQUIRE, L. (1980) Encoding in anterograde amnesia. *Neuropsychologia*, **18**, 177–184.

WETZEL, W., OTT, T. and MATTHIES, H. (1977) Post-training hippocampal rhythmic slow activity ('theta') elicited by septal stimulation improves memory consolidation in rats. *Behavioral Biology*, **21**, 32–40.

WHITELEY, A.M. and WARRINGTON, E.K. (1978) Selective impairment of topographical memory: a single case study. *Journal of Neurology, Neurosurgery and Psychiatry*, **41**, 575–578.

WHITELEY, A.M. and WARRINGTON, E.K. (1979) Category specific deficits of visual memory and visual perception. *The INS Bulletin*, June, 30.

WHITTY, C.W.M. and LEWIN, W. (1960) A Korsakoff syndrome in the post cingulectomy confusional state. *Brain*, **83**, 648–653.

WHITTY, C.W.M. and ZANGWILL, O.L. (1966) (Eds.) *Amnesia*. First Edition. Butterworth, London.

WICKLEGREN, W.A. (1979) Chunking and consolidation: a theoretical synthesis of semantic networks, configuring in conditioning, S–R versus cognitive learning, normal forgetting, the amnesic syndrome, and the hippocampal arousal system. *Psychological Review*, **86**, 44–60.

WILLIAMS, M. and SMITH, H.V. (1954) Mental disturbances in tuberculous meningitis. *Journal of Neurology, Neurosurgery and Psychiatry*, **17**, 173–182.

WINOCUR, G. (1979) A comment on hippocampal function in working and reference memory systems. *Behavioral and Brain Sciences*, **2**, 349–350.

WINOCUR, G. and BRECKENRIDGE, C.B. (1973) Cue-dependent behavior of hippocampally damaged rats in a complex maze. *Journal of Comparative and Physiological Psychology*, **82**, 512–522.

WINOCUR, G. and KINSBOURNE, M. (1978) Contextual cueing as an aid to Korsakoff amnesics. *Neuropsychologia*, **16**, 671–682.

WINOCUR, G., KINSBOURNE, M. and MOSCOVITCH, M. (in press) The effect of cueing on release from proactive interference in Korsakoff amnesic patients. *Journal of Experimental Psychology: Human Learning and Memory*.

WINOCUR, G. and OLDS, J. (1978) Effects of context manipulation on memory and reversal learning in rats with hippocampal lesions. *J. of Comparative and Physiological Psychology*, **92**, 312–321.

WINOCUR, G. and WEISKRANTZ, L. (1976) An investigation of paired associate learning in amnesic patients. *Neuropsychologia*, **14**, 97–110.

WINSON, J. (1978) Loss of hippocampal theta rhythm results in spatial memory deficit in the rat. *Science*, **201**, 160–163.

WOOD, F., ARMENTROUT, R., TOOLE, J.F., McHENRY, L. and STUMP, D. (1980) Regional cerebral blood flow response during rest and memory activation in a patient with global amnesia. *Brain and Language*, **9**, 129–136.

WOODS, R.T. and PIERCY, M. (1974) A similarity between amnesic memory and normal forgetting. *Neuropsychologia*, **12**, 437–445.

YUILLE, J.C. and HARE, R.D. (1980) A Psychophysiological study investigation of short-term memory. *Psychophysiology*, **17** (5), 423–436.

ZOLA-MORGAN, S., MISHKIN, M. and SQUIRE, L.R. (1981) The anatomy of amnesia: Hippocampus and amygdala vs. temporal stem. *Soc. Neuro. Abst.*, **7** (in press).

CHAPTER 7

Memory Processes Unique to Humans

Michael Gruneberg

7.1 Introduction

This chapter is concerned with the way in which strategies used by humans affect later memory performance in a wide range of tasks. As much of the material considered is verbal in nature, or the tasks involve making a subjective judgement of confidence in the accuracy of memory, this chapter can reasonably be taken to apply only to human memory performance. Specifically it will be concerned with strategies which individuals use to process incoming information, and to examine the way in which the individual's knowledge of his memory system affects the kind of memory processes which will be adopted. The final section will deal with specific mnemonic aids which have been devised to improve memory performance.

7.2 Rehearsal

7.2.1 The Nature of Rehearsal

One major strategy for improving memory involves rehearsal, that is, the overt or covert repetition of material by the individual after it has been presented and the material is no longer present. A typical example is the rehearsal of phone numbers newly heard, or reciting poetry to oneself with one's eyes closed in order to learn it. There is a substantial body of experimental evidence which shows that rehearsal is effective as a strategy for improving later retention. Rundus (1971), for example, showed that the more items in a list were rehearsed, the greater was later recall, and the facilitating effects of rehearsal on later retention, especially when rehearsal is delayed for a few seconds after material is presented, has been shown by Modigliani (1978). The fact is, however, that such a well known phenomenon is still not fully understood, and the actual interpretation of rehearsal effects is subject to some dispute.

One popular account of the nature of rehearsal is that it is a mechanism for transferring material from a labile short-term memory system to a permanent long-term memory system. Newly acquired material, according to this theory, first enters a short-term memory store where it is either rapidly forgotten or transferred rapidly for permanent storage to long-term memory. This is necessary because short-term memory has a severely limited storage capacity for newly acquired information; some five to nine items, so that newly arriving information can cause forgetting of material already in store. In addition some proponents of this theory argue that material in short-term store will decay of its own accord unless rapidly transferred to long-term memory (see, e.g. Murdock, 1967). On this view of memory, therefore, the function of rehearsal is to maintain material in short-term store so that it can be transferred to long-term memory.

One assumption of the theory outlined above is that the longer material is in the short-term store, the greater is the chance of it being transferred to long-term memory. A number of studies, e.g. Craik and Watkins (1973), Modigliani (1976), have, however, failed to find evidence for this. Their studies found that individuals who repeated items to themselves immediately after presentation did not recall more as a result of this rehearsal. Another example of a failure to find any effect of rehearsal on long-term retention comes from the study of Glanzer and Meinzer (1967). They presented a series of words to two different groups at the rate of one word every 6 s. One group was given no instruction about memorizing, the other group was asked to repeat each word as often as they could until the next word was presented. It was found that the group repeating the words memorized less well than the group given no instructions as to how to memorize. The assumption, therefore, that repetition of material *per se* is a mechanism for transferring from short- to long-term memory is clearly dubious.

Findings such as those of Craik and Watkins (1973) and Glanzer and Meinzer (1967) have prompted some psychologists to distinguish two processes of rehearsal. The first is maintenance rehearsal whose function is to keep newly acquired information circulating in a short-term memory store in order to prevent decay of the memory trace. The second form of rehearsal is elaborative rehearsal, whose function is to code material in greater depth through associative contact with related material. Thus in elaborating material, the subject may try to relate together items in the same semantic category, for example animals, or might attempt to relate incoming material to material already stored in 'long-term memory'.

Because maintenance rehearsal *per se* has not been shown to improve later retention, studies showing rehearsal to improve recall are, therefore, taken to be evidence of the effectiveness of elaborative rehearsal rather than maintenance rehearsal.

The assumption that rehearsal is effective because individuals impose meaning or relationships on newly acquired information has considerable implications for theories which assume a short-term temporary memory store separate from a permanent long-term memory store. Theorists who argue for a distinction between a short- and long-term store often argue that the short-term store involves storing verbal material in an acoustic form, without any semantic encoding taking place (e.g. Murdock, 1967). If, however, rehearsal is only effective when semantic processing is taking place, this entails new material having contact with the existing cognitive framework, namely long-term memory. Indeed it is only after contact with the existing cognitive framework that a decision can be made that material is meaningful. At the very least, therefore, evidence on the nature of rehearsal does not force the conclusion that rehearsal is a mechanism for transferring material out of a temporary, acoustic short-term store into a permanent store. One major alternative view of the role of rehearsal to that of transferring material from STM to LTM is the 'levels of processing' approach to the nature of memory processing (Craik & Lockhart, 1973). This approach to memory makes no assumptions about distinctive short-

and long-term memory stores, but rather regards future memory as being dependent on the depth to which newly acquired information is processed. New information which is only processed at a shallow, acoustic level will soon be forgotten relative to material which is processed to a greater depth by, for example, imposing meaning on the new material or enriching the new material with new associations. According to this view maintenance rehearsal is basically coding incoming material at a shallow level compared to elaborative encoding which involves processing material at a deeper semantic level.

Another view of rehearsal which does not entail viewing the process as one of transfer of material from short- to long-term memory, is that each rehearsal is equivalent to putting a further copy of the original into the memory store, thus strengthening the memory trace. The more copies in store, the greater is the likelihood of retention. According to this view, one way of accounting for the failure of some studies to find increased retention with maintenance rehearsal is to argue that multiple copies improve storage but do not improve the ability to find material in store (retrieval). If this were the case, one would expect maintenance rehearsal to improve recognition but not recall, arguably as recognition does not require such as extensive retrieval process as recall. This has in fact been found to be the case in a study by Glenberg *et al.* (1977).

Whatever the exact nature of rehearsal, there is little doubt that when used as a strategy for improving the meaningfulness of material, it improves recall. For this reason, as Wickelgren (1979) notes, rehearsal is of importance primarily for aiding the retention of unrelated, meaningless material. Indeed there is evidence (Morris *et al.*, 1981) that where apparently meaningless new material is nevertheless meaningful to the individual, retention can be very high even in the absence of rehearsal. They found that the correlation between knowledge of football as measured by a questionnaire, and actual retention of football scores (two digit pairs) which were read out by a BBC announcer was 0.81, and for those with the highest level of knowledge in the study there was perfect retention of all scores in the first and second division (44 digits). Presumably for those with a high degree of knowledge, results would be meaningful even before they come in, as it were. Thus a score of Arsenal 1, Liverpool 2, might indicate that the league champions had won a difficult away game, that Arsenal's home record had gone, that Liverpool were now only two points behind Ipswich, and that Arsenal were now out of the running for the championship. A score of Arsenal 1 Liverpool 5 would convey all these factors and the fact that it was an emphatic win, that it helped Liverpool's goal difference, etc. In other words, each score would be significant because of pre-processing which gives each digit a particular significance, even before it arrives, alleviating the need for much elaborative encoding of the material as it was coming in.

7.2.2 *Methodological and Developmental Implications of Subject Rehearsal*

As almost all adult subjects indulge in rehearsal of some sort when presented with new unrelated, meaningless material, it is important to prevent rehearsal when studying the nature of pure forgetting over time. For this reason a number of 'classical' experiments on the nature of forgetting over time deliberately attempt to prevent rehearsal of material being tested by giving unrelated interpolated activity between presentation and later recall.

Perhaps the best known experimental paradigm which attempts to prevent rehearsal in studying the time-course of forgetting is the so-called Peterson–Brown paradigm (Peterson & Peterson, 1959; Brown, 1958). In this experimental paradigm three unrelated letters are presented, followed immediately by a three digit number. The subject is requested to count backwards from this number for a few seconds until asked for the recall of the original letter sequence.

The assumption is that counting backwards after the three letter sequence is presented prevents rehearsal, so that 'pure' forgetting over time can be studied. However, as Wickelgren (1979) points out, there is considerable doubt as to whether rehearsal is in fact prevented. Our questioning of students who take part in this type of experiment reveals that many cannot help but 'switch back' to think about the original sequence, during and despite the counting task. There is indeed experimental evidence that the more difficult the interpolated counting backwards the greater is forgetting (Dillon & Reid, 1969), suggesting that the interpolated activity has a role to play in the observed forgetting, either by increasing the difficulty of rehearsal or by actively interfering with earlier material. As the interpolated material in the Dillon experiment differs only in difficulty and not in its similarity to the original material, the experiment does suggest that the more difficult the task, the less capacity is left for surreptitous rehearsal or elaborative encoding.

Earlier it was noted that rehearsal was something the great majority of adults employed when faced with a memory task. One interesting finding is that rehearsal develops with age, and is absent in young children. Flavell et al. (1966), for example, tested the memory of children of five, seven, and ten years old, who were shown a series of seven features of common objects. The experimenter pointed to three of the pictures and after a delay of 15 s, the child was asked to point to these three pictures in their correct order. The older children performed the task better than the younger children. For a variety of reasons rehearsal is implicated as the cause of this better performance. First, only 2 of the 20 five-year-olds, compared to 17 of the 20 older children gave evidence of verbal activity during the interpolated activity. Second, in a further experiment Keeney et al. (1967) found that where young children who had exhibited little evidence of rehearsal and had poor memory on this task were shown how to rehearse, then their performance rose to that of older children. Thus younger children have the capacity to utilize strategies such as rehearsal but have insufficient awareness of the role of such strategies in improving recall. This awareness of the nature and capacity of one's own memory system is termed metamemory.

The experiments of Flavell et al. and Keenan et al. used pictorial material, although the assumption is that verbal processes such as verbal labelling enabled improved recall to occur. Graeffe and Watkins (1980) conducted an experiment which seems to point to the possibility that pictorial rehearsal can take place without verbal rehearsal. Their subjects were asked to visualize pictures, or in some way imagine them visually. Retention was superior for these pictures compared to conditions where no such instruction was given.

In summary, rehearsal of material previously presented can have facilitating effects on subsequent recall. Such facilitating effects are, however, unlikely to be due to the effects of repetition *per se*, but rather to strategies which involve relating new incoming material to the existing cognitive framework. The following sections will examine the nature of strategies which are effective in improving retention.

7.3 Strategies for Improving Recall

As was noted above, rehearsal *per se* is probably not effective in improving recall. Rehearsal allows time for those processes which do improve recall to operate. Among such processes, those of establishing meaningful relationships between incoming items, or between incoming items and the existing cognitive framework seem paramount. Establishing meaningful relationships between incoming items can be undertaken either by identifying intrinsic relationships between the incoming items, for example identifying animals from a list of miscellaneous items and grouping them together, or by imposing, extrinsically, relationships on normally unrelated material. This can be done by using visual imagery, for example, where two items are imaged interacting in some way. If, for example, three 'to be remembered' items are 'car', 'dog' and 'house', then a car can be visualized running into a dog which then goes squealing off into a house.

There is considerable experimental evidence that both utilizing intrinsic organization and imposing organization on material facilitates recall. A number of experiments on children, for example, show that where they are required to sort items into categories, recall improves. In one study, by Moely and Jeffrey (1974) children were told to sort items according to whether they were alike in some way. Following a training session, recall of both items and the number of categories improved.

The effects of organization in improving recall have also been studied in adults. An early study by Cofer (1967), for example, of American college students, found recall to increase where items were presented in an organized fashion, with one group of items belonging to one class, followed by another group belonging to another class and so on. An interesting series of experiments reported by Cole and Scribner (1974) shows that dramatic improvements in recall can be obtained from individuals not normally used to organizing material for free recall. Their subjects were Kpelle tribesmen from Liberia, for whom free recall of unrelated items was presumably somewhat unusual. When they were required to organize material for recall, however, their performance improved considerably.

It is not entirely clear where the major benefit of organization of material operates. In the study of Cole and Scribner, it is likely that improvement is due almost entirely to the increased ease of retrieving material, as the organization was imposed at the time of retrieval.

As noted above, it is sometimes impossible to organize incoming material in terms of meaningful intrinsic relationships. In such a case, external relationships can be imposed. One such strategy involves imagining two or more unrelated items together such as 'car', 'dog' and 'house'. A study by Morris and Stevens (1974) found that when individual items were vividly imagined as they came in, recall did not improve. Only where one item was imagined as being linked interactively with the next was recall improved. The facilitating effects of imagery in improving recall will be discussed in Section 7.5.

It is not, however, necessary to use imagery to impose external memory

257

organization on to unrelated material. Some mnemonic aids use meaningful sentences to link together the first letter of unrelated words, such as 'Richard Of York Gave Battle In Vain' for the colours of the rainbow. Indeed unrelated items can be linked together by an elaborated story to help recall, such as 'A *Car* ran into a *Dog* which went squealing down the *Road* until it came to a *House*. In the House sat an old *Man*, smoking a *Cigarette* and eating an *Apple*', and so on. Bower and Clark (1969) found such a technique highly efficient in improving recall.

Why should the imposition of meaningfulness and organization improve recall? One factor is that organization makes it easier to retrieve what is in store but not being retrieved. A number of studies, e.g. Earhard (1967) have shown that considerably more is normally stored than is retrieved in free recall experiments. She showed that where individuals are cued with the first letter of words previously unrecalled, retrieval improves considerably, and a study of Tulving (1966) also shows that much more is stored than is recalled at any one time. He presented 36 words and asked for free recall on three successive occasions. Only 50% of words recalled were recalled on all occasions, in other words many words not recalled when first asked for were recalled on subsequent occasions. Presumably they were stored but not retrieved. By linking newly acquired material to other material which is easily retrieved by following some systematic search plan, it seems likely that organization would improve recall. The application of such retrieval plans to practical memory problems is considered in subsequent sections.

Another method of improving the retention of incoming material is to relate it to the existing cognitive framework by categorizing and processing the material according to its semantic characteristics. A number of experiments by psychologists of the 'levels of processing' school have shown that by subjecting incoming information to semantic as opposed to acoustic or structural processing, retention is much improved. Craik and Tulving (1975), for example, found that where individuals were required only to analyse items in structural terms, for example, Is the word 'HAMSTER' in capital letters — Yes/No? then retention was not as great as where they were required to answer such questions as 'Does the word "HAMSTER" fit the sentence, "The hamster bit the man".' In the latter case, semantic processing would be required in order to answer such a question. In fact in their experiment, Craik and Tulving found that only 20% of words given the answer 'Yes' were recognized subsequently in the structural condition compared to 80% in the semantic condition. Such findings do of course fit in well with our common-sense experience that the longer we think about a particular idea, say, and the more we relate it to other ideas, the more it is likely to be recalled in the future.

On the other hand, there is strong evidence that the processing of information which relates incoming material to the existing cognitive framework and hence makes it 'meaningful' and more easily retrievable does not have to occur at the point at which incoming material actually enters the memory system. It can occur before. Morris *et al.* (1981), for example, found a correlation of 0.81 between recall of football scores and knowledge of football as measured by an independent questionnaire. It appears, therefore, that where individuals have a knowledge of a particular area, they have in a sense 'pre-processed' incoming information, so that when the information does come in it is readily related to the cognitive framework. As noted earlier, a score of Liverpool 0 Leicester 1, for example, indicates to the individual who is knowledgeable about football that the European champions have been beaten at home, by the bottom club, that this is their third defeat in a row and so on. To those lacking in football knowledge, the score is just another of a large number of meaningless digit pairs on which some meaning has to be imposed — usually unsuccessfully.

7.4   Feeling of Knowing (FOK)

7.4.1   Developmental Aspects

This section examines one major factor which determines whether or not the individual will apply strategies for improving recall, namely the knowledge that the individual has about his memory system. This knowledge has been termed metamemory by developmental psychologists such as Flavell (1977). An example given in the previous section concerns the nature of rehearsal, where it has been found that young children do not realize the importance of rehearsal in improving memory performance. When they are taught to rehearse, then memory performance improves considerably (Keeney et al., 1967).

There is evidence that even very young children have an awareness that some material is easier to remember than others. Wellman et al. (1973), for example, found that three-year-old children who were asked to remember where a toy had been placed showed a higher level of memory than other children not asked to remember. Presumably the former group of children were aware of, and were using strategies which were effective in improving recall.

Certainly, by the time children reach the age of seven or eight, there is clear evidence that they possess metamemorial knowledge which is applied to improve memory performance. Rogoff et al. (1974) and Kreutzer et al. (1975) both found that young children of seven and eight years old realized that the longer the period of study, the greater was retention, but it is also clear that an awareness of the usefulness of strategies in improving recall increases continually with age and is certainly not complete even in student populations. Kreutzer et al. (1975) found 10- and 11-year-olds to be aware that related word pairs were easier to learn than unrelated' pairs, whereas seven-year-olds were not aware of this. They also found that the older the child, the more strategies they could name for aiding recall in a hypothetical situation.

That metamemorial knowledge is never really complete is evidenced from the failure of many students to use mnemonic aids such as imagery in word pair learning. In a recent first year psychology class, I asked students to learn a list of word pairs without giving instruction on strategies for list learning. Only 26 out of 45 used imagery in order to relate word pairs.

Not only strategies such as imagery, but other strategies such as the use of material grouping and retrieval aids increase with age (Harris, 1978). Furthermore young children can be taught successfully to utilize such aids, although they frequently abandon them if they are not continually instructed to use them, or if the situation changes. Such findings are also true of mentally retarded individuals (Belmont, 1978) which tends to indicate that one major problem with young children and retarded individuals is not a lack of structural memory capacity and not even a lack of capacity to put strategies into action, but a lack of metamemorial knowledge which results in a failure to appreciate how their memory systems function and how strategies of which they are capable can be applied.

The failure of younger children to apply strategies because of a lack of awareness of the workings in their memory systems is also reflected in their inability to make judgements in respect to the contents of their memory store. Wellman (1977), for example, found young children were poorer than older children at predicting whether they would be able to recognize items they were unable to recall, although even young children of six were able to make judgements at well above the chance level. The relationship between the degree of 'feeling of knowing' (FOK) for items not recallable and subsequent evidence of retention has also been investigated recently in a number of studies of adult subjects, and because of their theoretical and practical importance, these studies are now considered below.

7.4.2 *Feeling of Knowing Studies in Adults: Some Theoretical Implications*

While the failure to recall what is known to the individual has been of concern to psychologists for some time (e.g. James, 1890), within experimental psychology the seminal papers on the feeling of knowing phenomenon (FOK) were published by Brown and McNeil (1966) and Hart (1965, 1967). Brown and McNeil were interested in the extreme case of the FOK phenomenon, the 'tip of the tongue' phenomenon (TOT) where individuals are absolutely certain that they know an item, but the sought-for item will just not emerge, it is on the tip of the tongue. Brown and McNeil's experiment involved giving subjects a definition and requiring them to name the sought-for item. For example, 'An instrument used in navigation, for measuring the angular distance of objects by means of reflection' was presented, and subjects were required either to produce the item 'sextant' or to give as much information as they could about it, for example the length of the word, the first letter and so on. Brown and McNeil found that subjects could produce information on words for which they had a TOT, such as the first letter, the number of syllables and so on. The first letter, for example, was correctly supplied on 57% of occasions.

While there are a number of limitations to the Brown and McNeil study, the findings are of considerable importance in drawing attention to the fact that memory storage is a complex matter and not merely a question of storing words as whole units. On the contrary, the fact that on occasion we can recall practically everything about an item except the item itself indicates that items in memory must consist of a number of dimensions, some available, and some temporarily not available to the individual seeking to retrieve from memory store. Thus a sextant is a two syllable word, it begins with s, and so on. When a word is sought in memory, these dimensions are brought together.

It is not merely the structural characteristics which are the attributes of the sought-for items. Eysenck (1979) has shown that where memory fails then a considerable amount of semantic information is known about the item also. He reversed the Brown and McNeil paradigm, presenting words and asking for definitions, and found that even where the definition was not accurate, feeling of knowing was able to predict performance on a semantic-differential task and a related words task. Sought-for items in memory, therefore, appear to consist of a number of dimensions, some structural, some semantic, and in retrieving an item from memory the individual seeks to produce the acoustic or sensorimotor representation. Given this, it is perhaps not so mysterious that one can 'know' that one knows even though one cannot retrieve the sought-for item. Possibly what one knows is that one can produce a significant number of attributes of the sought-for item.

While the Brown and McNeil study is of importance in drawing our attention to the attributional nature of memory it has perhaps two limitations. In the first place individuals were asked to indicate the first letter and other information for items not recalled, but in a TOT state. Such instructions called attention of subjects to structural characteristics of sought-for items. It is possible that such information need not be available to individuals before making a judgement that they are in a TOT state. Indeed Gruneberg et al. (1973) found subjects to give an indication that they were in a TOT state and then, over an extended period, give attributes. In other words Brown and McNeil's study only shows a correlation between being in a TOT state and subject's ability to produce attributes, it does not show the direction of causality.

Evidence of a further limitation of the Brown and McNeil study comes from the later work of Koriat and Leiblich (1974) who showed that even where individuals did not know an item, they could still give information on it, for example, the first letter and word length, significantly above chance. Thus being able to give attributes of an item does not of itself indicate a TOT state. This said, it is clear as noted above, that the study of Brown and McNeil is of considerable importance in drawing attention to the importance of seeing memory storage in terms of a number of attributes, rather than in terms of little parcels of items stored in separate cells.

Brown and McNeil dealt with the TOT phenomenon, where individuals were absolutely sure they knew an item, to the extent that it usually produced emotional reactions such as frustration. However, this feeling of knowing that one has material in memory which one cannot immediately retrieve can vary from this kind of certainty, to being fairly sure one knows an item, to being absolutely sure one does not know an item. The first experiment aimed at examining the whole range of 'feeling of knowing' in relation to later evidence of retention was carried out by Hart (1965). In his experiment, Hart gave his subjects a number of questions such as 'On what sea does West Pakistan border?' and asked subjects either to supply the answer, or to rate on a six point scale how sure they were they knew the answer even if they could not recall it. There then followed a recognition test in order to establish whether the item was in fact memorized. Hart found a strong relationship between feeling of knowing and subsequent recognition. Thus where individuals claimed they were certain they knew the missing item 78% were later recognized, compared to 30% where subjects were certain they did not know the item.

A number of studies have since confirmed those of Hart (1965) in establishing a relationship between FOK and evidence of later retention. Hart himself (1967) confirmed his findings using paired-associate learning and Gruneberg and Monks (1974) found a significant relationship between FOK and later cued recall. Blake (1973) found a relationship between FOK and subsequent evidence of retention for nonsense syllables, and Yarmey (1973) found a relationship between FOK and later memory for famous faces. Finally Hart (1967) and Gruneberg and Sykes (1978) found a relationship between FOK and reminiscence. Thus for a wide variety of test materials and retention tests

261

it appears clear that the relationship between FOK and subsequent evidence of later retention is well established.

Despite the uniformity of findings, there are a number of methodological problems with FOK studies. Hart (1967), for example, does acknowledge that the relationship between FOK and subsequent recognition varies with the ease or difficulty of the recognition test. This of course is a perennial problem of recognition tests employing multiple distractors, and does mean that no generalization can be made on the magnitude of the FOK–retention relationship on the basis of this kind of study.

A further methodological problem in cued recall and reminiscence studies has been shown by Gruneberg et al. (1977a). In the original experiment of Gruneberg and Monks (1974) it was found that subjects spent longer searching for items they felt they knew but could not recall, compared to those they did not know. Greater recall of the former items could, therefore, have been due to a greater time being spent in searching for them. In fact, Gruneberg et al. (1977a) showed that greater search time for FOK rated items compared to items not known was not responsible for any differences in recall probability. They induced subjects to spend as much time searching for 'not known' as FOK items. This was done by offering a 5p reward for recall of items previously given a 'not known' rating compared to a FOK rating.

A further major methodological problem noted by Gruneberg and Sykes (1978) and Koriat and Leiblich (1977) is that FOK ratings are systematically influenced by the nature of the material used. Gruneberg and Sykes (1978) gave subjects three types of material, capitals of countries, definitions of rare words and general knowledge, and found significant differences between materials on the relationship between FOK and subsequent uncued recall on a second retrieval attempt. In a previous experiment Gruneberg et al. (1977a) had also shown that the relationship between FOK and subsequent cued recall varied with the nature of the material. Specifically, where material was well recalled by the group as a whole, FOK was more highly related to subsequent recall than where material was unknown. The different degrees of knowledge for different kinds of material, may in fact account for the differences reported by Gruneberg and Sykes (1978). As noted above, Koriat and Leiblich (1977) also noted that FOK ratings and indeed FOK accuracy are systematically affected by various factors. For example adding redundant information to a cue is likely to increase rated FOK without increasing the subsequent probability of recall.

Despite these various limitations on feeling of knowing studies outlined above, however, there is little dispute that the relationship between FOK and subsequent evidence of retention is well established, indeed the present writer knows of no failure to find such a relationship in the literature. Hart has used his findings to argue for a special memory device which he has termed a memory monitoring mechanism. This memory monitoring mechanism enables an individual to assess the probability that an item is in store. Only where the memory monitoring mechanism produces a positive result will the individual commence a memory search, and presumably the mechanism would indicate when an unsuccessful search should be terminated. Such a mechanism would be biologically useful in saving the individual from searching for material not in store, or not likely to be retrieved.

There certainly is support for the view that the individual's FOK does affect his willingness to search for an item not immediately retrievable. For example,

Gruneberg et al. (1977a) found that the greater the FOK, the greater the time spent searching for the missing item. Nevertheless, the memory-monitoring mechanism, if it exists, is far from perfect. Blake (1973) has noted how often FOK is inaccurate and Gruneberg and Monks (1974) found that items 'not known' were recalled on 16% of occasions following first letter cueing. This may not be an entirely fair argument against the biological utility of the memory-monitoring process, as it is not reasonable to expect perfect working. Perhaps a more serious question is whether such a mechanism is a necessary one, given the possibility, discussed later, that the FOK phenomenon can be accounted for in much simpler terms.

A more certain theoretical implication of FOK studies comes from the evidence that FOK can materially affect the kind of strategy which subjects use in memory experiments. As noted above, Gruneberg et al. (1977a) found that the greater the FOK, the longer the individual spent on a retrieval attempt, and the greater the time spent on a retrieval attempt the likelier it is that a retrieval will be forthcoming (Gruneberg et al., 1973). Again, as noted above, a knowledge of the workings of one's own memory considerably affects performance in, for example, children's use of rehearsal to improve recall, in the recall of the last items first in a free recall test (before they have time to 'slip away'), and in the use of imagery where individuals have experience of the facilitating effects of learning using imagery.

Clearly such findings are of considerable importance theoretically, as it is almost meaningless to seek to interpret memory performance without asking what the subject actually does in a memory task, rather than what he is asked to do. What the subject does depends critically on how aware he is of his own memory processes, including the relationship between feeling of knowing and subsequent successful retrieval.

7.4.3 The Nature of FOK

Most accounts of the nature of feeling of knowing assume that the individual in some way makes a preliminary estimate of the likelihood of an item being in store by assessing either the strength or the number of attributes of the missing item which are available. Eysenck (1979) notes that the strength of FOK is related to the amount of semantic information available on the item, the implication being that the individual uses this information to assess the strength of FOK.

The causal relationship, however, is not entirely clear, it may be that where the individual gives a high FOK, he can then go on to find more attributes following a search. Certainly in the Gruneberg et al. (1973) study, individuals reported that they were blocking on an item, and then proceeded over an extended period to provide attributes of the missing item. Koriat and Leiblich (1974) make the distinction between characteristics common to a class of items, and characteristics specific to an actual item. For example, the general characteristic of the capital of Denmark is that it is a Scandinavian capital. A brief search of Scandinavian capitals might indicate to the individual that he can recall the capital of Sweden, and therefore there is an inference that he is likely to know other Scandinavian capitals, such as that of Denmark. The individual may then make a FOK judgement on this basis. On the other hand, it may be that the individual 'knows' the first letter of the capital of Denmark starts with a

'C', and that if he knows so much about the sought-for item, he will have information on the whole item. In other words, it is possible, but not necessarily the case, that the ability of subjects to produce more information about items for which they have a strong feeling of knowing, shows that FOK judgements are based on partial information that the individual is aware of.

Koriat and Leiblich (1977) have in fact shown that FOK judgements are affected by the nature of information presented to individuals. Koriat and Leiblich, for example, have found that repeating or giving alternative specification for a missing item increases the strength of FOK without increasing the accuracy of FOK. For example, the cue Foxy, Cunning, Crafty, as specifications for vulpine, increases the level of expressed FOK above that obtained when only one specification is given; other factors involved in specifying a target word which appear to have the effect of increasing FOK, include increasing the number of words used to specify an item and providing specifications which might at first sight appear to indicate a number of potential target items. Koriat and Leiblich suggest that increased FOK occurs because subjects will feel that the larger the number of specifications, the more chance they have of hitting an associate which will allow the retrieval of the sought-for word. If this is a factor in individuals making FOK judgements, then clearly this is an alternative explanation to that based on an assessment of the strength of attributes for the sought-for item.

While factors such as increasing the number of words in the specification increase FOK, but not recall accuracy, other aspects of the specification of an item increase accuracy of FOK. In particular the more the cue delineates the sought-for item, the more this allows the individual an accurate assessment of whether he really does know the item. For example, 'A plant growing in SW United States, which has long pointed often rigid leaves and which bears a large cluster of white blossom' (*Yucca*) allows a very accurate assessment of whether the item is stored.

Koriat and Leiblich also note that target items themselves may be more or less likely to be retrieved. They suggest that abstract words have fewer 'tags' than concrete words, and are therefore more difficult to retrieve. Again, as noted earlier, Gruneberg and Sykes (1978) found that FOK accuracy was affected by the nature of the material used, which in turn is related to the extent of knowledge of the material. As Koriat and Leiblich note, those factors which make for the assessment of FOK strength are not necessarily those which make for FOK accuracy. If there is such a device as a memory-monitoring mechanism as suggested by Hart (1967) it may involve no more than a rapid and relatively inaccurate assessment of memory. This might involve making inferences on the basis of the nature of the cue, rather than by an initially extensive search of the contents of memory in order to assess the number of attributes, acoustic or semantic, associated with the target item. Such inferences based on cues might involve an awareness of knowledge of specific items in the class the cue is specifying, or might involve being able to eliminate items as the individual is aware of a lack of knowledge for a class of item. On the other hand it is possible that FOK is based on a knowledge of some specific aspects of a sought-for item. Again it is possible that FOK is a consequence of the individual's awareness of some kind of 'physiological' response blocking. If such is the case, then FOK would be neither an inference based on the nature of the cue, nor an assessment of item strength based on semantic and acoustic associations. Clearly, at present the nature of the FOK phenomenon is a matter of speculation, although there is no dispute that whatever its exact nature, the phenomenon is a robust one with considerable theoretical implications.

7.4.4   Practical Applications of FOK Research

(a)   Strategies of retrieval.   One of the major questions facing investigators of the FOK phenonmenon concerns what strategies are most successful in overcoming TOT states? Gruneberg *et al.* (1973) set out to examine this question by having subjects produce memory blocks in their own way, and then asking subjects to describe the ways in which they sought to retrieve the missing items. Subjects usually produced blocks by searching through categories such as old school friends, where they pictured a face they could not recall, or tried to recall capitals of countries, and so on. The majority of blocks produced (66%) were recovered following a memory search, although this search sometimes lasted for a considerable period of time before it was successful. For example, of 206 blocks reported, 29 were recalled after a search period of more than 30 s, a search time which is subjectively extremely long. Clearly one successful search strategy is to carry on searching for a subjectively considerable period of time, rather than giving up if the item will not come back almost immediately.

A second possible strategy is to leave the item after it has failed to be retrieved following a sustained retrieval attempt. It is sometimes suggested that such items will then be recovered spontaneously during other activity — the missing word will suddenly 'pop up'. In fact in the Gruneberg *et al.* experiment, subjects were contacted some 2 to 9 h after the experimental session and asked to attempt a further retrieval. About 20% of the outstanding blocks were recalled following such a second retrieval, but only four blocks were recovered between the two retrieval attempts. In all four of these cases, subjects admitted to an active self-initiated search. It appears that a second active retrieval attempt some time after retrieval failure is an effective strategy, but there is no evidence that leaving material alone without actually searching for it will lead to 'spontaneous' retrieval.

There are a number of activities in which subjects engage when searching for a missing item. One strategy successfully reported by a number of subjects involved trying to identify the first letter of the missing item, in the hope that this would cue the rest of the word. As noted earlier first letter cueing does seem effective in improving recall (e.g. Gruneberg & Monks, 1974) and it might well be that where individuals feel they have a memory block, then first letter cueing might be most effective. Gruneberg and Monks (1976) did investigate whether a first letter search strategy might be effective. Subjects were presented with capitals and asked to name countries or to give a FOK rating. They were then asked in a second recall trial, to try again to recall items previously unrecalled. On a third retrieval attempt subjects were asked to use a first letter search strategy, going through the alphabet to see if they could identify the first letter of the missing item. Recall on this third trial was significantly greater than recall on the previous uninstructed trial, and significantly greater than recall for a control group given no instruction on a third retrieval attempt. At first sight, therefore, it appears that the first letter search strategy is effective in increasing recall. Unfortunately it is not clear that the first letter search strategy *per se* is effective in improving recall, because subjects spent longer in the search for items when instructed to use a first letter search strategy than when not given any instruction. It could well be, therefore, that instruction to use a first letter search strategy induces individuals to spend longer on searching for the missing item than they otherwise would, and that unconscious search processes initiated by a further active search is what improves recall. Certainly there is evidence (e.g. Gruneberg *et al.*, 1973) that the longer the individual spends searching, the more is recalled.

There are clear indications from subjects that first letter searching *per se* was not always responsible for improved recall. Many subjects recalled items with first letters towards the end of the alphabet while they were still considering 'early' letters. Nevertheless, some kind of active search seems necessary for successful retrieval, whatever the exact nature of the search process, and the first letter search strategy at least induces individuals to search for longer than they otherwise would. To this extent, at least, therefore, it can be considered an effective strategy.

Another possible effective strategy involves shifting the perspective from which recall occurs. Anderson and Richert (1978), for example, found that when individuals were asked to recall their account of a burglary from the point of view of a home-buyer or the burglar, then a shift of perspective from one to the other resulted in increased recall of information that was important to the new perspective. Such a finding is suggestive that improved recall in blocking situation will result from changing the perspective or the strategy of search, although this writer is not aware of any experiment which actually shows this. Certainly, in the Gruneberg *et al.* study subjects frequently used visual and verbal associates as well as first letter search strategies and often used them successively until there was eventual success in retrieval. As Morris (1979) notes, the study of effective search strategies has been almost completely neglected by psychologists, at the expense of examining effective encoding strategies.

(b) Eyewitness testimony.   A third area in which the study of FOK is of considerable practical significance is that of eyewitness testimony, where a number of studies have recently claimed that there is no relationship between the accuracy of an eyewitness's memory, and the confidence that the witness has in the accuracy of the memory. Clifford and Scott (1978), for example, failed to find any correlation between eyewitness accuracy and confidence for recall of physical description or of physical actions of a witnessed 'crime', and Leippe *et al.* (1978) also failed to find a correlation between accuracy and confidence in a task involving facial recognition. Deffenbacher *et al.* (1978) report two studies which failed to find correlations between face recognition accuracy and confidence, although the study of Lipton (1977) on facial recognition has shown a significant correlation.

On the basis of results such as those described above, a number of writers have claimed that there is no relationship between witness confidence and witness accuracy. Bull and Clifford (1979) state 'Jurors ought to be aware that a witness's confidence or assurance in the accuracy of his testimony has repeatedly been found not to be related to the true accuracy of his testimony.' Similarly Deffenbacher *et al.* (1978) state 'Confident eyewitnesses are no more likely to be accurate than less confident ones, while a given witness will tend to

266

exhibit a particular level of confidence, whether right or wrong.'

Before such an important conclusion can be accepted, however, it really is necessary to establish that this does represent the true state of affairs. Fortunately, there are a number of reasons to suppose that the conclusion of Deffenbacher *et al.* and of Bull and Clifford may need considerable qualifying. First, as noted above, there are inconsistencies in the findings which make it unclear at present what the relationship is. Second, the experiments have been conducted on a somewhat narrow range of phenomena (facial recognition or recall for the most part). Third, the findings on 'eyewitness' studies are completely opposite to findings on 'Feeling of Knowing' studies which, as noted above, invariably find a significant relationship between confidence and later evidence of memory. It would be peculiar if one aspect of a memory mechanism involving confidence were invariably effective, another almost invariably ineffective. Perhaps the most important reason to doubt the conclusions of Bull and Clifford and Deffenbacher *et al.*, however, is that a between-subject single item correlational analysis is almost always used to analyse eyewitness data, a procedure which Leippe *et al.* (1978) point out may be inappropriate, because of a lack of variance in the ratings of confidence. In their study, for example, subjects were reluctant to make an identification until they were at least 70% certain they were correct.

Before any statement concerning the relationship between accuracy and confidence can be made, therefore, it is necessary to examine a number of different phenomena and to carry out different kinds of statistical analysis in addition to those simply using between-subject correlations for a single item. The present writer and his colleagues have in fact carried out a number of experiments which have done this, and which have shown considerable relationships between confidence and accuracy.

The first experiment (Gruneberg & Sykes, 1981) involved presenting a coloured picture to subjects for 15 s. The picture contained human figures in various postures, and after the presentation of the picture, subjects were asked to answer 10 questions, such as 'How many individuals were sitting?' and to give a rating of confidence in the accuracy of their answer. While the between-subject correlational analysis produced a sequence of inconsistent correlations, some significant, others not, a within-subject analysis which looked at the difference in confidence rating when an individual was correct compared to when he was wrong, was highly significant. In other words, the more confident an individual was that he was accurate, the more likely he was, in fact, to be accurate ($p < .0001$) — 26 out of 27 subjects produced ratings in the direction of the hypothesis.

It has to be said that others such as Deffenbacher *et al.* (1978) have carried out within-subject analysis. Deffenbacher *et al.*, for example, correlated the ratings of individuals when correct and when wrong and found a correlation of .7. In other words, individuals who rated high tended to rate high whether right or wrong, those who rated low, tended to rate low whether right or wrong. However, the conclusion that 'a witness will tend to exhibit a particular level of confidence whether right or wrong' is totally erroneous on the basis of a correlational analysis. For example subjects A, B and C might score 6, 5 and 4 on test x and 3, 2 and 1 on test y. The correlation would be 1, while the levels that individuals were operating on in the two tests might be quite different. Only those tests showing differences between ratings when accurate and when inaccurate are adequate tests of within-subject effects. As noted above, in the

Gruneberg and Sykes experiment this was highly significant.

The results of the Gruneberg and Sykes study, therefore, show that it is dangerous to make the generalization that there is no relationship between accuracy and confidence. Within-subject relationships have practical significance in practical situations such as interrogation, where an investigating officer might well place more weight on items where individuals were confident compared to where they were not. Finally, in finding significant within-subject differences, it is also interesting to note that the results of the Gruneberg and Sykes experiment reconcile findings from FOK studies with those of 'eyewitness' studies, suggesting that the same kind of memory processes are used in both cases.

Following the Gruneberg and Sykes study of picture identification, two more studies have been conducted on totally different kinds of material. The first study (Gruneberg et al., 1982) involved an experiment in which university students were required to listen to the Association Football results broadcast by the BBC on Saturday afternoon. Immediately after presentation, subjects were required to recall as many scores as they could and to rate how confident they were that they were correct.

The aim of the experiments was again to examine the relationship between knowledge and accuracy. A within-subject analysis revealed a strong and statistically significant relationship between degree of confidence and accuracy. Again, the between-subject correlations for individual items provided an erratic array of correlations with some correlations high and significant, some low and insignificant. At least some of the reasons for this erratic array of correlations may be due to the lack of variance in either confidence ratings or accuracy. For example, in some cases, only two or three individuals reported the correct result, in other cases no individuals were certain they were correct.

The correlation between the mean group rating of confidence for a particular item and the number of times that item was correctly recalled by the group as a whole was also obtained and the result was significant ($r = .51$ $p < .01$). In other words, the results show the higher the confidence rating of the group as a whole, the more likely the memory is to be accurate. This finding, like that for within-subject analysis, places a further limitation on the generalization that there is no relationship between confidence and accuracy.

The results of these experiments, therefore, cast considerable doubt on the general conclusion that there is no relationship between eyewitness confidence and accuracy. In experiments covering totally different experimental situations, there were highly significant within-subject differences between confidence ratings when correct and when incorrect. At present, therefore, conclusions covering the failure to find any relationship between accuracy and confidence should be confined to differences *between* individuals.

7.5 Mnemonic Aids

As the writer has noted elsewhere (Gruneberg, 1978), if psychology is going to make any contribution to the man in the street in helping him with his own memory problems, it will have to come through an understanding of processes over which the individual himself has control, in other words, strategies of learning and retrieval. Fortunately there are a number of such strategies which are useful, and which over the years have been formalized as mnemonic aids or techniques. Indeed the history of mnemonic aids stretches back to the Greeks. Yates (1966) recounts the story of how Simonedes was a guest at a banquet held to celebrate a wrestling match at the Olympic Games. During the banquet Simonedes was called outside and during his absence the banqueting hall collapsed, killing all those inside and causing such mutilation to the victims that they could not readily be identified. Simonedes, however, during his oration to the banquet had noticed the places in which each individual had been sitting and was able to identify the bodies for the relatives. Simonedes had in fact invented a mnemonic aid, later known as the method of loci, the principals of which form the basis of many mnemonic aids even today.

7.5.1   The Method of Loci

As noted above, the essence of the 'method of loci' is the association of a physical place with a 'to be remembered' object. The physical place is normally a familiar geographical location such as a bedroom with which the individual is familiar. Different parts of that location would then be isolated, such as the bed, the chest next to the bed, the window sill behind the chest, the wardrobe at the other end of the window sill, the chair next to the wardrobe, and so on. Items to be remembered are mentally 'placed' in each location, and the 'to be remembered item' is visualized as vividly as possible in association with its place. Suppose, for example, the first three words to be remembered were 'elephant', 'sugar' and 'mouse-trap'; the elephant might be visualized sitting on the bed, the sugar spilled all over the chest and the mouse trap placed on the window sill.

There is little doubt that this mnemonic system is highly effective in improving recall for lists of imageable material. In one experiment by Ross and Lawrence (1968), for example, 40 locations round a university campus were given to a group of students and they were required to learn a list of 40 words. Immediately after the list was presented, the students were asked for immediate recall. Recall averaged 37.5 words. After a day's delay, recall averaged 34 words. In a similar experiment Gronginger (1971) found that after 5 weeks, recall using the method of loci was 20 out of 25 words, compared to only 10 words for a group not using any mnemonic technique. While many of the studies on the method of loci have been conducted on university students, studies by Brown (1975) and Kobasigawa (1974) have shown that even young children perform at a significantly higher level when using the method of loci.

As far as this writer is aware no study has been reported which fails to show the effectiveness of the 'method of loci' in improving recall, so that the original findings of the ancient Greeks can be reasonably said to have been established by present-day cognitive psychologists.

The method of loci has perhaps two main aspects. First, the loci provide the individual with an easily retrieved set of ordered cues, so that he can move effortlessly from one cue to the next, considerably simplifying the memory search process. The second aspect is that the method of loci utilizes the power of imagery to improve recall. As noted previously many studies, e.g. Bower (1967) have found visualizing pairs of words together considerably improves recall.

This is particularly true when words are visualized as interacting together in some way. Morris and Stevens (1974) found that where individuals were asked to image each word as it was presented, this did not improve recall. Where one word was linked to the next, however, in an interacting way, the recall increased considerably. Clearly the method of loci involves interacting images.

Apart from having items interact, Higbee (1977) points out that it is useful to make the imaged picture as vivid as possible, a vivid image being one that is clear, distinct and strong. He quotes a number of studies which have found better retention following instruction to use vivid imagery. Among the techniques suggested for increasing vividness are motion, i.e. seeing the picture in action, and exaggeration, seeing huge dogs and small chairs perhaps, where the items to be remembered are dog and chair.

On the other hand one suggestion for improving the value of imagery which does not seem to have empirical support involves the suggestion of making images as bizzare as possible. A number of studies, e.g. Wood (1967) have failed to show the effects of bizzareness, and although there are studies which have found a facilitating effect (e.g. Delin, 1969), such findings might well be due to the fact that in some instances bizzareness is associated with vividness and it is this which is improving recall.

The method of loci then, is a technique which utilizes useful principles of memory facilitation, as established by independent experimentation, and the technique has been shown empirically to be effective in improving recall. While it might appear that the loci technique is limited by the number of loci that any individual is familiar with, two factors overcome this. First, it is quite feasible to go from one set of loci to another, for example from the bedroom to a favourite 18 hole golf course, to a well known street. Second it is quite possible to 'leave' more than one 'item' at a particular location. For example, if two items, 'comb' and 'fox' are to be left in location 1, say on the bed in the bedroom, a fox could be imagined jumping on the bed holding a comb in its mouth. Not only can these two techniques be used to increase the amount of material to be learned at any one time but also, as Higbee (1977) notes, they can be used to reduce interference for the memory of different lists learned at different times. Thus for list 1, the first set of loci can be used, for list 2 the second set, and so on. Again for a second list of items, the initial loci can be used by elaborating the first word on the first list with the first word on the second list. If, for example, the first word on list 1 is fish and on list 2 is cow, one can imagine a fish on the first set of loci (say a bed) with a cow eating its tail.

7.5.2 The Hook or Peg System

The hook or peg system is essentially a derivative of the method of loci, but in this system the 'pegs' are not physical places but items learned beforehand. The items form a series from 1 to 10, based on the following poem.

One is for bun
Two is for shoe
Three is for tree
Four is for door
Five is for hive
Six is for sticks
Seven is for heaven
Eight is for gate
Nine is for wine
Ten is for hen

When learning the poem, the individual is associating the appropriate number with an acoustically related word which is easily visualized. When learning a list of words, the first word to be remembered is linked in a vivid visual image to the first word in the poem. For example if the first three words to be learned are house, tie and knife, a bun might be imaged on top of a house, a tie round a shoe and a knife in a tree.

Like the method of loci, the peg system uses imagery and a plan for retrieving information in memory through a sequence of related cues. Again, as with the method of loci, there is considerable empirical evidence of its effectiveness in improving recall (e.g. Bugelski, 1968; Morris & Reid, 1970).

The pegword system has a slight advantage over the method of loci in allowing immediate access to the item and its position in a sequence, although the method of loci can allow this fairly rapidly also. Perhaps the major drawback to the pegword system, however, is that after the first 10 pegwords, it becomes difficult to find good words to rhyme with numbers. One solution to this, suggested by Higbee, is to use alphabetic rather than number hooks. For example

a — ape,
b — bee,
c — sea, and so on

7.5.3   The Digit–Letter Mnemonic System

Probably the most important extension of the method of loci system is the digit–letter system, in which letters are substituted for digits in the following way

0	1	2	3	4	5	6	7	8	9
s	t	n	m	r	e	j	k	g	p

In fact, many of the letters are physically or in some other way related to the digit which they represent. This substitution allows pegs to be constructed from 1 to 1000 or more, simply by substituting letters for numbers, and adding any meaningful vowels one chooses to the appropriate letter in order to make a meaningful word. For example, 1 = t to which can be added t(ea). The first peg, tea, is then associated with the first 'to be remembered' word, say elephant, in the same way that the first pegword of the pegword system is associated with the first 'to be remembered word'. Word 32 has the letters m, n which can become the pegword moon, and so on. When reaching the 32nd word, the individual generates m, n which readily generates moon and its visual associate. In principle, therefore, the digit letter system provides a set of ordered cues and a rule for generating the cue associated with each number. Second, the system uses imagery to relate pegwords to 'to be remembered' words in the same way as the method of loci. The major advance of the digit symbol technique over the method of loci is that a very long list of pegwords can be generated with relative ease.

As with the method of loci and the pegword system, there is strong empirical evidence that the digit–letter technique improves memory performance. Persensky and Senter (1969) found that those using the phonetic–letter system recalled double the number of items recalled by those not using the system and Foth (1973) found that all the mnemonic systems he examined, loci, pegword and the keyword method (the latter being the keywords of the digit–letter system) produced superior recall for concrete words to that of a fourth condition, where no mnemonic instruction was given.

7.5.4   Link System

While there is no doubt that the mnemonic techniques discussed above are all highly effective in improving memory, they all suffer from the one disadvantage of requiring preparation beforehand. The loci have to be identified and memorized, the poem has to be learned or the keywords have to be established. One technique which required no preparation beforehand is the link method, in which the first item is linked to the next item either through visual imagery or by means of a linking story. For example, if the first two words are 'car' and 'house', a car is visualized as driving through a house, or a story is made up in which a car drives through a house. The next word coming in, e.g. tree, is then linked to the previous word in the link, namely house, so that the next image is house and tree, or the next part of the story involves the tree falling on the house, and so on.

This link method has been shown to be highly effective in a study by Bower and Clark (1969). They required subjects to learn 12 lists of 10 words at their own pace by making up a story which linked the words. After all the lists were learned, subjects were required to recall all the words. For the mnemonic group 93% of words were recalled, compared to 14% for a control group given no instruction.

A number of studies have compared the relative merits of the method of loci, the link method and the peg system. One recent study by Roediger (1980) found that in terms of the number of items recalled there was little to choose between the three conditions. If account was taken of whether items were recalled in their correct order, however, then not surprisingly, the method of loci and pegword system were superior. This is because the link system only gives accurate order where every item is remembered.

7.5.5   The First Letter Mnemonic Aid

Unlike mnemonic systems which utilize imagery, the first letter mnemonic aid utilizes the cueing power of the first letter of the 'sought for' item in retrieving a whole item. As was noted earlier, where an individual has a memory block, then supplying the first letter of the missing item can result in recall in 50% of cases (Gruneberg & Monks, 1974). First letter mnemonics are very common in everyday life as in HMSO for Her Majesty's Stationery Office; CO for Commanding Officer and so on. They are also common as aids to remembering lists of items, such as ROYGBIV for the colours of the rainbow. Frequently such mnemonics are expanded into sentences in which the first letter of an item is connected into the first word of a sentence, such as Richard Of York Gave Battle In Vain for the colours of the rainbow. There are even books and dictionaries of mnemonics, e.g. Eyre-Methuen (1972) giving useful mnemonics for everyday life or for specialist disciplines such as medicine. For example, the phrase 'Every Good Boy Deserves Fun' gives the notes for the stave lines in music. Unlike the case of imagery mnemonics, however, the effectiveness of first letter mnemonics is far less clearly established empirically. While a number of small studies, e.g. Pash and Blick (1970), Manning and Bruning (1975), have found first letter mnemonics to be effective, a number of other studies, e.g. Nelson and Archer (1972), failed to find any effect on the number of items recalled. It is the case, however, that in the Nelson and Archer study and that of Morris and Cook (1978), the order of items was better recalled using first letter mnemonics.

One reason why first letter mnemonics may not work in some studies is that they may not be very effective in aiding memory for unrelated, poorly learned material. In one study using related lists of words, such as lists of birds, rivers, and so on, Gruneberg *et al.* (1977b) found a significant effect of using first letter mnemonics on both item and order recall. In their study, a large number of items (48) had to be learned and recall was delayed for 20 min after learning. As Gruneberg (1978) has argued, this perhaps more nearly represents the situation where students have to learn large amounts of related material and retain it for some time between learning and examination performance.

It has been argued that one disadvantage of using first letter mnemonics is that retention suffers because the mnemonic is often forgotten. In the Gruneberg *et al.* experiment there was certainly evidence that where the mnemonic was forgotten so were the associated words. Of the 130 mnemonics not recalled, only 16 associated word lists were correctly recalled. On 110 occasions the mnemonic was correctly recalled and in 92 of these occasions the associated word lists were also correctly recalled.

While the performance of the mnemonic group was superior to that of the non-mnemonic group, the mnemonic group took significantly longer to learn the word lists because they had to construct a mnemonic and relate it to the word list. It could be, therefore, that the superiority of the mnemonic condition was due to the greater time spent in learning, rather than the greater efficiency of the mnemonic *per se*. Nevertheless one can conclude that whatever the exact reason, the mnemonic instruction induced subjects to learn in such a way that overall recall was improved, a finding of considerable practical importance in examination situations for example. Again, as noted above, whatever the doubts about improved item recall, there is considerable evidence that the first letter mnemonic aid improves order recall.

7.5.6   *Problems of Mnemonic Aids*

It appears that while mnemonic aids, such as the first letter aid are used quite extensively by many individuals, techniques such as the method of loci and the peg system are rarely used. Harris (1978) carried out two interview studies in which he established that the use of internal memory aids such as the method of loci, first letter mnemonics and so on was extremely rare. For students, first letter mnemonics had, however, been used by 73% of the sample. This compares with 53% of students in a study by Gruneberg (1973). On the other hand, Harris reports that the method of loci had only ever been used by 13% and the peg by 7% of students. For housewives, the figures were 47% for first letter mnemonics, 17% for loci and 7% for the peg system. As the use of mnemonic aids such as the method of loci and the peg system has been established as of considerable use in improving recall, the question arises as to why such mnemonic aids are not in frequent use.

One major reason, probably, is that methods such as loci are seen to be of use for a very restricted range of materials, namely lists of concrete, unrelated words. A number of studies have shown, for example, that for 'naive' individuals, abstract words are not better memorized using imagery mnemonic techniques. As Higbee points out it is not difficult to overcome the problem of abstract words. It is only necessary to form a relationship with a concrete word and then relate the concrete word to the pegword. For example, if the first word on a list is 'arbitrary', then a similar sounding word might be harbour, and this could be visualized in conjunction with 'tea' or whatever the first keyword happened to be. On the other hand, as Higbee notes, such techniques do have their limitations in that for at least some abstract words it is hard to find substitute items. In such situations Higbee recommends that verbal linking might be a more appropriate technique.

A second major reason for mnemonics not being widely used is that they take time to apply. In some cases there is the time involved in making up lists of loci or learning pegwords, in addition to the extra time involved in linking words together in a visual image. For first letter mnemonics in which the first letters are transformed into a meaningful sentence, such as Richard Of York Gave Battle In Vain for the colours of the rainbow, the construction time for the mnemonic can be considerable. In one case in our experiment a subject took 20 min to make up one six letter mnemonic.

Apart from these reasons, a number of reasons have been advanced by individuals for not using mnemonics, which Higbee (1978) describes as 'Pseudo Limitations' on mnemonics. Among these are: (a) mnemonics are not suitable where understanding is required; (b) they are mental tricks; and (c) in any case they have no real practical application. The first argument that mnemonics involve an inferior form of learning devoid of understanding is put forward by Howe (1970) who states 'If something is worth learning, there is almost always a meaningful way of doing so'.

However, to take this position is to overlook the fact that in many situations rote learning has to take place prior to understanding. This is the case in learning a foreign vocabulary, for instance. Again, in high level examinations, Howe's argument is probably misconceived. Mnemonics in examinations cannot enable a student to do well where understanding is lacking. What mnemonics can do is to enable the student to give of his best by recalling what it is he does know despite the stress of examinations. If this is the case, then the argument that mnemonics are only 'tricks' seems irrelevant. Finally, the question of whether mnemonics are really practical is an empirical one, which is considered in the next section.

7.5.7   Practical Applications of Mnemonic Aids

(a)   Mnemonic aids in everyday life.   As noted above, one of the main arguments against the value of mnemonic aids is that they are useful only for the learning of lists of concrete, unrelated words, and the number of times that this is of use is strictly limited, especially as we often have the possibility of writing lists down on a piece of paper, when shopping, say. In fact, as Higbee notes, it is not the use of mnemonics which is limited, but the lack of foresight as to where mnemonics could be used which is limited. Apart from the fact that there are a number of situations in which mnemonics can aid list learning, such as in learning the States of the Union, the capitals of countries or the atomic weights of elements, mnemonic aids can be useful for making speeches, for remembering ideas late at night, for remembering cards played at bridge and other card games and for remembering the names of people to whom one has been recently introduced.

As far as learning useful lists is concerned, Higbee gives the example of teaching his young children the 10 commandments. He used the pegword system in which a concrete word represented each commandment. For example, a thief stealing a gate represented the eighth commandment (eight-gate). Unfortunately Higbee does not indicate what word he used for the commandment concerning adultery! The principle involved can of course be extended to remembering jokes, stories and so on.

As far as speech making is concerned, Higbee argues for the use of the link system, in which the main points you wish to make in the speech are linked together by imagery or story. This might of course involve some risk if any of the linking items were forgotten, so that at least for the unpractised, writing the keywords down might be a sensible precaution. Related to learning speeches is remembering speeches and indeed what is written in books. Higbee, for example, reports the case of a student who used the link system to complete a self-paced physics course which involved a 24 chapter book, a six-unit study guide and a series of films. The student linked the information under each unit to acquire a chain of information for each unit which was associated with the chain for the film. The student obtained 'A's on all examinations, and the course was completed in 2 weeks instead of one semester!

As far as card playing is concerned, the use of the digit–letter system can readily be adapted to memory for cards, once seen. One method for remembering cards involves the first letter of a keyword representing the suit, the last letter represents the number of the card. For example, eight of hearts would be h, g which would give the word hog, and so on. As Lorayne and Lucas (1974) note, once the card associations are learned it is a relatively easy matter to remember cards in sequence by the link method. However, the link system is probably not very useful for card games involving discarding cards, and for this Lorayne and Lucas recommend what they call the mutilation method. This involves mutilating in the mind's eye a card which has been discarded in some way. For example, if the eight of hearts is called, imagine a hog with blood spurting out of its head. When it comes to recalling which cards have not been discarded, it is only necessary to run through the cards to identify those not mutilated. For a more detailed account of the application of mnemonics to card playing, see Lorayne and Lucas (1974).

The question of how valuable mnemonics are for remembering faces has been investigated by Morris et al. (1978). The technique recommended by Lorayne and Lucas for remembering faces involves converting the person's name to some imageable substitute, such as Sykes to sex. A prominent feature of that individual, say the eyes, is chosen and exaggerated, and an image formed linking the eyes to the substitute word, so that Mr. Sykes's large eyes have in the centre of them a couple having sex. Morris et al. had subjects learn randomly chosen names assigned at random to photographs. Performance of the group using the mnemonic improved 80% compared with their earlier performance and with that of a control group not using a mnemonic to remember names. It should be added that this technique does sometimes have its dangers, especially where the substitute word is recalled instead of the 'real' name!

A further useful everyday application for the method of loci is in its use as a mental filing system. Higbee describes how the method can be used by associating an idea thought of with a locus. Ideas might occur at any time, when driving, or watching a film, or often when falling asleep at night. Often when this happens the idea is lost. Higbee suggests that the method of loci can be used by taking a concrete keyword from the idea, for example 'poisoning "mother-in-law" in the morning'. The thought of one's mother-in-law writhing in agony is associated with the first locus, say the bookshelf, so she is imagined writhing on top of the bookshelf. In the morning, one goes through the loci, imaging the ideas of the night before.

Finally mnemonics are useful for remembering telephone numbers. This is done through the use of the digit–letter system where numbers are substituted by letters. For example, if a girl friend called Pamela has a telephone number 8326593, this becomes g m n j l p m which in turn might be 'Go Man, Jail Pam'. My own personal experience is that the mnemonic does not have to be too meaningful in order to be effective.

(b) Mnemonics and educational applications.   Perhaps one of the best established uses of mnemonics is in foreign language learning. Two studies by Raugh and Atkinson (1975) and Atkinson and Raugh (1975) established that the use of the keyword method could considerably enhance vocabulary learning. Raugh and Atkinson substituted keywords which sounded like Spanish words which the individual had to remember. For example the Spanish for puddle is chirco. The word charcoal was substituted for chirco and charcoal imaged with puddle. In one experiment a group of students were given a list of 60 Spanish words to learn: 88% were remembered by those using a mnemonic compared to only 28% for the group not using mnemonics. In another experiment, on Russian words, the corresponding figures were 72% for the mnemonic and 46% for the control group. In these experiments, the foreign word is given and the subject has to produce the English equivalent. While there is little evidence that recall of the foreign equivalent, given the English word, is improved using the keyword method, at least it does not seem to be any worse than any other technique (Pressley *et al.*, 1980).

Pressley (1977) has, in fact, extended the findings on foreign language learning to young children. In one experiment he found that second grade children using the keyword mnemonic performed at a level 189% above those not using a mnemonic when tested on Spanish–English word association. On the other hand, there does seem to be some question about whether the findings of laboratory studies are always directly applicable to classroom situations. Levin *et al.* (1979) cite a study of the keyword method, in which there was no significant effect in a classroom situation, and Levin *et al.* show the keyword method to be best in situations where keywords are read aloud to relatively small groups of children, rather than have the children read the keyword for themselves. For the keyword method to be most successful the following rules seem to follow from the work of Pressley and Levin *et al.*

1.   Provide children with a visual picture which links the keyword with the English word.

2. Pronounce aloud the word and its association.
3. Allow a limited set time, perhaps 15 s between presentation of word pairs. This may well increase the attention that young children will give to the task.
4. Where possible, teach children in small groups, perhaps of between three and six individuals.

(c) Other educational uses of mnemonics. As indicated above, first letter mnemonics are quite frequently used by students when preparing for examination, and while the evidence for the efficiency of first letter mnemonics is somewhat ambiguous, there is no doubt that some students at least regard such mnemonics as essential aids to examination performance. One student, cited in Gruneberg (1978), used mnemonics so extensively that before looking at an examination paper, he would write down all the mnemonics he had learned for that particular course. Two other students who recently obtained first class degrees within the writer's department both used first letter mnemonics extensively and both claimed that the use of mnemonics gave them the confidence that they would be able to recall the enormous amount of material they had learned and thought about.

Within a non-examination context, Levin *et al.* report on a study in which the keyword mnemonic was used to teach children the definitions of different words and on events associated with fictitious people. Presumably such a technique could be adapted to help in the association of facts with real people! Finally, Higbee reports a number of studies which show that mnemonic techniques have helped in the teaching of reading and in the learning process for brain damaged, elderly and mentally retarded individuals.

It does seem reasonable to question the claim of critics of mnemonic aids, that they have no practical application.

Furthermore, there is every reason why they should work as they invariably employ principles shown by independent laboratory research to facilitate memory. Thus systems such as the method of loci and the peg, cue information with the aid of a retrieval plan which locates items in the memory store, and both mnemonic techniques also exploit the facilitating effects of imagery on memory. They also exploit two other principles, increasing the willingness of the individual to learn, and also forcing the individual to organize the material to be learned as well as possible. In organizing material to be learned for mnemonics, the individual has to think about it, and this too is likely to increase later recall. This in turn may well make the task more interesting to the individual, and as Morris *et al.* (1981) have shown, the more interested individuals are in material, the more likely they are to remember it later. While it is true, as both Morris (1978) and Higbee (1978) point out, that mnemonic aids do have limitations, it is quite clear that they also have their uses.

References

ANDERSON, R.C. and RICHERT, J.W. (1978) Recall of previously unrecallable information following a shift in perspective. *Journal of Verbal Learning and Verbal Behavior*, **17**, 1–12.

ATKINSON, R.C. and RAUGH, M.R. (1975) An application of the mnemonic keyword method to the acquisition of a Russian vocabulary. *Journal of Experimental Psychology: Human Learning and Memory*, **1**, 126–133.

BELMONT, J.M. (1978) Individual differences in memory: The cases of normal and retarded development. In: M.M. GRUNEBERG, and P.E. MORRIS (Eds.) *Aspects of Memory*, pp. 153–185. Methuen, London.

BLAKE, M. (1973) Prediction of recognition where recall fails: Exploring the feeling of knowing phenomenon. *Journal of Verbal Learning and Verbal Behavior*, **12**, 311–319.

BOWER, G.H. (1967) Mental imagery and memory. Cited in M.J. HOWE (Ed.) *Adult Learning*. John Wiley, New York.

BOWER, G.H. and CLARK, M.C. (1969) Narrative stories as mediators for serial learning. *Psychonomic Science*, **14**, 181–182.

BROWN, A.L. (1975) The development of memory: Knowing, knowing about knowing and knowing how to know. In: H.W. REESE (Ed.) *Advances in Child Development and Behavior*. Academic Press, New York.

BROWN, J. (1958) Some tests of the decay theory of immediate memory. *Quarterly Journal of Experimental Psychology*, **10**, 10–21.

BROWN, R. and MCNEIL, D. (1966) The 'Tip of the Tongue' phenomenon. *Journal of Verbal Learning and Verbal Behavior*, **5**, 325–337.

BUGELSKI, B.R. (1968) Images as a mediator in one trial paired associate learning. *Journal of Experimental Psychology*, **77**, 328–334.

BULL, R. and CLIFFORD, B. (1979) Eyewitness memory. In: M.M. GRUNEBERG and P.E. MORRIS (Eds.) *Applied Problems in Memory*, pp. 151–184. Academic Press, London.

CLIFFORD, B. and SCOTT, J. (1978) Individual and situational factors in eyewitness testimony. *Journal of Applied Psychology*, **63**, 352–359.

COFER, C. (1967) Does conceptual clustering influence the amount retained in immediate free recall? In: B. KLEINMUNTS (Ed.) *Concepts and the Structure of Memory*. John Wilet, New York.

COLE, M. and SCRIBNER, S. (1974) *Culture and Thought*. John Wiley, New York.

CRAIK, F.I.M. and LOCKHART, R.S. (1973) Levels of processing: A framework for memory research. *Journal of Verbal Learning and Verbal Behavior*, **11**, 671–684.

CRAIK, F.I.M. and TULVING, E. (1975) Depth of processing and the retention of words in episodic memory. *Journal of Experimental Psychology: General*, **104**, 268–294.

CRAIK, F.I.M. and WATKINS, M.J. (1973) The role of rehearsal in short-term memory. *Journal of Verbal Learning and Verbal Behavior*, **12**, 599–607.

DEFFENBACHER, K.A., BROWN, E.L. and STURGILL, W. (1978). Some predictors of eye witness memory accuracy. In: M.M. GRUNEBERG, P.E. MORRIS and R.N. SYKES (Eds.) *Practical Aspects of Memory*, pp. 219–226. Academic Press, London.

DELIN, P.S. (1969). The learning to criterion of a serial list with and without mnemonic instruction. *Psychonomic Science*, **16**, 169–170.

DILLON, R.F. and REID, L.S. (1969). Short-term memory as a function of information processing during the retention interval. *Journal of Experimental Psychology*, **81**, 261.

EARHARD, M. (1967). Cued recall and free recall as a function of the number of items percue. *Journal of Verbal Learning and Verbal Behavior*, **6**, 257–263.

EYRE-METHUEN (1972). *A Dictionary of Mnemonics*. Eyre-Methuen, London.

EYSENCK, M.W. (1979). The feeling of knowing a word's meaning. *British Journal of Psychology*, **70**, 243–251.

FLAVELL, J.H. (1977). *Cognitive Development*. Prentice Hall, Englewood Cliffs, New Jersey.

FLAVELL, J.H., BEACH, D.R. and CHINSKY, J.M. (1966). Spontaneous verbal rehearsal in a memory task as a function of age. *Child Development*, **37**, 283–299.

FOTH, D.L. (1973). Mnemonic technique effectiveness as a function of word abstractness and mediation instruction. *Journal of Verbal Learning and Verbal Behavior*, **12**, 239–245.

GLANZER, M. and MEINZER, A. (1967). The effects of intralist activity on free recall. *Journal of Verbal Learning and Verbal Behavior*, **6**, 928–935.

GLENBERG, A., SMITH, S.M. and GREEN, C. (1977). Type I rehearsal: Maintenance and move. *Journal of Verbal Learning and Verbal Behavior*, **16**, 339–352.

GRAEFE, T.M. and WATKINS, M.J. (1980). Picture rehearsal: An effect of selectively attending to pictures no longer in view. *Journal of Experimental Psychology, Human Learning and Memory*, **6**, 156–162.

GRONINGER, K.D. (1971). Mnemonic imagery and forgetting. *Psychonomic Science*, **23**, 161–163.

GRUNEBERG, M.M. (1973). The role of memorization techniques in finals examination preparation — a study of psychology students. *Educational Research*, **15**, 134–139.

GRUNEBERG, M.M. (1978). The feeling of knowing, memory blocks and memory aids. In: M.M. GRUNEBERG and P.E. MORRIS (Eds.) *Aspects of Memory*, pp. 186–209. Methuen, London.

GRUNEBERG, M.M. and MONKS, J. (1974) Feeling of knowing and cued recall. *Acta Psychologica*, **38**, 257–265.

GRUNEBERG, M.M. and MONKS, J. (1976). The first letter search strategy. *IRCS Medical Science: Psychology and Psychiatry*, **4**, 307.

GRUNEBERG, M.M., MONKS, J. and SYKES, R.N. (1977a). Some methodological problems with feeling of knowing studies. *Acta Psychologica*, **41**, 365–371.

GRUNEBERG, M.M., MONKS, J. and SYKES, R.N. (1977b). The first letter mnemonic aid. *IRCS Medical Science: Psychology and Psychiatry, Social and Occupational Medicine*, **5**, 304.

GRUNEBERG, M.M., MORRIS, P.E. and SYKES, R.N. (1982). The relationship between confidence and accuracy in the recall of football results. Submitted for publication.

GRUNEBERG, M.M. and SYKES, R.N. (1978). Knowledge and memory: The feeling of knowing and reminiscence. In: M.M. GRUNEBERG, P.E. MORRIS, and R.N. SYKES (Eds.) *Practical Aspects of Memory*, pp. 189–196. Academic Press, London.

GRUNEBERG, M.M. and SYKES, R.N. (1981). Eyewitness confidence and eyewitness accuracy for pictures. Submitted for publication.

GRUNEBERG, M.M. and SYKES, R.N. (1982). Eyewitness accuracy and feelings of certainty. Submitted for publication.

GRUNEBERG, M.M., WINFROW, P. and WOODS, R. (1973). An investigation into memory blocking. *Acta Psychologica*, **37**, 187–196.

HARRIS, J. (1978). External memory aids. In: M.M. GRUNEBERG, P.E. MORRIS and R.N. SYKES (Eds.) *Practical Aspects of Memory*. Academic Press, London.

HARRIS, P. (1978). Developmental aspects of children's memory. In: M.M. GRUNEBERG and P.E. MORRIS (Eds.) *Aspects of Memory*, pp. 132–152. Methuen, London.

HART, J.T. (1965). Memory and the feeling of knowing experience. *Journal of Educational Psychology*, **56**, 208–216.

HART, J.T. (1967). Memory and the memory monitoring process. *Journal of Verbal Learning and Verbal Behavior*, **6**, 685–691.

HIGBEE, K.L. (1977). *Your memory: How it works and how to improve it*. Prentice Hall, Englewood Cliffs, New Jersey.

HIGBEE, K.L. (1978). Some pseudo-limitations of mnemonics. In: M.M. GRUNEBERG, P.E. MORRIS and R.N. SYKES (Eds.) *Practical Aspects of Memory*. Academic Press, London.

HOWE, M.J.A. (1970). *Introduction to Human Memory*. Harper & Row, New York.

JAMES, W. (1890). *Principles of Psychology*. Harvey Holt, New York.

KEENEY, T.J., CANNIZZO, S.R. and FLAVELL, J.H. (1967). Spontaneous and induced verbal rehearsal in a recall task. *Child Development*, **38**, 953–966.

KOBASIGAWA, A. (1974). Utilization of retrieval cues of children in recall. *Child Development*, **45**, 127–134.

KORIAT, A. and LEIBLICH, I. (1974). What does a person in a TOT state know that a person in a 'don't know' state doesn't know? *Memory and Cognition*, **2**, 647–655.

KORIAT, A. and LEIBLICH, I. (1977). A study of memory pointers. *Acta Psychologica*, **41**, 151–164.

KREUTZER, M.A., LEONARD, C. and FLAVELL, J.H. (1975). An interview study of children's knowledge about memory. *Monographs of Society for Research in Child Development*, **40**, 1, Serial No. 159.

LEIPPE, M.R., WELLS, G.L. and OSTROM, T.M. (1978). Crime seriousness as a determinant of accuracy in eyewitness identification. *Journal of Applied Psychology*, **63**, 345–351.

LEVIN, J.R., PRESSLEY, M., MCCORMICK, C.B., MILLER, G.E. and STRIBERG, L.K. (1979). Assessing the classroom potential of the keyword method. *Journal of Educational Psychology*, **71**, 583–594.

LIPTON, J.P. (1977). On the psychology of eyewitness testimony. *Journal of Applied Psychology*, **62**, 90–95.

LORAYNE, H. and LUCAS, J. (1974). *The Memory Book*. Stein & Day, New York.

MANNING, B.A. and BRUNING, R.H. (1975). Interactive effects of mnemonic techniques and word list characteristics. *Psychological Reports*, **36**, 727–736.

MODIGLIANI, V. (1976). Effects on a later recall by delaying initial recall. *Journal of Experimental Psychology: Human Learning and Memory*, **2**, 609–622.

MODIGLIANI, V. (1978). Effects of initial testing on later retention as a function of the initial retention interval. In: M.M. GRUNEBERG, P.E. MORRIS and R.N. SYKES (Eds.) *Practical Aspects of Memory*, pp. 652–659. Academic Press, London.

MOELY, B.E. and JEFFREY, W. (1974). The effect of organization training on children's free recall of category items. *Child Development*, **45**, 135–134.

MORRIS, P.E. (1978). Sense and nonsense in traditional mnemonics. In: M.M. GRUNEBERG, P.E. MORRIS and R.N. SYKES (Eds.) *Practical Aspects of Memory*, pp. 155–163. Academic Press, London.

MORRIS, P.E. (1979). Strategies for learning and recall. In: M.M. GRUNEBERG and P.E. MORRIS (Eds.) *Applied Problems in Memory*, pp. 25–57. Academic Press, London.

MORRIS, P.E. and COOK, N. (1978). When do first letter mnemonics aid recall? *British Journal of Educational Psychology*, **48**, 22–28.

MORRIS, P.E., GRUNEBERG, M.M., SYKES, R.N. and MERRICK, A. (1981). Football scores: Knowledge and retention. *British Journal of Psychology* (in press).

MORRIS, P.E., JONES, S. and HAMPSON, P.J. (1978). An imagery mnemonic for the learning of people's names. *British Journal of Psychology*, **69**, 335–336.

MORRIS, P.E. and STEVENS, R. (1974). Linking images and free recall. *Journal of Verbal Learning and Verbal Behavior*, **13**, 310–315.

MORRIS, P.E. and REID, R.L. (1970). Repeated use of mnemonic imagery. *Psychonomic Science*, **20**, 337–338.

MURDOCK, B.B. (1967). Recent developments in short-term memory. *British Journal of Psychology*, **58**, 421–433.

NELSON, D.L. and ARCHER, C.S. (1972). The first letter mnemonic. *Journal of Educational Psychology*, **63**, 482–486.

PASH, J.R. and BLICK, K.A. (1970). The effect of a mnemonic device on retention of verbal material. *Psychonomic Science*, **19**, 203–204.

PERSENSKY, J.J. and SENTER, R.J. (1969). An investigation of bizarre imagery as a mnemonic device. *Psychological Record*, **20**, 145–150.

PETERSON, L.R. and PETERSON, M.J. (1959). Short-term retention of individual items. *Journal of Experimental Psychology*, **58**, 193–198.

PRESSLEY, G.M. (1977). Children's use of the keyword method to learn simple Spanish vocabulary words. *Journal of Educational Psychology*, **69**, 465–472.

PRESSLEY, M., LEVIN, J.R., HALL, J.W., MILLER, G.E. and BERRY, J.K. (1980). The keyword method and foreign word acquisition. *Journal of Experimental Psychology, Human Learning and Memory*, **6**, 163–173.

RAUGH, M.R. and ATKINSON, R.C. (1975). A mnemonic method for learning a second language vocabulary. *Journal of Educational Psychology*, **67**, 1–16.

ROEDIGER, H.L. (1980). The effectiveness of four mnemonics in ordering recall. *Journal of Experimental Psychology, Human Learning and Memory*, **6**, 555–567.

ROGOFF, B., NEWCOMBE, N. and HAGAN, J. (1974). Playfulness and recognition memory. *Child Development*, **45**, 972–977.

ROSS, J. and LAWRENCE, K.A. (1968). Some observations on memory artifice. *Psychonomic Science*, **13**, 107–108.

RUNDUS, O. (1971). Analysis of rehearsal processes in free recall. *Journal of Experimental Psychology*, **89**, 63–77.

TULVING, E. (1966). Theoretical issues in free recall. In: R. DIXON and D.L. HORTON (Eds.) *Verbal Behavior and General Behavior Theory*, pp. 2–36. Prentice Hall, Englewood Cliffs, New Jersey.

WELLMAN, H. (1977). Tip of the tongue and feeling of knowing experiments: A developmental study of memory monitoring. *Child Development*, **48**, 13–21.

WELLMAN, H.M., RITTER, K. and FLAVELL, J.H. (1975). Deliberate memory behavior in the delayed reactions of very young children. *Developmental Psychology*, **11**, 780–787.

WICKELGREN, W. (1979). *Cognitive Psychology*. Prentice Hall, Englewood Cliffs, New Jersey.

WOOD, G. (1967). Mnemonic systems in recall. *Journal of Educational Psychology*, Mono. 58, 6, Part 2.

YARMEY, A.D. (1973). I recognize your face, but I cannot remember your name: Further evidence on the tip of the tongue phenomenon. *Memory and Cognition*, **1**, 287–290.

YATES, F. (1966). *The Art of Memory*. Routledge & Kegan Paul, London.

CHAPTER 8

Individual Differences in Human Memory

Michael W. Eysenck

8.1 Introduction

It is one of the oddities of the development of psychology as a science that there is an almost complete schism between experimental psychology on the one hand and individual-difference psychology on the other hand. This schism has been widely deplored, most notably by Cronbach (1957) in his Presidential Address to the American Psychological Association concerning 'The two disciplines of scientific psychology'. Some of the reasons for the almost total lack of attempts to integrate the two disciplines are discussed below.

First, it has been argued that any individual differences in memorial functioning are modest in size, and thus may conveniently be ignored. The fallacy in this argument is that it is only true of certain limited situations. For example, behavioural differences between individuals high and low in trait anxiety are much greater when environmental stress is present than when it is not (Eysenck, 1979, 1981). The explanation is fairly straightforward: there are minimal differences in experienced anxiety as a function of trait anxiety in non-stressful conditions. The typical laboratory study of memory, where well-motivated subjects acquire information in a non-stressful environment which is relatively free of distracting stimuli, may well minimize individual differences. However, this is accomplished at a considerable cost in terms of ecological validity.

Second, it is frequently claimed that individual differences in behaviour are rather inconsistent. As Eysenck and Eysenck (1980) have argued, it is quite clear that consistent relationships can be (and have been) demonstrated when major dimensions are investigated via reliable measuring instruments. However, the position is quite different with respect to other dimensions of individual differences. Consider as an example the personality dimension of field dependence, two popular measures of which have been found to correlate approximately + .35 with each other. With such reliability of measurement, it should come as no surprise to discover that field dependence is not related to performance in a consistent fashion.

Third, many researchers have suggested that there is no need to consider individual differences, even if robust effects of individual differences on behaviour can be obtained. The argument is that the existence of reliable individual differences in learning and memory does not, in and of itself, enhance our understanding of memorial processes. Proponents of this view fail to distinguish among different possible behavioural outcomes. If some dimension of individual differences affects only the level of performance, then it may be reasonable to assume that different individuals or groups of individuals are using the same processes with varying degrees of efficiency. There would be some justification for disregarding individual differences under such circumstances.

However, interactions between dimensions of individual differences and task conditions have frequently been found. Such interactions may take two basic forms: (1) ordinal interaction, in which the rank ordering of performance in the various task conditions is the same at every level of the individual-difference dimension; and (2) disordinal interaction, in which the rank ordering is not invariant. When a disordinal interaction is obtained, the implication is that different individuals are using qualitatively different processes or strategies, so that the normal policy of pooling data across subjects would lead to erroneous conclusions.

A study by Howarth and Eysenck (1968) provides a good example of a disordinal interaction. They found that the paired-associate recall of extraverts declined considerably over time, whereas that of introverts increased substantially; this produced a theoretically important interaction between introversion–extraversion and retention interval. If personality had been ignored, they would have discovered only that paired-associate recall was apparently unaffected by the length of the retention interval! Given such findings, the prevalent refusal to consider individual differences at all seems obtuse.

It is not always necessary to discover disordinal interactions between dimensions of individual differences and task conditions in order to show that different individuals use qualitatively different processes. An alternative method is to compare different individuals in a *single* task condition, but to measure two or more aspects of their performance. If there are non-equivalent effects of individual differences on the various dependent variables, then we cannot account for the data on the assumption that some individuals are simply more efficient than others.

An example of individuals differing in their response patterning is to be found in work on the effects of introversion–extraversion on vigilance performance (Eysenck, 1981). Introverts make fewer false alarms than extraverts, and usually have a significantly higher response criterion. However, there is often no effect of introversion–extraversion on detection sensitivity. We are here dealing with something more than an effect of introversion–extraversion on the overall level of performance.

The thrust of the argument so far is that it is pointless to ignore individual differences unless we are confident that all our subjects are using exactly the same processes and strategies. The usual approach of relegating individual differences to the error term in an analysis of variance needlessly inflates the error term and reduces the information that can be extracted from the data.

It is also possible to investigate individual differences in ways having more direct relevance to theories of memory. Consider as an example the notion of a short-term store. This has been incorporated in several major theories of memory (e.g. Atkinson & Shiffrin, 1968; Baddeley & Hitch, 1974). Such theories sometimes make two assumptions which have rarely been tested empirically: (1) the various measures of short-term storage capacity (e.g. memory span and recency effect in free recall) are equivalent; and (2) there are a large number of tasks (e.g. mental arithmetic) which make demands on the short-term storage system.

These assumptions can readily be tested by means of an approach based on individual differences. Those individuals with large short-term storage capacity as indexed by one of the main measures of that capacity should tend to show large capacity on other measures of short-term storage capacity. They should also excel on tasks allegedly heavily dependent on maintaining information transiently in a short-term store.

When this approach has been adopted, it appears that the assumption that a single short-term storage system is used in the performance of several different tasks may be unwarranted. Martin (1978) found that individuals with a large digit span did not necessarily obtain a large recency effect in free recall. In fact, the mean correlation coefficient between the two measures was a non-significant + .15. When taken in conjunction with other findings, this result obviously calls for some kind of reappraisal of the concept of the short-term store (cf. Baddeley & Hitch, 1974).

Sternberg (1977) has argued convincingly that research in cognitive psychology can profit from an amalgamation of the information-processing and individual-difference approaches. An information-processing analysis often produces a reasonably accurate account of the component processes involved in the performance of a task, but it is difficult to assess the generality of these processes. In contrast, the individual-difference approach frequently produces constructs possessing generality, but it fails to specify with any precision what is involved in task performance.

Problems associated with the specificity of information-processing constructs and with the imprecision of the theoretical terms emerging from the individual-difference approach can be minimized by integrating the two approaches. For example, Sternberg (1980) used the information-processing approach to identify the various processing stages involved in linear syllogistic reasoning. According to one theoretical model, some of these stages involve linguistic processing, whereas others depend on spatial processing. Individual differences in verbal and spatial ability were found to correlate in predictable ways with speed of performance of the various component processes; the existence of these correlations supported the theoretical model, and also suggested that the processing stages identified have some general significance.

In sum, it turns out that none of the conventional arguments for ignoring individual differences carries much force. Indeed, one may go further and argue that memory research which disregards individual differences (probably more than 95% of published work) is necessarily inadequate. The basic point was expressed clearly by Vale and Vale (1969):

> If organisms are meaningfully different, they may be expected to react differentially to the same treatment, and the search for general, invariant relations between environmental treatments and behavioural responses may be foredoomed (p. 1094).

In the following sections of the chapter, we deal with various aspects of individual differences. In Section 8.2 the emphasis is on personality, i.e. the effects of individual differences in motivation and emotion. Section 8.3 deals with individual differences of a more cognitive kind, including factors of intelligence and memory ability. Section 8.4, the final section, presents various conclusions.

8.2 Personality and Memory

8.2.1 Introduction

While there has been quite a lot of research into the effects of personality on learning and memory, much of it is of poor quality. There are two main reasons for this: (1) minor personality dimensions have often been selected for study without an adequate theoretical rationale; and (2) far too many researchers in this area have been blissfully unaware of recent theoretical and empirical developments in the field of memory.

The emphasis in this section is largely on work which does not suffer from these deficiencies. There is strong evidence (e.g. Eysenck, 1967) that the orthogonal personality factors of neuroticism and introversion–extraversion constitute major, consistently replicable, personality dimensions. These two personality dimensions have emerged in numerous factor-analytic studies, and thus have claims to be regarded as more important than most others.

Are there any theoretical arguments to support the notion that the two-dimensional space defined by neuroticism and introversion–extraversion is of especial significance? There are several, but perhaps the most persuasive was suggested by Gray (1973). He argued that there is an anxiety dimension running from stable extraversion (low anxiety) to neurotic introversion (high anxiety). The systematic importance of this dimension is that it reflects individual differences in susceptibility to punishment. Orthogonal to the anxiety dimension is an impulsivity dimension, which runs from stable introversion (low impulsivity) to neurotic extraversion (high impulsivity); this is a dimension of susceptibility to reward.

There is both behavioural and physiological evidence to support Gray's theoretical contentions. In addition, the linking of personality factors to major classes of environmental events (i.e. reward and punishment) represents a desirable development in personality research.

8.2.2 Anxiety

There has been more research on the effects of anxiety on learning and memory than any other personality dimension. For many years the emphasis was on trait anxiety, which may be considered as a semi-permanent predisposition to experience anxiety. However, since experienced anxiety reflects both trait anxiety and the degree of environmental stress, there has more recently been increased interest in anxiety as a transient emotional mood. Anxiety in this sense is usually referred to as state anxiety, and it is commonly assumed that state anxiety (which reflects situational stress) is a better predictor of behaviour than is trait anxiety.

Much of the early work in this area was based on the theoretical ideas of Spence (e.g. Spence & Spence, 1966), who concentrated primarily on trait anxiety. He started with the Hullian assumption that habit strength (a measure of learning) multiplied by drive (a motivational measure) produces excitatory potential. Performance at any given moment would be determined by the habit having the greatest strength, provided that the level of excitatory potential produced by that habit when multiplied by drive exceeded the response threshold.

Anxiety (which was usually measured by means of the Manifest Anxiety Scale) was regarded as one of the determinants of drive level; in addition, the emotional response associated with anxiety was thought to produce drive stimuli which could lead to task-irrelevant behaviour. Since there is a multiplicative relationship between drive and habit strength, it follows that an increase in drive produced by anxiety should increase the difference in probability of two responses differing in response strength. When the correct response is already the strongest at the start of learning, then anxiety should improve performance. However, when the correct response has to be discriminated from incorrect competing responses which are stronger than it, then any increase in anxiety will make the incorrect responses even stronger relative to the correct response, and thus impair performance.

While the theory identifies the number and strength of competing responses as the prime determinant of the effects of anxiety on memory, it has often been supposed that the basic idea is that anxiety enhances performance on easy learning tasks but impairs it on difficult tasks. According to this revised conceptualization, there should be an interaction between anxiety and task difficulty. In fact, such an interaction has been obtained over 20 times, mostly in studies of paired-associate learning (see Eysenck, 1979, for a review).

In spite of this empirical support for the theory, there are a number of reasons for not accepting the findings at face value. First, subjects tend to experience more anxiety when engaged in a difficult learning task than an easy one, so there is a confounding between task difficulty and anxiety level (cf. Weiner & Schneider, 1971). Second, when task difficulty and degree of response competition are unconfounded (Saltz & Hoehn, 1957), anxiety tends to interact with task difficulty rather than with degree of response competition.

The astute reader may have noticed that Spence's theory makes the strong claim that anxiety affects retrieval but has no effect at all on learning. This follows from the assumption that anxiety plays no part in determining habit strength. Very surprisingly, most studies have failed to separate out the effects of anxiety on storage and on retrieval, so that the data obtained are equivocal. However, since high-anxiety subjects engage in more off-task glancing than low-anxiety subjects (Nottelman & Hill, 1977), and since high-anxiety subjects report that they spend a smaller proportion of the available time attending to the experimental task (Deffenbacher, 1978), it seems implausible that there are no effects of anxiety on learning.

More direct evidence was obtained by Straughan and Dufort (1969). They discovered that relaxation instructions given shortly before learning had beneficial effects on the subsequent recall performance of high-anxiety subjects but an adverse effect on low-anxiety subjects. The implication is that the amount of anxiety experienced at the time of storage affected what was learned.

A further problem for Spence's theory is posed by the findings from studies of free recall. According to the theory, high drive in the form of anxiety increases the excitatory potential of all responses; as a consequence, anxiety should improve free recall by raising additional responses above the response threshold. In fact, anxiety either has no effect on free recall, or actually reduces the number of words recalled (Mueller, 1977).

We must conclude that Spence's theory, in spite of its historical importance, is inadequate in many ways. An alternative approach was proposed by Easterbrook (1959), who contended that states of high emotionality, arousal and anxiety all produce a restriction in the range of cue utilization. In more contemporary terms, the basic idea is that arousal and anxiety produce a narrowing of attention.

If we assume that there are more cues associated with difficult tasks than with easy ones, we can then apply Easterbrook's hypothesis to the interaction which has often been obtained between anxiety and task difficulty. The narrowing of attention under high anxiety would obviously be more likely to impair performance on difficult tasks under this assumption, and this is, of course, what is usually found.

Easterbrook's hypothesis has been investigated most often in situations involving concurrent primary and subsidiary tasks. The primary task has usually involved intentional learning, whereas the subsidiary task has consisted of incidental learning. The prediction is that, since anxiety produces a narrowing of attention, any adverse effects of anxiety will be greater on the subsidiary task than on the primary task.

The relevant findings are discussed in detail by Eysenck (1979). There are 20 experimental comparisons in which the effects of anxiety have been studied in dual-task situations. Anxiety did not affect performance of the main task in 16 experiments, and impaired performance in only three cases. In contrast, anxiety significantly impaired performance on the subsidiary task in 15 experiments. The data thus provide support for Easterbrook's hypothesis; however, Easterbrook seems to have regarded attentional narrowing as a relatively passive and automatic reaction to high anxiety, whereas it is at least as likely that it represents an active coping response to information overload.

The weakest part of Easterbrook's hypothesis is the notion that anxiety impairs performance on difficult tasks by producing great concentration on only a few task elements. As we have already seen, anxiety seems to *reduce* rather than increase concentration on the experimental task (Deffenbacher, 1978; Nottelman & Hill, 1977). Furthermore, Easterbrook's hypothesis appears to generate the counter-intuitive prediction that high anxiety reduces the susceptibility to distraction. There is some scattered evidence in support of this prediction (e.g. Zaffy & Bruning, 1966), but there are several studies in which distractibility was found to be positively related to anxiety (e.g. Dornic, 1977).

Eysenck (1979, 1981) argued that the frequent finding that anxiety has non-significant effects on performance does not necessarily mean that anxiety is having no effect on internal processing mechanisms. He suggested that high-anxiety subjects achieve performance comparability with low-anxiety subjects at greater subjective cost to themselves. There is supporting evidence in the dual-task literature reviewed above. There were 16 cases in which anxiety had no effect on main-task performance; in the absence of a subsidiary task, the likely conclusion would be that anxiety did not affect internal processing. However, analysis of the subsidiary-task data refutes that conclusion, since anxiety significantly impaired performance in 11 out of the 16 cases. This is precisely the pattern of results to be expected if anxiety reduces the efficiency of processing so that reasonable main-task performance must be 'bought' at greater cost, thus reducing the resources available for the subsidiary task.

Dornic (1980) has investigated some of these theoretical issues. He found that neurotic introverts (i.e. high-anxiety subjects) performed various tasks as effectively as stable extraverts (i.e. low-anxiety subjects), but in some of the more demanding task conditions the neurotic introverts estimated that they had expended significantly more effort than stable extraverts. If we define processing efficiency as the ratio of performance effectiveness to effort investment, then anxiety reduced processing efficiency despite the absence of any effects of anxiety on performance.

Why does anxiety reduce processing efficiency? The answer may be that

287

anxiety leads to task-irrelevant cognitive activities which compete with task-relevant information for space in the processing system (Eysenck, 1979; Hamilton, 1975). Since worry has been identified as one of the major components of test anxiety (Liebert & Morris, 1967), these task-irrelevant cognitions may include concern about the level of performance, negative task expectations and negative self-evaluations.

Eysenck (1979) speculated that the part of the processing system most strongly implicated in concurrent processing of task-relevant and task-irrelevant information is working memory. The working memory system was described by Baddeley and Hitch (1974), who identified two components: (1) a modality-free limited capacity central processing space; and (2) an articulatory rehearsal loop with a capacity of approximately three items.

If task-irrelevant cognitive activities such as worry pre-empt some of the limited capacity of working memory, then the adverse effects of anxiety should be greatest on tasks making substantial demands on working memory. While there are undoubtedly many reasons why a task may be difficult, it seems reasonable to assume that difficult tasks typically make greater demands on working memory than do easy tasks. This could be used as a basis for understanding the typical interaction between anxiety and task difficulty.

Baddeley and Hitch (1974) argued that the working memory system is involved in the digit-span task, in which a string of random digits must be repeated back in the correct order. While trait anxiety usually has little or no effect on digit span, situational stress and state anxiety are usually negatively related to performance. Eysenck (1979) reviewed the relevant evidence; of 12 studies reporting a significant effect of state anxiety or environmental stress on digit span, anxiety reduced the span in 11 cases.

It is not clear from the literature which of the two components of working memory is primarily responsible for the adverse effects of anxiety on digit span. However, in recent unpublished work by one of my students (Anna Eliatamby) the detrimental effects of anxiety disappeared when subjects performed a simple articulatory suppression task (i.e. saying 'ABCDEF' rapidly and repeatedly). Since suppression tasks of this kind mainly use the resources of the articulatory loop, the implication is that anxiety affects the articulatory loop component of working memory more than the central processor on this task.

Eysenck (1979) assumed that anxious individuals are effectively in a divided-attention situation (i.e. attention has to be shared between task stimuli and anxiety-related information). This may resemble what happens when a non-anxious individual has to divide attention between a main task and an attentionally-demanding subsidiary task. Recent findings support this notion. Hitch and Baddeley (1976) found that speed of performance on a reasoning task was interactively determined by task complexity and by presence or absence of a subsidiary task (i.e. retaining six random digits). In this interaction, the adverse effects on reasoning speed of concurrent performance of the subsidiary task were greater on the more complex reasoning problems. Anna Eliatamby used the same reasoning task with no concurrent task, and obtained a significant interaction between anxiety and task complexity: high anxiety had a much greater detrimental effect on the more difficult problems. Thus anxiety may operate in a similar fashion to a subsidiary task, in that they both utilize some of the resources of working memory.

The hypothesis that anxiety reduces the available capacity of working

288

memory has been investigated in a direct fashion by Eysenck in recent unpublished work. Subjects low and high in trait anxiety performed a letter-transformation task in which between one and four letters required transformation. A sample one-letter problem is 'D + 4' for which the answer is 'H', and an example of a four-letter is 'FLCM + 3' for which the answer is 'IOFP'. Anxiety did not affect performance on one-letter problems but did greatly slow down performance speed on three- and four-letter problems. Since there is a progressive increase in the demands placed on working memory as the number of letters to be transformed goes up, the results indicate strongly that anxiety reduces working memory capacity.

There have been sporadic attempts in recent years to relate anxiety research to contemporary developments in theorizing on memory. One example concerns the levels of processing approach pioneered by Craik and Lockhart (1972). They argued that long-term retention depends on the depth of processing, by which they meant the amount of meaningfulness extracted from the stimulus. Since anxiety tends to reduce long-term memory, it is tempting to assume that anxiety impairs the ability to process at a deep or semantic level. Schwartz (1975) found that neurotic introverts (i.e. high-anxiety subjects) engaged in less semantic processing but more physical processing than stable extraverts (i.e. low-anxiety subjects), but it has proved difficult to replicate these findings (Craig et al., 1979).

Mueller (1979) has put forward the more plausible hypothesis that anxiety reduces the extensiveness or elaboration of encoding: this hypothesis seems consistent with the notion that anxiety leads to attentional narrowing. In a series of studies, Mueller usually found that anxiety produced a modest reduction in long-term retention, but this was certainly not because anxiety impaired semantic processing more than shallow processing: in eight out of nine experiments there were equivalent effects of anxiety on retention of semantic and shallow features or attributes. It seems that the quantity or amount of elaboration of processing is reduced under high anxiety, but there is no consistent effect on the kinds of processing which occur.

In sum, there is no clear theoretical understanding of the effects of anxiety on learning and memory. It is probable that anxiety is more likely to reduce the efficiency of internal processing operations than it is to impair performance. This reduction in processing efficiency is due to attentional narrowing and to a decrease in working memory capacity which may in turn be due to task-irrelevant cognitive activities. As a consequence of these effects of anxiety on processing efficiency, adverse effects of anxiety are most likely to be found when a learning task imposes great demands on working memory. Perhaps surprisingly, what limited evidence there is indicates that anxiety affects primarily the initial encoding of information; it has usually been found that retrieval *per se* is unaffected by anxiety, and the same is true for rate of forgetting over long retention intervals (Eysenck, 1977).

8.2.3 Introversion–Extraversion

Research on the effects of introversion–extraversion on memory has almost always relied on questionnaire assessment of the personality dimension by means of one of the tests devised by Eysenck and his associates (Maudsley Personality Inventory; Eysenck Personality Inventory; Eysenck Personality

Questionnaire). All of these questionnaires provide trait measures of introversion–extraversion; for reasons that are not altogether clear, a satisfactory state measure of introversion–extraversion has never been devised.

There are two related (but conceptually distinguishable) theoretical frameworks within which to evaluate the effects of introversion–extraversion. One was expressed in the following terms by Gray (1972):

> We may regard the dimension of introversion–extraversion as a dimension of susceptibility to punishment and non-reward: the greater the degree of introversion, the greater is this susceptibility (p. 194).

The alternative theoretical position was put forward by Eysenck (1967), who argued that introverts are chronically more cortically aroused than extraverts.

Gray's hypothesis has been investigated in a few studies of verbal operant conditioning. Introverts show more verbal conditioning than extraverts with negative reinforcement (Gupta, 1976; Gupta & Nagpal, 1978), suggesting that extraverts are more affected than introverts by the provision of reward.

There is other evidence to indicate that extraverts are more susceptible to reward than introverts (Eysenck, 1981), but most of this evidence has been obtained from tasks not involving memory processes to any great extent. For example, Corcoran (1962) investigated the effects of incentive on a letter-cancellation task. In the low-incentive condition there was a remarkably high correlation of + .90 between introversion and performance speed; the correlation was actually reversed in the high-incentive condition. The performance of introverts was almost unaffected by incentive, whereas extraverts manifested an improvement of approximately 80%.

Gray's theoretical ideas may well help to explain the well-known fact that introverts are characteristically more cautious than extraverts. The degree of caution is usually indexed by the signal-detection theory measure beta, which is based on the amount of information required for response emission. If, as Gray would argue, introverts attach more importance than extraverts to the potential costs of incorrect responding (i.e. false alarms), whereas extraverts attach more importance than introverts to the potential gains of correct responding, then it follows that introverts should adopt a more cautious response criterion than extraverts.

The predicted difference in response criterion or beta has been obtained several times in studies of vigilance (see Eysenck, 1981). In a study of continuous recognition memory, Gillespie and Eysenck (1980) analysed performance by means of the measures of signal-detection theory. Introverts adopted more stringent response criteria than extraverts, especially during the initial part of the task.

It is unfortunate that there has not been more research investigating the applicability of Gray's theory to memory phenomena, particularly in view of the encouraging nature of the findings to date. It would certainly be useful if more studies considered possible interactions between introversion and extraversion and environmental manipulations of reward and punishment.

Eysenck's (1967) claim that introverts are more cortically aroused than extraverts has not met with universal accord. A thorough review of the relevant EEG literature was carried out by Gale (1973); he assumed that high amplitude and low frequency of alpha reflect low arousal, whereas low amplitude and high frequency are indicative of high arousal. From a total of 16 studies, 7 suggested

290

that introverts were more aroused than extraverts, 3 supported the opposite hypothesis, and the rest found no effect of introversion–extraversion on the EEG. It is probably fair to conclude that there is modest support for the hypothesis that introverts are more physiologically aroused than extraverts; however, the opposite may be the case during the evening (Blake, 1967; Revelle *et al.*, 1980).

At the behavioural level, Eysenck's preferred strategy has been to consider known effects of arousal on memory, seeing whether or not these effects can be mimicked by the personality dimension of introversion–extraversion. The best example of this strategy in operation concerns the effects of arousal on memory as a function of retention interval: there is typically an interaction between arousal and retention interval, with high arousal (produced by white noise or other means) reducing memory at relatively short retention intervals but improving it at long intervals (see Eysenck, 1976b, for a review). Rather similar results have been obtained when introversion–extraversion has been investigated, with extraverts showing better short-term recall than introverts, but inferior long-term recall (e.g. Howarth & Eysenck, 1968; McLean, 1968).

While it is reasonably well established that high arousal produced in various different ways can slow down the rate of forgetting, the explanation of this effect is unclear. Eysenck (1973) based his interpretation on Walker's (1958) action decrement theory, according to which high arousal produces a longer-lasting active trace, leading to enhanced consolidation and long-term memory. While the process of consolidation is going on, there is a temporary inhibition of retrieval (or 'action decrement') which protects the trace from disruption. Since consolidation takes longer under high arousal, retention at shortish retention intervals is inversely related to arousal level.

Amelang *et al.* (1977) attempted to provide some more direct measures of the putative process of consolidation on a task involving retention of strings of consonants for a few seconds. A subsidiary visual reaction time task was used during the retention interval; it was assumed that slow reaction times indicated that the consolidation process was still continuing. Introverts had slower reaction times than extraverts early in the retention interval, but this difference disappeared later in the retention interval. Introverts had poorer memory performance than extraverts only at the shorter retention intervals. While Amelang *et al.* argued that their data mapped the time-course of consolidation, it must be noted that they used considerably shorter retention intervals than have customarily been used in studies of consolidation. In addition, long reaction times seem more likely to reflect the use of active rehearsal strategies than the process of consolidation.

Of the many difficulties with Walker's action decrement theory, the most serious is that it is by no means always the case that high arousal impairs short-term retention. Indeed, arousal has been found to enhance immediate free recall and recognition (Eysenck, 1976b). The best evidence in favour of Walker's theory has come from studies of paired-associate learning, but even there high arousal improves short-term retention under some circumstances (Hamilton *et al.*, 1972). At the present time there is no satisfactory explanation of the interaction between arousal and retention interval.

One of the most general effects of arousal on performance was originally enunciated by Yerkes and Dodson (1908), who argued that the optimal level of arousal is inversely related to task difficulty. If introverts are more aroused than extraverts, then it can be predicted that introversion–extraversion should interact with task difficulty, with introverts tending to cope less well than extraverts with highly demanding tasks. As we will see, task difficulty has usually been assessed in an informal way. A superior approach would be to measure spare processing capacity by using a subsidiary task concurrently with each learning task, but this has not been attempted as yet.

Broadly speaking, the available results provide quite strong support for the predicted differential effects of introversion–extraversion on easy and difficult learning tasks (Eysenck, 1976a). The first relevant study was carried out by Siegman (1957), who obtained a correlation of $+.34$ between extraversion and complex list learning and of $-.35$ between extraversion and simple list learning. Howarth (1969b) produced progressively more difficult learning lists by systematically increasing response competition on a paired-associate task. After an initial list had been thoroughly learned, the stimuli and responses from that list were re-paired to produce the second list. Following acquisition of the second list, a third list was formed by re-pairing the same stimuli and responses yet again. It was only on the final list, on which response competition was highest, that the learning rate of extraverts was significantly faster than that of introverts.

It has been found in a number of other studies (Bone, 1971; Eysenck, 1975; Jensen, 1964) that introverts are more adversely affected than extraverts by response competition. It is difficult to explain this phenomenon because the factors involved in response-competition effects are not well understood. However, it is likely that response competition reduces the speed of retrieval, and Eysenck (1975) found that there were more pronounced effects of introversion–extraversion on speed of recall than on probability of recall in conditions of response competition. He suggested that high arousal increases the tendency to retrieve readily accessible information, which is counter-productive when there are accessible but incorrect responses available, as happens in conditions of response competition.

It has sometimes been argued (e.g. Kahneman, 1973) that high arousal increases distractibility, and it is relevant in this connection to note that Broadbent (1971) has reported reduced ability to discriminate between task and non-task stimuli when arousal is high. A few studies have considered susceptibility to distraction among introverts and extraverts using the well-known Stroop test, in which subjects are shown cards containing colour names printed in inks of different colours (e.g. 'RED' printed in blue). The colour of the ink must be reported in each case, and distraction is present in the tendency to read the word itself. It has consistently been found that extraverts are less detrimentally affected than introverts by the distracting information presented on the Stroop test (Davies, 1967; Gulian, 1972).

Similar findings have been obtained in studies of learning and memory. Shanmugan and Santhanam (1964) presented a serial learning list under conditions of no interference or with competing stimuli presented at the marginal visual level. The correlation between extraversion and recall was $+.65$ with no interference, and it increased to $+.82$ when the distracting stimuli were additional words. However, the correlation dropped to $+.58$ when distraction was produced by both letters and numbers.

More convincing evidence that introverts are more susceptible to distraction was obtained by Howarth (1969a). There was no effect of introversion–

extraversion on serial learning when no distraction was present, but extraverts outperformed introverts under distraction conditions. A very similar pattern of results was obtained by Morgenstern *et al.* (1974). Words to be remembered were presented auditorily, and distracting stimuli consisted of extra auditorily presented words, a German prose passage, or an English prose passage. Introversion–extraversion had no effect on retention in the absence of distraction, but introverts were much more adversely affected than extraverts by distraction.

Why are introverts more susceptible to distraction than extraverts? In the present state of knowledge, there are several possible reasons consistent with the evidence. However, it is tempting to assume that introverts typically have less spare processing capacity than extraverts, and as a consequence they are less able to cope effectively with the increased processing demands imposed by the need to distinguish between task and non-task stimuli.

My main criticism of research in this area is that far too little has been done to identify the processing mechanisms primarily responsible for the observed effects of introversion–extraversion. It is often difficult to decide whether storage or retrieval processes are involved, and there have been practically no attempts to assess the effects of introversion–extraversion on theoretically important mechanisms (e.g. working memory). As Eysenck (1976a) concluded in his review of the literature:

> The major obstacle to future progress appears to be a marked reluctance on the part of researchers to use the information processing concepts being developed by memory theorists in the design and interpretation of their experiments (p. 87).

One way of clarifying matters is to use a paradigm which permits investigation of a single aspect of processing. This ideal can perhaps be approximated by focusing on the efficiency of retrieval of well-learned information from permanent storage. Vocabulary tests can be used to make sure that there is comparable storage of relevant information by introverts and extraverts; this permits the conclusion that any performance differences are attributable to effects of introversion–extraversion on the retrieval process.

A popular way of assessing retrieval efficiency has been to use a test of verbal or word fluency, with the subjects being required to write down as many words as possible fulfilling some criterion (e.g flower names). In the first such study, Cattell (1934) recorded the number of two-syllable words that were written down in 2½ min. Intelligence was not related to performance, but surgency (a personality trait resembling extraversion) correlated + .30 with the number of words produced.

In the years since then extraverts have been found to outperform introverts on fluency tasks in a number of studies. However, while these results clearly suggest that extraverts are more efficient that introverts at retrieving information from permanent storage, little can be said about the reasons for this superiority.

Eysenck (1974) tried to decide whether arousal was involved by asking all of his subjects to complete a self-report measure of experienced levels of activation or arousal (the general activation scale of Thayer's Activation–Deactivation Adjective Check List). In addition to the usual finding that extraverts are more proficient than introverts at retrieval from permanent storage, Eysenck also obtained an interaction between introversion–extraversion and general activation. High general activation or arousal enhanced retrieval among extraverts, but reduced introverts' retrieval performance. Since highly activated introverts recalled less than any of the other groups, it seems that high arousal has an adverse effect on retrieval from permanent storage.

In this study by Eysenck (1974), the task was to think of as many words as possible belonging to each of five categories. A serendipitous finding was that differences in recall between introverts and extraverts only became apparent after some time on the task. Since common category exemplars tend to be recalled initially, the implication is that the retrieval difficulty of introverts centres on relatively rare and non-dominant words.

Considerable support for the notion that the retrieval inefficiency of introverts is most obvious with relatively inaccessible information was obtained in a series of studies by Eysenck (reviewed by Eysenck, 1981). One important aspect of this work is the way in which the interaction between introversion and extraversion and accessibility of the information to be retrieved was replicated across a wide range of paradigms. In particular, retrieval from both episodic memory and semantic memory was investigated, and broadly similar results were found. The difference between these two kinds of memory was spelled out by Tulving (1972):

> Episodic memory refers to memory for personal experiences and their temporal relations, while semantic memory is a system for receiving, retaining, and transmitting information about meaning of words, concepts, and classification of concepts (p. 401).

One of the major limitations of this series of studies is that the primary emphasis is on semantically based retrieval. Accordingly, Eysenck and Eysenck (1979) compared the effects of introversion–extraversion on speed of retrieval under conditions requiring physical matching (i.e. is the probe word identical to one of the previously presented words?) or semantic matching (i.e. is the probe word a member of one of the previously presented category names?). A modified version of the Sternberg paradigm was used; this permits assessment of the speed with which the previously presented words are scanned. There was no difference between introverts and extraverts in speed of scanning on physical matching trials, but extraverts scanned faster than introverts on semantic matching trials.

Schwartz (1979) essentially replicated these findings using a somewhat different paradigm. It is tempting to conclude that introverts have more difficulty than extraverts in retrieving deep or semantic information from long-term store, but that there is no effect of introversion–extraversion on the retrieval of shallow or physical information. However, Schwartz also found that introverts were slower than extraverts in retrieving phonemic information (i.e. deciding whether two words are pronounced in the same way), which is inconsistent with that conclusion.

Eysenck (1976b) argued that most of the data were consistent with the following hypothesis:

> High arousal has the effect of biasing the subject's search process towards readily accessible, or functionally dominant, stored information more than is the case with lower levels of arousal (p. 401).

If introverts are more aroused than extraverts, they may be less able to process

294

in parallel (Walley & Weiden, 1973), and thus would be at a disadvantage in any task (e.g. retrieving relatively inaccessible information) requiring the processing of several different items of information.

A consideration of the effects of other arousers (e.g. monetary incentive, white noise) on retrieval suggests that matters are more complex than was previously supposed. As Eysenck (in press) has shown, incentive usually has no effect at all on the efficiency of retrieval, and white noise often increases rather than decreases retrieval speed.

What can we conclude about the effects of introversion–extraversion on memory? Matters are obviously clearer empirically than they are theoretically. It has been reasonably well established that there are a number of performance differences between introverts and extraverts, which are listed below for convenience:

1. Reward affects the performance of extraverts more than introverts, whereas punishment affects introverts more.
2. Introverts have a higher response criterion than extraverts.
3. Introverts are more adversely affected than extraverts by increasing task difficulty.
4. Introverts are more susceptible than extraverts to distraction.
5. Extraverts show more forgetting over time than introverts.
6. Introverts are less efficient than extraverts at retrieving information from long-term or permanent storage, especially relatively inaccessible information.

It would be agreeable to provide a theoretical integration of this gallimaufry of findings, but this cannot be done at present. A more achievable goal is to evaluate the degree of success of an arousal-based explanation (Eysenck, 1967). Three kinds of findings support the notion that behavioural differences between introverts and extraverts may depend on a chronically higher level of cortical arousal in introverts. First, in spite of some inconsistency in the data, introverts have fairly often been found to be more physiologically aroused than extraverts. This conclusion is strengthened by a number of drug studies. For example, Laverty (1958) found that injections of sodium amytal (a depressant) increased extraversion scores on a personality questionnaire, and also produced behavioural evidence of greater extraversion (e.g increased talkativeness and sociability). Furthermore, the amount of the drug sufficient to produce slurred speech (the so-called sedation threshold) was much greater for introverts than for extraverts.

Second, if introverts are actually more aroused than extraverts, then one might expect introversion–extraversion to interact with known arousers (e.g. white noise, caffeine, incentive, time of day) in predictable ways. Broadly speaking, such interaction effects have frequently been observed (see Eysenck, 1982).

Third, as we have been, the effects of introversion–extraversion on performance are often similar to the effects of other arousers. For example, the rate of forgetting is slower under high arousal, and it is slower in introverts than in extraverts. In addition, the adverse effects of increased task difficulty and/or distraction on performance are greater in states of high arousal, and they are also greater in introverts than in extraverts.

In spite of the fact that an arousal theory of introversion–extraversion has some successes to its credit, there are some other considerations which are more embarrassing for the theory. First, there is evidence (e.g. Blake, 1967; Revelle *et al.*, 1980) suggesting that introverts are more aroused than extraverts only during the morning and afternoon; the opposite appears to be the case in the evening. If these findings can be replicated, then the notion that introverts are *chronically* more aroused than extraverts will have to be abandoned.

Second, in some situations the effects of introversion–extraversion on performance are dissimilar to the effects of other arousers. For example, introversion generally impairs the efficiency of retrieval, whereas incentive and white noise do not. High arousal has often been found to be associated with fast and relatively inaccurate performance; in contrast, Eysenck (1967) concluded that, 'The studies . . . are remarkably unanimous in showing introverts to be slower and more careful and accurate than extraverts' (p. 162).

Third, detailed examination of the interactions between introversion and extraversion and other arousers reveals an intriguing state of affairs. If it is assumed that introverts are more affected physiologically than extraverts by arousing stimuli (Eysenck, 1967), and if the prevailing state of arousal is a major determinant of behaviour, then it is reasonable to predict that arousing stimuli will affect the performance of introverts more than that of extraverts. In fact, the opposite is usually the case, suggesting that the behaviour of introverts is less directly determined by the level of arousal than that of extraverts.

Fourth, the most fundamental weakness of the arousal theory is its vagueness. Even if it makes sense to explain behavioural differences between introverts and extraverts in terms of varying levels of arousal, this explanation provides little insight into the reasons *why* high arousal has its observed effects. More specifically, the crucial omission is a specification of the mediating mechanisms which determine the behavioural consequences of high arousal.

While it is hazardous to predict future theoretical developments in this area, some speculations are in order. It has often been noted that the behaviour of introverts is more consistent and unchanging than that of extraverts, and it has also been discovered that various arousing and de-arousing agents affect the performance of extraverts more than introverts. Perhaps introverts monitor themselves and their behaviour to a greater extent than extraverts, and this would account for the fact that introverts often appear to behave in a less spontaneous fashion than extraverts.

Presumably the self-monitoring of introverts uses some of their processing resources. This self-monitoring, perhaps combined with high arousal, would then explain why introverts sometimes have fewer processing resources available than extraverts for responding to task demands. This resource inferiority is manifested in the finding that introverts are less able than extraverts to cope effectively with increased processing demands (e.g. from distracting stimulation, from response competition, or from complex retrieval tasks).

Many of the situations in which the performance of introverts is worse than that of extraverts seem to involve two or more concurrent processing activities. The notion that introverts are less able than extraverts to engage in parallel or shared processing is an intriguing one, and it is consistent with some theoretical views of the effects of arousal on processing (e.g. Walley & Weiden, 1973). Some indirect support was obtained by Nideffer (1976), who made use of a self-report inventory called the Test of Attentional and Interpersonal Style. Extraverts claimed to be able to integrate many stimuli, to use effectively information or ideas from several different areas, and to process a great deal of information. In contrast, introverts reported a tendency to make mistakes and become confused as a consequence of thinking about too much at once.

The most direct investigation of the effects of introversion–extraversion on the ability to process in parallel was reported by Eysenck and Eysenck (1979). In their study a short list of words was followed by a probe word, and there were two possible relationships between the probe and one of the list words (i.e. physical match or physical match). In the dual-task conditions, both types of match had to be looked for, against only one in the single-task conditions. There were only small effects of introversion–extraversion on speed of responding in the single-task conditions, but introverts were significantly slower than extraverts in the dual-task conditions in which parallel processing was required.

In sum, the arousal-theory interpretation of the effects of introversion–extraversion on performance is only partially satisfactory. It accounts for most of the data only by remaining rather imprecise and by failing to spell out the mechanisms involved in mediating the effects of arousal on performance. Some possible mechanisms have been discussed above in a preliminary way.

8.3   Cognitive Abilities

8.3.1   Introduction

It seems entirely reasonable to assume that learning and memory depend substantially on a variety of cognitive processes and mechanisms. If so, one might expect that individual differences in cognitive abilities would be predictive of memory performance. This has been confirmed in a number of studies in which intelligence as measured by standardized tests has been correlated with learning scores. For example, Tilton (1949) obtained a correlation of $+.49$ between intelligence scores and the amount of learning shown by school-children taking specific courses.

There are various disadvantages associated with this kind of molar approach. One obvious problem is that it is not clear whether the level of intelligence determines the speed of learning, or whether learning speed affects intelligence. A second problem is that the use of measures of general intelligence is likely to be rather unrevealing as to the exact processes involved. A popular way of at least partially obviating this problem is to distinguish between two major factors of intelligence: verbal ability and spatial ability. While these two kinds of ability tend to be positively correlated, DiVesta et al. (1971) obtained evidence for a clear separation between them. In two factor-analytic experiments they identified verbal and spatial abilities as orthogonal factors. The relative importance of verbal and spatial ability in determining memory performance will depend upon factors such as the concreteness or imageability of the stimulus material and the processing instructions.

An alternative approach is to focus on individual differences in some of the component processes involved in learning and memory. For example, groups of people having high and low working memory capacities could be identified by the use of suitable criterion tasks. If, as Baddeley and Hitch (1974) claimed, working memory is importantly involved in a wide range of tasks, then this dimension of individual differences should have considerable predictive power with respect to memory performance.

These various approaches are discussed at some length below. Progress has been disappointingly slow, leading Carroll and Maxwell (1979) in their literature review to come to the following rather pessimistic conclusion:

> Relationships between learning performance and ability factors have thus continued to elude meaningful experimental analysis; the studies discussed here illustrate the need to consider both learning performance and ability measures as complex composites of pure components in order to establish interpretable relationships (p. 611).

8.3.2 Verbal Ability

The most thorough attempt to assess relationships between verbal ability and memory has been made by Hunt and his associates (e.g. Hunt *et al.*, 1973; Hunt *et al.*, 1975; Hunt, 1978). Verbal ability in most of their work has been measured by means of standard, group-administered verbal aptitude tests such as the Verbal Composite of the Scholastic Aptitude Test or the Verbal Composite of the Washington Pre-College Test.

Hunt *et al.* (1973) found that subjects of high verbal ability differed from those of low verbal ability on five out of the seven memory tasks which they studied. Subjects having high verbal ability showed greater release from proactive inhibition than those of low ability, they had a faster rate of search in the Sternberg paradigm, and they learned a list of paired associates faster. Of most interest in view of subsequent research findings, they discovered that verbal ability affected performance on the Posner in which two letters are presented. In the name match condition, the subject responds 'same' if both letters have the same name (e.g. AA or aA); in the physical match condition, the subject responds 'same' only if the two letters are physically identical (e.g. AA or aa). Verbal ability had no effect on speed of performance on the physical matching task, but was positively related to speed on the name matching task.

Hunt *et al.* (1973) concluded on the basis of these various findings that there was a relationship between verbal ability and speed of short-term memory processes. However, some of the key findings from this study have proved difficult to replicate (e.g. the beneficial effect of high verbal ability on rate of search in short-term memory as measured by the Sternberg paradigm), so this conclusion may be erroneous.

Hunt *et al.* (1975) replicated the findings of Hunt *et al.* (1973) with the Posner task. They also found that high verbal ability facilitated the learning of lists of words but not of lists of nonsense syllables, and that subjects of high verbal ability showed superior performance in the Brown–Peterson short-term memory paradigm. In a sentence–picture verification task, subjects read an assertion about a picture, then looked at a picture, and decided as rapidly as possible whether the assertion was true with respect to the picture. Verbal ability was primarily related to the time taken to comprehend, and to make a decision about, negative statements.

The fact that verbal ability affects performance on a wide range of memory tasks makes it difficult to specify the precise nature of the advantage conferred by high verbal ability on the processes involved in information processing. Hunt (1978) emphasized the robust finding that the time difference between name matching and physical matching on the Posner task correlates approximately – .30 with verbal ability even when a relatively homogeneous sample of subjects (e.g. university students) is used. He argued that this basic finding indicates that verbal ability affects the efficiency of the decoding process, using the term 'decoding' to refer to the activation of highly overlearned information in long-term memory. An alternative possibility is that verbal ability has the more general effect of determining the speed with which all kinds of information are retrieved, but there are at least two reasons why this interpretation seems implausible: (1) verbal ability does not correlate with speed of retrieval of recently acquired information; and (2) there is virtually no correlation between verbal ability and scanning rate in Sternberg's task (which involves accessing active memory).

The process of decoding is presumably relatively automatic and attentionally undemanding. What about the relationship between verbal ability and the limited capacity of short-term storage? Since successful linguistic processing often requires the integration of information presented over a period of time, it might be expected that large short-term storage capacity would be more prevalent among those of high verbal ability. In this connection, it is noteworthy that digit span (one index of short-term storage capacity) correlates approximately + .50 with overall intelligence.

A possible explanation for the correlation between short-term memory performance and verbal ability is that subjects of high verbal ability are more likely to use efficient coding strategies (e.g. grouping or chunking of information). However, this explanation seems untenable in view of the findings of Lyon (1977). He effectively eliminated the opportunity to use grouping strategies in a digit-span task by presenting the digits at an unusually rapid rate, but this failed to have much effect on individual differences in digit span.

It is more likely that performance on short-term memory tasks and on verbal problem-solving tasks depends on the same attentional resources. This view is supported by a study in which subjects performed a verbal reasoning task while concurrently holding additional information in short-term memory. Hitch and Baddeley (1976) discovered that the two tasks interfered with each other only when the number of items to be recalled approached the short-term memory span, presumably because under those circumstances the combined demands of the two tasks exceeded the available attentional resources.

An obvious prediction from the attentional hypothesis is that the advantage of high verbal ability will be most apparent when attentionally demanding tasks are used. When a series of mental addition problems of varying difficulty was used, it was the more difficult problems that differentiated between those of high and low verbal ability (Hunt, 1978).

The general strategy adopted by Hunt and his associates of attempting to locate behavioural patterns in which verbal ability affects performance on some tasks but not on others is a useful one. For example, the fact that verbal ability affects speed of name matching but not of physical matching in the Posner task clearly indicates that the additional decoding requirement of the name-matching task is affected by verbal ability. However, one of the problems with this strategy, which would become even more pronounced if individuals of greatly varying ability were used, is that verbal ability tends to correlate with performance on most tasks. While Hunt has emphasized the effects of verbal ability on decoding and on attentional capacity, it has not been shown that these two effects can account for the myriad behavioural differences between high and low verbals.

A further problem with Hunt's approach concerns the verbal aptitude tests which he has used to measure verbal ability. Tests of this type have been found to be substantially affected by educational and experiential factors. This then raises the question of the direction of causality: does verbal ability affect the mechanics of information processing, or is it not rather that the efficiency of information-processing activities determines verbal ability?

8.3.3 Spatial Ability

While individual differences in verbal ability may be of major importance in predicting learning and memory for certain kinds of information, it is likely that there are other kinds of learning material (e.g. pictorial stimuli) where spatial ability might be highly relevant. Spatial or imagery ability has typically been assessed by means of either a self-report questionnaire or objective tests of spatial ability.

The questionnaire method was initiated by Galton, who asked people to indicate how well they could form an image of their breakfast table. Betts (1909) developed the Questionnaire upon Mental Imagery from Galton's original procedure; this questionnaire measures the subjective vividness of a person's mental imagery in seven major sense modalities. It is not easy to assess the validity of such self-report techniques, but there has been a suspicion that the scores obtained may reflect social desirability effects (DiVesta et al., 1971) rather than experienced imagery. Ashton and White (1975) discovered that 'low motivating' instructions (associating vivid mental imagery with 'dull, uncreative people') reduced the imagery scores in all seven sensory modalities.

Attempts to relate individual differences in self-reported imagery to performance in learning and memory tasks have proved disappointing. Instructions to use imagery often improve memory for word lists, but the extent of the improvement does not depend on individual differences in the rated vividness of experienced imagery. In similar fashion, such individual differences do not affect the beneficial effects of concurrent presentation of relevant pictures on word learning, or the effects of stimulus imageability on recall (see Richardson, 1980, for further details).

Why are self-reports of imagery vividness so non-predictive of memory performance? One obvious problem is that imagery questionnaires require each individual to provide absolute ratings despite the fact that he or she can only experience his or her own mental images. It is hard to judge whether or not your own images are vivid in the absence of any suitable basis for comparison. A second potential problem is that the usual procedure of evaluating the vividness of each individual's evoked mental imagery by averaging across all seven sensory modalities is inappropriate when attempting to predict performance on memory tasks in which visual imagery is likely to be used far more than other kinds of imagery. However, attempts to predict memory performance on the basis of the Vividness of Visual Imagery Questionnaire (Marks, 1972) have not fared much better. It is also possible that the aspect of imagery which is most relevant in determining memory is not vividness at all; perhaps the ability to control one's own imagery is more important. Gordon (1949) devised a questionnaire concerned with imagery control, but it has not proved to have predictive power.

Some of the disadvantages associated with the questionnaire method can be obviated by the use of tests of spatial ability. Such tests frequently necessitate the mental rotation of objects, and it is assumed that spatial–imaginal ability rather than verbal ability determines speed of performance. It has usually been found that tests of spatial ability do not show any consistent relationship with questionnaire ratings; indeed, the two kinds of tests generally load on different factors (e.g. DiVesta *et al.*, 1971). Unfortunately there appears to be no consistent relationship between spatial ability and memory performance, in spite of some promising findings (e.g. Klee & Eysenck, 1973).

Richardson (1980) has made some interesting points in attempting to account for the various non-significant relationships. He noted that the emphasis in the literature has been heavily on individual differences in imagery ability rather than on individual differences in preference for using imagery; on the basis of remarkably little evidence, it has simply been assumed that the two are correlated. As Richardson concluded:

> If coding *preference* is the crucial determiner of performance in memory tasks, then this would explain why research employing measures of imagery *ability* has produced confusing, contradictory and unreplicable findings (p. 133).

An alternative possibility is that most of the studies have simply relied on too gross a level of measurement (e.g. total items recalled). There are so many factors determining the overall level of memory performance that the contribution made by imagery ability is difficult to identify. Some important recent research by Hunt and his associates (MacLeod *et al.*, 1978; Mathews *et al.*, 1980) has focused on coding preference, and has also provided a reasonably fine-grained analysis of performance.

In their research they have made use of a sentence–picture verification paradigm in which the task is to verify or reject a simple linguistic statement as being a description of a subsequently presented picture. There are two radically different ways in which the task can be formed. One strategy is based on imaginal processing; this involves reading the sentence, forming an image of the expected picture, and then comparing the presented picture to this image. The alternative strategy relies on verbal or linguistic processing; it involves retaining the sentence in verbal form, describing the picture in verbal terms, and then comparing the two verbal descriptions.

There are very pronounced performance differences between subjects following the two strategies. At a relatively global level, the imagery strategy leads to slower processing of the sentence than the verbal strategy, but to faster picture verification; at a more specific level, some aspects of the sentence (e.g. whether it is affirmative or negative) make more difference to the time taken on the task when the verbal strategy is adopted. However, in spite of these various effects, it is worth noting that the difference in total solution times for those using the two strategies was very small (only just over 10 %).

MacLeod *et al.* (1978) also asked the question whether these preferences in coding strategy were related to underlying abilities. They correlated verbal and spatial ability scores on the Washington Pre-College Test with speed of performance. For those using the verbal strategy, verbal ability correlated more than spatial ability with total verification time (– .52 v. – .32), and the opposite was the case for those using the imagery strategy (– .32 v. – .68).

Mathews *et al.* (1980) replicated these findings, and additionally considered how well subjects could perform the sentence–picture verification task when instructed to use the non-preferred strategy. Most of the subjects were adept at processing in the non-preferred way, thus demonstrating the existence of considerable flexibility in information processing.

These studies on the sentence–picture verification task provide an especially valuable example of the potential value of considering individual differences. Prior to the work of Hunt and his associates, the most popular theory of performance on this task was the verbal–linguistic theory proposed by Carpenter and Just (1975). The median correlation between individual performance across conditions and the predictions of their constituent comparison model was + .82 in the study by MacLeod *et al.* (1978), apparently providing strong supporting evidence. However, individual correlations ranged from + .998 to – .887, and indicated that the model only applied to some of the subjects. Indeed, it is now clear that no verbal–linguistic model can account for the performance of the minority of subjects (approximately 25%) who prefer to use an imagery strategy.

One reason for discussing the findings of MacLeod *et al.* (1978) and of Mathews *et al.* (1980) at length is because in some ways their research is a model for others to follow. In the first place, they used a well-understood task for which detailed mathematical models had previously been developed. In addition, they obtained separate measures of coding ability, coding preference and performance, so that they were able to look at the interrelationships among all three factors. Finally, they used a task that permits unequivocal identification of at least two qualitatively different processing strategies.

8.3.4 *Component Processes in Memory*

One of the lacunae in contemporary memory research is the failure to consider possible interrelationships among different memory tasks. For example, it would be useful to know the extent to which the same or similar processes are used in paired-associate learning and free recall, or the amount of involvement of the short-term storage system or working memory in the performance of other tasks. Such questions ultimately concern the degree of generality of the processes involved in the performance of any particular task, and a study of individual differences can provide relevant evidence in many cases. If it turned out that subjects performing well on paired-associate learning tasks showed no tendency to perform well on free-recall tasks, then it would seem improbable that the same cognitive processes are involved in the performance of the two kinds of tasks.

One method of attempting to delineate some of the major classes of processes involved in laboratory memory tasks is to carry out a factor analysis based on the performance of a group of subjects across a variety of learning and memory tests. This was done by Underwood *et al.* (1977), who performed a factor analysis on 22 variables derived from standard long-term memory tasks such as paired-associate learning, free recall, serial learning, and verbal discrimination, as well as memory span. Five rotated orthogonal factors resulted, all of which seem to be highly task specific. These five factors can be approximately identified as follows: Paired-Associate and Serial Learning; Free

Recall; Memory Span; Recognition Memory; and Verbal Discrimination. Although Carroll (1978) pointed out that the first two factors can be combined to form a second-order factor of Associative Memory, the results are still rather discouraging.

It probably makes more sense to apply the approach based on individual differences to more limited issues. For example, there has been much theoretical controversy over the degree of similarity between the processes involved in recall and those involved in recognition (see Eysenck, 1977, for a review). Tulving (1976) has consistently claimed that essentially the same processes are involved in recall and recognition, whereas two-stage theorists such as Kintsch (1970) and Anderson and Bower (1972) have argued that recall involves retrieval followed by discrimination, whereas recognition involves only the latter stage of discrimination. In this connection, Underwood (1969) distinguished between discriminative attributes (e.g. situational frequency, spatial attributes and temporal attributes) and retrieval attributes (e.g. attributes linking words with the context or words with one another).

All of these theorists would clearly anticipate that recall and recognition performance should be correlated, although the predicted strength of that correlation varies from theorist to theorist. In fact, Underwood (1972) found in a number of studies that the correlations between word recognition memory and word free recall for subjects given both types of tasks were positive, but surprisingly low. Similar results were obtained by Tversky (1973), who found only a small positive correlation between recognition and recall scores for pictures when the same subjects were tested on recall before recognition, and no correlation at all when the recognition test was given first.

It is important not to overinterpret these findings. It is likely that high correlations between recall and recognition would be obtained under some circumstances, and it might be worth while to discover the factors which determine the size of the correlation. Nevertheless, it remains a matter of some theoretical concern that the correlations between recall and recognition which have been obtained so far are much lower than most theorists would have guessed.

An approach based on individual differences has also proved useful in exploring the issue of the equivalence of different methods of assessing the capacity of short-term memory. Historically, the two main methods have been the span measure (i.e. immediate serial recall of a short list of items) and the recency effect in free recall (i.e. the superior retention of the last few items presented compared to recall from the middle of the list).

The notion that these two methods provide equivalent measures of short-term storage capacity has been convincingly refuted by various lines of evidence. Of particular importance at this point, Martin (1978) obtained a mean correlation coefficient of only + .15 between digit span and the recency effect in free recall; this strongly indicates that the two methods are by no means measuring the same thing. Byrne and Arnold (1981) obtained a similar non-significant correlation of + .134 between the recency effect and digit span. In addition, they compared performance of poor beginning readers with an IQ-matched group of good readers. The poor readers had a significantly inferior digit span, but there was no effect of reading ability on the recency effect. They concluded as follows:

The results demonstrate a degree of dissociation between the recency effect and

303

memory span, supporting arguments that the two aspects of performance are manifestations of different memory processes (p. 371).

The next step is obviously to discover what the span and recency effect are actually measuring. Martin (1978) found that digit span did not correlate with the long-term memory component of free recall; however, it did correlate highly with serial recall. She suggested that free recall is primarily a measure of item retention, whereas digit span (which uses overlearned items) provides an estimate of the ability to remember the order in which events occur. However, Craik (1971) found that word span correlated + .49 with the recency effect in free recall and + .72 with the long-term memory component of free recall. Perhaps word span and digit span are not equivalent measures, in that the former task places greater emphasis on the retention of item information.

An aspect of individual differences that attracted interest some years ago was subjective organization. This is a measure derived from performance in multi-trial free recall, and reflects the extent to which words are recalled in a stable order over trials. There appear to be consistent individual differences in the amount of subjective organization across different kinds of material (Gorfein et al., 1969), and such individual differences predict performance on various learning tasks. In particular, Earhard (1967) found that those subjects obtaining high subjective organization scores showed superior free recall and serial recall to those obtaining low scores, and Earhard and Endicott (1969) found that subjective organization correlated with serial anticipation and paired-associate learning.

Why are measures of subjective organization derived from free recall so successful in predicting performance in other learning situations? Transfer studies (e.g. Postman, 1972) have indicated that free recall and paired-associate learning both involve the formation of inter-item associations, and so it is possible that good subjective organizers have a greater ability to form associations between verbal items.

However, there is a fly in the ointment. Within free recall learning studies, subjective organization usually correlates positively with free recall performance; it may thus simply be that good learners in one situation (i.e. free recall) are likely to learn rapidly in other situations (e.g. serial recall; paired-associate learning). Gorfein (1971) explored this possibility. He discovered that high subjective organizers learned a paired-associate list much faster than low subjective organizers. However, there was a non-significant correlation between subjective organization and paired-associate learning when learning rate on the free recall task was partialed out. In contrast, free recall performance correlated + .45 with paired-associate learning performance when individual differences in subjective organization were partialed out. It is thus possible that learning rate in free recall rather than subjective organization is the crucial variable.

An issue in memory research which can fruitfully be explored by an approach based on individual differences is whether visual and verbal long-term memory involve different processing systems. Paivio (1971) put forward a dual coding hypothesis which emphasized qualitative differences between separate imaginal and verbal processing systems, whereas Anderson and Paulson (1978) argued that it was more economical to postulate a single abstract propositional system.

Woodhead and Baddeley (1981) investigated this area of controversy by looking at individual differences in memory performance. They selected people who had done especially well or badly on tests of facial recognition one year or more previously, and gave them three kinds of recognition task (based on faces, paintings and words). The good recognizers on the original tests outperformed the poor recognizers on recognition of faces and of paintings, but not on word recognition. Since there were no clear differences in reported processing strategy between the two groups, the results are clearly more consistent with the view that visual and verbal memory involve separate systems than the notion of a common abstract propositional system.

It may be instructive to evaluate the success of the individual-differences strategy in dealing with the four limited issues considered here: (1) similarity of recall and recognition; (2) measures of short-term storage capacity; (3) subjective organization and memory; and (4) similarity of visual and verbal long-term memory. In every case there was at least one theory apparently predicting that there would be consistent individual differences across two or more measures of memory performance. Correlational evidence indicated a lack of such consistent individual differences in every case except correlations of subjective organization with memory performance on various tasks, and yet that was the issue to which the individual-differences approach contributed the least.

Why should this be so? Part of the reason is that high correlations between performance on two memory tasks can be explained in several different ways. In the case of the work on subjective organization, it transpired that there was no causal relationship between subjective organization and paired-associate learning. In general terms, high correlations between two memory tasks may reflect similarities of stimulus material, processing, or retrieval strategy. Thus while high correlations may have been predicted by a particular theory, their presence does not provide very strong support for that theory.

In contrast, if a theory argues that precisely the same process plays a major role in determining performance in two different memory tasks, the discovery of a zero correlation is potentially very damaging. Of course, it can always be argued that variations in processing instructions, stimuli, or other factors are preventing the common process from producing sizeable correlations, but the fact remains that zero correlations obtained in well-designed studies can effectively destroy theories. In a nutshell, low correlations can disprove theories, but high correlations cannot prove them to be correct.

8.3.5 Conclusions

It is safe to conclude that relatively little progress has been made in understanding individual differences in memorial performance. It has usually been assumed, whether explicitly or implicitly, that any given individual will use a consistent learning strategy. If that assumption proves to be erroneous, then that would go some way towards explaining the lack of progress. It would also indicate the necessity of formulating theories based on within-individual differences as well as between-individual differences.

Some preliminary evidence on within-individual consistency was reported by Battig (1979), who discussed eight learning studies in which the learning strategies used by each subject on each item had been assessed, typically by means of post-experimental questioning. In spite of the fact that the items within each study were selected so as to be homogeneous with respect to word frequency, or meaningfulness, pleasantness and imagery, the mean percentage of items on which an individual's preferred strategy was used was only 55.2%.

One way of handling within-individual differences is to assume that such variability or flexibility is an important dimension of differences between individuals. Indeed, in some of the studies the number of different types of strategies reported by individual subjects was found to correlate approximately + .7 with recall performance. In other studies, however, much lower correlations were obtained, perhaps because strategy flexibility may be the product of confusion and lack of interest as well as of intelligent problem-solving activities.

What does the future hold? It must be hoped that the rather fragmentary nature of much of the research so far will be replaced by a more systematic approach, perhaps one based on contemporary theoretical views of memorial functioning. For example, Atkinson and Shiffrin (1968) proposed an influential structural model of memory that distinguished between modality-specific sensory registers, a short-term store and a long-term store. At the process level, Atkinson and Shiffrin argued that *attention* leads to some of the contents of the sensory registers receiving further processing in the short-term store; they also argued that information is transferred from the short-term store to the long-term store primarily as a result of *rehearsal*, and that information returns to the short-term store from the long-term store via *retrieval*.

Within the context of this model, one can enquire about individual differences in the capacities of the various stores, or alternatively focus on differences in the efficiency of the processes of attention, rehearsal and retrieval. Such a theory-driven approach might well pay dividends in terms of understanding the memory system better as well as accounting for individual differences in memory performance. Some of the relevant research has been referred to in this chapter; additional studies considering individual differences in learning and memory in the light of the theoretical position advocated by Atkinson and Shiffrin (1968) are discussed by MacLeod (1979).

8.4 General Conclusions

In this chapter we have considered the effects of various individual differences in cognitive ability and in personality on learning and memory. The preferred approach is one that attempts initially to identify some of the major processes and mechanisms involved in learning and memory; it is then assumed that individual differences, whether emotional, motivational or cognitive, are meaningfully related to these processes. The emphasis on internal processes was partly responsible for the selection of aspects of individual differences which clearly relate to internal states and abilities. Other individual-difference variables such as age, sex and social status would perhaps be more difficult to relate to the structures and processes postulated in contemporary theories of memory.

Most of the research to date has been more informative about individual differences than it has about models of memory. However, there are some cases in which research on individual differences has clarified theoretical controversies concerning memory, and future interdisciplinary research should strive to shed light both on individual differences in memory and on the basic architecture and processes of the memory system.

In spite of some notable successes, research on individual differences has had a chequered history. Nevertheless, the arguments put forward in favour of such research by Melton (1967) still seem sound today:

As long as we throw possible within-individual and between-individual differences together in a measurement, we have no way to think clearly about the effects of the variables in experiments . . . the sooner our experiments on human memory and human learning consider the differences between individuals in our experimental analyses of component processes in memory and learning, the sooner we will have theories and experiments that have some substantial probability of reflecting the fundamental characteristics of those processes (pp. 249–50).

Acknowledgements

Many thanks are due to the Social Science Research Council for their invaluable financial assistance during the preparation of this chapter.

References

AMELANG, M., WENDT, W. and FRÜNDT, H. (1977) Zum Einfluss von Extraversion/ Introversion auf Konsolidierungsprozesse beim Behalten verbalen Materials. *Zeitschrift für Experimentelle und Angewandte Psychologie*, **24**, 525–545.

ANDERSON, J.R. and BOWER, G.H. (1972) Recognition and retrieval processes in free recall. *Psychological Review*, **79**, 97–123.

ANDERSON, J.R. and PAULSON, R. (1978) Interference in memory for pictorial information. *Cognitive Psychology*, **10**, 178–202.

ASHTON, R. and WHITE, K. (1975) The effects of instructions on subjects' imagery questionnaire scores. *Social Behavior and Personality*, **3**, 41–43.

ATKINSON, R.C. and SHIFFRIN, R.M. (1968) Human memory: A proposed system and its control processes. In: K.W. SPENCE and J.T. SPENCE (Eds.) *The Psychology of Learning and Motivation*, vol. 2. Academic Press, London.

BADDELEY, A.D. and HITCH, G. (1974) Working memory. In G.H. BOWER (Ed.) *The Psychology of Learning and Motivation*, Vol. 8. Academic Press, London.

BATTIG, W.F. (1979) Are the important 'individual differences' between or within individuals? *Journal of Research in Personality*, **13**, 546–558.

BETTS, G.H. (1909) *The Distribution and Functions of Mental Imagery*. Columbia University Teachers Contributions to Education, No. 26.

BLAKE, M.J.F. (1967) Relationship between circadian rhythm of body temperature and introversion–extraversion. *Nature*, **215**, 896–897.

BONE, R.N. (1971) Interference, extraversion and paired-associate learning. *British Journal of Social and Clinical Psychology*, **10**, 284–285.

BROADBENT, D.E. (1971) *Decision and Stress*. London Academic Press, London.

BYRNE, B. and ARNOLD, L. (1981) Dissociation of the recency effect and immediate memory span: Evidence from beginning readers. *British Journal of Psychology*, **72**, 371–376.

CARPENTER, P.A. and JUST, M.A. (1975) Sentence comprehension: A psycholinguistic processing model of verification. *Psychological Review*, **82**, 45–73.

CARROLL, J.B. (1978) How shall we study individual differences in cognitive abilities? —Methodological and theoretical perspectives. *Intelligence*, **2**, 87–115.

CARROLL, J.B. and MAXWELL, S.E. (1979) Individual differences in cognitive abilities. *Annual Review of Psychology*, **30**, 603–640.

307

CATTELL, R.B. (1934) Temperament tests: II. Tests. *British Journal of Psychology*, **24**, 20–49.

CORCORAN, D.W.J. (1962) Individual differences in personality after loss of sleep. Unpublished Ph.D. thesis, University of Cambridge, England.

CRAIG, M.J., HUMPHREYS, M.S., ROCKLIN, T. and REVELLE, W. (1979) Impulsivity, neuroticism, and caffeine: Do they have additive effects on arousal? *Journal of Research in Personality*, **13**, 404–419.

CRAIK, F.I.M. (1971) Primary memory. *British Medical Bulletin*, **27**, 232–236.

CRAIK, F.I.M. and LOCKHART, R.S. (1972) Levels of processing: A framework for memory research. *Journal of Verbal Learning and Verbal Behavior*, **11**, 671–684.

CRONBACH, L.J. (1957) The two disciplines of scientific psychology. *American Psychologist*, **12**, 671–684.

DAVIES, A.D.M. (1967) Temperament and narrowness of attention. *Perceptual and Motor Skills*, **24**, 42.

DEFFENBACHER, J.L. (1978) Worry, emotionality, and task-generated interference in test anxiety: An empirical test of attentional theory. *Journal of Educational Psychology*, **70**, 248–254.

DiVESTA, F.J., and INGERSOLL, G. and SUNSHINE, P. (1971) A factor analysis of imagery tests. *Journal of Verbal Learning and Verbal Behavior*, **10**, 471–479.

DORNIC, S. (1977) Mental load, effort, and individual differences. *Reports from the Department of Psychology, The University of Stockholm*, No. 509.

DORNIC, S. (1980) Efficiency vs. effectiveness in mental work: The differential effect of stress. *Reports from the Department of Psychology, The University of Stockholm*, No. 568.

DORNIC, S. and FERNAEUS, S.-E. (1981) Individual differences in high-load tasks: The effect of verbal distraction. *Reports from the Department of Psychology, The University of Stockholm*, No. 569.

EARHARD, M. (1967) Subjective organization and list organization as determinants of free recall and serial recall memorization. *Journal of Verbal Learning and Verbal Behavior*, **6**, 501–507.

EARHARD, M. and ENDICOTT, O. (1969) Why are there individual differences in subjective sequential organization during free-recall memorization? *Journal of Verbal Learning and Verbal Behavior*, **8**, 316–319.

EASTERBROOK, J.A. (1959) The effect of emotion on cue utilization and the organization of behaviour. *Psychological Review*, **66**, - 3–201.

EYSENCK, H.J. (1967) *The Biological Basis of Personality*. C.C. THOMAS, Springfield, Ill.

EYSENCK, H.J. (1973) Personality, learning, and 'anxiety'. In: H.J. EYSENCK (Ed.) *Hand-book of Abnormal Psychology*, 2nd. edn. Pitman, London.

EYSENCK, M.W. (1974) Extraversion, arousal, and retrieval from semantic memory. *Journal of Personality*, **42**, 319–331.

EYSENCK, M.W. (1975) Arousal and speed of recall. *British Journal of Social and Clinical Psychology*, **14**, 269–277.

EYSENCK, M.W. (1976a) Extraversion, verbal learning and memory. *Psychological Bulletin*, **83**, 75–90.

EYSENCK, M.W. (1976b) Arousal, learning, and memory. *Psychological Bulletin*, **83**, 389–404.

EYSENCK, M.W. (1977) *Human Memory: Theory, Research, and Individual Differences*. Pergamon, Oxford.

EYSENCK, M.W. (1979) Anxiety, learning, and memory: A reconceptualization. *Journal of Research in Personality*, **13**, 363–385.

EYSENCK, M.W. (1981) Personality, learning and memory. In: H.J. EYSENCK (Ed.) *A Model for Personality*. Springer, Heidelberg.

EYSENCK, M.W. (1982) *Attention and Arousal: Cognition and Performance*. Springer, Heidelberg.

EYSENCK, M.W. and EYSENCK, H.J. (1980) Mischel and the concept of personality. *British Journal of Psychology*, **71**, 191–204.

308

EYSENCK, M.W. and EYSENCK, M.C. (1979) Memory scanning, introversion–extraversion, and levels of processing. *Journal of Research in Personality*, **13**, 305–315.

GALE, A. (1973) The psychobiology of individual differences: Studies of extraversion and the EEG. In: P. KLINE (Ed.) *New Approaches to Psychological Measurement*. Wiley, London.

GILLESPIE, C.R. and EYSENCK, M.W. (1980) Effects of introversion–extraversion on continuous recognition memory. *Bulletin of the Psychonomic Society*, **15**, 233–235.

GORDON, R. (1949) An investigation into some of the factors that favour the formation of stereotyped images. *British Journal of Psychology*, **39**, 156–167.

GORFEIN, D.S. (1971) Are good subjective organizers good paired-associate learners? *Psychonomic Science*, **22**, 340.

GORFEIN, D.S., BLAIR, C. and O'NEILL, C.R. (1969) A reanalysis of 'The generality of free recall: 1. Subjective organization as an ability factor.' *Psychonomic Science,* **17**, 110.

GRAY, J.A. (1972) The psychophysiological nature of introversion–extraversion: A modification of Eysenck's theory. In: V.D. NEBLITSYN and J.A. GRAY (Eds.) *Biological Bases of Individual Behaviour*. Academic Press, London.

GRAY, J.A. (1973) Causal theories and how to test them. In: J.R. ROYCE (Ed.) *Multivariate Analysis and Psychological Theory*. Academic Press, London.

GULIAN, E. (1972) Focusing of attention and arousal level under interaction of stressors in introverts and extraverts. *Revue Roumaine des Sciences Sociales*, **16**, 153–167.

GUPTA, B.S. (1976) Extraversion and reinforcement in verbal operant conditioning. *British Journal of Psychology*, **67**, 47–52.

GUPTA, B.S. and NAGPAL, M. (1978) Impulsivity/sociability and reinforcement in verbal operant conditioning. *British Journal of Psychology*, **69**, 203–206.

HAMILTON, P., HOCKEY, G.R.J. and QUINN, J.G. (1972) Information selection, arousal and memory. *British Journal of Psychology*, **63**, 181–190.

HAMILTON, V. (1975) Socialization anxiety and information processing: A capacity model of anxiety induced performance deficits. In: I.G. SARASON and C.D. SPIELBERGER (Eds.) *Stress and Anxiety*. Hemisphere, Washington, DC.

HITCH, G. and BADDELEY, A. (1976) Verbal reasoning and working memory. *Quarterly Journal of Experimental Psychology*, **28**, 603–621.

HOWARTH, E. (1969a) Personality differences in serial learning under distraction. *Perceptual and Motor Skills*, **28**, 379–382.

HOWARTH, E. (1969b) Extraversion and increased interference in paired-associate learning. *Perceptual and Motor Skills*, **29**, 403–406.

HOWARTH, E. and EYSENCK, H.J. (1968) Extraversion, arousal, and paired-associate recall. *Journal of Experimental Research in Personality*, **3**, 114–116.

HUNT, E. (1978) Mechanics of verbal ability. *Psychological Review*, **85**, 109–130.

HUNT, E., FROST, N. and LUNNEBORG, C. (1973) Individual differences in cognition: A new approach to intelligence. In G. BOWER (Ed.) *The Psychology of Learning and Motivation*, Vol. 7. Academic Press, London.

HUNT, E., LUNNEBORG, C. and LEWIS, J. (1975) What does it mean to be high verbal? *Cognitive Psychology*, **7**, 194–227.

JENSEN, A. (1964) Individual differences in learning: Interference factor. United States Department of Health, Education and Welfare, Project Report, No. 1867, Washington, DC.

KAHNEMAN, D. (1973) *Attention and Effort*. Prentice Hall, Englewood Cliffs, NJ.

KINTSCH, W. (1970) Models for free recall and recognition. In: D.A. NORMAN (Ed.) *Models of Human Memory*. Academic Press, London.

KLEE, H. and EYSENCK, M.W. (1973) Comprehension of abstract and concrete sentences. *Journal of Verbal Learning and Verbal Behavior*, **12**, 522–529.

LAVERTY, S.G. (1958) Sodium amytal and extraversion. *Journal of Neurology and Neurosurgery*, **21**, 50–54.

LIEBERT, R.M. and MORRIS, L.W. (1967) Cognitive and emotional components of test anxiety: A distinction and some initial data. *Psychological Reports*, **20**, 975–978.

LYON, D.R. (1977) Individual differences in immediate serial recall: A matter of mnemonics? *Cognitive Psychology*, **9**, 403–411.

MCLEAN, P.D. (1968) Paired-associate learning as a function of recall interval, personality and arousal. Unpublished Ph.D. thesis, University of London.

MACLEOD, C.M. (1979) Individual differences in learning and memory: A unitary information processing approach. *Journal of Research in Personality*, **13**, 530–545.

MACLEOD, C.M., HUNT, E.B. and MATHEWS, N.N. (1978) Individual differences in the verification of sentence-picture relationships. *Journal of Verbal Learning and Verbal Behavior*, **17**, 493–507.

MARKS, D.F. (1972) Individual differences in the vividness of visual imagery and their effect on function. In: P. SHEEHAN (Ed.) *The Function and Nature of Imagery*. Academic Press, London.

MARTIN, M. (1978) Memory span as a measure of individual differences in memory capacity. *Memory and Cognition*, **6**, 194–198.

MATHEWS, N.N., HUNT, E.B. and MACLEOD, C.M. (1980) Strategy choice and strategy training in sentence–picture verification. *Journal of Verbal Learning and Verbal Behavior*, **19**, 531–548.

MELTON, A.W. (1967) Individual differences and theoretical process variables: General comments on the conference. In: R.M. GANGNé (Ed.) *Learning and Individual Differences*. Merrill, Columbus, Oh.

MORGENSTERN, F.S., HODGSON, R.J. and LAW, L. (1974) Work efficiency and personality: A comparison of introverted and extraverted subjects exposed to conditions of distraction and distortion of stimulus in a learning task. *Ergonomics*, **17**, 211–220.

MUELLER, J.H. (1977) Test anxiety, input modality, and levels of organization in free recall. *Bulletin of the Psychonomic Society*, **9**, 67–69.

MUELLER, J.H. (1979) Test anxiety and the encoding and retrieval of information. In: I.G. SARASON (Ed.) *Test Anxiety: Theory, Research, and Applications*. Erlbaum, Hillsdale, NJ.

NIDEFFER, R.M. (1976) Test of attentional and interpersonal style. *Journal of Personality and Social Psychology*, **34**, 394–404.

NOTTELMAN, E.D. and HILL, K.T. (1977) Test anxiety and off-task behaviour in evaluative situations. *Child Development*, **48**, 225–231.

PAIVIO, A. (1971) *Imagery and Verbal Processes*. Holt, Rinehart, and Winston, New York.

POSTMAN, L. (1972) A pragmatic view of organization theory. In: E. TULVING and W. DONALDSON (Eds.) *Organization of Memory*. Academic Press, London.

REVELLE, W., HUMPHREYS, M.S., SIMON, L. and GILLILAND, K. (1980) The interactive effect of personality, time of day, and caffeine: A test of the arousal model. *Journal of Experimental Psychology: General*, **109**, 1–31.

RICHARDSON, J.T.E. (1980) *Mental Imagery and Human Memory*. Macmillan, London.

SALTZ, E. and HOEHN, A.J. (1957) A test of the Taylor–Spence theory of anxiety. *Journal of Abnormal and Social Psychology*, **54**, 114–117.

SCHWARTZ, S. (1975) Individual differences in cognition: Some relationships between personality and memory. *Journal of Research in Personality*, **9**, 217–225.

SCHWARTZ, S. (1979) Differential effects of personality on access to various long-term memory codes. *Journal of Research in Personality*, **13**, 396–403.

SHANMUGAN, T.E. and SANTHANAM, M.C. (1964) Personality differences in serial learning when interference is presented at the marginal visual level. *Journal of the Indian Academy of Applied Psychology*, **1**, 25–28.

SIEGMAN, A.W. (1957) Some relationships of anxiety and introversion–extraversion to serial learning. Unpublished doctoral dissertation, University of Michigan.

SPENCE, J.T. and SPENCE, K.W. (1966) The motivational components of manifest

310

anxiety: Drive and drive stimuli. In:C.D. SPIELBERGER (Ed.) *Anxiety and Behavior*. Academic Press, London.

STERNBERG, R.J. (1977) *Intelligence, Information Processing, and Analogical Reasoning: The Componential Analysis of Human Abilities*. Erlbaum, Hillsdale, NJ.

STERNBERG, R.J. (1980) Representation and process in linear syllogistic reasoning. *Journal of Experimental Psychology: General*, **109**, 119–159.

STRAUGHAN, J.H. and DUFORT, W.H. (1969) Task difficulty, relaxation, and anxiety level during verbal learning and recall. *Journal of Abnormal Psychology*, **74**, 621–624.

TILTON, J.R. (1949) A survey of the reliability, validity, and usefulness of the Cattell Culture-Free Test. *Persona*, **1**, 17–19.

TULVING, E. (1972) Episodic and semantic memory. In: E. TULVING and W. DONALDSON (Eds.) *Organization of Memory*. Academic Press, London.

TULVING, E. (1976) Ecphoric processes in recall and recognition. In: J. BROWN (Ed.) *Recall and Recognition*. WILEY, London.

TVERSKY, B. (1973) Encoding processes in recognition and recall. *Cognitive Psychology*, **5**, 275–278.

UNDERWOOD, B.J. (1969) Attributes of memory. *Psychological Review*, **76**, 559–573.

UNDERWOOD, B.J. (1972) Are we overloading memory? In: A.W. MELTON and E. MARTIN (Eds.) *Coding Processes in Human Memory*. Winston, Washington, DC.

UNDERWOOD, B.J., BORUCH, R.F. and MALMI, R.A. (1977) *The Composition of Episodic Memory*. Department of Psychology, Northwestern University.

VALE, J.R. and VALE, C.A. (1969) Individual differences and general laws in psychology. *American Psychologist*, **24**, 1093–1108.

WALKER, E.L. (1958) Action decrement and its relation to learning. *Psychological Review*, **65**, 129–142.

WALLEY, R.E. and WEIDEN, T.D. (1973) Lateral inhibition and cognitive masking: A neuropsychological theory of attention. *Psychological Review*, **80**, 284–302.

WEINER, B. and SCHNEIDER, K. (1971) Drive versus cognitive theory: A reply to Boor and Harmon. *Journal of Personality and Social Psychology*, **18**, 258–262.

WOODHEAD, M.M. and BADDELEY, A.D. (1981) Individual differences and memory for faces, pictures, and words. *Memory and Cognition*, **9**, 368–370.

YERKES, R.M. and DODSON, J.D. (1908) The relation of strength of stimulus to rapidity of habit-formation. *Journal of Comparative Neurology and Psychology*, **18**, 459–482.

ZAFFY, D.J. and BRUNING, J.L. (1966) Drive and the range of cue utilization. *Journal of Experimental Psychology*, **71**, 382–384.

CHAPTER 9

Overview: Problems and Perspectives in Memory Research

Andrew Mayes

9.1 Introduction

The diverse perpectives on memory processes, discussed in the earlier chapters of this book, illustrate the argument of the introductory chapter about the most fruitful way to explore such processes. In that chapter, it was urged that memory research should not be confined to one or two paradigms, but should instead examine the operation of memory in many circumstances, which differ except in so far as they reflect the operations of putative memory processes. Tests in these diverse situations should yield convergent implications about the postulated memory processes. If they do not, then either the processes have been basically misconstrued or their operation does not generalize to some of the situations examined.

An important aspect of this 'convergent operations' approach to memory is the use of animal models to elucidate the physiology of human memory and provide the basis for detailed information processing and storage theories, the predictions of which may need to be determined by computer-simulated models. The success of such models depends on careful identification of key memory processes in both humans and other species. These cross-species comparisons are hard to make because human memory is complicated by the effects of cognitive mediation, which may not occur in other species. This chapter considers some of the problems of cross-species comparisons as well as difficulties in identifying the effects of memory processes.

9.2 Registration and Memory Processes Unique to Human Beings

Retrieval of what Oakley calls representational and abstract memory is enhanced if relevant information is encoded in an elaborative fashion. Such encoding involves voluntary effort, requires considerable attentional capacity, and enables new information to be interpreted in ways which are more meaningful for the perceiver. This kind of encoding is most developed in humans, if it is not unique to them. Encoding in non-human animals is probably less flexible and more automatic. This contention is strengthened by observations that poor memory in young children and elderly adults may be partially caused by a failure to encode information in mnemonically effective ways. More automatic encoding processes seem less vulnerable to developmental changes (Hasher & Zacks, 1979).

Unfortunately, attempts to demonstrate deficient elaborative encoding, particularly in elderly adults, have yielded conflicting results. The studies concerned tried to influence the way in which subjects encoded information so as to improve or impair their memory. A major source of conflict may lie in the fact that elderly people fail to process information adequately for a variety of reasons. Some may be incapable of adequately encoding new material whereas others merely need encouragement or guidance. As attentional capacity is probably reduced with age, it is important not only to monitor whether subjects have encoded what was intended, but also that attentional capacity has not been overloaded by the orienting task, so that the encoding of other information is disrupted.

Little is known about the dynamics of information registration. It is, however, generally accepted that encoding information in terms of meaning improves later remembering, although Craik and Lockhart's (1972) original explanation of this effect in terms of the greater durability of semantic information is no longer accepted. Individual semantic features are lost as rapidly as less meaningful ones (Hunt & Elliot, 1980). The superiority of semantic encoding may depend on the creation of a memory clearly distinct from potential competitors. From a multifactorial viewpoint, the goodness of later memory is determined by how many features are encoded and how distinctive they make the memory, but also how effectively stored each of these features may be. Current theory fails to separate properly the encoding and storage stages. It is possible to imagine, however, successful registration which fails to lead to storage, as perhaps happens in organic amnesics and some elderly people.

There are no proper tests to reveal the full range of features encoded during learning. Such tests must minimize memory load. They may achieve a picture of the full range of encoded features by randomly sampling different ones. This procedure may help determine whether subjects are failing to register automatically encoded features or ones which require the organizing machinery of the frontal lobes. Encoding of complex stimuli, which requires the processing capacity of specialized neocortical systems, may use surprisingly little attentional capacity. For example, Kellogg (1980) found that reliable face recognition still occurred even when the original stimuli were viewed while subjects performed difficult mental arithmetic tasks and were not consciously trying to encode. Perhaps most encoding is relatively automatic like this, and attentional capacity is only heavily used when the frontal neocortex integrates the processing of several, specialized neocortical regions.

Warrington and Weistrantz (1982) have recently proposed that organic amnesia is caused by the disconnection of the memory structures in the medial temporal lobes from the processing capacities of the frontal neocortex. Several versions of this hypothesis are feasible, but one is that although the frontal neocortex encodes complex information, this information is not stably stored as it cannot access the limbic memory structures. As a result, memories involving effortful, planned encoding should be most affected in amnesia. It is indeed often reported that amnesics have more difficulty in learning new material than in reactivating memory for familiar things. These reports may, however, be artefacts caused by comparing strong and poor memory (see Chapter 6). Further, it is known that face recognition, which seems to depend on fairly automatic encoding, is very bad in amnesics.

It seems equally likely that amnesics have suffered from a general disconnection of their limbic memory systems from their neocortical processing systems. The anatomical aspects of this claim are best explored with animal models of amnesia, but its prediction for humans is that all information processed by specialized neocortical systems and integrated by frontal neocortex will be poorly remembered. This prediction presupposes that we have a clear understanding of what is processed by different neocortical systems — but unfortunately we do not. It is interesting to note that Squire (in press) has reported that alcoholic amnesics have *disproportionate* problems with recency judgements, and Hirst (1982) has described a similar deficit in anoxic amnesics. Whereas Squire argued that this was a problem incidental to frontal damage, Hirst believed it to be an essential feature of amnesia. The effect is interesting because it supports the position that parts of the frontal neocortex may be important in some kinds of automatic encoding. If Hirst is right, the problem will be one of storage, found in most if not all amnesics (as an effect of frontal-limbic disconnection) whereas, if Squire is correct, it will be an encoding problem confined to amnesics with direct frontal damage. Only careful tests of the encoding and storage of recency information can determine this issue.

Memory for stimuli, like faces, probably depends both on the processing efficiency of specialized neocortical regions and on the effectiveness of their links with the limbic memory structures. Despite Warrington and Weiskrantz's disconnection hypothesis, amnesics have probably also suffered destruction of these limbic structures, and it will need to be determined what exactly their memory functions are. Individual differences in specific kinds of memory may often reveal variations in the efficiency of neocortical processing or of limbic function. There are, however, many cases of exceptional memory for special material which do not reflect in a simple way on these probably inherited efficiency differences. Michael Gruneberg's report of football fans' excellent memory for scores is an example of such an ability, which clearly depends on the accumulation of specialist knowledge. Such knowledge seems to facilitate rich, but relatively automatic registration.

If conscious monitoring of effortful memory process is more important in humans, and the frontal cortex is centrally involved in such monitoring, then, on the frontal disconnection view of amnesia, humans should be more severely affected than other animals by limbic lesions. Michael Gruneberg makes clear that conscious mediation affects memory in a very general way. Knowledge of the limits of one's memory usually leads to the adoption of appropriate degrees of effort at learning and retrieval. This matching ability emerges slowly in children pari passu with the development of self-awareness.

Short-term memory abilities seem to develop in a similar way. The more automatic of these abilities appear early in development, whereas those implicating voluntary, conscious mediation emerge later. For example, recency effects are apparent in children when behaviour which depends on rehearsal is deficient. Similarly, Byrne and Arnold (1981) found that children who were poor readers showed normal recency effects but deficient digit spans. Digit span increases slowly with age and involves conscious mediation.

If apparently sophisticated abilities develop early, this suggests they may be more automatic than previously suspected. For example, Ceci, Caves and Howe (1981) found that when stories about famous characters, like James Bond, were read to children and their memories tested after 3 weeks, their memories were distorted if the picture painted in the original story did not correspond to the children's pre-existing knowledge. Even children aged seven seemed to reconstruct their memories on the basis of the schemata about well known characters. They were not aware that they were doing this. Indeed, seven-year-olds monitored their memories less than ten-years-olds. The older children showed little memory distortion when the stories contradicted established stereotypes on *several* points whereas the younger children still showed marked distortions. Older children seemed to be aware that the stories sometimes contradicted established knowledge and used this awareness to counteract the automatic reconstructive distortions which otherwise occurred.

The memory abilities of young children may serve as a heuristic for the kind of abilities likely to be seen in animals. In both cases, low levels of conscious mediation should lead one to expect relatively automatic encoding, retrieval and short-term memory processes. Claims that supposedly simple animals, like rats and pigeons, possess apparently sophisticated capacities, such as rehearsal, should be viewed cautiously. Rehearsal, of course, may be a set of heterogeneous abilities, some of which are more automatic.

Measures of consciousness in animals should be useful indicants of their mnemonic abilities. Although they are polemical, Gallup (1977) has argued that an animal's ability to use a mirror to identify otherwise invisible marks on its body is a valid measure of self-recognition and self-awareness. As only chimpanzees and orang-utans pass Gallup's test (even gorillas and humans under age two fail it), one might predict that these species and older humans will possess memory processes unknown in the rest of the animal kingdom. In a recent review of the self and memory, Greenwald (1981) discusses what these processes might be. He cites evidence that material which is encoded with reference to the self is more easily remembered and that ego-involvement with a persisting task gives rise to better recall. Frontal neocortex involvement with these processes remains a key issue.

9.3 Familiarity

A salient concomitant of consciousness is the feeling of familiarity that some memories have, particularly episodic or representational ones. It is hard to determine whether a similar effect occurs in other species. A potential lever on this problem is provided by the Claparède effect in human amnesia. In this effect, amnesics show evidence for a kind of memory (by, for example, playing a recently learnt piano tune) but experience no recognition or familiarity for that memory or how it was learned. Claims of similar dissociations in animals should be treated cautiously. For example, Susmann and Ferguson (1981) reported that young rats showed no savings when relearning avoidance tasks after a delay, whereas they did show activity changes, which suggests that there was retention of some aspects of the tasks. This type of dissociation probably occurs because classical conditioning emerges earlier than instrumental conditioning in ontogeny. This is consistent with the claim, discussed by Mayes, that ECS disrupts instrumental conditioning more readily than classical. In rats, neither kind of conditioning need depend on conscious mediation in the way that applies in complex human memory.

More convincingly, Gaffan (1972) has argued that fornix-lesioned monkeys, like human amnesics, cannot distinguish novel and familiar events, although

315

they can learn to associate events with reward. As the lesioned monkeys can associate an event with reward, yet fail to recognize it as familiar, this effect seems similar to the Claparède effect of human amnesia. Familiarity is indexed by the ability to discriminate novel and repeated events. Even so, the mechanisms of this ability may differ in humans and species that fail Gallup's test. There is some evidence favouring this possibility. Human amnesics are bad at making familiarity judgements whether they have to decide that an event is familiar in a given context or familiar from any context whatsoever — a distinction between relative and absolute familiarity. A person might be asked, for example, to decide whether they had seen a face before at their home, or whether they'd ever seen it before. Owen and Butler (1980) have shown, however, that fornix-lesioned monkeys are poor at relative familiarity judgements but not at absolute familiarity judgements.

It can be argued that the above finding does not show that the mechanisms of familiarity judgement in monkeys differ from those of humans. As discussed in Chapter 6, it is controversial whether the monkey fornix lesion constitutes an appropriate model of human amnesia. Even if it does not, however, Owen and Butler's result may mean that relative and absolute familiarity or recognition judgements require different memory processes. Relative familiarity judgements depend on the use of contextual information, whereas absolute familiarity judgements may generally depend on context-free processes. It is possible that relative familiarity judgements share many mediating operations with recency judgements, as the latter also involve the use of spatiotemporal information which is a form of contextual information. Indeed it is hard to know whether monkeys are making recency judgements or relative familiarity judgements when 'novel' objects have been shown on previous testing sessions. Only in research on humans has care been taken to distinguish between familiarity and recency judgements.

Tests of relative and absolute familiarity judgements and recency judgements on human amnesics and a range of animal models may show that different processes underlie each kind of judgement. The issue relates to the question of whether amnesia is caused by a selective context-free familiarity loss, unrelated to the use of contextual information, as suggested by Gaffan (1977a). The more popular view is that amnesia arises from poor use of contextual information. Contextual confusion causes high susceptibility to interference and only those kinds of memory that are minimally influenced by contextual manipulations will be spared. If this latter view is correct, then one should predict that artificially increasing the influence of contextual factors for those kinds of memory normally preserved in amnesia should disproportionately disrupt the performance of amnesics, and make them more susceptible to interference.

Attempts to model context-dependent forgetting and interference effects in animals must involve careful task selection as apparent similarities are often spurious. For example, Heinemann, Sage-Day and Brenners (1981) have reported that pigeons suffer devastatingly from retroactive interference in a discrimination task. This interference was caused, however, by non-specific responding to stimuli used in the task. In contrast, humans are little affected by such non-specific interference and are mainly susceptible to the acquisition of competing responses to common stimuli. The mechanisms of the two sorts of interference are likely to be different.

316

9.4   The Rate of Forgetting — An Animal Model?

In human memory, it has proved very difficult to demonstrate variations in the rate of forgetting. Most variables only seem to affect registration or retrieval processes, leaving storage uninfluenced. There are three exceptions. First, it is usually claimed that proactive interference speeds forgetting although it has been argued recently that proper controls show the effect is confined to the learning stage (see Crowder, 1982). Second, it has been reported that high levels of arousal are associated with normal or poor initial recall but superior delayed recall (for example, see Howarth & Eynsenck, 1968). Third, temporal lobe amnesics have been reported not only to learn slowly but to forget more rapidly (see Huppert & Piercy, 1979). If the reality of these phenomena is confirmed, the issue of whether they are related becomes important.

Thompson and Yang (1982) have recently developed an animal model of the rapid forgetting in temporal lobe amnesia. They trained rats on a series of position reversal problems and then tested their memory at delays of one day or more. Earlier work suggested that hippocampal lesions caused more rapid forgetting, but that mammillary body lesions did not (Thompson, 1981; Thompson et al., 1981). This effect was, however, probably caused by failure to control for poor initial learning. When this problem was circumvented, by adopting as a learning criterion the first appearance of a run of correct responses with a probability of less than 0.05, then hippocampal animals ceased to show rapid forgetting. In this, they also resembled animals with amygdala and reticular formation lesions.

In contrast, lesions of the parafascicular region of the posteromedial thalamus, of the substantia nigra and the caudate, all caused rats to forget the positional task more rapidly. No analogue for this effect has been found in humans although it raises the interesting question of whether extrapyramidal lesions in humans cause more rapid forgetting of spatial information. On the other hand, if Huppert and Piercy (1979) are correct, hippocampal lesions in rats should cause more rapid forgetting of spatial information. Failure to find such an effect raises doubts about this animal model. The lesion may be wrongly located, the hippocampus' functions may have changed or the apparently similar spatial task may involve different mechanisms than human spatial memory. Even so, exploration of the extrapyramidal lesion effect is important, as it may establish what is the role of the damaged structures in memory storage.

9.5   The Dorsomedial Thalamic Nucleus — More Animal Models

As discussed in Chapter 6, it remains controversial whether dorsomedial thalamic lesions are sufficient to cause permanent and severe amnesia in humans. It is therefore interesting that Isseroff et al. (1982) have reported that, in rhesus monkeys, these lesions caused impaired spatial delayed alternation and spatial delayed response performance. The lesions did not, however, impair object reversal or visual pattern discrimination learning. This report corroborates recent observations of Winocur et al. (in press) that bilateral thalamic lesions in humans can cause severe anterograde amnesia in the absence of intellectual loss. The animal model may be appropriate therefore, but it remains important to see whether human cases show the same pattern of impairment on the tasks used by Isseroff *et al*. It would, for example, be surprising if humans with bilateral thalamic lesions had an amnesia selective for spatial information, as seems to be the case with rhesus monkeys. Winocur *et al*'s case did, however, show little or no retrograde amnesia, and fewer problems with interference than other amnesics. The animal model may prove a valuable means of examining these effects and determining more precisely the locus of the lesion responsible.

One of David Oakley's criteria for distinguishing abstract from representational memory is that the former does not require the limbic memory structures. He also argues that learning set information is an animal equivalent of human abstract memory. Slotnick and Kaneks (1981) have reported, however, that dorsomedial thalamic lesions in rats drastically impair olfactory learning set formation for reversal learning, whereas lesions of the amygdala and lateral olfactory tract projection do not. Olfactory information is known to project divergently to the entorhinal cortex and amygdala, the hypothalamus, and the dorsomedial thalamic nucleus. The hypothalamus uses this information to modulate hormonal activity, the amygdala seems to use it to influence species-typical behaviours and pheromonal communication and the dorsomedial thalamic nucleus uses it for mediating kinds of learning, like olfactory reversal learning set formation.

Two points emerge from this study. First, it illustrates the notion that once sensory information has been encoded to some degree it is passed in parallel into modular systems, which then operate on the information in radically different ways. Second, it shows that abstract memory is likely to be a heterogeneous entity and that it must be specified more fully before animal models of it can be erected. Most forms of human abstract memory may turn out to require activity in the limbic memory systems. Indeed, only those forms, dubbed by Squire as 'procedural memory' (see Chapter 1 and 6) may function normally without limbic system involvement. In addition to these problems of heterogeneity, one must expect that abstract memory in humans will be mediated by processes unique to them, perhaps because they are associated with self- and other forms of consciousness.

9.6 Short-Term Memory Abilities

In Chapter 5, Graham Hitch argues that there are a number of short-term memory abilities in humans, which may be partially characterized in terms of the way information is encoded. Evidence for his position is drawn from several paradigms and received some support from observations of individual memory differences (see Chapter 8). It also has some support from observed neuropsychological dissociations. Despite these sources of support, it remains unknown whether such short-term memory abilities are based on specialized storage systems or on the dynamics of rapid registration with an associated poor long-term storage, interacting with later retrieval. Wickelgren (1974) has argued for the latter position on the ground that the forgetting curve of short-term forgetting fits the same equation as long-term forgetting. If he is correct then work using the experimental retrograde amnesia paradigm (see Chapter 4), which purports to show that the consolidation of long-term memory is a slow process, is irrelevant to the elucidation of the mechanisms of human short-term memory abilities. One interpretation of this work is that there are a number of storage systems with different life times and that such systems operate with both simple and complex kinds of memory. Normally, their life times overlap, so memory expression is continuously possible, and their activities do not correspond with the duration of human short-term memory abilities.

Animal models of human short-term memory abilities may offer valuable means of discovering whether such abilities are founded on specialized storage mechanisms or an interaction between registration and retrieval processes. They should also help determine how many such abilities there are and whether they apply to both simple and complex kinds of memory. In this connection, it is interesting to note that Maki (1979) found that factors which disturbed short-term memory (measured by ability to match after a delay) in pigeons, had no effect on the course of discrimination learning. This suggests that, contrary to some proposals, instrumental learning is not associated with short-term memory abilities.

As organic amnesia is normally associated with intact short-term memory, Warrington and Taylor (1973) interpreted their finding of an impairment in immediately tested amnesic memory for sequentially shown pictures as evidence that there is no short-term memory ability for this kind of material. Amnesics show intact short-term memory for simultaneously presented and randomly positioned dots (Warrington & Baddeley, 1974), so the argument might be extended to claim that there are short-term memory systems for variously coded verbal inputs and for simultaneously presented visual material.

Some support for the above position might be claimed from animal lesion studies. Thus, Gaffan (1977b) found that fornix-transected monkeys were impaired not only on longer-term recognition memory, but also on recognition after brief delays for short lists of colours or spatial positions. Gaffan presented his stimuli sequentially. In a recent study, Owen and Butler (1981) did find that fornix lesions left short-term memory unimpaired. They used a delayed non-matching to sample task in which the same two test objects were repeatedly used. The task could be interpreted as involving simultaneous visual presentation.

Once again, however, these animal observations must be interpreted cautiously. First, some evidence indicates that there may be short-term memory for sequentially shown visual material in humans, in which case fornix lesions should not affect such memory in monkeys. For example, Broadbent and Broadbent (1981) presenting abstract visual patterns in a paradigm similar to Gaffan's, not only reported recency effects but also showed that these effects reflected the operation of a short-term visual memory analogous to pre-categorical acoustic storage. Second, fornix lesions may not cause an amnesic syndrome in humans, but may cause an exaggerated need for perceptual novelty (see Squire & Zola-Morgan, in press), which perhaps arises from excessively rapid satiation. If this interpretation were correct, then fornix lesions might affect recognition differentially for reasons unconnected with memory.

Some of the above uncertainty arises because of disagreement about the role of fornix lesions in memory. If these lesions directly affect memory and leave memory for some tasks intact in the short term, then the effect is important, even if fornix lesions are not a suitable model of human amnesia. It is the directness of the effect on memory which must be resolved. Disagreement also arises because there is a lack of agreement specifically over the human evidence, including the proper criteria for indentifying short-term memory abilities. An essential requirement for animal modelling is that memory abilities have been clearly adumbrated in humans.

9.7 Biochemical Models of Memory

Identification of memory-controlling neural systems requires knowledge of the neurotransmitter systems involved. There has consequently been much research on biochemical correlates of memory and on drug effects. Recent evidence indicates that some kinds of complex memory in humans depend on the activity of cholinergic neurons. Some of this evidence is discussed in Chapter 6. First, Alzheimer's disease, in which an early presenting sign is often a selective amnesia, is believed by some researchers to be caused by atrophy of primitive isodendritic neurons, which project widely to the neocortex and hippocampus. These neurons are cholinergic. For example, Whitehouse et al. (1982) reported a massive cell loss of the cholinergic neurons in the substantia innominata in Alzheimer patients.

Second, anticholinergic drugs have been reported to cause a memory disturbance which closely resembles organic amnesia (Frith et al., 1980). It is significant, however, that a state which appears to be indistinguishable from the one caused by anticholinergic drugs is caused by injections of benzodiazepines (Frith et al., 1980; Brown et al., 1982). It is difficult or impossible with humans beings to determine whether this apparent commonality of effect is caused by the use of inappropriate tests, disturbances in the operation of parallel systems, or by the drugs acting on a common system such as the hippocampus. These possibilities may be assessed much more effectively by the appropriate use of animal models. Such models could avoid the insensitivity of the human work by microinjecting drugs into specific brain regions. Conversely, assays may be made to determine what biochemical activity in these regions correlates with changes in memory. In fact, there is already evidence from animal studies that cholinergic drugs, benzodiazepines and vasopressin interact in the hippocampus, and possibly in other limbic system structures. An explanation of these interactions requires a complex information processing theory, such as Jeffrey Gray's, as referred to in Chapter 1.

9.8 Arousal

The arousal of wakefulness is associated with the release of acetylcholine at forebrain sites. Both arousal and acetylcholine release are caused by selective stimulation of the midbrain reticular formation, which confirms that this structure contains an arousal system (see Vanderwolf & Robinson, 1981, for a discussion). It is possible therefore that some of the effects of arousal on memory, discussed by Michael Eysenck, are cholinergically mediated, and that part of mnemonically effective action of cholinergic stimulants is on this arousal system.

Unfortunately, despite its ubiquity as an explanatory concept, 'arousal' is still a vague notion. It is regarded as a non-specific process, variations in the intensity of which affect the whole gamut of performance, but for reasons, or by means, which have never convincingly been proposed. Measures of this process, such as the autonomic indices, are indirect, and although they avoid the charge of circularity (according to which performance changes are used to measure arousal) they produce other problems. For example, the autonomic measures correlate poorly with each other. This could be because they only index arousal indirectly and are influenced by other factors, or it could be because there is more than one form of arousal.

Problems like the above one can only be resolved finally through the use of animal models, which directly identify the arousal process(es) within the brain. Research on such models is in progress but has not yet reached universally agreed conclusions. For example, Vanderwolf and Robinson (1981) have argued that there is an aminergic reticulocortical system, the activity of which is essential for voluntary movements, and a second, cholinergic reticulocortical system, the activity of which is essential for the storage of new information. This proposal is, however, disputed.

Activity in the cholinergic arousal system may influence the way in which attention is distributed and also, possibly, the amount of attentional resources available. These influences may affect how appropriately complex information is encoded, as human studies suggest. They may also affect how strong is the storage of information that is encoded — perhaps by modulating neocortical-limbic circuits. Once more, these suggestions can only feasibly be tested with model systems in animals. Users of these models should view some effects of arousal on memory observed in humans with caution. For example, anxiety associated with arousal production in some circumstances can cause subjects to engage in distracting ruminations when confronting unpleasant facts. Poor performance on hard tasks, caused by high anxiety, can be reversed if subjects are given false (and encouraging) feedback about how they are doing (see Heckhousen and Weiner, 1980).

9.9 Conclusion

The examples discussed in the previous sections are intended to show the difficulty of making animal models of human memory processes and the potential value of such models. Not all human memory processes can be illuminated by such models. Furthermore, these uniquely human processes, which may comprise verbal memory and the effects of metamemory, probably dependent on sophisticated forms of consciousness, influence the way that other simpler forms of memory are achieved. In animals, such forms of mediation cannot occur. It is therefore essential to analyse carefully the component processes in human memory, if appropriate animal models are to be adopted. The use of a wide range of paradigms should help achieve this end. It is particularly important not only to adapt human memory tests to animals, but also to examine how humans perform memory tasks originally devised for animals.

Most of the major questions about memory, enumerated in Chapter 1, remain largely unanswered. There is, for example, little knowledge about where most kinds of memory are stored, let alone how such storage is organized. Controversies about the causes of forgetting still persist, swinging from the extreme of claiming that memory storage is permanent and unchanging to the view that forgetting is caused by the decay of memory storage. These questions can be resolved as improved techniques come to be applied to animal models of memory. Phenomena, like hippocampal long-term potentiation, may soon be discovered as the plastic changes underlying various kinds of memory. Their exploration will illuminate the processes of forgetting. The chances are that in 25 years' time a book of this kind will be able to sketch firmly the answers to the major questions concerning human and animal memory.

References

BROADBENT, D.E. and BROADBENT, M.H.P. (1981) Recency effects in visual memory. *Quarterly Journal of Experimental Psychology*, **33A**, 1-15.

BROWN, J., LEWIS, V., BROWN, M., HORN, G. and BOWES, J.B. (1982) A comparison between transient amnesias induced by two drugs (diazepam and lorazepam) and amnesia of organic amnesia. *Neuropsychologia*, **20**, 55-70.

BYRNE, B. and ARNOLD, L. (1981) Dissociation of the recency effect and immediate memory span: Evidence from beginning readers. *British Journal of Psychology*, **72**, 371-376.

CECI, S.J., and CAVES, R.D. and HOWE, M.J.A. (1981) Children's long-term memory for information that is incongruous with their prior knowledge. *British Journal of Psychology*, **72**, 443-450.

CRAIK, F.I.M. and LOCKHART, R.S. (1972) Levels of processing: A framework for memory research. *Journal of Verbal Learning and Verbal Behavior*, **11**, 671-684.

CROWDER, R.G. (1982) General forgetting theory and the locus of amnesia. In: L.S. CERMAK (Ed.) *Human Memory and Amnesia*, pp. 33-42. Lawrence Erlbaum Associates, Hillsdale, New Jersey.

FRITH, C.D., RICHARDSON, J.T.E., SCOTT, E., SAMUEL, M., CROW, T.T., CUNNINGHAM-OWENS, D. and MCKENNA, P.J. (1980) The effects of intravenous diazepam and hyoscine upon human memory. Paper given at the Exeter meeting of the Experimental Psychology Society, March.

GAFFAN, D. (1972) Loss of recognition memory in rats with lesions of the fornix. *Neuropsychologia*, **10**, 327-341.

GAFFAN, D. (1977a) Monkey's recognition memory for complex pictures and the effects of fornix transection. *Quarterly Journal of Experimental Psychology*, **29**, 505-514.

GAFFAN, D. (1977b) Recognition memory after short retention intervals in fornix-transected monkeys. *Quarterly Journal of Experimental Psychology*, **29**, 577-588.

GALLUP, G. (1977) Self-recognition in primates: A comparative approach to bidirectional properties of consciousness. *American Psychologist*, **32**, 329-338.

GREENWALD, A.G. (1981) Self and memory. *The Psychology of Learning and Motivation*, **15**, 201-236.

HASHER, L. and ZACKS, T.T. (1979) Automatic and effortful processes in memory. *Journal of Experimental Psychology (General)*, **108**, 356-388.

HECKHAUSEN, H. and WEINER, B. (1980) The emergence of a cognitive psychology of motivation. In: P.C. DODWELL (Ed.) *New Horizons in Psychology. 2. 2nd edition*, pp. 126-147. Penguin, Harmondsworth.

HEINEMANN, E.G., SAGE-DAY, J. and BRENNER, N. (1981) Retroactive interference in discrimination learning. *Science*, **214**, 1254-1256.

HIRST, W. (1982) The Amnesic Syndrome: Descriptions and explanations. *Psychological Bulletin*, **9**, 435-460.

HOWARTH, E. and EYSENCK, H.J. (1968) Extraversion and paired-associate recall. *Journal of Experimental Research in Personality*, **3**, 114-116.

HUNT, R.R. and ELLIOTT, J.M. (1980) The role of nonsemantic information in memory: Orthographic distinctiveness effects on retention. *Journal of Experimental Psychology (General)*, **109**, 49-74.

HUPPERT, F.A. and PIERCY, M. (1979) Normal and abnormal forgetting in amnesia: Effect of locus of lesion. *Cortex*, **15**, 385–390.

ISSEROFF, A., ROSVOLD, H.E., GALKIN, T.W. and GOLDMAN-RAKIC, P.S. (1982) Spatial memory impairments following damage to the mediodorsal nucleus of the thalamus in rhesus monkeys. *Brain Research*, **232**, 97–113.

KELLOGG, R.T. (1980) Is conscious attention necessary for long-term storage? *Journal of Experimental Psychology: Human Learning and Memory*, **6**, 379–390.

MAKI, W.S. (1979) Discrimination learning without short-term memory: Dissociation of memory processes in pigeons. *Science*, **204**, 83–85.

OWEN, M.J. and BUTLER, S.R. (1981) Amnesia after transection of the fornix in monkeys. Long-term memory impaired, short-term memory intact. *Behavioural Brain Research*, **3**, 115–123.

SLOTNICK, B.N. and KANEKO, N. (1981) Role of mediodorsal thalamic nucleus in olfactory discrimination learning in rats. *Science*, **214**, 91–92.

SQUIRE, L.R. (in press) Comparisons among forms of amnesia: Some deficits are unique to Korsakoff syndrome.

SQUIRE, L.R. and ZOLA-MORGAN, S. (in press) Neuropsychology of memory: Studies in man and sub-human primates. In: J.A. DEUTSCH (Ed.) *The Physiological Basis of Memory, 2nd edition*. Academic Press, New York.

SUSMANN, P.S. and FERGUSON, H.B. (1980) Retained elements of early avoidance training and relearning of forgotten operants. *Developmental Psychobiology*, **13**, 545–562.

THOMPSON, R. (1981) Rapid forgetting of a spatial habit in rats with hippocampal lesions. *Science*, **212**, 959–960.

THOMPSON, R., KAS, L. and YANG, S. (1981) Rapid forgetting of individual spatial reversal problems in rats with parafascicular lesions. *Behavioral and Neural Biology*, **33**, 1–16.

THOMPSON, R. and YANG, S. (1982) Retention of individual spatial reversal problems in rats with nigral, caudoputamenal, and reticular formation lesions. *Behavioral and Neural Biology*, **34**, 98–103.

VANDERWOLF, F.H. and ROBINSON, T.E. (1981) Reticulo-cortical activity and behaviour: A critique of the arousal theory and a new synthesis. *The Behavioral and Brain Sciences*, **4**, 459–514.

WARRINGTON, E.K. and BADDELEY, A.D. (1974) Amnesia and memory for visual location. *Neuropsychologia*, **12**, 257–263.

WARRINGTON, E.K. and TAYLOR, A.M. (1973) Immediate memory for faces: long- or short-term memory? *Quarterly Journal of Experimental Psychology*, **25**, 316–322.

WARRINGTON, E.K. and WEISKRANTZ, L. (1982) Amnesia: A disconnection syndrome? *Neuropsychologia*, **20**, 233–247.

WHITEHOUSE, P.J., PRICE, D.L., STRUBLE, R.G., CLARK, A.W., COYLE, J.T. and DE LONG, M.R. (1982) Alzheimer's disease and senile dementia: Loss of neurons in the basal forebrain. *Science*, **215**, 1237–1239.

WICKELGREN, W.A. (1974) Single trace fragility theory of memory dynamics. *Memory and Cognition*, **2**, 775–780.

WINOCUR, G., OXBURY, S., AGNETTI, V. and DAVIS, C. (in press) Amnesia in a patient with bilateral lesions to the thalamus.

Author Index

328

Ross, E.D., 8
Ross, J.E., 53, 54, 57, 269
Rossor, M.N., 144
Rosvold, H.E., 59
Rotter, J.B., 47
Routtenberg, A., 148, 153, 154
Rowe, E.J., 104, 111
Rowe, E.S., 111
Rozin, P., 207, 211
Ruggiero, F.T., 65
Rumbaugh, D.M., 53
Rundus, D., 189
Rundus, O., 253
Russell, I.S., 44, 59, 63, 70
Russell, W.R., 208
Rust, L.D., 114

Saffran, E.M., 185
Sage-Day, J., 316
Sahakian, B.J., 232, 233
Saltz, E., 286
Salzen, E.A., 31
Samuels, I., 9, 206, 214
Sanders, H.I., 119
Sands, S.F., 62, 190
Santhanam, M.C., 292
Saslove, 266
Schactel, E., 84
Scheibel, M.E., 100
Schiller, P.H., 136
Schlapfer, W.T., 135, 155, 165, 243
Schneider, A.M., 139, 145
Schneider, G.E., 149
Schneider, K., 286
Schneider, N.G., 114
Schnore, M.M., 104, 114
Schonfield, D., 87, 114, 115, 116
Schreiner, L., 59
Schulman, J., 160
Schulman, S., 235
Schwartz, B., 35
Schwartz, J.G., 156
Schwartz, S., 289, 294
Schwegler, H., 12
Scott, J., 266
Scott, M.S., 87
Scoville, W.B., 235
Scribner, S., 257
Seligman, M.E.P., 6, 34
Senter, R.J., 271
Shaffer, W.O., 183, 190
Shallice, T., 8, 53, 54, 68, 69, 70, 113, 179, 184, 185, 195
Shanmugan, T.E., 292
Shashoua, V.E., 153

Shavalia, D.A., 193
Shepard, R.N., 46
Shettleworth, S.J., 34
Shiffrin, R.M., 67, 178, 183, 186, 189, 190, 195, 283, 306
Shimp, C.P., 191, 195
Siegman, A.W., 292
Signoret, J.L., 9, 203, 204, 214, 230
Siipola, E.M., 41
Sime, M.E., 121, 122
Simon, E., 103, 106, 112, 115
Sinnamon, H.M., 66
Skinner, D.M., 142
Slater, P.C., 118, 119
Slobodkin, L.B., 47
Slotnick, B.N., 318
Smith, A.D., 106, 108, 115, 116
Smith, C.B., 100, 142
Smith, G., 94
Smith, N., 95
Smithson, B.L., 61
Smythe, W.E., 190, 191
Solheim, G.S., 95
Solomon, P.R., 239
Spear, N.E., 83, 90, 91, 92, 95, 140, 161, 162
Spence, J.T., 285
Spence, K.W., 285
Sperling, G., 181
Spiegel, E.A., 217, 230
Spiegler, B.J., 242
Squier, L.H., 61
Squire, L.R., 10, 99, 118, 119, 135, 140, 143, 144, 145, 146, 150, 151, 152, 154, 155, 156, 165, 166, 204, 206, 210, 216, 217, 218, 222, 223, 224, 225, 226, 227, 228, 229, 230, 231, 242, 243, 314, 319
Squire, S., 10, 11
Stahl, J., 48
Stamm, J.S., 235
Stanny, G.J., 183, 190
Starr, 219
Staubli, U., 167
Stea, D., 45
Stein, N.L., 87
Stern, W.C., 142
Sternberg, D.B., 146, 152
Sternberg, R.J., 284
Stettner L.H., 151
Stevens, R., 241, 257
Stoff, D.M., 103, 213
Stone, C.P., 122
Stones, M.J., 114, 115
Storandt, M., 97, 118

Wilcoxon, H.C., 34
Wilkie, D.M., 35, 64
Williams, 218
Williams, D.R., 35
Williams, H., 35
Williams, J.M., 5
Wilson, M., 15
Wimer, R.E., 114
Winocur, G., 92, 116, 214, 215, 219, 220, 222, 238, 239, 317
Winograd, E., 106
Winson, J., 237
Wishaw, I.Q., 93, 121
Wisniewski, H., 100
Wittee, K.L., 104
Wittles, I., 104
Wittman, T.K., 139
Wodinsky, J., 60
Wood, F., 224, 226, 270
Woodhead, M.M., 11, 304
Woods, R.T., 99, 210, 222
Worsham, R.W., 65
Wright, A.A., 62, 190
Wright, F.F., 160

Wright, M., 106

Yamamoto, T., 91
Yang, S., 317
Yarmey, A.D., 261, 266
Yates, A.J., 102
Yates, F., 269
Yerkes, R.M., 291
Young, J., 142
Yuille, J.C., 215

Zachs, R.T., 109, 111, 207, 216
Zacks, T.T., 312
Zaffy, D.J., 287
Zajonc, R.B., 210
Zangwill, O.L., 203
Zaretsky, H.H., 116
Zelinski, E.M., 106
Zentall, T.R., 60, 187, 194
Zinkin, S., 137
Zinober, J.W., 89
Zola-Morgan, S., 10, 214, 220, 231, 241, 242, 319
Zornetzer, S.F., 100, 101, 120, 147

Subject Index